IFIP Advances in Information and Communication Technology 323

IFIP – The International Federation for Information Processing

IFIP was founded in 1960 under the auspices of UNESCO, following the First World Computer Congress held in Paris the previous year. An umbrella organization for societies working in information processing, IFIP's aim is two-fold: to support information processing within its member countries and to encourage technology transfer to developing nations. As its mission statement clearly states,

> IFIP's mission is to be the leading, truly international, apolitical organization which encourages and assists in the development, exploitation and application of information technology for the benefit of all people.

IFIP is a non-profitmaking organization, run almost solely by 2500 volunteers. It operates through a number of technical committees, which organize events and publications. IFIP's events range from an international congress to local seminars, but the most important are:

- The IFIP World Computer Congress, held every second year;
- Open conferences;
- Working conferences.

The flagship event is the IFIP World Computer Congress, at which both invited and contributed papers are presented. Contributed papers are rigorously refereed and the rejection rate is high.

As with the Congress, participation in the open conferences is open to all and papers may be invited or submitted. Again, submitted papers are stringently refereed.

The working conferences are structured differently. They are usually run by a working group and attendance is small and by invitation only. Their purpose is to create an atmosphere conducive to innovation and development. Refereeing is less rigorous and papers are subjected to extensive group discussion.

Publications arising from IFIP events vary. The papers presented at the IFIP World Computer Congress and at open conferences are published as conference proceedings, while the results of the working conferences are often published as collections of selected and edited papers.

Any national society whose primary activity is in information may apply to become a full member of IFIP, although full membership is restricted to one society per country. Full members are entitled to vote at the annual General Assembly, National societies preferring a less committed involvement may apply for associate or corresponding membership. Associate members enjoy the same benefits as full members, but without voting rights. Corresponding members are not represented in IFIP bodies. Affiliated membership is open to non-national societies, and individual and honorary membership schemes are also offered.

Cristian S. Calude Vladimiro Sassone (Eds.)

Theoretical Computer Science

6th IFIP TC 1/WG 2.2 International Conference
TCS 2010, Held as Part of WCC 2010
Brisbane, Australia, September 20-23, 2010
Proceedings

Springer

Volume Editors

Cristian S. Calude
University of Auckland, Department of Computer Science
Private Bag 92019, Auckland, New Zealand
E-mail: cristian@cs.auckland.ac.nz

Vladimiro Sassone
University of Southampton, School of Electronics and Computer Science
Southampton, SO17 1BJ, UK
E-mail: vs@ecs.soton.ac.uk

CR Subject Classification (1998): F.2, F.3, F.1, C.2, D.2, G.2

ISSN 1868-4238
ISBN-10 3-642-42311-6 Springer Berlin Heidelberg New York
ISBN-13 978-3-642-42311-6 Springer Berlin Heidelberg New York

springer.com

Softcover re-print of the Hardcover 1st edition 2010

Typesetting: Camera-ready by author, data conversion by Scientific Publishing Services, Chennai, India
Printed on acid-free paper 06/3180

IFIP World Computer Congress 2010 (WCC 2010)

Message from the Chairs

Every two years, the International Federation for Information Processing (IFIP) hosts a major event which showcases the scientific endeavors of its over one hundred technical committees and working groups. On the occasion of IFIP's 50th anniversary, 2010 saw the 21st IFIP World Computer Congress (WCC 2010) take place in Australia for the third time, at the Brisbane Convention and Exhibition Centre, Brisbane, Queensland, September 20–23, 2010.

The congress was hosted by the Australian Computer Society, ACS. It was run as a federation of co-located conferences offered by the different IFIP technical committees, working groups and special interest groups, under the coordination of the International Program Committee.

The event was larger than ever before, consisting of 17 parallel conferences, focusing on topics ranging from artificial intelligence to entertainment computing, human choice and computers, security, networks of the future and theoretical computer science. The conference History of Computing was a valuable contribution to IFIPs 50th anniversary, as it specifically addressed IT developments during those years. The conference e-Health was organized jointly with the International Medical Informatics Association (IMIA), which evolved from IFIP Technical Committee TC-4 "Medical Informatics".

Some of these were established conferences that run at regular intervals, e.g., annually, and some represented new, groundbreaking areas of computing. Each conference had a call for papers, an International Program Committee of experts and a thorough peer reviewing process of full papers. The congress received 642 papers for the 17 conferences, and selected 319 from those, representing an acceptance rate of 49.69% (averaged over all conferences). To support interoperation between events, conferences were grouped into 8 areas: Deliver IT, Govern IT, Learn IT, Play IT, Sustain IT, Treat IT, Trust IT, and Value IT.

This volume is one of 13 volumes associated with the 17 scientific conferences. Each volume covers a specific topic and separately or together they form a valuable record of the state of computing research in the world in 2010. Each volume was prepared for publication in the Springer IFIP Advances in Information and Communication Technology series by the conference's volume editors. The overall Publications Chair for all volumes published for this congress is Mike Hinchey.

For full details of the World Computer Congress, please refer to the webpage at http://www.ifip.org.

June 2010

Augusto Casaca, Portugal, Chair, International Program Committee
Phillip Nyssen, Australia, Co-chair, International Program Committee
Nick Tate, Australia, Chair, Organizing Committee
Mike Hinchey, Ireland, Publications Chair
Klaus Brunnstein, Germany, General Congress Chair

Foreword

This volume contains the invited and regular papers presented at TCS 2010, the 6th IFIP International Conference on Theoretical Computer Science, organised by IFIP Technical Committee 1 (Foundations of Computer Science) and IFIP WG 2.2 (Formal Descriptions of Programming Concepts) in association with SIGACT and EATCS. TCS 2010 was part of the World Computer Congress held in Brisbane, Australia, during September 20–23, 2010 (`http://www.wcc2010.com`).

TCS 2010 is composed of two main areas: (A) Algorithms, Complexity and Models of Computation, and (B) Logic, Semantics, Specification and Verification.

The selection process led to the acceptance of 23 papers out of 39 submissions, each of which was reviewed by three Programme Committee members. The Programme Committee discussion was held electronically using Easychair.

The invited speakers at TCS 2010 are:

Rob van Glabbeek (NICTA, Australia)
Bart Jacobs (Nijmegen, The Netherlands)
Catuscia Palamidessi (INRIA and LIX, Paris, France)
Sabina Rossi (Venice, Italy)

James Harland (Australia) and Barry Jay (Australia) acted as TCS 2010 Chairs.

We take this occasion to thank the members of the Programme Committees and the external reviewers for the professional and timely work; the conference Chairs for their support; the invited speakers for their scholarly contribution; and of course the authors for submitting their work to TCS 2010.

May 2010

Cristian S. Calude
Vladimiro Sassone

Conference Organization

Local Organization

James Harland	RMIT University, Melbourne, Australia
Barry Jay	University of Technology, Sydney, Australia

Programme Chairs

Cristian Calude	University of Auckland, New Zealand
Vladimiro Sassone	University of Southampton, UK

Programme Committee

Area A

Valérie Berthé (Montpellier, France)
Cristian S. Calude (Auckland, New Zealand)
Cezar Câmpeanu (Charlottetown, Canada)
S. Barry Cooper (Leeds, UK)
Michael J. Dinneen (Auckland, New Zealand)
Rod Downey (Victoria, New Zealand)
Cunsheng Ding (Hong Kong)
Graham Farr (Melbourne, Australia)
Joachim Gudmundsson (Alexandria, Australia)
Lane A. Hemaspaandra (Rochester, USA)
Oscar H. Ibarra (Santa Barbara, USA)
Masami Ito (Kyoto, Japan)
Alexander Shen (Marseille, France)
Ludwig Staiger (Halle, Germany)
Frank Stephan (Singapore)
Ileana Streinu (Northampton, USA)
Kohtaro Tadaki (Tokyo, Japan)
Vincent Vajnovszki (Dijon, France)
Taso Viglas (Sydney, Australia)
Klaus Wagner (Würzburg, Germany)
Damien Woods (Seville, Spain)
Sheng Yu (London, Ont., Canada)

Area B

Stephen L Bloom (Stevens Institute, USA)
Roberto Bruni (Pisa, Italy)
Kostas Chatzikokolakis (CWI, The Netherlands)
Corina Cirstea (Southampton, UK)
Veronique Cortier (CNRS Loria, France)
Mariangiola Dezani (Turin, Italy)
Rob van Glabbeek (NICTA, Australia)
Atsushi Igarashi (Kyoto, Japan)
Alan Jeffrey (Bell Labs, USA)
He Jifeng (Shanghai, China)
Bartek Klin (Cambridge, UK)
Barbara König (Duisburg, Germany)
Dexter Kozen (Cornell, USA)
Marta Kwiatkowska (Oxford, UK)
Huimin Lin (Bejing, China)
Dale Miller (École Polytechnique, France)
Carroll Morgan (UNSW, Australia)
Doron Peled (Bar Ilan, Israel)
Sabina Rossi (Venice, Italy)
Vladimiro Sassone (Southampton, UK)
Thomas Schwentick (TU Dortmund, Germany)
Andrzej Tarlecki (Warsaw, Poland)
Yde Venema (Amsterdam, The Netherlands)

External Reviewers

Pieter Adriaans, George Barmpalias, Marta Bilkova, Filippo Bonchi, Andreas Brandstaedt, Doina Bucur, Haiming Chen, Vincenzo Ciancia, Qi Ge, Nils Gesbert, Silvia Ghilezan, Daniele Gorla, Nadia Kasto, Mark Kattenbelt, Yevgeny Kazakov Masoud Khosravani, Daisuke Kimura, Wojtek Kowalczyk, Benedikt Löwe, Satyaki Mahalanabis, Keiko Nakata, Lawrence Paulson, Gustavo Petri, Ilya Razenshteyn, Jan Rutten, Pawel Sobocinski, Frank Stephan, Santosh Vempala, Philipp Woelfel, Peng Wu.

Table of Contents

Convexity, Duality and Effects

Bart Jacobs

Institute for Computing and Information Sciences (iCIS),
Radboud University Nijmegen, The Netherlands
www.cs.ru.nl/B.Jacobs

Abstract. This paper describes some basic relationships between mathematical structures that are relevant in quantum logic and probability, namely convex sets, effect algebras, and a new class of functors that we call 'convex functors'; they include what are usually called probability distribution functors. These relationships take the form of three adjunctions. Two of these three are 'dual' adjunctions for convex sets, one time with the Boolean truth values $\{0, 1\}$ as dualising object, and one time with the probablity values $[0, 1]$. The third adjunction is between effect algebras and convex functors.

1 Introduction

A set X is commonly called convex if for each pair of elements $x, y \in X$ and each number $r \in [0, 1]$ in the unit interval of real numbers the 'convex' sum $rx + (1 - r)y$ is again in X. Informally this says that a whole line segment is contained in X as soon as the endpoints are in X. Convexity is of course a well-established notion that finds applications in for instance geometry, probability theory, optimisation, economics and quantum mechanics (with mixed states as convex combinations of pure states). The definition of convexity (as just given) assumes a monoidal structure $+$ on the set X and also a scalar multiplication $[0, 1] \times X \to X$. People have tried to capture this notion of convexity with fewer assumptions, see for instance [25], [27] or [12]. We shall use the latter source that involves a ternary operation $\langle -, -, - \rangle \colon [0, 1] \times X \times X \to X$ satisfying a couple of equations, see Definition 3. We first recall (see *e.g.* [28, 8, 20, 6, 11]) that such convex structures can equivalently be described uniformly as algebras of a monad, namely of the distribution monad $\mathcal{D}$, see Theorem 4. Such an algebra map gives an interpretation of each formal convex combination $r_1x_1 + \cdots + r_nx_n$, where $r_1 + \cdots + r_n = 1$, as a single element of X. This algebraic formulation of convexity yields a description of a familiar embedding construction as an adjunction between convex sets and modules, see Proposition 2 below.

The main part of this paper concerns duality for convex spaces. We shall describe two dual adjunctions:

$$\mathbf{PreFrm} \underset{Hom(-,\{0,1\})}{\overset{Hom(-,\{0,1\})}{\rightleftarrows}} \mathbf{Conv}^{\mathrm{op}} \underset{Hom(-,[0,1])}{\overset{Hom(-,[0,1])}{\leftrightarrows}} \mathbf{EA} \qquad (1)$$

namely in Theorems 9 and 17. This diagram involves the following structures.

C.S. Calude and V. Sassone (Eds.): TCS 2010, IFIP AICT 323, pp. 1–19, 2010.

- The category **Conv** of convex sets, with as special objects the two element set $2 = \{0, 1\}$ of Booleans and the unit interval $[0, 1]$ of probabilities—where $[0, 1] \cong \mathcal{D}(2)$.
- The category **PreFrm** of preframes: posets with directed joins and finite meets, distributing over these joins, see [19]. These preframes are slightly more general than frames (or complete Heyting algebras) that occur in the familiar duality with topological spaces, see [18].
- The category **EA** of effect algebras (from [9], see also [7] for an overview): effect algebras have arisen in the foundations of quantum mechanics and are used to capture quantum effects, as studied in quantum statistics and quantum measurement theory, see *e.g.* [4].

The diagram (1) thus suggests that convex sets form a setting in which one can study both Boolean and probabilistic logics. It opens up new questions, like: can the adjunctions be refined further so that one actually obtains equivalences, like between Stone spaces and Boolean algebras or between compact Hausdorff spaces and commutative C^*-algebras (see [18] for an overview). This is left to future work. Dualities are important in algebra, topology and logic, for transferring results and techniques from one domain to another. They are used in the semantics of computation (see *e.g.* [1, 29]), but are relatively new in a quantum setting. They may become part of what is called in [2] an "extensive network of interlocking analogies between physics, topology, logic and computer science".

In addition to the adjunctions in (1) another adjunction involving effect algebras is presented, namely a coreflection:

$$\mathbf{EA} \underset{F \mapsto F(2)}{\overset{\mathcal{D}}{\rightleftarrows}} \mathit{Conv}(\mathbf{Sets}) \quad (\bot) \tag{2}$$

between effect algebras and what we call convex endofunctors. These functors capture the essentials of the probability distribution functor (or monad), which is generalised here from taking probability values in $[0, 1]$ to taking values in an arbitrary effect algebra. We expect that the adjunction (2) can be used to build a "triangle of adjunctions" in the style of [5], relating scalars (or probabilities), convex monads, and Lawvere theories with partially additive structure.

The paper starts with a section on multiset and distribution monads over semirings, including an adjunction between their categories of algebras. Section 3 recalls in Theorem 4 how (real) convex sets can be described as algebras of the distribution monad. Subsequently, Section 4 describes the adjunction on the left in (1) between convex sets and preframes, via prime filters in convex sets and Scott-open filters in preframes. Both can be described via homomorphisms to the dualising object $\{0, 1\}$. The adjunction on the right in (1) requires that we first sketch the basics of effect algebras. This is done in Section 5. The unit interval $[0, 1]$ now serves as dualising object, where we note that effect algebra maps $E \to [0, 1]$ are commonly studied as states or measures in a quantum system. The paper concludes in Section 7 with the adjunction (2) between effect algebras and convex functors.

2 Multiset and Distribution Monads

This section describes the multiset monad $\mathcal{M}_S$, for a semiring S, and the distribution monad $\mathcal{D}$. The main result is an adjunction, in Proposition 2, between their categories of algebras. It is assumed that the reader is familiar with the basics of the theory of monads and their algebras. More information may be found in for instance [24, 3, 23].

Let S be a semiring, consisting of a commutative additive monoid $(S, +, 0)$ and a multiplicative monoid $(S, \cdot, 1)$, where multiplication distributes over addition. One can define a "multiset" functor $\mathcal{M}_S \colon \mathbf{Sets} \to \mathbf{Sets}$ by:

$$\mathcal{M}_S(X) \;=\; \{\varphi\colon X \to S \mid \operatorname{supp}(\varphi) \text{ is finite}\},$$

where $\operatorname{supp}(\varphi) = \{x \in X \mid \varphi(x) \neq 0\}$ is the support of φ. For a function $f\colon X \to Y$ one defines $\mathcal{M}_S(f)\colon \mathcal{M}_S(X) \to \mathcal{M}_S(Y)$ by:

$$\mathcal{M}_S(f)(\varphi)(y) \;=\; \textstyle\sum_{x\in f^{-1}(y)} \varphi(x). \tag{3}$$

Such a multiset $\varphi \in \mathcal{M}_s(X)$ may be written as formal sum $s_1x_1 + \cdots + s_kx_k$ where $\operatorname{supp}(\varphi) = \{x_1, \ldots, x_k\}$ and $s_i = \varphi(x_i) \in S$ describes the "multiplicity" of the element x_i. This formal sum notation might suggest an order $1, 2, \ldots k$ among the summands, but this sum is considered, up-to-permutation of the summands. Also, the same element $x \in X$ may be counted multiple times, but $s_1x + s_2x$ is considered to be the same as $(s_1 + s_2)x$ within such expressions. With this formal sum notation one can write the application of $\mathcal{M}_S$ on a map f as $\mathcal{M}_S(f)(\sum_i s_ix_i) = \sum_i s_if(x_i)$.

This multiset functor is a monad, whose unit $\eta\colon X \to \mathcal{M}_S(X)$ is $\eta(x) = 1x$, and multiplication $\mu\colon \mathcal{M}_S(\mathcal{M}_S(X)) \to \mathcal{M}_S(X)$ is $\mu(\sum_i s_i\varphi_i)(x) = \sum_i s_i \cdot \varphi_i(x)$.

For the semiring $S = \mathbb{N}$ one gets the free commutative monoid $\mathcal{M}_{\mathbb{N}}(X)$ on a set X. And if $S = \mathbb{Z}$ one obtains the free Abelian group $\mathcal{M}_{\mathbb{Z}}(X)$ on X. The Boolean semiring $2 = \{0, 1\}$ yields the finite powerset monad $\mathcal{P}_{fin} = \mathcal{M}_2$.

An (Eilenberg-Moore) algebra $\alpha\colon \mathcal{M}_S(X) \to X$ for the multiset monad corresponds to a monoid structure on X—given by $x + y = \alpha(1x + 1y)$—together with a scalar multiplication $\bullet\colon S \times X \to X$ given by $s \bullet x = \alpha(sx)$. It preserves the additive structure (of S and of X) in each coordinate separately. This makes X a module, for the semiring S. Conversely, such an S-module structure on a commutative monoid M yields an algebra $\mathcal{M}_S(M) \to M$ by $\sum_i s_ix_i \mapsto \sum_i s_i \bullet x_i$. Thus the category of algebras $Alg(\mathcal{M}_S)$ is equivalent to the category $\mathbf{Mod}_S$ of S-modules.

Analogously one defines the distribution monad $\mathcal{D}$ as:

$$\mathcal{D}(X) \;=\; \{\varphi\colon X \to [0,1] \mid \operatorname{supp}(\varphi) \text{ is finite and } \textstyle\sum_{x\in X} \varphi(x) = 1\}. \tag{4}$$

Elements of $\mathcal{D}(X)$ are convex combinations $s_1x_1 + \cdots + s_kx_k$, where the probabilities $s_i \in [0, 1]$ satisfy $\sum_i s_i = 1$. In Section 7 we shall see how one can generalise the set of probabilities from the unit interval $[0, 1]$ to an arbitrary effect algebra. Unit and multiplication making $\mathcal{D}$ a monad can be defined as for $\mathcal{M}_S$. This multiplication is well-defined since:

$$\sum_x \mu(\sum_i s_i\varphi_i)(x) = \sum_x \sum_i s_i \cdot \varphi_i(x) = \sum_i s_i \cdot \big(\sum_x \varphi_i(x)\big) = \sum_i s_i = 1.$$

The inclusion maps $\mathcal{D}(X) \hookrightarrow \mathcal{M}_{\mathbb{R}_{\geq 0}}(X)$, sending distributions to multisets over the non-negative real numbers $\mathbb{R}_{\geq 0}$, are natural and commute with the units and multiplications of the two monads, and thus form an example of a "map of monads".

We continue this section with a basic results, which is stated without proof, but with a few subsequent pointers.

Theorem 1. *For a monad T on* **Sets**, *the category $Alg(T)$ of algebras is:*

1. *both complete and cocomplete, so has all limits and colimits;*
2. *symmetric monoidal closed in case the monad T is "commutative".* □

A category of algebras is always "as complete" as its underlying category, see *e.g.* [23, 3]. Since **Sets** is complete, so is $Alg(T)$. Cocompleteness is special for algebras over **Sets** and follows from a result of Linton's, see [3, § 9.3, Prop. 4].

Monoidal structure in categories of algebras goes back to [22, 21]. Each monad on **Sets** is strong, via a "strength" map $\mathsf{st}\colon X \times T(Y) \to T(X \times Y)$ given as $\mathsf{st}(x, v) = T(\lambda y.\, \langle x, y\rangle)(v)$. There is also a swapped version $\mathsf{st}'\colon T(X) \times Y \to T(X \times Y)$ given by $\mathsf{st}'(u, y) = T(\lambda x.\, \langle x, y\rangle)(u)$. The monad T is called commutative if the two resulting maps $T(X) \times T(Y) \rightrightarrows T(X \times Y)$, obtained by either doing first st and st' or first st' and then st, are equal.

The multiset monad $\mathcal{M}_S$ is commutative if S is a (multiplicatively) commutative semiring. The distribution monad $\mathcal{D}$ is always commutative.

The next construction goes back to [27] and occurs in many places (see *e.g.* [26, 20]) but is usually not formulated in the following way. It can be understood as a representation theorem turning a convex set into a module over the nonnegative reals.

Proposition 2. *The functor* $\mathbf{Mod}_{\mathbb{R}_{\geq 0}} = Alg(\mathcal{M}_{\mathbb{R}_{\geq 0}}) \xrightarrow{U} Alg(\mathcal{D})$, *induced by the map of monads $\mathcal{D} \Rightarrow \mathcal{M}_{\mathbb{R}_{\geq 0}}$, has a left adjoint.*

Proof. We turn an algebra $\alpha\colon \mathcal{D}(X) \to X$ and into a module $F(X)$, where:

$$F(X) \;=\; \{0\} + \mathbb{R}_{>0} \times X,$$

with addition for $u, v \in F(X)$, in trivial cases given by $u + 0 = u = 0 + u$ and:

$$(s, x) + (t, y) \;=\; (s + t, \alpha(\tfrac{s}{s+t}x + \tfrac{t}{s+t}y))$$

A scalar multiplication $\bullet\colon \mathbb{R}_{\geq 0} \times F(X) \to F(X)$ is defined as:

$$s \bullet u \;=\; \begin{cases} 0 & \text{if } u = 0 \text{ or } s = 0 \\ (s \cdot t, x) & \text{if } u = (t, x) \text{ and } s \neq 0. \end{cases}$$

This makes $F(X)$ a module over $\mathbb{R}_{\geq 0}$. Next we show that F is left adjoint to $U\colon \mathit{Alg}(\mathcal{M}_{\mathbb{R}_{\geq 0}}) \to \mathit{Alg}(\mathcal{D})$, via the following bijective correspondence.

$$\frac{X \xrightarrow{\;f\;} U(Y) \qquad \text{in } \mathit{Alg}(\mathcal{D})}{F(X) \xrightarrow[\;g\;]{} Y \qquad \text{in } \mathit{Alg}(\mathcal{M}_{\mathbb{R}_{\geq 0}})}$$

It works as follows.

- Given $f\colon X \to U(Y)$ in $\mathit{Alg}(\mathcal{D})$ define $\overline{f}\colon F(X) \to Y$ by $\overline{f}(0) = 0$ and $\overline{f}(r, x) = r \bullet f(x)$ where $\bullet$ is scalar multiplication in Y. This yields a homomorphism of modules, *i.e.* a homomorphism of $\mathcal{M}_{\mathbb{R}_{\geq 0}}$-algebras.
- Conversely, given $g\colon F(X) \to Y$ take $\overline{g}\colon X \to U(Y)$ to be $\overline{g}(x) = g(1, x)$. This yields a map of $\mathcal{D}$-algebras.

Finally we check that we actually have a bijective correspondence:

$$\overline{\overline{f}}(x) = \overline{f}(1, x) = 1 \bullet f(x) = f(x).$$

Similarly, $\overline{\overline{g}}(0) = 0$ and:

$$\overline{\overline{g}}(r, x) = r \bullet \overline{g}(x) = r \bullet g(1, x) = g(r \bullet (1, x)) = g(r, x). \qquad \square$$

3 Convex Sets

This section introduces convex structures—or simply, convex sets—as described in [12] and recalls that such structures can also be described as algebras of the distribution monad $\mathcal{D}$.

Definition 3. *A convex set consists of a set X together with a ternary operation $\langle -, -, - \rangle\colon [0, 1] \times X \times X \to X$ satisfying the following four requirements,*

$$\begin{aligned} \langle r, x, x \rangle &= x & \langle r, x, y \rangle &= \langle 1 - r, y, x \rangle \\ \langle 0, x, y \rangle &= y & \langle r, x, \langle s, y, z \rangle\rangle &= \langle r + (1 - r)s,\ \langle \tfrac{r}{(r+(1-r)s)}, x, y \rangle,\ z \rangle, \end{aligned}$$

where $r \in [0, 1]$ and $x, y, z \in X$, and $(r + (1 - r)s) \neq 0$ in the last equation.

A morphism of convex structures $(X, \langle -, -, - \rangle_X) \to (Y, \langle -, -, - \rangle_Y)$ consists of an "affine" function $f\colon X \to Y$ satisfying $f(\langle r, x, x' \rangle_X) = \langle r, f(x), f(x') \rangle_Y$, for all $r \in [0, 1]$ and $x, x' \in X$. This yields a category **Conv**.

A convex set is sometimes called a barycentric algebra, using terminology from [27]. The tuple $\langle r, x, y \rangle$ can also be written as labeled sum $x +_r y$, like in [20], but the fourth condition becomes a bit difficult to read with this notation.

The next result recalls an alternative description of convex structures and their homomorphisms, namely as algebras of a monad. It goes back to [28] and also applies to compact Hausdorff spaces [20] or Polish spaces [6]. For convenience, a proof sketch is included.

Theorem 4. *The category* **Conv** *of convex sets is isomorphic to the category Alg($\mathcal{D}$) of Eilenberg-Moore algebras of the distribution monad.*

Proof. Given an algebra $\alpha\colon \mathcal{D}(X) \to X$ on a set X one defines an operation $\langle -,-,-\rangle\colon [0,1] \times X \times X \to X$ by $\langle r,x,y\rangle = \alpha(rx + (1-r)y)$. It is not hard to show that the four requirements from Definition 3 hold.

Conversely, given a convex set X with ternary operation $\langle -,-,-\rangle$ one defines a function $\alpha\colon \mathcal{D}(X) \to X$ inductively by:

$$\alpha(r_1x_1 + \cdots + r_nx_n) = \begin{cases} x_1 & \text{if } r_1 = 1, \text{ so } r_2 = \cdots = r_n = 0 \\ \langle r_1, x_1, \alpha(\frac{r_2}{1-r_1}x_2 + \cdots + \frac{r_n}{1-r_1}x_n)\rangle & \text{otherwise, } i.e.\ r_1 < 1. \end{cases} \tag{5}$$

Repeated application of this definition yields:

$$\alpha(r_1x_1 + \cdots + r_nx_n) = \langle r_1, x_1, \langle \tfrac{r_2}{1-r_1}, x_2, \langle \tfrac{r_3}{1-r_1-r_2}, x_3, \langle \ldots, \langle \tfrac{r_{n-1}}{1-r_1-\cdots-r_{n-2}}, x_{n-1}, x_n\rangle \ldots \rangle\rangle\rangle\rangle. \tag{6}$$

One first has to show that the function α in (5) is well-defined, in the sense that it does not depend on permutations of summands, see also [27, Lemma 2]. Via some elementary calculations one checks that exchanging the summands r_ix_i and $r_{i+1}x_{i+1}$ produces the same result. In a next step one proves the algebra equations: $\alpha \circ \eta = \mathrm{id}$ and $\alpha \circ \mu = \alpha \circ \mathcal{D}(\alpha)$. The first one is easy, since $\alpha(\eta(a)) = \alpha(1a) = a$, directly by applying (5). The second one requires more work. Explicitly, it amounts to:

$$\alpha\big(\textstyle\sum_{i\le n} r_i\alpha(\sum_{j\le m_i} s_{ij}x_{ij})\big) = \alpha\big(\sum_{i\le n}\sum_{j\le m_i}(r_is_{ij})x_{ij}\big). \tag{7}$$

For the proof the following auxiliary result is convenient. It handles nested tuples in the second argument of a triple $\langle -,-,-\rangle$, just like the fourth equation in Definition 3 deals with nested structure in the third argument. In a general convex structure one has $\langle r, \langle s,x,y\rangle, z\rangle = \langle rs, x, \langle \frac{r(1-s)}{1-rs}, y, z\rangle\rangle$, assuming $rs \neq 1$. The rest is then left to the reader. □

This theorem now allows us to apply Theorem 1 to the category **Conv** of (real) convex structures. First we may conclude that it is both complete and cocomplete; also, that the forgetful functor **Conv** $\to$ **Sets** has a left adjoint, giving free convex structures of the form $\mathcal{D}(X)$. And since $\mathcal{D}$ is a commutative monad, the category **Conv** is symmetric monoidal closed: maps $X \otimes Y \to Z$ in **Conv** correspond to functions $X \times Y \to Z$ that are "bi-homomorphisms", *i.e.* homomorphisms of convex structures in each variable separately. In this special case the tensor unit is the final (singleton) convex set, since $\mathcal{D}(1) \cong 1$. Hence one has "tensors with projections", see [15]. Closedness means that the functors $(-)\otimes Y$ have a right adjoint, given by $Y \multimap (-)$. Moreover, $\mathcal{D}(A \times B) \cong \mathcal{D}(A) \otimes \mathcal{D}(B)$, for sets A, B.

Remark 5. *We shall later use that a meet semilattice* $(L, \wedge, 0)$ *can be understood as a convex set* $\mathcal{D}(L) \to L$ *via:*

$$r_1 x_1 + \cdots + r_n x_n \longmapsto x_1 \wedge \cdots \wedge x_n,$$

where it is (implicitly) assume that $r_i \neq 0$. *This can be extended to a functor* **MSL** $\to$ **Conv**. *In particular, the two-element set* $2 = \{0, 1\}$ *of Booleans is a convex set.*

Remark 6. *The adjunction* **Conv** $= \mathit{Alg}(\mathcal{D}) \leftrightarrows$ **Sets** *induces a comonad on the category* **Conv**, *which is also written as* $\mathcal{D}$. *An Eilenberg-Moore coalgebra* $X \to \mathcal{D}(X)$ *of this comonad can be understood as spectral decomposition: it maps an element* x *in a convex set* X *to a formal convex combination* $\sum_i r_i x_i$, *which, when interpreted in* X, *is equal to* x. *For instance, the density matrices on a finite dimensional Hilbert space form a convex set and carry such a spectral decomposition coalgebra (depending on a choice of basis). See also [14] for similar decompositions involving atoms and compact elements in ordered sets captured via the comonad induced on a category of algebras.*

4 Prime Filters in Convex Sets

The next definition follows [8], but uses filters instead of ideals.

Definition 7. *Let* $\alpha \colon \mathcal{D}(X) \to X$ *be an algebra of the distribution monad* $\mathcal{D}$, *making* X *a convex set. We write* $(\sum_{i \leq n} s_i x_i) \in \mathcal{D}(X)$, *with* $s_i \neq 0$, *for an arbitrary formal convex combination. A subset* $U \subseteq X$ *is called a:*

- *subalgebra if* $\forall_{i \leq n}. x_i \in U$ *implies* $\alpha(\sum_i s_i x_i) \in U$;
- *filter if* $\alpha(\sum_i s_i x_i) \in U$ *implies* $x_i \in U$, *for each* i;
- *prime filter if it is both a subalgebra and a filter.*

It is not hard to see that subalgebras are closed under arbitrary intersections and under directed joins. Hence one can form the least subalgebra $\overline{V} \subseteq X$ containing an arbitrary set $V \subseteq X$, by intersection. Filters are closed under arbitrary intersections and joins, hence also prime filters are closed under arbitrary intersections and directed joins. We shall write $\mathit{pFil}(X)$ for the set of prime filters in a convex set X, ordered by inclusion.

Lemma 8. *Assume* X *is a convex set. A subset* $U \subseteq X$ *is a prime filter if and only if it is the "true kernel"* $f^{-1}(1)$ *of a homomorphism of convex sets* $f \colon X \to \{0, 1\}$. *It yields an order isomomorphism:*

$$\mathit{pFil}(X) \cong \mathit{Hom}(X, \{0, 1\}).$$

Here we consider $\{0, 1\}$ *as meet semilattice as described in Remark 5.*

Proof. Let $\alpha\colon \mathcal{D}(X) \to X$ be an algebra on X. Given a prime filter $U \subseteq X$, define $f_U(x) = 1$ iff $x \in U$. This yields a homormophism of algebras/convex sets, since for a convex sum $\sum_i s_i x_i$ with $s_i \neq 0$,

$$\begin{aligned}
(f_U \circ \alpha)(\textstyle\sum_i s_i x_i) = 1 &\iff \alpha(\textstyle\sum_i s_i x_i) \in U \\
&\iff \forall_i.\, x_i \in U \qquad \text{since } U \text{ is a prime filter} \\
&\iff \forall_i.\, f_U(x_i) = 1 \\
&\iff \textstyle\sum_i s_i f_U(x) = \bigwedge_i f_U(x_i) = 1 \\
&\iff (\beta \circ \mathcal{D}_S(f_U))(\textstyle\sum_i s_i x_i) = 1,
\end{aligned}$$

where $\beta\colon \mathcal{D}(\{0,1\}) \to \{0,1\}$ is the convex structure induced by the meet semilattice structure of $\{0,1\}$. Similarly one shows that such homomorphisms induce prime filters as their true-kernels. □

We write **PreFrm** for the category of preframes. They consist of a poset L with directed joins $\bigvee^{\uparrow}$ and finite meets $(1, \wedge)$ distributing over these joins: $x \wedge \bigvee^{\uparrow}_i y_i = \bigvee^{\uparrow}_i x \wedge y_i$. Morphisms in **PreFrm** preserve both finite meets and directed joins. The two-element set $\{0,1\}$ is obviously a preframe. Homomorphisms of preframes $L \to \{0,1\}$ correspond (as true-kernels) to Scott-open filters $U \subseteq L$, see [29]. They are upsets, closed under finite meets, with the property that if $\bigvee^{\uparrow}_i x_i \in U$ then $x_i \in U$ for some i.

We have seen so far that taking prime filters yields a contravariant functor $pFil = Hom(-,\{0,1\})\colon \mathbf{Conv} = Alg(\mathcal{D}) \to \mathbf{PreFrm}$. The main result of this section shows that this forms actually a (dual) adjunction.

Theorem 9. *There is a dual adjunction between convex sets and preframes:*

$$\mathbf{Conv}^{\mathrm{op}} \underset{Hom(-,\{0,1\})}{\overset{Hom(-,\{0,1\})}{\rightleftarrows}} \mathbf{PreFrm} \qquad (\bot)$$

Proof. For a preframe L the homset $Hom(L,\{0,1\})$ of Scott-open filters is closed under finite intersections: if $\bigvee^{\uparrow}_i x_i \in U_1 \cap \cdots \cap U_m$, then for each $j \leq m$ there is an i_j with $x_j \in U_{i_j}$. By directedness there is an i with $x_i \geq x_{i_j}$ for each j, so that x_i is in each U_j. Hence, $Hom(L,\{0,1\})$ carries a $\mathcal{D}$-algebra structure.

For a convex set X we need to construct a bijective correspondence:

$$\frac{X \longrightarrow Hom(L,\{0,1\}) \qquad \text{in } \mathbf{Conv}}{L \longrightarrow Hom(X,\{0,1\}) \qquad \text{in } \mathbf{PreFrm}}$$

It is given in the usual way by swapping arguments. □

Homomorphisms from convex sets to the set of Boolean values $\{0,1\}$ capture only a part of what is going on. Richer structures arise via homomorphisms to the unit interval $[0,1]$. They give rise to effect algebras, instead of preframes, as will be shown in the next two sections.

5 Effect Algebras

This section recalls the basic definition, examples and results of effect algebras. To start, we need the notion of partial commutative monoid (PCM). It consists of a set M with a zero element $0 \in M$ and a partial binary operation $\ovee\colon M \times M \to M$ satisfying the three requirements below—involving the notation $x \perp y$ for: $x \ovee y$ is defined.

1. Commutativity: $x \perp y$ implies $y \perp x$ and $x \ovee y = y \ovee x$;
2. Associativity: $y \perp z$ and $x \perp (y \ovee z)$ implies $x \perp y$ and $(x \ovee y) \perp z$ and also $x \ovee (y \ovee z) = (x \ovee y) \ovee z$;
3. Zero: $0 \perp x$ and $0 \ovee x = x$;

When $x \perp y$ we say that elements x, y are orthogonal. More generally, a subset of a PCM is called orthogonal if all its elements are pairwise orthogonal. In writing $x \ovee y$ it is usually implicitly assumed that $x \ovee y$ is defined, *i.e.* that x, y are orthogonal.

An example of a PCM is the unit interval $[0, 1]$ of real numbers, where $\ovee$ is the partially defined sum $+$. The notation $\ovee$ for the sum might suggest a join, but this is not intended, as the example $[0, 1]$ shows. We wish to avoid the notation $\oplus$ (and its dual $\otimes$) that is more common in the context of effect algebras because we like to reserve these operations $\oplus, \otimes$ for tensors on categories.

As an aside, for the more categorically minded, a PCM may also be understood as a monoid in the category of sets and partial functions. However, we shall use total maps as morphisms between PCMs (and effect algebras).

The notion of effect algebra is due to [9], see also [7] for an overview.

Definition 10. *An effect algebra is a partial commutative monoid $(E, 0, \ovee)$ with an orthosupplement. The latter is a unary operation $(-)^{\perp}\colon E \to E$ satisfying:*

1. $x^{\perp} \in E$ is the unique element in E with $x \ovee x^{\perp} = 1$, where $1 = 0^{\perp}$;
2. $x \perp 1 \Rightarrow x = 0$.

Example 11. *We briefly discuss several classes of examples.*

(1) A singleton set forms an example of a degenerate effect algebra, with $0 = 1$. A two element set $2 = \{0, 1\}$ is also an example.

(2) A more interesting example is the unit interval $[0, 1] \subseteq \mathbb{R}$ of real numbers, with $r^{\perp} = 1 - r$ and $r \ovee s$ is defined as $r + s$ in case this sum is in $[0, 1]$. In fact, for each positive number $M \in \mathbb{R}$ the interval $[0, M]_{\mathbb{R}} = \{r \in \mathbb{R} \mid 0 \leq r \leq M\}$ is an example of an effect algebra, with $r^{\perp} = M - r$.

Also the interval $[0, M]_{\mathbb{Q}} = \{q \in \mathbb{Q} \mid 0 \leq q \leq M\}$ of rational numbers, for positive $M \in \mathbb{Q}$, is an effect algebra. And so is the interval $[0, M]_{\mathbb{N}}$ of natural numbers, for $M \in \mathbb{N}$.

The general situation involves so-called "interval effect algebras", see e.g. [10] or [7, 1.4]. An Abelian group $(G, 0, -, +)$ is called ordered if it carries a partial order $\leq$ such that $a \leq b$ implies $a + c \leq b + c$, for all $a, b, c \in G$. A positive point is an element $p \in G$ with $p \geq 0$. For such a point we write $[0, p]_G \subseteq G$ for the "interval" $[0, p] = \{a \in G \mid 0 \leq a \leq p\}$. It forms an effect algebra with p as top, *orthosupplement* $a^\perp = p - a$, *and sum* $a + b$, *which is considered to be defined in case* $a + b \leq p$.

(3) *A separate class of examples has a join as sum* $\ovee$. *Let* $(L, \vee, 0, (-)^\perp)$ *be an ortholattice:* $\vee, 0$ *are finite joins and complementation* $(-)^\perp$ *satisfies* $x \leq y \Rightarrow y^\perp \leq x^\perp$, $x^{\perp\perp} = x$ *and* $x \vee x^\perp = 1 = 0^\perp$. *This* L *is called an orthomodular lattice if* $x \leq y$ *implies* $y = x \vee (x^\perp \wedge y)$. *Such an orthomodular lattice forms an effect algebra in which* $x \ovee y$ *is defined if and only if* $x \perp y$ *(i.e.* $x \leq y^\perp$, *or equivalently,* $y \leq x^\perp$*); and in that case* $x \ovee y = x \vee y$. *This restriction of* $\vee$ *is needed for the validity of requirements (1) and (2) in Definition 10.*

In particular, the lattice $\mathrm{KSub}(H)$ *of closed subsets of a Hilbert space* H *is an orthomodular lattice and thus an effect algebra. This applies more generally to the kernel subobjects of an object in a dagger kernel category [13]. These kernels can also be described as self-adjoint endomaps below the identity, see [13, Prop. 12]—in group-representation style, like in the above point 2.*

(4) *Since Boolean algebras are (distributive) orthomodular lattices, they are also effect algebras. By distributivity, elements in a Boolean algebra are orthogonal if and only if they are disjoint, i.e.* $x \perp y$ *iff* $x \wedge y = 0$. *In particular, the Boolean algebra of measurable subsets of a measurable space forms an effect algebra, where* $U \ovee V$ *is defined if* $U \cap V = \emptyset$, *and is then equal to* $U \cup V$.

An obvious next step is to organise effect algebras into a category **EA**.

Definition 12. *A homomorphism* $E \to D$ *of effect algebras is given by a function* $f \colon E \to D$ *between the underlying sets satisfying* $f(1) = 1$, *and if* $x \perp x'$ *in* E *then both* $f(x) \perp f(x')$ *in* D *and* $f(x \ovee x') = f(x) \ovee f(x')$.

Effect algebras and their homomorphisms form a category, called **EA**.

Homomorphisms are like measurable maps. Indeed, for the effect algebra Σ associated in Example 11 (4) with a measureable space (X, Σ), effect algebra homomorphisms $f \colon \Sigma \to [0, 1]$ satisfy $f(U \cup V) = f(U) + f(V)$ in case U, V are disjoint—because then $U \ovee V$ is defined and equals $U \cup V$. In general, effect algebra homomorphisms $E \to [0, 1]$ to the unit interval are often called states.

Homomorphisms of effect algebras preserve all the relevant structure.

Lemma 13. *Let* $f \colon E \to D$ *be a homomorphism of effect algebras. Then:*

$$f(x^\perp) = f(x)^\perp \quad \text{and thus} \quad f(0) = 0.$$

Proof. From $1 = f(1) = f(x \ovee x^\perp) = f(x) \ovee f(x^\perp)$ we get $f(x^\perp) = f(x)^\perp$ by uniqueness of orthosupplements. Hence: $f(0) = f(1^\perp) = f(1)^\perp = 1^\perp = 0$. □

Example 14. *It is not hard to see that the one-element effect algebra* 1 *is final, and the two-element effect algebra* 2 *is initial.*

Orthosupplement $(-)^\perp$ *is an isomorphism* $E \xrightarrow{\cong} E^{\mathrm{op}}$ *in* **EA**, *namely from* $(E, 0, \ovee, (-)^\perp)$ *to* $E^{\mathrm{op}} = (E, 1, \owedge, (-)^\perp)$, *where* $x \owedge y = (x^\perp \ovee y^\perp)^\perp$. *This makes* **EA** *and involutive category, see [16].*

An element (or point) $x \in E$ of an effect algebra E can be identified with a homomorphism $2 \times 2 \to E$ in **EA**, *as in:*

$$2 \times 2 = \mathsf{MO}(2) = \left(\begin{array}{c} \bullet \overset{1}{\underset{0}{\diamond}} \bullet^{\perp} \end{array} \right) \xrightarrow{\ \ x\ \ } E.$$

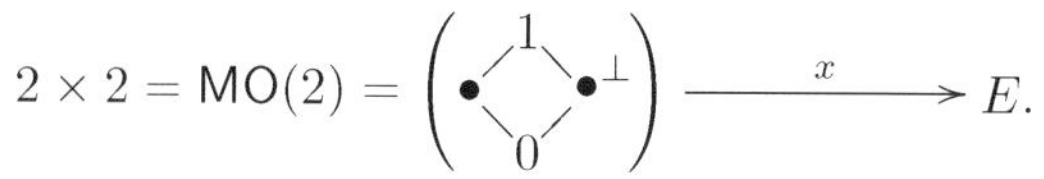

In [17] it shown that the category **EA** is complete and cocomplete, and has a symmetric monoidal structure.

6   Effect Algebras and Convex Sets

The aim in this section is to establish the dual adjunction between convex sets and effect algebras on the right in the diagram (1) in the introduction. As we have seen, the unit interval $[0,1]$ of real numbers is a prime example of a convex set. The set of states of an effect algebra—consisting of maps into $[0,1]$—is also convex, as noticed for instance in [10].

Lemma 15. *Taking states yields a functor $\mathcal{S} = \mathrm{Hom}(-, [0,1]) \colon \mathbf{EA} \to \mathbf{Conv}^{\mathrm{op}}$.*

Proof. Let E be an effect algebra with states $f_i \colon E \to [0,1]$ and $r_i \in [0,1]$ with $\sum_i r_i = 1$, then we can form a new state $f = r_1 f_1 + \cdots + r_n f_n$ by $f(x) = \sum_i r_i \cdot f_i(x)$, using multiplication $\cdot$ in $[0,1]$. This yields a homomorphism of effect algebras $E \to [0,1]$, since:

- $f(1) = \sum_i r_i \cdot f_i(1) = \sum_i r_i \cdot 1 = \sum_i r_i = 1$;
- if $x \perp x'$ in E, then in $[0,1]$:

$$
\begin{aligned}
f(x \varovee x') &= \sum_i r_i \cdot f_i(x \varovee x') &= \sum_i r_i \cdot (f_i(x) + f_i(x')) \\
&&= \sum_i r_i \cdot f_i(x) + r_i \cdot f_i(x') \\
&&= \sum_i r_i \cdot f_i(x) + \sum_i r_i \cdot f_i(x') \\
&&= f(x) + f(x').
\end{aligned}
$$

Further, for a map of effect algebras $g \colon E \to D$ the induced function $\mathcal{S}(g) = (-) \circ g \colon \mathrm{Hom}(D, [0,1]) \to \mathrm{Hom}(E, [0,1])$ is a map of convex sets:

$$
\begin{aligned}
\mathcal{S}(g)(\textstyle\sum_i r_i f_i) &= \lambda x.\, (\textstyle\sum_i r_i f_i)(g(x)) \\
&= \lambda x.\, \textstyle\sum_i r_i \cdot f_i(g(x)) \\
&= \lambda x.\, \textstyle\sum_i r_i \cdot \mathcal{S}(g)(f_i)(x) \\
&= \textstyle\sum_i r_i (\mathcal{S}(g)(f_i)).
\end{aligned}
$$

A set of state $\mathcal{S}(E) = \mathrm{Hom}(E, [0,1])$ is thus convex, but it does not have an underlying scalar multiplication $\bullet \colon [0,1] \times \mathcal{S}(E) \to \mathcal{S}(E)$, since $r \bullet f = \lambda x.\, r \cdot f(x)$ need not be a map of effect algebras: $(r \bullet f)(1) = r \cdot f(1) = r \cdot 1 = r \neq 1$, in general.

Interestingly, there is also a Hom functor in the other direction.

Lemma 16. *For each convex set X the homset $Hom(X, [0,1])$ of homomorphisms of convex sets is an effect algebra. In this way one gets a functor $Hom(-, [0,1])\colon \mathbf{Conv}^{\mathrm{op}} \to \mathbf{EA}$.*

Proof. Let X be a convex set. We define effect algebra structure on the homset $Hom(X, [0,1])$ in a pointwise manner. There is an obvious zero element, namely the zero function $\lambda x.\, 0$. A partial sum $f + f'$ is defined as $(f + f')(x) = f(x) + f'(x)$, provided $f(x) + f'(x) \leq 1$ for all $x \in X$. It is easy to see that this $f + f'$ is again a map of convex sets. Similarly, one defines $f^{\perp} = \lambda x.\, 1 - f(x)$, which is again a homomorphism since:

$$\begin{aligned} f^{\perp}(r_1x_1 + \cdots + r_nx_n) &= 1 - f(r_1x_1 + \cdots + r_nx_n) \\ &= (r_1 + \cdots + r_n) - (r_1 \cdot f(x_1) + \cdots + r_n \cdot f(x_n)) \\ &= r_1 \cdot (1 - f(x_1)) + \cdots + r_n \cdot (1 - f(x_n)) \\ &= r_1 \cdot f^{\perp}(x_1) + \cdots + r_n \cdot f^{\perp}(x_n). \end{aligned}$$

Functoriality is easy: for a map $g\colon X \to Y$ of convex sets we obtain a map of effect algebras $(-) \circ g\colon Hom(Y, [0,1]) \to Hom(X, [0,1])$ by precomposition. □

The next result is now an easy combination of the previous two lemmas.

Theorem 17. *There is a dual adjunction between convex sets and effect algebras:*

$$\mathbf{Conv}^{\mathrm{op}} \underset{Hom(-,[0,1])}{\overset{\mathcal{S}=Hom(-,[0,1])}{\rightleftarrows}} \mathbf{EA} \quad (\perp)$$

Proof. We need to check that the unit and counit

$$\begin{array}{rcl} E & \xrightarrow{\eta} & Hom(\mathcal{S}(E), [0,1]) \\ x & \longmapsto & \lambda f.\, f(x) \end{array} \qquad \begin{array}{rcl} X & \xrightarrow{\varepsilon} & \mathcal{S}(Hom(X, [0,1])) \\ x & \longmapsto & \lambda f.\, f(x) \end{array}$$

are appropriate maps. First we check that η is a morphism of effect algebras:

- $\eta(1) = \lambda f.\, f(1) = \lambda f.\, 1 = 1$;
- and if $x \perp x'$ in E, then:

$$\begin{aligned} \eta(x \ovee x') = \lambda f.\, f(x \ovee x') &= \lambda f.\, f(x) + f(x') \\ &= \lambda f.\, \eta(x)(f) + \eta(x')(f) \\ &= \eta(x) + \eta(x'). \end{aligned}$$

Similarly ε is a map of convex sets:

$$\begin{aligned} \varepsilon(r_1x_1 + \cdots + r_nx_n) &= \lambda f.\, f(r_1x_1 + \cdots + r_nx_n) \\ &= \lambda f.\, r_1 \cdot f(x_1) + \cdots + r_n \cdot f(x_n) \\ &= \lambda f.\, r_1 \cdot \varepsilon(x_1)(f) + \cdots + r_n \cdot \varepsilon(x_n)(f) \\ &= r_1\varepsilon(x_1) + \cdots + r_n\varepsilon(x_n). \end{aligned}$$

□

7 Effect Algebras and Convex Functors

Let **A** be an arbitrary category with finite limits and finite coproducts $(0, +)$ which are disjoint and universal. This means that coprojections κ_i are monic and form pullback squares as on the left below, and additionally that in a square as on the right below, the induced map $Z_1 + Z_2 \to Z$ is an isomorphism.

$$\begin{array}{ccc} 0 & \longrightarrow & Y \\ \downarrow & \lrcorner & \downarrow{\scriptstyle \kappa_2} \\ X & \xrightarrow[\kappa_1]{} & X+Y \end{array} \qquad\qquad \begin{array}{ccccc} Z_1 & \longrightarrow & Z & \longleftarrow & Z_2 \\ \downarrow & \lrcorner & \downarrow & \llcorner & \downarrow \\ X & \xrightarrow[\kappa_1]{} & X+Y & \xleftarrow[\kappa_2]{} & Y \end{array}$$

In this setting one can prove that diagrams of the form below are pullbacks.

$$\begin{array}{ccc} X & \xrightarrow{\kappa_1} & X+Z \\ {\scriptstyle f}\downarrow & \lrcorner & \downarrow{\scriptstyle f+g} \\ Y & \xrightarrow[\kappa_1]{} & Y+Z \end{array} \qquad\qquad \begin{array}{ccc} X+W & \xrightarrow{f+\mathrm{id}} & Y+W \\ {\scriptstyle \mathrm{id}+g}\downarrow & \lrcorner & \downarrow{\scriptstyle \mathrm{id}+g} \\ X+Z & \xrightarrow[f+\mathrm{id}]{} & Y+Z \end{array} \tag{8}$$

The final object $1 \in \mathbf{A}$ can be used to obtain (representations of) natural numbers $\underline{n} \in \mathbf{A}$, for $n \in \mathbb{N}$. One simply puts:

$$\underline{0} = 0 \qquad \text{and} \qquad \underline{n+1} = \underline{n} + 1.$$

We shall use these "numbers" $\underline{n} \in \mathbf{A}$ with coprojections $\kappa_i \colon 1 \to \underline{n}$ for $1 \le i \le n$. The following maps will be useful.

$$\underline{n+1} \xrightarrow{\nabla_i} \underline{2} \quad \text{where} \quad \nabla_i \circ \kappa_j = \begin{cases} \kappa_1 & \text{if } i = j \\ \kappa_2 & \text{otherwise} \end{cases} \tag{9}$$

(where $0 \le i \le n$ and $0 \le j \le n+1$). Writing the underlining gets tedious, so we often drop it when no confusion arises.

In **Sets** we identify n (to be more precise: $\underline{n}$) with the set $\{1, 2, \ldots, n\}$. The coprojection $\kappa_i \colon 1 \to n$ is then simply i. The maps $\nabla_i \colon n+1 \to 2$ from (9), for $1 \le i \le n$, satisfy $\nabla_i(j) = 1$ if $i = j$ and $\nabla_i(j) = 2$ if $i \ne j$.

We are now ready to introduce a new notion of convex functor. What we present is finitary version, because in the present context we only consider finite convex combinations, and correspondingly, finite (partial) sums in effect algebras.

Definition 18. *Let* **A** *be a category with disjoint and universal finite coproducts, and finite limits (as above). A functor $F \colon \mathbf{A} \to \mathbf{A}$ will be called* convex *if it satisfies the following three requirements.*

1. $F(1) \xrightarrow{\cong} 1$;
2. *F preserves the following three pullbacks, which are special instances of (8).*

$$\begin{array}{ccc} n & \xrightarrow{\kappa_1} & n+1 \\ {\scriptstyle !}\downarrow & \lrcorner & \downarrow{\scriptstyle !+\mathrm{id}} \\ 1 & \xrightarrow[\kappa_1]{} & 1+1=2 \end{array} \qquad \begin{array}{ccc} 1 & \xrightarrow{\kappa_1} & 1+n \\ \| & \lrcorner & \downarrow{\scriptstyle \mathrm{id}+!} \\ 1 & \xrightarrow[\kappa_1]{} & 1+1=2 \end{array} \qquad \begin{array}{ccc} n+m & \xrightarrow{!+\mathrm{id}} & 1+m \\ {\scriptstyle \mathrm{id}+!}\downarrow & \lrcorner & \downarrow{\scriptstyle \mathrm{id}+!} \\ n+1 & \xrightarrow[!+\mathrm{id}]{} & 1+1=2 \end{array} \tag{10}$$

3. the following tuple is monic, involving the maps ∇_i *from (9).*

$$F(\underline{n+1}) \xrightarrow{\langle F(\nabla_1),\ldots,F(\nabla_n)\rangle} F(2) \times \cdots \times F(2). \tag{11}$$

*We shall write CNV(***A***) for the category of convex endofunctors on* **A***, and natural transformations between them.*

Convexity can in principle also be defined for functors $\mathbf{A} \to \mathbf{B}$ between different categories, but such generality is not needed here. A functor F satisfying the first requirement $F(1) \cong 1$ is sometimes called *affine*, see *e.g.* [21, 15].

Example 19. *We shall shortly see a general construction to obtain convex functors in the form of probability distribution functors. But it is instructive to see a non-example first. The non-empty powerset functor* $\mathcal{P}^+ \colon \mathbf{Sets} \to \mathbf{Sets}$ *is a possible candidate for a convex functor because* $\mathcal{P}^+(1) \cong 1$*. We shall skip the second condition in Definition 18 and show why the third one fails. The maps* $\mathcal{P}^+(\nabla_i) \colon \mathcal{P}^+(n+1) \to \mathcal{P}^+(2)$ *are given by:*

$$\mathcal{P}^+(\nabla_i)(U) \;=\; \{1 \mid i \in U\} \cup \{2 \mid U - i \neq \emptyset\}.$$

If $U, V \in \mathcal{P}^+(n+1)$ *satisfy* $\mathcal{P}^+(\nabla_i)(U) = \mathcal{P}^+(\nabla_i)(V)$*, then we have* $i \in U \Leftrightarrow i \in V$ *for* $1 \leq i \leq n$*. But we have no information about whether or not* $n+1$ *is in* U *or* V*. Hence we don't have enough information to conclude* $U = V$*.*

The following construction gives an important class of examples of convex functors on the category of sets. It generalises the construction of the distribution functor $\mathcal{D}$ in (4) from the unit interval $[0,1]$ to an arbitrary effect algebra.

Definition 20. *For an effect algebra* E *define a functor* $\mathcal{D}_E \colon \mathbf{Sets} \to \mathbf{Sets}$ *by:*

$$\mathcal{D}_E(X) \;=\; \{\varphi \colon X \to E \mid \mathrm{supp}(\varphi) \textit{ is finite and orthogonal, and } \textstyle\bigovee_{x\in E} \varphi(x) = 1\}.$$

For a function $f \colon X \to Y$ *one gets* $\mathcal{D}_E(f) \colon \mathcal{D}_E(X) \to \mathcal{D}_E(Y)$ *by:*

$$\mathcal{D}_E(f)(\varphi)(y) \;=\; \bigovee_{x \in f^{-1}(y)} \varphi(x).$$

Proposition 21. *Functors* $\mathcal{D}_E$ *are convex, and satisfy* $\mathcal{D}_E(2) \cong E$*. The mapping* $E \mapsto \mathcal{D}_E$ *yields a functor* $\mathbf{EA} \to Conv(\mathbf{Sets})$*.*

Proof. We begin by describing what the sets $\mathcal{D}_E(1)$ and $\mathcal{D}_E(2)$ are. An element $\varphi \in \mathcal{D}_E(1)$ is a map $\varphi \colon \{1\} \to E$ with $\bigovee_{x\in\{1\}}\varphi(x) = 1$. Hence φ is completely determined as $\varphi(1) = 1$. Thus $\mathcal{D}_E(1) \cong 1$, making $\mathcal{D}_E$ an affine functor.

An element $\varphi \in \mathcal{D}_E(2)$ is a map $\varphi \colon \{1,2\} \to E$ satisfying $\varphi(1) \perp \varphi(2)$ and $\varphi(1) \ovee \varphi(2) = 1$. Hence $\varphi(2) = \varphi(1)^\perp$, so that φ is determined by $\varphi(1) \in E$. Thus $\mathcal{D}_E(2) \cong E$.

If we have two elements $\varphi, \psi \in \mathcal{D}_E(n+1)$ satisfying $\mathcal{D}_E(\nabla_i)(\varphi) = \mathcal{D}_E(\nabla_i)(\psi)$, for $1 \leq i \leq n$, then $\varphi(i) = \mathcal{D}_E(\nabla_i)(\varphi)(1) = \mathcal{D}_E(\nabla_i)(\psi)(1) = \psi(i)$. But then

$\varphi = \psi$, as required in point 3 in Definition 18, since the remaining value at $n+1$ is determined by the others (unlike in Example 19):

$$\varphi(n+1) = \big(\varphi(1) \ovee \cdots \ovee \varphi(n)\big)^{\perp} = \big(\psi(1) \ovee \cdots \ovee \psi(n)\big)^{\perp} = \psi(n+1).$$

We turn to point 2 and check that the functor $\mathcal{D}_E$ preserves the three pullbacks (10). For the first one, assume $\varphi \in \mathcal{D}_E(n+1)$ satisfies $\mathcal{D}_E(!+\mathrm{id})(\varphi) = \mathcal{D}_E(\kappa_1)(*)$, where $\kappa_1 \colon 1 \to 1+1$ and $*$ is the single element $* = \lambda x.\,1 \in \mathcal{D}_E(1)$. This means that $\varphi(1) \ovee \cdots \ovee \varphi(n) = \mathcal{D}_E(!+\mathrm{id})(\varphi)(1) = \mathcal{D}_E(\kappa_1)(*)(1) = 1$, and thus $\varphi(n+1) = 0$. Hence there is a unique element $\varphi' \in \mathcal{D}_E(n)$ with $\mathcal{D}_E(\kappa_1)(\varphi') = \varphi$, namely $\varphi'(i) = \varphi(i)$ for $1 \le i \le n$.

Preservation of the second pullback is left to the reader. For the third one, assume $\varphi \in \mathcal{D}_E(n+1)$ and $\psi \in \mathcal{D}_E(1+m)$ satisfying $\mathcal{D}_E(!+\mathrm{id})(\varphi) = \mathcal{D}_E(\mathrm{id}+!)(\psi)$. This means:

$$\varphi(1) \ovee \cdots \ovee \varphi(n) \;=\; \psi(1) \qquad \varphi(n+1) \;=\; \psi(2) \ovee \cdots \ovee \psi(m+1).$$

The $\chi \in \mathcal{D}_E(n+m)$ that we are looking for must satisfy $\varphi = \mathcal{D}_E(\mathrm{id}+!)(\chi)$ and $\psi = \mathcal{D}_E(!+\mathrm{id})(\chi)$. That is:

$$\begin{array}{rclrcl} \varphi(i) & = & \chi(i), \text{ for } 1 \le i \le n, & \varphi(n+1) & = & \chi(n+1) \ovee \cdots \ovee \chi(n+m) \\ \psi(1) & = & \chi(1) \ovee \cdots \ovee \chi(n) & \psi(j+1) & = & \chi(n+j-1), \text{ for } 2 \le j \le m+1. \end{array}$$

Hence there is a precisely one choice for such a χ, so that $\mathcal{D}_E$ applied the last pullback in (10) is again a pullback.

Finally we have to check that the mapping $E \mapsto \mathcal{D}_E$ is functorial. Given a map $g \colon E \to D$ in **EA**, there is a natural transformation $g \circ (-) \colon \mathcal{D}_E \Rightarrow \mathcal{D}_D$, that is well-defined and natural because g is a homomorphism. □

The next step is to show that, in the reverse direction, a convex functor (on **Sets**) gives rise to an effect algebra.

Proposition 22. *Let $F \colon$ **Sets** $\to$ **Sets** be a convex functor. Then $F(2)$ is an effect algebra, with the following structure:*

$$0 = \Big(1 \xrightarrow{\cong} F(1) \xrightarrow{F(\kappa_2)} F(2)\Big) \qquad 1 = \Big(1 \xrightarrow{\cong} F(1) \xrightarrow{F(\kappa_1)} F(2)\Big)$$
$$(-)^{\perp} = \Big(F(2) \xrightarrow[\cong]{F([\kappa_2,\kappa_1])} F(2)\Big) \tag{12}$$

For $a, b \in F(2)$ we say $a \perp b$ if there is a 'bound' $\beta \in F(3)$ such that $F(\nabla_1)(\beta) = a$ and $F(\nabla_2)(\beta) = b$, with ∇_i as in (9). In that case we define:

$$a \ovee b \;=\; F(!+\mathrm{id})(\beta) \;\in\; F(2),$$

where $!+\mathrm{id} \colon 2+1 \to 2$ sends $1, 2 \mapsto 1$ and $3 \mapsto 2$.

*Further, the mapping $F \mapsto F(2)$ yields a functor $CNV($**Sets**$) \to$ **EA**.*

It may be instructive to see what this partial sum $\ovee$ on $F(2)$ means for the convex functors $F = \mathcal{D}_E$ from Proposition 21. So assume $\varphi, \psi \in \mathcal{D}_E(2)$ have bound $\beta \in \mathcal{D}_E(3)$. The equations $\varphi = F(\nabla_1)(\beta)$ and $\psi = F(\nabla_2)(\beta)$ yield:

$$\varphi(1) = \beta(1) \qquad \varphi(2) = \beta(2) \ovee \beta(3) \qquad \psi(1) = \beta(2) \qquad \psi(2) = \beta(1) \ovee \beta(3).$$

In particular, the elements $\varphi(1), \psi(1)$ can be added, since $\varphi(1) \ovee \psi(1) \ovee \beta(3) = 1$. Thus, the sum $\varphi \ovee \psi = \mathcal{D}_E(! + \mathrm{id})(\beta) \in \mathcal{D}_E(2)$ satisfies:

$$\begin{array}{c} (\varphi \ovee \psi)(1) = \beta(1) \ovee \beta(2) = \varphi(1) \ovee \psi(1) \\ (\varphi \ovee \psi)(2) = \beta(3) = (\beta(1) \ovee \beta(2))^{\perp} = (\varphi(1) \ovee \psi(1))^{\perp} = (\varphi \ovee \psi)(1)^{\perp}. \end{array}$$

Proof. We check some of the requirements that must hold for effect algebras.

The partial sum $\ovee$ is commutative, since if $\beta \in F(3)$ is a bound for $a, b \in F(2)$, then $\beta' = F([\kappa_2, \kappa_1] + \mathrm{id}) \in F(3)$ is a bound for b, a, with the same sum:

$$b \ovee a = F(! + \mathrm{id})(\beta') = F((! + \mathrm{id}) + ([\kappa_2, \kappa_1] + \mathrm{id}))(\beta) = F(! + \mathrm{id})(\beta) = a \ovee b.$$

The 0 defined in (12) is a zero element for $\ovee$, since for an arbitrary element $a \in F(2)$ there is a bound $\alpha = F(\kappa_2)(a) \in F(1 + 2)$ for $0, a$ with sum a.

Associativity of $\ovee$ requires more work. Assume $a, b, c \in F(2)$ are given with $a \perp b$, say with bound $\alpha \in F(3)$, and $(a \ovee b) \perp c$, with bound $\beta \in F(3)$. The latter means $F(\nabla_1)(\beta) = a \ovee b = F(! + \mathrm{id})(\alpha)$. Thus we have a situation:

$$\begin{array}{ccc} F(2+2) & \xrightarrow{F(\mathrm{id}+!)} & F(2+1) \ni \alpha \\ {\scriptstyle F(!+\mathrm{id})}\downarrow \lrcorner & & \downarrow{\scriptstyle F(!+\mathrm{id})} \\ \beta \in F(1+2) & \xrightarrow[F(\mathrm{id}+!) = F(\nabla_1)]{} & F(2) \end{array}$$

Because this is a pullback that is preserved by F, see (10), there is a (unique) element $\gamma \in F(2+2)$ with $F(\mathrm{id}+!)(\gamma) = \alpha$ and $F(!+\mathrm{id})(\gamma) = \beta$. We first consider the function $h\colon 4 \to 3$ given by $h(1) = h(4) = 3$, $h(2) = 1$, and $h(3) = 2$. It yields $\gamma' = F(h)(\gamma) \in F(3)$, which is a bound for b, c with sum $b \ovee c$. We next take the function $k\colon 4 \to 3$ defined by $k(1) = 1$, $k(2) = k(3) = 2$, and $k(4) = 3$. Now $\gamma'' = F(k)(\gamma) \in F(3)$ is a bound for a and $b \ovee c$. Finally we get:

$$\begin{array}{rcl} a \ovee (b \ovee c) & = & F(! + \mathrm{id})(\gamma'') \;=\; F((! + \mathrm{id}) \circ k)(\gamma) \\ & & \phantom{F(! + \mathrm{id})(\gamma'')} \;=\; F((! + \mathrm{id}) \circ (! + \mathrm{id}))(\gamma) \\ & & \phantom{F(! + \mathrm{id})(\gamma'')} \;=\; F(! + \mathrm{id})(\beta) \;=\; (a \ovee b) \ovee c. \end{array}$$

The equation $a^{\perp} \ovee a = 1$ can be proven via the bound $\alpha = F(h)(a) \in F(3)$ for $h\colon 2 \to 3$ defined by $h(1) = 2$ and $h(2) = 1$.

We leave it to the reader to check that $a^{\perp}$ is the only element $b \in F(2)$ with $b \ovee a = 1$, and proceed by showing $1 \perp a \Rightarrow a = 0$. Assume thus $1 \perp a$, say via a bound $\alpha \in F(3)$ satisfying $F(\nabla_1)(\alpha) = 1 = F(\kappa_1)(*)$ and $F(\nabla_2)(\alpha) = a$. The first equation allows us to use preservation by F of the second pullback in (10), since $\nabla_1 = \mathrm{id} + !$. Hence we get $\alpha = F(\kappa_1)(*)$ for $\kappa_1 \colon 1 \to 1 + 2$, and thus:

$$a = F(\nabla_2)(\alpha) = F(\nabla_2 \circ \kappa_1)(*) = F(\kappa_2)(*) = 0.$$

Finally we have to prove functoriality of the mapping $F \mapsto F(2)$. If we have a natural transformation $\sigma \colon F \Rightarrow G$ between convex functors F, G, then the component $\sigma_2 \colon F(2) \to G(2)$ is a map of effect algebras. It is easy to see that it preserves $0, 1 \in F(2)$. Next, assume $a, b \in F(2)$ are orthogonal, via bound $\alpha \in F(3)$ satisfying $F(\nabla_1)(\alpha) = a$ and $F(\nabla_2)(\alpha) = b$. Then $\sigma_3(\alpha) \in G(3)$ is a bound for $\sigma_2(a), \sigma_2(b) \in G(2)$ by naturality. Hence $\sigma_2(a) \perp \sigma_2(b)$. Further,

$$\sigma_2(a) \ovee \sigma_2(b) = G(! + \mathrm{id})(\sigma_3(\alpha)) = \sigma_2(F(! + \mathrm{id})(\alpha)) = \sigma_2(a \ovee b). \qquad \square$$

The main result is then the adjointness of these functors between effect algebras and convex functors.

Theorem 23. *The functor* $\mathbf{EA} \to \mathit{CNV}(\mathbf{Sets})$ *from Proposition 21 given by* $E \mapsto \mathcal{D}_E$ *is left adjoint to the functor* $F \mapsto F(2)$ *from Proposition 22.*

Proof. For an effect algebra E and a convex endofunctor F on **Sets** we have to prove that there is a bijective correspondence:

$$\begin{array}{cl} E \xrightarrow{\;f\;} F(2) & \text{in } \mathbf{EA} \\ \hline\hline \mathcal{D}_E \underset{\sigma}{\Longrightarrow} F & \text{in } \mathit{Conv}(\mathbf{Sets}) \end{array}$$

The upward direction is easy: one maps $\sigma \colon \mathcal{D}_E \Rightarrow F$ to:

$$\overline{\sigma} = \Big(E \xrightarrow{\cong} \mathcal{D}_E(2) \xrightarrow{\;\sigma_2\;} F(2)\Big)$$

It is not hard to see that this is a map of effect algebras.

The other direction requires more work. So suppose we have $f \colon E \to F(2)$ in **EA**. We have to define a natural transformation $\overline{f} \colon \mathcal{D}_E \Rightarrow F$. So assume $\varphi \in \mathcal{D}_E(X)$, say with $\mathrm{supp}(\varphi) = \{x_1, \ldots, x_n\}$. The elements $\varphi(x_i) \in E$ are pairwise orthogonal, and thus so are $f(\varphi(x_i)) \in F(2)$. This means that there is a (unique) bound $\beta \in F(n+1)$ with $F(\nabla_i)(\beta) = f(\varphi(x_i))$, and also:

$$F(! + \mathrm{id})(\beta) = \ovee_i f(\varphi(x_i)) = f(\ovee_i \varphi(x_i)) = f(1) = 1 = F(\kappa_1)(*).$$

Now we need to use that pullbacks of the following form are preserved by F.

$$\begin{array}{ccc} n & \xrightarrow{\;\kappa_1\;} & n+1 \\ {\scriptstyle !}\downarrow & \lrcorner & \downarrow{\scriptstyle ! + \mathrm{id}} \\ 1 & \xrightarrow[\;\kappa_1\;]{} & 1 + 1 = 2 \end{array}$$

This yields a unique $\beta' \in F(n)$ with $F(\kappa_1)(\beta') = \beta$. Finally we put:

$$\overline{f}_X(\varphi) = \Big(F(n \xrightarrow{\;[x_1, \ldots, x_n]\;} X)(\beta')\Big) \in F(X).$$

Remaining details are left to the reader. $\square$

An obvious next step is to extend this result to an adjunction between effect algebras with multiplication—like $[0, 1]$ has—and convex monads. It can form part of a "triangle of adjunctions", like in [5]. This will be elaborated elsewhere.

Acknowledgements. Thanks to Dion Coumans, Chris Heunen, Bas Spitters and Jorik Mandemaker for feedback and/or helpful discussions.

References

[1] Abramsky, S.: Domain theory in logical form. Ann. Pure & Appl. Logic 51(1/2), 1–77 (1991)
[2] Baez, J.C., Stay, M.: Physics, topology, logic and computation: A Rosetta stone (2009), arxiv.org/abs/0903.0340
[3] Barr, M., Wells, C.: Toposes, Triples and Theories. Springer, Berlin (1985); Revised and corrected version, `www.cwru.edu/artsci/math/wells/pub/ttt.html`
[4] Busch, P., Grabowski, M., Lahti, P.: Operational Quantum Physics. Springer, Berlin (1995)
[5] Coumans, D., Jacobs, B.: Scalars, monads and categories (2010), arxiv.org/abs/1003.0585
[6] Doberkat, E.-E.: Eilenberg-Moore algebras for stochastic relations. Inf. & Comp. 204(12), 1756–1781 (2006); Erratum and addendum 206(12), 1476–1484 (2008)
[7] Dvurečenskij, A., Pulmannová, S.: New Trends in Quantum Structures. Kluwer Acad. Publ., Dordrecht (2000)
[8] Flood, J.: Semiconvex geometry. Journ. Austr. Math. Soc., Series A 30, 496–510 (1981)
[9] Foulis, D.J., Bennett, M.K.: Effect algebras and unsharp quantum logics. Found. Physics 24(10), 1331–1352 (1994)
[10] Foulis, D.J., Greechie, R.J., Bennett, M.K.: The transition to unigroups. Int. Journ. Theor. Physics 37(1), 45–63 (1998)
[11] Fritz, T.: Convex spaces I: Definition and examples (2009), arxiv.org/abs/0903.5522
[12] Gudder, S.: A general theory of convexity. Milan Journal of Mathematics 49(1), 89–96 (1979)
[13] Heunen, C., Jacobs, B.: Quantum logic in dagger kernel categories. Order (2010) doi:10.1007/s11083-010-9145-5
[14] Jacobs, B.: Coalgebras and approximation. In: Nerode, A., Matiyasevich, Y.V. (eds.) LFCS 1994. LNCS, vol. 813, pp. 173–183. Springer, Heidelberg (1994)
[15] Jacobs, B.: Semantics of weakening and contraction. Ann. Pure & Appl. Logic 69(1), 73–106 (1994)
[16] Jacobs, B.: Involutive categories and monoids, with a GNS-correspondence. In: Quantum Physics and Logic, QPL (2010)
[17] Jacobs, B., Mandemaker, J.: Coreflections in algebraic quantum logic. In: Quantum Physics and Logic, QPL (2010)
[18] Johnstone, P.T.: Stone Spaces. Cambridge Studies in Advanced Mathematics, vol. 3. Cambridge Univ. Press, Cambridge (1982)
[19] Johnstone, P.T., Vickers, S.: Preframe presentations present. In: Carboni, A., Pedicchio, M.C., Rosolini, G. (eds.) Como Conference on Category Theory. Lect. Notes Math., vol. 1488, pp. 193–212. Springer, Berlin (1991)

[20] Keimel, K.: The monad of probability measures over compact ordered spaces and its Eilenberg-Moore algebras. Topology and its Applications 156, 227–239 (2008)
[21] Kock, A.: Bilinearity and cartesian closed monads. Math. Scand. 29, 161–174 (1971)
[22] Kock, A.: Closed categories generated by commutative monads. Journ. Austr. Math. Soc. XII, 405–424 (1971)
[23] Manes, E.G.: Algebraic Theories. Springer, Berlin (1974)
[24] Mac Lane, S.: Categories for the Working Mathematician. Springer, Berlin (1971)
[25] von Neumann, J., Morgenstern, O.: Theory of Games and Economic Behavior. Princeton University Press, Princeton (1944)
[26] Pulmannová, S., Gudder, S.: Representation theorem for convex effect algebras. Commentationes Mathematicae Universitatis Carolinae 39(4), 645–659 (1998), http://dml.cz/dmlcz/119041
[27] Stone, M.H.: Postulates for the barycentric calculus. Ann. Math. 29, 25–30 (1949)
[28] Swirszcz, T.: Monadic functors and convexity. Bull. de l'Acad. Polonaise des Sciences. Sér. des sciences math., astr. et phys. 22, 39–42 (1974)
[29] Vickers, S.: Topology Via Logic. Tracts in Theor. Comp. Sci, vol. 5. Cambridge Univ. Press, Cambridge (1989)

A Calculus for Power-Aware Multicast Communications in Ad Hoc Networks

Lucia Gallina and Sabina Rossi

Dipartimento di Informatica, Università Ca' Foscari, Venezia (Italy)
{lgallina,srossi}@dsi.unive.it

Abstract. We present CMN$^{\#}$, a process calculus for formally modelling and reasoning about Mobile Ad Hoc Networks (MANETs) and their protocols. Our calculus naturally captures essential characteristics of MANETs, including the ability of a MANET node to broadcast a message to any other node within its physical transmission range, and to move in and out of the transmission range of other nodes in the network. In order to reason about cost-effective ad hoc routing protocols, we also allow unicast and multicast communications as well as the possibility for a node to control the transmission radius of its communications. We show how to use our calculus to prove some useful connectivity properties which can be exploited to achieve low-cost routing solutions.

1 Introduction

A Mobile Ad Hoc Network (MANET) is a self-configuring network of mobile devices connected by wireless links. Each device in a MANET is free to move independently in any direction, and will therefore change its links to other devices frequently. Each node must forward traffic unrelated to its own usage, and then be a router. The primary challenge in building a MANET is equipping each device to continuously maintain the information required to properly route traffic. The devices communicate with each other via radio transceivers through the protocol IEEE 802.11 (WiFi) [9]. This type of communication has a physical scope, because a radio transmission spans over a limited area. Different protocols are evaluated based on the packet drop rate, the routing overhead, the power control, and other measures.

As mobile ad hoc networks communicate in a self organized way without depending on any fixed infrastructure, they are the best solution for various applications, ranging from the monitoring of herds of animals to supporting communications in military battlefields and civilian disaster recovery scenarios. Many of these applications require that nodes be mobile and be deployed with little network planning. The mobility of nodes limits their size, which in turn limits the energy reserves available to them. Moreover, in wireless networks, bandwidth is precious and scarce. Thus energy and bandwidth conservation is a key requirement in the design of MANETs.

Routing in ad hoc networks faces extreme challenges due to node mobility/dynamics and limited communication resources (energy and bandwidth).

C.S. Calude and V. Sassone (Eds.): TCS 2010, IFIP AICT 323, pp. 20–31, 2010.

Table 1. Syntax

Networks		**Processes**	
M,N ::= $\mathbf{0}$	Empty network	P,Q,R ::= $\mathbf{0}$	Inactive process
$\mid M_1 \mid M_2$	Parallel composition	$\mid c(\tilde{x}).P$	Input
$\mid (\nu c)M$	Channel restriction	$\mid \bar{c}_L\langle\tilde{w}\rangle.P$	Output
$\mid n[P]^{\mu}_{l,r}$	Node (or device)	$\mid [w_1 = w_2]P, Q$	Matching
		$\mid A\langle\tilde{w}\rangle$	Recursion

The routing protocols for mobile ad hoc networks have to adapt quickly to frequent and unpredictable topology changes and must be parsimonious of communication and processing resources. Moreover, since radio signals are likely to overlap with others in a geographical area, a straightforward broadcasting by flooding is usually very costly and will result in serious redundancy, contention, and collision. For this reason, modern ad hoc routing protocols use unicast and multicast communications to reduce the number of control packets (see, e.g., [1,2,7]). In addition, power aware protocols reduce the total energy consumption by adjusting each node's transmission power (e.g., radius) just enough to reach up to the intended receivers only (see, e.g., [10]).

In this paper we present a calculus, named CMN$^{\#}$, for formally modelling and reasoning about mobile ad hoc networks and their protocols. This is an extension of CMN (Calculus of Mobile Ad Hoc Networks), proposed by Merro in [4]. It naturally captures essential characteristics of MANETs, including the ability of a MANET node to broadcast a message to any other node within its physical transmission range, and to move in and out of the transmission range of other nodes in the network. In our model the connectivity of a node is represented by a location and a transmission radius. Broadcast communications are limited to the transmission cell of the sender. Unicast and multicast communications are modelled by specifying, for each output action, the addresses of the intended recipients of the message. Moreover, the arbitrary and unexpected connections and disconnections of nodes as well as the possibility for a node to dynamically adjust its transmission power are represented by enabling nodes to modify the corresponding transmission radius through internal actions.

We show how to use our calculus to prove some useful connectivity properties of MANETs which can be exploited to control power/energy consumption. For instance, we can determine the minimum transmission radius ensuring the connectivity of a node with all the intended recipients of its transmissions, thus reducing power consumption.

2 The Calculus

We introduce the language CMN$^{\#}$, an extension of CMN (Calculus of Mobile Ad Hoc Networks) [4], that models mobile ad hoc networks as a collection of nodes, running in parallel, and using channels to broadcast messages. Our calculus extends CMN to support multicast and unicast communications. Moreover, it allows one to model the arbitrary and unexpected connections and disconnections of nodes in a network as well as the possibility for a node to administrate power control by choosing the optimal transmission radius to communicate with the desired receivers.

We use letters c and d for *channels*; m and n for *nodes*; l, k and h for *locations*; r for *transmission radii*; x, y and z for *variables*. *Closed values* contain nodes, locations, transmission radii and any basic value (booleans, integers, ...). *Values* include also variables. We use u and v for closed values and w for (open) values. We denote by $\tilde{v}$, $\tilde{w}$ tuples of values.

The syntax of CMN$^{\#}$ is shown in Table 1. This is defined in a two-level structure: the lower one for processes, the upper one for networks. Networks are collections of nodes (which represent devices), running in parallel, using channels to communicate messages. As usual, **0** denotes the empty network and $M_1|M_2$ represents the parallel composition of two networks. The restriction in $(\nu c)M$ acts as the standard CCS restriction (i.e., it does not perform any channel creation). Processes are sequential and live within the nodes. Process **0** denotes the inactive process. Process $c(\tilde{x}).P$ can receive a tuple $\tilde{w}$ of (closed) values via channel c and continue as $P\{\tilde{w}/\tilde{x}\}$, i.e., as P with $\tilde{w}$ substituted for $\tilde{x}$ (where $|\tilde{x}| = |\tilde{w}|$). Process $\bar{c}_L\langle\tilde{w}\rangle.P$ can send a tuple of (closed) values $\tilde{w}$ via channel c and continue as P. The tag L is used to maintain the set of locations of the intended recipients: $L = \infty$ represents a broadcast transmission, while a finite set of locations L denotes a multicast communication (unicast if L is a singleton). Syntactically, L may be a variable, but it must be a set of locations when the output prefix is ready to fire. Process $[w_1 = w_2]P, Q$ behaves as P if $w_1 = w_2$, and as Q otherwise. We write $A\langle\tilde{w}\rangle$ to denote a process defined via a (possibly recursive) definition $A(\tilde{x}) \stackrel{\text{def}}{=} P$, with $|\tilde{x}| = |\tilde{w}|$, where $\tilde{x}$ contains all channels and variables that appear free in P.

Each node, if connected, has a location and a transmission radius. Nodes cannot be created or destroyed. We write $n[P]^{\mu}_{l,r}$ for a node named n (this is the logic location of the device in the network), located at l, with transmission radius r, mobility tag μ, and executing a process P. The tag μ is $\mathtt{m}$ for mobile nodes, and $\mathtt{s}$ for stationary nodes; l denotes the physical location of the node. To each node n is associated a maximum transmission radius r_n; nodes may control power consumption by dynamically adjusting their transmission radius r provided that $r \in [0, r_n]$. Notice that if $r = 0$ then the node is disconnected.

In the process $c(\tilde{x}).P$, the tuple $\tilde{x}$ is bound in P; while in $(\nu c)M$, the channel name c is bound in M. We denote by $fv(\cdot)$ and $fc(\cdot)$ free variables and channels, respectively, and identify processes and networks up to α-conversion. Parallel composition of networks has lower precedence with respect to restriction. We denote by $\prod_{i \in I} M_i$ the parallel composition of networks M_i, for $i \in I$. We write $(\nu\tilde{c})M$ as an abbreviation for $(\nu c_1)...(\nu c_k)M$. To denote unicast communication, we write c_l for $c_{\{l\}}$. We write $\bar{c}_L\langle w\rangle$ for $\bar{c}_L\langle w\rangle.\mathbf{0}$, $\mathbf{0}$ for $n[\mathbf{0}]^{\mu}_{l,r}$ and $[w_1 = w_2]P$ for $[w_1 = w_2]P, \mathbf{0}$. We assume that there are no free variables in a network (while there can be free channels). Moreover, we assume that networks are *well-formed*, i.e., each node identifier is unique and the corresponding transmission

Table 2. Structural Congruence

$n[[v = v]P, Q]^{\mu}_{l,r} \equiv n[P]^{\mu}_{l,r}$	(Struct Then)
$n[[v_1 = v_2]P, Q]^{\mu}_{l,r} \equiv n[Q]^{\mu}_{l,r} \quad v_1 \neq v_2$	(Struct Else)
$n[A\langle\tilde{v}\rangle]^{\mu}_{l,r} \equiv n[\{\tilde{v}/\tilde{x}\}P]^{\mu}_{l,r}$ if $A(\tilde{x}) \stackrel{\text{def}}{=} P \wedge \lvert\tilde{x}\rvert = \lvert\tilde{v}\rvert$	(Struct Rec)
$M \vert N \equiv N \vert M$	(Struct Par Comm)
$(M \vert N) \vert M' \equiv M \vert (N \vert M')$	(Struct Par Assoc)
$M \vert \mathbf{0} \equiv M$	(Struct Zero Par)
$(\nu c)\mathbf{0} \equiv \mathbf{0}$	(Struct Zero Res)
$(\nu c)(\nu d)M \equiv (\nu d)(\nu c)M$	(Struct Res Res)
$(\nu c)(M \vert N) \equiv M \vert (\nu c)N$ If $c \notin fc(M)$	(Struct Res Par)
$M \equiv M$	(Struct Refl)
$N \equiv M$ if $M \equiv N$	(Struct Symm)
$M \equiv M''$ if $M \equiv M' \wedge M' \equiv M''$	(Struct Trans)
$M \vert M' \equiv N \vert M' \quad \forall M'$ if $M \equiv N$	(Struct Cxt Par)
$(\nu c)M \equiv (\nu c)N \quad \forall c$ if $M \equiv N$	(Struct Cxt Res)

radius is compatible with the node's power capacity. Formally, a network $M \equiv n_1[P_1]^{\mu_1}_{l_1,r_1} \mid n_2[P_2]^{\mu_2}_{l_2,r_2} \cdots \mid n_k[P_k]^{\mu_k}_{l_k,r_k}$ is *well-formed* if for $i, j \in \{1, \ldots, k\}$ it holds that $n_i \neq n_j$ when $i \neq j$ and $r_i \in [0, r_{n_i}]$.

Reduction Semantics. The dynamics of the calculus is specified by the *reduction relation* over networks ($\longrightarrow$), described in Table 3. As usual, it relies on an auxiliary relation, called structural congruence ($\equiv$), defined in Table 2. We assume the possibility of comparing locations in order to determine whether a node lies or not within the transmission cell of another node. This is done through function $d(\cdot, \cdot)$ which takes two locations and returns their distance.

Rule (R-Bcast) models the transmission of a tuple $\tilde{v}$ through a channel c_L. The set L associated to channel c indicates the locations of the intended recipients, even if broadcast communications are indeed performed. If $L = \infty$ then the recipients set is the whole network (broadcast transmission), while a finite set L (resp., a singleton) is used to denote a multicast (resp., a unicast) communication. In our calculus transmission is a *non-blocking action*: transmission proceeds even if there are no nodes listening for messages. The messages transmitted will be received only by those nodes which lie in the transmission area of the sender. It may occur that some receivers within the range of the transmitter do not receive the message. This may be due to several reasons that concern the instability and dynamism of the network. In terms of observation this corresponds to a local activity of the network which an observer is not party to. Rule (R-Rad) models the possibility for a node n to control power consumption by changing its transmission radius r into r' provided that $r' \in [0, r_n]$. Rule (R-Move) models arbitrary and unpredictable movements of mobile nodes. δ denotes the maximum distance that a node can cover in a computational step. Notice that a node is disconnected when its radius is set to 0. We denote by $\longrightarrow^*$ the reflexive and transitive closure of $\longrightarrow$.

Table 3. Reduction Semantics

(R-Bcast) $$\frac{r \neq 0,\ \forall i \in I. d(l, l_i) \leq r,\ r_i \neq 0,\ |\tilde{x_i}| = |\tilde{v}|}{n[\bar{c}_L\langle\tilde{v}\rangle.P]^{\mu}_{l,r} \mid \prod_{i\in I} n_i[c(\tilde{x_i}).P_i]^{\mu_i}_{l_i,r_i} \rightarrow n[P]^{\mu}_{l,r} \mid \prod_{i\in I} n_i[P_i\{\tilde{v}/\tilde{x_i}\}]^{\mu_i}_{l_i,r_i}}$$

(R-Rad) $$\frac{r' \in [0, r_n]}{n[P]^{\mu}_{l,r} \rightarrow n[P]^{\mu}_{l,r'}}$$ (R-Move) $$\frac{d(l,k) \leq \delta}{n[P]^{\mathtt{m}}_{l,r} \rightarrow n[P]^{\mathtt{m}}_{k,r}}$$

(R-Par) $$\frac{M \rightarrow M'}{M|N \rightarrow M'|N}$$ (R-Res) $$\frac{M \rightarrow M'}{(\nu c)M \rightarrow (\nu c)M'}$$

(R-Struct) $$\frac{M \equiv N\ N \rightarrow N'\ N' \equiv M'}{M \rightarrow M'}$$

Behavioral Semantics. The central actions of our calculus are transmission and reception of messages. However, only the transmission of messages (over unrestricted channels) can be observed. An observer cannot be sure whether a recipient actually receives a given value. Instead, if a node receives a message, then surely someone must have sent it. As usual, we adopt the term *barb* as a synonymous of observable. In our definition of barb a transmission is considered an observable action only if at least one location in the set of the intended recipients is able to receive the message.

Definition 1 (Barb). *We write* $M \downarrow_c$ *if* $M \equiv (\nu\tilde{d})(n[\bar{c}_L\langle\tilde{v}\rangle.P]^{\mu}_{l,r}|M')$, *with* $c \notin \tilde{d}$ *and* $\exists k \in L \wedge d(l,k) \leqslant r$. *We write* $M \Downarrow_c$ *if* $M \longrightarrow^* M' \downarrow_c$.

Notice that, if $M \equiv (\nu\tilde{d})(n[\bar{c}_L\langle\tilde{v}\rangle.P]^{\mu}_{l,r}|M')$ and $M \downarrow_c$ then at least one of the locations in L is actually able to receive the message.

To define our observation equivalence we will ask for the largest relation which satisfies the following properties. Let $\mathcal{R}$ be a relation over networks:

Barb preservation. $\mathcal{R}$ is *barb preserving* if $M \mathcal{R} N$ and $M \downarrow_c$ implies $N \Downarrow_c$.

Reduction closure. $\mathcal{R}$ is *reduction closed* if $M \mathcal{R} N$ and $M \longrightarrow M'$ implies that there exists N' such that $N \longrightarrow^* N'$ and $M' \mathcal{R} N'$.

Contextuality. $\mathcal{R}$ is *contextual* if $M \mathcal{R} N$ implies $\mathcal{C}[M] \mathcal{R} \mathcal{C}[N]$ for any context $\mathcal{C}[\cdot]$, where a context is a network term with a hole $[\cdot]$ defined by:

$$\mathcal{C}[\cdot] ::= [\cdot] \mid [\cdot]|M \mid M|[\cdot] \mid (\nu c)[\cdot]$$

Definition 2 (Reduction barbed congruence). *Reduction barbed congruence, written* $\cong$, *is the largest symmetric relation over networks, which is reduction closed, barb preserving, and contextual.*

Table 4. LTS rules for Processes

$$\text{(Output)}\ \frac{-}{\bar{c}_L\langle\tilde{v}\rangle.P \xrightarrow{\bar{c}_L\tilde{v}} P} \qquad \text{(Input)}\ \frac{-}{c(\tilde{x}).P \xrightarrow{c\tilde{v}} P\{\tilde{v}/\tilde{x}\}}$$

$$\text{(Then)}\ \frac{P \xrightarrow{\eta} P'}{[\tilde{v} = \tilde{v}]P, Q \xrightarrow{\eta} P'} \qquad \text{(Else)}\ \frac{Q \xrightarrow{\eta} Q' \quad \tilde{v_1} \neq \tilde{v_2}}{[\tilde{v_1} = \tilde{v_2}]P, Q \xrightarrow{\eta} Q'}$$

$$\text{(Rec)}\ \frac{P\{\tilde{v}/\tilde{x}\} \xrightarrow{\eta} P' \quad A(\tilde{x}) \stackrel{\text{def}}{=} P}{A\langle\tilde{v}\rangle \xrightarrow{\eta} P'}$$

3 Bisimulation-Based Proof Method

In this section we develop a proof technique for the relation $\cong$. More precisely, we define a LTS semantics for CMN$^{\#}$ terms, which is built upon two sets of rules: one for processes and one for networks. Table 4 presents the LTS rules for processes. Transitions are of the form $P \xrightarrow{\eta} P'$, where η ranges over input and output actions of the form $c\tilde{v}$ and $\bar{c}_L\tilde{v}$, respectively. Table 5 presents the LTS rules for networks. Transitions are of the form $M \xrightarrow{\gamma} M'$, where γ is as follows:

$$\gamma ::= c?\tilde{v}@l \mid c_L!\tilde{v}[l, r] \mid c!\tilde{v}@K \mid \tau.$$

Rules for processes are simple and they do not need deeper explanations. Let us illustrate the rules for networks. Rule (Snd) models the sending, with transmission radius r, of the tuple $\tilde{v}$ through channel c to a specific set L of recipients, while rule (Rcv) models the reception of $\tilde{v}$ at l via channel c. Rule (Bcast) models the broadcast message propagation: all the nodes lying within the transmission cell of the sender may receive the message, regardless of the fact that they are in L. Rule (Obs) models the observability of a transmission: every output action may be detected (and hence *observed*) by any node located within the transmission cell of the sender. The action $c!\tilde{v}@K$ represents the transmission of the tuple $\tilde{v}$ of messages via c to a set K of recipients in L, located within the transmission cell of the transmitter. When $K \neq \emptyset$ this is an observable action corresponding to the barb $\downarrow_c$. Rule (Lose) models both message loss and a local activity of the network which an observer is not party to. As usual, τ-transitions are used to denote non-observable actions. Rule (Move) models migration of a mobile node from a location l to a new location k, where δ represents the maximum distance that a node can cover in a single computational step. Rule (Rad) models the possibility for a node n to change its transmission radius, provided that it is within $[0, r_n]$. Finally (Par) and (Res) are standard. Notice that since we do not transmit channels, in our calculus there is no scope extrusion.

The following relationships between the LTS semantics and the reduction one hold.

Table 5. LTS rules for Networks

$$(\text{Snd})\ \frac{P \xrightarrow{\bar{c}_L \tilde{v}} P'}{n[P]^{\mu}_{l,r} \xrightarrow{c_L!\tilde{v}[l,r]} n[P']^{\mu}_{l,r}}\ r \neq 0 \qquad (\text{Rcv})\ \frac{P \xrightarrow{c\tilde{v}} P'}{n[P]^{\mu}_{l,r} \xrightarrow{c?\tilde{v}@l} n[P']^{\mu}_{l,r}}\ r \neq 0$$

$$(\text{Bcast})\ \frac{M \xrightarrow{c_L!\tilde{v}[l,r]} M' \quad N \xrightarrow{c?\tilde{v}@l'} N' \quad d(l,l') \leq r}{M|N \xrightarrow{c_L!\tilde{v}[l,r]} M'|N'}$$

$$(\text{Obs})\ \frac{M \xrightarrow{c_L!\tilde{v}[l,r]} M' \quad K \subseteq \{k : d(l,k) \leq r \wedge k \in L\} \quad K \neq \emptyset}{M \xrightarrow{c!\tilde{v}@K} M'}$$

$$(\text{Lose})\ \frac{M \xrightarrow{c_L!\tilde{v}[l,r]} M'}{M \xrightarrow{\tau} M'} \qquad (\text{Move})\ \frac{d(l,k) \leq \delta}{n[P]^{\mathtt{m}}_{l,r} \xrightarrow{\tau} n[P]^{\mathtt{m}}_{k,r}}$$

$$(\text{Rad})\ \frac{r' \in [0, r_n]}{n[P]^{\mu}_{l,r} \xrightarrow{\tau} n[P]^{\mu}_{l,r'}}$$

$$(\text{Par})\ \frac{M \xrightarrow{\gamma} M'}{M|N \xrightarrow{\gamma} M'|N} \qquad (\text{Res})\ \frac{M \xrightarrow{\gamma} M' \quad c \notin fc(\gamma)}{(\nu c)M \xrightarrow{\gamma} (\nu c)M'}$$

Lemma 1. *Let M be a network.*

1. *If $M \xrightarrow{c?\tilde{v}@l} M'$, then there are n, P, μ, l, r, M_1 and $\tilde{d}$, with $c \notin \tilde{d}$, such that $M \equiv (\nu\tilde{d})(n[c(\tilde{x}).P]^{\mu}_{l,r}|M_1)$ and $M' \equiv (\nu\tilde{d})(n[P\{\tilde{v}/\tilde{x}\}]^{\mu}_{l,r}|M_1)$.*
2. *If $M \xrightarrow{c_L!\tilde{v}[l,r]} M'$, then there are n, P, μ, l, r, M_1, I (possibly empty), and $\tilde{d}$, with $c \notin \tilde{d}$, and n_i, P_i, μ_i, l_i, r_i, with $d(l,l_i) \leq r$ for all $i \in I$, such that: $M \equiv (\nu\tilde{d})(n[\bar{c}_L\langle\tilde{v}\rangle.P]^{\mu}_{l,r}|\prod_{i\in I} n_i[c(\tilde{x}_i).P_i]^{\mu_i}_{l_i,r_i}|M_1)$ and $M' \equiv (\nu\tilde{d})(n[P]^{\mu}_{l,r}|\prod_{i\in I} n_i[P_i\{\tilde{v}/\tilde{x}_i\}]^{\mu_i}_{l_i,r_i}|M_1)$.*

Lemma 2. *Let M be a network. It holds that (i) $M \downarrow_c$ if and only if $M \xrightarrow{c!\tilde{v}@K}$ for some tuple of values $\tilde{v}$ and set of locations K; (ii) if $M \xrightarrow{\tau} M'$ then $M \longrightarrow M'$; (iii) if $M \longrightarrow M'$ then $M \xrightarrow{\tau}\equiv M'$.*

We now introduce a labelled bisimilarity that is a complete characterization of our notion of reduction barbed congruence. We adopt the metavariable α to range over those actions that will be used in the definition of labelled bisimilarity:

$$\alpha ::= c?\tilde{v}@l \ \mid\ c!\tilde{v}@K \ \mid\ \tau.$$

Since we are interested in weak behavioral equivalences, that abstract over τ-actions, we introduce the notion of *weak action*. We denote by $\Rightarrow$ the reflexive and transitive closure of $\xrightarrow{\tau}$; we use $\xRightarrow{c?\tilde{v}@l}$ to denote $\Rightarrow\xrightarrow{c?\tilde{v}@l}\Rightarrow$; we use $\xRightarrow{c?\tilde{v}@F}$ to denote

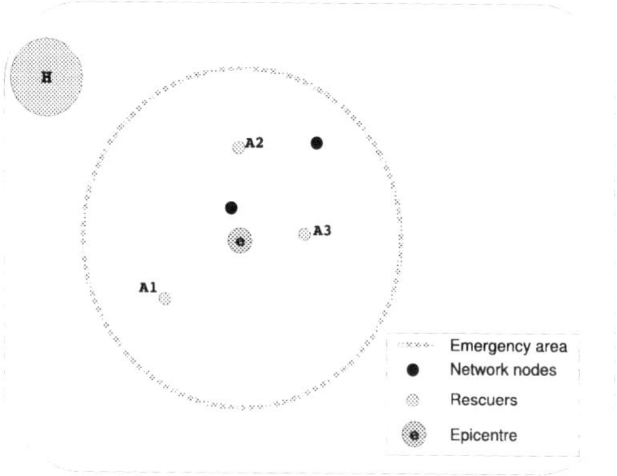

Fig. 1. A mobile ad hoc network in an earthquake area

$\stackrel{c?\tilde{v}@l_1}{\Longrightarrow} \dots \stackrel{c?\tilde{v}@l_n}{\Longrightarrow}$ for $F = \{l_1, \dots, l_n\}$; we use $\stackrel{c!\tilde{v}@K}{\Longrightarrow}$ to denote $\stackrel{c?\tilde{v}@F_1}{\Longrightarrow} \xrightarrow{c!\tilde{v}@K_1} \stackrel{c?\tilde{v}@F'_1}{\Longrightarrow} \dots \stackrel{c?\tilde{v}@F_n}{\Longrightarrow} \xrightarrow{c!\tilde{v}@K_n} \stackrel{c?\tilde{v}@F'_n}{\Longrightarrow}$ for $K = \bigcup_{i=1}^{n} K_i$, $F = \bigcup_{i=1}^{n} (F_i \cup F'_i)$ and $F \cap K = \emptyset$; finally, $\stackrel{\hat{\alpha}}{\Longrightarrow}$ denotes $\Rightarrow$ if $\alpha = \tau$ and $\stackrel{\alpha}{\Longrightarrow}$ otherwise.

Notice that $\stackrel{c!\tilde{v}@K}{\Longrightarrow}$ means that a distributed observer receiving an instance of message $\tilde{v}$, at each location in K, in several computational steps, cannot assume that those messages belong to the same broadcast transmission, but they may be different transmissions of the same message. The presence of the weak input actions $\stackrel{c?\tilde{v}@F_i}{\Longrightarrow}$ are due to the fact that we want to ignore all the inputs executed by each location which is not included in the set of the intended receivers.

Definition 3 (Labelled bisimilarity). *A binary relation $\mathcal{R}$ over networks is a* simulation *if $M \mathcal{R} N$ implies:*

- *If $M \xrightarrow{\alpha} M'$, $\alpha \neq c?\tilde{v}@l$, then there exists N' such that $N \stackrel{\hat{\alpha}}{\Longrightarrow} N'$ with $M' \mathcal{R} N'$;*
- *If $M \xrightarrow{c?\tilde{v}@l} M'$ then there exists N' such that either $N \stackrel{c?\tilde{v}@l}{\Longrightarrow} N'$ with $M' \mathcal{R} N'$ or $N \Rightarrow N'$ with $M' \mathcal{R} N'$.*

We say that N simulates *M if there is some simulation $\mathcal{R}$ such that $M \mathcal{R} N$. A relation $\mathcal{R}$ is a* bisimulation *if both $\mathcal{R}$ and its converse are simulations.* Labelled bisimilaty, *written $\approx$, is the largest bisimulation over networks.*

Labeled bisimilarity is a valid proof method for reduction barbed congruence.

Theorem 1. *Let M and N be two well-formed networks. Then, $M \cong N$ if and only if $M \approx N$.*

4 Properties of Mobile Ad Hoc Networks

In this section we use $\text{CMN}^{\#}$ to define and prove some useful properties of mobile ad hoc networks.

We consider a running example, depicted in Figure 1, describing the case of an emergency due to an earthquake. The hospital (H) sends three ambulances (A1, A2, A3) to the emergency area. An ad hoc network is installed to manage the communication between the ambulances, placing a router near the epicenter (e) of the earthquake.

We assume that for each process P executed by a network node, it is possible to identify the set of all the intended recipients that may appear in an output action performed by P. We denote by $\mathtt{rcv}(P)$ the minimum set of locations ensuring that for each output action $\bar{c}_L\langle\tilde{w}\rangle$ performed by P it holds that $L \subseteq \mathtt{rcv}(P)$. Indeed, the tag L associated to an output action occurring in P can be either a variable or a set of locations, then we are not able to statically calculate $\mathtt{rcv}(P)$. However, since an ad hoc network is usually designed to guarantee the communications within a specific area, we can reasonably assume that the underling protocol will always multicast messages to recipients located within the interested area and we can abstractly represent them by a finite set of locations.

Radius of maximum observability. We can define a "*radius of maximum observability*", that is a radius ensuring the correct reception of a message from all the locations in the recipients set. In particular, we define the "*minimum radius of maximum observability*", which corresponds to the distance between the sender of the message and the most distant recipient. Clearly, this property is relevant only for stationary nodes, since mobile nodes can always move within the transmission cell of the transmitter to receive the communication.

Consider two different static devices lying at the same location and executing the same code, but with different power capacities. The behaviour of those devices will be different only if they are able to reach distinct sets of intended receivers. The next theorem shows that if a device can reach all its intended receivers, then it behaves as every other device lying at the same location and executing the same code, but with a larger transmission radius.

Theorem 2 (Radius of maximum observability). *Let $n[P]^{\mathsf{s}}_{l,r}$ be a stationary node located at l such that $\mathtt{rcv}(P) = L$ and $d(l,k) \leqslant r_n$ for all $k \in L$. Then $n[P]^{\mathsf{s}}_{l,r} \approx m[P]^{\mathsf{s}}_{l,r'}$ for every node m such that $r_m \geq r_n$. In this case, we say that r_n is a radius of maximum observability for $n[P]^{\mathsf{s}}_{l,r}$.*

The *minimum radius of maximum observability* can be defined as the smallest radius a node can choose in order to reach all its intended recipients.

Definition 4 (Minimum radius of maximum observability). *Let $n[P]^{\mathsf{s}}_{l,r}$ be a stationary node such that $\mathtt{rcv}(P) = L$ and r_n is a radius of maximum observability for $n[P]^{\mathsf{s}}_{l,r}$. A radius r' is said the minimum radius of maximum observability for $n[P]^{\mathsf{s}}_{l,r}$ if $r' \leq r_n$ and for all $k \in L$ it holds that $d(l,k) \leq r'$ and for all $r'' < r'$ there exists $k' \in L$ such that $d(l,k') \geq r''$.*

In our example, we can assume that the earthquake has damaged a delimited area and the rescuers need to communicate only within this emergency area. We can then determine the minimum transmission radius which ensures the central server of the hospital to be able to communicate with the ambulances sent for assistance in the disaster area.

The notion of minimum radius of maximum observability is relevant when dealing with the problem of power saving, since it provides us a with way of reducing the transmission power of a node without loosing connectivity within the whole network.

Simulation of stationary nodes in different locations. The tag L associated to each output action allows us to express a property of simulation for stationary devices in different locations. Indeed, two stationary nodes, placed at different locations (with therefore different neighbors), but communicating with the same set of intended recipients, result to be observational equivalent.

Theorem 3 (Simulation of stationary nodes at different locations). *Let $n[P]^{\mathsf{s}}_{l_n,r}$ and $m[P]^{\mathsf{s}}_{l_m,r'}$ be two stationary nodes located at l_n and l_m, respectively. Assume $\mathtt{rcv}(P) = L$, $K = \{k \mid d(l_n, k) \leq r_n \wedge k \in L\}$ and $K' = \{k \mid d(l_m, k) \leq r_m \wedge k \in L\}$. It holds that*

1. *If $K' \subseteq K$, then $n[P]^{\mathsf{s}}_{l_n,r}$ simulates $m[P]^{\mathsf{s}}_{l_m,r'}$;*
2. *If $K = K'$, then $n[P]^{\mathsf{s}}_{l_n,r} \approx m[P]^{\mathsf{s}}_{l_m,r'}$.*

This property is useful, e.g., to minimize the number of routers within a network area while ensuring the correct communication between a given set of locations. If two different routers result to exhibit the same behaviour, then one of them can be turn off, thus allowing us to save both power and physical resources.

Range repeaters. Range repeaters are devices which regenerate a network signal in order to extend the range of the existing network infrastructure. Here we generalize the definition of repeater given in [4] and introduce a notion of *complete* range repeater. We consider range repeaters with both one and two channels.

Definition 5. *Let c and d be two channels, l_{rr} be a fixed location, r_{rr} be a transmission radius and L be a set of locations. A repeater with two channels relative to L is a stationary device, denoted by $rr[c \hookrightarrow_L d]^{\mathsf{s}}_{l_{rr},r}$, where $c \hookrightarrow_L d$ is the recursive process defined by:*

$$c \hookrightarrow_L d \stackrel{\text{def}}{=} c(x).\bar{d}_L\langle x\rangle.c \hookrightarrow_L d.$$

A range repeater with two channels receives values through the input channel and retransmits them through the output channel. A range repeater with one channel operates likewise, but input and output channels coincide.

Range repeaters are usually exploited to enlarge the transmission cell of a stationary node and, if such a node always communicates with the same set of devices, each time through the same channel, by using a range repeater we can simulate the presence of the sender in the location of the repeater. In our running example, if we consider the distance between the hospital and the earthquake area, we may have that this is too large to guarantee the correct communication with the ambulances running up in the emergency area. It could be necessary to employ a range repeater powerful enough to cover all the area and, at the same

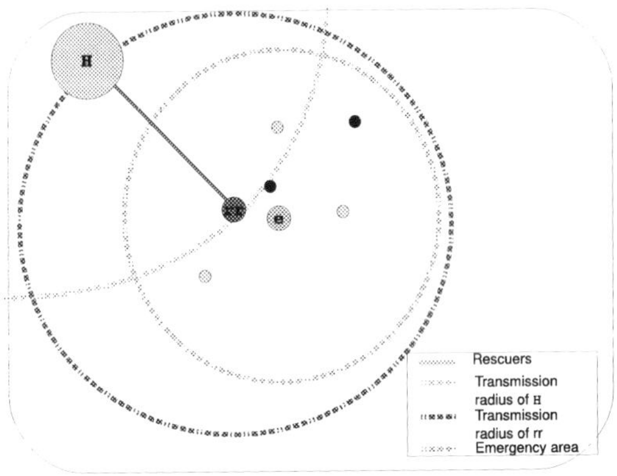

Fig. 2. A range repeater in the earthquake area

time, to be reachable by the central server of the hospital. If the earthquake epicenter is too distant from the hospital we can install a series of consecutive repeaters, which will connect the central server to the disaster area.

Theorem 4 (Range repeaters with one channel). *Let* $n[P]^{\mathtt{s}}_{l,r}$ *be a stationary node such that* $fc(P) \subseteq \{c\}$ *for some channel* c *and* $\mathtt{rcv}(P) = L$. *Let* $rr[c \hookrightarrow_L c]^{\mathtt{s}}_{l_{rr},r'}$ *be a range repeater with* $d(l, l_{rr}) \leq r_n \leq r_{rr}$. *Then:*

$$n[P]^{\mathtt{s}}_{l,r} \mid rr[c \hookrightarrow_L c]^{\mathtt{s}}_{l_{rr},r'} \quad \textit{simulates} \quad n[P]^{\mathtt{s}}_{l_{rr},r}.$$

The simulation just described can be realized also with a two-channels range repeater. Using two channels, however, two range repeaters are needed, one for input ($\mathtt{in}[d \hookrightarrow_L c]^{\mathtt{s}}_{l,r'}$) and one for output ($\mathtt{out}[c \hookrightarrow_L d]^{\mathtt{s}}_{l,r''}$) management.

Theorem 5 (Range repeaters with two channels). *Let* $n[P]^{\mathtt{s}}_{l,r}$ *be a stationary node such that* $fc(P) \subseteq \{c\}$ *for some channel* c *and* $\mathtt{rcv}(P) = L$. *Let* $\mathtt{in}[d \hookrightarrow_L c]^{\mathtt{s}}_{k,r'}$ *and* $\mathtt{out}[c \hookrightarrow_L d]^{\mathtt{s}}_{k,r''}$ *be two range repeaters with* $d(l,k) \leq r_{\mathtt{in}} \leq r_n \leq r_{\mathtt{out}}$. *Then:*

$$n[P]^{\mathtt{s}}_{l,r} \mid \mathtt{in}[d \hookrightarrow_L c]^{\mathtt{s}}_{k,r''} \mid \mathtt{out}[c \hookrightarrow_L d]^{\mathtt{s}}_{k,r'} \; \textit{simulates} \; n[P\{d/c\}]^{\mathtt{s}}_{k,r}.$$

We introduce the notion of *complete range repeater*, that is a repeater which has a radius large enough to reach all its intended recipients.

Definition 6 (Complete range repeater). *A range repeater* $rc[c \hookrightarrow_L c]^{\mathtt{s}}_{l_{rc},r}$ *is said* complete *with respect to* L *if* $L \subseteq K$ *where* $K = \{k : d(l_{rc}, k) \leqslant r_{rc}\}$.

Consider our running example and suppose that a repeater is installed to allow the central server of the hospital to communicate with the ambulances dispatched in the emergency area (see Figure 2). The repeater can be chosen in such a way to guarantee that its transmission radius covers the complete area of the disaster. This is an example of a complete range repeater, whose radius is a radius of maximum observability for the entire earthquake area.

Theorem 6 (Complete range repeaters). *Let* $n[P]^{\mathtt{s}}_{l,r}$ *be a stationary node such that* $fc(P) \subseteq \{c\}$ *for some channel* c *and* $\mathtt{rcv}(P) = L$*. Let* $rc[c \hookrightarrow_L c]^{\mathtt{s}}_{l_{rc},r'}$ *be a complete range repeater with respect to* L *and* $d(l, l_{rc}) \leq r_n$*. Then all the recipients in* L *are reachable by* n*, i.e.,* $\forall k \in L$*, it holds that* $d(k, l) \leqslant (r_n + r_{rc})$*.*

5 Conclusion

Ad hoc networks is a new area of mobile communication networks that has attracted significant attention due to its challenging research problems. Many researchers have proposed formal models, such as a process calculus, in order to reason on their properties and problems (see, e.g., [8,3,5,6]).

In this paper we extended CMN by associating a tag to each transmission; the tag represents a set of nodes (message receivers) and enables us to prove some important properties concerning the observability of transmissions. For example we have defined the *minimum radius of maximum observability*, that is the minimum radius ensuring that a packet is reachable by all its receivers; moreover we proved that, under some specific conditions, stationary nodes lying in different locations might have the same behavior. Such properties can be used to reduce the transmission power of a node without loosing connectivity within the whole network.

References

1. Ad hoc on-demand distance vector routing protocol, `http://moment.cs.ucsb.edu/AODV`
2. Chakeres, I.D., Belding-Royer, E.M.: Aodv routing protocol implementation design. In: Proc. of 24th International Conference on Distributed Computing Systems Workshops - W7: EC (ICDCSW'04), vol. 7, pp. 698–703. IEEE Press, Los Alamitos (2004)
3. Godskesen, J.C.: A calculus for mobile ad hoc networks. In: Murphy, A.L., Vitek, J. (eds.) COORDINATION 2007. LNCS, vol. 4467, pp. 132–150. Springer, Heidelberg (2007)
4. Merro, M.: An observational theory for mobile ad hoc networks. Information and Computation 207(2), 194–208 (2009)
5. Nanz, S., Hankin, C.: A framework for security analysis of mobile wireless networks. Theoretical Computer Science 367(1), 203–227 (2006)
6. Prasad, K.V.S.: A calculus of broadcasting systems. Science of Computer Programming 25(2-3), 285–327 (1995)
7. Royer, E.M., Perkins, C.E.: Multicast operation of the ad-hoc on-demand distance vector routing protocol. In: Proc. of the 5th annual ACM/IEEE International Conference on Mobile Computing and Networking, pp. 207–2018 (1999)
8. Singh, A., Ramakrishnan, C.R., Smolka, S.A.: A process calculus for mobile ad hoc networks. In: Lea, D., Zavattaro, G. (eds.) COORDINATION 2008. LNCS, vol. 5052, pp. 296–314. Springer, Heidelberg (2008)
9. IEEE 802.11 official website, `http://www.ieee802.org/11`
10. Zhang, B., Mouftah, H.T.: Energy-aware on-demand routing protocols for wireless ad hoc networks. Wireless Networks 12(4), 481–494 (2006)

The Coarsest Precongruences Respecting Safety and Liveness Properties

Robert Jan van Glabbeek[1,2]

[1] NICTA, Sydney, Australia
[2] School of Computer Sc. and Eng., Univ. of New South Wales, Sydney, Australia

Abstract. This paper characterises the coarsest refinement preorders on labelled transition systems that are precongruences for renaming and partially synchronous interleaving operators, and respect all safety, liveness, and conditional liveness properties, respectively.

1 Introduction

The goal of this paper is to define and characterise certain semantic equivalences $\equiv$ and refinement preorders $\sqsubseteq$ on processes. The idea is that $p \equiv q$ says, essentially, that for practical purposes processes p and q are equally suitable, i.e. one can be replaced for by the other without untoward side effects. Likewise, $p \sqsubseteq q$ says that for all practical purposes under consideration, q is at least as suitable as p, i.e. it will never harm to replace p by q. Thus, one should have that $p \equiv q$ iff both $p \sqsubseteq q$ and $q \sqsubseteq p$.

Naturally, the choice of $\equiv$ and $\sqsubseteq$ depends on how one models a process, and what range of practical purposes one considers. I this paper I restrict myself to one of the most basic process models: *labelled transition systems.* I study processes that merely perform actions $a, b, c, \ldots$ which themselves are not subject to further investigations. These actions may be instantaneous or durational, but they may not last forever; moreover, in a finite amount of time only finitely many actions can be carried out. I distinguish between *visible* actions, that can be observed by the environment of a process, and whose occurrence can be influenced by this environment, and *invisible* actions, that cannot be observed of influenced. Since there is no need to distinguish different invisible actions, I can just as well consider all of them to be occurrences of the same invisible action, which is traditionally called τ. Furthermore, I abstract from real-time and probabilistic aspects of processes.

This choice of process model already rules out many practical purposes for which one process could be more suitable than another. I can for instance not compare processes on speed, since this is an issue that my process model has already abstracted from. In fact, the only aspects of processes that are captured by such a model and that may matter in practical applications, are the sequences of actions that a process may perform in a, possibly infinite, run, performed in, or in collaboration with, a certain environment. As the invisible action is by definition unobservable, it moreover suffices to consider sequences of *visible*

C.S. Calude and V. Sassone (Eds.): TCS 2010, IFIP AICT 323, pp. 32–52, 2010.

actions. A sequence of visible actions that a process p may perform is called a *trace* of p; it is a *complete trace* if it is performed during a maximal run of p, one that cannot be further extended. Obviously, the traces of p are completely determined by the complete traces of p, namely as their prefixes.

Based on the considerations above, it is tempting to postulate that the relevant behaviour of a process, as far as discernible in terms of labelled transition systems, is completely determined by its set of complete traces; hence two processes should be equivalent if they have the same competed traces. However, this argument bypasses the role of the environment in influencing the behaviour of a process. Often, one allows the actions a process performs to be synchronisations with the environment, and the environment can influence the course of action of a process by synchronising with some actions but not with others. Therefore, a safe over-approximation of the relevant behaviour of a process is not merely its set of complete traces, but rather its set of complete traces obtained as a function of the environment the process is running in.

In this paper I consider a neutral environment in which all courses of action are possible and the behaviour of a process is indeed determined by its complete traces. All other ways in which the environment may influence the behaviour of a process are given in terms of *contexts* build from other processes and certain composition operators. It could for instance be that in the neutral environment there is no way to tell the difference between processes p and q; maybe because they have the same set of complete traces. However, for a suitable parallel composition operator $\|$ and other process r it may be that there is a manifest practical difference between $p\|r$ and $q\|r$, so that one has $p\|r \not\equiv q\|r$. Now that fact alone is taken to be enough reason to postulate that $p \not\equiv q$. Namely the difference between p and q can be spotted by placing them in a context $\_\|r$. This context can be regarded as an environment in which the behaviours of p and q differ.

Following this programme, a suitable semantic equivalence on processes is defined in terms of two requirements. First of all the behaviour of processes is compared in the neutral environment. This entails isolating a class $\mathcal{C}$ of properties φ of processes that are deemed relevant in a given range of applications. One then requires for $p \equiv q$ to hold that p and q have the same properties from this class:

$$p \equiv q \quad \Rightarrow \quad \forall \varphi \in \mathcal{C}.\ (p \models \varphi \Leftrightarrow q \models \varphi) \tag{1}$$

where $p \models \varphi$ denotes that process p has the property φ. An equivalence $\equiv$ that satisfies this last requirement is said to *respect* or *preserve* the properties in $\mathcal{C}$. The second requirement entails selecting a class $\mathcal{O}$ of useful operators for combining processes. One then requires that for any context $C[\_]$ (such as $\_\|r$) built from operators from $\mathcal{O}$ and arbitrary processes, that

$$p \equiv q \quad \Rightarrow \quad C[p] \equiv C[q]. \tag{2}$$

An equivalence $\equiv$ that satisfies this last requirement is called a *congruence* for $\mathcal{O}$. For the sake of intuition it may help to consider the contrapositive formulation of these implications: if there exists a property φ in $\mathcal{C}$ that holds for p but not for q, or vice versa, then p and q cannot be considered equivalent. Likewise $C[p] \not\equiv C[q]$ implies $p \not\equiv q$.

These two requirements merely insist that the desired equivalence $\equiv$ does not identify processes that in some context differ on their relevant properties. They are satisfied by many equivalence relations, including the identity relation, that distinguishes all processes. In order to characterise precisely when two systems have the same relevant properties in any relevant context, one takes the *coarsest* equivalence satisfying (1) and (2); the one making the most identifications. This equivalence is called *fully abstract* w.r.t. $\mathcal{C}$ and $\mathcal{O}$. It always exists, and, as is straightforward to check, is characterised by

$$p \equiv q \quad \Leftrightarrow \quad \forall \mathcal{O}\text{-context } C[\_].\ \forall \varphi \in \mathcal{C}.\ (C[p] \models \varphi \Leftrightarrow C[q] \models \varphi).$$

When, for a certain application, the choice of $\mathcal{C}$ and $\mathcal{O}$ is clear, the unique equivalence relation that is fully abstract w.r.t. $\mathcal{C}$ and $\mathcal{O}$ is the right semantic equivalence for that application. However, when the choice of $\mathcal{C}$ and $\mathcal{O}$ is not clear, or when proving results that may be re-used in future applications that may call for extending $\mathcal{C}$ or $\mathcal{O}$, it is better to err on the side of caution, and use equivalences that satisfy (1) and (2) but need not be fully abstract; instead the finest equivalence $\equiv_{\mathit{fine}}$ for which a result $p \equiv_{\mathit{fine}} q$ can be proved is often preferable, because this immediately entails that $p \equiv q$ for any coarser equivalence relation $\equiv$, in particular for an $\equiv$ that may turn out to be fully abstract for some future choice of $\mathcal{C}$ and $\mathcal{O}$. It is for this reason that much actual verification work employes the finest equivalences that lend themselves for verification purposes, such as the various variants of bisimulation equivalence [12], see e.g. [1]. Nevertheless, this paper is devoted to the characterisation of fully abstract equivalences, and preorders, for a few suitable choices of $\mathcal{C}$ and $\mathcal{O}$.

The programme for refinement preorders proceeds along the same lines, but here it is important to distinguish between good and bad properties of processes. The counterpart of (1) is

$$p \sqsubseteq q \quad \Rightarrow \quad \forall \varphi \in \mathcal{G}.\ (p \models \varphi \Rightarrow q \models \varphi) \tag{3}$$

where $\mathcal{G}$ is the set of *good* properties within $\mathcal{C}$, those that for some applications may be required of a process. If this holds, $\sqsubseteq$ *respects* or *preserves* the properties in $\mathcal{G}$. When dealing with *bad* properties, those that in some applications should be avoided, the implication between $p \models \varphi$ and $q \models \varphi$ is oriented in the other direction. Since every bad property φ can be reformulated as a good property $\neg\varphi$, there is no specific need add a variant of (3) for the bad properties. The counterpart of (2) is simply

$$p \sqsubseteq q \quad \Rightarrow \quad C[p] \sqsubseteq C[q]. \tag{4}$$

and a preorder $\sqsubseteq$ that satisfies this requirement is called a *precongruence* for $\mathcal{O}$. Now the preorder that is *fully abstract* w.r.t. $\mathcal{G}$ and $\mathcal{O}$ always exists, and is characterised by

$$p \sqsubseteq q \quad \Leftrightarrow \quad \forall \mathcal{O}\text{-context } C[\_].\ \forall \varphi \in \mathcal{G}.\ (C[p] \models \varphi \Rightarrow C[q] \models \varphi).$$

It is the coarsest precongruence for $\mathcal{O}$ that respects the properties in $\mathcal{G}$. A characterisation of the preorder $\sqsubseteq$ that is fully abstract w.r.t. a certain $\mathcal{G}$ and $\mathcal{O}$ automatically yields a characterisation of the equivalence $\equiv$ that is fully abstract w.r.t. $\mathcal{G}$ and $\mathcal{O}$, as one has $p \equiv q$ iff both $p \sqsubseteq q \wedge q \sqsubseteq p$.

In this paper I will propose three main candidates for the set $\mathcal{G}$ of good properties: *safety properties* in Section 3, *liveness properties* in Section 4 and *conditional liveness properties* in Section 5. For the sake of theoretical completeness I moreover address general *linear time properties* in Section 6.

In Section 2 I will define my model of labelled transition systems and propose a class of $\mathcal{C}$ of operators that appear useful in applications to combine processes. My favourite selection contains

- the *partially synchronous interleaving operator* of CSP [15],
- *abstraction* or *concealment* [3,15]
- and the *state operator* [2],

or any other basis that is equally expressive. With each of the four choices for $\mathcal{G}$ this set of operators determines a fully abstract preorder, which will be characterised in Sections 3, 4, 5 and 6. It turns out that the resulting preorders are somewhat robust under the precise choice of operators for which one imposes a precongruence requirement: the same ones are obtained already without using concealment, and using merely injective renaming instead of the more general state operator. In the other direction, I could just as well have used all operators of CSP.

2 Labelled Transition Systems and a Selection of Composition Operators

Let Σ^* denote the set of finite sequences over a given set Σ, and Σ^∞ the set of infinite ones; $\Sigma^\omega := \Sigma^* \cup \Sigma^\infty$. Write ϵ for the empty sequence, $\sigma\rho$ for the concatenation of sequences $\sigma \in \Sigma^*$ and $\rho \in \Sigma^\omega$, and a for the sequence consisting of the single symbol $a \in \Sigma$. Write $\sigma \leq \rho$ for "σ is a prefix of ρ", i.e. "$\rho = \sigma \vee \exists \nu \in \Sigma^*.\sigma\nu = \rho$", and $\rho < \sigma$ for "$\sigma \leq \rho$ and $\sigma \neq \rho$".

I presuppose an infinite action alphabet A, not containing the *silent* action τ, and set $A_\tau = A \cup \{\tau\}$.

Definition 1. A *labelled transition system* (LTS) is a pair $(\mathbb{P}, \rightarrow)$, where $\mathbb{P}$ is a class of *processes* or *states* and $\rightarrow \subseteq \mathbb{P} \times A_\tau \times \mathbb{P}$ is a set of *transitions*, such that for each $p \in \mathbb{P}$ and $\alpha \in A_\tau$ the class $\{q \in \mathbb{P} \mid (p, \alpha, q) \in \rightarrow\}$ is a set.

Assuming a fixed transition system $(\mathbb{P}, \rightarrow)$, I write $p \xrightarrow{\alpha} q$ for $(p, \alpha, q) \in \rightarrow$; this means that process p can evolve into process q, while performing the action α. The ternary relation $\Longrightarrow \subseteq \mathbb{P} \times A^* \times \mathbb{P}$ is the least relation satisfying

$$p \stackrel{\epsilon}{\Longrightarrow} p\ , \qquad \frac{p \xrightarrow{\tau} q}{p \stackrel{\epsilon}{\Longrightarrow} q}\ , \qquad \frac{p \xrightarrow{a} q,\ a \neq \tau}{p \stackrel{a}{\Longrightarrow} q} \qquad \text{and} \qquad \frac{p \stackrel{\sigma}{\Longrightarrow} q \stackrel{\rho}{\Longrightarrow} r}{p \stackrel{\sigma\rho}{\Longrightarrow} r}\ .$$

This enables a formalisation of the concepts of traces and complete traces from the introduction.

Definition 2. Let $p \in \mathbb{P}$.

- p is *deterministic* if, for any $\sigma \in A^*$, $p \stackrel{\sigma}{\Longrightarrow} q_1$ and $p \stackrel{\sigma}{\Longrightarrow} q_2$ implies that $q_1 = q_2$ and $q_1 \stackrel{\tau}{\not\longrightarrow} r$.
- p *deadlocks*, notation $p \not\longrightarrow$, if there are no $\alpha \in A_\tau$ and $q \in \mathbb{P}$ with $p \stackrel{\alpha}{\longrightarrow} q$.
- p is *locked* if it can never do a visible action, i.e. if $p \stackrel{a}{\Longrightarrow} q$ for no $a \in A$ and $q \in \mathbb{P}$.
- p *diverges*, notation $p\Uparrow$, if there are $p_i \in \mathbb{P}$ for all $i > 0$ such that $p \stackrel{\tau}{\longrightarrow} p_1 \stackrel{\tau}{\longrightarrow} p_2 \stackrel{\tau}{\longrightarrow} \cdots$.
- $a_1 a_2 a_3 \cdots \in A^\infty$ is an *infinite trace* of p if there are $p_1, p_2, \ldots \in \mathbb{P}$ such that $p \stackrel{a_1}{\Longrightarrow} p_1 \stackrel{a_2}{\Longrightarrow} p_2 \stackrel{a_3}{\Longrightarrow} \cdots$.
- $\mathit{inf}(p)$ denotes the set of infinite traces of p.
- $\mathit{ptraces}(p) := \{\sigma \in A^* \mid \exists q.\ p \stackrel{\sigma}{\Longrightarrow} q\}$ is the set of *partial traces* of p.
- $\mathit{traces}(p) := \mathit{inf}(p) \cup \mathit{ptraces}(p)$ is the set of *traces* of p.
- $\mathit{deadlocks}(p) := \{\sigma \in A^* \mid \exists q.\ p \stackrel{\sigma}{\Longrightarrow} q \not\longrightarrow\}$ is the set of *deadlock traces* of p.
- $\mathit{diverg}(p) := \{\sigma \in A^* \mid \exists q.\ p \stackrel{\sigma}{\Longrightarrow} q\Uparrow\}$ is the set of *divergence traces* of p.
- $\mathit{CT}(p) := \mathit{inf}(p) \cup \mathit{diverg}(p) \cup \mathit{deadlocks}(p)$ is the set of *complete traces* of p.

Note that $\mathit{traces}(p) = \{\sigma \in A^\omega \mid \exists \rho \in \mathit{CT}(p).\ \sigma \leq \rho\}$.

To justify that $\mathit{CT}(p)$ is indeed a correct formalisation of the set of complete traces of p, I postulate that in a neutral environment, if a process $p \in \mathbb{P}$ has any outgoing transition $p \stackrel{\alpha}{\longrightarrow} q$, then within a finite amount of time it will do one its outgoing transitions. This is called a *progress property*; it says that a process will continue to make progress if possible.

As explained in the introduction, whether a fully abstract equivalence identifies processes p and q may depend on the existence of a third process r such that $p\|r$ can be distinguished from $q\|r$. When restricting attention to a particular labelled transition system $(\mathbb{P}, \rightarrow)$ it might happen that a perfectly reasonable candidate r happens not to be a member of $\mathbb{P}$, and thus that the conclusion $p \equiv q$ is arrived at solely as a result underpopulation of $\mathbb{P}$. To obtain the most robust notions of equivalence, I therefore assume my LTS to be *universal*, in the sense that up to isomorphism it contains *any* process one can imagine.

Definition 3. An LTS $(\mathbb{P}, \rightarrow_{\mathbb{P}})$ is *universal* if for any other LTS $(\mathbb{Q}, \rightarrow_{\mathbb{Q}})$ there exists an injective mapping $f : \mathbb{Q} \rightarrow \mathbb{P}$, called an *embedding*, such that, for any $q \in \mathbb{Q}$ and $p' \in \mathbb{P}$ one has $f(q) \stackrel{\alpha}{\longrightarrow}_{\mathbb{P}} p'$ iff $p' \in \mathbb{P}$ has the form $f(q')$ for some $q' \in Q$ with $q \stackrel{\alpha}{\longrightarrow}_{\mathbb{Q}} q'$.

The existence of a universal LTS has been established in [7]. Here one needs $\mathbb{P}$ to be a proper class. All preorders $\sqsubseteq$ that I consider in this paper are defined on arbitrary LTSs and have the property that $q \sqsubseteq q' \Leftrightarrow f(p) \sqsubseteq f(q')$, for any embedding f. This means that they are precongruences for isomorphism, and only take into account the future behaviour of processes, i.e. in determining whether $p \sqsubseteq q$ transitions leading to p or q play no rôle. Thus, a definition of such a preorder on a universal LTS, implicitly also defines it on any other LTS.

I will now do a proposal for the set $\mathcal{O}$ that will be my default choice in this paper. It consists of three operators for combining processes that appear useful in practical applications.

Table 1. Partially synchronous interleaving, abstraction, and the state operator

$$\frac{p \stackrel{\alpha}{\longrightarrow} p'}{p\|_S q \stackrel{\alpha}{\longrightarrow} p'\|_S q}\ (\alpha{\notin}S) \qquad \frac{q \stackrel{\alpha}{\longrightarrow} q'}{p\|_S q \stackrel{\alpha}{\longrightarrow} p\|_S q'}\ (\alpha{\notin}S) \qquad \frac{p \stackrel{a}{\longrightarrow} p' \quad q \stackrel{a}{\longrightarrow} q'}{p\|_S q \stackrel{a}{\longrightarrow} p'\|_S q'}\ (a{\in}S)$$

$$\frac{p \stackrel{\alpha}{\longrightarrow} p'}{\tau_I(p) \stackrel{\alpha}{\longrightarrow} \tau_I(p')}\ (\alpha{\notin}I) \qquad \frac{p \stackrel{a}{\longrightarrow} p'}{\tau_I(p) \stackrel{\tau}{\longrightarrow} \tau_I(p')}\ (a{\in}I)$$

$$\frac{p \stackrel{\tau}{\longrightarrow} p'}{\lambda_s^m(p) \stackrel{\tau}{\longrightarrow} \lambda_s^m(p')} \qquad \frac{p \stackrel{a}{\longrightarrow} p'}{\lambda_s^m(p) \stackrel{a(m,s)}{\longrightarrow} \lambda_{s(m,a)}^m(p')}$$

The first is the *partially synchronous interleaving operator* of CSP [15]. It is parametrised with a set $S \subseteq A$ of visible actions on which it synchronises: the composition $p\|_S q$ can perform an action from S only when both p and q perform it. All other actions from p and q are interleaved: whenever one of the two components can perform such an action, so can the composition, while the other component doesn't change its state. Formally, for any choice of $S \subseteq A$, $\|_S : \mathbb{P} \times \mathbb{P} \rightarrow \mathbb{P}$ is a binary operator on $\mathbb{P}$ such that a process $p\|_S q$ can make an α-transition iff this can be inferred by the first three rules of Table 1 from the transitions that p and q can make. Here a ranges over A and α over A_τ.

A context $\_\|_S r$ is widely regarded as a plausible way of modelling an environment that partially synchronises with processes under investigation. It is for this reason I include it in $\mathcal{O}$. This argument does not hold for many other process algebraic operators, such as the choice operator $+$ of CCS [12]. This is an example of an operator that is useful for *describing* particular processes, but a context $\_+r$ does not really model a reasonable environment in which one wants to run processes under investigation. For reasons of algebraic convenience, being a precongruence for the $+$ is an optional desideratum of refinement preorders, but it is not such an overriding requirement as being a precongruence for $\|_S$.

The second operator nominated for membership of $\mathcal{O}$ is the unary *abstraction operator* τ_I of ACP$_\tau$ [3], also known as the *concealment* operator of CSP [4,15]. This operator models a change in the level of abstraction at which processes are regarded, by reclassifying visible actions as hidden ones. It is parametrised with the set $I \subseteq A$ of visible actions that one chooses to abstract from, and formally defined by the next two rules of Table 1. Abstraction from internal actions by such a mechanism is an essential part of most work on verification in a process algebraic setting, and a context $\tau_I(\_)$ represents a reasonable environment in which to evaluate processes.

My final nominee for the set $\mathcal{O}$ of useful composition operators is the *state operator* λ_s^m of [2]. This unary operator formalises an interface between a process and its environment that is able to rename actions: if its argument process performs an action b, the interface $\lambda_s^m(\_)$ may pass on this action to the environment as c, thereby opening up the possibility of synchronisation with another occurrence of c when using a composed context $\lambda_s^m(\_)\|_S r$. Furthermore, the interface may remember the actions that have been performed to far, and make its renaming behaviour dependent on this history. For instance, if its argument p performs two a-actions in a row, $\lambda_s^m(p)$ may pass these on to the environment as a_1 and a_2, respectively.

The state operator λ_s^m is parametrised with an *interface specification* $m = (\mathcal{S}, \text{ACTION}, \text{EFFECT})$, consisting of set $\mathcal{S}$ of *internal states*, and functions $\text{ACTION} : \mathcal{S} \times A \rightarrow A$ and $\text{EFFECT} : \mathcal{S} \times A \rightarrow \mathcal{S}$, as well as a *current state* $s \in \mathcal{S}$. Here ACTION is a function that renames actions performed by an argument process p into actions performed by the interface $\lambda_s^m(p)$; the renaming depends on the internal state of the state operator, and thus is of type $\mathcal{S} \times A \rightarrow A$. EFFECT specifies the transformation of one internal state of the state operator into another, as triggered by the the encounter of an action of its argument process; it thus is of type $\mathcal{S} \times A \rightarrow \mathcal{S}$. Traditionally, one writes $a(m, s)$ for $\text{ACTION}(s, a)$ and $s(m, a)$ for $\text{EFFECT}(s, a)$. So $a(m, s)$ denotes the action a, as modified by the interface m in state s, whereas $s(m, a)$ denotes the internal state s, as modified by the occurrence of action a of the argument process within the scope of the interface m. With this notation, the formal definition of the state operator is given by the last two rules of Table 1.

The special case of a state operator with a singleton set of internal states is known as a *renaming operator*. Renaming operators occur in the languages CCS [12] and CSP [4,15]. Here I denote a renaming operator as λ^m, where the redundant subscript s is omitted, and m trivialises to a function $\text{ACTION} : A \rightarrow A$. I speak of an *injective* renaming operator if $\text{ACTION}(a) = \text{ACTION}(b)$ implies $a = b$. For any injective renaming operator λ^m there exists an inverse renaming operator λ^{-m} (not necessarily injective) such that for all $p \in \mathbb{P}$, the process $\lambda^{-m}(\lambda^m(p))$ behaves exactly the same as p—they are equivalent under all notions of equivalence considered in this paper.

3 Safety Properties

A *safety property* [9] is a property that says that

something bad will never happen.

To formulate a canonical safety property, assume that my alphabet of visible actions contains one specific action b, whose occurrence is *bad.* The canonical safety property now says that b **will never happen**.

Definition 4. A process p satisfies the *canonical safety property*, notation $p \models \mathit{safety}(b)$, if no trace of p contains the action b.

To arrive at a general concept of safety property for labelled transition systems, assume that some notion of *bad* is defined. Now, to judge whether a process p satisfies this safety property, one should judge whether p can reach a state in which one would say that something bad had happened. But all observable behaviour of p that is recorded in a labelled transition system until one comes to such a verdict, is the sequence of visible actions performed until that point. Thus the safety property is completely determined by the set sequences of visible actions that, when performed by p, lead to such a judgement. Therefore one can just as well define the concept of a safety property in terms of such a set.

Definition 5. A *safety property* of processes in an LTS is given by a set $B \subseteq A^*$. A process p *satisfies* this safety property, $p \models \mathit{safety}(B)$, when $\mathit{ptraces}(p) \cap B = \emptyset$.

This formalisation of safety properties is essentially the same as the one in [9] and all subsequent work on safety properties; the only, non-essential, difference is that I work with transition systems in which the transitions are labelled, whereas [9] and most related work deals with state-labelled transition systems.

A property is called *trivial* if it either always holds or always fails. Trivial properties are respected by any equivalence. The sets $B := \emptyset$ and $B := \{\epsilon\}$ specify trivial safety properties.

Theorem 1. A precongruence for the state operator respects every safety property iff it respects the canonical safety property.

Proof: "*Only if*" follows because the canonical safety property is in fact a safety property, namely the one with B being the set of those sequences that contain the action b.

"*If*": I use here a state operator that remembers exactly what sequence of actions has occurred so far. Thus the set of internal states of its interface specification m is A^*, and furthermore $\sigma(m,a) := \sigma a$ for all $\sigma \in A^*$ and $a \in A$. Now given a safety property $B \subseteq A^*$, let $b \in A$ be the special "bad" action, and $d \in A$ be a different "neutral" action. Define $a(m,\sigma) := \begin{cases} b \text{ if } \sigma a \in B \\ d \text{ otherwise.} \end{cases}$
Then $\lambda^m_\epsilon(p) \models \mathit{safety}(b)$ iff $p \models \mathit{safety}(B)$. Thus, if $p \sqsubseteq q$ and $p \models \mathit{safety}(B)$, then $\lambda^m_\epsilon(p) \sqsubseteq \lambda^m_\epsilon(q)$ and $\lambda^m_\epsilon(p) \models \mathit{safety}(b)$. Hence $\lambda^m_\epsilon(q) \models \mathit{safety}(b)$, so $q \models \mathit{safety}(B)$. □

Being locked (see Definition 2) is a safely property, namely with B the set of all sequences over A^* of length 1. It can be understood this way by regarding any occurrence of an action as bad.

Theorem 2. A precongruence for abstraction that respects the property of being locked, respects the canonical safety property.

Proof: Let $\sqsubseteq$ be a precongruence for abstraction that respects the property of being locked, and suppose that $p \sqsubseteq q$. Let $I := A \setminus \{b\}$. Then τ_I is an operator that renames all actions other than b into τ; thus if a process of the form $\tau_I(r)$ ever performs a visible action, it must be b. Now $p \models \mathit{safety}(b) \Leftrightarrow \tau_I(p) \models \mathit{safety}(b) \Leftrightarrow \tau_I(p)$ is locked $\Rightarrow \tau_I(q)$ is locked $\Leftrightarrow \tau_I(q) \models \mathit{safety}(b) \Leftrightarrow q \models \mathit{safety}(b)$. □

By combining Theorems 1 and 2 one obtains:

Corollary 1. A precongruence for abstraction and for the state operator that respects the property of being locked, respects all safety properties.

Theorem 3. Any precongruence for $\mathcal{O}$ that respects a single nontrivial safety property, respects every safety property.

Proof: Let $\sqsubseteq$ be a precongruence for $\mathcal{O}$ that respects *safety*(B), where $B \subseteq A^*$, $B \neq \emptyset$ and $\epsilon \notin B$. Let $\sigma \in A^*$ and $a \in A$ be such that $\sigma a \in B$, and no prefix $\rho \leq \sigma$ of σ is in B. Let *safety*(a) be the canonical safety property, but with a playing the role of b. Naturally, Theorem 1 holds for this renamed canonical safety property as well. Hence it suffices to show that $\sqsubseteq$ respects the property *safety*(a). Let $I := A \backslash \{a\}$. Then τ_I is an operator that renames all actions other than a into τ; thus if a process of the form $\tau_I(s)$ ever performs a visible action, it must be a. Let r_σ be a process with $CT(r) = \{\sigma\}$ and $r_{\sigma a}$ be a process with $CT(r) = \{\sigma a\}$. Then, for any choice of $s \in \mathbb{P}$, $(\tau_I(s)\|_\emptyset r_\sigma)\|_A r_{\sigma a}$ is a process all of whose traces are prefixes of σa, with $\sigma a \in ptraces((\tau_I(s)\|_\emptyset r_\sigma)\|_A r_{\sigma a})$ iff $a \in ptraces(\tau_I(s))$, which is the case iff $s \not\models$ *safety*(a). Suppose $p \sqsubseteq q$. Then $(\tau_I(p)\|_\emptyset r_\sigma)\|_A r_{\sigma a} \sqsubseteq (\tau_I(q)\|_\emptyset r_\sigma)\|_A r_{\sigma a}$ and

$$\begin{array}{l} p \models \mathit{safety}(a) \Leftrightarrow (\tau_I(p)\|_\emptyset r_\sigma)\|_A r_{\sigma a} \models \mathit{safety}(B) \Rightarrow \\ (\tau_I(q)\|_\emptyset r_\sigma)\|_A r_{\sigma a} \models \mathit{safety}(B) \Leftrightarrow q \models \mathit{safety}(a). \end{array} \qquad \square$$

Let $\sqsubseteq_{safety}$ denote the preorder that is fully abstract w.r.t. the class of safety properties and $\mathcal{O}$. The following, well-known, theorem characterises this preorder as *reverse partial trace inclusion.*

Theorem 4. $p \sqsubseteq_{safety} q \Leftrightarrow ptraces(p) \supseteq ptraces(q)$.

Proof: Define reverse partial trace inclusion, $\sqsubseteq_T^{-1}$, by $p \sqsubseteq_T^{-1} q$ iff $ptraces(p) \supseteq ptraces(q)$.

"$\Leftarrow$": It suffices to establish that $\sqsubseteq_T^{-1}$ is a precongruence for $\mathcal{O}$ that respects all safety properties.

That $\sqsubseteq_T^{-1}$ is a precongruence for $\mathcal{O}$ follows immediately from the following observations:

$$\begin{aligned} ptraces(p\|_S q) &= \{\sigma \in \nu\|_S\xi \mid \nu \in ptraces(p) \wedge \xi \in ptraces(q)\} \\ ptraces(\tau_I(p)) &= \{\tau_I(\sigma) \mid \sigma \in ptraces(p)\} \\ ptraces(\lambda_s^m(p)) &= \{\lambda_s^m(\sigma) \mid \sigma \in ptraces(p)\}. \end{aligned}$$

Here $\nu\|_S\xi$ denotes the set of sequences of actions for which is it possible to mark each action occurrence as *left*, *right* or both, obeying the restriction that an occurrence of action a is marked both *left* and *right* iff $a \in S$, such that the subsequence of all *left*-labelled action occurrences is ν and the subsequence of all *right*-labelled action occurrences is ξ. Furthermore, the operators τ_I and λ_s^m on A^* are uniquely determined by

$$\begin{array}{rclrcl} \tau_I(\epsilon) &=& \epsilon & \tau_I(a\sigma) &=& \begin{cases} \tau_I(\sigma) & \text{if } a \in I \\ a\tau_I(\sigma) & \text{otherwise} \end{cases} \\ \lambda_s^m(\epsilon) &=& \epsilon & \lambda_s^m(a\sigma) &=& a(m,s)\lambda_{s(m,a)}^m(\sigma). \end{array}$$

To show that $\sqsubseteq_T^{-1}$ respects all safety properties, let $B \subseteq A^*$, $p \sqsubseteq_T^{-1} q$, and suppose $p \models$ *safety*(B). Then $ptraces(q) \subseteq ptraces(p)$ and $ptraces(p) \cap B = \emptyset$. Thus $ptraces(q) \cap B = \emptyset$, i.e. $q \models$ *safety*(B), which had to be shown.

"⇒": Let $\sqsubseteq$ be any precongruence for $\mathcal{O}$ that respects all safety properties, and suppose $p \sqsubseteq q$. I have to establish that $p \sqsubseteq_T^{-1} q$. Let $B := A^* \setminus ptraces(p)$. Then $p \models safety(B)$. Thus $q \models safety(B)$, i.e. $ptraces(q) \cap (A^* \setminus ptraces(p)) = \emptyset$. This yields $ptraces(q) \subseteq ptraces(p)$. □

The above characterisation as reverse partial trace inclusion of the coarsest congruence for $\mathcal{O}$ that respects all safety properties, is rather robust under the choice of $\mathcal{O}$. It holds already for the empty class of operators, and it remains true when adding in all operators of CSP [4], CCS [12] or ACP$_\tau$ [3], as $\sqsubseteq_T^{-1}$ is known to be a precongruence for all of them.

By Theorem 3, the characterisation also remains valid when requiring respect for one arbitrary safety property only, instead of all of them, but to this end all three operators of $\mathcal{O}$ are needed. If we just retain the state operator, by Theorem 1 it suffices to require respect for the canonical safety property only.

4 Liveness Properties

A *liveness property* [9] is a property that says that

something good will eventually happen.

To formulate a canonical liveness property, assume that the alphabet A contains one specific action g, whose occurrence is *good*. The canonical liveness property now says that g **will eventually happen**.

Definition 6. A process p satisfies the *canonical liveness property*, notation $p \models liveness(g)$, if every complete trace of p contains the action g.

To arrive at a general concept of liveness property for labelled transition systems, assume that some notion of *good* is defined. Now, to judge whether a process p satisfies this liveness property, one should judge whether p can reach a state in which one would say that something good had happened. But all observable behaviour of p that is recorded in a labelled transition system until one comes to such a verdict, is the sequence of visible actions performed until that point. Thus the liveness property is completely determined by the set sequences of visible actions that, when performed by p, lead to such a judgement. Therefore one can just as well define the concept of a liveness property in terms of such a set.

Definition 7. A *liveness property* of processes in an LTS is given by a set $G \subseteq A^*$. A process p *satisfies* this liveness property, notation $p \models liveness(G)$, when each complete trace of p has a prefix in G.

This formalisation of liveness properties is essentially different from the one in [9] and most subsequent work on liveness properties; this point is discussed in Section 6.

Just as for safety properties, the sets $G := \emptyset$ and $G := \{\epsilon\}$ specify trivial liveness properties.

Theorem 5. A precongruence for the state operator respects every liveness property iff it respects the canonical liveness property.

Proof: Just like the proof of Theorem 1. □

A process p has the *initial progress* property if it cannot immediately diverge or deadlock, i.e. if $\epsilon \notin \mathit{diverg}(p) \cup \mathit{deadlocks}(p)$. This is a liveness property, namely with G the set of all sequences over A^* of length 1. It can be understood this way by regarding any occurrence of an action as good.

Theorem 6. A precongruence for abstraction that respects the initial progress property, respects the canonical liveness property.

Proof: Just like the proof of Theorem 2. □

By combining Theorems 5 and 6 one obtains:

Corollary 2. A precongruence for abstraction and for the state operator that respects the initial progress property, respects all liveness properties.

Conjecture 1. Any precongruence for $\mathcal{O}$ that respects a single nontrivial liveness property, respects every liveness property.

Let $\sqsubseteq_{liveness}$ denote the preorder that is fully abstract w.r.t. the class of liveness properties and $\mathcal{O}$. I will proceed to characterise $\sqsubseteq_{liveness}$ as the preorder $\sqsubseteq_{FDI}^{\perp}$ based on failures, divergences and infinite traces that is also used in the work on CSP [15]. *Failures* of a process p are defined below; they are pairs $\langle \sigma, X \rangle$ such that p can perform the sequence of visible actions σ and then reach a state in which no further progress can be made in case the environment allows only those visible actions to occur that are listed in X. The preorder $\sqsubseteq_{FDI}^{\perp}$ does not take into account any information about the behaviour of processes that can be thought of as taking place after a divergence. One of the ways to erase this information from the set of failures, divergences and infinite traces of a process is by means of *flooding*. Flooded sets of failures, divergences and infinite traces are indicated by the subscript $_\perp$.

Definition 8. Let $p \in \mathbb{P}$.

- $\mathit{initials}(p) := \{\alpha \in A_\tau \mid \exists q.\ p \stackrel{\alpha}{\longrightarrow} q\}$.
- $\mathit{failures}(p) := \{\langle \sigma, X \rangle \in A^* \times \mathcal{P}(A) \mid \exists q.\ p \stackrel{\sigma}{\Longrightarrow} q \wedge \mathit{initials}(q) \cap (X \cup \{\tau\}) = \emptyset\}$.
- $\mathit{diverg}_\perp(p) := \{\sigma\rho \mid \sigma \in \mathit{diverg}(p) \wedge \rho \in A^*\}$.
- $\mathit{inf}(p) \cup \{\sigma\rho \mid \sigma \in \mathit{diverg}(p) \wedge \rho \in A^\infty\}$.
- $\mathit{failures}(p) \cup \{\langle \sigma\rho, X \rangle \mid \sigma \in \mathit{diverg}(p) \wedge \rho \in A^* \wedge X \subseteq A\}$.

So $\mathit{deadlocks}(p) = \{\sigma \mid \langle \sigma, A \rangle \in \mathit{failures}(p)\}$
and $\mathit{ptraces}(p) = \mathit{diverg}(p) \cup \{\sigma \mid \langle \sigma, \emptyset \rangle \in \mathit{failures}(p)\}$.

Theorem 7. $p \sqsubseteq_{liveness} q \quad \Leftrightarrow \quad \begin{array}{rcl} \mathit{diverg}_\perp(p) & \supseteq & \mathit{diverg}_\perp(q) \wedge \\ \mathit{inf}_\perp(p) & \supseteq & \mathit{inf}_\perp(q) \wedge \\ \mathit{failures}_\perp(p) & \supseteq & \mathit{failures}_\perp(q). \end{array}$

Proof: Let $\sqsubseteq_{FDI}^{\perp}$ be the preorder defined by: $p \sqsubseteq_{FDI}^{\perp} q$ iff the right-hand side of Theorem 7 holds.

"$\Leftarrow$": It suffices to establish that $\sqsubseteq_{FDI}^{\perp}$ is a liveness respecting precongruence.

To show that $\sqsubseteq_{FDI}^{\perp}$ respects liveness, let $G \subseteq A^*$, $p \sqsubseteq_{FDI}^{\perp} q$, and suppose $p \models \mathit{liveness}(G)$. I need to show that $q \models \mathit{liveness}(G)$. So suppose $\sigma \in CT(q)$. Then either $\sigma \in \mathit{diverg}(g) \subseteq \mathit{diverg}_\perp(g) \subseteq \mathit{diverg}_\perp(p)$ or $\sigma \in \mathit{inf}(q) \subseteq \mathit{inf}_\perp(q) \subseteq \mathit{inf}_\perp(p)$ or $\langle\sigma, A\rangle \in \mathit{failures}(q) \subseteq \mathit{failures}_\perp(q) \subseteq \mathit{failures}_\perp(q)$. In the first case $\rho \in \mathit{diverg}(p) \subseteq CT(p)$ for some $\rho \leq \sigma$; in the second case either $\sigma \in \mathit{inf}(p) \subseteq CT(p)$ or $\rho \in \mathit{diverg}(p) \subseteq CT(p)$ for some $\rho < \sigma$; and in the third case either $\langle\sigma, A\rangle \in \mathit{failures}(p)$ or $\rho \in \mathit{diverg}(p) \subseteq CT(p)$ for some $\rho \leq \sigma$. In all three cases $\rho \in CT(p)$ for some $\rho \leq \sigma$. Since $p \models \mathit{liveness}(G)$, there must be a $\nu \leq \rho$ with $\nu \in G$. As $\nu \leq \sigma$ it follows that $q \models \mathit{liveness}(G)$.

That $\sqsubseteq_{FDI}^{\perp}$ is a precongruence for $\|_S$ and τ_I has been established in [15] by means of the following observations:

$$
\begin{aligned}
\mathit{diverg}_\perp(p\|_S q) &= \{\sigma\rho \mid \exists\langle\nu, X\rangle \in \mathit{failures}_\perp(p), \xi \in \mathit{diverg}_\perp(q).\\
&\qquad\qquad \sigma \in \nu\|_S\xi \wedge \rho \in A^*\}\\
&\quad \cup \{\sigma\rho \mid \exists\nu \in \mathit{diverg}_\perp(p), \langle\xi, X\rangle \in \mathit{failures}_\perp(q).\\
&\qquad\qquad \sigma \in \nu\|_S\xi \wedge \rho \in A^*\}\\
\mathit{inf}_\perp(p\|_S q) &= \{\sigma \mid \exists\nu \in \mathit{inf}_\perp(p), \xi \in \mathit{inf}_\perp(q).\ \sigma \in \nu\|_S\xi\} \cup\\
&\quad \{\sigma \mid \exists\langle\nu, X\rangle \in \mathit{failures}_\perp(p), \xi \in \mathit{inf}_\perp(q).\ \sigma \in \nu\|_S\xi\} \cup\\
&\quad \{\sigma \mid \exists\nu \in \mathit{inf}_\perp(p), \langle\xi, X\rangle \in \mathit{failures}_\perp(q).\ \sigma \in \nu\|_S\xi\} \cup\\
&\quad \{\sigma\rho \mid \sigma \in \mathit{diverg}_\perp(p\|_S q) \wedge \rho \in A^\infty\}\\
\mathit{failures}_\perp(p\|_S q) &= \{\langle\sigma, X \cup Y\rangle \mid \exists\langle\nu, X\rangle \in \mathit{failures}_\perp(p), \langle\xi, Y\rangle \in \mathit{failures}_\perp(q).\\
&\qquad\qquad X \setminus S = Y \setminus S \wedge \sigma \in \nu\|_S\xi\}\\
&\quad \cup \{\langle\sigma, X\rangle \mid \sigma \in \mathit{diverg}_\perp(p\|_S q) \wedge X \subseteq A\}.\\
\mathit{diverg}_\perp(\tau_I(p)) &= \{\tau_I(\sigma)\rho \mid \tau_I(\sigma), \rho \in A^* \wedge \sigma \in \mathit{inf}_\perp(p) \cup \mathit{diverg}_\perp(p)\}\\
\mathit{inf}_\perp(\tau_I(p)) &= \{\tau_I(\sigma) \mid \tau_I(\sigma) \in A^\infty \wedge \sigma \in \mathit{inf}_\perp(p)\}\\
&\quad \cup \{\sigma\rho \mid \sigma \in \mathit{diverg}_\perp(\tau_I(p)) \wedge \rho \in A^\infty\}\\
\mathit{failures}_\perp(\tau_I(p)) &= \{\langle\tau_I(\sigma), X\rangle \mid \langle\sigma, X \cup I\rangle \in \mathit{failures}_\perp(p)\}\\
&\quad \cup \{\langle\sigma, X\rangle \mid \sigma \in \mathit{diverg}_\perp(\tau_I(p)) \wedge X \subseteq A\}.
\end{aligned}
$$

Here $\tau_I(\sigma)$ for $\sigma \in A^\infty$ is the supremum, w.r.t. the prefix order $\leq$ on A^ω, of the set $\{\tau_I(\rho) \mid \rho < \sigma\}$.

Likewise, $\sqsubseteq_{FDI}^{\perp}$ is a congruence for λ_s^m:

$$
\begin{aligned}
\mathit{diverg}_\perp(\lambda_s^m(p)) &= \{\lambda_s^m(\sigma)\rho \mid \sigma \in \mathit{diverg}_\perp(p) \wedge \rho \in A^*\}\\
\mathit{inf}_\perp(\lambda_s^m(p)) &= \{\lambda_s^m(\sigma) \mid \sigma \in \mathit{inf}_\perp(p)\}\\
&\quad \cup \{\sigma\rho \mid \sigma \in \mathit{diverg}_\perp(\lambda_s^m(p)) \wedge \rho \in A^\infty\}\\
\mathit{failures}_\perp(\lambda_s^m(p)) &= \{\langle\lambda_s^m(\sigma), X\rangle \mid \langle\sigma, \lambda_s^{-m}(X)\rangle \in \mathit{failures}_\perp(p)\}\\
&\quad \cup \{\langle\sigma, X\rangle \mid \sigma \in \mathit{diverg}_\perp(\lambda_s^m(p)) \wedge X \subseteq A\}.
\end{aligned}
$$

Here $\lambda_s^{-m}(X) := \{a \in A \mid a(m, s) \in X\}$.

"$\Rightarrow$": Let $\sqsubseteq$ be any liveness respecting precongruence, and suppose $p \sqsubseteq q$. I have to establish that $p \sqsubseteq_{FDI}^{\perp} q$. W.l.o.g. I may assume that neither p nor q has any trace containing the action g. For let λ^m be an injective renaming operator such that g is not in the image of λ^m. Then $\lambda^m(p) \sqsubseteq \lambda^m(q)$. Suppose one can establish $\lambda^m(p) \sqsubseteq_{FDI}^\perp \lambda^m(q)$. Since $\sqsubseteq_{FDI}^\perp$ is a precongruence for renaming, this yields $p \equiv_{FDI}^\perp \lambda^{-m}(\lambda^m(p)) \sqsubseteq_{FDI}^\perp \lambda^{-m}(\lambda^m(p)) \equiv_{FDI}^\perp q$.

Suppose $\mathit{diverg}_\perp(p) \not\supseteq \mathit{diverg}_\perp(q)$; say $\sigma \in \mathit{diverg}_\perp(q) \setminus \mathit{diverg}_\perp(p)$. So there is no $\rho \leq \sigma$ with $\rho \in \mathit{diverg}(p)$. Let r be a deterministic process such that $CT(r) = \{\rho g \mid \rho \leq \sigma\}$. Then each complete trace of $p\|^g r$ contains g. Here I write $\|^g$ for $\|_{A\setminus\{g\}}$, the interleaving operator that synchronises on all visible actions except g. As $\sqsubseteq$ is a precongruence, $p \sqsubseteq q$ implies $p\|^g r \sqsubseteq q\|^g r$, and since $\sqsubseteq$ respects the canonical liveness property, I obtain that each complete trace of $q\|^g r$ must contain g. However, $\rho \in \mathit{diverg}(q)$ for some $\rho \leq \sigma$. So $\rho \in CT(q\|^g r)$, although ρ does not contain g.

Suppose $\mathit{inf}_\perp(p) \not\supseteq \mathit{inf}_\perp(q)$; say $\sigma \in \mathit{inf}_\perp(q) \setminus \mathit{inf}_\perp(p)$. So $\sigma \notin \mathit{inf}(p)$ and there is no $\rho < \sigma$ with $\rho \in \mathit{diverg}(p)$. Let r be a deterministic process such that $CT(r) = \{\rho g \mid \rho < \sigma\} \cup \{\sigma\}$. Then each complete trace of $p\|^g r$ contains g. As $\sqsubseteq$ is a precongruence, $p \sqsubseteq q$ implies $p\|^g r \sqsubseteq q\|^g r$, and since $\sqsubseteq$ respects the canonical liveness property, I obtain that each complete trace of $q\|^g r$ must contain g. However, either $\sigma \in \mathit{inf}(q)$ or $\rho \in \mathit{diverg}(q)$ for some $\rho < \sigma$. So either $\sigma \in CT(q\|^g r)$ or $\rho \in CT(q\|^g r)$, and neither σ nor ρ contains g.

Suppose $\mathit{failures}_\perp(p) \not\supseteq \mathit{failures}_\perp(q)$; say $\langle\sigma, X\rangle \in \mathit{failures}_\perp(q) \setminus \mathit{failures}_\perp(p)$. So $\langle\sigma, X\rangle \notin \mathit{failures}(p)$ and there is no $\rho \leq \sigma$ with $\rho \in \mathit{diverg}(p)$. Let r be a deterministic process with $CT(r) = \{\rho g \mid \rho < \sigma\} \cup \{\sigma a \mid a \in X\}$, and consider the liveness property given by $G := \{\rho g \mid \rho < \sigma\} \cup \{\sigma a \mid a \in X\}$. Then $p\|^g r \models \mathit{liveness}(G)$. As $\sqsubseteq$ is a precongruence, $p \sqsubseteq q$ implies $p\|^g r \sqsubseteq q\|^g r$, and since $\sqsubseteq$ respects liveness properties, also $q\|^g r \models \mathit{liveness}(G)$. However, either $\langle\sigma, X\rangle \in \mathit{failures}(q)$ or there is an $\rho \leq \sigma$ with $\rho \in \mathit{diverg}(q)$. So either $\sigma \in CT(q\|^g r)$ or $\rho \in CT(q\|^g r)$ for some $\rho \leq \sigma$, contradicting that $q\|^g r \models \mathit{liveness}(G)$. □

The standard refinement preorder used in CSP is in fact the *failures-divergences* preorder $\sqsubseteq_{FD}$, defined exactly like $\sqsubseteq_{FDI}^\perp$, but abstracting from the infinite traces. As remarked in [15], this can be done because in CSP one normally restricts attention to processes p with the property that for any $\sigma \in A^*$ either $\sigma \in \mathit{diverg}_\perp(p)$ or there are only finitely many processes q with $p \stackrel{\sigma}{\Longrightarrow} q$. For such processes the set $\mathit{inf}_\perp(p)$ is, with Königs Lemma, completely determined by $\mathit{failures}_\perp(p)$ and $\mathit{diverg}_\perp(p)$, and thus need not be explicitly recorded. When extending CSP to processes not having this property, the component $\mathit{inf}_\perp$ should be added to the semantics of processes [15]. In fact, $\sqsubseteq_{FDI}^\perp$ is the coarsest precongruence for $\mathcal{O}$ contained in $\sqsubseteq_{FD}$: if p, q and r are the processes used in the $\mathit{inf}_\perp$-case of the above proof, and $I := A \setminus \{g\}$, then $\epsilon \in \mathit{diverg}_\perp(\tau_I(q\|^g r)) \setminus \mathit{diverg}_\perp(\tau_I(p\|^g r))$.

The above characterisation as $\sqsubseteq_{FDI}^\perp$ of the coarsest congruence for $\mathcal{O}$ that respects all liveness properties, is somewhat robust under the choice of $\mathcal{O}$. It holds already with just $\|^g$ and injective renaming (for these are the only two operators that are used in the proof), and it remains true when adding in all operators of CSP [4], as $\sqsubseteq_{FDI}^\perp$ is known to be a precongruence for all of them [15].

By Corollary 2, the above characterisation also remains valid when requiring respect for the initial progress property only, but to this end all three operators of $\mathcal{O}$ are needed. This result has in essence been obtained already by Bill Roscoe in [15]. The state operator does not feature in [15]; its rôle in this full abstraction result is taken over by a renaming operator that allows renaming an action a into a choice between two actions b and c. When ignoring this difference in syntax, Theorem 7 can be obtained as an immediate corollary of Corollary 2 and that result. The main reason for using the above proof instead is to show that the concealment or abstraction operator is not needed here.

By Theorem 5, $\sqsubseteq_{FDI}^{\perp}$ is even fully abstract w.r.t. the partially synchronous interleaving and state operators, and the canonical liveness property. This result, like the full abstraction result of [15], does not hold without the state operator, or something equally powerful, even if renaming and abstraction is allowed to be used. Namely, as pointed out by Antti Puhakka [13], one would fail to distinguish the following two processes:

5 Conditional Liveness Properties

Figure 1 presents two processes that have the same liveness properties in any CSP-context. The fact that only the left-hand process *can* do something good doesn't matter here, as neither of the two processes is *guaranteed* to do something good: they may never proceed beyond their initial τ-loops. Nevertheless, from a practical point of view, the difference between these two processes may be enormous. It could be that the action c comes with a huge cost, that is only worth making when something good happens afterwards. Only the right-hand side process is able to incur the cost without any benefits, and for this reason it lacks an important property that the left-hand process has. I call such properties *conditional liveness properties* [6,11]. A *conditional liveness property* is a property that says that

under certain conditions something good will eventually happen.

To formulate a canonical conditional liveness property, assume that the alphabet A contains two specific action c and g, where the occurrence of c is the condition, and the occurrence of g is *good*. The canonical conditional liveness property now says that **if c occurs then g will eventually happen**.

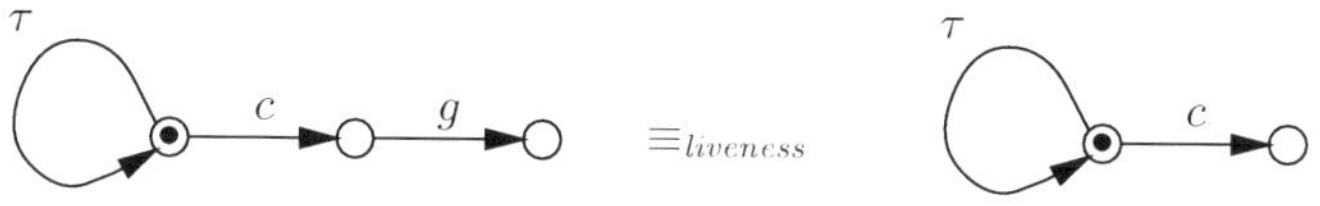

Fig. 1. Two processes with the same liveness properties but different conditional liveness properties

Definition 9. A process p satisfies the *canonical conditional liveness property*, notation $p \models \mathit{liveness}_c(g)$, if every complete trace of p that contains the action c also contains the action g.

To arrive at a general concept of conditional liveness property for labelled transition systems, assume that some condition, and some notion of *good* is defined. Now, to judge whether a process p satisfies this conditional liveness property, one should judge first of all in which states the condition is fulfilled. All observable behaviour of p that is recorded in a labelled transition system until one comes to such a verdict, is the sequence of visible actions performed until that point. Thus the condition is completely determined by the set sequences of visible actions that, when performed by p, lead to such a judgement. Next one should judge whether p can reach a state in which one would say that something good had happened. Again, this judgement can be expressed in terms of the sequences of visible actions that lead to such a state.

Definition 10. A *conditional liveness property* of processes in an LTS is given by two sets $C, G \subseteq A^*$. A process p *satisfies* this conditional liveness property, notation $p \models \mathit{liveness}_C(G)$, when each complete trace of p that has a prefix in C, also has prefix in G.

For the sake of added generality, one could make the notion of success dependent on the particular sequence of actions that fulfilled the condition. This would make G a function from C to $\mathcal{P}(A^*)$ and the requirement would be that each complete trace of p that has a prefix $\sigma \in C$, also has prefix in $G(\sigma)$. However, such a generalised conditional liveness property can be expressed as a conjunction of standard ones, and a preorder that respects a given collection of properties also respects their conjunction.

Theorem 8. A precongruence for the state operator respects every conditional liveness property iff it respects the canonical conditional liveness property.

Proof: "*Only if*" follows because the canonical conditional liveness property is in fact a conditional liveness property, namely the one with C being the set of those sequences that contain the action c, and G the set of those sequences that contain the action g.

"*If*": Again I use a state operator that remembers exactly what sequence of actions has occurred so far. Thus the set of internal states of its interface specification m is A^*, and $\sigma(m, a) := \sigma a$ for all $\sigma \in A^*$ and $a \in A$. Note that the properties $\mathit{liveness}_C(G)$ and $\mathit{liveness}_{C \setminus G}(G)$ are satisfied by the same processes, so w.l.o.g. I may restrict attention to properties $\mathit{liveness}_C(G)$ with $C \cap G = \emptyset$. Given such a property, define

$$a(m, \sigma) := \begin{cases} c \text{ if } \sigma a \in C \\ g \text{ if } \sigma a \in G \\ d \text{ otherwise.} \end{cases}$$

Then $\lambda^m_\epsilon(p) \models \mathit{liveness}_c(g)$ iff $p \models \mathit{liveness}_C(G)$. Thus, if $p \sqsubseteq q$ and $p \models \mathit{liveness}_C(G)$, then $\lambda^m_\epsilon(p) \sqsubseteq \lambda^m_\epsilon(q)$ and $\lambda^m_\epsilon(p) \models \mathit{liveness}_c(g)$. Hence $\lambda^m_\epsilon(q) \models \mathit{liveness}_c(g)$, so $q \models \mathit{liveness}_C(G)$. □

An element $\sigma \in \mathit{diverg}(p) \cup \mathit{deadlocks}(p)$ is called a *deadlock/divergence trace* of a process p. For any $\sigma \in A^*$, not having a deadlock/divergence trace σ is a conditional liveness property, namely with $C := \{\sigma\}$ and $G := \{\sigma a \mid a \in A\}$. Using similar techniques as for Corollary 1, one can establish:

Corollary 3. A precongruence for abstraction and for the state operator that respects the property of having no deadlock/divergence trace c, respects all liveness properties.

Let $\sqsubseteq_{\mathit{cond.\ liveness}}$ denote the preorder that is fully abstract w.r.t. the class of conditional liveness properties and $\mathcal{O}$. Furthermore, write $\sqsubseteq_{d/d}$ for the coarsest precongruence for $\mathcal{O}$ such that $q \sqsubseteq_{d/d} p$ implies $\mathit{deadlocks}(q) \cup \mathit{diverg}(q) \subseteq \mathit{deadlocks}(p) \cup \mathit{diverg}(p)$.

Corollary 4. $p \sqsubseteq_{\mathit{cond.\ liveness}} q$ iff $q \sqsubseteq_{d/d} p$.

Proof: "*If*" follows immediately from Corollary 3. "*Only if*" follows from the observation that the absence of any deadlock/divergence trace σ is a conditional liveness property. □

Antti Puhakka [13] has given a characterisation of the coarsest congruence that preserves deadlock/divergence traces, $\equiv_{d/d}$. His arguments easily extend to a characterisation of $\sqsubseteq_{d/d}$ and hence, using Corollary 4, of $\sqsubseteq_{\mathit{cond.\ liveness}}$. Below I will give a direct proof of the same result. It shows that this characterisation is already valid when merely requiring the precongruence property for $\|_S$ and injective renaming.

As for $\sqsubseteq_{\mathit{liveness}}$, the characterisation of $\sqsubseteq_{\mathit{cond.\ liveness}}$ is in terms of failures, divergences and infinite traces, and again some information needs to be erased, but less than in the case of $\sqsubseteq_{\mathit{liveness}}$. This time we need to forget about failures $\langle \sigma, X\rangle \in \mathit{failures}(p)$ such that $\sigma \in \mathit{diverg}(p)$, and about infinite traces of p that have arbitrary long prefixes in $\mathit{diverg}(p)$. In [13] this is achieved by removal of such failures and infinite traces; here, in order to stress the similarity with the refinement preorder of CSP, I equivalently apply the method of flooding.

Definition 11. Let $p \in \mathbb{P}$.

- $\mathit{inf}_d(p) := \mathit{inf}(p) \cup \{\sigma \in A^\infty \mid \forall \rho < \sigma \exists \nu \in \mathit{diverg}(p).\ \rho \leq \nu < \sigma\}$.
- $\mathit{failures}_d(p) := \mathit{failures}(p) \cup \{\langle \sigma, X\rangle \mid \sigma \in \mathit{diverg}(p) \wedge X \subseteq A\}$.

Theorem 9. $p \sqsubseteq_{\mathit{cond.\ liveness}} q \quad \Leftrightarrow \quad \mathit{diverg}(p) \supseteq \mathit{diverg}(q) \wedge \mathit{inf}_d(p) \supseteq \mathit{inf}_d(q) \wedge \mathit{failures}_d(p) \supseteq \mathit{failures}_d(q)$.

Proof: Let $\sqsubseteq^d_{FDI}$ be the preorder defined by: $p \sqsubseteq^d_{FDI} q$ iff the right-hand side of Theorem 7 holds.

"$\Leftarrow$": It suffices to establish that $\sqsubseteq^d_{FDI}$ is a precongruence for $\mathcal{O}$ that respects all conditional liveness properties.

To show that $\sqsubseteq^d_{FDI}$ respects conditional liveness properties, let $C, G \subseteq A^*$, $p \sqsubseteq^d_{FDI} q$, and suppose $p \models \mathit{liveness}_C(G)$. I need to show that $q \models \mathit{liveness}_C(G)$. So suppose $\sigma \in CT(q)$ and $\rho \in C$ for some prefix $\rho \leq \sigma$. Then one out of three possibilities must apply: either $\sigma \in \mathit{diverg}(g) \subseteq \mathit{diverg}(p)$ or $\sigma \in \mathit{inf}(q) \subseteq \mathit{inf}_d(q) \subseteq \mathit{inf}_d(p)$ or $\langle \sigma, A \rangle \in \mathit{failures}(q) \subseteq \mathit{failures}_d(q) \subseteq \mathit{failures}_d(p)$. In the first and last case, one has $\sigma \in CT(p)$. Since $p \models \mathit{liveness}_C(G)$, there must be a $\xi \leq \sigma$ with $\xi \in G$, which had to be shown. In the second case either $\sigma \in \mathit{inf}(p) \subseteq CT(p)$, in which case the argument proceeds as above, or $\exists \nu \in \mathit{diverg}(p) \subseteq CT(p)$ with $\rho \leq \nu < \sigma$. In the latter case, there must be a $\xi \leq \nu$ with $\xi \in G$, and as $\nu < \sigma$ it follows that $q \models \mathit{liveness}_C(G)$.

That $\sqsubseteq^d_{FDI}$ is a precongruence for $\|_S$, τ_I and λ^m_s follows from the following observations:

$$\begin{aligned}
\mathit{diverg}(p\|_S q) &= \{\sigma \mid \exists\langle \nu, X\rangle \in \mathit{failures}_d(p), \xi \in \mathit{diverg}(q).\ \sigma \in \nu\|_S\xi\} \cup \\
&\quad\ \{\sigma \mid \exists \nu \in \mathit{diverg}(p), \langle \xi, X\rangle \in \mathit{failures}_d(q).\ \sigma \in \nu\|_S\xi\} \\
\mathit{inf}_d(p\|_S q) &= \{\sigma \mid \exists \nu \in \mathit{inf}_d(p), \xi \in \mathit{inf}_d(q).\ \sigma \in \nu\|_S\xi\} \cup \\
&\quad\ \{\sigma \mid \exists\langle \nu, X\rangle \in \mathit{failures}_d(p), \xi \in \mathit{inf}_d(q).\ \sigma \in \nu\|_S\xi\} \cup \\
&\quad\ \{\sigma \mid \exists \nu \in \mathit{inf}_d(p), \langle \xi, X\rangle \in \mathit{failures}_d(q).\ \sigma \in \nu\|_S\xi\} \cup \\
&\quad\ \{\sigma \in A^\infty \mid \forall \rho < \sigma \exists \nu \in \mathit{diverg}(p\|_S q).\ \rho \leq \nu < \sigma\} \\
\mathit{failures}_d(p\|_S q) &= \{\langle \sigma, X \cup Y\rangle \mid \exists\langle \nu, X\rangle \in \mathit{failures}_d(p), \langle \xi, Y\rangle \in \mathit{failures}_d(q). \\
&\qquad\qquad X \setminus S = Y \setminus S \wedge \sigma \in \nu\|_S\xi\} \\
&\quad\ \cup \{\langle \sigma, X\rangle \mid \sigma \in \mathit{diverg}(p\|_S q) \wedge X \subseteq A\}. \\
\mathit{diverg}(\tau_I(p)) &= \{\tau_I(\sigma) \mid \tau_I(\sigma) \in A^* \wedge \sigma \in \mathit{inf}_d(p) \cup \mathit{diverg}(p)\} \\
\mathit{inf}_d(\tau_I(p)) &= \{\tau_I(\sigma) \mid \tau_I(\sigma) \in A^\infty \wedge \sigma \in \mathit{inf}_d(p)\} \\
&\quad\ \cup \{\sigma \in A^\infty \mid \forall \rho < \sigma \exists \nu \in \mathit{diverg}(\tau_I(p)).\ \rho \leq \nu < \sigma\} \\
\mathit{failures}_d(\tau_I(p)) &= \{\langle \tau_I(\sigma), X\rangle \mid \langle \sigma, X \cup I\rangle \in \mathit{failures}_d(p)\} \\
&\quad\ \cup \{\langle \sigma, X\rangle \mid \sigma \in \mathit{diverg}(\tau_I(p)) \wedge X \subseteq A\} \\
\mathit{diverg}(\lambda^m_s(p)) &= \{\lambda^m_s(\sigma) \mid \sigma \in \mathit{diverg}(p)\} \\
\mathit{inf}_d(\lambda^m_s(p)) &= \{\lambda^m_s(\sigma) \mid \sigma \in \mathit{inf}_d(p)\} \\
&\quad\ \cup \{\sigma \in A^\infty \mid \forall \rho < \sigma \exists \nu \in \mathit{diverg}(\lambda^m_s(p)).\ \rho \leq \nu < \sigma\} \\
\mathit{failures}_d(\lambda^m_s(p)) &= \{\langle \lambda^m_s(\sigma), X\rangle \mid \langle \sigma, \lambda^{-m}_s(X)\rangle \in \mathit{failures}_d(p)\} \\
&\quad\ \cup \{\langle \sigma, X\rangle \mid \sigma \in \mathit{diverg}(\lambda^m_s(p)) \wedge X \subseteq A\}.
\end{aligned}$$

"$\Rightarrow$": Let $\sqsubseteq$ be any precongruence for $\mathcal{O}$ that respects conditional liveness properties, and suppose $p \sqsubseteq q$. I have to establish that $p \sqsubseteq^d_{FDI} q$. W.l.o.g. I may assume that neither p nor q has any trace containing the actions c or g. The argument for this is as in the proof of Theorem 7.

Suppose $\mathit{diverg}(p) \not\supseteq \mathit{diverg}(q)$; say $\sigma \in \mathit{diverg}(q) \setminus \mathit{diverg}(p)$. Let r be a deterministic process such that $CT(r) = \{\sigma c g\}$. Then each complete trace of $p\|^{c,g}r$ that contains c also contains g. Here I write $\|^{c,g}$ for $\|_{A\setminus\{c,g\}}$, the interleaving operator that synchronises on all visible actions except c and g. As $\sqsubseteq$ is a precongruence, $p \sqsubseteq q$ implies $p\|^{c,g}r \sqsubseteq q\|^{c,g}r$, and since $\sqsubseteq$ respects the canonical conditional liveness property, I obtain that each complete trace of $q\|^{c,g}r$ that contains c must also contain g. However, as $\sigma \in \mathit{diverg}(q)$, $\sigma c \in \mathit{diverg}(q\|^{c,g}r) \subseteq CT(q\|^{c,g}r)$, although σc does not contain g.

Suppose $\mathit{inf}_d(p) \not\supseteq \mathit{inf}_d(q)$; say $\sigma \in \mathit{inf}_d(q) \setminus \mathit{inf}_d(p)$. So $\sigma \notin \mathit{inf}(p)$ and there is a $\rho < \sigma$ such that $\rho \leq \rho\nu < \sigma$ for no sequence $\rho\nu \in \mathit{diverg}(p)$. Let r be a deterministic process such that $CT(r) = \{\rho c \nu g \mid \rho\nu < \sigma\} \cup \{\sigma\}$. Then each complete trace of $p\|^g r$ that contains c, must also contain g. As $\sqsubseteq$ is a precongruence, $p \sqsubseteq q$ implies $p\|^{c,g} r \sqsubseteq q\|^{g,c} r$, and since $\sqsubseteq$ respects the canonical conditional liveness property, I obtain that each complete trace of $q\|^{c,g} r$ that contains c must also contain g. However, either $\sigma \in \mathit{inf}(q)$ or $\rho\nu \in \mathit{diverg}(q)$ for some $\rho \leq \rho\nu < \sigma$. In each case $q\|^{c,g} r$ has a complete trace that contains c but not g.

Suppose $\mathit{failures}_d(p) \not\supseteq \mathit{failures}_d(q)$; say $\langle\sigma, X\rangle \in \mathit{failures}_d(q) \setminus \mathit{failures}_d(p)$. So $\langle\sigma, X\rangle \notin \mathit{failures}(p)$ and $\sigma \notin \mathit{diverg}(p)$. Let r be a deterministic process with $CT(r) = \{\sigma c a \mid a \in X\}$, let C be the set of sequences containing c, and consider the conditional liveness property given by C and $G := \{\sigma c a \mid a \in X\}$. Then $p\|^c r \models \mathit{liveness}_C(G)$. As $\sqsubseteq$ is a precongruence, $p \sqsubseteq q$ implies $p\|^c r \sqsubseteq q\|^c r$, and since $\sqsubseteq$ respects conditional liveness properties, also $q\|^g r \models \mathit{liveness}_C(G)$. However, either $\langle\sigma, X\rangle \in \mathit{failures}(q)$ or $\sigma \in \mathit{diverg}(q)$. So $\sigma c \in CT(q\|^g r)$, contradicting that $q\|^c r \models \mathit{liveness}_C(G)$. □

In [14], Bill Roscoe has shown that $\sqsubseteq^d_{FDI}$ is a precongruence for all operators of CSP; he also developed a new fixed point theory that shows that it is a congruence for recursion as well.

6 Linear Time Properties

Safety, liveness, and conditional liveness properties, as studied in the previous sections, are special cases of *linear time properties.* A linear time property can be thought of as any requirement on the observable content of the runs of a process. The property is satisfied by a process when the observable content of all its maximal runs satisfy this requirement. Hence a linear time property can be formalised by the set of sequences over A^ω that, when performed in a maximal run of a process, meet the requirement.

Definition 12. A *linear time property* of processes in an LTS is given by a set $P \subseteq A^\omega$. A process p *satisfies* this property, notation $p \models P$, when $CT(p) \subseteq P$.

A safety property is a special kind of linear time property, namely $\mathit{safety}(B) = \{\sigma \in A^\omega \mid \neg\exists\rho \in B.\ \rho \leq \sigma\}$. Likewise, $\mathit{liveness}(G) = \{\sigma \in A^\omega \mid \exists\rho \in G.\ \rho \leq \sigma\}$, and $\mathit{liveness}_C(G) = \{\sigma \in A^\omega \mid (\exists\rho \in C.\ \rho \leq \sigma) \Rightarrow (\exists\nu \in G.\ \nu \leq \sigma)\}$.

In [9] and most subsequent work, liveness properties are formalised in a different way than in this paper. For the canonical liveness property it is fundamentally impossible to ever tell that it is not going to be satisfied when one has only observed a finite prefix of a maximal run of a process. For if "something good" is promised to happen, it is always possible to assume it will be further in the future. In [9], this is taken to be the defining characteristic of liveness properties, and a property P is called a liveness property iff $\forall\rho \in A^*.\exists\sigma \in P.\ \rho \leq \sigma$.

The property $\mathit{liveness}(G)$ with $G = \{a\}$ for instance says that the first visible action of a process should be an a. It is a liveness property in my sense, since the first action being an a can be thought of as a good thing that happened eventually; here the requirement that it has to happen as first action could be part of one's concept of *good*. However, it is not a liveness property as formalised in [9] and subsequent work, since the occurrence of a $b \neq a$ as first action proves that the property will never be satisfied.

The property that from some point onwards all visible actions a process performs should be g's, is an example of a liveness property in the sense of [9] that is not a liveness property in my sense. Namely, at no point can one ever tell that something good has happened.

A well know theorem [9] says that any linear time property P can be written as the conjunction $\mathit{safety}(B) \cap P_{liveness}$ of a safety property and a liveness property in the sense of [9]. Namely,

$$B := \{\rho \in A^* \mid \neg\exists\sigma \in P.\ \rho \leq \sigma\} \quad \text{and} \quad P_{liveness} := P \cup (A^\omega \setminus \mathit{safety}(B)).$$

Such a theorem does not hold for my liveness properties.

My characterisation of $\sqsubseteq_{liveness}$ would still be valid if I would have taken as class of liveness properties the intersection of mine and the ones from [9]. This follows immediately from Theorem 5, as the canonical liveness property is in this intersection. So the extra generality in my definition is harmless. However, the extra restriction makes a difference, as the canonical conditional liveness property, for instance, is a liveness property in the sense of [9].

Liveness properties in the sense of [9] are studied because proving them requires a different tool set than proving safety properties. However, as far as practical applications are concerned, one is mostly interested in conjunctions of safety and liveness properties, i.e. general linear time properties. I will therefore not try to characterise coarsest congruences that respect just the liveness properties in the sense of [9].

The coarsest congruence respecting all linear time properties has been characterised as *NDFD-equivalence* by Roope Kaivola and Antti Valmari in [8]; this results extends to preorders in a straightforward way. The NDFD preorder can be defined just like $\sqsubseteq^d_{FDI}$, except that $\inf(\_)$ is used instead of $\mathit{inf}_\perp(\_)$. In fact, this result can also be obtained as corollary of what we have seen so far.

Theorem 10. $p \sqsubseteq_{lt\text{-}properties} q \quad \Leftrightarrow \quad$
$$\begin{aligned} \mathit{diverg}(p) &\supseteq \mathit{diverg}(q) \wedge \\ \mathit{inf}(p) &\supseteq \mathit{inf}(q) \wedge \\ \mathit{failures}_d(p) &\supseteq \mathit{failures}_d(q). \end{aligned}$$

Proof: Let $\sqsubseteq_{NDFD}$ be the preorder defined by: $p \sqsubseteq_{NDFD} q$ iff the right-hand side of Theorem 10 holds.

"$\Leftarrow$": It suffices to establish that $\sqsubseteq_{NDFD}$ is a precongruence for $\mathcal{O}$ that respects all linear time properties.

To show that $\sqsubseteq_{NDFD}$ respects linear time properties, let $P \subseteq A^\omega$, $p \sqsubseteq_{NDFD} q$, and suppose $p \models P$. I need to show that $q \models P$. So suppose $\sigma \in CT(q)$. Then either $\sigma \in \mathit{diverg}(g) \subseteq \mathit{diverg}(p)$ or $\sigma \in \mathit{inf}(q) \subseteq \mathit{inf}(q)$ or $\langle\sigma, A\rangle \in \mathit{failures}(q) \subseteq \mathit{failures}_d(q) \subseteq \mathit{failures}_d(p)$. In the last case, one has either $\langle\sigma, A\rangle \in \mathit{failures}(p)$ or $\sigma \in \mathit{diverg}(p)$. So in all cases $\sigma \in CT(p)$. Since $p \models P$, it must be that $\sigma \in P$. It follows that $CT(q) \subseteq P$, i.e. $q \models P$.

That $\sqsubseteq^d_{FDI}$ is a precongruence for $\|_S$, τ_I and λ^m_s follows from similar, but simpler, observations as in the proof of Theorem 9.

"$\Rightarrow$": Let $\sqsubseteq$ be any precongruence for $\mathcal{O}$ that respects linear time properties, and suppose $p \sqsubseteq q$. I have to establish that $p \sqsubseteq_{NDFD} q$. That $diverg(p) \supseteq diverg(q)$ and $failures_d(p) \supseteq failures_d(q)$ follows immediately from Theorem 9, using that conditional liveness properties are linear time properties. That $inf(p) \supseteq inf(q)$ follows immediately by considering the linear time property $CT(p)$. □

To obtain this result it suffices to define $\sqsubseteq_{lt\text{-}properties}$ as the coarsest precongruence w.r.t. $\|_S$ and injective renaming that respects all linear time properties. However, it happens to also be a precongruence for all operators of CSP.

Linear time properties do not capture the entire observable behaviour or processes in the neutral environment. Orthogonal to them are *possibility properties*, such as: a process *may* do an action g. As argued by Leslie Lamport, "verifying possibility properties tells you nothing interesting about a system" [10]. Nevertheless, it is not hard to characterise the coarsest precongruence for $\mathcal{O}$ that respects linear time properties as well as all possibility properties, and thereby arguably the entire observable behaviour of a processes in a neutral environment. It is $\equiv_{NDFD}$, the symmetric closure of $\sqsubseteq_{NDFD}$.

7 Concluding Remark

The methodology of the paper is close in spirit to the work on testing equivalences by Rocco De Nicola and Matthew Hennessy [5], and the results in Sections 3 and 4 are comparable as well. The notion of *must testing* of [5] could be reinterpreted as a way to test liveness properties, and hence, unsurprisingly, my preorder $\sqsubseteq_{liveness}$ is exactly the must-testing preorder of [5]. However, my safety preorder is exactly the *inverse* of the *may testing* preorder of [5]. This can be explained by thinking, in the context of may testing, of the "success"-action ω as marking a state of *failure*, rather than one of *success*. Now the property of whether a process may reach ω is exactly the negation of whether it will always avoid ω. This turns may-testing around, from testing certain possibility properties, to testing safety properties. It remains to elaborate a theory of testing that captures the concept of conditional liveness.

References

1. Alexander, M., Gardner, W. (eds.): Process Algebra for Parallel and Distributed Processing. Chapman & Hall, Boca Raton (2008)
2. Baeten, J.C.M., Bergstra, J.A.: Global renaming operators in concrete process algebra. Information and Computation 78(3), 205–245 (1988)
3. Bergstra, J.A., Klop, J.W.: Algebra of communicating processes with abstraction. Theoretical Computer Science 37(1), 77–121 (1985)
4. Brookes, S.D., Hoare, C.A.R., Roscoe, A.W.: A theory of communicating sequential processes. Journal of the ACM 31(3), 560–599 (1984)

5. De Nicola, R., Hennessy, M.: Testing equivalences for processes. Theoretical Computer Science 34, 83–133 (1984)
6. van Glabbeek, R.J., Voorhoeve, M.: Liveness, Fairness and Impossible Futures. In: Baier, C., Hermanns, H. (eds.) CONCUR 2006. LNCS, vol. 4137, pp. 126–141. Springer, Heidelberg (2006)
7. van Glabbeek, R.J.: The Linear Time – Branching Time Spectrum I; The Semantics of Concrete, Sequential Processes. In: Bergstra, J.A., Ponse, A., Smolka, S.A. (eds.) Handbook of Process Algebra, ch.1, pp. 3–99. Elsevier, Amsterdam (2001)
8. Kaivola, R., Valmari, A.: The Weakest Compositional Semantic Equivalence Preserving Nexttime-less Linear Temporal Logic. In: Cleaveland, W.R. (ed.) CONCUR 1992. LNCS, vol. 630, pp. 207–221. Springer, Heidelberg (1992), `http://dx.doi.org/10.1007/BFb0084793`
9. Lamport, L.: Proving the correctness of multiprocess programs. IEEE Transactions on Software Engineering 3(2), 125–143 (1977)
10. Lamport, L.: Proving Possibility Properties. Theoretical Computer Science 206(1-2), 341–352 (1998), `http://research.microsoft.com/en-us/um/people/lamport/pubs/pubs.html#lamport-possibility`
11. Levy, P.B.: Infinite trace equivalence. Annals of Pure and Applied Logic 151(2-3), 170–198 (2008), `http://dx.doi.org/10.1016/j.apal.2007.10.007`
12. Milner, R.: Operational and algebraic semantics of concurrent processes. In: van Leeuwen, J. (ed.) Handbook of Theoretical Computer Science, ch.19, pp. 1201–1242. Elsevier Science Publishers B.V, North-Holland (1990); Alternatively see Communication and Concurrency. Prentice-Hall, Englewood Cliffs, (1989), an earlier version appeared as A Calculus of Communicating systems. LNCS, vol. 92. Springer, Heidelberg (1980)
13. Puhakka, A.: Weakest Congruence Results Concerning "Any-Lock". In: Kobayashi, N., Pierce, B.C. (eds.) TACS 2001. LNCS, vol. 2215, pp. 400–419. Springer, Heidelberg (2001)
14. Roscoe, A.W.: Seeing Beyond Divergence. In: Abdallah, A.E., Jones, C.B., Sanders, J.W. (eds.) Communicating Sequential Processes. LNCS, vol. 3525, pp. 15–35. Springer, Heidelberg (2005)
15. Roscoe, A.W.: The Theory and Practice of Concurrency. Prentice-Hall, Englewood Cliffs (1997), `http://www.comlab.ox.ac.uk/bill.roscoe/publications/68b.pdf`

Entropy and Attack Models in Information Flow
(Invited Talk)

Mário S. Alvim[1], Miguel E. Andrés[2], and Catuscia Palamidessi[1]

[1] INRIA and LIX, École Polytechnique, Palaiseau, France
[2] University of Nijmegen, The Netherlands

In recent years, there has been a growing interest in considering the quantitative aspects of Information Flow, partly because often the a priori knowledge of the secret information can be represented by a probability distribution, and partly because the mechanisms to protect the information may use randomization to obfuscate the relation between the secrets and the observables.

Several works in literature use an Information Theoretic approach to model the problem and define the leakage in a quantitative way, see for example [17,4,9,10,13,12,2]. The idea is that the system is seen as a *channel*. The input represents the secret, the output represents the observable, and the correlation between the input and output (*mutual information*) represents the information leakage. The worst case leakage corresponds then to the *capacity* of the channel, which is by definition the maximum mutual information that can be obtained by varying the input distribution.

In the works mentioned above, the notion of mutual information is based on *Shannon entropy*, which (because of its mathematical properties) is the most established measure of uncertainty. From the security point of view, this measure corresponds to a particular model of attack and a particular way of estimating the security threat (vulnerability of the secret). Other notions have been considered, and argued to be more appropriate for security in certain scenarios. These include: *Rényi min-entropy* [1,16], *Bayes risk* [3], *guessing entropy* [11], and *marginal guesswork* [14]. Köpf and Basin discuss the relation between brute-force guessing attacks and entropy in [8], in the context of information flow induced by a deterministic program, and define the information leakage as difference between the input entropy and the conditional one, namely the entropy based on the a priori input distribution, and the entropy of the a posteriori distribution (i.e. after observing teh output), respectively. One of their main results is that, in their framework, the notion of leakage under the various notions of attacks considered in their paper is always non-negative.

In this talk, we extend the analysis of Köpf and Basin to the probabilistic scenario, and we consider also other notions of entropy, including the family of entropies proposed by Rényi [15]. We argue that in the probabilistic case the notion of information leakage needs to be revised. In fact, when the same secret can give different observables (according to a probability distribution), the difference between a priori and a posteriori entropy may be negative. This is due to the fact that the notion of entropy uses the probability distribution in two different ways: for averaging and for representing the belief of the attacker. While the leakage should depend on the difference induced by the belief change

C.S. Calude and V. Sassone (Eds.): TCS 2010, IFIP AICT 323, pp. 53–54, 2010.

due to the observation, the averaging probability should remain the same. (A similar concern has also inspired the works of [5] and [7].) In order to avoid the unnatural consequence of a negative leakage, we propose to base the notion of leakage directly on the (more primitive) notion of mutual information. We consider some cases of entropy, in particular the Rényi's entropies, for which the corresponding notion of mutual information has been investigated in [6], and we show that in this way the property of non-negativeness is ensured.

References

1. Cachin, C.: Entropy Measures and Unconditional Security in Cryptography. PhD thesis (1997)
2. Chatzikokolakis, K., Palamidessi, C., Panangaden, P.: Anonymity protocols as noisy channels. Inf. and Comp. 206(2-4), 378–401 (2008)
3. Chatzikokolakis, K., Palamidessi, C., Panangaden, P.: On the Bayes risk in information-hiding protocols. Journal of Computer Security 16(5), 531–571 (2008)
4. Clark, D., Hunt, S., Malacaria, P.: Quantitative information flow, relations and polymorphic types. J. of Logic and Comp. 18(2), 181–199 (2005)
5. Clarkson, M.R., Myers, A.C., Schneider, F.B.: Belief in information flow. Journal of Computer Security 17(5), 655–701 (2009)
6. Csiszár, I.: Generalized cutoff rates and Rényi's information measures. Transactions on Information Theory 41(1), 26–34 (1995)
7. Hamadou, S., Sassone, V., Palamidessi, C.: Reconciling belief and vulnerability in information flow. In: Proc. of the IEEE Symposium on Security and Privacy. IEEE, Los Alamitos (to appear, 2010)
8. Köpf, B., Basin, D.A.: An information-theoretic model for adaptive side-channel attacks. In: Proc. of CCS, pp. 286–296. ACM, New York (2007)
9. Malacaria, P.: Assessing security threats of looping constructs. In: Proc. of POPL, pp. 225–235. ACM, New York (2007)
10. Malacaria, P., Chen, H.: Lagrange multipliers and maximum information leakage in different observational models. In: Proc. of PLAS, pp. 135–146. ACM, New York (2008)
11. Massey: Guessing and entropy. In: Proceedings of the IEEE International Symposium on Information Theory, p. 204. IEEE, Los Alamitos (1994)
12. Moskowitz, I.S., Newman, R.E., Crepeau, D.P., Miller, A.R.: Covert channels and anonymizing networks. In: Proc. of PES, pp. 79–88. ACM, New York (2003)
13. Moskowitz, I.S., Newman, R.E., Syverson, P.F.: Quasi-anonymous channels. In: Proc. of CNIS, pp. 126–131. IASTED (2003)
14. Pliam, J.O.: On the incomparability of entropy and marginal guesswork in brute-force attacks. In: Roy, B., Okamoto, E. (eds.) INDOCRYPT 2000. LNCS, vol. 1977, pp. 67–79. Springer, Heidelberg (2000)
15. Rényi, A.: On Measures of Entropy and Information. In: Proc. of the 4th Berkeley Symposium on Mathematics, Statistics, and Probability, pp. 547–561 (1961)
16. Smith, G.: On the foundations of quantitative information flow. In: de Alfaro, L. (ed.) FOSSACS 2009. LNCS, vol. 5504, pp. 288–302. Springer, Heidelberg (2009)
17. Zhu, Y., Bettati, R.: Anonymity vs. information leakage in anonymity systems. In: Proc. of ICDCS, pp. 514–524. IEEE, Los Alamitos (2005)

Safe Equivalences for Security Properties

Mário S. Alvim[1], Miguel E. Andrés[2], Catuscia Palamidessi[1], and Peter van Rossum[2]

[1] INRIA and LIX, École Polytechnique Palaiseau, France
[2] Institute for Computing and Information Sciences, The Netherlands

Abstract. In the field of Security, process equivalences have been used to characterize various information-hiding properties (for instance secrecy, anonymity and non-interference) based on the principle that a protocol P with a variable x satisfies such property if and only if, for every pair of secrets s_1 and s_2, $P[^{s_1}/_x]$ is equivalent to $P[^{s_2}/_x]$. We argue that, in the presence of nondeterminism, the above principle relies on the assumption that the scheduler "works for the benefit of the protocol", and this is usually not a safe assumption. Non-safe equivalences, in this sense, include complete-trace equivalence and bisimulation. We present a formalism in which we can specify admissible schedulers and, correspondingly, safe versions of these equivalences. We prove that safe bisimulation is still a congruence. Finally, we show that safe equivalences can be used to establish information-hiding properties.

1 Introduction

One of the fundamental problems in computer security is the protection from information leaks, namely how to make sure that a system does not reveal, by observations that can be made during the execution, some information that we wish to maintain secret.

One way to prevent an attacker to infer the secret from the observables is to create *noise*, namely to make sure that for every execution in which a given secret produces a certain observable, there is at least another execution in which a different secret produces the same observable. In practice this is often done by using randomization, see for instance the DCNet [10] and the Crowds [23] protocols.

In the literature about the foundations of Computer Security, however, the quantitative aspects are often abstracted away, and probabilistic behavior is replaced by nondeterministic behavior. Correspondingly, there have been various approaches in which information-hiding properties are expressed in terms of equivalences based on nondeterminism, especially in a concurrent setting. For instance, [24] defines *anonymity* as follows[1]: A protocol S is anonymous if, for every pair of culprits a and b, $S[^a/_x]$ and $S[^b/_x]$ produce the same observable traces. A similar definition is given in [1] for *secrecy*, with the difference that $S[^a/_x]$ and $S[^b/_x]$ are required to be bisimilar. In [13], an electoral system S preserves the *confidentiality of the vote* if for any voters v and w, the observable behavior of S is the same if we swap the votes of v and w. Namely, $S[^a/_v \,|^b/_w] \sim S[^b/_v \,|^a/_w]$, where $\sim$ represents bisimilarity.

[1] The actual definition of [24] is more complicated, but the spirit is the same.

C.S. Calude and V. Sassone (Eds.): TCS 2010, IFIP AICT 323, pp. 55–70, 2010.

These proposals are based on the implicit assumption that *all the nondeterministic executions present in the specification of S will always be possible under every implementation of* S. Or at least, that the adversary will believe so. In concurrency, however, as argued in [8], nondeterminism has a rather different meaning: if a specification S contains some nondeterministic alternatives, typically it is because we want to abstract from specific implementations, such as the scheduling policy. A specification is considered correct, with respect to some property, if every alternative satisfies the property. Correspondingly, an implementation is considered correct if all executions are among those possible in the specification, i.e. if the implementation is a refinement of the specification. There is no expectation that the implementation will actually make possible all the alternatives indicated by the specification.

We argue that the use of nondeterminism in concurrency corresponds to a *demonic* view: the scheduler, i.e. the entity that will decide which alternative to select, may try to choose the worst alternative. Hence we need to make sure that "all alternatives are good", i.e. satisfy the intended property. In the above mentioned approaches to the formalization of security properties, on the contrary, the interpretation of nondeterminism is *angelic*: the scheduler is expected to actually help the protocol to confuse the adversary and thus protect the secret information.

There is another issue, orthogonal to the angelic/demonic dichotomy, but relevant for the achievement of security properties: the scheduler *should not be able to make its choices dependent on the secret*, or else nearly every protocol would be insecure, i.e. the scheduler would always be able to leak the secret to an external observer (for instance by producing different interleavings of the observables, depending on the secret). This remark has been made several times already, and several approaches have been proposed to cope with the problem of full-information scheduler (aka almighty, omniscient, clairvoyant, etc.), see for example [6,7,9,8,3].

The risk of a naive use of nondeterminism to specify a security property, is not only that it may rely on an implicit assumption that the scheduler behaves angelically, but also that it is clairvoyant (fully-informed), i.e. that it peeks at the secrets (that it is not supposed to be able to see) to achieve its angelic strategy.

Example 1. Consider the following system, in a CCS-like syntax: $S \stackrel{\text{def}}{=} (c)(A \parallel H_1 \parallel H_2 \parallel Corr)$, with $A \stackrel{\text{def}}{=} \overline{c}\langle sec\rangle$, $H_1 \stackrel{\text{def}}{=} c(s).\overline{out}\langle a\rangle$, $H_2 \stackrel{\text{def}}{=} c(s).\overline{out}\langle b\rangle$, $Corr \stackrel{\text{def}}{=} c(s).\overline{out}\langle s\rangle$. Here $\parallel$ is the parallel operator, $\overline{c}\langle sec\rangle$ is a process that sends sec on channel c, $c(s).P$ is a process that receives s on channel c and then continues as P, and (c) is the restriction operator, enforcing synchronization on c. The name sec represents a secret.

It is easy to see that we have $S\left[{}^{a}/_{sec}\right] \sim S\left[{}^{b}/_{sec}\right]$. Note that, in order to simulate the third branch in $S\left[{}^{a}/_{sec}\right]$, the process $S\left[{}^{b}/_{sec}\right]$ needs to select its first branch. Viceversa, in order to simulate the third branch in $S\left[{}^{b}/_{sec}\right]$, the process $S\left[{}^{a}/_{sec}\right]$ needs to select its second branch. This means that, in order to achieve bisimulation, the scheduler needs to know the secret, and change its choice accordingly.

This example shows a system that intuitively is not secure, because the third component, *Corr*, reveals whatever secret it receives. However, according to the equivalence-based notions of security discussed above, *it is secure*. But it is secure thanks to a scheduler that angelically helps the system to protect the secret, and it does so by making its choices dependent on the secret. We consider these assumptions on the scheduler excessively strong.

We do not claim, however, that we should rule out the use of angelic nondeterminism in security: on the contrary, angelic nondeterminism can be a powerful specification concept. We only advocate a cautious use of this notion. In particular, it should not be used in a context in which the scheduler may be in collusion with the attacker. The goal of this paper is to define a framework in which we can combine both angelic and demonic nondeterminism in a setting in which also probabilistic behavior may be present, and in a context in which the scheduler is restricted (i.e. not fully-informed). We define "safe" variant of typical equivalence relations (complete traces and bisimulation), and we show how to use them to characterize information-hiding properties.

1.1 Contribution

The main novelties of our work can be articulated as follows:

- We propose a formalism for concurrent systems which accounts for both probabilistic and nondeterministic behaviour, and in which the latter is of two kinds: *global* and *local*. The first represents the possible interleavings produced by the parallel components, which may be influenced by the attacker. The second is associated to the possible choices internal to each component, which may depend on the secrets or other unknown parameters, not controlled by the attacker. Correspondingly, we split the scheduler in two constituents: global and local. The latter is actually a tuple of local schedulers, one for each component of the system.
- We propose a notion of *admissible scheduler* for the above systems, in which the global constituent is not allowed to see the secrets, and each local constituent is not allowed to see any information about the other components. We then generalize the standard definition of strong (probabilistic) information hiding (such as no-interference and strong anonymity) to the case in which also nondeterminism is present, under the assumption that the schedulers are admissible.
- We use admissible schedulers to define safe versions of complete-trace equivalence and bisimilarity especially tuned for security (in this paper we often refer to complete traces as simply traces). This means that we account for the possibility that the global constituent of the scheduler is in collusion with the attacker, and therefore does not necessarily help the system to obfuscate the secret. We show that the latter is still a congruence, like in the classical case.
- We finally show that our notions of safe trace equivalence and bisimilarity imply strong information hiding in the above sense.

2 Probabilistic Automata

In this section we gather preliminary notions and results related to probabilistic automata [26,25].

A function $\mu\colon Q \to [0,1]$ is a *discrete probability distribution* on a set Q if the support of μ is countable and $\sum_{q\in Q}\mu(q) = 1$. The set of all discrete probability distributions on Q is denoted by $\mathcal{D}(Q)$.

A *probabilistic automaton* is a quadruple $M = (Q, \Sigma, \hat{q}, \alpha)$ where Q is a countable set of *states*, Σ a finite set of *actions*, $\hat{q}$ the *initial* state, and α is a *transition function* $\alpha : Q \to \mathcal{P}(\Sigma \times \mathcal{D}(Q))$. Here $\mathcal{P}(X)$ is the set of all finite subsets of X. If $\alpha(q) = \emptyset$ then q is a *terminal* state. We write $q \xrightarrow{a} \mu$ for $(a, \mu) \in \alpha(q)$. Moreover, we write $q \xrightarrow{a} r$ whenever $q \xrightarrow{a} \mu$ and $\mu(r) > 0$. A *fully probabilistic automaton* is a probabilistic automaton satisfying $|\alpha(q)| \leq 1$ for all states. In case $\alpha(q) \neq \emptyset$ in a fully probabilistic automaton, we will overload notation and use $\alpha(q)$ to denote the distribution outgoing from q. A *path* in a probabilistic automaton is a sequence $\sigma = q_0 \xrightarrow{a_1} q_1 \xrightarrow{a_2} \cdots$ where $q_i \in Q$, $a_i \in \Sigma$ and $q_i \xrightarrow{a_{i+1}} q_{i+1}$. A path can be *finite* in which case it ends with a state. A path is *complete* if it is either infinite or finite ending in a terminal state. Given a path σ, *first*(σ) denotes its first state, and if σ is finite then *last*(σ) denotes its last state. Let $\mathrm{Paths}_q(M)$ denote the set of all paths, $\mathrm{Paths}^\star_q(M)$ the set of all finite paths, and $\mathrm{CPaths}_q(M)$ the set of all complete paths of an automaton M, starting from the state q. We will omit q if $q = \hat{q}$. Paths are ordered by the prefix relation, which we denote by $\leq$. The *trace* of a path is the sequence of actions in $\Sigma^\infty = \Sigma^* \cup \Sigma^\omega$ obtained by removing the states, hence for the above path σ we have $\mathit{trace}(\sigma) = a_1 a_2 \ldots$. We denote by $\mathit{Traces}(M)$ the complete traces of M, i.e. $\mathit{Traces}(M) \stackrel{\text{def}}{=} \{\mathit{trace}(\sigma) \mid \sigma \in \mathrm{CPaths}(M)\}$. If $\Sigma' \subseteq \Sigma$, then $\mathit{trace}_{\Sigma'}(\sigma)$ is the projection of $\mathit{trace}(\sigma)$ on the elements of Σ'.

Let $M = (Q, \Sigma, \hat{q}, \alpha)$ be a (fully) probabilistic automaton, $q \in Q$ a state, and let $\sigma \in \mathrm{Paths}^\star_q(M)$ be a finite path starting in q. The *cone* generated by σ is the set of complete paths $\langle\sigma\rangle = \{\sigma' \in \mathrm{CPaths}_q(M) \mid \sigma \leq \sigma'\}$. Given a fully probabilistic automaton $M = (Q, \Sigma, \hat{q}, \alpha)$ and a state q, we can calculate the *probability value*, denoted by $\mathbf{P}_q(\sigma)$, of any finite path σ starting in q as follows: $\mathbf{P}_q(q) = 1$ and $\mathbf{P}_q(\sigma \xrightarrow{a} q') = \mathbf{P}_q(\sigma)\cdot\mu(q')$, where $\mathit{last}(\sigma) \xrightarrow{a} \mu$. Let $\Omega_q \stackrel{\text{def}}{=} \mathrm{CPaths}_q(M)$ be the sample space, and let $\mathcal{F}_q$ be the smallest σ-algebra generated by the cones. Then $\mathbf{P}_q$ induces a unique *probability measure* on $\mathcal{F}_q$ (which we will also denote by $\mathbf{P}_q$) such that $\mathbf{P}_q(\langle\sigma\rangle) = \mathbf{P}_q(\sigma)$ for every finite path σ starting in q. For $q = \hat{q}$ we write $\mathbf{P}$ instead of $\mathbf{P}_{\hat{q}}$.

A scheduler for a probabilistic automaton M is a function $\zeta\colon \mathrm{Paths}^\star(M) \to (\Sigma \times \mathcal{D}(Q) \cup \{\bot\})$ such that for all finite path σ, if $\alpha(\mathit{last}(\sigma)) \neq \emptyset$ then $\zeta(\sigma) \in \alpha(\mathit{last}(\sigma))$, and $\zeta(\sigma) = \bot$ otherwise. Hence, a scheduler ζ selects one of the available transitions in each state, and determines therefore a fully probabilistic automaton, obtained by pruning from M the alternatives that are not chosen by ζ. A scheduler is history dependent since it takes into account the path and not only the current state. It may be partial, i.e. it may halt the execution at any time [2].

3 Systems

In this section we describe the kind of systems we are dealing with. We start by introducing a variant of probabilistic automata, that we call *Tagged Probabilistic Automata*

[2] In this paper, however, we will consider only total schedulers, to be more in line with the standard semantics of CCS.

(TPA). These systems are parallel compositions of probabilistic processes, called *components*. Each component is equipped with a unique identifier, called *tag*. Whenever a component (or a pair of components in case of synchronization) makes a step, the corresponding transition will be decorated with the associated tag (or pair of tags).

Similar systems have been already introduced in [3]. The main differences are that here the components may contain nondetermism, and a secret can label any transition.

3.1 Tagged Probabilistic Automata

We now formalize the notion of TPA.

Definition 1. *A* Tagged Probabilistic Automaton *is a tuple* $(Q, L, \Sigma, \hat{q}, \alpha)$*, where* Q *is a set of* states, L *is a set of* tags, Σ *is a set of* actions, $\hat{q} \in Q$ *is the* initial state, $\alpha\colon Q \to \mathcal{P}(L \times \Sigma \times \mathcal{D}(Q))$ *is a* transition function.

In the following we write $q \xrightarrow{l:a} \mu$ for $(\ell, a, \mu) \in \alpha(q)$, and we use $enab(q)$ to denote the tags of the components that are enabled to make a transition. Namely, $enab(q) \stackrel{\text{def}}{=} \{\ell \in L \mid \textit{there exists } a \in \Sigma, \mu \in \mathcal{D}(Q) \textit{ such that } q \xrightarrow{l:a} \mu\}$. In these systems, we can decompose the scheduler in two: a *global scheduler*, which decides which component or pair of components makes the move next, and a *local scheduler*, which solves the internal nondeterminism of the selected component.

We assume that the local scheduler can only select enabled transitions, and that the global scheduler can only select enabled components. This means that the execution does not stop unless all components are blocked. This is in line with the tradition of process algebra and of Markov Decision Processes, but contrasts with that of Probabilistic Automata [26]. However, the results in this paper do not depend on this assumption.

Definition 2. *Let* $M = (Q, L, \Sigma, \hat{q}, \alpha)$ *be a Tagged Probabilistic Automaton.*

- *A global scheduler for* M *is a function* $\zeta\colon \text{Paths}^\star(M) \to (L \cup \{\bot\})$ *such that for all finite paths* σ*, if* $enab(last(\sigma)) \neq \emptyset$ *then* $\zeta(\sigma) \in enab(last(\sigma))$*, and* $\zeta(\sigma) = \bot$ *otherwise.*
- *A local scheduler for* M *is a function* $\xi\colon \text{Paths}^\star(M) \to (L \times \Sigma \times \mathcal{D}(Q) \cup \{\bot\})$ *such that, for all finite paths* σ*, if* $\alpha(last(\sigma)) \neq \emptyset$ *then* $\xi(\sigma) \in \alpha(last(\sigma))$*, and* $\xi(\sigma) = \bot$ *otherwise.*
- *A global scheduler* ζ *and a local scheduler* ξ *for* M *are* compatible *if, for all finite paths* σ*,* $\xi(\sigma) = (\ell, a, \mu)$ *implies* $\zeta(\sigma) = \ell$*, and* $\xi(\sigma) = \bot$ *implies* $\zeta(\sigma) = \bot$*.*
- *A scheduler is a pair* (ζ, ξ) *of compatible global and local schedulers.*

3.2 Components

We are going to use a simple probabilistic process calculus (a sort of probabilistic version of CCS [20,21]) to specify the components.

We assume a set of *actions* or *channel names* Σ with elements $a, a_1, a_2, \cdots$, including the special symbol τ denoting a *silent step*. Except τ, each action a has a co-action $\bar{a} \in \Sigma$ and we assume $\bar{\bar{a}} = a$. Components are specified by the following grammar:

$$q \;::=\; 0 \quad | \quad a.q \quad | \quad q_1 + q_2 \quad | \quad \sum_i p_i : q_i \quad | \quad q_1 | q_2 \quad | \quad (a)q \quad | \quad A$$

The constructs 0, $a.q$, $q_1 + q_2$, $q_1|q_2$ and $(a)q$ represent termination, prefixing, nondeterministic choice, parallel composition, and the restriction operator, respectively. $\sum_i p_i : q_i$ is a probabilistic choice, where p_i represents the probability of the i-th branch and must satisfy $0 \leq p_i \leq 1$ and $\sum_i p_i = 1$. The process call A is a simple process identifier. For each identifier, we assume a corresponding unique process declaration of the form $A \stackrel{\text{def}}{=} q$. The idea is that, whenever A is executed, it triggers the execution of q. Note that q can contain A or another process identifier, which means that our language allows (mutual) recursion. We will denote by $fn(q)$ the *free channel names* occurring in q, i.e. the channel names not bound by a restriction operator.

Components' semantics: The operational semantics consists of probabilistic transitions of the form $q \xrightarrow{a} \mu$ where $q \in Q$ is a process, $a \in \Sigma$ is an action and $\mu \in \mathcal{D}(Q)$ is a distribution on processes. They are specified by the following rules:

$$\text{PRF}\ \frac{}{a.q \xrightarrow{a} \delta_q} \qquad \text{NDT}\ \frac{q_1 \xrightarrow{a} \mu}{q_1 + q_2 \xrightarrow{a} \mu}$$

$$\text{PRB}\ \frac{}{\sum_i p_i : q_i \xrightarrow{\tau} \sum_i p_i \cdot \delta_{q_i}} \qquad \text{PAR}\ \frac{q_1 \xrightarrow{a} \mu}{q_1 \mid q_2 \xrightarrow{a} \mu \mid q_2}$$

$$\text{CALL}\ \frac{q \xrightarrow{a} \mu}{A \xrightarrow{a} \mu}\ \text{if } A \stackrel{\text{def}}{=} q \qquad \text{COM}\ \frac{q_1 \xrightarrow{a} \delta_{r_1} \quad q_2 \xrightarrow{\bar{a}} \delta_{r_2}}{q_1 \mid q_2 \xrightarrow{\tau} \delta_{r_1|r_2}} \qquad \text{RST}\ \frac{q \xrightarrow{a} \mu}{(b)q \xrightarrow{a} (b)\mu}\ a,\bar{a} \neq b$$

We assume also the symmetric versions of the rules NDT, PAR and COM. The symbol δ_q is the delta of Dirac, which assigns probability 1 to q and 0 to all other processes. The symbol $\sum_i$ is the summation on distributions. Namely, $\sum_i p_i \cdot \mu_i$ is the distribution μ such that $\mu(x) = \sum_i p_i \cdot \mu_i(x)$. The notation $\mu \mid q$ represents the distribution μ' such that $\mu'(r) = \mu(q')$ if $r = q' \mid q$, and $\mu'(r) = 0$ otherwise. Similarly, $(b)\mu$ represents the distribution μ' such that $\mu'(q) = \mu(q')$ if $q = (b)q'$, and $\mu'(q) = 0$ otherwise.

3.3 Systems

A system has the form $(A)\ q_1 \parallel q_2 \parallel \cdots \parallel q_n$, where the q_i's are components and $A \subseteq \Sigma$. The restriction on A enforces synchronization on the channel names belonging to A, in accordance with the CCS spirit.

Systems' semantics The semantics of a system gives rise to a TPA, where the states are terms representing systems during their evolution. A transition now is of the form $q \xrightarrow{\ell:a} \mu$ where $a \in \Sigma$, $\mu \in \mathcal{D}(Q)$, and $\ell \in L$ is either the tag of the component which makes the move, or a (unordered) pair of tags representing the two partners of a synchronization. We can simply define L as $L = I \cup I^2$ where $I = \{1, 2, \ldots, n\}$.

$$\text{Interleaving}\ \frac{q_i \xrightarrow{a} \sum_j p_j \cdot \delta_{q_{ij}}}{(A)\ q_1 \parallel \cdots \parallel q_i \parallel \cdots \parallel q_j \parallel \cdots \parallel q_n \xrightarrow{i:a} \sum_j p_j \cdot \delta_{(A) q_1 \parallel \cdots \parallel q_{ij} \parallel \cdots \parallel q_n}}\ a \notin A$$

where i is the tag indicating that the component i is making the step. Note that we assume that probabilistic choices are finite. This implies that every transition $q \xrightarrow{\ell:a} \mu$ can be written $q \xrightarrow{\ell:a} \sum_i p_i \cdot \delta_{q_i}$, and justifies the notation used in the interleaving rule.

$$\text{Synchronization} \quad \frac{q_i \xrightarrow{a} \delta_{q'_i} \qquad q_j \xrightarrow{\bar{a}} \delta_{q'_j}}{(A)\, q_1 \parallel \cdots \parallel q_i \parallel \cdots \parallel q_j \parallel \cdots \parallel q_n \xrightarrow{\{i,j\}:\tau} \delta_{(A) q_1 \parallel \cdots \parallel q'_i \parallel \cdots \parallel q'_j \parallel \cdots \parallel q_n}}$$

here $\{i, j\}$ is the tag indicating that the components making the step are i and j. Note that it is an unordered pair. Sometimes we will write i, j instead of $\{i, j\}$, for simplicity.

Example 2. Consider the systems of Example 1. Figures 1(a) and 1(b) show the TPAs of $S\left[{}^{a}/_{sec}\right]$ and of $S\left[{}^{b}/_{sec}\right]$ respectively. For simplicity we do not write the restriction on channels c and out, and the termination symbol 0. We use '$-$' to denote a component that is stuck. The corresponding tags are indicated in the figure with numbers above the components. The set of enabled transitions should be clear from the figures. For instance, we have $enab(S\left[{}^{b}/_{sec}\right]) = \{\{1,2\},\{1,3\},\{1,4\}\}$ and $enab(\,-\parallel \overline{out}\langle a\rangle \parallel - \parallel -\,) = \{2\}$. The scheduler ζ defined as

$$\zeta(\sigma) \stackrel{\text{def}}{=} \begin{cases} \{1,4\} & if\ \sigma = S\left[{}^{a}/_{sec}\right], \\ 2 & if\ \sigma = S\left[{}^{a}/_{sec}\right] \xrightarrow{1,2:\tau} (\,-\parallel \overline{out}\langle a\rangle \parallel - \parallel -\,), \\ 3 & if\ \sigma = S\left[{}^{a}/_{sec}\right] \xrightarrow{1,3:\tau} (\,-\parallel - \parallel \overline{out}\langle b\rangle \parallel -\,), \\ 4 & if\ \sigma = S\left[{}^{a}/_{sec}\right] \xrightarrow{1,4:\tau} (\,-\parallel - \parallel - \parallel \overline{out}\langle a\rangle\,), \\ \bot & otherwise, \end{cases}$$

is a global scheduler for $S\left[{}^{a}/_{sec}\right]$.

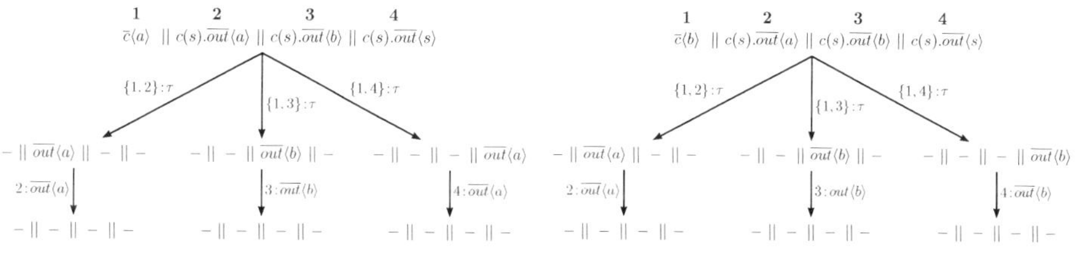

1(a) 1(b)

Fig. 1. Automata $S\left[{}^{a}/_{sec}\right]$ and $S\left[{}^{b}/_{sec}\right]$

4 Admissible Schedulers

In this section we restrict the discerning power of the global and local schedulers in order to avoid the problem of the information leakage induced in security by clairvoyant schedulers. We impose two kinds of restrictions: For the global scheduler, following [3], we assume that it can only see, and keep memory of, the observable actions and the components that are enabled, but not the secret actions. As for the local scheduler, we assume that the local nondeterminism of each component is solved on the basis of the view of the history local to that component, i.e. the projection of the history of the system on that component. In other words, each component has to make decisions based only on the history of its own execution; it cannot see anything of the other components.

4.1 Restricting Global Schedulers

We assume that the set of actions Σ is divided in two parts, the *secret actions* $\mathcal{S}$ and the *observable actions* $\mathcal{O}$. The secret actions are supposed to be invisible to the global scheduler. Formally, this can be achieved using a function *sift* with $sift(a)$ equals τ if $a \in \mathcal{S}$ and equals a otherwise. Then, we restrict the power of the global scheduler by forcing it to make the same decisions on paths he cannot tell apart.

Definition 3. *Given a TPA M, a global scheduler ζ for M is admissible if for all paths σ_1 and σ_2 we have $t(\sigma_1) = t(\sigma_2)$ implies $\zeta(\sigma_1) = \zeta(\sigma_2)$, where* $t\left(\hat{q} \xrightarrow{l_1:a_1} q_1 \xrightarrow{l_2:a_2} \cdots \xrightarrow{l_n:a_n} q_{n+1}\right) \stackrel{\text{def}}{=} (enab(\hat{q}), sift(a_1), l_1)(enab(q_1), sift(a_2), l_2) \cdots (enab(q_n), sift(a_n), l_n)$.

The idea is that t sifts the information of the path that the scheduler can see. Since *sift* "hides" the secrets, the scheduler cannot take different decisions based on secrets.

4.2 Restricting Local Schedulers

The restriction on the local scheduler is based on the idea that a step of the component i of a system can only be based on the view that i has of the history, i.e. its own history. In order to formalize this restriction, it is convenient to introduce the concept of i-view of a path σ, or *projection* of σ on i, which we will denote by $\sigma_{\upharpoonright i}$. We define it inductively:

$$(\sigma \xrightarrow{\ell:a} \mu)_{\upharpoonright i} = \begin{cases} \sigma_{\upharpoonright i} \xrightarrow{i:b} \delta_{q_i} & \text{if } \ell = \{i, j\} \text{ and } \mu = \delta_{(A)\ q_1 \| \ldots \| q_i \| \ldots \| q_j \| \ldots \| q_n} \\ \sigma_{\upharpoonright i} \xrightarrow{i:a} \mu & \text{if } \ell = i \\ \sigma_{\upharpoonright i} & \text{otherwise} \end{cases}$$

In the above definition, the first line represents the case of a synchronization step involving the component i, where we assume that the premise for i is of the form $q'_i \xrightarrow{b} \delta_{q_i}$. The second line represents an interleaving step in which i is the active component. The third line represents step in which the component i is idle.

The restriction to the local scheduler can now be expressed as follows:

Definition 4. *Given a TPA M and a local scheduler ξ for M, we say that ξ is admissible if for all paths σ and σ', if $\xi(\sigma) = (\ell, a, \mu)$, and $\xi(\sigma') = (\ell', a', \mu')$ we have:*

- *if $\ell = \ell' = i$ and $\sigma_{\upharpoonright i} = \sigma'_{\upharpoonright i}$, then $\xi(\sigma) = \xi(\sigma')$,*
- *if $\ell = \ell' = \{i, j\}$, $\sigma_{\upharpoonright i} = \sigma'_{\upharpoonright i}$, and $\sigma_{\upharpoonright j} = \sigma'_{\upharpoonright j}$ then $\xi(\sigma) = \xi(\sigma')$.*

A pair of compatible schedulers (ζ, ξ) is called *admissible* if ζ and ξ are admissible.

5 Safe Equivalences

In this section we revise process equivalence notions to make them safe for security.

5.1 Safe Complete Traces

We define here a safe version of complete-trace semantics. The idea is that we compare two processes based not only on their traces, but also on the choices that the global scheduler makes at every step. We do this by recording explicitly the tags in the traces.

Definition 5

- *Given a TPA $M = (Q, L, \Sigma, \hat{q}, \alpha)$, the (complete) safe traces of M, denoted here by $Traces_s$, are defined as the probabilities of sequences of tags and actions corresponding to all possible complete executions, i.e.*

$$\begin{aligned} Traces_s(M) = \{f : (L \times \Sigma)^\infty \to [0,1] \mid \\ \text{there exists an admissible scheduler } (\zeta, \xi) \text{ s.t.} \forall t \in (L \times \Sigma)^\infty \\ f(t) = \mathbf{P}_{M,\zeta,\xi}(\{\sigma \in \mathrm{CPaths}(M) \mid trace_s(\sigma) = t\}) \} \end{aligned}$$

  where $\mathbf{P}_{M,\zeta,\xi}$ is the probability measure in M under (ζ, ξ), and $trace_{ta}$ extracts from a path the sequence of tags and actions, i.e. $trace_{ta}(\epsilon) = \epsilon$ (on the empty path $trace_{ta}$ gives the empty string) and $trace_{ta}(q \xrightarrow{\ell:a} \sigma) = \ell : a \cdot trace_{ta}(\sigma)$.
- *We denote by $Traces_s(q)$ the safe traces of the automaton associated to a system q.*
- *Two systems q_1 and q_2 are safe-trace equivalent, denoted by $q_1 \simeq_s q_2$, if and only if $Traces_s(q_1) = Traces_s(q_2)$.*

The following example points out the difference between $\simeq_s$ and the standard (complete) trace equivalence.

Example 3. Consider the TPAs of Example 2. The two TPAs have the same complete traces. In fact $Traces(S\,[^a/_{sec}]) = \{\tau \cdot \overline{out}\langle a\rangle\ ,\ \tau \cdot \overline{out}\langle b\rangle\} = Traces(S\,[^b/_{sec}])$. On the other hand, we have $Traces_s(S\,[^a/_{sec}]) = \{f_1, f_2, f_3\}$ where $f_1(\{1,2\} : \tau \cdot 2 : \overline{out}\langle a\rangle) = f_2(\{1,3\} : \tau \cdot 3 : \overline{out}\langle b\rangle) = f_3(\{1,4\} : \tau \cdot 4 : \overline{out}\langle a\rangle\}) = 1$, and $f_i(t) = 0$ otherwise (for $i \in \{1,2,3\}$), while $Traces_s(S\,[^b/_{sec}]) = \{f_1, f_2, f_4\}$ with f_1, f_2 as above, and $f_4(\{1,4\} : \tau \cdot 4 : \overline{out}\langle b\rangle) = 1$, $f_4(t) = 0$ otherwise.

5.2 Safe Bisimilarity

In this section we propose a security-safe version of strong bisimulation, that we call *safe bisimulation*. This is an equivalence relation stricter than safe-trace equivalence, with the advantage of being a congruence. Since in this paper schedulers can always observe which component is making a step (even a silent step), it does not seem natural to consider weak bisimulation.

We start with some notation. Given a TPA $M = (Q, L, \Sigma, \hat{q}, \alpha)$, and a global scheduler ζ, we write $q \xrightarrow{a}_{\zeta} \mu$ if there exists $\sigma \in \mathrm{Paths}^{\star}(M)$ such that $\zeta(\sigma) \neq \bot$, $(\zeta(\sigma), a, \mu) \in \alpha(q)$, and $q = \mathit{last}(\sigma)$. Note that the restriction to ζ still allows non-determinism, i.e. there may be μ_1, μ_2, such that $q \xrightarrow{a_1}_{\zeta} \mu_1$ and $q \xrightarrow{a_2}_{\zeta} \mu_2$ (with either $a_1 = a_2$ or $a_1 \neq a_2$).

We now define the notion of safe bisimulation. The idea is that, if q and q' are bisimilar states, then every move from q should be mimicked by a move from q' *using the same (admissible) scheduler*.

Definition 6. *Given a TPA $M = (Q, L, \Sigma, \hat{q}, \alpha)$, we say that a relation $\mathcal{R} \subseteq Q \times Q$ is a safe bisimulation if, whenever $q_1 \mathcal{R} q_2$, then $\mathit{enab}(q_1) = \mathit{enab}(q_2)$, and for all admissible global schedulers ζ for M such that $\zeta(\sigma_1) = \zeta(\sigma_2)$ whenever $\mathit{last}(\sigma_1) = q_1$ and $\mathit{last}(\sigma_2) = q_2$:*

- *if $q_1 \xrightarrow{a}_{\zeta} \mu_1$, then there exists μ_2 such that $q_2 \xrightarrow{a}_{\zeta} \mu_2$ and $\mu_1 \mathcal{R} \mu_2$, and*
- *if $q_2 \xrightarrow{a}_{\zeta} \mu_2$, then there exists μ_1 such that $q_1 \xrightarrow{a}_{\zeta} \mu_1$ and $\mu_1 \mathcal{R} \mu_2$,*

where $\mu_1 \mathcal{R} \mu_2$ means that for all equivalence classes $X \in Q_{\hat{\mathcal{R}}}$, we have $\mu_1(X) = \mu_2(X)$, where $\hat{\mathcal{R}}$ is the smallest equivalence class induced by $\mathcal{R}$.

The following result is analogous to the case of standard bisimulation:

Proposition 1. *The union of all the safe bisimulations is still a safe bisimulation.*

Therefore the largest safe bisimulation exists, and coincides with the union of all safe bisimulations. We call it *safe bisimilarity*, and we denote it by $\sim_s$.

Given two TPAs on the same L and Σ, $M_1 = (Q_1, L, \Sigma, \hat{q}_1, \alpha_1)$ and $M_2 = (Q_2, L, \Sigma, \hat{q}_2, \alpha_2)$, we can define bisimulation and bisimilarity across their states, i.e. as relations on $(Q_1 \cup Q_2)$, in the obvious way, by constructing the TPA M with a new initial state $\hat{q}$ and two transitions to $\delta_{\hat{q}_1}$ and to $\delta_{\hat{q}_2}$, respectively.

Given two components or systems, q_1 and q_2, we will say that q_1 and q_2 are safely bisimilar, denoted by $q_1 \sim_s q_2$, if the initial states of the corresponding TPAs are safely bisimilar. Note that $q_1 \sim_s q_2$ is possible only if q_1 and q_2 have the same number of active components, where "active", for a component, means that during the execution of the system it will make at least one step. Note that in the case of components, or of systems constituted by one component only, safe bisimulation and safe bisimilarity coincide with standard bisimulation and bisimilarity (denoted by $\sim$), respectively. This is not the case for systems, as shown by the following example:

Example 4. Consider again the TPAs of Example 2. As pointed out in the introduction, we have $S\left[{}^{a}/_{sec}\right] \sim S\left[{}^{b}/_{sec}\right]$. However $S\left[{}^{a}/_{sec}\right] \not\sim_s S\left[{}^{b}/_{sec}\right]$. To show this, let us construct a new TPA (as described before) with initial state $\hat{q}$ such that $\hat{q} \xrightarrow{\ell:\tau} S\left[{}^{a}/_{sec}\right]$ and $\hat{q} \xrightarrow{\ell:\tau} S\left[{}^{b}/_{sec}\right]$. Now consider the (admissible) global scheduler ζ such that

$$\zeta(\sigma) \stackrel{\text{def}}{=} \begin{cases} \ell & if\ \sigma = \hat{q}, \\ \{1,4\} & if\ \sigma = \hat{q} \xrightarrow{\ell:\tau} S\left[{}^{a}/_{sec}\right], \\ 2 & if\ \sigma = \hat{q} \xrightarrow{\ell:\tau} S\left[{}^{a}/_{sec}\right] \xrightarrow{1,2:\tau} (\, - \,||\, \overline{out}\langle a\rangle \,||\, - \,||\, - \,), \\ 3 & if\ \sigma = \hat{q} \xrightarrow{\ell:\tau} S\left[{}^{a}/_{sec}\right] \xrightarrow{1,3:\tau} (\, - \,||\, - \,||\, \overline{out}\langle b\rangle \,||\, - \,), \\ 4 & if\ \sigma = \hat{q} \xrightarrow{\ell:\tau} S\left[{}^{a}/_{sec}\right] \xrightarrow{1,4:\tau} (\, - \,||\, - \,||\, - \,||\, \overline{out}\langle a\rangle \,), \\ \{1,4\} & if\ \sigma = \hat{q} \xrightarrow{\ell:\tau} S\left[{}^{b}/_{sec}\right], \\ 2 & if\ \sigma = \hat{q} \xrightarrow{\ell:\tau} S\left[{}^{b}/_{sec}\right] \xrightarrow{1,2:\tau} (\, - \,||\, \overline{out}\langle a\rangle \,||\, - \,||\, - \,), \\ 3 & if\ \sigma = \hat{q} \xrightarrow{\ell:\tau} S\left[{}^{b}/_{sec}\right] \xrightarrow{1,3:\tau} (\, - \,||\, - \,||\, \overline{out}\langle b\rangle \,||\, - \,), \\ 4 & if\ \sigma = \hat{q} \xrightarrow{\ell:\tau} S\left[{}^{b}/_{sec}\right] \xrightarrow{1,4:\tau} (\, - \,||\, - \,||\, - \,||\, \overline{out}\langle b\rangle \,), \\ \bot & otherwise. \end{cases}$$

It is easy to see that $S\left[{}^{b}/_{sec}\right]$ cannot mimic the transition $4 : \overline{out}\langle a\rangle$ produced by $S\left[{}^{a}/_{sec}\right]$ using the same scheduler ζ.

It turns out that safe bisimulation is a congruence with respect to all the operators of our language, as expressed by the following theorem. (Statements $2(a)$ and $2(b)$ are just the standard compositionality result for probabilistic bisimulation.)

Theorem 1

1. $\sim_s$ is an equivalence relation.
2. Let $a \in \Sigma$ and $A, B, B' \subseteq \Sigma$. Let $p_1, \ldots, p_n$ be probability values, and let $q, q_1, q_2, \ldots, q_n, q'_1, q'_2, \ldots, q'_n$ be components.
   (a) If $q_1 \sim_s q_2$, then $a.q_1 \sim_s a.q_2$, $q_1 + q \sim_s q_2 + q$, $(a)q_1 \sim_s (a)q_2$, and $q_1 \mid q \sim_s q_2 \mid q$.
   (b) If $q_1 \sim_s q'_1, \ldots, q_n \sim_s q'_n$, then $\sum_i p_i : q_i \sim_s \sum_i p_i : q'_i$.
   (c) If $(B)\, q_1 \,||\, \ldots \,||\, q_n \sim_s (B')\, q'_1 \,||\, \ldots \,||\, q'_n$, and $fn(q) \notin B \cup B'$, then

$$(A \cup B)\, q_1 \,||\, \ldots \,||\, q \,||\, \ldots \,||\, q_n \sim_s (A \cup B')\, q'_1 \,||\, \ldots \,||\, q \,||\, \ldots \,||\, q'_n.$$

The following property shows that bisimulation is stronger than safe-trace equivalence, like in the standard case.

Proposition 2. *If $q_1 \sim_s q_2$ then $q_1 \simeq_s q_2$.*

Like in the standard case, the vice-versa does not hold, and safe-trace equivalence is not a congruence[3].

6 Safe Nondeterministic Information Hiding

In this section we define the notion of information hiding under the most general hypothesis that the nondeterminism is handled partly in a demonic way and partly in an

[3] This is because we are considering the *complete* traces.

angelic way. We assume that the demonic part is in the realm of the global scheduler, while the angelic part is controlled by the local scheduler. The motivation is that in a protocol the local components can be thought of as programs running locally in a single machine, and locally predictable and controllable, while the network can be subject to attacks that make the interactions unpredictable.

We recall that, in a purely probabilistic setting, the absence of leakage, such as no-interference and strong anonymity, is expressed as follows (see for instance [5]). Given a purely probabilistic automaton M, and a sequence $\tilde{a} = a_1 a_2 \ldots a_n$, let $\mathbf{P}_M([\tilde{a}])$ represent the probability measure of all complete paths with trace $\tilde{a}$ in M. Let S be a protocol containing a variable action $secr$, and let s be secret actions. Let M_s be the automaton corresponding to $S[^{s}/_{secr}]$. Define $Pr(\tilde{a} \mid s)$ as $\mathbf{P}_{M_s}([\tilde{a}])$. Then S is leakage-free if for every observable trace $\tilde{a}$, and for every secret s_1 and s_2, we have $Pr(\tilde{a} \mid s_1) = Pr(\tilde{a} \mid s_2)$.

In a purely nondeterministic setting, on the other hand, the absence of leakage has been characterized in the literature by the property $S[^{s_1}/_{secr}] \cong S[^{s_2}/_{secr}]$, where $\cong$ is an equivalence relation like trace equivalence, or bisimulation. As we have argued in the introduction, this definition assumes an angelic interpretation of nondeterminism.

We want to combine the above notions so to cope with both probability and nondeterminism. Furthermore, we want to extend it to the case in which part of the nondeterminism is interpreted demonically. Let us first introduce some notation.

Let S be a system containing a variable action $secr$. Let s be a secret action. Let M_s be the TPA associated to $S[^{s}/_{secr}]$ and let (ζ, ξ) be a compatible pair of global and local schedulers for M_s. The probability of an observable trace $\tilde{a}$ given s is defined as $Pr_{\zeta,\xi}(\tilde{a} \mid s) = \mathbf{P}_{M_s,\zeta,\xi}([\tilde{a}])$.

The global nondeterminism is interpreted demonically, and therefore we need to ensure that the conditional of an observable, given the two secrets, are calculated with respect to the same global scheduler. On the other hand, the local scheduler is interpreted angelically, and therefore we can compare the conditional probabilities generated by the two secrets as sets under different schedulers. In other words, we have the freedom to match conditional probability from the first set with one of the other set, without requiring the local scheduler to be the same.

Either angelic or demonic, we want to avoid the clairvoyant schedulers, i.e. a scheduler should not be able to use the secret information to achieve its goals. For this purpose, we require both the global and the local scheduler to be admissible.

Definition 7. *A system is leakage-free if, for every secrets s_1 and s_2, every admissible global scheduler ζ, and every observable trace $\tilde{a}$, $\{Pr_{\zeta,\xi}(\tilde{a} \mid s_1) \mid \xi$ admissible and compatible with $\zeta\} = \{Pr_{\zeta,\xi}(\tilde{a} \mid s_2) \mid \xi$ admissible and compatible with $\zeta\}$.*

The safe equivalences defined in Section 5 imply the absence of leakage:

Theorem 2. *Let S be a system with a variable action $secr$ and assume $S[^{s_1}/_{secr}] \simeq_s S[^{s_2}/_{secr}]$ for every pair of secrets s_1 and s_2. Then S is leakage-free.*

Note that the vice versa is not true, i.e. it is not the case that the leakage-freedom of S implies $S[^{s_1}/_{secr}] \simeq_s S[^{s_2}/_{secr}]$. This is because in the definition of safe-trace equivalence we compare the set of probability functions (determined by the schedulers) on traces, while in the definition of leakage-freedom we compare the set of probabilities of each trace, which may come from different functions. This additional degree of freedom generated by the local scheduler helps the system to obfuscate the secret, and provides further justification for the adjective "angelic" for the local nondeterminism.

From the above theorem and from Proposition 2, we also have the following corollary (with the same premises as the previous theorem):

Corollary 1. *If* $S[^{s_1}/_{secr}] \sim_s S[^{s_2}/_{secr}]$ *for every pair of secrets* s_1 *and* s_2*, then* S *is leakage-free.*

7 Related Work

The problem of deriving correct implementations from secrecy specifications has received a lot of attention already. One of the first works to address the problem was [18], which showed that the fact that an implementation is a consistent refinement w.r.t. a specification does not imply that the (information-flow) security properties are preserved. More recently, [2] has proposed a notion of secrecy-preserving refinement, and a simulation-based technique for proving that a system is the refinement of another. [11] argues that important classes of security policies such as noninterference and average response time cannot be expressed by traditional notion of *properties*, which consist of sets of traces, and proposes to use *hyperproperties* (sets of properties) instead. [14] addresses the problem of supervisory control, i.e, given a critical system G that may leak confidential information, how to design a controller C so that the system $G|C$ dos not leak. An effective algorithm is presented to compute the most permissible controller such that the system is still opaque w.r.t. a secret.

Concerning angelic and demonic nondeterminism, there are various works which investigate their relation and possible combination. In [4] it is shown that angelic and demonic nondeterminism are dual. [19] uses multi-relations to express specifications involving both angelic and demonic nondeterminism. There are two kinds of agents, demonic and angelic ones, and there is the point of view of the internal system and the one of the external adversary. [22] considers the problem of refining specifications while preserving ignorance. While the focus is on the reduction of demonic nondeterminism of the specification, the hidden values are treated essentially in a angelic way.

The problem of the leakage caused by full-information schedulers has also been investigated in literature. [6] and [7] work in the framework of probabilistic automata and introduce a restriction on the scheduler to the purpose of making them suitable to applications in security protocols. Their approach is based on dividing the actions of each component of the system in equivalence classes (*tasks*). The order of execution of different tasks is decided in advance by a so-called *task scheduler*, which is history-independent and therefore much more restricted than our notion of global scheduler. [3] proposes a notion of system and admissible scheduler very similar to our notion of system and admissible global scheduler. The main difference is that in that work the components are deterministic and therefore there is no notion of local scheduler.

The work in [9,8] is similar to ours in spirit, but in a sense *dual* from a technical point of view. Instead of defining a restriction on the class of schedulers, they provide a way to specify that a choice is transparent to the scheduler. They achieve this by introducing labels in process terms, used to represent both the states of the execution tree and the next action or step to be scheduled. They make two states indistinguishable to schedulers, and hence the choice between them private, by associating to them the same label. We believe that every scheduler in our formalism can be expressed in theirs, too. In [8] they also consider the problem of defining a safe version of bisimulation for expressing security properties. They call it *demonic bisimulation*. The main difference with our work is that we consider a combination of angelic and demonic nondeterminism, and this affects also the definition of bisimulation. Similarly, our definition of leakage-freedom reflects this combination. In [8] the aspect of angelicity is not considered, although they may be able to simulate it with an appropriate labeling.

The fact that full-information schedulers are unrealistic has also been observed in fields other than security. First attempts used restricted schedulers in order to obtain rules for compositional reasoning [12]. The justification for those restricted schedulers is the same as for ours, namely, that not all information is available to all entities in the system. However that work considers a synchronous parallel composition, so the setting is rather different from ours. Later on, it was shown that model checking is unfeasible in its general form for the restricted schedulers in [12] (see [16] and, more recently, [15]). Despite of undecidability, not all results concerning such schedulers have been negative as, for instance, the technique of partial-order reduction can be improved by assuming that schedulers can only use partial information [17].

8 Conclusion and Future Work

We have observed that some definitions of security properties based on process equivalences may be too naive, in that they assume the scheduler to be angelic, and, worse yet, to achieve its angelic strategy by peeking at the secrets. We have presented a formalism allowing us to specify a demonic constituent of the scheduler, possibly in collusion with the attacker, and an angelic one, under the control of the system. We have also considered restrictions on the schedulers to limit the power of what they can see, and extended to our nondeterministic framework the (probabilistic) information-hiding properties like non interference and strong anonymity. We then have defined "safe" equivalences. In particular we have defined the notions of safe trace equivalence and safe bisimilarity, and we have shown that the latter is still a congruence. Finally, we have shown that the safe equivalences can be used to prove information-hiding properties.

For the future, we plan to extend our framework to quantitative notions of information leakage, possibly based on information theory. We also plan to implement model checking techniques to verify information hiding properties for our kind of systems. A natural candidate for the implementation would be PRISM. Of course, we would need to restrict the class of schedulers in PRISM so to meet the admissibility criteria.

Acknowledgement. The authors wish to thank the anonymous reviewers for their useful comments, and Pedro D'Argenio for helpful discussion.

References

1. Abadi, M., Gordon, A.D.: A calculus for cryptographic protocols: The spi calculus. Inf. and Comp. 148(1), 1–70 (1999)
2. Alur, R., Zdancewic, S.: Preserving secrecy under refinement. In: Bugliesi, M., Preneel, B., Sassone, V., Wegener, I. (eds.) ICALP 2006. LNCS, vol. 4052, pp. 107–118. Springer, Heidelberg (2006)
3. Andrés, M.E., Palamidessi, C., van Rossum, P., Sokolova, A.: Information hiding in probabilistic concurrent systems, `http://www.cs.ru.nl/M.Andres/downloads/SAuN.pdf`
4. Back, R.J.R., von Wright, J.: Combining angels, demons and miracles in program specifications. TCS 100(2), 365–383 (1992)
5. Bhargava, M., Palamidessi, C.: Probabilistic anonymity. In: Abadi, M., de Alfaro, L. (eds.) CONCUR 2005. LNCS, vol. 3653, pp. 171–185. Springer, Heidelberg (2005)
6. Canetti, R., Cheung, L., Kaynar, D., Liskov, M., Lynch, N., Pereira, O., Segala, R.: Task-structured probabilistic i/o automata. In: Proc. of WODES (2006)
7. Canetti, R., Cheung, L., Kaynar, D.K., Liskov, M., Lynch, N.A., Pereira, O., Segala, R.: Time-bounded task-PIOAs: A framework for analyzing security protocols. In: Dolev, S. (ed.) DISC 2006. LNCS, vol. 4167, pp. 238–253. Springer, Heidelberg (2006)
8. Chatzikokolakis, K., Norman, G., Parker, D.: Bisimulation for demonic schedulers. In: de Alfaro, L. (ed.) FOSSACS 2009. LNCS, vol. 5504, pp. 318–332. Springer, Heidelberg (2009)
9. Chatzikokolakis, K., Palamidessi, C.: Making random choices invisible to the scheduler. In: Caires, L., Vasconcelos, V.T. (eds.) CONCUR 2007. LNCS, vol. 4703, pp. 42–58. Springer, Heidelberg (2007)
10. Chaum, D.: The dining cryptographers problem: Unconditional sender and recipient untraceability. Journal of Cryptology 1, 65–75 (1988)
11. Clarkson, M.R., Schneider, F.B.: Hyperproperties. In: CSF, pp. 51–65. IEEE, Los Alamitos (2008)
12. de Alfaro, L., Henzinger, T.A., Jhala, R.: Compositional methods for probabilistic systems. In: Larsen, K.G., Nielsen, M. (eds.) CONCUR 2001. LNCS, vol. 2154, p. 351. Springer, Heidelberg (2001)
13. Delaune, S., Kremer, S., Ryan, M.: Verifying privacy-type properties of electronic voting protocols. Journal of Computer Security 17(4), 435–487 (2009)
14. Dubreil, J., Darondeau, P., Marchand, H.: Supervisory control for opacity. IEEE Transactions on Automatic Control 55(5), 1089–1100 (2010)
15. Giro, S.: Undecidability results for distributed probabilistic systems. In: Oliveira, M.V.M., Woodcock, J. (eds.) SBMF 2009. LNCS, vol. 5902, pp. 220–235. Springer, Heidelberg (2009)
16. Giro, S., D'Argenio, P.R.: Quantitative model checking revisited: Neither decidable nor approximable. In: Raskin, J.-F., Thiagarajan, P.S. (eds.) FORMATS 2007. LNCS, vol. 4763, pp. 179–194. Springer, Heidelberg (2007)
17. Giro, S., D'Argenio, P.R., Fioriti, L.M.F.: Partial order reduction for probabilistic systems: A revision for distributed schedulers. In: Bravetti, M., Zavattaro, G. (eds.) CONCUR 2009. LNCS, vol. 5710, pp. 338–353. Springer, Heidelberg (2009)
18. Jacob, J.: On the derivation of secure components. In: S&P, pp. 242–247. IEEE, Los Alamitos (1989)
19. Martin, C.E., Curtis, S.A., Rewitzky, I.: Modelling angelic and demonic nondeterminism with multirelations. Science of Computer Programming 65(2), 140–158 (2007)
20. Milner, R.: Communication and Concurrency. Series in Comp. Sci. Prentice Hall, Englewood Cliffs (1989)

21. Milner, R.: Communicating and mobile systems: the π-calculus. CUP (1999)
22. Morgan, C.: The shadow knows: Refinement and security in sequential programs. Science of Computer Programming 74(8), 629–653 (2009)
23. Reiter, M.K., Rubin, A.D.: Crowds: anonymity for Web transactions. ACM Transactions on Information and System Security 1(1), 66–92 (1998)
24. Schneider, S., Sidiropoulos, A.: CSP and anonymity. In: Martella, G., Kurth, H., Montolivo, E., Bertino, E. (eds.) ESORICS 1996. LNCS, vol. 1146, pp. 198–218. Springer, Heidelberg (1996)
25. Segala, R.: Modeling and Verification of Randomized Distributed Real-Time Systems. PhD thesis, Tech. Rep. MIT/LCS/TR-676 (1995)
26. Segala, R., Lynch, N.: Probabilistic simulations for probabilistic processes. Nordic Journal of Computing 2(2), 250–273 (1995)

On Probabilistic Alternating Simulations

Chenyi Zhang[1,2] and Jun Pang[1]

[1] Faculty of Sciences, Technology and Communication
University of Luxembourg, Luxembourg
[2] School of Computer Science and Engineering
University of New South Wales, Australia

Abstract. This paper presents simulation-based relations for probabilistic game structures. The first relation is called probabilistic alternating simulation, and the second called probabilistic alternating forward simulation, following the naming convention of Segala and Lynch. We study these relations with respect to the preservation of properties specified in probabilistic alternating-time temporal logic.

1 Introduction

Simulation relations [15] have proved to be useful for comparing the behavior of concurrent systems, which can be formally interpreted as labeled transition systems. The study of logic characterization of simulation is to build its connection to a modal or temporal logic which can be used to formulate some interesting properties. Soundness of logic characterization requires simulation preserve the satisfaction of logic formulas, while completeness shows the relation has the same strength as the logic. Intuitively, the fact that one state s_1 simulates another state s_2 can be used to establish the relation that any possible behavior of s_1 is also possible on s_2. Thus it can preserve certain desirable properties formulated in temporal logics like CTL [11]. Simulation relations have set up the foundations for constructing correct abstractions.

Related work. Segala and Lynch [21] extend the classical notions of simulation for probabilistic automata [20], a general extension of labeled transition systems which admits both probabilistic and nondeterministic behaviors. Their main idea is to relate probability distributions over states, instead of relating individual states. They show soundness of the logical characterization of probabilistic simulation, which preserves probabilistic CTL formulas [12] without negation and existential quantification. Segala introduces probabilistic forward simulation, which relates states to probability distributions over states and is sound and complete for trace distribution precongruence [19,13]. Logic characterization of strong and weak probabilistic bisimulation has been studied in [10,17].

Alur, Henzinger and Kupferman [1,2] define ATL (alternating-time temporal logic) to generalize CTL for game structures by requiring each path quantifier to be parametrized with a set of agents. Game structures are more general than LTS, in the sense that they allow both collaborative and adversarial behaviors

C.S. Calude and V. Sassone (Eds.): TCS 2010, IFIP AICT 323, pp. 71–85, 2010.

of individual agents in a system, and ATL can be used to express properties like "a set of agents can enforce a specific outcome of the system". Alternating refinement relations, in particular alternating simulation, are introduced later in [3]. Alternating simulation is a natural game-theoretic interpretation of the classical simulation in two-player games. Logic characterization of this relation concentrates on a subset of ATL* formulas where negations are only allowed at proposition level and all path quantifiers are parametrized by a predefined set of agents A. This sublogic of ATL* contains all formulas expressing the properties that agents in A can enforce no matter what the other agents do. Alur et al. [3] have proved both soundness and completeness of their characterization.

Our contribution. Extending game structures with probabilistic behaviors of players gives rise to a more expressive framework for modeling (open) systems. Mixed strategies, which allow for players to randomly select their actions, are often necessary for the players to achieve their expected rewards [16]. As the papers [3,2] only focuse on pure strategies, it is a natural step to study the corresponding notion of simulation in a probabilistic game-based setting.

In this paper, we introduce two notions of simulation for probabilistic game structures — probabilistic alternating simulation and forward simulation, following the aforementioned results [19,21,3]. We prove the soundness of logical characterization of probabilistic alternating simulation relations, by showing that they preserve a fragment of a probabilistic extension of ATL.

Outline. The rest of the paper is organized as follows. We briefly explain some basic notations that are used throughout the paper in Sect. 2. Sect. 3 introduces the notion of probabilistic game structures and the definition of probabilistic executions. In Sect. 4 we present PATL an extension of the alternating-time temporal logic [2] for probabilistic systems, and roughly discuss its model checking problem. We define probabilistic alternating simulation and forward simulation in Sect. 5, and show their soundness for preserving properties specified in PATL in Sect. 6. Probabilistic alternating bisimulation is shortly discussed in Sect. 7. We conclude the paper with some future research topics in Sect. 8.

2 Preliminaries

This section contains basic notions that are used in the technical part. Let S be a set, then a discrete probabilistic distribution Δ over S is a function of type $S \to [0,1]$, satisfying $\sum_{s\in S}\Delta(s) = 1$. We write $\mathcal{D}(S)$ for the set of all such distributions. For a set $S' \subseteq S$, define $\Delta(S') = \sum_{s\in S'}\Delta(s)$. Given two distributions Δ_1, Δ_2 and $p \in [0,1]$, $\Delta_1 \oplus_p \Delta_2$ is a function of type $S \to [0,1]$ defined as $\Delta_1 \oplus_p \Delta_2(s) = p\cdot\Delta_1(s) + (1-p)\cdot\Delta_2(s)$ for all $s \in S$. Obviously, $\Delta_1 \oplus_p \Delta_2$ is also a distribution. We further extend this notion by combining a set of distributions $\{\Delta_i\}_{i\in I}$ ordered by an indexed set $\{p_i\}_{i\in I}$ into a distribution $\sum_{i\in I} p_i\Delta_i$, where $p_i \in [0,1]$ for all $i \in I$ and $\sum_{i\in I} p_i = 1$. $\overline{s}$ is called a point distribution satisfying $\overline{s}(s) = 1$ and $\overline{s}(t) = 0$ for all $t \neq s$. Let $\Delta \in \mathcal{D}(S)$, write $\lceil\Delta\rceil$ for the *support* of Δ as the set $\{s \in S \mid \Delta(s) > 0\}$.

Let $S = S_1 \times S_2 \times \cdots \times S_n$, then $\boldsymbol{s} \in S$ is a vector of length n. We may also write $\boldsymbol{s} = \langle s_1, s_2, \ldots, s_n \rangle$, with $\boldsymbol{s}(i) = s_i \in S_i$. Given a finite sequence $\alpha = s_1 s_2 \ldots s_n \in S^*$, write $last(\alpha)$ for s_n. Let $S' \subseteq S$, then $\alpha \mid S'$ is a subsequence of α with exactly the elements not in S' removed. Given $L \subseteq S^*$, write $L \mid S'$ for the set $\{(\alpha \mid S') \mid \alpha \in L\}$.

3 Probabilistic Game Structures

Assume a set of players $\Sigma = \{1, 2, \ldots, \mathtt{k}\}$. A probabilistic game structure (PGS) $\mathcal{G}$ is defined as a tuple $\langle S, s_0, \mathcal{L}, \mathtt{Act}, \delta \rangle$, where

- S is a finite set of states, with s_0 the initial state,
- $\mathtt{Act} = \mathtt{Act}_1 \times \mathtt{Act}_2 \times \cdots \times \mathtt{Act}_\mathtt{k}$ is a set of joint actions, where $\mathtt{Act}_i$ is the set of actions for player $i = 1, \ldots, \mathtt{k}$,
- $\mathcal{L} : S \to 2^{\mathtt{Prop}}$ is the labeling function,
- $\delta : S \times \mathtt{Act} \to \mathcal{D}(S)$ is a transition function.

A play ρ is a (finite or infinite) sequence $s_0 \boldsymbol{a}_1 s_1 \boldsymbol{a}_2 s_2 \ldots$, such that $\boldsymbol{a}_i \in \mathtt{Act}$ and $\delta(s_{i-1}, \boldsymbol{a}_i)(s_i) > 0$ for all i. Write $|\rho|$ for the length of a run ρ, which is the number of transitions in ρ, and $|\rho| = \infty$ if ρ is infinite. We write $\rho(i)$ for the i-th state in ρ starting from 0, and $\rho[i, j]$ for the subsequence starting from i-th state and ending at the j-th state, provided $0 \leq i \leq j \leq |\rho|$. Note that the players choose their next moves simultaneously, but their moves may or may not be cooperative. If on state s each player i performs action a_i, then $\delta(s, \langle a_1, a_2, \ldots a_k \rangle)$ is the distribution for the next reachable states. In the following discussion, we fix a probabilistic game structure $\mathcal{G}$.

We assume that the transition function δ is total on the set $\mathtt{Act}$. Note that this does not pose any limitation on the expressiveness of the model. If an action $c \in \mathtt{Act}_i$ of player i is not supposed to be enabled on state s for player i, we may find another action $c' \in \mathtt{Act}_i$ and define c to have the same effect as c' on s. Since player i knows the current state, he also knows the set of actions available to him, so that as a rational player he will not choose actions that are not enabled. This allows such models to express systems in which on some states the available (joint) actions are proper subsets of $\mathtt{Act}$.[1] We may even disable a particular player on a state. A player i is disabled on s if $\delta(s, \boldsymbol{a}) = \delta(s, \boldsymbol{a}')$ for all action vectors $\boldsymbol{a}, \boldsymbol{a}' \in \mathtt{Act}$ satisfying $\boldsymbol{a}(j) = \boldsymbol{a}'(j)$ for all $j \neq i$. A PGS is *turn-based* if all but one player is disabled on s for all $s \in S$.

A strategy of a player $i \in \Sigma$ is a function of type $S^+ \to \mathcal{D}(\mathtt{Act}_i)$. We write $\Pi_i^{\mathcal{G}}$ for the set of strategies of player i in $\mathcal{G}$. A play ρ is compatible with an i-strategy π_i, if $\boldsymbol{a}_k(i) \in \lceil \pi_i(\rho[0, k-1] | S) \rceil$ for all $k \leq |\rho|$. Given a vector of strategies $\boldsymbol{\pi} \in \Pi_1^{\mathcal{G}} \times \Pi_2^{\mathcal{G}} \times \cdots \times \Pi_{|\Sigma|}^{\mathcal{G}}$, a run ρ is compatible with $\boldsymbol{\pi}$ if $\boldsymbol{a}_k(i) \in \lceil \boldsymbol{\pi}(i)(\rho[0, k-1] | S) \rceil$ for all $k \leq |\rho|$ and $i = 1, \ldots, \mathtt{k}$. Write $\mathcal{G}(\boldsymbol{\pi}, s)$ for the set of infinite plays compatible with every strategy in $\boldsymbol{\pi}$ starting from $s \in S$, and $\mathcal{G}^*(\boldsymbol{\pi}, s)$ the set of finite plays in $\mathcal{G}$ that are compatible with $\boldsymbol{\pi}$ starting from s.

[1] In the literature some authors encode available actions for player i as a function of type $S \to 2^{\mathtt{Act}_i} \setminus \{\emptyset\}$.

The set of finite plays compatible to strategy vector $\boldsymbol{\pi}$ is also called a set of *cones* [20], with each finite play α representing the set of infinite plays prefixed by α. Given a state $s_0 \in S$, we can derive the probability for every member in S^+ compatible with $\boldsymbol{\pi}$, by recursively defining a function $Pr_{\mathcal{G}(\boldsymbol{\pi},s_0)}$ from S^+ to $[0,1]$ as follows. This function $Pr_{\mathcal{G}(\boldsymbol{\pi},s_0)}$ can be further generalized as the probability measure to the σ-field $\mathcal{F}_{\mathcal{G},\boldsymbol{\pi},s_0} \subseteq \mathcal{G}(\boldsymbol{\pi}, s_0)$ which is a unique extension from the set of cones $\mathcal{G}^*(\boldsymbol{\pi}, s)$ closed by countable union and complementation, in a way similar to [20]:

- $Pr_{\mathcal{G}(\boldsymbol{\pi},s_0)}(s_0) = 1$,
- $Pr_{\mathcal{G}(\boldsymbol{\pi},s_0)}(\alpha \cdot s) = Pr_{\mathcal{G}(\boldsymbol{\pi},s_0)}(\alpha) \cdot \overline{\delta}(last(\alpha), \langle \boldsymbol{\pi}(1)(\alpha), \boldsymbol{\pi}(2)(\alpha), \ldots, \boldsymbol{\pi}(\mathtt{k})(\alpha)\rangle)(s)$,

where $\overline{\delta}(s, \langle \Delta_1, \Delta_2, \ldots, \Delta_\mathtt{k}\rangle)$ is a distribution over states derived from δ and the vector of action distributions defined by

$$\overline{\delta}(s, \langle \Delta_1, \ldots, \Delta_\mathtt{k}\rangle) = \sum_{i\in\{1,\ldots,\mathtt{k}\}, a_i \in \lceil \Delta_i \rceil} \Delta_1(a_1) \cdot \ldots \cdot \Delta_\mathtt{k}(a_\mathtt{k}) \cdot \delta(s, \langle a_1, \ldots, a_\mathtt{k}\rangle).$$

Given $A \subseteq \Sigma$, sometimes we write $\boldsymbol{\pi}(A)$ for a vector of $|A|$ strategies $\{\pi_i\}_{i\in A}$, and $\Pi(A)$ for the set of all such strategy vectors. Write $\overline{A}$ for $\Sigma \setminus A$. Given $A \cap A' = \emptyset$, strategy vectors $\boldsymbol{\pi} \in \Pi(A)$ and $\boldsymbol{\pi}' \in \Pi(A')$, $\boldsymbol{\pi} \cup \boldsymbol{\pi}'$ is the vector of strategies $\{\pi_i\}_{i\in A} \cup \{\pi'_j\}_{j\in A'}$ that combines $\boldsymbol{\pi}$ and $\boldsymbol{\pi}'$.

We also define strategies of *finite depth* by restricting the size of their domains, by writing $\pi \in \Pi_i^{\mathcal{G},n}$ as a *level-n* strategy, i.e., π is a function from traces of states with length up to n (i.e., the set $\bigcup_{m\in\{1,2,\ldots,n\}} S^m$) to $\mathcal{D}(\mathtt{Act}_i)$. Given a set of strategies $\{\pi_i\}_{i\in I}$ of the same domain, and $\{p_i\}_{i\in I}$ with $\sum_{i\in I} p_i = 1$, let $\pi = \sum_{i\in I} p_i \cdot \pi_i$ be a (combined) strategy, by letting $\pi(\gamma) = \sum_{i\in I} p_i \cdot \pi_i(\gamma)$ for all γ in the domain.

We overload the function $\overline{\delta}$ as from a state in S and a vector of strategies (of any depth n) $\boldsymbol{\pi} \in \Pi_1^{\mathcal{G},n} \times \Pi_2^{\mathcal{G},n} \times \cdots \times \Pi_{|\Sigma|}^{\mathcal{G},n}$ to $\mathcal{D}(S)$, by $\overline{\delta}(s, \boldsymbol{\pi}) = \overline{\delta}(s, \boldsymbol{a})$, where $\boldsymbol{a}(i) = \boldsymbol{\pi}(i)(s)$ for all $i \in \Sigma$. Note each $\boldsymbol{a}(i)$ is a distribution over $\mathtt{Act}_i$. We further lift $\overline{\delta}$ to be a transition function from state distributions and strategy vectors to state distributions, by

$$\overline{\delta}(\Delta, \boldsymbol{\pi}) = \sum_{s\in\lceil \Delta \rceil} \Delta(s) \cdot \overline{\delta}(s, \boldsymbol{\pi})$$

Probabilistic Executions

We settle the nondeterminism in a probabilistic game structure by fixing the behaviors of all players represented as strategies. Let $\mathcal{G} = \langle S, s_0, \mathcal{L}, \mathtt{Act}, \delta\rangle$ be a PGS, define a *probabilistic execution* $\mathcal{E}$ as in the form of $\langle E, \Delta, \mathcal{L}^\mathcal{E}, \delta^\mathcal{E}\rangle$, where

- $E \subseteq S^+$ is the set of finite plays starting form a state in the initial distribution and compatible with $\delta^\mathcal{E}$, i.e., $s_0 s_1 \ldots s_n \in E$ if $s_0 \in \lceil \Delta \rceil$, and $\delta^\mathcal{E}(s_0 \ldots s_i)(s_0 \ldots s_{i+1}) > 0$ for all $0 \le i < n$,
- $\Delta \in \mathcal{D}(S)$ an (initial) distribution,

- $\mathcal{L}^{\mathcal{E}}$ is the labeling function defined as $\mathcal{L}^{\mathcal{E}}(e) = \mathcal{L}(last(e))$ for all $e \in E$,
- $\delta^{\mathcal{E}} : E \to \mathcal{D}(E)$ is a (deterministic) transition relation, satisfying for all $e \in E$ there exists a (level 1) strategy vector $\boldsymbol{\pi}_e$, such that $\delta^{\mathcal{E}}(e)(e \cdot t) = \overline{\delta}(last(e), \boldsymbol{\pi}_e)(t)$ if $t \in \lceil \overline{\delta}(last(e), \boldsymbol{\pi}_e) \rceil$, and 0 otherwise.

A probabilistic execution of $\mathcal{G}$ can be uniquely determined by a strategy vector $\boldsymbol{\pi}$ and a state distribution. Given $\Delta \in \mathcal{D}(S)$, define $\mathcal{E}(\mathcal{G}, \boldsymbol{\pi}, \Delta)$ as the probabilistic execution $\langle E^{\boldsymbol{\pi}}, \Delta, \mathcal{L}^{\boldsymbol{\pi}}, \delta^{\boldsymbol{\pi}} \rangle$, with $E^{\boldsymbol{\pi}} = \bigcup_{s \in \lceil \Delta \rceil} \mathcal{G}^*(\boldsymbol{\pi}, s) \mid S$ for the set of compatible finite plays, $\mathcal{L}^{\boldsymbol{\pi}}$ defined as $\mathcal{L}^{\boldsymbol{\pi}}(e) = \mathcal{L}(last(e))$ for all $e \in E^{\boldsymbol{\pi}}$, and $\delta^{\boldsymbol{\pi}}(e) = \overline{\delta}(last(e), \boldsymbol{\pi}_e)$ for all $e \in E^{\boldsymbol{\pi}}$, where $\boldsymbol{\pi}_e(i) = \boldsymbol{\pi}(i)(e)$ for all $i \in \Sigma$. Intuitively, a probabilistic execution resembles the notion of the same name proposed by Segala and Lynch [20,21], and in this case the strategies of the players altogether represent a single adversary of Segala and Lynch.

4 Probabilistic Alternating-Time Temporal Logic

In this section we introduce a probabilistic version of alternating-time temporal logic [2], which focuses on the players ability to enforce a property with an expected probability. Let $\texttt{Prop}$ be a nonempty set of propositions. Probabilistic alternating-time temporal logic (PATL) was initially proposed by Chen and Lu [7]. Here we show its original syntax can be slightly simplified. PATL formulas are defined as follows.

$$\phi := p \mid \neg\phi \mid \phi_1 \wedge \phi_2 \mid \langle\langle A \rangle\rangle^{\bowtie\alpha} \psi$$

$$\psi := \bigcirc\phi \mid \phi_1 \mathtt{U}^{\leq k} \phi_2$$

where $A \subseteq \Sigma$ is a set of players, $\bowtie \in \{<, >, \leq, \geq\}$, $k \in \mathbb{N} \cup \{\infty\}$, $p \in \texttt{Prop}$, and $\alpha \in [0,1]$. We also write $\psi_1 \mathtt{U}\, \psi_2$ for $\psi_1 \mathtt{U}^{\leq\infty} \psi_2$ as 'unbounded until'. The symbols ϕ, ϕ_1, ϕ_2 are state formulas, and ψ is a path formula. We omit the syntactic sugars in our definition, such as $true \equiv p \vee \neg p$ and $false \equiv p \wedge \neg p$ for some $p \in \texttt{Prop}$, $\phi_1 \vee \phi_2 \equiv \neg(\neg\phi_1 \wedge \neg\phi_2)$ for state formulas. The path modality $\mathtt{R}$ can be expressed by $\mathtt{U}$ without introducing negations into path formulas, as we will show later in this section. One may also define $\Box^{\leq k}\psi \equiv false\ \mathtt{R}^{\leq k}\psi$, and $\Diamond^{\leq k}\psi \equiv true\ \mathtt{U}^{\leq k}\psi$, where $k \in \mathbb{N} \cup \{\infty\}$. The set of PATL formulas $\mathbb{L}$ are the set of state formulas as defined above. We have the semantics of the path formulas and the state formulas defined as follows.

- $\rho \models \phi$ iff $\mathcal{G}, \rho(0) \models \phi$ where ϕ is a state formula,
- $\rho \models \bigcirc\phi$ iff $\rho(1) \models \phi$,
- $\rho \models \phi_1 \mathtt{U}^{\leq k} \phi_2$ iff there exists $i \leq k$ such that $\rho(j) \models \phi_1$ for all $0 \leq j < i$ and $\rho(i) \models \phi_2$,
- $\mathcal{G}, s \models p$ iff $p \in \mathcal{L}(s)$,
- $\mathcal{G}, s \models \neg\phi$ iff $\mathcal{G}, s \not\models \phi$,
- $\mathcal{G}, s \models \phi_1 \wedge \phi_2$ iff $\mathcal{G}, s \models \phi_1$ and $\mathcal{G}, s \models \phi_2$,
- $\mathcal{G}, s \models \langle\langle A \rangle\rangle^{\bowtie\alpha}\, \psi$ iff there exists a vector of strategies $\boldsymbol{\pi} \in \Pi(A)$, such that for all vectors of strategies $\boldsymbol{\pi}' \in \Pi(\overline{A})$ for players in $\overline{A}$, we have $Pr_{\mathcal{G}(\boldsymbol{\pi} \cup \boldsymbol{\pi}', s)}(\{\rho \in \mathcal{G}(\boldsymbol{\pi} \cup \boldsymbol{\pi}', s) \mid \rho \models \psi\}) \bowtie \alpha$,

where ρ is an infinite play in $\mathcal{G}$, $\alpha \in [0,1]$, ϕ, ϕ_1, ϕ_2 are state formulas, and ψ is a path formula. Equivalently, given S the state space of a probabilistic game structure $\mathcal{G}$, we write $[\![\phi]\!]$ for $\{s \in S \mid s \models \phi\}$ for all PATL (state) formulas ϕ. For $\Delta \in \mathcal{D}(S)$, we write $\Delta \models \phi$ iff $\lceil \Delta \rceil \subseteq [\![\phi]\!]$. Intuitively, $\mathcal{G}, s \models \langle\!\langle A \rangle\!\rangle^{\geq \alpha}\psi$ ($\mathcal{G}, s \models \langle\!\langle A \rangle\!\rangle^{\leq \alpha}\psi$) describes the ability of players in A to cooperatively enforce ψ with probability at least (at most) α in s.

The following lemma is directly from the PATL semantics. If a group of users A can enforce a linear-time temporal logic formula ψ to hold with probability at least α with strategies $\boldsymbol{\pi} \in \Pi(A)$, then at the same time $\boldsymbol{\pi}$ enforces the formula $\neg\psi$ to hold with probability at most $1-\alpha$. To simplify the notation, we let '$\sim$' denote changes on directions of the symbols in $\{<, >, \leq, \geq\}$, e.g., symbol $\widetilde{\geq}$ for $\leq$, $\widetilde{\leq}$ for $\geq$, $\widetilde{>}$ for $<$, and $\widetilde{<}$ for $>$.

Lemma 1. $\mathcal{G}, s \models \langle\!\langle A \rangle\!\rangle^{\bowtie \alpha}\psi$ *iff* $\mathcal{G}, s \models \langle\!\langle A \rangle\!\rangle^{\widetilde{\bowtie} 1-\alpha}\neg\psi$

Therefore, the path quantifier $\mathtt{R}$ (release) can be expressed by the existing PATL syntax, in the way that $\langle\!\langle A \rangle\!\rangle^{\bowtie \alpha}\phi_1 \mathtt{R}^{\leq k}\phi_2 \equiv \langle\!\langle A \rangle\!\rangle^{\widetilde{\bowtie} 1-\alpha}(\neg\phi_1)\mathtt{U}^{\leq k}(\neg\phi_2)$, where both $\neg\phi_1$ and $\neg\phi_2$ are state formulas.

On Model Checking of PATL

In this section we briefly survey the results in the literature related to PATL model checking. Given a PATL formula in the form of $\langle\!\langle A \rangle\!\rangle^{\bowtie \alpha}\psi(\phi_1, \ldots, \phi_n)$, a standard way to solve this problem is to determine the maximal or minimal probability that the players in A can enforce the LTL formula $\psi(\phi_1, \ldots, \phi_n)$. In the following we write ψ for $\psi(\phi_1, \ldots, \phi_n)$ without further confusions.

LTL properties are special cases of ω-regular winning objectives [22] in two-player concurrent (zero-sum) games [9,6]. In such games one may group a set of players $A \subseteq \Sigma$ into a single protagonist and $\overline{A}$ into a single antagonist. Given an ω-regular winning objective ξ and starting from a state $s \in S$, the protagonist plays with a strategy trying to maximize the probability for a play to satisfy ξ while the antagonist tries to minimize the probability. In such a game there always exists a unique value in $[0,1]$, on which both players have strategies to guarantee (or infinitely approach) their best performances, regardless of the strategies played by their opponents. Such a supremum value (or infinum value, as for the antagonist) is called the *value of the game* [14,9]. In a probabilistic multi-player game, we let a group of players $A \subseteq \Sigma$ be a single player, and $\overline{A}$ be the other, and the supremal probability for A to enforce an LTL formula ψ starting from a given state $s \in S$ can be uniquely determined, as defined by

$$\langle A \rangle \psi(s) = \bigsqcup_{\pi \in \Pi(A)} \bigsqcap_{\pi' \in \Pi(\overline{A})} Pr_{\mathcal{G}(\pi \cup \pi', s)}(\{\rho \in \mathcal{G}(\pi \cup \pi', s) \mid \rho \models \psi\})$$

A vector of strategies, which does not necessarily exist, is *optimal* for a group of players, if it enforces the *value of the game* for that group.

Example 1. Fig. 1 gives a PGS with two players $\{\mathtt{I}, \mathtt{II}\}$, initial state s_0, $\mathtt{Act}_\mathtt{I} = \{a_1, a_2\}$ and $\mathtt{Act}_\mathtt{II} = \{b_1, b_2\}$. Note that this PGS is deterministic, i.e, no probabilities in its transitions. We assume that the only available transitions from

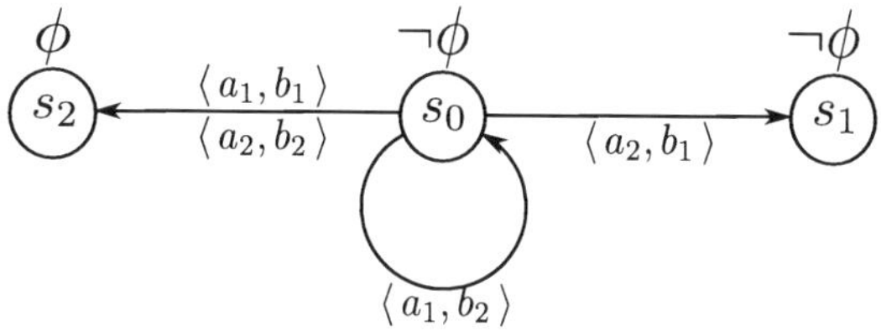

Fig. 1. An example showing that player I can guarantee to satisfy $\Diamond\phi$ with probability α for all $0 \le \alpha < 1$, but he cannot ensure that property with probability 1

s_1 and s_2 are self-loops, and the other transition relations are as depicted in the graph. Suppose player I wants to maximize the probability to enforce the property $\Diamond\phi$, and player II aims to minimize it.

Since the strategies applied on s_1 and s_2 do not matter, we focus on the choices of actions from both players on s_0. We first focus on memoryless strategies, and let player I's strategy π_1 gives $\pi_1(\gamma)(a_1) = p$ and $\pi_1(\gamma)(a_2) = 1 - p$ for all $\gamma \in S^+$. Similarly we let II assign probability q to b_1 and $1 - q$ to b_2 all the time. This produces an infinite tree, on which we write $x_{s_0}(\mathtt{I})$ for the actual probability I can achieve $\Diamond\phi$ from s_0, given the above memoryless strategies. (Note that $x_{s_1}(\mathtt{I}) = 0$ and $x_{s_2}(\mathtt{I}) = 1$ in all cases.) This establishes an equation which further derives $x_{s_0}(\mathtt{I}) = \frac{(1-p)+(2p-1)q}{(1-p)+pq}$. A simple analysis shows that when p approaches 1, the minimal value of $x_{s_0}(\mathtt{I})$ approaches 1 as well, for all choices of q. That is, there exists a strategy for player I to enforce $\Diamond\phi$ with probability $1 - \varepsilon$ for all $\varepsilon > 0$. However, if player I chooses $p = 1$, player II may set $q = 0$ so that a play will be trapped in s_0 for ever that yields $x_{s_0}(\mathtt{I}) = 0$. The result of [9] shows that in this case player I cannot do better even with general (history dependent) strategies. In fact there are no strategies for player I to enforce $\Diamond\phi$ with probability 1. $\square$

Indeed, $\langle A\rangle\psi(s)$ can be *almost* the best, i.e., we have $\mathcal{G}, s \models \langle\langle A\rangle\rangle^{\ge \langle A\rangle\psi(s)-\varepsilon}\psi$ for all $\varepsilon > 0$ [8]. Nevertheless, the quantitative version of determinacy [14] ensures that for all LTL formulas ψ and $s \in S$, we have

$$\langle A\rangle\psi(s) + \langle\overline{A}\rangle\neg\psi(s) = 1$$

The PATL model checking problems can be solved by calculating the values $\langle A\rangle\psi_s(s)$ for each state s, where each local objective ψ_s related to s might be distinct. The algorithms of [9] define monotonic functions of type $(S \to [0,1]) \to (S \to [0,1])$ to arbitrarily approach a vector $\{\langle A\rangle\psi_s(s)\}_{s\in S}$ in a game structure with finite state space S with respect to an ω-regular winning objective ψ. Within each step one has to go through $\mathcal{O}(|S|)$ matrix games, and each iteration produces a unique fixed point. The algorithms on safety and reachability objectives are special cases of solving stochastic games [18]. More complex properties can be expressed as nested fixed points [9]. Therefore, the upper bound complexities become exponential to the size of the winning objectives translated from

LTL formulas. More recently, alternative algorithms proposed in [6] prove that for quantitative games with ω-regular winning objectives expressed as parity conditions, whether the values of a game is within $[r-\epsilon, r+\epsilon]$ can be decided in $NP \cap coNP$ for all rational $r \in [0,1]$ and $\epsilon > 0$, which improves the theoretical upper bound for estimating the optimal values.

It has been shown in [9] that for *safety* games there always exist optimal strategies for the protagonists, however for *reachability* games it is not always the case. We generalise results on the *existence* of optimal strategies for PATL path formulas as follows. Note that the result for unbounded release R has not been studied in the literature, to the authors' knowledge, and the rest of the lemma is derivable from [9].

Lemma 2. *Let s be a state, ψ be a path formula, and A the set of protagonists.*

1. *If ψ is of the form $\bigcirc\phi$, $\phi_1 \mathtt{U}^{\leq k}\phi_2$, $\phi_1 \mathtt{R}^{\leq k}\phi_2$, or $\phi_1 \mathtt{R}\phi_2$ with $k \in \mathbb{N}$, there always exists a joint optimal strategy for A that enforces ψ on s with probability at least $\langle A\rangle\psi(s)$.*
2. *If ψ is of the form $\phi_1 \mathtt{U}\phi_2$, there always exists a joint ϵ-optimal strategy for A that enforces ψ on s with probability at least $\langle A\rangle\psi(s) - \epsilon$, for all $\epsilon > 0$.*

The next results prove the existence of a joint A strategy to enforce an PATL path formula with probability greater than α if there exists a joint strategy to enforce that formula with probability greater than α against an optimal $\overline{A}$ strategy. These two lemmas are essential for the proof of the main result (Theorem 1).

Lemma 3. *Let ψ be a PATL path formula and π' be a joint optimal strategy for the antagonists $\overline{A}$ on state s, if there exists a joint strategy π for the protagonists A such that $Pr_{\mathcal{G}(\pi\cup\pi',s)}(\{\rho \in \mathcal{G}(\pi\cup\pi',s) \mid \rho \models \psi\}) > \alpha$, then $\mathcal{G}, s \models \langle\langle A\rangle\rangle^{>\alpha}\psi$.*

Proof. Since π' is the optimal strategy for the antagonists, we have for all joint strategies π'', $Pr_{\mathcal{G}(\pi''\cup\pi',s)}(\{\rho \in \mathcal{G}(\pi''\cup\pi',s) \mid \rho \models \psi\}) \leq \langle A\rangle\psi(s)$, then we have $\langle A\rangle\psi(s) > \alpha$. If there exists an optimal joint strategy for A then we have $s \models \langle\langle A\rangle\rangle^{\geq\langle A\rangle\psi(s)}\psi$, which implies $s \models \langle\langle A\rangle\rangle^{>\alpha}\psi$. Otherwise by Lemma 2 there exists an ϵ-optimal joint strategy for A with small $\epsilon > 0$ to enforce ψ with probability at least $\langle A\rangle\psi(s) - \epsilon > \alpha$. This also gives us $s \models \langle\langle A\rangle\rangle^{>\alpha}\psi$. □

This result does not hold if we replace the operator "$>$" by "$\geq$" for unbounded until U. This is because if there does not exist a joint optimal strategy for A to enforce $\phi_1 \mathtt{U}\phi_2$ with probability $\geq \alpha$, we have no space to insert a tiny $\epsilon > 0$ as we did in the above proof. For the fragment of path formulas without unbounded until, we extend the results for $\geq$, by the fact that optimal joint strategies for A always exist for these path modalities, as stated by the following lemma.

Lemma 4. *For path formulas ψ in the form of $\bigcirc\phi$ or $\phi_1 \mathtt{U}^{\leq k}\phi_2$ and optimal strategies π' of $\overline{A}$ for the antagonists $\overline{A}$ on state s, if there exists a joint strategy π for the protagonists A such that $Pr_{\mathcal{G}(\pi\cup\pi',s)}(\{\rho \in \mathcal{G}(\pi\cup\pi',s) \mid \rho \models \psi\}) \bowtie \alpha$, then $\mathcal{G}, s \models \langle\langle A\rangle\rangle^{\bowtie\alpha}\psi$, where $k \in \mathbb{N}$ and $\bowtie \in \{>, \geq\}$.*

***A*-PATL**

We define a sublogic of PATL by focusing on a particular set of players. Similar to the approach of [3], we only allow negations to appear on the level of propositions. Let $A \subseteq \Sigma$, an A-PATL formula ϕ is a state formula defined as follows:

$$\phi := p \mid \neg p \mid \phi_1 \wedge \phi_2 \mid \phi_1 \vee \phi_2 \mid \langle\langle A' \rangle\rangle^{\bowtie\alpha} \bigcirc \phi \mid \langle\langle A' \rangle\rangle^{\bowtie\alpha} \phi_1 \mathtt{U}^{\leq k} \phi_2 \mid \langle\langle A' \rangle\rangle^{>\alpha} \phi_1 \mathtt{U} \phi_2$$

where $k \in \mathbb{N}$, $\bowtie \in \{>, \geq\}$ and $A' \subseteq A$. Write $\mathbb{L}_A$ for the set of A-PATL formulas. An A-PATL formula describes a property that players in A are able to ensure with a minimal expectation by their joint strategies. Note that we only allow '$> \alpha$' in the construction of unbounded until.

5 Probabilistic Alternating Simulation Relations

We define probabilistic versions of alternating simulation [3]. An alternating simulation is a two-step simulation. For a sketch, suppose state s is simulated by state t. In the first step the protagonists choose their actions on t to simulate the behavior of the protagonists on s, and in the second step the antagonists choose actions on s to respond to the behavior of the antagonists on t. This somehow results in a simulation-like relation, so that for a certain property the protagonists can enforce on s, they can also enforce it on t. To this end we split Σ into two groups of players — one group of protagonist and the other group of antagonist. Subsequently, we consider only the two-player case in a probabilistic game structure — player $\mathtt{I}$ for the protagonist and player $\mathtt{II}$ for the antagonist, since what we can achieve in the two-player case naturally extends to a result in systems with two complementary sets of players, i.e., $A \cup \overline{A} = \Sigma$. For readability we also write the transition functions as $\delta(s, a_1, a_2)$ and $\overline{\delta}(s, \pi_1, \pi_2)$ for $\delta(s, \langle a_1, a_2 \rangle)$ and $\overline{\delta}(s, \langle \pi_1, \pi_2 \rangle)$, respectively.

Let S, T be two sets and $\mathcal{R} \subseteq S \times T$ be a relation, then $\overline{\mathcal{R}} \subseteq \mathcal{D}(S) \times \mathcal{D}(T)$ is defined by $\Delta \overline{\mathcal{R}} \Theta$ if there exists a weight function $w : S \times T \to [0, 1]$ satisfying

- $\sum_{t \in T} w(s, t) = \Delta(s)$ for all $s \in S$,
- $\sum_{s \in S} w(s, t) = \Theta(t)$ for all $t \in T$,
- $s \mathcal{R}\, t$ for all $s \in S$ and $t \in T$ with $w(s, t) > 0$.

Based on the notion of lifting, we define the probabilistic alternating simulation relation for player $\mathtt{I}$ that extends the alternating simulation relation of [3]. The definition for player $\mathtt{II}$ can be made in a similar way.

Definition 1. *Consider $\mathcal{G}, \mathcal{G}'$ as two probabilistic game structures. A probabilistic alternating $\mathtt{I}$-simulation $\sqsubseteq \subseteq S \times S'$ is a relation satisfying if $s \sqsubseteq s'$, then*

- *$\mathcal{L}(s) = \mathcal{L}'(s')$,*
- *for all $\pi_1 \in \Pi_{\mathtt{I}}^{\mathcal{G},1}$, there exists $\pi_1' \in \Pi_{\mathtt{I}}^{\mathcal{G}',1}$, such that for all $\pi_2' \in \Pi_{\mathtt{II}}^{\mathcal{G}',1}$, there exists $\pi_2 \in \Pi_{\mathtt{II}}^{\mathcal{G},1}$, such that $\overline{\delta}(s, \pi_1, \pi_2) \overline{\sqsubseteq}\, \overline{\delta'}(s', \pi_1', \pi_2')$.*

Note we use level-1 strategies instead of actions (or distributions on actions) on establishing simulations, as in a game structure it is more natural to define simulation in a *behavior*-based way. Also note that a distribution on level-1 strategies yields a level-1 strategy.

Next we propose the notion of probabilistic alternating forward simulation, as per Segala [19], which relates a state to a distribution of states. This requires a different way of lifting. Let $\mathcal{R} \subseteq S \times \mathcal{D}(S)$ be a relation, write $\overline{\mathcal{R}}$ for the smallest relation satisfying $\Delta\overline{\mathcal{R}}\Theta$ if there exists an index set $\{p_i\}_{i\in I}$ satisfying $\Sigma_{i\in I}p_i = 1$, such that $\Delta = \Sigma_{i\in I}p_i \cdot \overline{s_i}$, $\Theta = \Sigma_{i\in I}p_i \cdot \Theta_i$ and $s_i\mathcal{R}\Theta_i$ for all i. Now we define the probabilistic alternating forward simulation relation for player $\mathtt{I}$, and the definition for player $\mathtt{II}$ can be made in a similar way.

Definition 2. *Consider two probabilistic game structures $\mathcal{G} = \langle S, s_0, \mathcal{L}, \mathtt{Act}, \delta\rangle$ and $\mathcal{G}' = \langle S', s_0', \mathcal{L}', \mathtt{Act}', \delta'\rangle$. A probabilistic alternating forward $\mathtt{I}$-simulation $\sqsubseteq_{\mathsf{f}} \subseteq S \times \mathcal{D}(S')$ is a relation satisfying if $s \sqsubseteq_{\mathsf{f}} \Delta'$, then*

- *$\mathcal{L}(s) = \mathcal{L}'(s')$ for all $s' \in \lceil \Delta' \rceil$,*
- *for all $\pi_1 \in \Pi_{\mathtt{I}}^{\mathcal{G},1}$, there exists $\pi_1' \in \Pi_{\mathtt{I}}^{\mathcal{G}',1}$, such that for all $\pi_2' \in \Pi_{\mathtt{II}}^{\mathcal{G}',1}$, there exists $\pi_2 \in \Pi_{\mathtt{II}}^{\mathcal{G},1}$, such that $\delta(s, \pi_1, \pi_2)\overline{\sqsubseteq_{\mathsf{f}}}\ \overline{\delta'}(\Delta', \pi_1', \pi_2')$.*

Lemma 5. *$s \sqsubseteq t$ implies $s \sqsubseteq_{\mathsf{f}} \overline{t}$.*

This lemma says that every probabilistic alternating simulation is a probabilistic forward simulation with a point distribution on the right hand side of the relation. The other way does not hold, i.e., probabilistic alternating forward simulation relates strictly more game structures than probabilistic alternating simulation. In Fig. 2 (which is essentially of [20]), we assume $\mathtt{Act}_{\mathtt{I}}$ and $\mathtt{Act}_{\mathtt{II}}$ are both singleton sets. One may find that there are no states in the set $\{s_2', s_3', s_4', s_5'\}$ in Fig. 2(b) that can simulate states s_3 and s_5 in Fig. 2(a). Therefore, we cannot establish a probabilistic alternating simulation from s_1 to s_1'. However, s_1 is related to s_1' by probabilistic alternating forward simulation, since s_3 (s_5) can be related to a uniform distribution over s_2' and s_3' (s_4' and s_5'). The next result shows that the definition of forward simulation also works on the lifted relation.

Lemma 6. *If $\Delta\overline{\sqsubseteq_{\mathsf{f}}}\Theta$, then for all $\pi_1 \in \Pi_{\mathtt{I}}^{\mathcal{G},1}$, there exists $\pi_2 \in \Pi_{\mathtt{I}}^{\mathcal{G}',1}$, such that for all $\pi_2' \in \Pi_{\mathtt{II}}^{\mathcal{G}',1}$, there exists $\pi_1' \in \Pi_{\mathtt{II}}^{\mathcal{G},1}$, such that $\overline{\delta}(\Delta, \pi_1, \pi_1')\overline{\sqsubseteq_{\mathsf{f}}}\ \overline{\delta}(\Theta, \pi_2, \pi_2')$.*

Consequently, we are able to show that lifted probabilistic alternating forward simulations are transitive.

Corollary 1. *(Transitivity of alternating forward simulation) Let $\sqsubseteq_{\mathsf{f}}$ be a probabilistic alternating forward $\mathtt{I}$-simulation, then $\Delta_1\overline{\sqsubseteq_{\mathsf{f}}}\Delta_2$ and $\Delta_2\overline{\sqsubseteq_{\mathsf{f}}}\Delta_3$ implies $\Delta_1\overline{\sqsubseteq_{\mathsf{f}}}\Delta_3$.*

6 Forward I-Simulation Is Sound for I-PATL

This section establishes the main result of the paper: a relationship between probabilistic forward $\mathtt{I}$-simulation and $\mathtt{I}$-PATL formulas. Recall that a $\mathtt{I}$-PATL

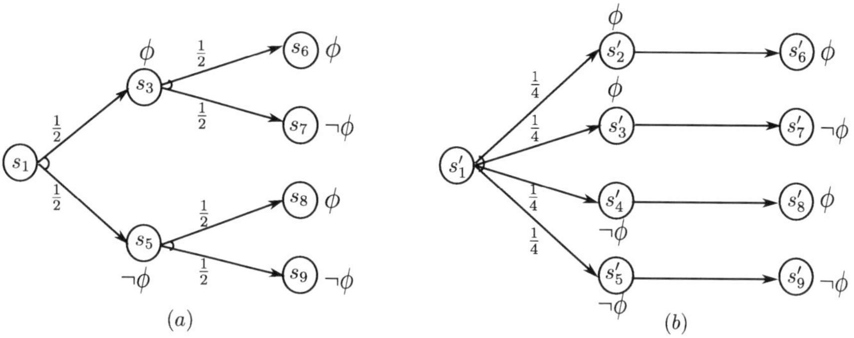

Fig. 2. An example showing that probabilistic alternating forward simulation is strictly weaker than probabilistic alternating simulation

formula has only strategy modalities $\langle\langle \mathtt{I} \rangle\rangle$ and $\langle\langle \emptyset \rangle\rangle$, and negations are only allowed to appear immediately before the propositions. For readability we write $\langle\langle \mathtt{I} \rangle\rangle$ for $\langle\langle \{\mathtt{I}\} \rangle\rangle$. Let $\mathcal{G}$ and $\mathcal{G}'$ be two PGSs, $\Delta \in \mathcal{D}(S)$ and $\Delta' \in \mathcal{D}(S')$ such that $\Delta \overline{\sqsubseteq}_{\mathsf{f}} \Delta'$ by a probabilistic alternating forward I-simulation. We need to show that $\Delta \models \phi$ implies $\Delta' \models \phi$ for all I-PATL formula ϕ.

Our proof relies on the existence of player II's optimal strategies for path formulas as winning objectives (as shown in Sect. 4). Suppose π_1 is a I strategy that enforces ϕ, we construct another I strategy π_1' that simulates π all along the way, in the sense that provided the optimal II strategy π_2' there exists another II strategy π_2 such that the probabilistic execution $\mathcal{E}(\mathcal{G}, \langle \pi_1, \pi_2 \rangle, \Delta)$ will be "simulated" by the probabilistic execution $\mathcal{E}(\mathcal{G}', \langle \pi_1', \pi_2' \rangle, \Delta')$. Since π_1 enforces ϕ, $\mathcal{E}(\mathcal{G}, \langle \pi_1, \pi_2 \rangle, \Delta)$ satisfies ϕ, and we show that it is also the case of $\mathcal{E}(\mathcal{G}', \langle \pi_1', \pi_2' \rangle, \Delta')$.

Let $\mathcal{E} = \langle E, \Delta, \mathcal{L}^{\mathcal{E}}, \delta^{\mathcal{E}} \rangle$ and $\mathcal{E}' = \langle E', \Delta', \mathcal{L}^{\mathcal{E}'}, \delta^{E'} \rangle$ be probabilistic executions of $\mathcal{G}$ and $\mathcal{G}'$, respectively. Also let $\sqsubseteq_{\mathsf{f}} \subseteq S \times \mathcal{D}(S')$ be a probabilistic alternating forward I-simulation. We say the pair $(\mathcal{E}, \mathcal{E}')$ is an *instance of simulation*, by writing $\mathcal{E} \sqsubseteq \mathcal{E}'$, if there exists a (simulation) relation $\sqsubseteq' \subseteq E \times \mathcal{D}(E')$, such that

- $\Delta \overline{\sqsubseteq}' \Delta'$,
- if $e \sqsubseteq' \Theta$ then $last(e) \sqsubseteq_{\mathsf{f}} last(\Theta)$,
- if $e \sqsubseteq' \Theta$ then $\delta^{\mathcal{E}}(e) \overline{\sqsubseteq} \delta^{\mathcal{E}'}(\Theta)$,

where $last(\Theta)$ is a distribution satisfying $last(\Theta)(s) = \sum_{last(e)=s} \Theta(e)$. A few properties of the relation $\sqsubseteq'$ are as follows.

Lemma 7. *1. $\Delta \overline{\sqsubseteq}' \Theta$ implies $\delta^{\mathcal{E}}(\Delta) \overline{\sqsubseteq}' \delta^{\mathcal{E}'}(\Theta)$.*
2. $\Delta \overline{\sqsubseteq}' \Theta$ and $\Delta = \Delta_1 \oplus_\alpha \Delta_2$ with $\alpha \in [0, 1]$, then there exist Θ_1, Θ_2 such that $\Delta_1 \overline{\sqsubseteq}' \Theta_1$, $\Delta_2 \overline{\sqsubseteq}' \Theta_2$, and $\Theta = \Theta_1 \oplus_\alpha \Theta_2$.

Let Δ be a state distribution of $\mathcal{G}$, Δ' be a state distribution of $\mathcal{G}'$, and $\Delta \overline{\sqsubseteq}_{\mathsf{f}} \Delta'$. Suppose π_1 is a I strategy in $\mathcal{G}$ that enforces ϕ with probability at least α, and π_2'

is a $\mathtt{II}$ strategy in $\mathcal{G}'$, step-by-step we establish a $\mathtt{I}$ strategy π_1' and a $\mathtt{II}$ strategy π_2, so that the probabilistic executution decided by π_1 and π_2 from Δ will be simulated by the probabilistic executution decided by π_1' and π_2' from Δ'.

Lemma 8. *Let $\mathcal{G} = \langle S, s_0, \mathcal{L}, \mathtt{Act}, \delta\rangle$ and $\mathcal{G}' = \langle S', s_0', \mathcal{L}', \mathtt{Act}', \delta'\rangle$ be two PGSs. If $\Delta \overline{\sqsubseteq}_{\mathsf{f}} \Delta'$, then for all $\pi_1 \in \Pi_{\mathtt{I}}^{\mathcal{G}}$ and $\pi_2' \in \Pi_{\mathtt{II}}^{\mathcal{G}'}$, there exists $\pi_1' \in \Pi_{\mathtt{I}}^{\mathcal{G}'}$ and $\pi_2 \in \Pi_{\mathtt{II}}^{\mathcal{G}}$, such that $\mathcal{E}(\mathcal{G}, \langle \pi_1, \pi_2\rangle, \Delta) \sqsubseteq \mathcal{E}'(\mathcal{G}', \langle \pi_1', \pi_2'\rangle, \Delta')$.*

In order to measure the probability of a path formula to be satisfied when the strategies from both player $\mathtt{I}$ and player $\mathtt{II}$ are fixed, we define a relation $\models^{\bowtie\alpha}$ for probabilistic executions.

Definition 3. *Let $\mathcal{G}$ be a probabilistic game structure, $\mathcal{E}(\Delta) = \langle E, \Delta, \mathcal{L}^{\mathcal{E}}, \delta^{\mathcal{E}}\rangle$ a probabilistic execution determined by a vector $\boldsymbol{\pi}_{\mathcal{E}}$, and ψ a path formula, define*

$$\mathcal{E}(\Delta) \models^{\bowtie\alpha} \psi \quad \text{iff} \quad Pr_{\mathcal{E}}^{\Delta}(\{\rho \in \bigcup_{s \in \lceil \Delta \rceil} \mathcal{G}(\boldsymbol{\pi}_{\mathcal{E}}, s) \mid \rho \models \psi\}) \bowtie \alpha$$

It is conceivable that in a probabilistic execution every finite or infinite trace in $E^* \cup E^\omega$ maps to a trace in $\mathcal{G}$, in the way that $\rho = e_1 e_2 e_3 \ldots$ is a trace in $\mathcal{E}$ implies that $proj(\rho) = last(e_1)last(e_2)last(e_3)\ldots$ is a play in $\mathcal{G}$, where the function $proj$ projects every finite sequence of states in E into its last state in S. Consequently, we let $Pr_{\mathcal{E}}^{\Delta}$ be a probabilistic measure over E^ω, such that for the cone sets (of finite traces), we have $Pr_{\mathcal{E}}^{\Delta}(e) = \Delta(last(e))$, and $Pr_{\mathcal{E}}^{\Delta}(\gamma \cdot e_1 \cdot e_2) = Pr_{\mathcal{E}}^{\Delta}(\gamma \cdot e_1) \cdot \delta^{\mathcal{E}}(e_1)(e_2)$, for $\gamma \in E^*$ and $e_1, e_2 \in E$. Let ρ be an infinite trace in $\mathcal{E}$, we write $\rho \models \psi$ iff $proj(\rho) \models \psi$. Similarly, for a state formula ϕ and $e \in E$, write $e \in [\![\phi]\!]$ iff $last(e) \in [\![\phi]\!]$. In the following we study the properties of the satisfaction relation for a probabilistic execution to satisfy a $\mathtt{I}$-PATL path formula by means of unfolding.

Lemma 9. *Let ϕ, ϕ_1 and ϕ_2 be $\mathtt{I}$-PATL (state) formulas, and $\bowtie \in \{>, \geq\}$ then*

1. *$\mathcal{E}(\Delta) \models^{\bowtie\alpha} \bigcirc\phi$ iff there exists $\alpha' \bowtie \alpha$, such that $\delta^{\mathcal{E}}(\Delta) = \Delta_1 \oplus_{\alpha'} \Delta_2$ with $\lceil \Delta_1 \rceil \cap \lceil \Delta_2 \rceil = \emptyset$, and $\Delta_1 \models \phi$.*
2. *$\mathcal{E}(\Delta) \models^{\bowtie\alpha} \phi_1 \mathcal{U}^{\leq k} \phi_2$ iff there exists a finite sequence of triples $\{\langle(\Delta_{i,0}, \alpha_{i,0}), (\Delta_{i,1}, \alpha_{i,1}), (\Delta_{i,2}, \alpha_{i,2})\rangle\}_{0 \leq i \leq j}$ for some $j \leq k$, with $\lceil \Delta_{i,\ell} \rceil \cap \lceil \Delta_{i,\ell'} \rceil = \emptyset$ for all distinct $\ell, \ell' \in \{0, 1, 2\}$ and $0 \leq i \leq j$, such that*

$$(1) \sum_{i \in [0 \ldots j]} \left(\alpha_{i,1} \cdot \prod_{i' \in [0 \ldots i-1]} \alpha_{i',0} \right) \bowtie \alpha,$$

   (2) $\Delta = \sum_{\ell \in \{0,1,2\}} \alpha_{0,\ell} \cdot \Delta_{0,\ell}$, and $\delta^{\mathcal{E}}(\Delta_{i,0}) = \sum_{\ell \in \{0,1,2\}} \alpha_{i+1,\ell} \cdot \Delta_{i+1,\ell}$ for all $0 \leq i < j$, (3) $\Delta_{i,0} \models \phi_1$ and $\Delta_{i,1} \models \phi_2$ for all $0 \leq i \leq j$.
3. *$\mathcal{E}(\Delta) \models^{\bowtie\alpha} \phi_1 \mathcal{U}\, \phi_2$ iff there exists a finite or infinite sequence of triples $\{\langle(\Delta_{i,0}, \alpha_{i,0}), (\Delta_{i,1}, \alpha_{i,1}), (\Delta_{i,2}, \alpha_{i,2})\rangle\}_{0 \leq i < j}$ for some $j \in \mathbb{N}^+ \cup \{\infty\}$, with $\lceil \Delta_{i,\ell} \rceil \cap \lceil \Delta_{i,\ell'} \rceil = \emptyset$ for all distinct $\ell, \ell' \in \{0, 1, 2\}$ and $0 \leq i < j$, such that*

$$(1) \sum_{0 \leq i < j} \left(\alpha_{i,1} \cdot \prod_{i' \in [0 \ldots i-1]} \alpha_{i',0} \right) \bowtie \alpha,$$

(2) $\Delta = \sum_{\ell \in \{0,1,2\}} \alpha_{0,\ell} \cdot \Delta_{0,\ell}$, *and* $\delta^{\mathcal{E}}(\Delta_{i,0}) = \sum_{\ell \in \{0,1,2\}} \alpha_{i+1,\ell} \cdot \Delta_{i+1,\ell}$ *for all* $0 \leq i < j$, (3) $\Delta_{i,0} \models \phi_1$ *and* $\Delta_{i,1} \models \phi_2$ *for all* $0 \leq i < j$.

Theorem 1. *Let* $\mathcal{G} = \langle S, s_0, \mathcal{L}, \mathtt{Act}, \delta \rangle$ *and* $\mathcal{G}' = \langle S', s_0', \mathcal{L}', \mathtt{Act}', \delta' \rangle$ *be two PGSs,* $\sqsubseteq_{\mathsf{f}} \subseteq S \times \mathcal{D}(S')$ *a probabilistic alternating forward* I*-simulation. If* $\Delta \overline{\sqsubseteq_{\mathsf{f}}} \Delta'$, *then* $\mathcal{G}, \Delta \models \phi$ *implies* $\mathcal{G}', \Delta' \models \phi$ *for all* $\phi \in \mathbb{L}_{\mathtt{I}}$.

Proof. (sketch) We prove by induction on the structure of a I-PATL formula ϕ. Base case: suppose $\Delta \models p$, then $s \models p$ for all $s \in \lceil \Delta \rceil$. By $\Delta \overline{\sqsubseteq_{\mathsf{f}}} \Delta'$, there exists an index set $\{q_i\}_{i \in I}$ satisfying $\sum_{i \in I} q_i = 1$, $\Delta = \sum_{i \in I} q_i \overline{s_i}$, $\Delta' = \sum_{i \in I} q_i \Delta_i$, and $s_i \sqsubseteq_{\mathsf{f}} \Delta_i$. Therefore $\mathcal{L}(s_i) = \mathcal{L}'(t)$ for all $t \in \lceil \Delta_i \rceil$. So $t \models p$ for all $t \in \lceil \Delta_i \rceil$ for all i. Therefore $\Delta' \models p$. The case of $\neg p$ is similar.

We show the case when $\phi = \langle\langle \mathtt{I} \rangle\rangle^{>\alpha} \phi_1 \mathtt{U} \phi_2$, and the proof methods for the other PATL path constructors are similar. Since for all $t \in \lceil \Delta' \rceil$ there exists an optimal strategy π^t for the winning objective $\neg\phi_1 \mathcal{R} \neg\phi_2$ by Lemma 2(1), and we combine these strategies into a single strategy π_2' satisfying $\pi_2'(t \cdot \alpha) = \pi^t(t \cdot \alpha)$ for all $t \in \lceil \Delta' \rceil$ and $\alpha \in S^*$. Then π_2' is optimal for $\neg\phi_1 \mathcal{R} \neg\phi_2$ on Δ'. Then by Lemma 8, there exist $\pi_2 \in \Pi_{\mathtt{II}}^{\mathcal{G}}$ and $\pi_1' \in \Pi_{\mathtt{I}}^{\mathcal{G}'}$ such that $\mathcal{E}(\mathcal{G}, \langle \pi_1, \pi_2 \rangle, \Delta) \sqsubseteq \mathcal{E}'(\mathcal{G}', \langle \pi_1', \pi_2' \rangle, \Delta')$. Since π_1 enforces $\phi_1 \mathtt{U} \phi_2$ with probability greater than α, we have $\mathcal{E}(\Delta) \models^{>\alpha} \phi_1 \mathtt{U} \phi_2$. By Lemma 9(3) there exists a sequence of triples $\{\langle (\Delta_{i,0}, \alpha_{i,0}), (\Delta_{i,1}, \alpha_{i,1}), (\Delta_{i,2}, \alpha_{i,2}) \rangle\}_{0 \leq i < j}$ for some $j \in \mathbb{N}^+ \cup \{\infty\}$ satisfying the properties as stated in Lemma 9(3). By repetitively applying Lemma 7 we establish another sequence of triples $\{\langle (\Delta_{i,0}', \alpha_{i,0}), (\Delta_{i,1}', \alpha_{i,1}), (\Delta_{i,2}', \alpha_{i,2}) \rangle\}_{0 \leq i < j}$, such that (1) $\sum_{0 \leq i < j} (\alpha_{i,1} \cdot \prod_{i' \in [0 \dots i-1]} \alpha_{i',0}) > \alpha$, (2) $\Delta' = \sum_{\ell \in \{0,1,2\}} \alpha_{0,\ell} \cdot \Delta_{0,\ell}'$, and $\delta^{\mathcal{E}}(\Delta_{i,0}') = \sum_{\ell \in \{0,1,2\}} \alpha_{i+1,\ell} \cdot \Delta_{i+1,\ell}'$ for all $0 \leq i < j$, (3) $\Delta_{i,0} \overline{\sqsubseteq_{\mathsf{f}}} \Delta_{i,0}'$ and $\Delta_{i,1} \overline{\sqsubseteq_{\mathsf{f}}} \Delta_{i,1}'$ for all $0 \leq i < j$. By induction hypothesis we have $\Delta_{i,0}' \models \phi_1$ and $\Delta_{i,1}' \models \phi_2$ for all $0 \leq i < j$. Therefore $\mathcal{E}(\Delta') \models^{>\alpha} \phi_1 \mathtt{U} \phi_2$ by Lemma 9(3). Since π_2' is an optimal strategy of II, we have $\Delta' \models \langle\langle \mathtt{I} \rangle\rangle^{>\alpha} \phi_1 \mathtt{U} \phi_2$ by Lemma 3.

For a formula $\langle\langle \emptyset \rangle\rangle^{\bowtie\alpha} \psi$ we apply the same proof strategies as for $\langle\langle \mathtt{I} \rangle\rangle^{\bowtie\alpha} \psi$, except that player I does not need to enforce ψ with a certain probability $\bowtie \alpha$ since every probabilistic execution generated by a pair of I and II strategies will enforce ψ with that probability. □

7 Probabilistic Alternating Bisimulation

If a probabilistic alternating simulation is symmetric, we call it a probabilistic alternating bisimulation.

Definition 4. *Consider two probabilistic game structures* $\mathcal{G} = \langle S, s_0, \mathcal{L}, \mathtt{Act}, \delta \rangle$ *and* $\mathcal{G}' = \langle S', s_0', \mathcal{L}', \mathtt{Act}', \delta' \rangle$. *A probabilistic alternating* I*-bisimulation* $\simeq \subseteq S \times S'$ *is a symmetric relation satisfying if* $s \simeq s'$, *then*

- $\mathcal{L}(s) = \mathcal{L}'(s')$,
- *for all* $\pi_1 \in \Pi_{\mathtt{I}}^{\mathcal{G},1}$, *there exists* $\pi_1' \in \Pi_{\mathtt{I}}^{\mathcal{G}',1}$, *such that for all* $\pi_2' \in \Pi_{\mathtt{II}}^{\mathcal{G}',1}$, *there exists* $\pi_2 \in \Pi_{\mathtt{II}}^{\mathcal{G},1}$, *such that* $\delta(s, \pi_1, \pi_2) \overline{\simeq} \delta'(s', \pi_1', \pi_2')$,

where $\overline{\simeq}$ *is a lifting of* $\simeq$ *by weight functions.*

Since every probabilistic alternating I-simulation is also a probabilistic alternating forward I-simulation by treating the right hand side state as a point distribution (Lemma 5), the lifted probabilistic alternating I-simulation is also a lifted probabilistic alternating forward I-simulation. This fact extends for bisimulation. A probabilistic alternating I-bisimulation also preserves formulas in $\mathbb{L}_{\mathtt{I}}$. Moreover, we write $\mathbb{L}_{\mathtt{I}}^{+}$ for the set of formulas defined as follows, which allows negations to appear anywhere in a formula, and further we are able to show that probabilistic alternating bisimulation preserves all properties expressed in $\mathbb{L}_{\mathtt{I}}^{+}$.

$$\phi := p \mid \neg\phi \mid \phi_1 \wedge \phi_2 \mid \langle\langle A' \rangle\rangle^{\bowtie\alpha} \bigcirc \phi \mid \langle\langle A' \rangle\rangle^{\bowtie\alpha} \phi_1 \mathtt{U}^{\leq k} \phi_2 \mid \langle\langle A' \rangle\rangle^{>\alpha} \phi_1 \mathtt{U} \phi_2$$

Theorem 2. *Let* $\mathcal{G} = \langle S, s_0, \mathcal{L}, \mathtt{Act}, \delta \rangle$ *and* $\mathcal{G}' = \langle S', s_0', \mathcal{L}', \mathtt{Act}', \delta' \rangle$ *be two PGSs,* $\simeq \subseteq S \times S'$ *is a probabilistic alternating* I*-bisimulation. For all* $s \in S$ *and* $s' \in S'$ *with* $s \simeq s'$ *and* $\phi \in \mathbb{L}_{\mathtt{I}}^{+}$*, we have* $\mathcal{G}, s \models \phi$ *iff* $\mathcal{G}', s' \models \phi$*.*

The proof methodology basically follows that of Theorem 1, besides that whenever $\Delta \overline{\simeq} \Delta'$ and $\Delta \models \neg\phi$, we show that if there were $s' \in \lceil \Delta \rceil'$ such that $\mathcal{G}', s' \models \phi$ then we would also have $\mathcal{G}, s \models \phi$ for some $s \in \lceil \Delta \rceil$, which is a contradiction. And from that we have $\Delta' \models \neg\phi$ as well.

8 Conclusion and Future Work

We report our first results on probabilistic alternating simulation relations. We have introduced two notions of simulation for probabilistic game structures — probabilistic alternating simulation and probabilistic alternating forward simulation, following the seminal works of Segala and Lynch [19,21] on probabilistic simulation relations and the work of Alur et al. [3] on alternating refinement relations for non-probabilistic game structures. Our main effort has been devoted to a logical characterization for probabilistic alternating simulation relations, by showing that they preserve a fragment of PATL formulas. It is worth noting that on our way to the main result, we find that the proof strategy accommodated in [3] no longer applies, due to the failure in reconstructing a strategy from sub-strategies when the system transitions become probabilistic. We circumvent this problem by incorporating the results of probabilistic determinacy [14] and the existence of optimal strategies [9] in stochastic games. A full version of the paper is available as a technical report [23].

There are several ways to proceed. We want to study the *completeness* of logical characterization for probabilistic alternating forward simulation. It is also of our interest to investigate the *complexity* for checking probabilistic alternating simulation relations by studying the results in the literature [3,5]. Our work was partially motivated by the paper [4], where PATL is used to formalize a *balanced* property for a probabilistic contract signing protocol. Here, a balanced protocol means that a dishonest participant never has a strategy to unilaterally determine the outcome of the protocol. It is interesting to see how much the development of simulation relations for probabilistic game structures can help the verification of such kind of security protocols.

References

1. Alur, R., Henzinger, T.A., Kupferman, O.: Alternating-time temporal logic. In: Proc. FOCS, pp. 100–109. IEEE CS, Los Alamitos (1997)
2. Alur, R., Henzinger, T.A., Kupferman, O.: Alternating-time temporal logic. J. ACM 49(5), 672–713 (2002)
3. Alur, R., Henzinger, T.A., Kupferman, O., Vardi, M.Y.: Alternating refinement relations. In: Sangiorgi, D., de Simone, R. (eds.) CONCUR 1998. LNCS, vol. 1466, pp. 163–178. Springer, Heidelberg (1998)
4. Aizatulin, M., Schnoor, H., Wilke, T.: Computationally sound analysis of a probabilistic contract signing protocol. In: Backes, M., Ning, P. (eds.) ESORICS 2009. LNCS, vol. 5789, pp. 571–586. Springer, Heidelberg (2009)
5. Baier, C., Engelen, B., Majster-Cederbaum, M.E.: Deciding bisimilarity and similarity for probabilistic processes. J. Comput. Syst. Sci. 60(1), 187–231 (2000)
6. Chatterjee, K., de Alfaro, L., Henzinger, T.A.: The complexity of quantitative concurrent parity games. In: Proc. SODA, pp. 678–687. ACM, New York (2006)
7. Chen, T., Lu, J.: Probabilistic alternating-time temporal logic and model checking algorithm. In: Proc. FSKD, pp. 35–39. IEEE CS, Los Alamitos (2007)
8. de Alfaro, L., Henzinger, T.A., Kupferman, O.: Concurrent reachability games. In: Proc. FOCS, pp. 564–575. IEEE CS, Los Alamitos (1998)
9. de Alfaro, L., Majumdar, R.: Quantitative solution of omega-regular games. J. Comput. Syst. Sci. 68(2), 374–397 (2004)
10. Desharnais, J., Gupta, V., Jagadeesan, R., Panangaden, P.: Weak bisimulation is sound and complete for PCTL*. In: Brim, L., Jančar, P., Křetínský, M., Kucera, A. (eds.) CONCUR 2002. LNCS, vol. 2421, pp. 355–370. Springer, Heidelberg (2002)
11. Emerson, E.A.: Temporal and modal logic. In: Handbook of Theoretical Computer Science (B), pp. 955–1072. MIT Press, Cambridge (1990)
12. Hansson, H.: Time and Probability in Formal Design of Distributed Systems. Elsevier, Amsterdam (1994)
13. Lynch, N.A., Segala, R., Vaandrager, F.W.: Observing branching structure through probabilistic contexts. SIAM J. Comput. 37(4), 977–1013 (2007)
14. Martin, D.A.: The determinacy of Blackwell games. J. Symb. Log. 63(4), 1565–1581 (1998)
15. Milner, R.: Communication and Concurrency. Prentice-Hall, Englewood Cliffs (1989)
16. von Neumann, J., Morgenstern, O.: Theory of Games and Economic Behavior. Princeton University Press, Princeton (1947)
17. Parma, A., Segala, R.: Logical characterizations of bisimulations for discrete probabilistic systems. In: Seidl, H. (ed.) FOSSACS 2007. LNCS, vol. 4423, pp. 287–301. Springer, Heidelberg (2007)
18. Raghavan, T.E.S., Filar, J.A.: Algorithms for stochastic games – A survey. Mathematical Methods of Operations Research 35(6), 437–472 (1991)
19. Segala, R.: A compositional trace-based semantics for probabilistic automata. In: Lee, I., Smolka, S.A. (eds.) CONCUR 1995. LNCS, vol. 962, pp. 234–248. Springer, Heidelberg (1995)
20. Segala, R.: Modeling and Verification of Randomized Distributed Real-Time Systems. PhD thesis, MIT (1995)
21. Segala, R., Lynch, N.A.: Probabilistic simulations for probabilistic processes. Nord. J. Comput. 2(2), 250–273 (1995)
22. Thomas, W.: Automata on infinite objects. In: Handbook of Theoretical Computer Science (B), pp. 133–192. MIT Press, Cambridge (1990)
23. Zhang, C., Pang, J.: On probabilistic alternating simulations. Tech. Rep .(2010), http://arxiv.org/abs/1003.0788

Probabilistic Mobility Models for Mobile and Wireless Networks*

Lei Song and Jens Chr. Godskesen

IT University of Copenhagen
Rued Langgaards Vej 7
DK-2300 Copenhagen S, Denmark
{leis,jcg}@itu.dk

Abstract. In this paper we present a probabilistic broadcast calculus for mobile and wireless networks whose connections are unreliable. In our calculus, broadcasted messages can be lost with a certain probability, and due to mobility the connection probabilities may change. If a network broadcasts a message from a location, it will evolve to a network distribution depending on whether nodes at other locations receive the message or not. Mobility of nodes is not arbitrary but guarded by a *probabilistic mobility function* (PMF), and we also define the notion of a weak bisimulation given a PMF. It is possible to have weak bisimular networks which have different probabilistic connectivity information. We furthermore examine the relation between our weak bisimulation and a minor variant of PCTL* [1]. Finally, we apply our calculus on a small example called the Zeroconf protocol [2].

1 Introduction

Mobile and wireless networks have gained in popularity in recent years, and the application area is broad, spanning from ambient intelligence, wireless local area networks, sensor networks, and cellular networks for mobile telephony. The key communication primitive in wireless communication is message broadcast but, differently from wired local area networks, broadcast in wireless networks is *local*, hence only nodes within the communication range of the emitting node can receive the message, and due to mobility the communication area may change over time.

Mobility and local wireless broadcast has been studied in the calculi: CBS♯[3], the ω-calculus[4], CMN[5], RBPT[6], and CMAN[7,8]. All these calculi only deal with connectivity in two modes: either two nodes are connected or disconnected. It is often assumed that when a node at location l is within the transmission range of another node at location k, then the node at l can receive messages broadcasted from k with probability 1, otherwise with probability 0. Here we refine this assumption and equip a connection with a probability, since in an unreliable medium we cannot guarantee that the broadcasted messages will always be received even within the transmission range. For example, in Fig. 1 the dashed circle denotes the transmission range of k, every node at a location within the circle, such as l and m, may receive the messages broadcasted

* Supported by the VKR Centre of Excellence MT-LAB.

C.S. Calude and V. Sassone (Eds.): TCS 2010, IFIP AICT 323, pp. 86–100, 2010.

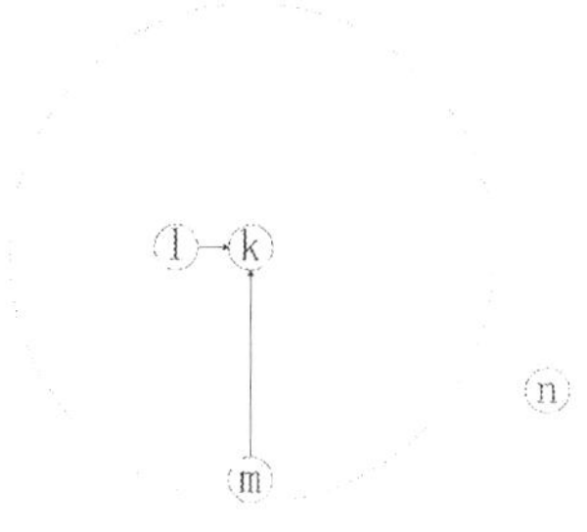

Fig. 1. Connectivity example

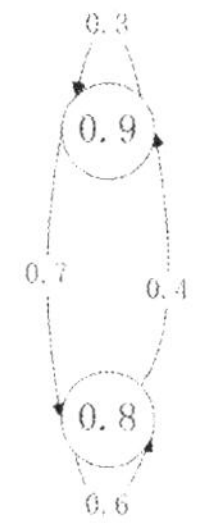

Fig. 2. Equivalent connection probabilities

from k, but the node at n outside the circle cannot. Intuitively, although both l and m are in the transmission range of k, it is more reasonable to let nodes there receive messages from k with different probabilities since m is further away from k than l. In our calculus, the connectivity of this network can be denoted as $\{\{(0.9, l), (0.5, m), (0, n)\} \longmapsto k\}$ if nodes at l, m, n can receive messages from k with probability 0.9, 0.5, and 0 respectively.

In order to model mobility we let connection probabilities between locations change, and the changes are also probabilistic. For instance, the nodes at location m in Fig. 1 may move closer to location k with a certain probability in which case the nodes at m will be able to receive messages from k with a higher probability.

In practice, when verifying properties of a mobile network it will be reasonable to assume that mobility within a network is not arbitrarily but respects certain rules or distributions. Therefore we introduce a *probabilistic mobility function* (PMF) which defines the mobility rules of all the connections. A PMF returns the probability for a connection evolving from one value into another. For example, if in a PMF the connection probability from l to k is given by Fig. 2, then we know that it can change to 0.8 with probability 0.7 or stay at 0.9 with probability 0.3, that is:

$$\{\{(0.9, l), (0.5, m), (0, n)\} \longmapsto k\} \longrightarrow \begin{cases} 0.7 : \{\{(0.8, l), (0.5, m), (0, n)\} \longmapsto k\} \\ 0.3 : \{\{(0.9, l), (0.5, m), (0, n)\} \longmapsto k\} \end{cases}$$

Hence we equip mobility with probabilities, and after each mobility action the network will evolve into a distribution with the probabilities specified by the given PMF. We expect that usually a PMF can be obtained based on measurement of case studies.

Our network calculus consists of concurrent processes (nodes) communicating internally over channels at (logical) locations and broadcasting messages to processes at neighboring locations over probabilistic connections that may change probabilistically over time as outlined above. The semantics is a combination of probability, concurrency, and non-determinism. Formally the labeled transition system semantics gives rise to a *simple probabilistic automata* as outlined in [9], which allows us to use a labeled variant of PCTL*[1] to reason about properties of networks specified in our calculus. We also define a (weak) bisimulation along the lines of [1] and show that it is sound and complete for our version of PCTL*. In our bisimulation, we abstract from mobility as in the other calculi for mobile and wireless systems mentioned above.

As a novelty a bisimulation is parameterized by a PMF, and since we abstract from mobility we consider two probabilities of a connection to be equivalent if they can evolve into each other eventually with probability 1 after a number of mobility steps. Intuitively, it means that a connection due to mobility can take any of the equivalent probabilities. For example, given the PMF in Fig. 2 the state 0.8 can evolve into 0.9 with probability 1 after an infinite number of steps. Furthermore, two locations l and m are considered equivalent if any other location k is connected to them by equivalent probabilities, because then nodes at k can with probability 1 receive messages from l and m with the same probability.

Another important contribution is the introduction of *unknown probabilities*. Since we are dealing with open systems where contexts may contain new nodes and information about connection probabilities, we cannot in a network expect to know the probability of all possible connections. We integrate unknown probabilities in our theory to deal with these cases. Intuitively a connection with an unknown probability means that the probability for the connection can be any value.

The paper is organized as follows: the syntax of our calculus is presented in the next section and in Section 3 we give the Labeled Transition System for it. In Section 4 a weak bisimulation is defined and we also prove it to be a congruence. PCTL* and its relation with weak bisimulation is given in Section 5. We illustrate the application of our calculus with a simple protocol called Zeroconf in Section 6. Finally, we end by a conclusion and future works.

2 The Calculus

Before introducing our calculus, we first give the following general definitions. A *probability space* is a triplet $\mathcal{P} = (\Omega, F, \eta)$ where Ω is a set, F is a collection of subsets of Ω closed under complement and countable union that includes Ω. $\eta : F \to [0, 1]$ is a probability distribution such that $\eta(\Omega) = 1$, and for any collection $\{C_i\}_i$ of at most countably many pairwise disjoint elements of F, $\eta(\cup_i C_i) = \sum_i \eta(C_i)$. A probability space (Ω, F, η) is discrete if Ω is countable and $F = 2^{\Omega}$, and hence abbreviated as (Ω, η). Given probability spaces $\{\mathcal{P} = (\Omega_i, \eta_i)\}_{i\in I}$ and weights $w_i > 0$ for each i such that $\sum_{i\in I} w_i = 1$, the *convex combination* $\sum_{i\in I} w_i \mathcal{P}_i$ is defined as the probability space (Ω, η) such that $\Omega = \bigcup_{i\in I} \Omega_i$ and for each set $Y \subseteq \Omega$, $\eta(Y) = \sum_{i\in I} w_i \eta_i(Y \cap \Omega_i)$. We let $\{\rho_i : N_i\}_{i\in I}$ denote the discrete probability space $(\{N_{i\in I}\}, \eta)$ where $\eta(\{N_i\}) = \rho_i$.

We presuppose a countably infinite set N of names, ranged over by x, y, z and a finite set L of location names, ranged over by k, l, m, n. The variables $\tilde{k}, \tilde{l} \ldots$ are used to denote a set of locations. In addition, we also suppose a finite set of probabilities $\wp$ including 0 and 1 ranged over by $\rho, \rho', \rho_1 \ldots$. We define a *location connection set*, ranged over by $\mathbb{L}, \mathbb{K} \ldots$, as a subset of $\{(\rho, l) \mid \rho \in \wp, l \in L\}$. We use $l(\mathbb{L}) = \{l \mid (\rho, l) \in \mathbb{L}\}$ to denote all the locations in $\mathbb{L}$. The syntax of processes is defined by the following grammar:

$$p, q ::= 0 \quad | \quad Act.p \quad | \quad \text{if}\,(x = y)\,\text{then}\; p\;\text{else}\; q \quad | \quad \nu x p \quad | \quad p \| q \quad | \quad !p$$

$$Act ::= \langle x \rangle \quad | \quad \bar{y}\langle x \rangle \quad | \quad (x) \quad | \quad y(x)$$

Action $\langle x \rangle$ represents broadcasting a message x, while the reception of a broadcasted message is denoted by (x); $\bar{y}\langle x \rangle$ denotes sending a message x via the channel y and in

Table 1. Structural congruence

$\lfloor 0 \rfloor_l \equiv 0$	$\lfloor !p \rfloor_l \equiv \lfloor p \| !p \rfloor_l$	$\nu x E \| E' \equiv \nu x(E \| E')$, if $x \notin fn(E')$
$E \| 0 \equiv E$	$\lfloor p \| q \rfloor_l \equiv \lfloor p \rfloor_l \| \lfloor q \rfloor_l$	$\lfloor \text{if } (x = x) \text{ then } p \text{ else } q \rfloor_l \equiv \lfloor p \rfloor_l$
$\lfloor \nu x.p \rfloor_l \equiv \nu x \lfloor p \rfloor_l$	$(E \| E') \| E'' \equiv E \| (E' \| E'')$	$\lfloor \text{if } (x = y) \text{ then } p \text{ else } q \rfloor_l \equiv \lfloor q \rfloor_l, x \neq y$
$\nu x \nu y E = \nu y \nu x E$	$E \| F \equiv F \| E$	$\{\mathbb{L}_1 \longmapsto k\} \| \{\mathbb{L}_2 \longmapsto k\} \equiv \{\mathbb{L}_1 \cup \mathbb{L}_2 \longmapsto k\}, l(\mathbb{L}_1) \cap l(\mathbb{L}_2) = \emptyset$

contrast $y(x)$ represents receiving a message x on channel y. Process 0 is the deadlocked process; $Act.p$ is the process that can perform action Act and then behave as p; if $(x = y)$ then p else q behaves as p if names x and y match and as q otherwise; νxp means that name x is bounded in the process p; in composition $p\|q$, the processes p and q can proceed in parallel and can also interact via shared names; $!p$ means an unbounded number of parallel compositions of process p. As usual we often leave out a trailing 0.

The set of networks $\mathcal{N}$ is defined by the grammar:

$$E, F ::= 0 \quad | \quad \lfloor p \rfloor_l \quad | \quad \{\mathbb{L} \longmapsto l\} \quad | \quad \nu x E \quad | \quad E \| F$$

Here $\lfloor p \rfloor_l$ is a process p at location l; $\nu x E$ and $E\|F$ are restriction and parallel composition respectively which have the standard meaning; $\{\mathbb{L} \longmapsto l\}$ denotes connection information, i.e. if $(\rho, k) \in \mathbb{L}$, the node at location k is connected to l and can receive messages from l with probability ρ. We use $E, F, G \ldots$ to range over $\mathcal{N}$.

We define a *network distribution* as a probability space $\mathbb{E} = \{(\rho_i : E_i)\}_{i \in I}$ meaning that a network can evolve into E_i with probability ρ_i. We use $\mathbb{E}, \mathbb{F}, \mathbb{G} \ldots$ to range over network distributions ND. If a network distribution consists of a single network, such as $\{(1 : E)\}$, then we denote it as E directly. Parallel composition of network distributions is defined by:

$$\mathbb{E} \| \mathbb{F} = \{(\rho \times \rho' : E \| F) \mid (\rho : E) \in \mathbb{E}, (\rho' : F) \in \mathbb{F}\}$$

A substitution $\{y/x\}$ can be applied to a node, network or network distribution. When applied to a network distribution, it means applying this substitution to each network within this distribution. The set of free names and bound names in E, denoted by $fn(E)$ and $bn(E)$ respectively, are defined as expected. Structural congruence, $\equiv$, is the least equivalence relation and congruence closed by the rules in Table 1 and α-conversion. $\equiv$ is extended to network distributions as expected.

In the following, we use $\rho_{k \longmapsto l}$ as an abbreviation of the probability from which k can receive messages from l. As mentioned, we assume that mobility is not arbitrary but respects certain rules. These rules are given by a function $pf : L \times L \times \wp \times \wp \rightarrow \wp$ called a *probabilistic mobility function* (PMF), the probability for $\rho_{k \longmapsto l}$ changing from ρ to ρ' is given by $pf(k, l, \rho, \rho')$. Let $G^{pf}_{k \longmapsto l}$ be the underlying directed graph for $\rho_{k \longmapsto l}$ given pf, where vertices are possible values of $\rho_{k \longmapsto l}$ and where there is an edge from state ρ to ρ' iff $pf(k, l, \rho, \rho') \in (0, 1]$, and we ignore nodes with 0 in-degree and 0 out-degree. Without causing any confusion, sometimes we also use $G^{pf}_{k \longmapsto l}$ to denote the set of nodes in the graph called the *support* of $\rho_{k \longmapsto l}$. A PMF pf is valid if for all $G^{pf}_{k \longmapsto l}$, $G^{pf}_{k \longmapsto l} \neq \emptyset$ and for each $\rho \in G^{pf}_{k \longmapsto l}$, $\sum_{\rho' \in G^{pf}_{k \longmapsto l}} pf(k, l, \rho, \rho') = 1$. In the following, we only consider valid PMFs.

A *well-formed network* under a given *pf* is defined inductively by: 0 and $\lfloor p \rfloor_l$ are well-formed, and $\nu x E$ is well-formed if E is well-formed; $\{\mathbb{L} \longmapsto l\}$ is well-formed if all location names in $\mathbb{L}$ are distinct and for each $(\rho, k) \in \mathbb{L}$, $\rho \in G^{pf}_{k \longmapsto l}$; $E \| F$ is well-formed if both E, F are well-formed and for any $l, k \in L$ with $l \neq k$, there does not exist E', F' such that $E \equiv \{\{(\rho, k)\} \longmapsto l\} \| E'$ and $F \equiv \{\{(\rho', k)\} \longmapsto l\} \| F'$. In the sequel given a *pf* we only consider the set of well-formed networks $\mathcal{N}_{pf}$. We assume that every node can receive messages broadcasted by itself with probability 1, but for simplicity we often denote this implicitly.

We use $\rho_{k \longmapsto l}(E)$ to denote the connection probability from k to l in network E, when the requested probability occurs in E it returns this value otherwise it returns $\theta_{k \longmapsto l}$ to denote an *unknown probability*, i.e.

$$\rho_{k \longmapsto l}(E) = \begin{cases} \rho & \text{if there exists } E' \text{ s.t. } E \equiv \{\mathbb{L} \longmapsto l\} \| E' \text{ and } (\rho, k) \in \mathbb{L} \\ \theta_{k \longmapsto l} & \text{otherwise} \end{cases}$$

We use $\mathfrak{D}_l(E)$ to denote the set of all connection probabilities from some locations to l in E, that is $\mathfrak{D}_l(E)$ is the smallest set such that $(\rho_{k \longmapsto l}(E), k) \in \mathfrak{D}_l(E)$ if $\rho_{k \longmapsto l}(E) \in \wp$.

We generalize network distributions to contain unknown probabilities. Let $\hat{\theta}_{k \longmapsto l}$ denote $\theta_{k \longmapsto l}$ or $1 - \theta_{k \longmapsto l}$. We let p range over *generalized probabilities*, i.e. expressions being a finite sequence $\hat{\theta}_{k_0 \longmapsto l_0} \times \ldots \times \hat{\theta}_{k_i \longmapsto l_i} \times \rho$. We say that a generalized probability $\hat{\theta}_{k_0 \longmapsto l_0} \times \ldots \times \hat{\theta}_{k_i \longmapsto l_i} \times \rho$ is 0 if $\rho = 0$. A *generalized network distribution*, GND, is defined inductively as follows: A network distribution is a GND, if $\mathbb{G} = \{(\mathrm{p}_i : E_i)\}_{i \in I}$ is a GND then $(\theta_{k \longmapsto l} \times \mathbb{G}) + ((1 - \theta_{k \longmapsto l}) \times \mathbb{G}) = \{(\theta_{k \longmapsto l} \times \mathrm{p}_i : E_i), (1 - \theta_{k \longmapsto l} \times \mathrm{p}_i : E_i)\}_{i \in I}$ is a GND. We may substitute unknown probabilities in a GND with known probabilities, e.g. $\mathbb{E} \circ \mathfrak{D}_l(E)$ means replacing each unknown probability $\theta_{k \longmapsto l}$ in $\mathbb{E}$ with the known probability $\rho_{k \longmapsto l}(E)$ if $(\rho_{k \longmapsto l}(E), k) \in \mathfrak{D}_l(E)$.

3 Label Transition System

In this section we introduce the labeled transition system semantics for our calculus; the semantics is parameterized by a given PMF which is denoted by *pf* and left implicit throughout the rest of this section.

First we define a set of actions $\mathcal{A}$, ranged over by α, by:

$$\alpha ::= \nu\tilde{x}\langle x, \mathbb{K}\rangle @ l \mid (x, \mathbb{K}) \triangleleft l \mid \nu\tilde{x}\bar{y}\langle x\rangle @ l \mid y(x) @ l \mid \tau$$

$\nu\tilde{x}\langle x, \mathbb{K}\rangle @ l$ denotes that a node at location k receives the message x broadcasted from l with probability ρ if $(\rho, k) \in \mathbb{K}$; $(x, \mathbb{K}) \triangleleft l$ means that the node at location k receives the message x from location l with probability ρ if $(\rho, k) \in \mathbb{K}$; $\nu\tilde{x}\bar{y}\langle x\rangle @ l$ means sending x on channel y at the location l (i.e.unicast), on the contrary $y(x) @ l$ means that x can be received on the channel y at location l. $\tilde{x}$ is either a singleton set $\{x\}$ or empty, if $\tilde{x}$ is empty then x is free else it is bounded.

The labeled transition system is defined in Table 2; notice that the semantics is late, i.e. the bound names of an input become instantiated only when inferring a communication. Rules $out, in, com, par, res, open, str$ are either standard or trivial and need no more comments; *brd* means that a process at a location can broadcast a message to the

Table 2. Labeled transition system

$$(\text{par})\ \frac{E \xrightarrow{\alpha} \mathbb{E}}{E\|F \xrightarrow{\alpha} \mathbb{E}\|F} \quad \alpha \notin ((x) \lhd l, \nu\tilde{x}\langle x\rangle @ l), bn(\alpha) \cap fn(F) = \emptyset$$

$$(\text{out})\ \frac{}{\lfloor \bar{y}\langle x\rangle.p\rfloor_l \xrightarrow{\bar{y}\langle x\rangle @ l} \lfloor p\rfloor_l} \qquad (\text{open})\ \frac{E \xrightarrow{\alpha} \mathbb{E}'}{\nu x E \xrightarrow{\nu x \alpha} \mathbb{E}'} \quad \alpha \in \{\bar{y}\langle x\rangle @ l, \langle x\rangle @ l\}, x \neq y$$

$$(\text{in})\ \frac{}{\lfloor y(x).p\rfloor_l \xrightarrow{y(x) @ l} \lfloor p\rfloor_l} \qquad (\text{com})\ \frac{E \xrightarrow{\nu\tilde{z}\bar{y}\langle z\rangle @ l} E' \quad F \xrightarrow{y(x) @ l} F'}{E\|F \xrightarrow{\tau} \nu\tilde{z}(E'\|F'\{z/x\})} \quad \tilde{z} \cap fn(F) = \emptyset$$

$$(\text{res})\ \frac{E \xrightarrow{\alpha} \mathbb{E}'}{\nu x E \xrightarrow{\alpha} \nu x \mathbb{E}'} \quad x \notin n(\alpha) \qquad (\text{pro})\ \frac{}{\{\mathbb{K} \longmapsto k\} \xrightarrow{(x,\mathbb{K}) \lhd k} \{\mathbb{K} \longmapsto k\}}$$

$$(\text{los})\ \frac{}{\lfloor Act.p\rfloor_k \xrightarrow{(x,\emptyset) \lhd l} \lfloor Act.p\rfloor_k} \quad Act \neq (y) \text{ and } x \notin fn(\lfloor Act.p\rfloor_k)$$

$$(\text{rec1})\ \frac{}{\lfloor (x).p\rfloor_k \xrightarrow{(x,\emptyset) \lhd l} \{(\theta_{k\longmapsto l} : \lfloor p\rfloor_k), (1 - \theta_{k\longmapsto l} : \lfloor (x).p\rfloor_k)\}}$$

$$(\text{brd})\ \frac{}{\lfloor \langle x\rangle.p\rfloor_l \xrightarrow{\langle x,\emptyset\rangle @ l} \lfloor p\rfloor_l} \qquad (\text{rec2})\ \frac{E \xrightarrow{(x,\mathbb{L}) \lhd l} \mathbb{E} \quad F \xrightarrow{(x,\mathbb{K}) \lhd l} \mathbb{F}}{E\|F \xrightarrow{(x,\mathbb{L}\cup\mathbb{K}) \lhd l} (\mathbb{E} \circ \mathfrak{D}_l(F))\|(\mathbb{F} \circ \mathfrak{D}_l(E))}$$

$$(\text{syn})\ \frac{E \xrightarrow{\nu\tilde{y}\langle y,\mathbb{L}\rangle @ l} \mathbb{E} \quad F \xrightarrow{(x,\mathbb{K}) \lhd l} \mathbb{F}}{E\|F \xrightarrow{\nu\tilde{y}\langle y,\mathbb{L}\cup\mathbb{K}\rangle @ l} ((\mathbb{E} \circ \mathfrak{D}_l(F))\|(\mathbb{F}\{y/x\} \circ \mathfrak{D}_l(E)))} \quad \tilde{y} \cap (\{x\} \cup fn(F)) = \emptyset$$

$$(\text{con})\ \frac{}{\{\{(\rho, l)\} \longmapsto k\} \xrightarrow{\tau} \{pf(l, k, \rho, \rho') : \{\{(\rho', l)\} \longmapsto k\}\}} \qquad (\text{str})\ \frac{E \equiv F \xrightarrow{\alpha} \mathbb{F} \equiv \mathbb{E}}{E \xrightarrow{\alpha} \mathbb{E}}$$

network it belongs to; *rec*1 states that nodes might evolve with unknown probability when they are ready to receive messages; *rec*2 allows to combine two networks which can receive a broadcasted message in parallel, and notice that unknown probabilities may be substituted by known ones. The union $\mathbb{L} \cup \mathbb{K}$ denotes that in a parallel composition the message can arrive at locations in both $\mathbb{L}$ and $\mathbb{K}$ with specific probabilities; *syn* deals with synchronization and broadcast, in that a network can broadcast a message to any neighbor network where each location may receive with a certain probability. For the same reason as in *rec*2, the location connection set in the resulting action is the union of the two location connection sets in the synchronizing actions. Notice that some processes must discard broadcasted messages as explained by the rules *los*.

In the rules *rec*2 and *syn*, we have that when parallelizing two networks, they can get connection information from each other and update the correspondent unknown probabilities. Note here that when there is a message broadcasted from l, we only need to update possibly unknown probabilities with probabilities from connections to l, that is why we only need $\mathcal{D}_l(E)$ and $\mathcal{D}_l(F)$ to update the unknown probabilities in *rec*2 and *syn*. The rule *con* changes the connection probabilities in a network depending on the PMF parameterizing the semantics, and the rule *pro* contributes by revealing the current probabilistic connectivity information.

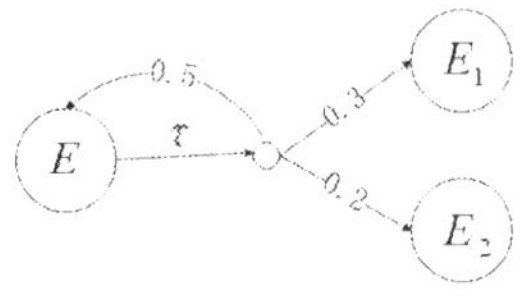

Fig. 3. A mobility transition

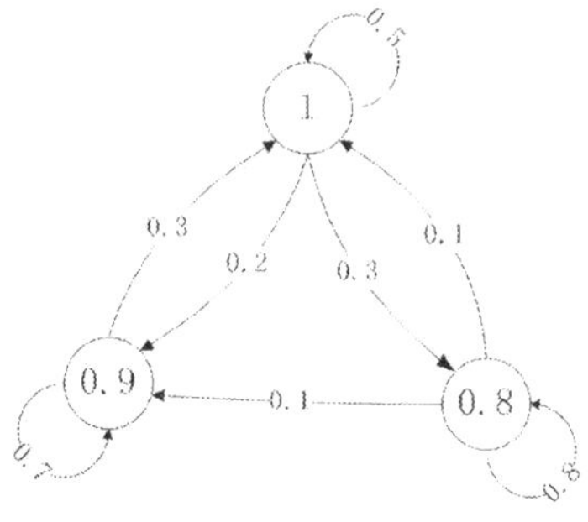

Fig. 4. A bottom strongly connected component

Example 1. Suppose we have a network E with $\rho_{l\longmapsto k}(E) = 0.8$ and we also know from the given PMF pf that $pf(l, k, 0.8, 0.9) = 0.3$, $pf(l, k, 0.8, 0.7) = 0.2$ and $pf(l, k, 0.8, 0.8) = 0.5$, then we have the derivation in Fig. 3 with $\rho_{l\longmapsto k}(E_1) = 0.9$, $\rho_{l\longmapsto k}(E_2) = 0.7$.

4 Weak Bisimulation

In this section we provide a weak bisimulation for our calculus.

A broadcast action, $\langle x, \mathbb{K}\rangle @l$, contains the name of the broadcasting location, the broadcasted message, and a location connection set which denotes locations receiving the message with specific probabilities. We want to allow a network to simulate such an action by $\langle x, \mathbb{K}\rangle @m$, if l and m are *mobility equivalent*. Intuitively, two locations are mobility equivalent if any of their connection probabilities, say $\rho_{k\longmapsto l}$ and $\rho_{k\longmapsto m}$, are able to evolve into each other eventually with probability 1, in which case the node at location k can with probability 1 receive messages from l and m with the same probability. For example, if the mobility of $\rho_{k\longmapsto l} = 0.8$ and $\rho_{k\longmapsto m} = 0.9$ is given by Fig. 4, then $\rho_{k\longmapsto l}$ can evolve into $\rho_{k\longmapsto m}$ and vice versa. Otherwise, if the mobility of $\rho_{k\longmapsto l} = 0.6$ and $\rho_{k\longmapsto m} = 0.5$ is given by Fig. 5 then $\rho_{k\longmapsto m}$ may evolve into $\rho_{k\longmapsto l}$ but not the other way around.

The following definitions are used to define mobility equivalence between two locations in their respective networks.

A subgraph SG of $G^{pf}_{l\longmapsto k}$ is called *strongly connected* if for each pair (ρ, ρ') of states in SG there exists a path fragment $\rho_0\rho_1 \ldots \rho_i$ such that $\rho_j \in SG$ and $pf(l, k, \rho_j, \rho_{j+1}) > 0$ for $0 \leq j < i$ with $\rho = \rho_0$ and $\rho' = \rho_i$. A *strongly connected component* (SCC) denotes a strongly connected set of states such that no proper superset of it is strongly connected. A *bottom* SCC (BSCC) is an SCC from which no state outside this SCC is reachable. If probabilities are in the same BSCC, they can for sure evolve into each other, or in probabilistic terms they can evolve into each other eventually with probability 1. For example, Fig. 4 is a BSCC whereas Fig. 5 and 6 are not. If two probabilities ρ and ρ' are in the same BSCC within $G^{pf}_{l\longmapsto k}$, then we write $pf(l, k, \rho, \rho')^* = 1$.

The *eventual support* of $\rho_{l\longmapsto k}$ under a given PMF pf, denoted by $ES^{pf}(l, k)$, is the set of all nodes (probabilities) which belong to a BSCC in $G^{pf}_{l\longmapsto k}$.

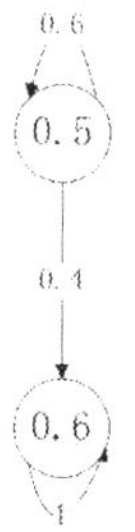

Fig. 5. A non-SCC

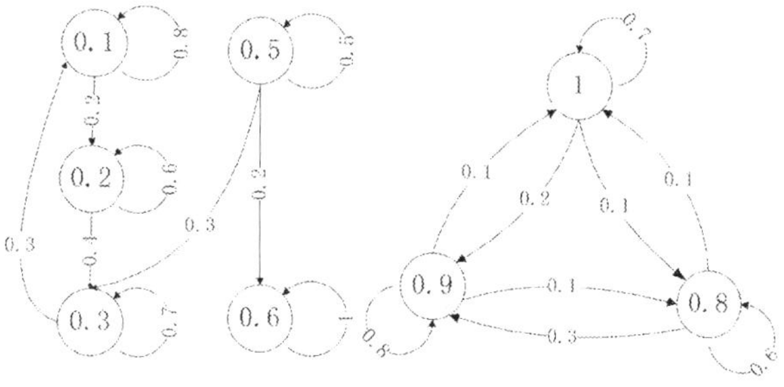

Fig. 6. A non-BSCC

Definition 1. *$ES^{pf}(l,k)$ is consistent if $G^{pf}_{l\longmapsto k}$ is a BSCC.*

In the following, we use $[\![\rho]\!]_{ES^{pf}(l,k)}$ to denote the set of nodes of the BSCC of $G^{pf}_{l\longmapsto k}$ which contains the node ρ if $\rho \in ES^{pf}(l,k)$, here $[\![\theta_{l\longmapsto k}]\!]_{ES^{pf}(l,k)} = ES^{pf}(l,k)$ if $ES^{pf}(l,k)$ is consistent, otherwise $[\![\theta_{l\longmapsto k}]\!]_{ES^{pf}(l,k)} = \{\theta_{l\longmapsto k}\}$.

Definition 2. *Let pf be a PMF, then l in E and m in F are* mobility equivalent, *denoted by $l_E \asymp^{pf} m_F$, if for any $k \in L$, either i) $l = m$ with $\rho_{k\longmapsto l}(E) = \rho_{k\longmapsto m}(F)$, or ii) $\rho_{k\longmapsto l}(E) \in ES^{pf}(k,l) \cup \{\theta_{k\longmapsto l}\}$ and $\rho_{k\longmapsto m}(F) \in ES^{pf}(k,m) \cup \{\theta_{k\longmapsto m}\}$ such that $[\![\rho_{k\longmapsto l}(E)]\!]_{ES^{pf}(k,l)} = [\![\rho_{k\longmapsto m}(F)]\!]_{ES^{pf}(k,m)}$.*

That is, two locations l and m in E and F respectively are mobility equivalent if either a) the locations are identical and all other locations are connected to them in E and F with the the same (possibly unknown) connection probabilities, b) the probability for a connection to l belongs to a BSCC and the probability for the similar connection to m belongs to a BSCC with the same probabilities, if the probability for the connection to m is unknown in F, the eventual support for the connection must be consistent, or c) the probability for a connection to l is unknown in E, the eventual support ES for the connection is consistent, and the probability for the corresponding connection to m belongs to a BSCC with the same values as in ES. Intuitively, for the cases b) and c) it means that even though the connection probabilities for connections to l and m are not the same, then they eventually with probability 1 can evolve into each other by a number of mobility steps.

Example 2. Suppose the mobility rules for $\rho_{l\longmapsto k}$ and $\rho_{m\longmapsto k}$ are given by Fig. 6 and 4 respectively and let all other connection probabilities be permanently 1. Assume we are given two networks E and F such that $\rho_{l\longmapsto k}(E) = 0.9$, $\rho_{m\longmapsto k}(F) = \theta_{m\longmapsto k}$. Then $l_E \asymp^{pf} m_F$, but if $\rho_{l\longmapsto k}(E) = 0.3$ then $l_E \not\asymp^{pf} m_F$, since there is no way for $\rho_{m\longmapsto k}(F)$ to become 0.3.

It follows immediately from the definition of $\asymp^{pf}$ that it is an equivalence relation. Observe also that whenever $ES^{pf}(l,k)$ is consistent, then the unknown connection probability $\theta_{l\longmapsto k}$ can be assigned with any value in $ES^{pf}(l,k)$ while still preserving mobility equivalence.

In our weak bisimulation equivalence, we as usual abstract from internal steps which in our case also involve the probabilistic mobility steps changing connection probabilities. In order to capture that a connection probability for sure (with probability 1) can evolve into another, we introduce the relation $\rightarrow$. Let $\rightarrow$ be the least relation closed by parallel composition, restriction and structural congruence and such that $\{\{(\rho, l)\} \longmapsto k\} \rightarrow \{\{(\rho', l)\} \longmapsto k\}$ if $pf(l, k, \rho, \rho')^* = 1$.

We use $E \stackrel{\alpha}{\Longrightarrow} \mathbb{E}$ to denote that a distribution $\mathbb{E}$ is reached through a finite sequence of steps some of which are internal. Formally $\stackrel{\alpha}{\Longrightarrow}$ is the least relation such that, $E \stackrel{\alpha}{\Longrightarrow} \mathbb{E}$ iff (i) $\alpha = \tau$ and $E = \mathbb{E}$, (ii) $\alpha = \tau$ and $E \rightarrow \mathbb{E}$, or (iii) there exists a step $E \stackrel{\beta}{\rightarrow} \mathbb{E}'$ such that $\mathbb{E} = \sum_{(\rho:E')\in\mathbb{E}'} \rho\mathbb{E}_{E'}$, where $E' \stackrel{\tau}{\Longrightarrow} \mathbb{E}_{E'}$ if $\beta = \alpha$, otherwise $E' \stackrel{\alpha}{\Longrightarrow} \mathbb{E}_{E'}$ and $\beta = \tau$.

Since there might occur unknown probabilities during the evolution of networks, we have to resolve this in order to define our bisimulation. For that we introduce a set of networks denoted by Σ^{pf} and ranged over by σ^{pf}. The networks in Σ^{pf} only contain connection information for a given pf and it is defined by:

$$\Sigma^{pf} = \{ \prod_{l\in L} \{\{(\rho, k) \mid k \in L\} \longmapsto l\} \mid \rho \in G^{pf}_{k\longmapsto l}\}$$

We write $E \bullet \sigma^{pf}$ to denote a network behaving like E but obtaining new connection information from σ^{pf}, that is,

$$E \bullet \{\emptyset \longmapsto l\} = E$$

$$E \bullet \{\{(\rho, k)\} \cup \mathbb{L} \longmapsto l\} = \begin{cases} E \bullet \{\mathbb{L} \longmapsto l\} & \rho_{k\longmapsto l}(E) \neq \theta_{k\longmapsto l} \\ (E \| \{\{(\rho, k)\} \longmapsto l\}) \bullet \{\mathbb{L} \longmapsto l\} & otherwise \end{cases}$$

The importance of mobility equivalence can be illustrated by the following lemma.

Lemma 1. *For each $\sigma^{pf} \in \Sigma^{pf}$, if $E \bullet \sigma^{pf} \xrightarrow{(x,\mathbb{K})\triangleleft l} \mathbb{E}$ and $l_E \asymp^{pf} m_E$ then $E \bullet \sigma^{pf} \stackrel{(x,\mathbb{K})\triangleleft m}{\Longrightarrow} \mathbb{E}$.*

We lift the notion of equivalence relation to distributions in the usual way.

Definition 3. *Let $\mathcal{R}$ be an equivalence relation over N_{pf}. Two (non-generalized) network distributions $\mathbb{E}_1 = (N_{pf}, \eta_1)$ and $\mathbb{E}_2 = (N_{pf}, \eta_2)$ are $\mathcal{R}$-equivalent, written $\mathbb{E}_1 \,\mathcal{R}\, \mathbb{E}_2$, if $\eta_1(C) = \eta_2(C)$ for each equivalence class C in $N_{pf}/\mathcal{R}$.*

Below follows our definition of weak bisimulation.

Definition 4. *Given a PMF pf, an equivalence relation $\mathcal{S} \subseteq N_{pf} \times N_{pf}$ is a weak bisimulation under pf if $E \,\mathcal{S}\, F$ implies $l_E \asymp^{pf} l_F$ for any $l \in L$ and for each $\sigma^{pf} \in \Sigma^{pf}$ whenever $E \bullet \sigma^{pf} \stackrel{\alpha}{\rightarrow} \mathbb{E}$ then:*

1. *if $\alpha = y(x)@l$ then there exists $F \bullet \sigma^{pf} \stackrel{\alpha}{\Longrightarrow} \mathbb{F}$ s.t. for each $z \in N$, $\mathbb{E}\{z/x\} \,\mathcal{S}\, \mathbb{F}\{z/x\}$.*
2. *if $\alpha = (x, \mathbb{L}) \triangleleft l$ then there exists $F \bullet \sigma^{pf} \stackrel{(x,\mathbb{L})\triangleleft m}{\Longrightarrow} \mathbb{F}$ s.t. for each $z \in N$, $\mathbb{E}\{z/x\} \,\mathcal{S}\, \mathbb{F}\{z/x\}$ and $l_E \asymp^{pf} m_F$.*
3. *if $\alpha = \langle x, \mathbb{L}\rangle@l$ then there exists $F \bullet \sigma^{pf} \stackrel{\langle x,\mathbb{L}\rangle@m}{\Longrightarrow} \mathbb{F}$ s.t. $\mathbb{E} \,\mathcal{S}\, \mathbb{F}$ and $l_E \asymp^{pf} m_F$.*
4. *otherwise there exists $F \bullet \sigma^{pf} \stackrel{\alpha}{\Longrightarrow} \mathbb{F}$ and $\mathbb{E} \,\mathcal{S}\, \mathbb{F}$.*

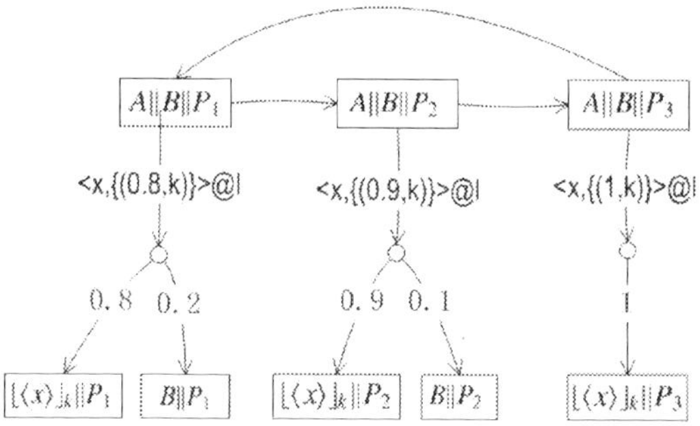

Fig. 7. Network derivations

Two networks E and F are weak bisimular under a given PMF pf, written $E \approx_{pf} F$, if $E\ \mathcal{S}\ F$ for some weak bisimulation $\mathcal{S}$ under pf.

Clauses 1 and 4 in Definition 4 are standard. Clause 2 requires that if nodes at locations $l(\mathbb{L})$ in network E can receive a message from location l with specific probabilities, then nodes at locations $l(\mathbb{L})$ in F must be able to receive the same message from some location m with the same probabilities which is mobility equivalent to l. Clause 3 means that if E can broadcast a message from l with receivers at locations $l(\mathbb{L})$, then F can also broadcast the same message from some location m to $l(\mathbb{L})$ with the same probabilities. In addition, l and m are required to be mobility equivalent. Notice that none of the resulting distributions in a bisimulation contains unknown probabilities because of σ^{pf}, and observe that all possible σ^{pf} are taken into account and hence all possible values of otherwise unknown connection information are considered.

Theorem 1. *$\approx_{pf}$ is a congruence.*

To illustrate our weak bisimulation we give the following example.

Example 3. Suppose two nodes $A = \lfloor\langle x\rangle\rfloor_l$, $B = \lfloor(y).\langle y\rangle\rfloor_k$ and connection information: $P_1 = \{\{0.8, k\} \longmapsto l\}$, $P_2 = \{\{0.9, k\} \longmapsto l\}$, $P_3 = \{\{1, k\} \longmapsto l\}$. Let the mobility of $\rho_{k\mapsto l}$ be given by pf in Fig. 6. It is then not hard to see that $A||B||P_1 \approx_{pf} A||B||P_2 \approx_{pf} A||B||P_3$. The derivation is shown in Fig. 7 where we only show the essential transitions and omit others. Observe that in each of the three networks B can always receive the message from A with probability 0.8, 0.9, or 1.

5 Characterization

In this section we will examine the relation between our calculus and a variant of PCTL* [1] which is a standard modal logic used for expressing properties of probabilistic systems. We use $\mathbb{E}(E)$ to denote the probability of the equivalence class which contains E in a distribution $\mathbb{E}$ and define the (weak) infinite *paths* of a network E under a given pf by: [1]

$$\Omega_E = \{E_0\alpha_0E_1 \ldots \mid \exists\sigma^{pf}.E_0 = E \bullet \sigma^{pf} \wedge \forall i \geq 0\ \exists\mathbb{E}_{i+1}.\ E_i \overset{\alpha_i}{\Longrightarrow} \mathbb{E}_{i+1} \wedge \mathbb{E}_{i+1}(E_{i+1}) \neq 0\}$$

[1] Notice that no path from a network E needs to be finite.

For $\omega = E_0\alpha_0E_1\alpha_1... \in \Omega_E$ we denote by $\omega|_i$ the finite path $E_0\alpha_0E_1...\alpha_{i-1}E_i$ in which case we let $\omega|^i = E_i$, and we define $\Omega_E|_i = \{\omega|_i \mid \omega \in \Omega_E\}$. Notice that as usual due to non-determinism we cannot define a probability measure on Ω_E. To resolve this we, like in e.g.[9,10], define a *policy*. An *i-level policy* for Ω_E is a partial function

$$\pi_i : \Omega_E|_i \times \mathcal{A} \hookrightarrow ND$$

defined by $\pi_i(\omega|_i, \alpha) = \mathbb{E}$ if there exists $\omega|^i \stackrel{\alpha}{\Longrightarrow} \mathbb{E}$. A policy π for Ω_E is a pair consisting of a tuple of i-level policies one for each $i \geq 0$ and $\sigma^{pf} \in \Sigma^{pf}$. It defines a subset of Ω_E denoted by Ω^π_E such that

$$\Omega^\pi_E = \{\omega \in \Omega_{E\bullet\sigma^{pf}} \mid \forall i \geq 0\ \exists\mathbb{E}, \alpha, E.\ \pi_i(\omega|_i, \alpha) = \mathbb{E} \wedge \mathbb{E}(E) \neq 0 \wedge \omega|_{i+1} = \omega|_i\alpha E\}$$

where $\pi = ((\pi_0, \pi_1, \ldots), \sigma^{pf})$. The probability of a path $E_0\alpha_0E_1\alpha_1 \ldots \in \Omega^\pi_E$ is defined by $\rho_0 \times \rho_1 \times \ldots$ where for all i, $\pi_i(E_0\alpha_0E_1\alpha_1 \ldots E_i, \alpha_i) = \mathbb{E}$ for some $\mathbb{E}$ and $\rho_i = \mathbb{E}(E_{i+1})$.

Let $\mathcal{B}^\pi_E$ be the smallest algebra of subsets of Ω^π_E that contains all the *basic cylinder sets* $\{\omega \in \Omega^\pi_E \mid \omega|^0 = E_0 \wedge ... \wedge \omega|^i = E_i\}$ for all $i \geq 0$ that is closed under complement and countable unions. [2] The measure on paths of Ω^π_E, written as $\mu_{\pi,E}$, gives a unique measure on $\mathcal{B}^\pi_E$.

Below we give the syntax and the semantics for our logic.

Syntax. There are two kinds of formulas: state formulas *Stat* ranged over by ϕ, ϕ' and sequence formulas *Seq* ranged over by ψ, ψ'. The grammar is as follows:

$$\phi ::= \top \mid a \mid \neg\phi \mid \phi \wedge \phi' \mid \exists\psi \mid P_{\bowtie q}\psi$$

$$\psi ::= \alpha \mid \phi \mid \neg\psi \mid \psi \wedge \psi' \mid \bigcirc\psi \mid \psi\mathcal{U}\psi'$$

In the above, $\bowtie$ stands for one of $=, \leq, \geq, <, >$, q is a rational in [0,1] and $\alpha \in \mathcal{A}$. $a \in \mathsf{AP}$ where AP is the set of atomic propositions. Here we omit the details of AP and only assume that weak bisimular networks satisfy the same atomic propositions. These atomic propositions should also cover the connectivity of networks and be able to distinguish networks with non-equivalent connectivity. For example, if we have a network E such that $\rho_{l\mapsto k}(E) = 0.8$ then we could say that E satisfy proposition $\rho_{l\mapsto k} = 0.8$.

Semantics. For a formula $\phi \in Stat$, we indicate by $E \models_{pf} \phi$ its satisfaction on network E, and for $\psi \in Seq$ its satisfaction on the path ω is denoted by $\omega \models_{pf} \psi$ under a given PMF pf. The semantics of the logical connectives are defined in the usual way; the semantics of the remaining operators is defined below:

$$\omega \models_{pf} \alpha \text{ iff } \omega = E_0\alpha_0E_1 \ldots \wedge \alpha_0 =_{pf} \alpha$$
$$\omega \models_{pf} \bigcirc\psi \text{ iff } \omega = E_0\alpha_0E_1 \ldots \wedge E_1\alpha_1 \ldots \models_{pf} \psi$$
$$\omega \models_{pf} \psi\mathcal{U}\psi' \text{ iff } \omega = E_0\alpha_0E_1 \ldots \wedge \exists i \geq 0.(E_i\alpha_i \ldots \models_{pf} \psi' \wedge \forall 0 \leq j < i.E_j\alpha_j \ldots \models_{pf} \psi)$$
$$E \models_{pf} \exists\psi \text{ iff } \exists\pi, \omega \in \Omega^\pi_E.\ \omega \models_{pf} \psi$$
$$E \models_{pf} P_{\bowtie q}\psi \text{ iff } \forall\pi.\ \mu_{\pi,E}(\{\omega \in \Omega^\pi_E \mid \omega \models_{pf} \psi\}) \bowtie q$$

[2] By standard measure theory this algebra is the *Borel σ-algebra* and all its elements are the measurable sets of paths.

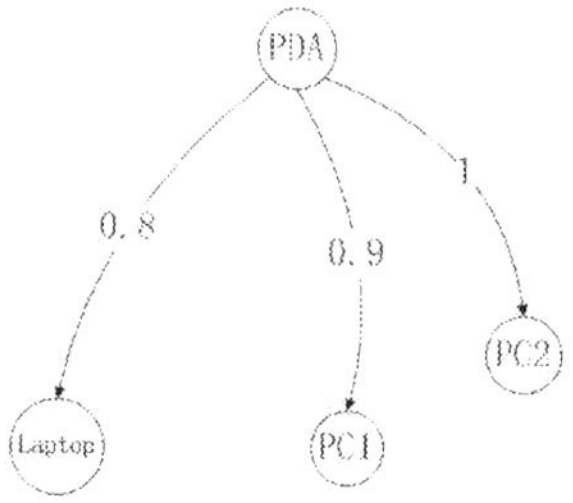

Fig. 8. A home network

In the above $\langle x, \mathbb{L}\rangle@l =_{pf} \langle x, \mathbb{L}\rangle@m$ iff $l \asymp^{pf} m$, it is similar for receptions. Intuitively, $E \models_{pf} P_{\bowtie q}\psi$ denotes the probability for the path from E satisfying ψ is $\bowtie q$. With this we can express many kinds of properties such as greatest and lowest bounds and intervals. For example, $P_{\geq q}\psi$ can be used to denote that the lowest bound is q while $P_{\geq q_1}\psi \wedge P_{<q_2}\psi$ guarantees that the probability is in interval $[q_1, q_2)$ with $q_1 < q_2$.

The following are the main results of this section which show the soundness and completeness of weak bisimulation with respect to PCTL*.

Theorem 2. *If $E \approx_{pf} F$ then for all $\phi \in Stat$, $E \models_{pf} \phi$ iff $F \models_{pf} \phi$.*

Theorem 3. *If for all $\phi \in Stat$, $E \models_{pf} \phi$ iff $F \models_{pf} \phi$, then $E \approx_{pf} F$.*

6 The Zeroconf Protocol

The Zeroconf protocol is designed for self-configuring home local networks. For example, Fig. 8 gives a typical home local network which contains four nodes: PC1, PC2, Laptop, and PDA. The arrows indicate that PC1, PC2, and Laptop can receive messages from PDA with probability 0.9, 1, and 0.8 respectively. Here we assume that all other connections have probability 1.

In order to ensure mutual communication, each node must have an unique IP address, so when a new node joins a network it must be assigned an unused IP address. The Zeroconf protocol solves this in the following way:

1. The new node selects an IP address out of all available IP addresses randomly;
2. It broadcasts a message to other nodes to probe if the selected IP address is in use or not;
3. If the new node receives a message indicating the IP address is already taken, then it returns to step 1 and restarts the process;
4. Due to unreliable connections, messages can be lost with a certain probability. To increase the reliability of the protocol, the new node is required to send several probes for the same IP address;
5. If no error message has been received after these probes, the selected IP address will be used by the new node.

Table 3. The Zeroconf protocol

$$oldnode_{ip} = !((x).(if\ x = ip\ then\ \langle error\rangle\ else\ 0))$$
$$newnode_i^p = \langle p\rangle.waitawk_i^p$$
$$newnode_0^p = \langle success\rangle$$
$$waitawk_i^p = (x).(if\ x = error\ then\ newnode\ else\ waitawk_i^p) + newnode_{i-1}^p$$
$$newnode = \nu y(y(p).\langle p\rangle.waitawk_{pn}^p \| \textstyle\prod_{ip\in IP} \bar{y}\langle ip\rangle)$$

Note that after running the protocol it is indeed possible for a new node to use an IP address that is already used by another node. This is called address collision and is highly undesirable.

In the following, we model and analyse the Zeroconf protocol, the model of the protocol is given in Table 3.[3] We use $oldnode_{ip}$ to denote an existing network node, i.e. a process with IP address *ip* running at a location; $oldnode_{ip}$ repeatedly receives messages and compare these messages with its own IP address *ip*. If a message is identical to *ip*, it will broadcast an error message, *error*, informing the new node that the selected IP address is being used already; $newnode_i^p$ denotes a process which will probe *i* times before assuming that the selected IP address *p* is not used by other nodes. It will evolve into process $waitawk_i^p$ after broadcasting a probe. $newnode_0^p$ is a special process which denotes that the protocol succeeded in finding an unused IP address *p* (although this might not be true with a certain probability); $waitawk_i^p$ waits for the responses from other nodes. If it receives an *error* message because the selected IP address is not valid, it will restart the whole process, otherwise it will recurse and become $waitawk_i^p$ again. The summation here is used to denote timeout from waiting for responses and then start a new round of probing. *newnode* starts the protocol by selecting an IP address from *IP* randomly, here *IP* is the set of all available addresses and $\prod$ means parallel composition of processes. In the above, we use *pn* to denote the maximum number of probes for the same IP address.

The behavior of the network in Fig. 8 can be represented as follows:

$$E = \lfloor newnode\rfloor_k \,\|\, \lfloor oldnode_{ip_1}\rfloor_l \,\|\, \lfloor oldnode_{ip_2}\rfloor_m \,\|\, \lfloor oldnode_{ip_3}\rfloor_n$$

We assume Laptop, PC1, and PC2 are existing nodes which are located at *l*, *m*, and *n* respectively, and PDA at *k* is a node that wants to join the network; here ip_1, ip_2, and ip_3 are used to denote IP addresses in *IP* already in use. Concerning mobility we assume a PMF *pf* such that the mobility rules of $\rho_{k\longmapsto l}$ and $\rho_{k\longmapsto m}$ are given by Fig. 4 and the mobility rule of $\rho_{k\longmapsto n}$ is given by Fig. 6, in addition all the other connections are always equal to 1.

In the following, we use $\langle x\rangle@\tilde{l}$ as a shorthand of $\vee_{l\in\tilde{l}}\langle x, \mathbb{L}\rangle@l$ where $\mathbb{L}$ ranges over all the location connection sets. With the PCTL* logic introduced in the above section, we can denote the obvious property that "if an unused IP address is selected by the new node then the probability of this IP address being allocated to the new node is equal to 1", formally we have:

$$\phi = P_{=1}(\vee_{ip\in IP\setminus\{ip_1,ip_2,ip_3\}}\langle ip\rangle@k \rightarrow \diamond(\neg\langle error\rangle@\{l,m,n\} \wedge \langle success\rangle@k))$$

[3] Summation is defined by: $P + Q = \nu x(\bar{x}\langle y\rangle \| x(y).P \| x(y).Q)$.

letting $\diamond\psi \stackrel{def}{=} \top\mathcal{U}\psi$. Clearly $E \models \phi$. We may also specify the property: "if an used IP address is selected by the new node then the probability of address collision is less than q". Formally we have:

$$\phi_q = P_{\leq q}(\vee_{i\in\{1,2,3\}}\langle ip_i\rangle@k\mathcal{U} \vee_{i\in\{1,2,3\}} \langle ip_i\rangle@k \rightarrow \diamond(\neg\langle error\rangle@\{l,m,n\} \wedge \langle success\rangle@k))$$

Assuming the maximum number of probes pn to be 3 it turns out that $E \not\models \phi_{0.001}$ while $E \models \phi_{0.008}$. Intuitively, if the new node selects an used IP address such as ip_1, then among all policies to consider there exists a worst case policy under which $oldnode_{ip_1}$ may fail to receive the probe from the new node for three times with probability $(1 - 0.8)^3 = 0.008$.

In order to illustrate analysis through the use of weak bisimulation we may define

$$F \equiv \lfloor newnode \rfloor_k \parallel \lfloor oldnode_{ip_1} \rfloor_l \parallel \lfloor oldnode_{ip_3} \rfloor_m \parallel \lfloor oldnode_{ip_2} \rfloor_n$$

i.e. compared to E in the network F the two old nodes PC1 and PC2 have swapped their locations m and n. Further let

$$E' \equiv \{\{(k,0.8)\} \longmapsto l\} ||| \{\{(k,1)\} \longmapsto m\} ||| \{\{(k,0.9)\} \longmapsto n\}$$

and let

$$F' \equiv \{\{(k,1)\} \longmapsto l\} ||| \{\{(k,0.9)\} \longmapsto m\} ||| \{\{(k,0.8)\} \longmapsto n\}$$

then because $m_{E'} \asymp^{pf} n_{F'}$ we infer

$$E \| E' \approx_{pf} F \| F'$$

Intuitively, by the given pf locations m and n are mobility equivalent and furthermore they can always receive messages from other locations with the same probability. If the new node selecting an used IP address such as ip_2 broadcasts a probe, then the node at location m in E can receive it with probability 1 and then broadcast an *error* message. The node at location n in F can simulate this by performing the same actions in addition with some mobility transitions. In both E and F, the *newnode* can receive the *error* message with the same probability. A similar argument holds for other transitions.

7 Conclusion and Future Works

The main contribution of this paper is the development of a probabilistic broadcast calculus for mobile and wireless networks with unreliable connections in that broadcasted messages can be lost with a certain probability. Moreover, due to a *probabilistic mobility function* connections between locations may change with certain probabilities.

We have given a labeled transition system semantics for our calculus on which we define a probabilistic weak bisimulation equivalence parameterized by a probabilistic mobility function. Two bisimular networks need not have the same connectivity information and also they may broadcast the same messages from different locations. To the best of our knowledge, the integration of bisimulation, probabilistic loss of broadcasted messages, and probabilistic mobility functions is a novel contribution. Also, we have characterized our weak bisimulation by a variant of PCTL*.

A number of further developments are possible. One of them is that we could enrich the calculus by adding probability at the process level. This would allows to model e.g. randomized backoff protocols for wireless systems. Also the Zeroconf protocol example could be improved by having a randomized timeout instead of just using non-determinism. Since time is important for wireless network, another extension is to consider a timed version of our calculus like in [11].

References

1. Desharnais, J., Gupta, V., Jagadeesan, R., Panangaden, P.: Weak Bisimulation is Sound and Complete for PCTL*. In: Brim, L., Jančar, P., Křetínský, M., Kucera, A. (eds.) CONCUR 2002. LNCS, vol. 2421, pp. 355–370. Springer, Heidelberg (2002)
2. Baier, C., Katoen, J.P.: Principles of Model Checking. MIT Press, Cambridge (2008)
3. Nanz, S., Hankin, C.: A Framework for Security Analysis of Mobile Wireless Networks. Theoretical Computer Science 367(1-2), 203–227 (2006)
4. Singh, A., Ramakrishnan, C.R., Smolka, S.A.: A Process Calculus for Mobile Ad Hoc Networks. In: Olso, Lea, D., Zavattaro, G. (eds.) COORDINATION 2008. LNCS, vol. 5052, pp. 296–314. Springer, Heidelberg (2008)
5. Merro, M.: An Observational Theory for Mobile Ad-hoc Networks. Electronic Notes in Theoretical Computer Scienc, vol. 173, pp. 275–293. Elsevier, Amsterdam (2007)
6. Ghassemi, F., Fokkink, W., Movaghar, A.: Restricted Broadcast Process Theory. In: Proceedings of 6th Conference on Software Engineering and Formal Methods (SEFM'08), pp. 345–354. IEEE Press, Los Alamitos (2008)
7. Godskesen, J.C.: A Calculus for Mobile Ad-hoc Networks. In: Murphy, A.L., Vitek, J. (eds.) COORDINATION 2007. LNCS, vol. 4467, pp. 132–150. Springer, Heidelberg (2007)
8. Godskesen, J.C.: A Calculus for Mobile Ad-hoc Networks with Static Location Binding. In: 15th International Workshop on Expressiveness in Concurrency (2008)
9. Segala, R., Lynch, N.: Probabilistic Simulations for Probabilistic Processes. In: Uppsala, Jonsson, B., Parrow, J. (eds.) CONCUR 1994. LNCS, vol. 836, pp. 481–496. Springer, Heidelberg (1994)
10. Philippou, A., Lee, I., Sokolsky, O.: Weak Bisimulation for Probabilistic Systems. In: Palamidessi, C. (ed.) CONCUR 2000. LNCS, vol. 1877, pp. 334–349. Springer, Heidelberg (2000)
11. Merro, M., Sibilio, E.: A Timed Calculus for Wireless Systems. In: Arbab, F., Sirjani, M. (eds.) FSEN 2009. LNCS, vol. 5961, pp. 228–243. Springer, Heidelberg (2010)

On Packing Splittable Items with Cardinality Constraints

Fouad B. Chedid

Department of Computer Science, Notre Dame University
P.O.Box: 72 Zouk Mikael, Zouk Mosbeh, Lebanon
fchedid@ndu.edu.lb

Abstract. This paper continues the study of the the allocation of memory to processors in a pipeline problem. This problem can be modeled as a variation of bin packing where each item corresponds to a different type and the normalized weight of each item can be greater than 1, which is the size of a bin. Furthermore, in this problem, items may be split arbitrarily, but each bin may contain at most k types of items, for any fixed integer $k \geq 2$. The case of $k = 2$ was first introduced by Chung *el al.* who gave a 3/2-approximation asymptotically. In this paper, we generalize the result of Chung *et al.* to higher k. We show that NEXT FIT gives a $\left(1 + \frac{1}{k}\right)$-approximation asymptotically, for $k \geq 2$. Also, as a minor contribution, we rewrite the strong NP-hardness proof of Epstein and van Stee for this problem for $k \geq 3$.

1 Introduction

An important issue in parallel processing is the allocation of memory to processors. In principle, each processor should have enough memory with little memory waste. In 2006, Chung *et al.* [1] studied this problem in the context of designing fast IP lookup schemes where the processors are arranged as a pipeline. Knowing that most existing IP lookup schemes traverse some kind of a tree [6] (lookup time is proportional to the height of the tree), a simple way to statically pipeline a tree is to place all nodes at height i in memory unit i which is then made accessible only to processor numbered i. Obviously, while this design prevents memory contention, it is not very efficient in terms of memory utilization. The question at hand then is how to assign memory to processors so that both memory contention and memory waste are minimized. According to [1], this problem was first raised and left as an open problem in [7]. To deal with this problem, the authors of [1] proposed to allocate memory dynamically rather than statically. Consequently, they proposed an architecture that connects processors to multiple two-port memories using a crossbar switch interconnection network [2]. This allows each processor to be connected to multiple memories, but allows at most two processors to be connected to a single memory. As observed in [1], the crossbar needs only be configured at allocation time, which is generally orders of magnitude less stringent than lookup times. The formulation of the problem

C.S. Calude and V. Sassone (Eds.): TCS 2010, IFIP AICT 323, pp. 101–110, 2010.

as proposed by Chung *et al.* gives the following definition, which we term the two-port memory allocation problem:

The Two-Port Memory Allocation Problem:
INPUT: A number of processors n, a number of memories m, and a collection of memory requests per processor.
OUTPUT: A way to satisfy each processor's request such that no more than two processors are allocated to any one memory.

The authors of [1] abstracted this problem as a variant of bin packing, where the bins are the memories and the items to be packed are the memory requirements of the processors, where each processor corresponds to a different type. Thus, the two-port constraint is abstracted as a two-type constraint. Moreover, since processors may require memory of any size (its normalized value can be larger than 1, which is the size of a bin), this version of bin packing allows items to be split arbitrarily, but each bin may contain at most two types of items. The authors of [1] showed that this problem is NP-hard in the strong sense. They used a reduction from the 3-Partition problem [4]. They also gave a $O(n)$ time 3/2-approximation asymptotically. Moreover, this approximation is optimal if $m > n$.

In 2007, Epstein and van Stee proposed a generalization of the solution proposed by Chung *et al.* In particular, they proposed to allow each memory to be accessed by at most k processors, for any fixed integer $k \geq 2$. We term this generalization the k-port Memory Allocation Problem, which can be similarly defined.

The k-Port Memory Allocation Problem:
INPUT: A number of processors n, a number of memories m, and a collection of memory requests per processor.
OUTPUT: A way to satisfy each processor's request such that no more than k processors are allocated to any one memory. Here, k is any fixed integer greater than or equal to 2.

Modeled as a bin packing problem, this generalization still allows items to be split arbitrarily, but now each bin may contain at most k types of items for any fixed integer $k \geq 2$. The authors of [3] showed that this generalization is also NP-hard in the strong sense. They used a reduction from the 3-Partition problem. They also showed that a straightforward generalization of NEXT FIT gives a $\left(2 - \frac{1}{k}\right)$-approximation.

In this paper, we generalize the approximation result of Chung *et al.* to the k-Port Memory Allocation Problem. We show that NEXT FIT gives a $\left(1 + \frac{1}{k}\right)$-approximation asymptotically, for $k \geq 2$. Also, we rewrite the NP-hardness proof of Epstein and van Stee for this problem for $k \geq 3$.

The rest of the paper is organized as follows. Section 2 reviews basic definitions and relevant results from the literature. Our contributions are included in sections 3. Section 4 is the conclusion.

2 Preliminaries

Let P be a minimization problem and let I be an instance of P. Let A be an algorithm for P and let $A(I)$ be the cost of algorithm A on the input I. Let $OPT(I)$ be the cost of an optimal algorithm for P on the input I. We define the approximation ratio $R_A(I)$ by

$$R_A(I) = \frac{A(I)}{OPT(I)}.$$

The absolute approximation ratio R_A for the algorithm A for P is given by [4]

$$R_A = \inf\{r \geq 1 : R_A(I) \leq r, \forall I\}.$$

Thus, for all inputs I of P, $A(I) \leq R_A \cdot OPT(I)$. In this case, the algorithm A is called an R_A-approximation for P. This means that the algorithm A guarantees a solution for P that is within a factor of R_A of the optimum.

We next give the definitions of five problems:

The Partition Problem. Given a set of items of total size B, the partition problem asks for a way to partition these items into two subsets of size $B/2$. This problem is known to be NP-hard [4].

The 3-Partition Problem. Given a set of $3m$ positive numbers $s_1, s_2, \ldots, s_{3m}$ such that $\sum_{j=1}^{3m} s_j = mB$ and each s_i satisfies $B/4 < s_i < B/2$, the 3-partition problem asks for a way to partition the $3m$ numbers into m sets of size 3 such that the sum of the elements of each set is exactly B. This problem is known to be NP-hard in the strong sense [4].

The Classical Bin Packing Problem. Given an infinite number of bins each of capacity 1, and a list of items of weights $\{w_1, w_2, \ldots, w_n\}$, where $w_i \in (0, 1]$, the classical bin packing problem asks for a way to pack these items into a minimum number of bins. A simple reduction from the 3-partition problem shows that bin packing is NP-hard. This reduction also shows that no polynomial-time algorithm for bin packing can have an approximation ratio better than $3/2$ unless P=NP [4]. A simple online 2-approximation for bin packing is NEXT FIT [5]. Recall that in the NEXT FIT heuristic, an item is placed in the current bin if it fits. If the item does not fit, the current bin is closed, and another bin is considered.

The 2-Way Splittable Bin Packing Problem. In [1], the authors introduced a variation of bin packing, where each item corresponds to a different type and the normalized weight of each item can be greater than 1, which is the size of a bin. Furthermore, in this problem, items may be split arbitrarily, but each bin may contain at most two types of items. Hereafter, we refer to this problem as the 2-way Splittable Bin Packing problem (2-SBP for short). The authors of [1] showed that 2-SBP is NP-hard in the strong sense. They used a reduction from the 3-partition problem. They also gave a 3/2-approximation, asymptotically, for 2-SBP. In particular, the approximation ratio of Chung *et al.*'s algorithm for 2-SBP is $\frac{3}{2}(1+o(1))$ as the sum of weights of the items tends to infinity.

The k-Way Splittable Bin Packing Problem. In [3], the authors introduced a generalization of 2-SBP, where items can still be split arbitrarily, but each bin may contain at most k types of items, for any fixed integer $k \geq 2$. We refer to this problem as k-SBP. Epstein and van Stee [3] showed that k-SBP is NP-hard in the strong sense. They used a reduction from the 3-partition problem. They also showed that a straightforward generalization of NEXT FIT gives a $(2-1/k)$-approximation for k-SBP.

3 Our Contribution

3.1 A Generalization of the Result of Chung *et al.*

The following generalization of NEXT FIT for k-SBP is quoted from [3]: An item is packed (partially) in the current bin if the bin is not full and the bin contains less than k types of items so far. If the item does not fill entirely in the current bin, the current bin is filled, closed, and as many new bins are opened as necessary to contain the item.

We prove the following theorem:

Theorem 1. *The approximation ratio of NEXT FIT for k-SBP is* $1+\frac{1}{k}$ *asymptotically.*

Proof. This proof is inspired by the proof of Theorem 2 from [1]. Let the sizes of the items to be packed be $W = \{w_1, w_2, \ldots, w_n\}$ with the understanding that w_i is the size of the item of type i $(1 \leq i \leq n)$. Recall that each item corresponds to a different type. Let $w = \sum_{i=1}^{n} w_i$ and $w^* = \sum_{i=1}^{n} \lceil w_i \rceil$. Let NF and OPT denote the number of bins needed in NEXT FIT and the optimum packing, respectively. We develop our proof in three steps.

Lemma 1. *For* $k \geq 2$,
$$OPT \geq \max\{w, w^*/k\}.$$

Proof. Clealy, $OPT \geq w$. It remains to show that $OPT \geq w^*/k$. For each item i, there are at least $\lceil w_i \rceil$ parts of item i. Since, there can be at most k parts of items per bin, it follows that

$$OPT \geq \frac{1}{k}\sum_{i=1}^{n}\lceil w_i \rceil = w^*/k.$$

Lemma 2. *For* $k \geq 2$,

$$\frac{w + w^* + k - 1}{k} \leq \left(1 + \frac{1}{k}\right)(1 + o(1)) \max\{w, w^*/k\}$$

as $w \to \infty$.

Proof. We consider two cases:
Case a: If $w \leq w^*/k$, then $\frac{w+w^*+k-1}{k} \leq \frac{(1+k)w^*+k^2-k}{k^2} = \left(1+\frac{1}{k}\right)\left(1+\frac{k(k-1)}{(k+1)w^*}\right)\frac{w^*}{k}$ $= \left(1+\frac{1}{k}\right)(1+o(1))\frac{w^*}{k}$, as $w \to \infty$.
Case b: If $w^*/k < w$, then $\frac{w+w^*+k-1}{k} < \frac{(k+1)w+k-1}{k} = \left(1+\frac{1}{k}\right)\left(1+\frac{k-1}{(k+1)w}\right)w =$ $\left(1+\frac{1}{k}\right)(1+o(1))w$, as $w \to \infty$.

Lemma 3. *For any* $k \geq 2$,

$$NF \leq \frac{w + w^* + k - 1}{k}.$$

Proof. First, we show that we may assume that each bin completely filled by NEXT FIT contains exactly k types of items for any $k \geq 2$.

Our proof proceeds by induction on NF. Suppose that NEXT FIT has a bin B which is completely filled with at most α types of items for $1 \leq \alpha \leq k-1$. Denote these types of items by $t_1, t_2, \ldots, t_\alpha$. W.l.o.g., assume that these types appear in B in the order $t_1, t_2, \ldots, t_\alpha$ with the (part of) item of type t_1 at the bottom of B and the (part of) item of type t_α on top of B. Observe that items of types $t_2, \ldots, t_{\alpha-1}$ are not split by NEXT FIT. Let s_1 and s_α denote the sizes of the (parts of) items of types t_1 and t_α in B, respectively. Let W' denote a variation of W in which the items of types $t_2, \ldots, t_{\alpha-1}$ are removed, and the items of types t_1 and t_α have their sizes reduced by s_1 and s_α, respectively. Let NF' denote the number of bins needed in NEXT FIT to pack W'. Let $w' = \sum_{i\in W'} w_i$ and $w'^* = \sum_{i\in W'} \lceil w_i \rceil$. Recall that $w = \sum_{i\in W} w_i$ and $w^* = \sum_{i\in W} \lceil w_i \rceil$. We have

$$w' = w - \left(\sum_{j=2}^{\alpha-1} w_{t_j}\right) - s_1 - s_\alpha = w - 1.$$

This is true because $\sum_{j=2}^{\alpha-1} w_{t_j} + s_1 + s_\alpha = 1$.

Also, we have

$$w'^* \leq w^* - \sum_{j=2}^{\alpha-1} \lceil w_{t_j} \rceil \leq w^* - (\alpha - 2) \leq w^* + 1.$$

In this equation, we used the fact that $\lceil w'_{t_1} \rceil \leq \lceil w_{t_1} \rceil$, since $0 < s_1 < 1$ (and similarly for w'_{t_α}) and the fact that $\alpha \geq 1$.

Now, since the packing of instance W' uses a smaller number of bins ($NF' = NF - 1$), by the induction hypothesis, we have

$$NF' \leq \frac{w' + w'^* + k - 1}{k}.$$

Since $NF' = NF - 1$, $w' = w - 1$ and $w'^* \leq w^* + 1$, we have

$$NF \leq \frac{w + w^* + k - 1}{k}.$$

This completes the proof that each bin completely filled by NEXT FIT may be assumed to contain exactly k types of items.

Next, and following [3], we define a block as a maximal set of bins which were consecutively filled by NEXT FIT in which each pair of consecutive bins contains parts of the same item. Denote the list of blocks by $\{B_1, B_2, \ldots, B_m\}$, and let b_i denote the number of bins in block B_i $(1 \leq i \leq m)$. As observed in [3], in each block, all bins are completely filled except perhaps for the last bin, which contains k (parts of) items (except perhaps for block B_m). For a given block B_j $(1 \leq j \leq m)$, we use the notation $\sum_{i \in B_j} w_i$ to indicate the sum of weights of the items packed in bins pertaining to block B_j. Let $w_{B_j} = \sum_{i \in B_j} w_i$ and $w^*_{B_j} = \sum_{i \in B_j} \lceil w_i \rceil$. To prove Lemma 3, it is enough to show that the number of bins b_j in block B_j is at most $\frac{w_{B_j} + w^*_{B_j} + k - 1}{k}$, for $1 \leq j \leq m$.

First, we consider blocks B_j, for $1 \leq j \leq m - 1$. Here, we consider two cases. First, we consider the case where the last bin of B_j is full. In this case,

$$b_j = w_{B_j} \tag{1}$$

Let n_j denote the total number of items in bins $1, \ldots, b_j$ of block B_j. Then

$$w^*_{B_j} = \sum_{i \in B_j} \lceil w_i \rceil \geq n_j.$$

Since we may assume that each bin in B_j contains exactly k types of items, we have the following about block B_j:

- There are exactly $k - 1$ unsplit items in each of the bins numbered 1 and b_j of B_j.
- There are exactly $k - 2$ unsplit items in each of the bins numbered $2, \ldots, (b_j - 1)$ of B_j.
- There are exactly $b_j - 1$ items whose parts extend bin i into bin $(i + 1)$ of B_j for $1 \leq i \leq b_j - 1$.

Thus, the total number of items in B_j is

$$n_j = 2(k - 1) + \sum_{i=2}^{b_j - 1} (k - 2) + b_j - 1.$$

Thus

$$w^*_{B_j} \geq n_j = kb_j - b_j + 1 \tag{2}$$

Equations 1 and 2 imply

$$w_{B_j} + w^*_{B_j} \geq b_j + kb_j - b_j + 1 = kb_j + 1.$$

Thus

$$b_j \leq \frac{w_{B_j} + w^*_{B_j} - 1}{k} \leq \frac{w_{B_j} + w^*_{B_j} + k - 1}{k}.$$

Next, we consider the case where the last bin of B_j, which contains k types of items, is partially filled. In this case, we have

$$w_{B_j} \geq b_j - 1 \tag{3}$$

This is true since there are at least $b_j - 1$ filled bins in B_j. Equations 2 and 3 imply

$$w_{B_j} + w^*_{B_j} \geq b_j - 1 + kb_j - b_j + 1 = kb_j.$$

Thus

$$b_j \leq \frac{w_{B_j} + w^*_{B_j}}{k} \leq \frac{w_{B_j} + w^*_{B_j} + k - 1}{k}.$$

This is true because $k \geq 2$. This completes the proof for all blocks B_j, for $1 \leq j \leq m - 1$.

Next, we consider the case of block B_m. The last bin of this block may not contain any unsplit items at all. That is, the last bin of B_m may contain only a part of item that was extended into it from the previous bin. In this case, the total number of items in block B_m is

$$n_m \geq kb_m - b_m + 1 - (k - 1).$$

Thus

$$w^*_{B_m} \geq n_m = kb_m - b_m - k + 2 \tag{4}$$

Equations 1 and 4 imply

$$w_{B_m} + w^*_{B_m} \geq b_m - 1 + kb_m - b_m - k + 2 = kb_m - k + 1.$$

Thus

$$b_m \leq \frac{w_{B_j} + w^*_{B_j} + k - 1}{k}.$$

This completes the proof of Lemma 3.

Finally, putting Lemmas 1, 2, and 3 together gives, as $w \to \infty$

$$NF \leq \frac{w + w^* + k - 1}{k} \leq \left(1 + \frac{1}{k}\right)(1+o(1))\max\{w, w^*/k\} \leq \left(1 + \frac{1}{k}\right)(1+o(1))\cdot OPT.$$

This completes the proof of Theorem 1.

3.2 The NP-Hardness Proof of k-SBP Revisited

The Original Proof: The following theorem appears in [3]:

Theorem 2. *Packing splittale items with a cardinality constraint of k parts of items per bin is NP-hard in the strong sense for any fixed $k \geq 3$.*

Proof. Given an instance of 3-partition and a fixed $k \geq 3$, an instance of k-SBP is constructed as follows. There are $m(k-3)$ items, called padding items, all of size $\frac{3k-1}{3k(k-3)}$ (for $k = 3$, no items are defined at this point). In addition, there are $3m$ items, called adapted items, where item j has size $s_j/(3kB)$ (for $k = 3$, the size is defined to be s_j/B). The goal is to find a packing with exactly m bins. Since there are mk items, a solution in m bins contains exactly k items per bin. Since the sum of items is exactly m, all bins in such a solution are completely filled.

(*only if*) If there exists a partition of the numbers into m sets of sum B each, then there is a partition of the adapted items into m sets of sum $1/(3k)$ each (the sum is 1 for $k = 3$). Each bin is packed with $k-3$ padding items and one such triple of adapted items, giving m sets of k items, each set of sum exactly 1.

(*if*) If there is a packing into exactly m bins, no items are split and each bin must contain exactly k items. It is shown that for $k \geq 4$ each bin contains exactly $k-3$ padding items, and therefore contains exactly 3 adapted items, whose total size is exactly $1/(3k)$ (the sum is 1 for $k = 3$). These three adapted items correspond to three numbers in the instance of the 3-partition problem whose sum is exactly B. Thus, a solution in m bins implies a partition.

Our Version of the Proof: Given an instance of the 3-partition problem and a fixed $k \geq 3$, we define an instance of k-SBP as follows. There are $m(k-3)$ items, called padding items, all of size $1/k$. In addition, there are $3m$ items, called adapted items, where item j has size $3s_j/(kB)$. The goal is to find a packing with exactly m bins. Since there are mk items, a solution in m bins contains exactly k items per bin. Since the sum of items is exactly m $(= m(k-3) \cdot (1/k) + 3/(kB) \cdot mB)$, all bins in such a solution are completely filled. Next, we show that there is a partition if and only if there is a solution in m completely occupied bins.

(*only if*) If there exists a partition of the numbers into m sets of sum B each, then there is a partition of the adapted items into m sets of sum $3/k$ each. Each bin is packed with $k-3$ padding items and one such triple of adapted items, giving m sets of k items, each set of sum exactly 1 $(= (k-3) \cdot (1/k) + 3/k)$.

(*if*) If there is a packing into exactly m bins, no items are split and each bin must contain exactly k items. If $k = 3$, then the k-SBP instance has no padding items. Each bin contains exactly 3 adapted items, whose total size is exactly 1. These three adapted items correspond to three numbers in the instance of the 3-partition problem whose sum is exactly B. Thus, a solution in m bins implies a partition. Consider the case of $k \geq 4$. First, we prove that each bin contains exactly $k-3$ padding items. For $1 \leq i \leq m$, let x_a^i and x_p^i be the numbers of adapted and padding items in the ith bin, respectively. Moreover, for $1 \leq j \leq x_a^i$, let a_{ij} be the size of the jth adapted item in the ith bin. By construction, we have the following, for all $1 \leq i \leq m$:

$$x_a^i + x_p^i = k \tag{5}$$

$$\sum_{j=1}^{x_a^i} a_{ij} + \frac{x_p^i}{k} = 1 \tag{6}$$

$$\frac{3x_a^i}{4k} < \sum_{j=1}^{x_a^i} a_{ij} < \frac{3x_a^i}{2k} \tag{7}$$

Equation 5 states that the total number of items per bin is exactly k. Equation 6 states that the total size of adapted and padding items per bin is exactly 1. Equation 7 enforces proper bounds on the total size of adapted items per bin. These bounds are due to the bounds defined on the numbers in the instance of the 3-partition problem. Solving equations 5, 6, and 7 gives $x_a^i \leq 2k/3$ and $x_p^i \geq k/3 \geq 1$, since $k \geq 4$. Thus, for $k \geq 4$, each bin must contain at least 1 padding item. Given this information, the problem now reduces to packing $3m$ adapted items and $m(k-4)$ padding items into exactly m bins where each bin contains exactly $k-1$ items whose total size is exactly $1 - 1/k$. Repeating the above calculations on this new instance gives $x_a^i \leq 2(k-1)/3$ and $x_p^i \geq (k-1)/3 \geq 1$, since $k-1 \geq 4$. Thus, each bin in this new instance must contain at least 1 padding item. Repeating this argument again and again (as long as the exact number of items to be packed per bin is ≥ 4) distributes the $m(k-3)$ padding items of the original instance evenly across the m bins. Thus, each bin contains exactly $k-3$ padding items. Equivalently, each bin contains exactly 3 adapted items, whose total size is exactly $1 - \frac{k-3}{k} = 3/k$. These three adapted items correspond to three numbers in the instance of the 3-partition problem whose sum is exactly B. Thus, a solution in m bins implies a partition.

4 Conclusion

In this paper, we continued the study of the the allocation of memory to processors in a pipeline problem. This problem is modeled as a variant of bin packing named k-way splittable bin packing (k-SBP for short). In k-SBP, each item corresponds to a different type and items may be split arbitrarily but each bin may contain at most k types of items, for any fixed integer $k \geq 2$. We generalized the result of Chung *et al.* for 2-SBP to k-SBP. In particular, we showed that a straightforward generalization of NEXT FIT gives a $\left(1 + \frac{1}{k}\right)$-approximation asymptotically. Also, we rewrote the NP-hardness proof of Epstein and van Stee for k-SBP for $k \geq 3$.

References

1. Chung, F., Graham, R., Mao, J., Varghese, G.: Parallelism Versus Memory Allocation in Pipelined Router Forwarding Engines. Theory of Computing Systems 39(6), 829–849 (2006)
2. Culler, D., Singh, J., Gupta, A.: Parallel Computer Architecture, A Hardware/Software Approach. Morgan Kaufman, San Mateo (1999)
3. Epstein, L., van Stee, R.: Improved Results for a Memory Allocation Problem. In: Dehne, F., Sack, J.-R., Zeh, N. (eds.) WADS 2007. LNCS, vol. 4619, pp. 362–373. Springer, Heidelberg (2007)
4. Garey, M.R., Johnson, D.S.: Computers and Intractability: A Guide to the Theory of NP-Completeness. W. H. Freeman and Company, New York (1979)
5. Johnson, D.S.: Fast Algorithms for Bin Packing. Journal of Computer and System Sciences 8(3), 272–314 (1974)
6. Ruiz-Sanchez, M., Biersack, E., Dabbous, W.: Survey and Taxonomy of IP Address Lookup Algorithms. IEEE Network Magazine 15(2), 8–23 (2001)
7. Sikka, S., Varghese, G.: Memory Efficient State Lookups With Fast Updates. In: Applications, Technologies, Architectures, and Protocols for Computer Communication. ACM SIGCOMM, pp. 335–347 (2000)

Deterministic Computations in Time-Varying Graphs: Broadcasting under Unstructured Mobility

Arnaud Casteigts[1], Paola Flocchini[1], Bernard Mans[2], and Nicola Santoro[3]

[1] University of Ottawa, Ottawa, Canada
{casteig,flocchin}@site.uottawa.ca
[2] Macquarie University, Sydney, Australia
bernard.mans@mq.edu.au
[3] Carleton University, Ottawa, Canada
santoro@scs.carleton.ca

Abstract. Most highly dynamic infrastructure-less networks have in common that the assumption of *connectivity* does not necessarily hold at a given instant. Still, communication routes can be available between any pair of nodes over time and space. These networks (variously called delay-tolerant, disruptive-tolerant, challenged) are naturally modeled as *time-varying graphs* (or *evolving graphs*), where the existence of an edge is a function of time. In this paper we study *deterministic* computations under *unstructured* mobility, that is when the edges of the graph appear infinitely often but without any (known) pattern. In particular, we focus on the problem of *broadcasting with termination detection*. We explore the problem with respect to three possible metrics: the date of message arrival (*foremost*), the time spent doing the broadcast (*fastest*), and the number of hops used by the broadcast (*shortest*). We prove that the solvability and complexity of this problem vary with the metric considered, as well as with the type of knowledge a priori available to the entities. These results draw a complete computability map for this problem when mobility is unstructured.

1 Introduction

1.1 The Framework

The past few years have seen increasing research efforts devoted to the study of infrastructure-less highly dynamic networks, whose topologies change as a function of time. Most of these networks, variously called *delay-tolerant*, *disruptive-tolerant*, *challenged*, *opportunistic*, have in common that the assumption of *connectivity* does not necessarily hold at a given instant. The network may even be disconnected at every time instant. Still, communication routes can be available over time and space, and make broadcast and routing feasible. Indeed an extensive amount of research has been devoted, mostly by the engineering community, to the problems of broadcast and routing in such highly dynamical environment (*e.g.* [3,4,14,15,16,20,22,23,24,25]).

The highly dynamic features of these networks can be described by means of *time-varying* graphs (also called *evolving* graphs), where links exist only at some times, a priori unknown to the algorithm designer (see [2,8,10,13]). Thus, in these graphs, the set of edges existing at a given time might not form a connected graph. Due to the

C.S. Calude and V. Sassone (Eds.): TCS 2010, IFIP AICT 323, pp. 111–124, 2010.

complexity of these systems, it is not surprising that very few analytical results exist, all obtained under a set of restrictive assumptions that make the investigated problems amenable to analysis. An example of basic assumption is that the existence of these graphs is continuous over time; that is, the network does not suddenly cease forever to exist.

Almost all the work in this area considers these computations in time-varying graphs from a *probabilistic* standpoint [7,8,9,17], assuming e.g. that the edge schedule obeys a Markovian process. The design and analysis of *deterministic* solutions has been carried out under very strong assumptions. For example, knowing the complete edge schedule ahead of time in a central entity allows to compute optimum solutions to the broadcast and routing problems [2]. Intermediate assumptions have been investigated, such as the fact that the network is always connected [21]. A hierarchy of basic assumptions for distributed algorithms in dynamic networks is discussed in [5].

Clearly any a-priori knowledge about the edge schedule can be employed in the design and analysis of (possibly deterministic) solutions. This is also true from a practical point of view, and indeed an intensive investigation exists on *mobility patterns* [1,19,18,11]. Some classes of infrastructure-less networks have indeed specific mobility patterns. For example, in networks such as public transports with fixed timetables, low earth orbiting (LEO) satellite systems, security guards' tours, etc. the edge-schedule is *periodic*, and deterministic protocols for routing and exploration of such networks have been devised (e.g., [13,12,20]). Periodicity is interesting not only because it models several classes of dynamic systems, but also because the infinite mobility pattern defining it is highly *structured*. The existing results show that the existence of such a structure allows the development of deterministic solutions to fundamental problems.

The question immediately arises of what happens when the mobility is *unstructured*. More precisely, what happens if encounters between mobile entities occur infinitely often but without any (known) pattern? what happens if there is no known pattern but there is a time bound on the re-appearance of edges? What can be done *deterministically* in such cases?

In this paper we address these questions and provide some answers on the computability and complexity aspects with regards to the basic problem of *broadcasting with termination detection*.

1.2 Problems and Contributions

Consider the class $\mathcal{R}$ of *recurrent* time-varying graphs whose edges appear infinitely often; that is if an edge (x, y) between nodes x and y exists at time t (i.e., entities x and y are able to communicate at time t), then there exists a time $t' > t$ when (x, y) also exists (let us assume the set of apparition of a given edge as *enumerable*). Let $\mathcal{B} \subset \mathcal{R}$ be the class of time-bounded recurrent time-varying graphs, where two successive appearance of a same edge is bounded by some duration. We consider the basic problem of *broadcasting with termination detection* in $\mathcal{R}$ and in $\mathcal{B}$: there is a node (the source, also called *emitter*) that has a message that must be distributed to all other nodes; the source must be notified when the entire process has been completed. This problem is more difficult than simple broadcast, and is required in more complex operations, e.g. *sequence transmission*, where the i-th sequence item must only be transmitted after the $(i-1)^{th}$ item has been received by all nodes.

Table 1. Summary of contributions - Solvability

Metric	Class	Knowledge	Feasibility
Foremost	$\mathcal{R}$	$\emptyset$	no
		n	yes
	$\mathcal{B}$	$\emptyset$	no
		n	yes
		Δ	yes

Metric	Class	Knowledge	Feasibility
Shortest	$\mathcal{R}$	$\emptyset$	no
		n	no
	$\mathcal{B}$	$\emptyset$	no
		n	no
		Δ	yes
Fastest	$\mathcal{R}$ or $\mathcal{B}$	n or Δ	no

Table 2. Summary of contributions - Complexity (for solvable cases)

Metric	Class	Knowl.	Time	Info. msgs (1st run)	Control msgs (1st run)	Info. msgs (next runs)	Control msgs (next runs)
Foremost	$\mathcal{R}$	n	unbounded	$O(m)$	$O(n^2)$	$O(m)$	$O(n)$
	$\mathcal{B}$	n	$O(n\Delta)$	$O(m)$	$O(n^2)$	$O(m)$	$O(n)$
		Δ	$O(n\Delta)$	$O(m)$	$O(n)$	$O(m)$	0
		$n\&\Delta$	$O(n\Delta)$	$O(m)$	0	$O(m)$	0
Shortest	$\mathcal{B}$	Δ	$O(n\Delta)$	$O(m)$	$O(n) : 2n-2$	$O(n)$	0
either of {		$n\&\Delta$	$O(n\Delta)$	$O(m)$	$O(n) : n-1$	$O(n)$	0
		$n\&\Delta$	$O(n\Delta)$	$O(m)$	0	$O(m)$	0

We explore the problem with respect to the three possible metrics discussed in [2]: the date of message arrival (*foremost*); the number of hops used (*shortest*); and the time spent doing the effective broadcast (*fastest*). Interestingly, the solvability and complexity of the problem vary with the type of metric considered, as well as with the knowledge available to the nodes. Note that broadcasting with termination detection involves two processes: the actual dissemination of information achieved by exchange of *information messages*, and termination detection achieved by exchange of (typically smaller) *control messages*. In the paper we make a distinction between these two types of messages and we analyze them separately. Also notice that a byproduct of a broadcast algorithm might be the construction of a (delay-tolerant) spanning tree of the underlying graph, which could possibly be reused for subsequent broadcasts, sometimes for the dissemination process (thus reducing the information messages), sometimes for termination detection (impacting the number of control messages), or for both. In each setting we discuss also the consequences on subsequent broadcasts in order to highlight the variation of benefits in reusability.

We first provide some impossibility results showing that broadcasting with termination detection cannot be solved in $\mathcal{R}$ without any knowledge of the underlying graph, nor in $\mathcal{B}$ without either the same knowledge or a bound on the recurrence time. We then analyze solvability and complexity of the problem in the various settings providing algorithms when it can be solved. The solvability results are summarized in Table 1 and the complexity results in Table 2, where n is the number of nodes, and Δ a bound on the recurrence time. Due to space limitations some proofs are sketched, some omitted. The interested reader is refered to [6] for more details.

2 Model and Basic Properties

2.1 Definitions and Terminology

Consider a system composed of a set of entities V that interact with each other over a (possibly infinite) time interval $\mathbb{T}$, called *lifetime* of the system (a subset of either $\mathbb{Z}$ (*discrete* time) or $\mathbb{R}$ (*continuous* time); our results hold in either case). The set of the times when the entities are in contact defines a *time-varying graph* (*TVG*, for short) $\mathcal{G} = (V, E, \rho)$, with $E \subseteq V \times V$ being the set of *intermittently available* edges such that $(u, v) \in E \Leftrightarrow u$ and v have at least one contact overlapping with $\mathbb{T}$, and $\rho : E \times \mathbb{T} \to \{0, 1\}$ indicates whether a given edge is *present* at a given time. In the following the terms entity and node will be used interchangeably.

This model is equivalent in substance to that of *evolving graphs* [10], where $\mathcal{G}$ is represented by the sequence of graphs $G_1, G_2, ..., G_i, ...$ each providing a *snapshot* of the system whenever a change (edge appearance/disappearance) takes place. In comparison, the definition used in this paper offers an *interaction-centric* view of the network evolution (the evolution of each edge can be considered irrespective of the global time sequence), which proves more convenient to express several properties.

An edge $e \in E$ is said to be *recurrent* if it appears infinitely often; that is, for any date t, $\rho(e, t) = 0 \implies \exists t' > t \mid \rho(e, t') = 1$. When all the edges of a TVG $\mathcal{G}$ are recurrent, we say that $\mathcal{G}$ is *recurrent*. Let $\mathcal{R}$ denote the class of recurrent TVGs. The recurrence of an edge e is said to be *time-bounded* (or simply *bounded*), if there exists a constant $\Delta(e)$ such that the time between any two successive appearances of e is at most $\Delta(e)$. When the recurrence of all the edges of a graph $\mathcal{G}$ is time-bounded, we say that $\mathcal{G}$ is *time-bounded recurrent*, call $\Delta(\mathcal{G}) = \max\{\Delta(e) : e \in E\}$, and denote by $\mathcal{B} \subset \mathcal{R}$ the class of time-bounded recurrent TVGs.

Given a TVG $\mathcal{G} = (V, E, \rho)$, the underlying graph $G = (V, E)$ is assumed simple (no self-loop nor multiple edges) and connected[1]. Each node v has a local function λ_v associating labels (or *port numbers*), to its incident edges (or *ports*). For each edge e there are two labels: $\lambda_u(e)$ local to u and $\lambda_v(e)$, local to v. These labels are locally unique and do not change from one appearance to another. The set of edges being incident to a node u at time t is noted $I_t(u)$ (or simply I_t, when the node is implicit). Finally, we note $\mathcal{G}_{[t_a, t_b)}$ the temporal subgraph of a TVG $\mathcal{G}$ with restricted lifetime $[t_a, t_b)$.

When an edge $e = (x, y)$ appears, the entities x and y can communicate. The time ζ necessary to transmit a message on any edge is called *crossing delay*, and is known by the nodes. The TVGs in the rest of this paper are assumed to have recurrent edges with a minimal duration of $2 \times \zeta$ for every edge presence (long enough for a back and forth exchange of message). This last assumption implies that

[1] Broadcast, as well as any other global computation, would be impossible otherwise.

Property 1

1. If a message is sent just after an edge has appeared, the message and a potential answer are guaranteeed to be successfully transmitted.
2. If the recurrence of an edge is bounded by some Δ, then this edge cannot disappear for more than $\Delta - 2 \times \zeta$.

The appearances and disappearances of edges are instantaneously detected by the two adjacent nodes (they are notified of such an event without delay). If a message is sent less than ζ before the disappearance of an edge, the message is lost. However, since the disappearance of an edge is detected instantaneously, and the crossing delay ζ is known, the sending node can locally determine whether the message has arrived or not. We thus authorize the special primitive $send\_retry$ as a facility to specify that if the message is lost, then it is automatically re-sent on the next appearance of the edge, and this sending is necessarily successful (Property 1). Note that nothing precludes this primitive to be called while the corresponding edge is absent.

A sequence of couple $\mathcal{J} = \{(e_a, t_a), (e_b, t_b), ...\}$, with $e_i \in E$ and $t_i \in \mathbb{T}$ for all i, is called a *journey* in $\mathcal{G}$ iff $\{e_a, e_b, ...\}$ is a walk in G and for all t_i, $\rho(e_i)_{[t_i, t_i+\zeta)} = 1$ and $t_{i+1} \geq t_i + \zeta$, where ζ is the time required to transmit a message on an edge, called *crossing delay*. Journeys can be thought of as *paths over time* from a source node to a destination node (if the journey is finite). Let us denote by $\mathcal{J}^*_{\mathcal{G}}$ the set of all possible journeys in a graph $\mathcal{G}$. We will say that $\mathcal{G}$ *admits* a journey from a node u to a node v, and note $\exists \mathcal{J}_{(u,v)} \in \mathcal{J}^*_{\mathcal{G}}$, if there exists at least one possible journey from u to v in $\mathcal{G}$. Note that the notion of journey is asymmetrical ($\exists \mathcal{J}_{(u,v)} \in \mathcal{J}^*_{\mathcal{G}} \nRightarrow \exists \mathcal{J}_{(v,u)} \in \mathcal{J}^*_{\mathcal{G}}$), regardless of whether edges are directed or undirected.

Because no end-to-end connectivity is assumed, the very notion of distance must incorporate the time factor. In fact, at least three notions of *length* can be defined for journeys (adapted from [2]): the *hop-count*, the *arrival date*, and the *duration* of a journey. Given a journey $\mathcal{J} = \{(e_1, t_1), (e_2, t_2) \ldots, (e_k, t_k)\}$, its *hop-count* $|\mathcal{J}|_h$, is the number of couples in $\mathcal{J}$ (that is, k). The *arrival date* of $\mathcal{J}$, noted $|\mathcal{J}|_a$, is $t_k + \zeta$. Finally, the *duration* of $\mathcal{J}$, noted $|\mathcal{J}|_t$, is $|\mathcal{J}|_a - t_1$. Each of these metrics gives rise to a distinct definition of *distance* in $\mathcal{G}$.

- The *topological distance* between a node u and a node v, noted $d_h(u, v)$, is defined as $min\{|\mathcal{J}_{(u,v)}|_h : \mathcal{J}_{(u,v)} \in \mathcal{J}^*_{\mathcal{G}}\}$. A journey $\mathcal{J}_{(u,v)}$ whose length is $d_h(u, v)$ is qualified as *shortest* ;
- The *earliest arrival date* between u and v, noted $d_a(u, v)$ is defined as $min\{|\mathcal{J}_{(u,v)}|_a : \mathcal{J}_{(u,v)} \in \mathcal{J}^*_{\mathcal{G}}\}$. A journey $\mathcal{J}_{(u,v)}$ whose arrival date is $d_a(u, v)$ is qualified as *foremost* ;
- Finally, the *smallest delay* between u and v, noted $d_t(u, v)$ is $min\{|\mathcal{J}_{(u,v)}|_t : \mathcal{J}_{(u,v)} \in \mathcal{J}^*_{\mathcal{G}}\}$, and a journey $\mathcal{J}_{(u,v)}$ whose duration is $d_t(u, v)$ is qualified as *fastest*.

The *eccentricity* of a node u is defined as $max\{d_x(u, v) : v \in V\}$, where x is either h, a, or t, depending on the type of distance considered, and noted $\mathcal{E}_h(u)$, $\mathcal{E}_a(u)$, and $\mathcal{E}_t(u)$, respectively. Similarly, three notions of *diameter* of a graph $\mathcal{G} = (V, E, \rho)$ can be defined as $max(d_x(u, v) : u, v \in V)$, and noted $D_h(\mathcal{G})$, $D_a(\mathcal{G})$, or $D_t(\mathcal{G})$. Notice that D_h is closer to the usual notion of diameter (in hop-count) than D_a or D_t, which are both in the temporal domain. Observe also that all these notions are time-dependent in the sense that they may vary according to the time when they are considered.

2.2 Problems and Basic Limitations

The problem of *broadcast with termination detection*, `TDBroadcast`, requires all nodes to receive a message with some information initially held by a single node x, called *source* or *emitter*, and the source to enter a terminal state after all nodes have received the information, within finite time. A protocol solves `TDBroadcast` in $\mathcal{G} \in \mathcal{R}$ if it solves it for any source $x \in V$ and time t. We say that it solves `TDBroadcast` in $\mathcal{R}$ if it solves `TDBroadcast` for any $\mathcal{G} \in \mathcal{R}$.

We are interested in three variations of the `TDBroadcast` problem, following the notions of distance defined above: `TDBroadcast`[*foremost*], where *each* node must receive the information at the *earliest* possible date following its *creation* at the emitter; `TDBroadcast`[*shortest*], where each node must receive the information within a minimal number of hops from the emitter, and `TDBroadcast`[*fastest*], where each node must receive the information at the *earliest* possible date following the beginning of its *emission*. For each of these problems, we require that the emitter detects termination, but this detection is not subjected to the same foremost, shortest, or fastest constraint.

Some *knowledge* of G, the underlying graph, is necessary even for simple broadcast in recurrent TVGs. In fact we have:

Theorem 2. *Without any knowledge of the underlying graph,* `TDBroadcast` *in* $\mathcal{R}$ *cannot be solved.*

Proof. By contradiction, let $\mathcal{A}$ be a algorithm that solves `TDBroadcast` in $\mathcal{R}$. Consider an arbitrary $\mathcal{G} = (V, E, \rho) \in \mathcal{R}$ and $x \in V$. Execute $\mathcal{A}$ in $\mathcal{G}$ starting at time t_0 with x as the source. Let t_f be the time when the source terminates (and thus all nodes have received the information). Let $\mathcal{G}' = (V', E', \rho') \in \mathcal{R}$ such that $V' = V \cup \{u\}$, $E' = E \cup \{(u, v) : v \in V\}$, $\rho'(e, t) = \rho(e, t)$ for all $e \in E, t \in \mathbb{T}$, $\rho'((u, v), t) = 0$ for all $t_0 \leq t < t_f$, and $\rho'((u, v), t) = 1$ for $t > t_f$. Consider the execution of $\mathcal{A}$ in $\mathcal{G}'$ starting at time t_0 with x as the source. Since (u, v) does not appear from t_0 to t_f, the execution of $\mathcal{A}$ at every node in $\mathcal{G}'$ will be exactly as at the corresponding node in $\mathcal{G}$. In particular, node x will have entered a terminal state at time t_f with node v not having received the information, contradicting the correctness of $\mathcal{A}$.

Indeed, as we will discuss later, some *metric* knowledge such as knowing the number of nodes $n = |V|$ or, in the case of bounded TVGs (class $\mathcal{B}$), knowing an upper bound Δ on the recurrence time $\Delta(\mathcal{G})$, can play an important role.

Theorem 3. *Without any knowledge of the underlying graph nor of* Δ*,* `TDBroadcast` *in* $\mathcal{B}$ *cannot be solved.*

Finally, let us conclude with a general impossibility result for fastest broadcast with termination, which cannot be solved even if both n and Δ are known.

Theorem 4. TDBroadcast[fastest] *is not solvable in* $\mathcal{R}$*, nor in* $\mathcal{B}$*, regardless of the fact that* n *or* Δ *are known.*

Because of the impossibility of fastest broadcast, the rest of the paper focuses on TDBroadcast[*foremost*] and TDBroadcast[*shortest*] only, and on the impact on solvability and complexity of being in $\mathcal{R}$ or $\mathcal{B}$, and knowing n or Δ (if in $\mathcal{B}$).

3 TDBroadcast[*foremost*]

The objective is to have all the nodes receive the information at the *earliest* possible date following its creation at the emitter (*foremost* broadcast), then have the emitter detect termination. Clearly, achieving a foremost broadcast requires to use a flooding-based mechanism. Indeed, the very fact of probing a neighbor to determine whether it already has the information compromises the possibility of sending it in a foremost fashion (in addition to risking the disappearance of the edge between the probe and the real sending). The problem thus comes to minimize the number of messages and detect when all the nodes are informed. As we have seen in Theorem 2, the problem cannot be solved without any metric knowledge. We show that it becomes possible in the general class $\mathcal{R}$ if the number of nodes $n = |V|$ is known. Knowing n is however not required in the more specific case of $\mathcal{B}$, where the knowledge of an upper bound Δ on the recurrence time $\Delta(\mathcal{G})$ can also be used to solve the problem. If both n and Δ are known in $\mathcal{B}$, the termination detection can even become implicit, thereby saving a number of control messages.

3.1 TDBroadcast[*foremost*] in $\mathcal{R}$

In this section we discuss only knowledge of n since Δ cannot be known being the recurrent time unbounded by definition.

The problem is solvable when n is known, by using Algorithm 1, informally described as follows. Every time a new edge appears locally to an informed node, the node sends the information on this edge and remembers it. The first time a node receives the information, it chooses the sender as parent, transmits the information on its available edges, and sends back a notification message to the parent. Note that these notifications create a parent-relation and thus a converge-cast tree. The notification messages are sent using the special primitive $send\_retry$ discussed in Section 2.1, to ensure that the parent eventually receives it even if the edge disappears during the first attempt. Each notification is then individually forwarded in the converge-cast tree using the $send\_retry$ primitive, and eventually collected by the emitter. When the emitter has received $n-1$ notifications, it knows that all the nodes are informed (and the next broadcast can start, for example).

Theorem 5. *When* n *is known,* TDBroadcast[foremost] *can be solved in* $\mathcal{R}$ *exchanging* $O(m)$ *information messages and* $O(n^2)$ *control messages, in unbounded time. (We call* m *the number of edges* $|E|$*).*

Algorithm 1. Foremost broadcast in $\mathcal{R}$, knowing n

1: $Edge\ parent \leftarrow nil$ // edge the information was received from (for non-emitter nodes).
2: $Integer\ nbNotifications \leftarrow 0$ // number of notifications received (for the emitter).
3: $Set<Edge>\ informedNeighbors \leftarrow \emptyset$ // neighbors known to have the information.
4: $Status\ myStatus \leftarrow \neg\texttt{informed}$ // status of the node (informed or non-informed).

5: **initialization:**

6:      **if** $isEmitter()$ **then**
7:          $myStatus \leftarrow \texttt{informed}$
8:          $send(information)\ on\ I_{now()}$ // sends the information on all its present edges.
9: **onAppearance** of an edge e:

10:     **if** $myStatus == \texttt{informed}$ **and** $e \notin informedNeighbors$ **then**
11:         $send(information)\ on\ e$
12:         $informedNeighbors \leftarrow informedNeighbors \cup \{e\}$ // (see Prop. 1).

13: **onReception** of a message msg from an edge e:

14:     **if** $msg.type == Information$ **then**
15:         $informedNeighbors \leftarrow informedNeighbors \cup \{e\}$
16:         **if** $myStatus == \neg\texttt{informed}$ **then**
17:             $myStatus \leftarrow \texttt{informed}$
18:             $parent \leftarrow e$
19:             $send(information)\ on\ I_{now()} \setminus informedNeighbors$ // propagates.
20:             $send\_retry(notification)\ on\ e$ // notifies that a new node got the info.
                                  (this message is to be resent upon the next appearance, in case of failure).
21:     **else if** $msg.type == Notification$ **then**
22:         **if** $isEmitter()$ **then**
23:             $nbNotifications \leftarrow nbNotifications + 1$
24:             **if** $nbNotifications == n - 1$ **then**
25:                 terminate   // at this stage, the emitter knows that all nodes are informed.
26:         **else**
27:             $send\_retry(notification)\ on\ parent$

Proof sketch. Since a node sends the information to each new appearing edge, it is easy to see, by connectivity of the underlying graph, that all nodes will receive the information. As for termination detection: every node identifies a unique parent and a converge-cast spanning tree directed towards the source is implicitly constructed; since every node notifies the source (through the tree) and the source knows the total number of nodes, termination is guaranteed. Since information messages might traverse every edge in both directions, and an edge cannot be traversed twice in the same direction, we have that the number of *information* messages is in the worst case $2m$. Since every node but the emitter induces a notification that is forwarded up the converge-cast tree to the emitter. The number of *notification* messages is the sum of distances in converge-cast tree between all nodes and the emitter, $\sum_{v \in V \setminus \{emitter\}} d_{h\_tree}(v, emitter)$. The worst case is when the graph is a line where we have $\frac{n^2 - n}{2}$ control messages. Note that the dissemination of information itself is performed in optimal time: $\mathcal{E}_a(emitter)$ in $\mathcal{G}_{[t,+\infty)}$, because the information is either directly relayed on edges that are present, or sent as soon as a new edge appears. However, since the recurrence of the edges is unbounded, this time, as well as the time required for termination detection, is necessarily unbounded.

Reusability for the subsequent broadcasts. By nature, a foremost tree is transient and cannot be re-used as such in subsequent broadcasts. However, it can be re-used by subsequent broadcasts as a converge-cast tree for the notification process where, instead of sending a notification as soon as a node is informed, each node notifies its parent in the converge-cast tree if and only if it is itself informed and has received a notification from each of its children. This would allow to reduce the number of control messages from $O(n^2)$ to $O(n)$, having only one notification per edge of the converge-cast tree.

3.2 TDBroadcast[*foremost*] in $\mathcal{B}$

If the recurrence is bounded, then either the knowledge of n or an upper bound Δ on the recurrence time $\Delta(\mathcal{G})$ can be used to detect termination.

3.2.1 Knowledge of n

Using the same algorithm as for class $\mathcal{R}$ (Algorithm 1) we can obviously solve the problem in $\mathcal{B}$ with the same message complexity, but bounded time. Moreover, the same observations regarding reusability for the subsequent broadcasts apply.

Theorem 6. *When n is known,* TDBroadcast[foremost] *can be solved in $\mathcal{B}$ exchanging $O(m)$ information messages and $O(n^2)$ control messages, in $O(n\Delta)$ time.*

Proof sketch. The arrival-date-based eccentricity of the emitter ($\mathcal{E}_a(emitter)$ in $\mathcal{G}_{[t,+\infty)}$), which is itself bounded by the arrival-date-based diameter of the graph ($D_a(\mathcal{G}_{[t,+\infty)})$), is now clearly bounded by $\Delta(n-1)$ (the worst case is when the foremost tree is a line). The detection of termination by the emitter may require an additional $\Delta(n-1)$ for the propagation of the last notification. The overall time required for the emitter to detect termination is thus at most $\mathcal{E}_a(emitter)$ in $\mathcal{G}_{[t,+\infty)} + \Delta(n-1)$, bounded by $\Delta(2n-2)$.

3.2.2 Knowledge of Δ

The information dissemination is performed as in Algorithm 1, termination detection is however achieved differently and is based on knowledge of Δ.

Due to the time-bounded recurrence, no node can discover a new neighbor after a duration of Δ. Knowing Δ can thus be used by the nodes to determine whether they are a leaf in the broadcast tree (if they have not informed any other node after the date they were informed at, plus Δ). This allows the leaves to terminate spontaneously while notifying their parent, which recursively terminate as they receive the notifications from all their children. Everytime a new edge appears locally to an informed node, this node sends the information on this edge, and remembers it. The first time a node receives the information, it chooses the sender as parent, memorizes the current time (say, in a variable $firstRD$), transmits the information on its available edges, and returns an *affiliation* message to its parent using the $send\_retry$ primitive (starting to build the converge-cast tree). This affiliation message is not relayed upward in the tree, but only intended to inform the direct parent about the existence of a new child (so that it knows it will have to wait for a notification by this node during the hierarchical notification). If an informed node has not received any affiliation message after a duration of $\Delta + \zeta$ it sends a *notification* message to its parent using the $send\_retry$ primitive. If a node has one or several children, it waits until having received a notification message from each of them, then notifies its parent in the converge-cast tree in turn (using $send\_retry$ again). When the emitter has received a notification from each of its children, it knows that all nodes have received the information.

Theorem 7. *When Δ is known,* `TDBroadcast`[foremost] *can be solved in $\mathcal{B}$ exchanging $O(m)$ information messages and $O(n)$ control message, in $O(n\Delta)$ time.*

Proof sketch. Correctness follows the same lines of the proof of Theorem 5, where however the correct construction of a converge-cast spanning tree is guaranteed by knowledge of Δ (the leaves of the tree recognize to be so because no new edges appear within Δ time) and where notification starts from the leaves and is aggregated before reaching the source. The number of information messages is $O(m)$ as the exchange of information messages is the same as in Algorithm 1. However, the number of notification and affiliation messages decrease to $2(n-1)$. Each node but the emitter sends a single affiliation message; as for the notification messages, instead of sending a notification as soon as it is informed, each node notifies its parent in the converge-cast tree if and only if it has received a notification from each of its children resulting in one notification message per edge of the tree. The time complexity of the dissemination itself is the same as for the version where n is known, that is, optimal with $\mathcal{E}_a(emitter)$ in $\mathcal{G}_{[t,+\infty)}$. The time required for the emitter to subsequently detect termination is an additional $\Delta + \zeta + \Delta(n-1)$ (the value $\Delta + \zeta$ corresponds to the time needed by the last informed node to detect that it is a leaf, and $\Delta(n-1)$ corresponds to the worst case of the notification process, chained from that node to the emitter).

Reusability for the subsequent broadcasts. Clearly, the number of nodes n, which is not *apriori* known here, can be obtained through the notification process of the first broadcast (by having nodes reporting their number of descendants in the tree, while notifying hierarchically). All subsequent broadcasts can thus behave as if both n and Δ were known, which is discussed next and allows solving the problem with $O(m)$ information messages and no control messages.

3.2.3 Knowledge of Both n and Δ

In this case, the emitter knows an upper bound on the broadcast termination date; in fact, the broadcast cannot last longer than $n\Delta$ (the worst case is when the foremost tree is a line). The termination detection can thus become implicit after this amount of time, which allows us to do without any control message (whether of affiliation or notification kinds). Note that subsequent broadcasts will have the same complexity.

Theorem 8. *When Δ and n are known,* `TDBroadcast`[foremost] *can be solved in $\mathcal{B}$ exchanging $O(m)$ info. messages and no control messages, in $O(n\Delta)$ time.*

4 `TDBroadcast`[*shortest*]

The objective is to have all nodes receive the information within a minimal *number of hops* from the emitter (*shortest* broadcast), then have the emitter detect termination. We show below that contrarily to the foremost case, knowing n is not enough to perform a shortest broadcast (even in $\mathcal{B}$). Considering only the two kind of knowledge we considered in this paper, it requires Δ to be known (and thus also to be in $\mathcal{B}$). In the following we then consider only the case of $\mathcal{B}$. Note that, contrarily to the foremost case, if a given tree is shortest for some particular emission date, then it is also shortest for any other emission dates (thanks to the recurrence of edges). Put it differently, the shortest quality of a tree is not time-dependent in recurrent TVGs. This allows shortest trees to be reused as is in subsequent broadcasts.

4.1 `TDBroadcast`[*shortest*] in $\mathcal{B}$

We first show that knowledge of n is not sufficient to perform shortest broadcast with termination detection in $\mathcal{B}$; and we then describe how to solve the problem when Δ is know, and when both n and Δ are.

4.1.1 Knowledge of n

Theorem 9. *If n is the only knowledge available* `TDBroadcast`*[shortest] cannot be solved in $\mathcal{B}$.*

Proof. By contradiction, let $\mathcal{A}$ be a algorithm that solves `TDBroadcast`[*shortest*] in $\mathcal{B}$ with knowledge of n only. Consider an arbitrary $\mathcal{G} = (V, E, \rho) \in \mathcal{R}$ and $x \in V$. Execute $\mathcal{A}$ in $\mathcal{G}$ starting at time t_0 with x as the source obtaining a shortest tree T. Let t_f be the time when the algorithm terminates and all nodes have entered the terminal state. Let $\mathcal{G}' = (V', E', \rho') \in \mathcal{R}$ such that $V' = V$, $E' = E \cup \{(x, v) : v \in V, (x, v) \notin E\}$, $\rho'(e, t) = \rho(e, t)$ for all $e \in E, t \in \mathbb{T}$, $\rho'((u, v), t) = 0$ for all $t_0 \leq t < t_f$, and $\rho'((u, v), t) = 1$ for $t > t_f$. Consider the execution of $\mathcal{A}$ in $\mathcal{G}'$ starting at time t_0 with x as the source. Since (u, v) does not appear from t_0 to t_f, the execution of $\mathcal{A}$ at every node in $\mathcal{G}'$ will be exactly as at the corresponding node in $\mathcal{G}$ and terminate with v having received the information in more than one hop, contradicting the correctness of $\mathcal{A}$.

4.1.2 Knowledge of Δ

The idea is to propagate the message along the edges of a breadth-first spanning tree of the underlying graph. Assuming that the message is created at some date t, the mechanism consists of authorizing nodes at level i in the tree to inform new nodes only between time $t+i\Delta$ and $t+(i+1)\Delta$ (doing it sooner would lead to a non-shortest tree, while doing it later is pointless because all the edges have necessarily appeared within one Δ). So the broadcast is confined into rounds of duration Δ as follows: whenever a node sends the information to another, it sends a time value that indicates the remaining duration of its round, that is, the starting date of its own round plus Δ minus the current time minus the crossing delay, so that the receiving node knows when to start informing new nodes in turn (if it had not the information yet). If a node has not informed any other node during its round, it notifies its parent. When a node has been notified by all its children, it notifies its parent. Note that this requires parents to keep track of the number of children they have, and thus children need to send *affiliation* messages when they select a parent. Finally, when the emitter has been notified by all its children, it knows that the broadcast is terminated.

Theorem 10. *When Δ is known,* `TDBroadcast`[shortest] *can be solved in $\mathcal{B}$ exchanging $O(m)$ info. messages and $O(n)$ control messages, in $O(n\Delta)$ time.*

Reusability for subsequent broadcasts. Since shortest trees remain shortest regardless of the emission date, all subsequent broadcasts can be performed within the tree built during the first broadcast, which reduces the number of information message from $O(m)$ to $O(n)$ in these subsequent broadcasts (assuming the nodes memorized the set of their children during the first broadcast). Moreover, if the depth d of the tree is reported through the first notification process, then all subsequent broadcasts can have an implicit termination detection which is optimal in time (after $d\Delta$ time), and no control message is needed.

4.1.3 Knowledge of n and Δ

When both n and Δ are known the same dissemination procedure as in the previous section can be applied and, since $n\Delta$ is an upper bound on the termination time, an implicit termination detection can be used. This allows the nodes to exchange no control messages at all.

Theorem 11. *When n and Δ are known,* `TDBroadcast`[shortest] *can be solved in $\mathcal{B}$ exchanging $O(m)$ info. messages and no control messages, in $O(n\Delta)$ time.*

Reusability for subsequent broadcasts. Note that the solution discussed above offers no gain on the number of information messages in the subsequent broadcasts. An alternative solution would be to achieve explicit termination for the first broadcast in order to build a reusable broadcast tree (and learn its depth d in the process). In this case, dissemination is achieved with $O(m)$ information messages, termination detection is achieved similarly to the algorithm where only Δ is known with $O(n)$ control messages (where however affiliation messages are not necessary, and the number of control messages would decrease to $n-1$). In this way the control messages would increase, but subsequent broadcasts could reuse the tree for dissemination with $O(n)$ information messages, and termination detection could be implicit with no exchange of control message at all after $d\Delta$ time. The choice of either solution may depend on the size of an information message and the expected number of broadcasts planned.

References

1. Bettstetter, C., Resta, G., Santi, P.: The node distribution of the random waypoint mobility model for wireless ad hoc networks. IEEE Trans. on Mobile Comp. 2(3), 257–269 (2003)
2. Bui-Xuan, B., Ferreira, A., Jarry, A.: Computing shortest, fastest, and foremost journeys in dynamic networks. Intl. J. of Foundations of Comp. Science 14(2), 267–285 (2003)
3. Burgess, J., Gallagher, B., Jensen, D., Levine, B.N.: Maxprop: Routing for vehicle-based disruption-tolerant networks. In: Proc. of the 25th Conference on Computer Communications (INFOCOM'06), pp. 1–11 (2006)
4. Cardei, I., Liu, C., Wu, J.: Routing in Wireless Networks with Intermittent Connectivity. In: Encyclopedia of Wireless and Mobile Communications. CRC Press, Taylor & Francis (2007)
5. Casteigts, A., Chaumette, S., Ferreira, A.: Characterizing topological assumptions of distributed algorithms in dynamic networks. In: Kutten, S., Žerovnik, J. (eds.) SIROCCO 2009. LNCS, vol. 5869, pp. 126–140. Springer, Heidelberg (2010)
6. Casteigts, A., Flocchini, P., Mans, B., Santoro, N.: Deterministic computations in time-varying graphs: Broadcasting under unstructured mobility. Technical report, University of Ottawa (May 2010)
7. Clementi, A., Macci, C., Monti, A., Pasquale, F., Silvestri, R.: Flooding time in edge-markovian dynamic graphs. In: Proc. of the 27th Annual ACM Symposium on Principles of Distributed Computing (PODC), pp. 213–222. ACM, New York (2008)
8. Clementi, A., Monti, A., Pasquale, F., Silvestri, R.: Information spreading in stationary markovian evolving graphs. In: Proc. of the 23rd IEEE International Parallel and Distributed Processing Symposium (IPDPS), pp. 1–12. IEEE Computer Society, Los Alamitos (2009)
9. Dimitriou, T., Nikoletseas, S., Spirakis, P.: The infection time of graphs. Discrete Applied Mathematics 154(18), 2577–2589 (2006)
10. Ferreira, A.: Building a reference combinatorial model for MANETs. IEEE Network 18(5), 24–29 (2004)
11. Fiore, M., Härri, J.: The networking shape of vehicular mobility. In: Proc. of the 9th ACM intl. symposium on Mobile ad hoc networking and computing, pp. 261–272. ACM, New York (2008)
12. Flocchini, P., Kellett, M., Mason, P., Santoro, N.: Mapping an unfriendly subway system. In: Proc. 5th International Conference on Fun with Algorithms (to appear, 2010)
13. Flocchini, P., Mans, B., Santoro, N.: Exploration of periodically varying graphs. In: Dong, Y., Du, D.-Z., Ibarra, O. (eds.) ISAAC 2009. LNCS, vol. 5878. Springer, Heidelberg (2009)
14. Guo, S., Keshav, S.: Fair and efficient scheduling in data ferrying networks. In: Proceedings of the 2007 ACM CoNEXT conference. ACM, New York (2007)
15. Jacquet, P., Mans, B., Rodolakis, G.: Information propagation speed in mobile and delay tolerant networks. In: Proc. of the 28th Conference on Computer Communications (INFOCOM'09), Rio de Janeiro, Brazil (2009)
16. Jain, S., Fall, K., Patra, R.: Routing in a delay tolerant network. In: Proceedings of the 2004 conference on Applications, technologies, architectures, and protocols for computer communications, pp. 145–158. ACM, New York (2004)
17. Kempe, D., Kleinberg, J.: Protocols and impossibility results for gossip-based communication mechanisms. In: 43rd Symp. on Found. of Comp. Sci (FOCS), pp. 471–480 (2002)
18. Kim, M., Kotz, D., Kim, S.: Extracting a mobility model from real user traces. In: Proceedings of IEEE Infocom, vol. 6, pp. 1–13 (2006) (Citeseer)
19. Leguay, J., Friedman, T., Conan, V.: Evaluating mobility pattern space routing for DTNs. In: 25th IEEE Int. Conf. on Computer Communications (INFOCOM'06), p. 18 (2006)
20. Liu, C., Wu, J.: Scalable routing in cyclic mobile networks. IEEE Trans. Parallel Distrib. Syst. 20(9), 1325–1338 (2009)

21. O'Dell, R., Wattenhofer, R.: Information dissemination in highly dynamic graphs. In: DIALM-POMC '05: Proceedings of the 2005 joint workshop on Foundations of mobile computing, pp. 104–110. ACM, New York (2005)
22. Spyropoulos, T., Psounis, K., Raghavendra, C.S.: Spray and wait: an efficient routing scheme for intermittently connected mobile networks. In: Proceedings of the 2005 ACM SIGCOMM workshop on Delay-tolerant networking, p. 259. ACM, New York (2005)
23. Zhang, X., Kurose, J., Levine, B.N., Towsley, D., Zhang, H.: Study of a bus-based disruption-tolerant network: mobility modeling and impact on routing. In: Proc. of 13th ACM intl. conf. on Mobile computing and networking, pp. 195–206. ACM, New York (2007)
24. Zhang, Z.: Routing in intermittently connected mobile ad hoc networks and delay tolerant networks: Overview and challenges. IEEE Comm. Surveys & Tutorials 8(1), 24–37 (2006)
25. Zhao, W., Ammar, M., Zegura, E.: A message ferrying approach for data delivery in sparse mobile ad hoc networks. In: MobiHoc '04: Proc. of the 5th ACM intl. symposium on Mobile ad hoc networking and computing, pp. 187–198. ACM, New York (2004)

Slicing Behavior Tree Models for Verification

Nisansala Yatapanage[1], Kirsten Winter[2], and Saad Zafar[3]

[1] Institute for Integrated and Intelligent Systems, Griffith University, Nathan, QLD 4111, Australia
[2] School of Information Technology and Electrical Engineering, The University of Queensland, St.Lucia, QLD 4072, Australia
[3] Riphah International University, Rawalpindi, Pakistan

Abstract. Program slicing is a reduction technique that removes irrelevant parts of a program automatically, based on dependencies. It is used in the context of documentation to improve the user's understanding as well as for reducing the size of a program when analysing. In this paper we describe an approach for slicing not program code but models of software or systems written in the graphical Behavior Tree language. Our focus is to utilise this reduction technique when model checking Behavior Tree models. Model checking as a fully automated analysis technique is restricted in the size of the model and slicing provides one means to improve on the inherent limitations. We present a Health Information System as a case study. The full model of the system could not be verified due to memory limits. However, our slicing algorithm renders the model to a size for which the model checker terminates. The results nicely demonstrate and quantify the benefits of our approach.

1 Introduction

Detecting problems early in the software life cycle, in the modelling and design phase, would greatly reduce the costs involved. Formal models of systems allow for rigorous analyses to be conducted. The Behavior Tree graphical modelling language [1, 2], which has a formal semantics, has been proposed as a support for engineers handling the complexity of large systems. Behavior Tree models maintain a strong connection with the original textual requirements of the system. Behavior Trees can be automatically translated into model checking languages for verification [3–5].

Model checking [6] is an automated verification technique that exhaustively searches the state space to determine whether or not a given property holds for the system. A major limitation of model checking is what is known as the *state explosion problem*. It refers to the possibly exponential number of states produced from even a small number of system components. This prevents model checking from being applied to larger systems. The model checker may run out of memory resources before providing a result, or may take a prohibitively large amount of time to solve the verification problem.

This paper describes a technique for reducing Behavior Tree models prior to model checking, in order to reduce the time and memory resources required. We propose using a technique known as *slicing* [7], which has been traditionally applied to programs to aid in understanding and debugging (see [8] and [9] for comprehensive surveys).

C.S. Calude and V. Sassone (Eds.): TCS 2010, IFIP AICT 323, pp. 125–139, 2010.

The objective of this technique is to eliminate those parts of the program that are not relevant in the current context. In doing so slicing can significantly reduce the size of the investigated program.

Although most applications of slicing have been programs, slicing has also been applied to specifications. In particular, slices have been created from Z specifications [10, 11], hierarchical state machines in the RSML specification language [12] and Extended Finite State Machines [13]. The aim of these approaches is to support understanding.

Slicing in the context of automated analysis aims at eliminating those parts of the model that have no effect on whether the property to be checked is satisfied by the model or not. Thus, the approach requires a new type of *slicing criterion* which is derived from the property, often given as a temporal logic formula. This criterion may not refer to a specific program statement; instead several statements could be the slicing targets. In [14], Hatcliff et al. present the foundations of "property-directed" slicing in which formulas given in linear temporal logic (LTL) [15] without using the next state operator provide the slicing criteria.

Whereas Hatcliff et al. apply their technique to Java code, other approaches propose slicing for models of software or systems given in, e.g., the SPIN input language Promela [16], the SAL language [17] and timed automata as used by the UPPAAL tool [18]. Leuschel et al. [19] apply slicing to CSP models and Brückner and Wehrheim [20] investigate models written in CSP-OZ-DC, a language that combines Communicating Sequential Processes, Object-Z and Duration Calculus. Each of these approaches caters for the intricacies of the given modelling language. In our approach the characteristics of Behavior Trees define the avenue of how slicing can be defined such that properties are preserved. A major benefit of slicing is that it requires very little computational resources, as the slicing algorithm runs in close to linear time.

We have applied our slicing algorithm to the Behavior Tree model of a Health Information System in order to evaluate its effectiveness. The results are presented in this paper in the following way: Section 2 provides the reader with preliminaries on the Behavior Tree notation and on slicing in general. In Section 3 we define the main ingredients for Behavior Tree slicing. We introduce our case study in Section 4 and present the results of Behavior Tree slicing and the improvements gained when model checking in Section 5. Section 7 summarises and gives an outlook on future work.

2 Preliminaries

2.1 Behavior Trees

The *Behavior Tree* (BT) notation [1, 2] is a graphical notation to capture the functional requirements of a system provided in natural language. The strength of the BT notation is two-fold: Firstly, the graphical nature of the notation provides the user with an intuitive understanding of a BT model - an important factor especially for use in industry. Secondly, the process of capturing requirements is performed in a stepwise fashion. That is, single requirements are modelled as single BTs, called *individual requirements trees*. In a second step these individual requirement trees are composed into one BT, called the *integrated requirements tree*. Composition of requirements trees is done on the graphical level: an individual requirements tree is merged with a second tree (which can be another individual requirements tree or an already integrated tree) if its root node matches one of the nodes of the second tree. Intuitively, this merging step is based on the matching node providing the point at which the preconditions of the merged requirement trees are satisfied. This structured process provides a successful solution for handling very large requirements specifications [1, 21].

The syntax of the BT notation comprises nodes and edges. A node can be either a state realisation describing a state change of a component or one of its attributes, or a selection, guard, or event, guarding the control flow within the BT. A node is specialised by its *Component name C*, *Behavior B*, *Type*, and set of *Flags*.

The *Behavior* is an identifier (describing a state, an event, or a channel name), or an expression (referring to component attributes).

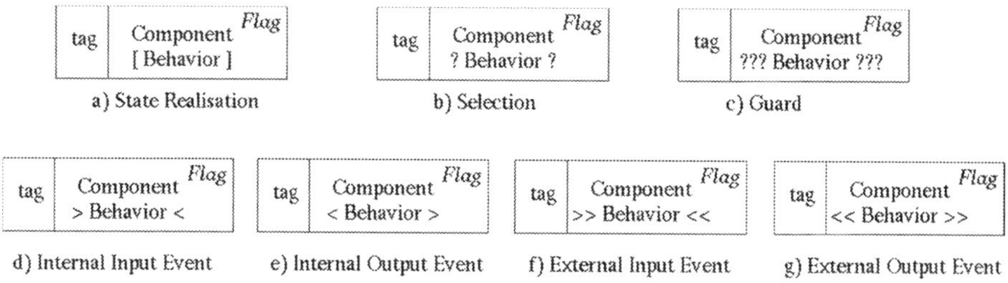

Fig. 1. Different node types of the BT syntax

The *Type* of a BT node can be (c.f., Figure 1)

(a) a state realisation, modelling C being in a state if B is a state name, or updating C's attribute if B is an update expression over the attribute;
(b) a selection (or condition) on C's state if B is a state name, or a selection on the state of one of C's attributes if B is an expression over the attribute; in both cases, the control flow terminates if the condition is not satisfied;
(c) a guard; the control flow can pass the guard when C is in state B if B is a state name, or when the expression B over one of C's attributes is satisfied if B is an expression over the attribute; otherwise it is blocked until the state realisation occurs;
(d-e) an internal event modelling communication and data flow between components within the system, where B specifies an event; the control flow can pass the internal input/output event node when the event occurs (the message is sent), otherwise it is blocked until it occurs;
(f-g) an external event modelling communication and data flow between the system and its environment, where B specifies an event; the control flow can pass the external input/output event node when the event occurs (the message is sent), otherwise it is blocked until it occurs.

The control flow of the system is modelled by either a normal or a branching edge. A normal arrowed edge models *sequential flow* between two steps. If two nodes are connected by a line without an arrow head the two steps occur together atomically.

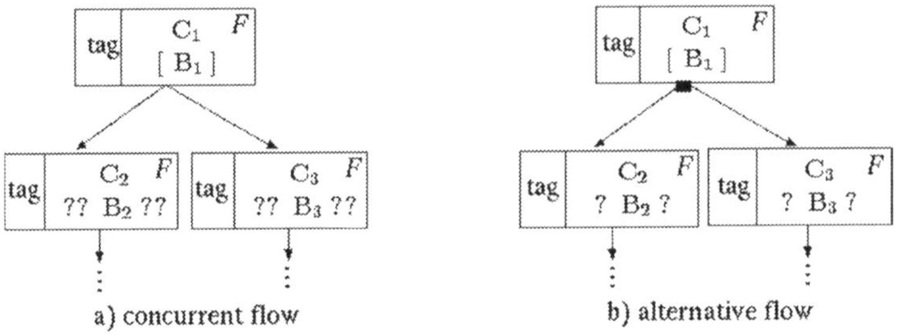

Fig. 2. Branching structures in the BT syntax

Figure 2 shows the two types of branching edges: concurrent and alternative. *Concurrent branching* (Figure 2a) models threads running in parallel. As an example the threads in the figure start with a guard node. The branches, however, can start with any node type. We show only two sub-trees in the branching, although in general there may be more.

In *alternative branching* (Figure 2b), the control flow follows only one of the branches. Alternative branches can comprise either selections only (for example, as shown in Figure 2b) or only other node types but no selections. Alternative branching over selections operates as a non-deterministic choice over the branches with a satisfied selection condition B_i. If none of the selections is satisfied the behaviour terminates. Alternative branching over non-selections behaves like a non-deterministic choice that is unguarded.

Flags in a BT node can specify: (a) a *reversion* node, marked by '^', if the node is a leaf node, indicating that the control flow loops back to the closest matching ancestor node (a matching node is a node with the same component name, type and behaviour) and all behaviour started after the matching ancestor node is terminated; (b) a *referring* node, marked by '=>', indicating that the flow continues from the matching node; (c) a *thread kill* node, marked by '−−', which kills the thread that starts with the matching node, or (d) a *synchronisation* node, marked by '=', where the control flow waits until all other threads with a matching synchronisation node have reached the synchronisation point.

As described in [22], the BT syntax also includes notation for standard set operations, some of which are shown in Figure 3 on page 128 (for a complete description of the syntax see [23]): Assume C has an attribute S which is a set, then a) models adding

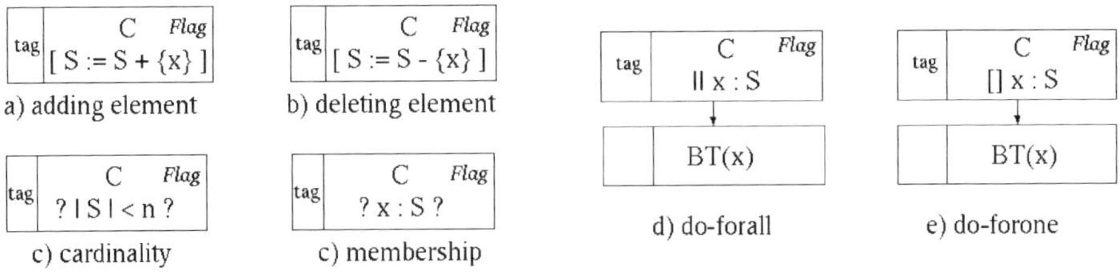

Fig. 3. Set Operations and Parametrisation of BTs

element x to S, b) removing element x from S, c) queries the cardinality of S, and d) queries membership of x in S. Union, difference and intersection of two sets S and T can be specified using the following syntax: $S := S{+}T$, $S := S{-}T$, and $S := S \rtimes\!\!\!\ltimes T$.

In addition to standard set operations, the syntax also provides constructs for parameterisation such that a sub-BT is to be performed on all members or one member of a reference set S. Figure 3d) models execution of a sub-tree BT(x) for all members x of set S, and Figure 3e) models execution of BT(x) for some member x of set S (where x is chosen non-deterministically). These constructs are referred to as *do-forall* and *do-forone*, respectively. The component name can also be omitted.

Type declarations and other structural information about the system model are captured in a *Composition Tree* (CT). We do not introduce the notion of CTs here but refer the interested reader to [23].

The semantics of BTs is formalised in [24] using CSP_σ [25] which is an extension of CSP with state. An automated translation [3, 4] provides an interface to the model checker SAL [26], allowing for fully automated analysis of BT models.

2.2 Program Slicing

Program slicing is a technique which removes irrelevant parts of a program based on the dependencies between the program statements. The program is first transformed into a Control Flow Graph (CFG). The nodes in the CFG represent the program statements and the edges correspond to control flow. There is a single entry node and a single exit node for each graph. Branching statements, such as if or while statements, are represented as nodes in the CFG with two successors representing the true and false paths. All other statements are represented as nodes with a single successor. In many approaches to slicing, a structure known as a Program Dependence Graph (PDG) [27, 28] is then created using the CFG. The PDG is a directed graph with vertexes representing program statements and edges representing dependencies, such as control-flow and data dependencies. To determine the set of statements that may directly or indirectly affect a specified criterion, a simple reachability analysis is performed on the graph. The statements that were found to be irrelevant to the criterion can then be removed, producing the slice. The slice will always be a subset of or equal to the original program.

A formal foundation of control dependencies and slicing correctness can be found in the work by Ranganath et al. [29].

3 Slicing of Behavior Trees

Slicing of BTs is performed in a similar manner as program slicing. We utilise this technique to reduce the size of a BT model when applying model checking. Model checking is a fully automated process which, in our case, checks whether a BT model satisfies a given temporal logic property. We assume the property is specified in LTL_X [6], which is linear temporal logic (LTL) [15] minus the next step operator X. A slice of a model wrt. a given property is created in such a way that it preserves the property. Assuming this, it suffices to model check the smaller slice instead of the full model.

The first step in the overall slicing process is to create a *Behavior Tree Dependence Graph* (BTDG) from the given BT. The BTDG indicates all the dependencies that exist between the nodes of the BT. Each BT will have only one *general* BTDG which is independent of the property to be verified but covers *all* dependencies between all components and attributes. Therefore this step only needs to be performed once per BT and the resulting BTDG can be used for creating slices for any LTL_X property as well as for any other analysis technique that relies on dependency graphs. The set of nodes that are relevant for a specific property are then identified using the BTDG. Finally, these nodes are re-formed into a tree, producing the *BT slice* for the given property.

3.1 Creating the BT Dependence Graph

The BTDG is similar to a Program Dependence Graph [27, 28]. Each node in a BTDG represents a node in the BT and each edge represents a dependency between two nodes. There are several types of dependencies that might be present in a BT, specifically: control, data, interference, synchronisation, message and alternative choice branching dependencies.

A BTDG is created not from the BT directly but from the *control flow graph of a BT* (CFG-BT). In the context of program slicing, a control flow graph indicates the flow of control between single program statements. A BT is almost a like a control flow graph as it shows the flow of control via sequential and branching edges. However, some parts of the control flow are denoted by boxes rather than edges, e.g. reversion and reference nodes. These have to be replaced by edges linking the predecessor node in the BT with its successor node. Moreover, selection, guard and (internal/external) input event nodes in a BT do not explicitly show the flow of control in the case where this respective condition fails (i.e., the behaviour in the negative case). We add edges to represent these cases: (a) each selection node has an additional outgoing edge to a terminal node representing termination when the selection condition is not satisfied, (b) guard and input event nodes have an additional edge that loops back to itself representing blocking behaviour (i.e., waiting) in the case where the guard or event is not available.

A *path* in a CFG-BT is a sequence of nodes. Let $Path(p,q)$ represent the path from node p to node q. If $k \in Path(p,q)$, then k is a node on the path. A path is called *maximal* if it either terminates (i.e. it has no successors) or contains an infinite loop (this definition was adapted from [29]).

We call two nodes p and q *matching*, denoted as $Matching(p,q)$, if they have the same component name, behavior and type. If $Concurrent(p,q)$ then nodes p and q are in concurrent threads of the CFG-BT. If $Alternate(p,q)$ then nodes p and q are in alternate branches of the same thread of the CFG-BT.

We now define the notion of *definition set* and *reference set* for BT nodes which are used to define dependencies between nodes. Intuitively, if a node updates/queries a component or attribute, the component or attribute is a member of the definition/reference set for that node. Assume in the following that C is a component, a and b are attributes of the component, s is a behavior, g is a guard, S and T are sets, x denotes an element of S, and m is a natural number.

Definition 1. (Definition Set)
$DEF(n)$ represents the set of components and attributes defined *at node n. Specifically, if n is of the form*

(a) *(state-realisation) C[s] then* $C \in DEF(n)$,
(b) *(state-realisation of attributes) C[a := s] then* $a \in DEF(n)$,
(c) *(adding/removing an element from a set) C[S := S + x] or C[S := S - x] then* $S \in DEF(n)$,
(d) *(union, subtraction, intersection of sets) C[S := S + T] or C[S := S - T] or C[S := S $\times$ T] then* $S \in DEF(n)$.

Definition 2. (Reference Set)
Let $REF(n)$ represent the set of components and attributes referenced at node n. Specifically, if n is of the form

(a) *(selection/guard) C?g? or C???g??? then* $C \in REF(n)$,
(b) *(selection/guard over attributes) C?a = exp? or C???a = exp??? where exp is an expression or a behavior, then* $a \in REF(n)$,
(c) *(state-realisation of attribute) C[a := f(b)], where $f(b)$ is an expression over b, then* $b \in REF(n)$,
(d) *(selection over set predicates) C?x : S? or C?S = {}? or C?|S| $\bowtie$ m? where* $\bowtie \in \{=, <, >, <=, >=\}$, *then* $S \in REF(n)$.

Based on these preliminary definitions we now define various types of dependencies between BT nodes from which the BTDG is built.

Control dependencies arise if a BT node controls the execution of another node. A node p in a BT is control-dependent on a node q if and only if there are two possible outcomes after executing node p: in one scenario all paths of execution lead to q and in the other scenario, there exists a path on which node q is never executed. This situation occurs when node p is either a guard, a selection or an external input event. For instance, in the case of a selection, if the selection is satisfied then the control flow proceeds to subsequent nodes, but if the selection is not satisfied then the control flow terminates. Thus, the execution of the subsequent nodes are controlled by the selection node. We exclude dependencies between nodes from alternative and concurrent branches as those are handled separately.

Definition 3. (Control Dependency)
For two nodes p and q in a CFG-BT, node q is control-dependent *on node p, denoted as* $p \xrightarrow{cd} q$, *iff:*

(i) *node p has at least two successors m and n, where NOT(Alternate(m, n)) and NOT(Concurrent(m, n)),*
(ii) *for all maximal paths from node m, node q always occurs and*
(iii) *there exists a maximal path from node n on which node q never occurs.*

If a node q in a BT queries the state of a component or attribute, it is *data-dependent* on any node p that updates the state of that component or attribute. That is, if for a node p a component or attribute c is in $REF(p)$, then p is data-dependent on a node q for which c is a member of $DEF(q)$, assuming c is not re-defined by another node on the path between p and q. This dependency occurs within a single thread as well as between parallel threads. In the latter case it is often also referred to as *interference dependence*.

These two dependencies are differentiated because interference dependency is intransitive (in contrast to all other dependencies). This results in slices that are not optimal as they contain nodes that are not relevant for the property and could have been sliced away. Krinke in [30] introduces the notion of *threaded witness* to determine whether a path in the dependency graph shows a true dependency. In our approach it remains future work to include a strategy for optimising the slicing algorithm that handles this problem.

The following definition combines data and interference dependency as both notions differ only in one condition: $NOT(Concurrent(p, q)$ for data dependency and $Concurrent(p, q)$ for interference dependency.

Definition 4. (Data and Interference Dependency)
For two nodes p and q in a CFG-BT, node q is data- or interference-dependent *on node p, denoted as* $p \xrightarrow{dd/id} q$*, iff:*

(i) $\exists c \in DEF(p)$ *such that* $c \in REF(q)$ *and*
(ii) $\forall k \in Path(p, q)$, $c \notin DEF(k)$.

Message dependence is similar to data dependence. All internal input nodes are message-dependent on internal output nodes with the same message name. (Note that for external input/output nodes we do not have a similar dependency as the sender/receiver of the message is outside the scope to the system (i.e., external).)

Definition 5. (Message Dependency)
For two nodes p and q in a CFG-BT, node q is message-dependent *on node p, denoted as* $p \xrightarrow{md} q$*, iff:*

(i) $Type(p) = InternalOutput$ *and* $Behavior(p) = m$ *and*
(ii) $Type(q) = InternalInput$ *and* $Behavior(q) = m$.

All sets of synchronising nodes are dependent on each other, because each node must wait for all the others before proceeding.

Definition 6. (Synchronisation Dependency)
For two nodes p and q in a CFG-BT, node q is synchronisation-dependent *on node p, denoted as* $p \xrightarrow{sd} q$*, iff:*

(i) $Flag(p) = Synchronisation$ *and* $Flag(q) = Synchronisation$ *and*
(ii) $Matching(p, q)$.

For BTs an extra dependency type arises that is not normally found in program slicing. A BT can have alternative choice branching points. At each of these points, each branch is dependent on whether or not the other branches have executed. If one branch executes then all others are terminated. Therefore, there is a dependency between the root nodes of all branches in an alternative branching construct.

Definition 7. (Alternative Dependency)
For two nodes p and q in a CFG-BT, node q is alternative-dependent *on node p, denoted as* $p \xrightarrow{ad} q$*, iff nodes p and q:*

(i) have the same parent node and
(ii) are connected by an alternative choice branching point.

Note that synchronisation as well as alternative dependency are symmetrical relations between BT nodes.

3.2 Creating the Slice

After the BTDG has been created for a given BT, it can be used to create the slice for any given LTL_X property. The *slicing criterion* consists of all state-realisation nodes which update the state of one of the components or attributes mentioned in the temporal logic property. If we lift the notion of reference set to temporal logic formulas such that for any formula p, $REF(p)$ denotes the set of components and component attributes that are mentioned in p, then the set of nodes building the slicing criterion for p is characterised as $SliceCrit(p) = \{n : BTNode \mid \exists c \in REF(p) \cdot c \in DEF(n)\}$. Starting from each of these nodes in $SliceCrit$, the BTDG is traversed in reverse, collecting every node that is encountered via dependency edges. During the traversal we check if a node has been visited already in order to avoid an infinite traversal due to symmetric or circular dependencies. The algorithm is in most cases linear and in the worst, but unrealistic, case quadratic in the number of nodes of the BTDG. Any nodes that were not encountered during the traversals can be removed from the BT, because they are irrelevant for the property.

The final set of relevant nodes is often a disjoint set of sub-trees. These must be reformed into a tree. Every node that is missing its parent node is joined to its closest remaining ancestor, becoming one of its children. However, if the node was originally part of an alternative or concurrent branch and one or more of the other branches are still present in the tree, then the root nodes of each branch are joined to a $blanknode$. A $blanknode$ is a place-holder for the concurrent or alternative branching construct of the original BT and is used in order to preserve the structure. The $blanknode$ then becomes a child of the closest remaining ancestor of the branching nodes.

The reversion and reference nodes are then added back to the slice. These nodes represent jumps to other locations in the tree. The nodes are placed at the bottom of the same threads that they belonged to in the original BT. However, if an entire sub-tree no longer exists in the slice, then any reversions/reference nodes in that sub-tree are left out.

If the BT contains *do-forall* and *do-forone* nodes, then these are added back to the slice, unless these nodes are no longer relevant. The nodes become obsolete if the sub-tree below no longer mentions the member of the reference set (i.e., the parameter).

The final slice can only be used in place of the original BT for model checking the desired property if our slicing algorithm, which is based on the above definitions, is correct. We have formally proved the correctness of our approach and summarise the proof idea in the following. Similar to [29] we base our proof on the notion that nodes in the slicing criterion of a property p, $SliceCrit(p)$, are *observable* steps whereas nodes not in the slicing criterion are silent or *stuttering* steps. The idea of our proof is to show that our algorithm produces a slice that is stuttering-equivalent to the original BT. We base our proof on the theorem on stutter equivalence and LTL_X equivalence

([6], chapter 7) which states that for any paths σ_1, σ_2 and any LTL_X formula φ (over the same set of atomic propositions) $\sigma_1 \hat{=} \sigma_2 \implies \sigma_1 \models \varphi$ *iff* $\sigma_2 \models \varphi$, where $\hat{=}$ denotes stuttering equivalence between two paths. That is, if two models are stuttering equivalent we can imply that both of them satisfy or dissatisfy the same properties.

Using these results it suffices in our context to show that for any behaviour in the original BT there exists a stuttering equivalent behaviour in the slice that is generated wrt. a formula φ. With the definitions as given in Section 3.1 a proof by contradiction provides the desired result. We assume that there exists an execution trace in the original BT for which there does not exist a stuttering-equivalent trace in the slice. Therefore the trace of the original BT must at some point contain an observable node that is not able to execute at the equivalent point in any of the traces of the slice. However, we have shown that such a node cannot exist according to the definitions of slicing and dependencies. We then assume that the converse is true: that there exists an execution trace in the slice that does not have a stuttering-equivalent trace in the original BT. We have also shown this to be impossible. Thus, a generated slice is always stuttering-equivalent to the original BT.

4 Case Study: The e-Health System

The e-Health system presented here has been adapted from a real case study presented in [31]. It is based on the automation requirements for an aged care facility. The facility provides accommodation and care for elderly residents. The facility is administered by a manager. The residents are visited by doctors regularly. Managers, residents and doctors can view and edit relevant electronic records. The resident's data is made up of the following elements. (1) At the time of admission the personal details of the residents are entered. These details include basic personal data (name, sex, etc.), medical details (blood group, allergies, etc.) and details of any nominated responsible person. (2) Before admission a legal agreement must also be signed electronically. (3) A care plan is initiated after he/she has been admitted to the facility. (4) Past medical records are entered by the manager of the facility. After each examination the doctor adds an entry to the medical records of the residents. The doctor can also add private notes to the medical records.

We have created a BT model of the e-Health system. Fig 4 shows an overview of the model, which is too large to be shown in further detail here. The BT describes the behaviour of the nominated responsible people, the managers, the doctors and the residents, each in a separate thread. A responsible person can give consent to add a doctor or sign an agreement on behalf of the patient. A manager can perform various tasks, including adding or viewing a patient's personal details, managing care plans, adding medical records and deleting data. A doctor can view or add medical records if he/she has permission to do so. Doctors, residents and temporary doctors can be added to the various access control lists, thereby granting them access to a patient's files.

In order to provide the reader with an idea of the structure of the tree, a section of the manager thread is shown in greater detail in Figure 5. The manager thread begins with "for all managers", "choose a resident", followed by "choose a data set". At this point there is an alternative choice between each of the possible actions that a manager can perform. We show only the action of the manager viewing personal details. If the

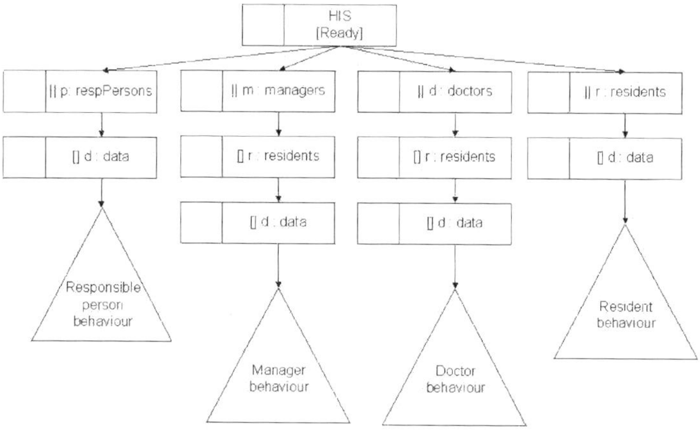

Fig. 4. Overview of the e-Health System BT

current data belongs to the current resident, then the manager can view the data. The behaviour then reverts to a higher node, to allow managers to perform other actions.

A number of access control requirements have been defined for the security of electronic records and to ensure the privacy of the residents. We have formulated these requirements as LTL theorems, shown below. To comply with different regulations, the resident records must be kept for a period of nine years. After the completion of the nine year period the record can be deleted. This requirement is formalised as theorem 1. The LTL operator, G(p), is used to state that p is always true. The second requirement concerns the ability of managers to add medical records. To protect the privacy of the residents, the access to medical records is limited only to the residents themselves or to the nominated doctors. However, the manager is allowed to enter past medical records at the time of admission to the facility. After the admission, the manager is not allowed to add or view the records. The formula states that medical records can only be added by a manager if the patient associated with the data has not yet been admitted. The last property states that a resident can view his/her private notes only if he/she has been assigned to the record's access control list (ViewNotesACL).

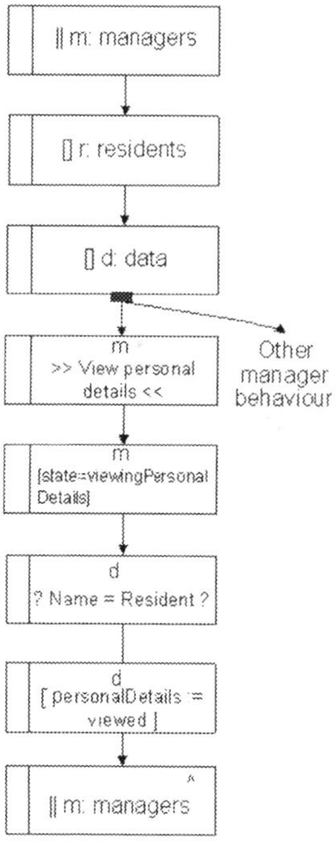

Fig. 5. Manager thread

1. Data can only be deleted by the manager if its leave date is greater than nine years.
   $\forall d : data, \forall m : managers,$
   $G\ ((d.deleted = true\ \wedge\ m.state = deletingData)$
   $\implies\ d.leaveDate = greaterThanNineYears)$

2. Medical records can only be added by the manager if the patient associated with the data has not yet been admitted. $\forall d : data, \forall m : managers,$
$\mathrm{G}\ ((d.medicalRecords = added\ \wedge\ m.state = addingMedicalRecords)$
$\implies d.admitted = false)$

3. A resident can only view his/her private notes if he/she is in the set ViewNotesACL.
$\forall d : data, \forall r : residents,$
$\mathrm{G}\ ((d.privateNotes = viewed\ \wedge\ r.state = viewingPrivateNotes)$
$\implies (r : d.ViewNotesACL).$

5 Slicing the Model of the e-Health System

In this section we compare the execution times for model checking the e-Health system BT with the slices for each property listed in Section 4. First, the BTDG for the e-Health system is created, according to the procedure outlined in Section 3. This BTDG is then used for creating each of the slices. The slicing criterion for each case is derived from the variables mentioned in the property. For example, the slicing criterion for theorem 1 is the set $\{d.deleted, m.state, d.leaveDate \mid d \in data \wedge m \in manager\}$. Starting from each of the state-realisation nodes that involve these components/attributes, the BTDG is traversed in reverse, collecting all relevant nodes.

The size of the resulting slices varies depending on the property. The only relevant part for theorem 1 is the manager's behaviour, so a significant proportion of the BT can be sliced away. The other two properties involve several parts of the BT, so the corresponding slices are larger than for theorem 1. For example, theorem 3 involves the set ViewNotesACL. This set is referred to in several places in the resident behaviour thread. However, the set is updated in the doctor behaviour thread, so the validity of the property is dependent on both parts of the BT. Table 1 lists the number of nodes in each of the slices compared to the original BT.

Table 1. Number of nodes in the original BT and each slice

	Original BT	Slice Th1	Slice Th2	Slice Th3
No. of nodes	125	36	116	73

The e-Health system BT utilises set constructs, so the BT is expanded before model checking. Whenever a *do-forall* or *do-forone* node is encountered, its sub-tree is replicated for each element in the set. We have compared the execution times for model checking the original BT vs. the slices, for increasing cardinality of the sets. The results are presented in Table 2. The system maintains sets of doctors, residents, responsible persons, managers, data and logs.

The checks were run on a 1.2GHz UltraSPARC processor with 24GB of RAM, running Solaris 10. The original model could not be verified. Even with only a single user in each set, i.e. the smallest possible model, the model checker ran out of memory before providing a result. However, using the slices, verification was possible. For all three theorems, the model checker provided a result in only seconds when the sets contained one element each. As the number of elements were increased, the execution times

Table 2. Execution times for model checking the original BT and slices, where: MEM = out of memory, n All = n elements in each user set, 2 D = 2 doctors, 2 R = 2 residents, 2 M = 2 managers, 2 RP = 2 responsible people, 1 data = 1 data set and 1 log, 2 data = 2 data sets and 2 logs; and if a set is not specified then it contained 1 element.

	1 All	2 D	2 M	2 R	2 RP	2 D, 2 M
Original Th1	MEM	-	-	-	-	-
Slice Th1	2.2s	2.4s	11.4s	8.7s	2.4s	11.4s
Original Th2	MEM	-	-	-	-	-
Slice Th2	70.8s	10.6hrs	35.4mins	1.2hrs	16.9mins	MEM
Original Th3	MEM	-	-	-	-	-
Slice Th3	10.7s	6.2mins	1.1min	8.9mins	19.4s	31.6mins

	2D, 2 R	2 M, 2 R	2 All, 1 data	2 All, 2 data	3 All, 1 data
Original Th1	-	-	-	-	-
Slice Th1	9.0s	1.4mins	1.8mins	23.5mins	2.1hrs
Original Th2	-	-	-	-	-
Slice Th2	MEM	MEM	MEM	-	-
Original Th3	-	-	-	-	-
Slice Th3	MEM	4.1hrs	18.6hrs	-	-

increased, but a result could still be obtained for most combinations in which there were two elements in one or more of the sets.

The slice for theorem 1 did not contain any nodes involving doctors or responsible persons, so increasing these sets did not affect the execution time. When the number of managers and residents were increased, the execution time increased, reaching 11 seconds with 2 managers and 1-2 minutes with 2 managers and 2 residents. Even with 3 elements in each of the sets a result was obtained in 2 hours.

The size of the slice for theorem 2 is almost the same as the original BT. However, there was still significant improvement in model checking. It was possible to obtain a result with one element in each set in only 71 seconds. With two elements in a set, the execution times varied between 17 minutes for 2 responsible persons and 10.6 hours for 2 doctors. If two sets contained two elements, such as 2 doctors and 2 residents, the model checker ran out of memory.

Model checking the slice for theorem 3 took only 11 seconds for one element in each set and less than 10 minutes for two elements in a set. With 2 elements in each of the user sets, the model was still able to be verified although the execution time reached 18.6 hours.

6 Discussion

Slicing can be considered to be complementary to other state-space reduction techniques. The low computational cost needed for slicing makes it ideal to be performed as an initial step prior to applying other reduction techniques. The extent to which slicing can reduce the verification time depends on both the model and the property. The more dependencies that exist between the components in the formula, the larger the slice. Despite this, in many cases slicing can improve the verification time. In particular, in concurrent models it is often the case that each thread represents a separate component that operates independently. In such cases, slicing is very effective as it reduces the parallelism in the model, which is one of the most computationally expensive aspects in model checking. Due to the low cost for applying slicing, it is worthwhile to try it, especially if the model is infeasible for a model checker.

7 Conclusion

We have developed a method for automatically reducing Behavior Tree models using the slicing. Slices of a BT model can be used for aiding in understanding and also for reducing models prior to verification. The case study we have presented in this paper demonstrates the benefits of slicing a model before model checking. The results show the improvements in execution time and memory usage. This enables the verification of models for which model checking was previously infeasible. Although the shape and size of a slice depend on the property to be checked, the low computational resources needed to compute a slice makes it ideal for aiding in model checking.

For future work, we plan to extend the slicing procedure to enable slicing wrt. full LTL (including X operator) and to explore further optimisations which could produce greater reductions in the model size.

References

1. Dromey, R.G.: From requirements to design: Formalizing the key steps. In: Proc. of Software Engineering and Formal Methods (SEFM 2003), pp. 2–13. IEEE Computer Society, Los Alamitos (2003)
2. Dromey, R.G.: Genetic design: Amplifying our ability to deal with requirements complexity. In: Leue, S., Systä, T.J. (eds.) Scenarios: Models, Transformations and Tools. LNCS, vol. 3466, pp. 95–108. Springer, Heidelberg (2005)
3. Grunske, L., Lindsay, P.A., Yatapanage, N., Winter, K.: An automated failure mode and effect analysis based on high-level design specification with behavior trees. In: Romijn, J.M.T., Smith, G.P., van de Pol, J. (eds.) IFM 2005. LNCS, vol. 3771, pp. 129–149. Springer, Heidelberg (2005)
4. Grunske, L., Winter, K., Yatapanage, N.: Defining the abstract syntax of visual languages with advanced graph grammars-a case study based on Behavior Trees. Journal of Visual Language and Computing 19(3), 343–379 (2008)
5. Colvin, R., Grunske, L., Winter, K.: Timed behavior trees for failure mode and effects analysis of time-critical systems. Journal of Systems and Software 81(12), 2163–2182 (2008)
6. Baier, C., Katoen, J.-P.: Principles of Model Checking. MIT Press, Cambridge (2008)
7. Weiser, M.: Program slicing. In: Proc. of Int. Conf. on Software Engineering (ICSE'81), pp. 439–449 (1981)
8. Tip, F.: A survey of program slicing techniques. Journal of Programming Languages 3(3), 121–189 (1995)
9. Xu, B., Qian, J., Zhang, X., Wu, Z., Chen, L.: A brief survey of program slicing. SIGSOFT Softw. Eng. Notes 30(2), 1–36 (2005)
10. Oda, T., Araki, K.: Specification slicing in formal methods of software development. In: Proc. of Computer Software and Applications Conference (COMSAC 93), pp. 313–319. IEEE, Los Alamitos (2005)

11. Wu, F., Yi, T.: Slicing Z specifications. ACM SIGPLAN Notices 39(8), 39–48 (2004)
12. Heimdahl, M., Whalen, M.: Reduction and slicing of heirarchical state machines. In: Jazayeri, M., Schauer, H. (eds.) ESEC 1997 and ESEC-FSE 1997. LNCS, vol. 1301, pp. 450–467. Springer, Heidelberg (1997)
13. Dorel, B., Singh, I., Tahat, L., Vaysburg, S.: Slicing of state-based models. In: Proc. of Int. Conf. on Software Maintenance (ICSM 2003), pp. 34–43. IEEE, Los Alamitos (2003)
14. Hatcliff, J., Dwyer, M., Zheng, H.: Slicing software for model construction. Higher-Order and Symbolic Computation 13(4), 315–353 (2000)
15. Emerson, E.A.: Temporal and modal logic. In: van Leeuwen, J. (ed.) Handbook of Theoretical Coomputer Science, vol. B. Elsevier Science Publishers, Amsterdam (1990)
16. Millett, L., Teitelbaum, T.: Slicing promela and its applications to model checking, simulation and protocol understanding. In: Proc. of Int. SPIN Workshop (1998)
17. Ganesh, V., Saidi, H., Shankar, N.: Slicing SAL. Technical report, Computer Science Laboratory (1999)
18. Thrane, C.: Slicing for UPPAAL. In: Ann. IEEE Conf. (Student Paper), pp. 1–5. IEEE, Los Alamitos (2008)
19. Leuschel, M., Llorens, M., Olivier, J., Silva, J., Tamarit, S.: The MEB and CEB static analysis for CSP specifications. In: Hanus, M. (ed.) LOPSTR 2008. LNCS, vol. 5438, pp. 103–118. Springer, Heidelberg (2009)
20. Brückner, I., Wehrheim, H.: Slicing an integrated formal method for verification. In: Lau, K.-K., Banach, R. (eds.) ICFEM 2005. LNCS, vol. 3785, pp. 360–374. Springer, Heidelberg (2005)
21. Wen, L., Dromey, R.G.: From requirements change to design change: A formal path. In: Proc. of Int. Conf. on Software Engineering and Formal Methods (SEFM 2004), pp. 104–113. IEEE Computer Society, Los Alamitos (2004)
22. Zafar, S., Colvin, R., Winter, K., Yatapanage, N., Dromey, R.G.: Early validation and verification of a distributed role-based access control model. In: Proc. of Asia-Pacific Software Engineering Conference (APSEC 2007), pp. 430–437. IEEE Computer Society, Los Alamitos (2007)
23. Dromey, G.R.: Behavior Engineering, `http://www.behaviorengineering.org`
24. Colvin, R., Hayes, I.J.: A semantics for Behavior Trees. Technical Report SSE-2010-03, The University of Queensland (May 2010), `http://espace.library.uq.edu.au/view/UQ:204809`
25. Colvin, R., Hayes, I.J.: Csp with hierarchical state. In: Leuschel, M., Wehrheim, H. (eds.) IFM 2009. LNCS, vol. 5423, pp. 118–135. Springer, Heidelberg (2009)
26. de Moura, L., Owre, S., Rueß, H., Rushby, J., Shankar, N., Sorea, M., Tiwari, A.: SAL 2. In: Alur, R., Peled, D.A. (eds.) CAV 2004. LNCS, vol. 3114, pp. 496–500. Springer, Heidelberg (2004)
27. Ottenstein, K.J., Ottenstein, L.M.: The program dependence graph in a software development environment. SIGSOFT Softw. Eng. Notes 9(3), 177–184 (1984)
28. Ferrante, J., Ottenstein, K.J., Warren, J.D.: The program dependence graph and its use in optimization. ACM Trans. Program. Lang. Syst. 9(3), 319–349 (1987)
29. Ranganath, V.P., Amtoft, T., Banerjee, A., Hatcliff, J., Dwyer, M.B.: A new foundation for control dependence and slicing for modern program structures. ACM Trans. Program. Lang. Syst. 29(5), 27 (2007)
30. Krinke, J.: Static slicing of threaded programs. SIGPLAN Notices 33(7), 35–42 (1998)
31. Evered, M., Bögeholz, S.: A case study in access control requirements for a health information system. In: Proc. of Workshop on Australasian Information Security, Data Mining and Web Intelligence, and Software Internationalisation, vol. 32, pp. 53–61. Australian Computer Society, Inc. (2004)

Optimization of the Anisotropic Gaussian Kernel for Text Segmentation and Parameter Extraction

Darko Brodić

University of Belgrade, Technical Faculty Bor, V.J. 12, 19210 Bor, Serbia
dbrodic@tf.bor.ac.rs

Abstract. In this paper, extended approach to Gaussian kernel algorithm for text segmentation, reference text line and skew rate extractions is presented. It assumes creation of boundary growing area around text based on Gaussian kernel algorithm extended by anisotropic approach. Those boundary growing areas form control image with distinct objects that are prerequisite for text segmentation. After text segmentation, text parameters such as reference text line and skew rate are calculated based on numerical method. Algorithm quality is examined by experiments. Results are evaluated by RMS method. Obtained results are compared with isotropic Gaussian kernel method. All results are examined, analyzed and summarized. Furthermore, optimal parameter values are suggested leading to anisotropic kernel optimization.

Keywords: Image processing, Document image processing, OCR, Text segmentation, Text parameters extraction, Isotropic Gaussian kernel.

1 Introduction

Printed and handwritten text is characterized by its attributes and features diversity. Hence, text parameter extraction procedure can be quite dissimilar one. However, its algorithm should be valid for printed as well as for handwritten text. To finish the task efficiently algorithm should be robust enough as well.

Prior to text parameters extraction, text line segmentation should be done. It is an important step in document processing. Although some text line detection techniques are successful in printed documents, processing of handwritten documents has remained a key problem in optical character recognition (OCR) [1,2]. Most text line segmentation methods are based on the assumptions that distance between neighboring text lines is significant as well as that text lines are reasonably straight. However, these assumptions are not always valid for handwritten documents. Hence, text line segmentation is a leading challenge in document image analysis [3].

Later, text parameters extraction from scanned documents is primary OCR goal. Reference text line and skew rate identification is mandatory. Their validity is of major importance for OCR process. Various reasons exist for appearance of multi-skewed lines in text, but two are most common [1]. Firstly, during scanning a misalignment degrees of the document made is unavoidable. All printed

C.S. Calude and V. Sassone (Eds.): TCS 2010, IFIP AICT 323, pp. 140–152, 2010.

text lines in the scanned document are uniformly skewed. Secondly, text lines in original document are differently skewed due to individual handwriting. Hence, text lines are made under different orientation. To enhance the ability of document analysis system, robust algorithm for text segmentation and parameters extraction is needed.

Previous work on text line segmentation can be categorized in few directions [2]: histogram analysis, k-nearest neighbor clustering, projection profile, Fourier transform, cross-correlation and other models.

In [1] is mentioned previously proposed and accepted technique of reference line extraction based on identifying valleys of horizontal pixel density histogram. It failed due to multi skewed text lines. Hence, it is not suitable for handwriting text.

K-nearest neighbor clustering method [2] is by product of a larger page layout analysis system, which assumed only text is being processed. The connected components formed by the nearest neighbors clustering are characters based only. Method is suitable for finding skew angle, but it is limited to Roman languages [2].

Method in [4] deals with "simple" multi skewed text. It uses as a basis Hough transform for straight lines. But, it is too specific and computationally expensive.

Method of identifying words contour area as a start of detecting baseline is proposed in [5]. The assumptions made on the word elements definition are specific.

Method [1] hypothetically assumed a flow of water in a particular direction across image frame in a way that it faces obstruction from the characters of the text lines. This method is adopted in [6]. To be totally robust it needs some further adaptation.

Algorithm proposed by [7] model text line detection as an image segmentation problem by enhancing text line structure using a Gaussian window and adopting the level set method to evolve text line boundaries. Method is specified as robust, but rotating text by an angle of (from -10° to 10°) has significant impact on it. In the paper, modification of this method is proposed, analyzed [8] and compared. Algorithm is evaluated by different sample text examples. Furthermore, optimal parameter values are suggested leading to anisotropic Gaussian kernel optimization.

Organization of the paper is as follows. In Section 2 information on proposed Gaussian kernel algorithm is given. In Section 3 experiments are described. Obtained results are analyzed, examined and discussed as well. In Section 4 conclusion is made.

2 Proposed Algorithm

Although document conversion system incorporates scanning, binarization, region segmentation, text recognition and document analysis, its procedure can be divided into three main stages as shown in Fig. 1.

In the first stage, algorithm for document text image binarization and normalization is applied. After preprocessing stage, text is prepared for segmentation,

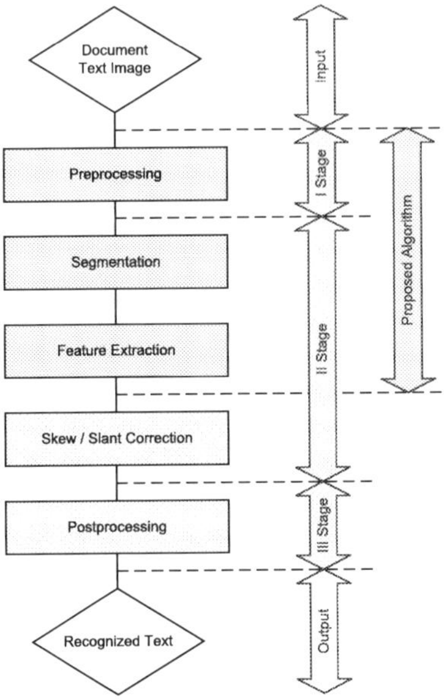

Fig. 1. Document text image identification procedure

feature extraction and character recognition. During the second stage, algorithm for text segmentation as well as for skew and reference text line identification is enforced. Also, reference text based on skew and stroke angle, is straightened and repaired. Finally, in third stage character recognition process is applied. As a result of scanning process, document text image is obtained. It is an input of text grayscale image described by following intensity matrix [9]:

$$D(i,j) \in [0,\ldots,255] \ , \tag{1}$$

where $i \in [1,\ldots,M]$ and $j \in [1,\ldots,N]$. After applying intensity segmentation with binarization, intensity function is converted into binary form given by:

$$X(i,j) = \begin{cases} 1 & \text{for } D(i,j) \geq D_{\text{th}} \\ 0 & \text{for } D(i,j) < D_{\text{th}} \end{cases} \ , \tag{2}$$

where D_{th} is given by Otsu algorithm [10]. It represents the threshold sensitivity decision value.

Document text image is black and white image represented by matrix $\mathbf{X}$. Each character or word consists of the only black pixels. Hence, every point $X(i,j)$ i.e. $X_{i,j}$ is represented by number of coordinate pairs $(0,1)$, where $i = 1,\ldots,M$, and $j = 1,\ldots,N$ of matrix $\mathbf{X}$ [9]. It is represented by document text image fragment as in Fig. 2.

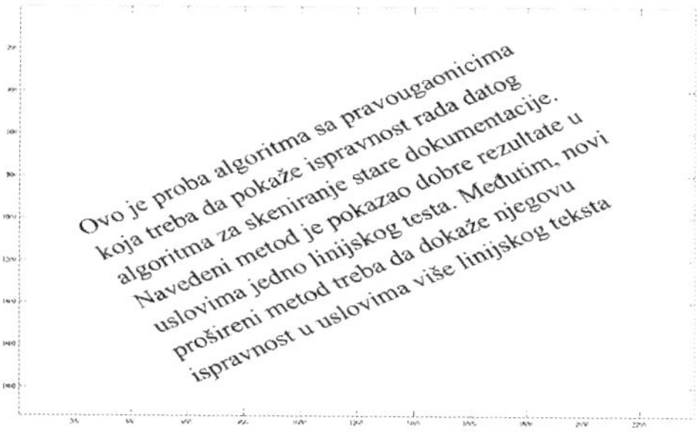

Fig. 2. Document text image fragment represented by matrix $\mathbf{X}$

2.1 Morphological Preprocessing

Prior to processing stage, document text image needs additional preparation. It is assumed text area is extracted by any appropriate method. Further, morphological preprocessing is performed to make document text image "noiseless". The morphological preprocessing was defined in [11] by following steps:

- Document image erosion by $\mathbf{X} \ominus \mathbf{S}_1$,
- Document image opening by $\mathbf{X} \circ \mathbf{S}_1$,
- Dilatation of the opening the document image by $(\mathbf{X} \circ \mathbf{S}_1) \ominus \mathbf{S}_1$,
- Closing of the opening the document image by $(\mathbf{X} \circ \mathbf{S}_1) \bullet \mathbf{S}_1$.

For the above operations, structuring element $\mathbf{S}_1$ dimension 3x3 is used [9].

2.2 Linear Bounding Containers

All text parameters extraction algorithms more or less depend on resolution and size of text letters. Consequently, algorithm's parameters are closely related to it. To be efficient, algorithm should choose optimal parameters from the entire set. Linear containers or its modifications are one of the tools for letter size estimation [11].

Linear container and its interior are specified by a finite number of linear inequalities. In our case linear container is assumed to be special case of the convex polygon i.e. bounding box. Special case of the box is a rectangular region whose edges are parallel to the coordinate axes. Furthermore, it is defined by its maximum and minimum extents for all axes. Hence, each pixel $X_{i,j}$ belonging to box is given by:

$$x_{\min} \leq i \leq x_{\max} \ , \tag{3}$$

and

$$y_{\min} \leq j \leq y_{\max} \ . \tag{4}$$

Hence, bounding box is defined by its endpoints $x_{\min}, x_{\max}, y_{\min}, y_{\max}$. Inclusion of the point $X_{i,j}$ in a box is tested by verifying these four inequalities. If any

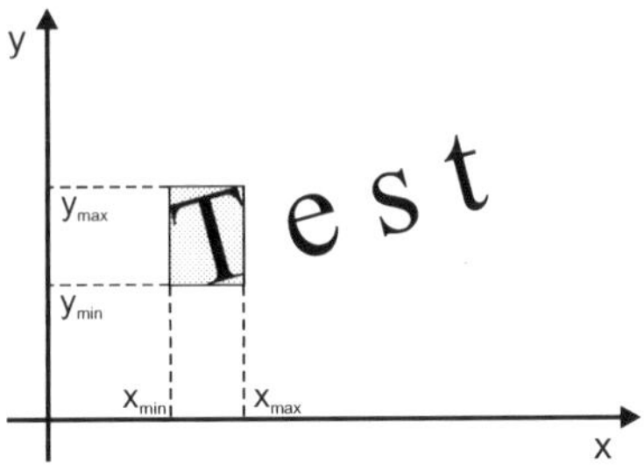

Fig. 3. Bounding box definition

one of them fails, then the point is not inside. Bounding box definition is given in Fig. 3.

The bounding box is the computationally simplest of all linear containers. Hence, it is one of the most frequently used in many applications due to its simplicity and computationally inexpensiveness [12]. Although the bounding box is not precise method for letter size estimation, it is simple and in many cases adequate to evaluate those values. All text elements like letters, part of words or words are surrounded by bounding boxes. Their heights represent the height of letters. To reduce the error, median height of all bounding boxes is used. Median is the middle value in a set of values. Hence, it is less sensitive to extreme values. Boundary box objects are defined by O_u, where $u = 1, \ldots, V$ and V is the total number of boundary box objects over sample text. If V is the number of objects and u is object index, reorder initial set of values h_u so that $g_1 < g_2 < \ < g_u$ and currently g_u is called u-th order statistic [13]. Hence, following is valid: $g_1 \equiv min(h_u)$ and $g_V \equiv min(h_u)$. Median is defined by [13] as:

$$h_{\text{median}} = \begin{cases} g_{\frac{(u+1)}{2}} & \text{if } u \text{ is odd} \\ \frac{1}{2}(g_{\frac{u}{2}} + g_{1+\frac{u}{2}}) & \text{if } u \text{ is even} \end{cases}, \tag{5}$$

After h_{median} of the letter heights set is obtained, typical letter height is annotated. It is prerequisite for algorithm's parameter optimization decision.

2.3 Anisotropic Gaussian Kernel

For the processing stage Gaussian kernel algorithm is used. It is based on two-dimensional Gaussian function given by [14]:

$$f(x,y) = Ae^{-\frac{(x-b_x)^2+(y-b_y)^2}{2\sigma^2}}, \tag{6}$$

where b_x is shift along x-axis, b_y is shift along y-axis, σ is standard deviation defining curve spread parameter and A is the amplitude of the function given as $A = 1/(2\pi\sigma^2)^{\frac{1}{2}}$. From (10) it is obvious that curve spread parameter σ is equal for x as well for y-axis. This way, Gaussian function is isotropic. Converting

Gaussian function into point spread function, Gaussian kernel is obtained. Hence, algorithm using Gaussian kernel expands black pixel area by scattering every black pixel in its neighborhood. Around every black pixel new pixels are non-uniformly dispersed. These pixels have lower intensity of black. Hence, they are grayscale. Their intensity depends on position or distance from original black pixel. Now, document image matrix is represented as grayscale image. Intensity pertains in level region $(0 - 255)$. Our black pixel of interest has coordinate $X_{i,j}$ and intensity of 255, while neighbor pixels have intensity smaller than 255. So, after applying Gaussian kernel, equal to $2R + 1$ in x-direction as well as in y-direction, text is scattered forming enlarged area around it. Converting all non black pixels in the same area, as well as inverting image, forms the black pixel expanded areas. Those areas named boundary growing areas.

In our case isotropic approach is less efficient. Alternatively in some cases, it is not suitable due to its possibility of merging different text lines. Using different curve spread parameter σ in x and y direction i.e. σ_x and σ_y respectively, extends (10) as follows [13,14]:

$$f(x, y) = Ae^{-\left[\frac{(x-b_x)^2}{2\sigma_x^2} + \frac{(y-b_y)^2}{2\sigma_y^2}\right]}. \tag{7}$$

This extension of the previous i.e. isotropic Gaussian function lead to image kernel equal to $2S + 1$ in x-direction and $2R + 1$ in y-direction. Due to relations $R \neq S$, Gaussian kernel is anisotropic [8]. Additionally, ratio parameter $\lambda = S/R$ completely defines Gaussian anisotropic condition. Example of the isotropic and anisotropic Gaussian kernel for $R = 10$, $\lambda = 1$ and $\lambda = 5$ is given in Fig. 4.

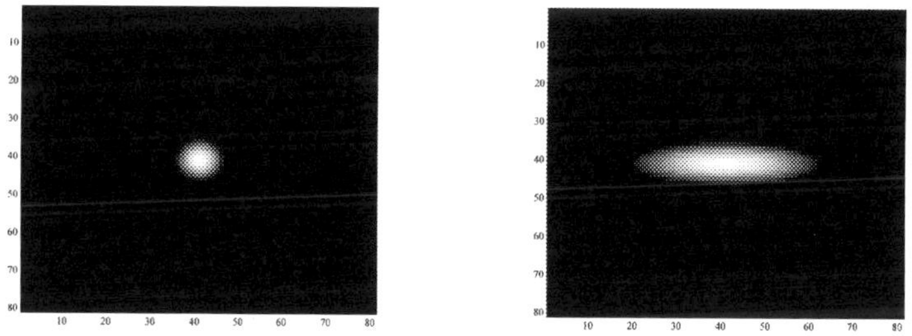

Fig. 4. Gaussian kernel: isotropic (left), anisotropic $\Rightarrow \lambda > 1$ (right)

Created boundary growing areas form control image with objects that are prerequisite for document image text segmentation [8]. These black objects represent different text lines needful for text segmentation. Hence, their basic task is text lines splitting. Example of the boundary growing areas is given in Fig. 5.

2.4 Reference Text Line

After text segmentation, primary task is reference text line and skew rate extraction. Their identification is based on information obtained from black pixel

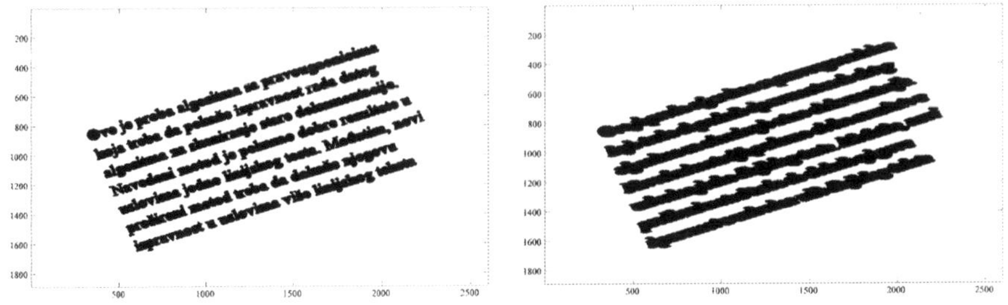

Fig. 5. Boundary growing areas over text: isotropic (left), anisotropic (right)

contained in boundary growing areas. Reference text line estimation is average position calculation of black pixels in every column of document image. It is calculated as [1,9]:

$$x_i = \frac{\sum_{j=1}^{L} y_j}{L} \quad {}_{i=1,\ldots,K} \ , \tag{8}$$

where x_i is point position of calculated reference text line, i is number of column position of calculated reference text, y_j is position of black pixel in column j and L is sum of black pixel number in specified column j of an image.

After calculation, sub-image matrix with only one black pixel per column is obtained. This black pixel defines estimated reference text line. Such reference text line forms continuous or discontinuous line partly "representing" reference text line. To form continuous reference text line, some numerical method could be used.

3 Experiments, Results and Discussion

Algorithm quality evaluation consists of two text experiments. First experiment represents text segmentation estimation. It is inevitable in algorithm segmentation quality assessment. Consequently, it is prerequisite for obtaining other text parameters. If segmentation experiment miscarry, other examination process will be meaningless. Hence, its importance is critical. Second experiment is mainly concerned with skew rate identification. Its task is algorithm performance evaluation of the skew rate tracking succeed. This experiment is primarily based on printed text, but it is good prerequisite for testing handwritten text. Obtained results are linked.

3.1 Text Segmentation Experiment and Results

In the first experiment text segmentation quality is examined. For this purpose multi line text is used. It is given in Fig. 6.

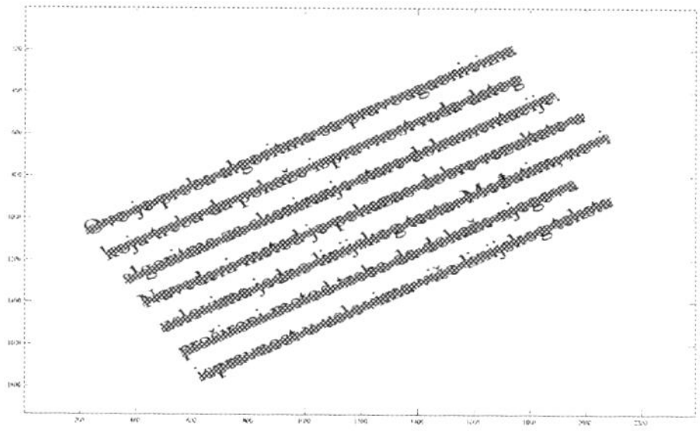

Fig. 6. Sample text for text segmentation experiment

Number of existing text objects relate to text segmentation quality success. Hence, the less objects the better segmentation process, except the number may not be less than text lines number. The quality is measured by RMS_{seg} calculated as [13,14]:

$$RMS_{\text{seg}} = \sqrt{\frac{1}{Q}\sum_{i=1}^{Q}(O_{i,\text{ref}} - O_{i,\text{est}})^2}\ , \tag{9}$$

where $i = 1, \ldots, Q$ is the number of examined text samples, $O_{i,\text{ref}}$ is number of referent objects in text i.e. number of text lines, and $O_{i,\text{est}}$ is number of obtained objects in text by the applied algorithm for each examined text sample.

Character height $H_{\text{ch}} \approx 100$ pixels (px) obtained as h_{median} is assumed. From [11] parameter R value may not exceed 20% of H_{ch}. In fact, bigger R could lead to text lines merging. Hence, algorithm is examined for $R = (5, 10, 15, 20)$. First part of experiment examined text segmentation through RMS_{seg} for angle range $(0° - 30°)$, while further angle range $(0° - 80°)$ is used. Results are given in Table 1 and Table 2.

Table 1. Text segmentation results: RMS_{seg1} for angle range $(0° - 30°)$ (less values are better ones)

Angle Range	λ	R			
$0° - 30°$	S/R	5	10	15	20
Isotropic	1	180.36	65.77	36.00	32.82
Anisotropic	2	79.86	48.15	3.63	0.00
	3	63.01	14.68	0.44	-
	4	55.40	9.21	-	-
	5	40.73	8.70	-	-

Table 2. Text segmentation results: RMS_{seg2} for angle range ($0^\circ - 80^\circ$) (less values are better ones)

Angle Range	λ	R			
$0^\circ - 80^\circ$	S/R	5	10	15	20
Isotropic	1	181.05	59.22	36.00	33.01
Anisotropic	2	105.34	42.52	20.87	6.90
	3	70.07	25.18	9.20	-
	4	59.18	15.70	-	-
	5	48.94	11.34	-	-

From Table 1 and 2, it is obvious that anisotropic approach is advantageous. Nevertheless, it is true for $\lambda > 1$. Under this condition, kernel is stretched in x-direction by parameter λ. Furthermore, segmentation experiment proved to be eligible for optimal parameters selection such as R and λ. This way, each parameter R can be paired with optimal parameter λ. From the above tables those pairs (R, λ) are following: $(5,5), (10,5), (15,3), (20,2)$ as well as $(5,4), (10,4), (10,3)$, and $(15,2)$. However, the best choice is $(20,2)$ from Table 1. All listed paired values are invaluable for further examination process i.e. for other text experiments.

3.2 Skew Rate Text Experiment and Results

Second experiment is mainly concerned with text skew rate. It examines algorithm quality to follow text skewing. In this case, sample printed text rotated by angle β up to 80° by step of 5° around x-axis is used. This is given in Fig. 7.

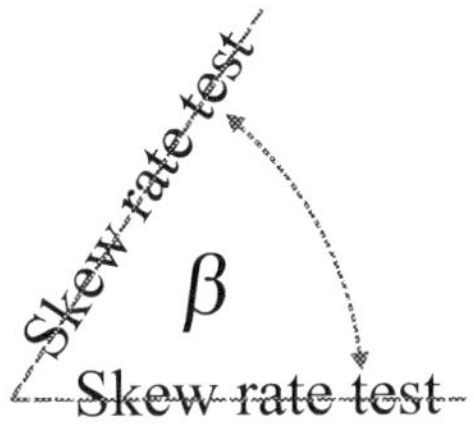

Fig. 7. Sample text rotating for the angle β up to 80°

Reference line of the sample text is represented by:

$$y = ax + b \, . \tag{10}$$

After applying algorithm to sample text, reference text line is calculated by (8). To achieve continuous linear reference text line, least square method is used. Function approximation by first degree polynomial is given as:

$$y = ax' + b' \, . \tag{11}$$

Then number of data points i.e. ndp is used and the slope a', and the y-intercept b' are calculated as [14]:

$$a' = \frac{\sum y \sum xy - ndp \sum xy}{(\sum x)^2 - ndp \sum x^2} \ , \tag{12}$$

and

$$b' = \frac{\sum x \sum xy - \sum y \sum x^2}{(\sum x)^2 - ndp \sum x^2} \ . \tag{13}$$

Further, referent line hit rate i.e. $RLHR$ is defined as [8]:

$$RLHR = 1 - \frac{\beta_{\mathrm{ref}} - \beta_{\mathrm{est}}}{\beta_{\mathrm{ref}}} \ , \tag{14}$$

where β_{ref} is arctangent from origin (10) i.e. a and β_{est} is arctangent from calculated i.e. estimated (11) i.e. a'. Then, RMS_{skew} values are calculated by [13,14]:

$$RMS_{\mathrm{skew}} = \sqrt{\frac{1}{P}\sum_{i=1}^{P}(x_{i,\mathrm{ref}} - x_{i,\mathrm{est}})^2} \ , \tag{15}$$

where $i = 1, \ldots, P$ is number of examined text rotating angles up to 80°, $x_{i,\mathrm{ref}}$ is $RLHR$ for β_{est} equal to β_{ref}, due to normalization equal to 1, and $x_{i,\mathrm{est}}$ is $RLHR$.

Again, $H_{\mathrm{ch}} \approx 100$ px is assumed. Algorithm is examined for $R = (5, 10, 15, 20)$ and $\lambda = (1, 2, 3, 4, 5)$. Quality of skew rate identification is obtained by $RLHR$ value as in (14). Furthermore, level of spreading results is obtained by RMS_{skew} value given in (15) for two angle ranges: $(0° - 30°)$ and $(0° - 80°)$. These results are given in Fig. 8. Isotropic results are given on the left side of the chart on Fig. 8 - 11. Unlike, anisotropic results are shown in the rest of the each chart.

It can be noted, anisotropic approach leads to quite better results. Still, it should be cautious on interpreting presented results. Namely, high S values should be avoided. These values contribute to faulty text segmentation process. So, it is recommended to match results from this experiment and previous one. This way, parameter pairs (R, λ) obtained from previous experiments is optimized ones. Still, from the optimized parameter pairs, set members $(R, \lambda) = (15, 45)$ and $(20, 40)$ are the best ones for $H_{\mathrm{ch}} \approx 100$ px. Hence, from the previous statements and claims, it can be concluded on optimal parameter values of R and λ. These optimal values are $K \approx$ 15-20% of H_{ch} as well as $\lambda \approx$ 2-3, leading to anisotropic approach.

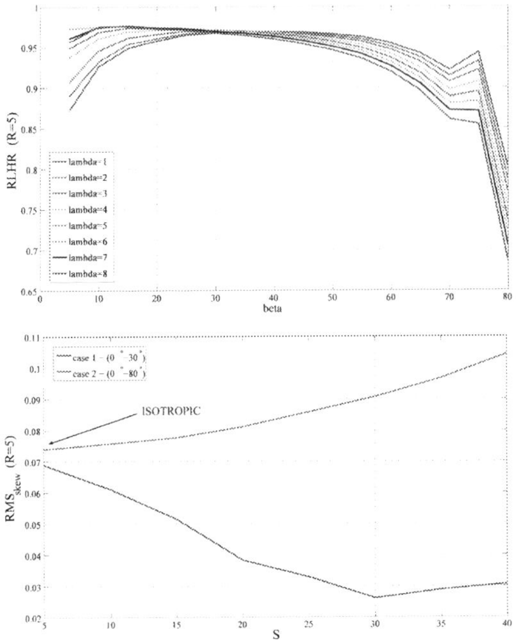

Fig. 8. Skew rate test for R=5, λ=(1, ..., 8): $RLHR$ (top), RMS_{skew} (bottom)

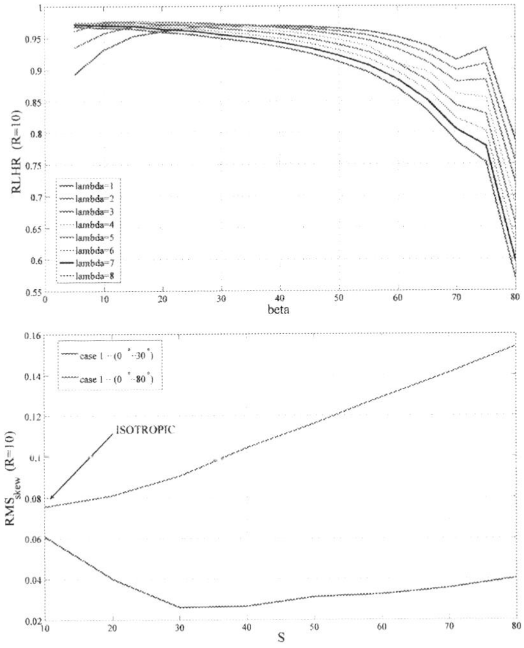

Fig. 9. Skew rate test R=10, λ=(1, ..., 8): $RLHR$ (top), RMS_{skew} (bottom)

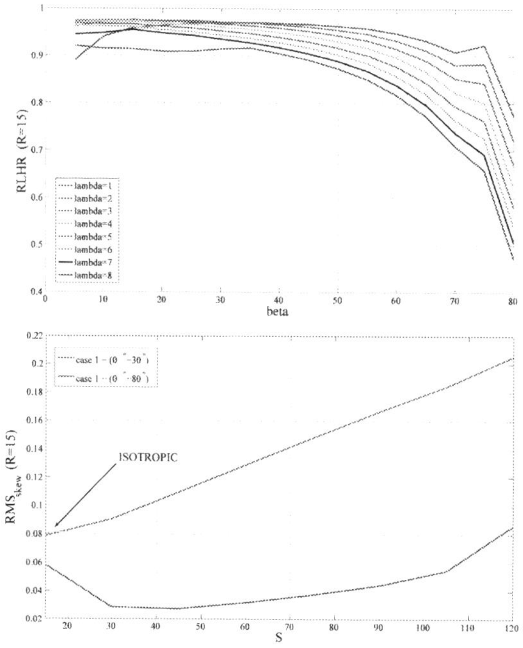

Fig. 10. Skew rate test R=15, λ=(1, ..., 8): $RLHR$ (top), $RMS_{\rm skew}$ (bottom)

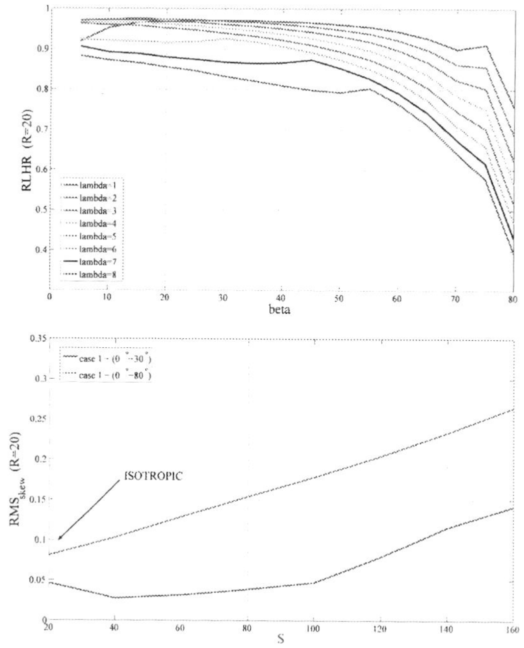

Fig. 11. Skew rate test R=20, λ=(1, ..., 8): $RLHR$ (top), $RMS_{\rm skew}$ (bottom)

4 Conclusions

Anisotropic Gaussian kernel algorithm proved to be advanced in the domain of text segmentation, which is of primary importance. Due to isotropic approach faulty results from segmentation experiment, all it's slightly better results in skew rate experiments are completely irrelevant. Still, text segmentation is primary goal. It is prerequisite for reference text line and skew rate identification. Slightly weaker results of anisotropic approach in some part of text parameter estimation are in the background. This way, anisotropic Gaussian kernel and its optimized parameter pairs proved to be useful and robust method which is promising. Consequently, for higher angles some modification of the anisotropic approach is recommended.

References

1. Basu, S., Chaudhuri, C., Kundu, M., Nasipuri, M., Basu, D.K.: Text Line Extraction from Multi-Skewed Handwritten Documents. Pattern Recognition 40, 1825–1839 (2006)
2. Amin, A., Wu, S.: Robust Skew Detection in Mixed Text/Graphics Documents. In: Proceedings of ICDAR'05, Seoul, Korea, pp. 247–251 (2005)
3. Likforman-Sulem, L., Zahour, A., Taconet, B.: Text Line Segmentation of Historical Documents: A Survey. International Journal on Document Analysis and Recognition (IJDAR) 9(2-4), 123–138 (2007)
4. Louloudis, G., Gatos, B., Pratikakis, I., Halatsis, C.: Text Line Detection in Handwritten Documents. Pattern Recognition 41, 3758–3772 (2008)
5. Wang, J., Mazlor, K.H.L., Hui, S.C.: Cursive Word Reference Line Detection. Pattern Recognition 30(3), 503–511 (1997)
6. Brodić, D., Milivojević, Z.: An Approach to Modification of Water Flow Algorithm for Segmentation and Text Parameters Extraction. In: Camarinha-Matos, L.M., Pereira, P., Ribeiro, L. (eds.) Emerging Trends in Technological Innovation. IFIP AICT, vol. 314, pp. 324–331. Springer, Heidelberg (2010)
7. Li, Y., Zheng, Y., Doermann, D., Jaeger, S.: A New Algorithm for Detecting Text Line in Handwritten Documents. In: Proceedings of 18th International Conference on Pattern Recognition, Hong Kong, China, vol. 2, pp. 1030–1033 (2006)
8. Brodić, D., Milivojević, Z.: Using Anisotropic Gaussian Window for Printed and Handwritten Text Parameters Extraction. In: Proceedings of 9th International Scientific Conference UNITECH, Gabrovo, Bulgaria, vol. 1, pp. 453–460 (2009)
9. Gonzalez, R.C., Woods, R.E.: Digital Image Procesing, 2nd edn. Prentice-Hall, Eaglewoods Cliffs (2002)
10. Draganov, I.V., Popova, A.A.: Rotation Angle Estimation of Scanned Handwritten Cursive Text Documents. In: Proceedings of ICEST '06, Sofia, Bulgaria (2006)
11. Brodić, D., Dokić, B.: Initial Skew Rate Detection Using Rectangular Hull Gravity Center. In: Proceedings of 14th International Conference of Electronics, Kaunas, Lithuania (2010)
12. Chang, C.M.: Detecting Ellipses via Bounding Boxes. Asian Journal of Health and Information Sciences 1(1), 73–84 (2006)
13. Qui, P.: Image Processing and Jump Regression Analysis. John Wiley & Sons, New Jersey (2005)
14. Bolstad, W.M.: Introduction to Bayesian Statistics. John Wiley and Sons, New Jersey (2005)

Online Dictionary Matching for Streams of XML Documents

Panu Silvasti[1], Seppo Sippu[2], and Eljas Soisalon-Soininen[1]

[1] Aalto University, School of Science and Technology, Finland
{ess,psilvast}@cs.hut.fi
[2] University of Helsinki, Finland
sippu@cs.helsinki.fi

Abstract. We consider the online multiple-pattern matching problem for streams of XML documents, when the patterns are expressed as linear XPath expressions containing child operators (/), descendant operators (//) and wildcards ($*$) but no predicates. For each document in the stream, the task is to determine all occurrences in the document of all the patterns. We present a general multiple-pattern-matching algorithm that is based on a backtracking deterministic finite automaton derived from the classic Aho–Corasick pattern-matching automaton. This automaton is of size linear in the sum of the sizes of the XPath patterns, and the worst-case time bound of the algorithm is better than the time bound of the simulation of linear-size nondeterministic automata. In addition to the worst-case-efficient general solution we present an algorithm with a simple backtracking mechanism that works extremely well for cases in which the backtracking stack remains low. Our experiments show that, when applied to filtering, this simple algorithm scales well as regards the number of patterns (or filters) and is competitive with YFilter, a widely accepted software for XML filtering.

1 Introduction

String-pattern matching with wildcards has been considered in various contexts and for various types of wildcards in the pattern [1,2,3,4,5,6]. The simplest approach is to use the single-character wildcard ($*$), a character that can appear in any position of the string pattern and matches any character of the input alphabet Σ. Generalizations of this are the various ways in which "variable-length gaps" in the patterns are allowed, implemented, for example, by the single-character wildcard and by Σ^* that denotes an unlimited gap [4,5].

Our goal in this article is to transfer the methodology of efficient string-pattern matching with wildcards and gaps to matching tree-structured text, especially one composed of a stream of XML documents. The patterns are given as linear XPath expressions with child operators (/), descendant operators (//), and wildcards ($*$), defined on paths of XML-document trees. Here the child and descendant operators correspond, respectively, to the concatenation and unlimited-gap operators of linear text.

C.S. Calude and V. Sassone (Eds.): TCS 2010, IFIP AICT 323, pp. 153–164, 2010.

Given a set of linear XPath expressions without predicates (the *patterns*) and a stream of XML documents (the *input documents*), we determine, for each document in the stream, all occurrences of all the patterns in an online fashion. Each matched occurrence is identified by the pattern and its last element position in the document. Because of the descendant operator "//", there can be more than one, actually an exponential number of occurrences of the same pattern at the same element position, but we avoid this possible explosion of the number of occurrences by reporting only one occurrence in such situations.

Our pattern-matching algorithm performs a single left-to-right scan of each document and reports each pattern occurrence once its end position is reached. Our strategy here is that we decompose each pattern into "keywords" that are maximal substrings of XML elements only containing child operators "/". Then we are able to consider the patterns as sequences composed of keywords and gaps that are maximal sequences of wildcards "$*$" and descendant operators "//". The basic idea of our algorithm is to recognize the keywords of the patterns using the Aho–Corasick pattern-matching automaton [7], and to build matches of the patterns upon these occurrences. The key feature of our algorithm is that we do not recognize those keyword occurrences about which we know that there cannot be a matching prefix with this keyword occurrence. Moreover, because matching of the patterns is performed against paths of the trees induced by XML documents, we need a backtracking mechanism in order to avoid repeated traversals of common path prefixes.

Our algorithm can also be used for filtering, in which only the first occurrence of each pattern needs to be reported. Related approaches to filtering are those of the NFA-based XFilter by Altinel and Franklin [8] and YFilter by Diao et al. [9,10], and the lazy DFA construction by Green et al. [11], only to mention the best-known ones. Compared to these methods our algorithm has a superior worst-case time bound. However, for practical XML documents, the tree paths remain quite short implying that our general approach with a worst-case-efficient backtracking strategy is slower than the above mentioned filtering algorithms. We noticed this when we performed our experimental comparisons with YFilter, which is a widely accepted software for filtering and transformation for high-volume XML-message brokering [9]; YFilter has been programmed with Java, as is our system.

Because of the inefficiency of the general approach we also designed a simple backtracking strategy, which allows the matching algorithm to return to a previous state at the end of the current path by just popping a state from the backtracking stack. This approach implies a higher worst-case time bound, but indeed makes our approach competitive with YFilter. Moreover, our algorithm outperforms YFilter in the case of data whose XML schema or DTD is not heavily recursive.

The contributions of the present paper are essential extensions of our previous results [12], where a worst-case-efficient algorithm was presented in the case in which descendant operators, but no wildcards, were allowed in the patterns.

2 Linear XML Patterns with Gaps and Wildcards

The problem of online dictionary matching of XML is stated as follows: Given a set of linear XPath expressions without predicates (the *patterns*) and a stream of XML documents (the *input documents*), the task is to determine, for each document in the stream, all occurrences of all the patterns. An occurrence is reported by the pattern number and the element position of its last element in the current document. Different instances of the same pattern at the same position are reported as a single occurrence.

We decompose each pattern into keywords and gaps as follows. First, we remove all child operators "/" from the pattern. Then we define the *keywords* of the pattern to be maximal substrings consisting of XML elements only. The *gaps* of the patterns are defined to be maximal substrings consisting of descendant operators "//" and wildcards "$*$". If the pattern ends at a nonempty gap, then we assume that the last keyword of the pattern is the empty string ϵ. Each pattern is considered to begin with a gap, which thus may be ϵ.

We number the patterns and their gaps and keywords consecutively, so that the ith pattern P_i can be represented as

$$P_i = \mathit{gap}(i,1)\mathit{keyword}(i,1)\ldots\mathit{gap}(i,m_i)\mathit{keyword}(i,m_i),$$

where $\mathit{gap}(i,j)$ denotes the jth gap and $\mathit{keyword}(i,j)$ denotes the jth keyword of pattern P_i. For example, the pattern $//a/b/*/c//*/d/*/*$ consists of four gaps, namely $//$, $*$, $//*$, and $**$, and of four keywords, namely ab, c, d, and ϵ. The pattern $/a/b/*/c//*/d$ consists of three gaps, namely ϵ, $*$, and $//*$, and three keywords, namely ab, c, and d.

For pattern P_i, we denote by $\mathit{mingap}(i,j)$ and $\mathit{maxgap}(i,j)$, respectively, the minimum and maximum lengths of element strings that can be matched by $\mathit{gap}(i,j)$. The length of the jth keyword of pattern P_i is denoted by $\mathit{length}(i,j)$. We also assume that $\#\mathit{keywords}(i)$ gives m_i, the number of keywords in pattern P_i, and that $\#\mathit{keywords}$ denotes the number of keywords altogether.

For example, if the pattern $//a/b/*/c//*/d/*/*$ is the ith pattern, we have

$\mathit{mingap}(i,1) = 0$, $\mathit{maxgap}(i,1) = \infty$, $\mathit{length}(i,1) = 2$,
$\mathit{mingap}(i,2) = 1$, $\mathit{maxgap}(i,2) = 1$, $\mathit{length}(i,2) = 1$,
$\mathit{mingap}(i,3) = 1$, $\mathit{maxgap}(i,3) = \infty$, $\mathit{length}(i,3) = 1$,
$\mathit{mingap}(i,4) = 2$, $\mathit{maxgap}(i,4) = 2$, $\mathit{length}(i,4) = 0$.

If the pattern $/a/b/*/c//*/d$ is the ith pattern, we have

$\mathit{mingap}(i,1) = 0$, $\mathit{maxgap}(i,1) = 0$, $\mathit{length}(i,1) = 2$,
$\mathit{mingap}(i,2) = 1$, $\mathit{maxgap}(i,2) = 1$, $\mathit{length}(i,2) = 1$,
$\mathit{mingap}(i,3) = 1$, $\mathit{maxgap}(i,3) = \infty$, $\mathit{length}(i,3) = 1$.

In the case of XPath patterns, we have, for all i and j, either $\mathit{mingap}(i,j) = \mathit{maxgap}(i,j)$ or $\mathit{maxgap}(i,j) = \infty$, because in any XPath expression the number of wildcards is fixed. However, as will be evident from the presentation below, our algorithm can also handle any variable-length gaps with $\mathit{mingap}(i,j) < \mathit{maxgap}(i,j) < \infty$.

3 The Matching Algorithm

For the set of all keywords in the patterns, we construct a backtracking Aho–Corasick pattern-matching automaton [7] with a dynamically changing output set *current-output* containing tuples of the form (q, i, j, b, e), where $q = state(keyword(i, j))$, the state reached from the initial state upon reading the jth keyword of pattern P_i, and b and e are the earliest and latest element positions on a path in the input document at which some partial match of pattern P_i up to and including the jth keyword can possibly be found. The latest possible element position e may be ∞, meaning the end of the path.

Initially, the set *current-output* contains all output tuples for the first keywords in the patterns, that is, tuples $(q, i, 1, b, e)$, where q is the state reached from the initial state upon reading the first keyword of pattern P_i,

$$b = mingap(i, 1) + length(i, 1), \text{ and}$$
$$e = maxgap(i, 1) + length(i, 1)$$

Here $e = \infty$ if $maxgap(i, 1) = \infty$.

The operating cycle of the PMA is given as Alg. 1. The SAX-parser [13] call *scan-next*(*token*) returns the next XML token from the input stream. The functions *goto* and *fail* are the goto and fail functions of the standard Aho–Corasick PMA, that is, $goto(state(y), a) = state(ya)$, where ya is a prefix of some keyword and a is an XML element, and $fail(state(uv)) = state(v)$, where uv is a prefix of some keyword and v is the longest proper suffix of uv such that v is also a prefix of some keyword.

Denote by $string(q)$ the unique element string y with $state(y) = q$. The function *output-fail*(q) used in Alg. 3 to traverse the *output path* for state q is defined by: $output\text{-}fail(q) = fail^k(q)$, where k is the greatest integer less than or equal to the length of $string(q)$ such that $string(fail^m(q))$ is not a keyword for any $m = 1, \ldots, k-1$. Here $fail^m$ denotes the *fail* function applied m times. Thus, the output path for state q includes those states in the fail path from q that have a nonempty set of output tuples.

The *backtracking stack* contains information about states visited and output tuples inserted into and deleted from the current output during traversing a root-to-leaf path in the current input document. The PMA backtracks when an end-element tag is scanned; then elements from the stack are popped, insertions and deletions of output tuples are undone, and the control of the PMA is returned to the state that was entered when scanning the previous start-element tag (see the procedure *backtrack* given as Alg. 4).

When visiting state q, the current output of the PMA is checked for possible matches of keywords in the procedure call *traverse-output-path*(q) (see Alg. 3). A current output tuple (q, i, j, b, e) is found to represent a match of the jth keyword of pattern P_i, if $b \leq path\text{-}length \leq e$, where *path-length* is a global variable that maintains the number of elements scanned from the current path in the input document. Now if the jth keyword is the last one in pattern P_i, then this indicates a match of the entire pattern P_i. Otherwise, an output tuple $(q', i, j+1, b', e')$ for the $(j+1)$st keyword of pattern P_i is inserted into the set *current-output*, where q' is the state reached from the intitial state upon reading the $(j+1)$st keyword of pattern P_i,

$$b' = \textit{path-length} + \textit{mingap}(i, j+1) + \textit{length}(i, j+1), \text{ and}$$
$$e' = \textit{path-length} + \textit{maxgap}(i, j+1) + \textit{length}(i, j+1).$$

Here $e' = \infty$ if $\textit{maxgap}(i, j+1) = \infty$. If $e' = \infty$, we could delete from *current-output* all output tuples (q'', i, j'', b'', e'') with $j'' \leq j$. However, since tuples (q'', i, j'', b'', e'') with $e'' < \textit{path-length}$ are eventually deleted by the procedure *clean-current-output* (see Alg. 2), we only delete here tuples $(q'', i, j'', b'', \infty)$ with $j'' \leq j$ (which can be done efficiently, see below).

The set of current output tuples is organized as two balanced binary search trees, both containing exactly the same information, namely, the current output tuples (q, i, j, b, e). One of the search trees is indexed by ordered triples (e, i, j), so that the node for key value (e, i, j) contains a pointer to a list of tuples (q, b). The other search tree is indexed by ordered pairs (q, b), so that the node for key value (q, b) contains a pointer to a list of tuples (e, i, j).

In the procedure *clean-current-output*, outdated output tuples (q, i, j, b, e) with $e < \textit{path-length}$ are first located and deleted from the former search tree, and then sorted by (q, b) and deleted from the latter search tree, in both cases using a bulk-deletion algorithm.

In the procedure *traverse-output-path*, when visiting state q, the latter search tree is used to locate the output tuples (q, i, j, b, e) with $b \leq \textit{path-length} \leq e$. Deletions of tuples $(q'', i, j'', b'', \infty)$ with $j'' \leq j$ are first performed on the latter search tree, and then sorted by (q'', b'') and deleted from the former search tree, again using a bulk-deletion algorithm. Every insertion into *current-output* goes to both search trees.

For pattern P_i, *#maxmatches*(i) denotes the maximum number of matches searched for i; this is specified by the user and may be a positive integer or ∞. For example, if we wish to solve only the filtering problem, we set *#maxmatches*$(i) = 1$ for all patterns P_i. The counter *#matches*(i) records the number of matches found for pattern P_i.

4 Correctness and Complexity

Whenever a prefix $P_{i,j}$ of P_i that ends with *keyword*(i, j) has been recognized at some element position (indicated by the variable *element-count* in the algorithm), a new output tuple $(q', i, j+1, b', e')$ will be inserted into the current output in Alg. 3. We have:

Lemma 1. At the point when a new tuple $(q', i, j+1, b', e')$ will be inserted into the current output in Alg. 3, an occurrence of a pattern prefix $P_{i,j}$ has been recognized. Conversely, for each occurrence of $P_{i,j}$, $j < m_i$, a tuple (q, i, j, b, e) with $b \leq \textit{path-length} \leq e$ is found in the current output and a new tuple $(q', i, j+1, b', e')$ is inserted into the current output.

For a set S of keywords or pattern prefixes, denote by *occ*(S) the number of occurrences in the input document of elements of S. Lemma 1 implies that

Algorithm 1. Operating cycle of the backtracking PMA

```
document-count ← 0
element-count ← 0
scan-next(token)
while token was found do
   element-count ← element-count + 1
   if token is a start-document tag then
      document-count ← document-count + 1
      initialize()
      path-length ← 0
      state ← initial-state
      push-onto-stack(state)
      traverse-output-path(state)
   else if token is an end-document tag then
      element-count ← 0
   else if token is the start-element tag of element E then
      path-length ← path-length + 1
      push-onto-stack(state)
      while goto(state, E) = fail do
         state ← fail(state)
      end while
      state ← goto(state, E)
      traverse-output-path(state)
      clean-current-output()
   else if token is an end-element tag then
      backtrack()
      path-length ← path-length − 1
   end if
   scan-next(token)
end while
```

Algorithm 2. Procedure *clean-current-output*()

```
for all tuples (q, i, j, b, e) ∈ current-output with e < path-length do
   delete (q, i, j, b, e) from current-output
   if #matches(i) < #maxmatches(i) then
      push-onto-stack(deleted⟨q, i, j, b, e⟩)
   end if
end for
```

the algorithm has the lower time bound $\Omega(occ(\{P_{i,j} \mid i \geq 1, j \geq 1\}))$. Moreover, processing the input document requires additionally at most $O(K \cdot n)$ time, where n is the length of the input document and K denotes the maximum number of proper suffixes of any keyword that are also keywords. The multiplier K is due to the fact that tuples to be inserted into the current output are created only for states *state*(*keyword*(i, j)) and thus all states in the output path must be traversed in order to check all possibilities to continue the currently matched pattern prefix. Observe that the backtracking approach using a stack allows to

Algorithm 3. Procedure *traverse-output-path(state)*

```
q ← state
traversed ← false
while not traversed do
  for all (q, i, j, b, e) ∈ current-output with b ≤ path-length ≤ e do
    if #matches(i) = #maxmatches(i) then
      delete (q, i, j, b, e) from current-output
    else if j = #keywords(i) then
      report a match of pattern P_i at position element-count in document
      document-count
      #matches(i) ← #matches(i) + 1
      if #matches(i) = #maxmatches(i) then
        delete (q, i, j, b, e) from current-output
        for all (q', i, j', b', ∞) ∈ current-output do
          delete (q', i, j', b', ∞) from current-output
        end for
      end if
    else
      q' ← state(keyword(i, j + 1))
      b' ← path-length + mingap(i, j + 1) + length(i, j + 1)
      e' ← path-length + maxgap(i, j + 1) + length(i, j + 1)
      insert (q', i, j + 1, b', e') into current-output
      push-onto-stack(inserted⟨q', i, j + 1, b', e'⟩)
      if e' = ∞ then
        for all (q'', i, j'', b'', ∞) ∈ current-output with j'' ≤ j do
          delete (q'', i, j'', b'', ∞) from current-output
          push-onto-stack(deleted⟨q'', i, j'', b'', ∞⟩)
        end for
      end if
    end if
  end for
  if q = initial-state then
    traversed ← true
  else
    q ← output-fail(q)
  end if
end while
```

Algorithm 4. Procedure *backtrack()*

```
pop the topmost element s from the stack
while s is not a state do
  if s is inserted⟨q, i, j, b, e⟩ then
    delete (q, i, j, b, e) from current-output
  else if s is deleted⟨q, i, j, b, e⟩ then
    insert (q, i, j, b, e) into current-output
  end if
  pop the topmost element s from the stack
end while
state ← s
```

relate the processing time to input length even though patterns are matched against tree paths. Some extra cost is due to maintaining the set *current-output*. Lemma 1 implies:

Lemma 2. The outermost **for** loop of Alg. 3 will be performed as many times as there are different occurrences of nonempty prefixes $P_{i,j}$ of pattern P_i, $j < m_i$, for all i. Moreover, for each iteration of the **while** loop, when performing the **for** loop of Alg. 3, the condition of the **for** loop will be tested unsuccessfully only once.

Output tuples (q, i, j, b, e) created in Alg. 3 become outdated when *path-length* advances beyond e, and should then be deleted. This is performed by the procedure *clean-current-output* (see Alg. 2). Also we have:

Lemma 3. After inserting tuple $(q', i, j+1, b', \infty)$ into the current output it is correct to delete all tuples of the form $(q'', i, j'', b'', \infty)$, where $j'' \leq j$.

Lemmas 1 and 3 imply:

Theorem 1. The multiple-pattern-matching algorithm given as Algs. 1–4 correctly reports all occurrences in the input document of all patterns P_i.

By Lemmas 1 and 2, and the discussion above we conclude:

Theorem 2. Excluding preprocessing that includes the construction of the Aho–Corasick PMA and only takes time linear in the total size of the patterns, the multiple-pattern-matching algorithm given in the previous section as Algs. 1–4 runs in time

$$O(K \times n + \log(L \times \#\mathit{keywords}) \times \mathit{occ}(\{P_{i,j} \mid i \geq 1, j \geq 1\})),$$

where n denotes the number of XML elements in the input document, K is the maximum number of proper suffixes of a keyword that are also keywords, and L is the depth of input document, that is, the maximum length of a path in the input document.

The logarithm term in the time bound of Theorem 2 is due to maintaining the binary trees as defined at the end of Sec. 3. The extreme worst case of the time bound occurs when all keywords that appear in the patterns are the same and all pattern prefixes match at every position in the input text. However, when the number of patterns is large we can safely assume that such a situation is very rare. If, on the contrary, $\#\mathit{keywords} = cN$, where N denotes the number of different keywords and c is a constant, the bound takes the form $O(Kn \times \log(L \times \#\mathit{keywords}))$.

5 Fast Backtracking

Our experiments have shown that in practice the tasks involved in backtracking the PMA constitute a performance bottleneck of our general algorithm presented in Sec. 3. The paths in XML documents tend to be quite short, so that backtracking happens often, and output tuples inserted into the current output and recorded into the backtracking stack are soon deleted from the current output because the path ends and backtracking must be performed.

We now present an organization for the current output tuples that allows for very fast backtracking. The current output set is stored in a *stack of blocks*, where each block is an array of $\#states$ entries, one for each state. The stack grows and shrinks in parallel with a stack used to store the states entered when reading start-element tags from the input document. The stack may grow up to a height of $maxdepth$ blocks, where $maxdepth$ is the length of the longest path in any input document in the stream. The block at height h stores the output tuples inserted when $h = \textit{path-length}$. Memory for the stack of blocks is allocated dynamically, so that $maxdepth$ need not be known beforehand. Backtracking now involves only popping a state from the stack of states and forgetting the topmost block of the stack of blocks of output tuples.

The stack of blocks is implemented as a single dynamically growing array *current-output* of at most $O(\#states \times maxdepth)$ entries, so that the index of the entry for state q in block h is obtained as $k = (h - 1) \times \#states + q$ (states q are numbered consecutively $1, 2, \ldots, \#states$). The array entry $\textit{current-output}[k]$ stores a tuple (t, d, v), where t is (a pointer to) a balanced binary search tree (a red-black tree) of output tuples (q, i, j, b, e) inserted into the current output when $\textit{path-length} = h$, $\textit{document-count} = d$, and $\textit{element-count} = v$. The binary search tree is indexed by the element positions b.

The pairs (d, v) act as version numbers of the entries in the array *current-output* and they relieve us from the need to deallocate an entire block when backtracking and from the need to reinitialize a block whose space is reused. When inserting a new output tuple (q, i, j, b, e) into the binary search tree t given in the entry $\textit{current-output}[k] = (t, d, v)$, we first check whether or not $d = \textit{document-count}$ and $v = \textit{element-count}$; if not, the entry contains outdated information and hence must be reinitialized: the tree rooted at t is forwarded to a garbage collector, t is initialized as empty, and d and v are set to the current values of *document-count* and *element-count*. When traversing an output path and finding out which output tuples for state q stored in block h match, we first check whether or not $d = \textit{document-count}$ and $v = \textit{element-count}$ for the entry in *current-output*; if so, the entry is current and the output tuples (q, i, j, b, e) stored in the search tree of the entry are checked for the condition $b \leq \textit{path-length} \leq e$.

The backtracking stack that in the algorithm of Sec. 3 contained, besides states pushed there when reading start-element tags, also logging information about output tuples inserted or deleted from the current output, is now reduced to a stack of pairs (q, v), where q is the state and d is the value of *element-count* that were current at the time the pair was pushed onto the stack.

A downside of this algorithm is that the current output for state q is now dispersed in h blocks, where h is *path-length*, the length of the current path. The traversal of the output path for a state involves searches on $h \times K$ different search trees, where K is the length of the output path. This means that the term $K \times n$ in the complexity bound stated in Theorem 2 is changed to $maxdepth \times K \times n$.

6 Experimental Analysis

We have implemented (in Java) various versions of our pattern-matching algorithm, including the one described in Sec. 5 and denoted by "PMA2" in Fig. 1. The performances of PMA2 and YFilter [10] were evaluated with sets of patterns generated for two publicly available data sets: the slightly recursive NASA data set [14] and the highly recursive NewsML [15] data set. We also experimented with the basic version of our algorithm described in Sec. 3, whose asymptotic complexity is lower than that of the PMA2 version, but as its performance turned out to be inferior to that of PMA2, we only report results for PMA2 here.

Workloads of 10 000 to 100 000 linear XPath patterns without predicates were generated using the XPath query generator described by Diao et al. [10], parameterized with the maximum depth of XPath patterns and with the probabilities of the occurrences of the descendant operator ($prob(//)$) and of the wildcard ($prob(*)$). For each pattern workload the maximum depth of XPath patterns was set to the depth of the XML input document, that is, 8 for the 23.8 MB NASA document and 10 for the 2.6 MB NewsML document. For 10 000 patterns, our PMA has 671 states in the case of NASA and 1576 states in the case of NewsML.

All our tests were run on a Dell PowerEdge SC430 server with 2.8 GHz Pentium 4 processor, 3 GB of main memory, and 1 MB of on-chip cache. The computer was running the Debian Linux 2.6.18 operating system with the Sun Java virtual machine 1.6.0_16 installed. In the tests the input document was read from the disk, but the overhead of the disk operations should be fairly small. The disk-read speed of the test hardware is more than 50 MB/sec. The throughput of the Java JAXP SAX parser (run in non-validating mode) on the input documents was 25–28 MB/sec.

Fig. 1 shows the running times of PMA2 and YFilter on the NASA and NewsML data sets for the filtering problem (that is, $\#maxmatches(i) = 1$ for each pattern P_i). The workloads of 10 000 to 100 000 linear XPath patterns without predicates were generated with $prob(*) = prob(//) = 0.2$. As is seen from the graphs, our algorithm clearly outperforms YFilter in the case of the

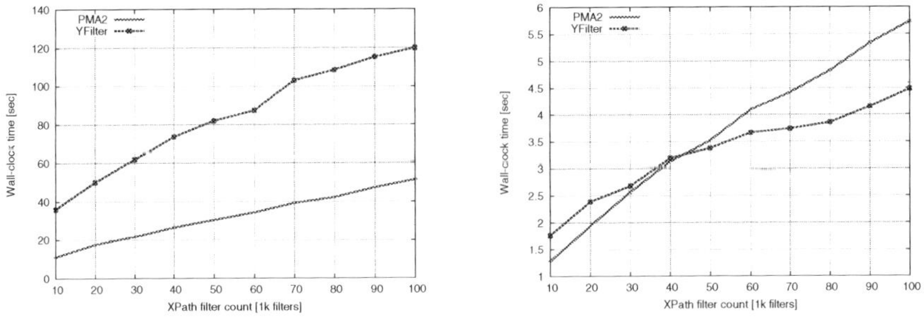

(a) NASA (b) NewsML

Fig. 1. Filtering times for two XML data sets

workloads for the slightly recursive NASA data set, but for NewsML workloads greater than 50 000 filters, our algorithm is slightly inferior to YFilter.

Besides these filtering tests we also run with our algorithm some tests in which all occurrences of all patterns were determined. Tests with the two data sets and with 10 000 or 20 000 patterns show that the running time of PMA2 is 5.7- to 6.2-fold for the NASA data and 1.7-fold for the NewsML data when compared to the time spent on determining only the first occurrences. When all the occurrences are stored, the space consumption is 290-fold and 7-fold, respectively. The high space consumption and speed degradation in the case of the NASA data set is mainly due to the great number of pattern occurrences.

7 Conclusion

Our main contribution is a new algorithm for online multiple-pattern matching of tree-structured text, where the patterns are given as path expressions composed of keywords and variable-length gaps. When applied to streams of XML documents, the patterns are linear XPath expressions without predicates, the keywords are maximal substrings of XML elements and child operators "/", and the gaps are maximal substrings of descendant operators "//" and wildcards "*".

Our algorithm is based on methodology previously applied to dictionary matching of linear text. We construct the Aho–Corasick pattern-matching automaton for the set of all keywords in the patterns, and we use this automaton for recognizing the occurrences of the keywords. From these we build occurrences of prefixes of patterns by checking that a candidate continuation of an already found prefix yields a new longer prefix, until an occurrence of a complete pattern is found. Our algorithm avoids recognizing occurrences of keywords that do not yield a proper continuation of any already found occurrence of a prefix of a pattern.

The use of the designed algorithm for matching patterns on paths of XML-document trees implies that a backtracking mechanism must be included, so that common prefixes of paths need not be traversed several time. However, worst-case-efficient backtracking, when tree paths are short as in typical XML documents, did not give good performance in practice. Therefore, we also designed a very simple backtracking strategy, which is not as good in the worst case, but allows for a considerable performance gain when tree paths remain short. We compared this simplified algorithm, when applied to filtering (in which only the first occurrences of the patterns are determined) with YFilter [10]. Our conclusion was that our method is better than YFilter, when the XML documents are not, as is usual in practice, deeply recursive.

Acknowledgement

The financial support of the Academy of Finland is gratefully acknowledged.

References

1. Cole, R., Gottlieb, L.A., Lewenstein, M.: Dictionary matching and indexing with errors and don't cares. In: Proc. of the 36th Annual ACM Symposium on Theory of Computing, pp. 90–100 (2004)
2. Fischer, M., Paterson, M.: String matching and other products. In: Proc. of the 7th SIAM-AMS Complexity of Computation, pp. 113–125 (1974)
3. Gusfield, D.: Algorithms on Strings, Trees, and Sequences. Cambridge University Press, Cambridge (1997)
4. Kucherov, G., Rusinowitch, M.: Matching a set of strings with variable length don't cares. Theor. Comput. Sci. 178, 129–154 (1997)
5. Navarro, G., Raffinot, M.: Flexible Pattern Matching in Strings. Cambridge University Press, Cambridge (2002)
6. Pinter, R.Y.: Efficient string matching. In: Apostolico, A., Galil, Z. (eds.) Combinatorial Algorithms on Words. NATO Advanced Science Institute Series F: Computer and System Sciences, vol. 12, pp. 11–29 (1985)
7. Aho, A.V., Corasick, M.J.: Efficient string matching: an aid to bibliographic search. Communcations of the ACM 18, 333–340 (1975)
8. Altinel, M., Franklin, M.J.: Efficient filtering of XML documents for selective dissemination of information. In: VLDB 2000, Proc. of 26th Internat. Conf. on Very Large Data Bases, pp. 53–64 (2000)
9. YFilter: Filtering and transformation for high-volume XML message brokering, Department of Computer Science, University of Massachusetts, Amherst, `http://yfilter.cs.umass.edu`
10. Diao, Y., Altinel, M., Franklin, M.J., Zhang, H., Fischer, P.M.: Path sharing and predicate evaluation for high-performance XML filtering. ACM Trans. Database Syst. 28, 467–516 (2003)
11. Green, T.J., Gupta, A., Miklau, G., Onizuka, M., Suciu, D.: Processing XML streams with deterministic automata and stream indexes. ACM Trans. Database Syst. 29, 752–788 (2004)
12. Silvasti, P., Sippu, S., Soisalon-Soininen, E.: Schema-conscious filtering of XML documents. In: EDBT 2009, Proc. of the 12th Internat. Conf. on Extending Database Technology, pp. 970–981 (2009)
13. Sax Project Organization: Simple API for XML (2001), `http://www.saxproject.org`
14. Suciu, D.: XML data repository. The Database Research Group, University of Washington (2006), `http://www.cs.washington.edu/research/xmldatasets/`
15. NewsML: News exchange format (International Press Telecommunications Council), `http://www.newsml.org`

The Duality of Computation under Focus

Pierre-Louis Curien[1] and Guillaume Munch-Maccagnoni[2]

[1] CNRS, Paris 7, and INRIA
[2] Paris 7, and INRIA

Abstract. We review the relationship between abstract machines for (call-by-name or call-by-value) λ-calculi (extended with Felleisen's $\mathcal{C}$) and sequent calculus, reintroducing on the way Curien-Herbelin's syntactic kit of the duality of computation. We provide a term language for a presentation of LK (with conjunction, disjunction, and negation), and we transcribe cut elimination as (non confluent) rewriting. A key slogan, which may appear here in print for the first time, is that commutative cut elimination rules are explicit substitution propagation rules. We then describe the focalised proof search discipline (in the classical setting), and narrow down the language and the rewriting rules to a confluent calculus (a variant of the second author's focalising system L). We then define a game of patterns and counterpatterns, leading us to a fully focalised finitary syntax for a synthetic presentation of classical logic, that provides a quotient on (focalised) proofs, abstracting out the order of decomposition of negative connectives.

1 Introduction

This paper on one hand has an expository purpose and on the other hand pushes further the syntactic investigations on the duality of computation undertaken in [3].

Section 2 discusses the relation between *abstract machines* for the λ-calculus (extended with control) and (classical) *sequent calculus*. Section 3 presents a language (with a one-to-one correspondence between well-typed terms and proof trees) for a version of LK in which we choose to give a dissymetric presentation for the conjunction on the left and for the disjunction on the right, anticipating a key ingredient of focalisation. We recall the non-confluence of unconstrained classical cut-elimination.

In Section 4, we present the *focalised proof search discipline* (for *classical logic*), and adapt the syntactic framework of Section 3 to get a confluent system whose normal forms are precisely the terms denoting (cut-free) focalised proofs. The system we arrive at from these proof-search motivations is (a variant of) the second author's *focalising system* L (L_{foc}) [19] We prove the completeness of L_{foc} with respect to LK for provability. In Section 5, we define some simple encodings having L_{foc} as source or target, indicating its suitability as an intermediate language.

Finally, in Section 6, further reinforcing of the focalisation discipline leads us to *synthetic system* L ($\mathsf{L}_{\text{synth}}$), a logic of synthetic connectives in the spirit of Girard's ludics and Zeilberger's CU, for which we offer a syntactic account based on a simple game of patterns and counterpatterns. We show that the synthetic system L is complete with respect to focalising system L.

Notation. We shall write $t\{v/x\}$ the result of substituting v for x at all (free) occurrences of x in t, and $t[v/x]$ for an explicit operator (as in [1]) added to the language together with rules propagating it.

C.S. Calude and V. Sassone (Eds.): TCS 2010, IFIP AICT 323, pp. 165–181, 2010.

2 Abstract Machines and Sequent Calculus

In this section, we would like to convey the idea that sequent calculus could have arisen from the goal of providing a typing system for the states of an abstract machine for the "mechanical evaluation of expressions" (to quote the title of Landin's pioneering [15]).

Here is Krivine machine, a simple device for call-by-name λ-calculus [13]:

$$\langle MN \mid E\rangle \to \langle M \mid N\cdot E\rangle \qquad \langle \lambda x.M \mid N\cdot E\rangle \to \langle M\{N/x\} \mid E\rangle$$

A state of the machine is thus a pair $\langle M \mid E\rangle$ where M is "where the computation is currently active", and E is the stack of things that are waiting to be done in the future, or the continuation, or the evaluation context. In λ-calculus litterature, contexts are more traditionally presented as terms with a hole: with this tradition, $\langle M \mid E\rangle$ (resp. $M \cdot E$) reads as $E[M]$ (resp. $E[[\,]M]$), or "fill the hole of E with M (resp. $[\,]M$)".

How can we type the components of this machine? We have three categories of terms and of typing judgements:

Expressions	Contexts	Commands
$M ::= x \mid \lambda x.M \mid MM$	$E ::= [\,] \mid M\cdot E$	$c ::= \langle M \mid E\rangle$
$(\Gamma \vdash M : A)$	$(\Gamma \mid E : A \vdash R)$	$c : (\Gamma \vdash R)$

where R is a (fixed) type of *final results*. The type of an expression (resp. a context) is the type of the value that it is producing (resp. expecting). The typing rules for contexts and commands are as follows:

$$\frac{}{\Gamma \mid [\,] : R \vdash R} \qquad \frac{\Gamma \vdash M : A \quad \Gamma \mid E : B \vdash R}{\Gamma \mid M\cdot E : A \to B \vdash R} \qquad \frac{\Gamma \vdash M : A \quad \Gamma \mid E : A \vdash R}{\langle M \mid E\rangle : (\Gamma \vdash R)}$$

and the typing rules for expressions are the usual ones for simply typed λ-calculus. Stripping up the term information, the second and third rules are rules of *sequent calculus* (left introduction of implication and cut).

We next review Griffin's typing of Felleisen's control operator $\mathcal{C}$. As a matter of fact, the behaviour of this constructor is best expressed at the level of an abstract machine:

$$\langle \mathcal{C}(M) \mid E\rangle \to \langle M \mid E^* \cdot [\,]\rangle \qquad \langle E^* \mid N\cdot E'\rangle \to \langle N \mid E\rangle$$

The first rule explains how the continuation E gets *captured*, and the second rule how it gets *restored*. Griffin [9] observed that the typing constraints induced by the well-typing of these four commands are met when $\mathcal{C}(M)$ and E^* are typed as follows:

$$\frac{\Gamma \vdash M : (A \to R) \to R}{\Gamma \vdash \mathcal{C}(M) : A} \qquad \frac{\Gamma \mid E : A \vdash R}{\Gamma \vdash E^* : A \to R}$$

These are the rules that one adds to intutionistic natural deduction to make it classical, if we interpret R as $\bot$ (false), and if we encode $\neg A$ as $A \to R$. Hence, Griffin got no less than Curry-Howard for classical logic! But how does this sound in sequent calculus style? In classical sequent calculus, sequents have several formulas on the right and $\Gamma \vdash \Delta$ reads as "if all formulas in Γ hold, then at least one formula of Δ holds".

Then it is natural to associate continuation variables with the formulas in Δ: a term will depend on its input variables, and on its output continuations. With this in mind, we can read the operational rule for $\mathcal{C}(M)$ as " $\mathcal{C}(M)$ is a map $E \mapsto \langle M \mid E^* \cdot [\,]\rangle$", and write it with a new binder (that comes from [23]): $\mathcal{C}(M) = \mu\beta.\langle M \mid \beta^* \cdot [\,]\rangle$, where $[\,]$ is now a continuation variable (of "top-level" type R). Likewise, we synthesise $E^* = \lambda x.\mu\alpha.\langle x \mid E\rangle$, with α, x fresh, from the operational rules for E^* and for $\lambda x.M$.

The typing judgements are now: $(\Gamma \vdash M : A \mid \Delta)$, $(\Gamma \mid E : A \vdash \Delta)$, $c : (\Gamma \vdash \Delta)$. The two relevant new typing rules are (axiom, right *activation*):

$$\frac{}{\Gamma \mid \alpha : A \vdash \alpha : A, \Delta} \qquad \frac{c : (\Gamma \vdash \alpha : A, \Delta)}{\Gamma \vdash \mu\alpha.c : A \mid \Delta}$$

plus a reduction rule: $\langle \mu\alpha.c \mid E\rangle \to c\{E/\alpha\}$.

Note that in this setting, there is no more need to "reify" a context E into an expression E^*, as it can be directly substituted for a continuation variable.

Similarly, we can read off a (call-by-name) definition of MN from its operational rule: $MN = \mu\beta.\langle M \mid N.\beta\rangle$. Hence we can remove application from the syntax and arrive at a system in sequent calculus style *only* (no more elimination rule). This yields Herbelin's $\overline{\lambda}\mu$-calculus [10]:

Expressions	Contexts	Commands
$M ::= x \mid \lambda x.M \mid \mu\alpha.c$	$E ::= \alpha \mid M \cdot E$	$c ::= \langle M \mid E\rangle$

which combines the first two milestones above: "sequent calculus", "classical".

Let us step back to the λ-calculus. The following describes a call-by-value version of Krivine machine:

$$\langle MN \mid e\rangle \to \langle N \mid M \odot e\rangle \qquad \langle V \mid M \odot e\rangle \to \langle M \mid V \cdot e\rangle$$

(the operational rule for $\lambda x.M$ is unchanged)[1]. Here, V is a *value*, defined as being either a variable or an abstraction (this goes back to [24]). Again, we can read $M \odot e$ as "a map $V \mapsto \langle M \mid V \cdot e\rangle$", or, introducing a new binder $\tilde{\mu}$ (binding now ordinary variables): $M \odot e = \tilde{\mu}x.\langle M \mid x \cdot e\rangle$. The typing rule for this operator is (left activation): $\dfrac{c : (\Gamma, x : A \vdash \Delta)}{\Gamma \mid \tilde{\mu}x.c : A \vdash \Delta}$, and the operational rule is $\langle V \mid \tilde{\mu}x.c\rangle \to c\{V/x\}$ (V value).

Finally, we get from the rule for MN a call-by-value definition of application: $MN = \mu\alpha.\big\langle N \,\big|\, \tilde{\mu}x.\langle M \mid x \cdot \alpha\rangle\big\rangle$.

We have arrived at Curien and Herbelin's $\overline{\lambda}\mu\tilde{\mu}_Q$-calculus [3]:

Expressions	Values	Contexts	Commands
$M ::= V^\diamond \mid \mu\alpha.c$	$V ::= x \mid \lambda x.M$	$e ::= \alpha \mid V \cdot e \mid \tilde{\mu}x.c$	$c ::= \langle M \mid e\rangle$
$\Gamma \vdash M : A \mid \Delta$	$\Gamma \vdash V : A\,;\,\Delta$	$\Gamma \mid e : A \vdash \Delta$	$c : (\Gamma \vdash \Delta)$

with a new judgement for values (more on this later) and an explicit coercion from values to expressions. The syntax for contexts is both extended ($\tilde{\mu}x.c$) and restricted ($V \cdot e$ instead of $M \cdot e$). The reduction rules are as follows:

$$\begin{array}{l} \langle (\lambda x.M)^\diamond \mid V \cdot e\rangle \to \langle M\{V/x\} \mid e\rangle \\ \langle \mu\alpha.c \mid e\rangle \to c\{e/\alpha\} \qquad \langle V^\diamond \mid \tilde{\mu}x.c\rangle \to c\{V/x\} \end{array}$$

[1] The reason for switching notation from E to e will become clear in Section 5.

3 A Language for LK Proofs

In this section, we use some of the kit of the previous section to give a term language for classical sequent calculus LK, with negation, conjunction, and disjunction as connectives. Our term language is as follows:

$$\begin{array}{ll}\text{Commands} & c ::= \langle x \,|\, \alpha\rangle \mid \langle v \,|\, \alpha\rangle \mid \langle x \,|\, e\rangle \mid \langle \mu\alpha.c \,|\, \tilde{\mu}x.c\rangle \\ \text{Expressions} & v ::= (\tilde{\mu}x.c)^{\bullet} \mid (\mu\alpha.c, \mu\alpha.c) \mid inl(\mu\alpha.c) \mid inr(\mu\alpha.c) \\ \text{Contexts} & e ::= \tilde{\mu}\alpha^{\bullet}.c \mid \tilde{\mu}(x_1, x_2).c \mid \tilde{\mu}[inl(x_1).c_1|inr(x_2).c_2]\end{array}$$

(In $\langle v \,|\, \alpha\rangle$ (resp. $\langle x \,|\, e\rangle$), we suppose α (resp. x) fresh for v (resp. e).) A *term* t is a command, an expression, or a context. As in section 2, we have three kinds of sequents: $(\Gamma \vdash \Delta)$, $(\Gamma \vdash A \,|\, \Delta)$, and $(\Gamma \,|\, A \vdash \Delta)$. We decorate LK's inference rules with terms, yielding the following typing system (one term construction for each rule of LK):

(axiom and cut/contraction)

$$\frac{}{\langle x \,|\, \alpha\rangle : (\Gamma, x : A \vdash \alpha : A, \Delta)} \qquad \frac{c : (\Gamma \vdash \alpha : A, \Delta) \qquad d : (\Gamma, x : A \vdash \Delta)}{\langle \mu\alpha.c \,|\, \tilde{\mu}x.d\rangle : (\Gamma \vdash \Delta)}$$

(right)

$$\frac{c : (\Gamma, x : A \vdash \Delta)}{\Gamma \vdash (\tilde{\mu}x.c)^{\bullet} : \neg A \,|\, \Delta} \qquad \frac{c_1 : (\Gamma \vdash \alpha_1 : A_1, \Delta) \qquad c_2 : (\Gamma \vdash \alpha_2 : A_2, \Delta)}{\Gamma \vdash (\mu\alpha_1.c_1, \mu\alpha_2.c_2) : A_1 \wedge A_2 \,|\, \Delta}$$

$$\frac{c_1 : (\Gamma \vdash \alpha_1 : A_1, \Delta)}{\Gamma \vdash inl(\mu\alpha_1.c_1) : A_1 \vee A_2 \,|\, \Delta} \qquad \frac{c_2 : (\Gamma \vdash \alpha_2 : A_2, \Delta)}{\Gamma \vdash inr(\mu\alpha_2.c_2) : A_1 \vee A_2 \,|\, \Delta}$$

(left)

$$\frac{c : (\Gamma \vdash \alpha : A, \Delta)}{\Gamma \,|\, \tilde{\mu}\alpha^{\bullet}.c : \neg A \vdash \Delta} \qquad \frac{c : (\Gamma, x_1 : A_1, x_2 : A_2 \vdash \Delta)}{\Gamma \,|\, \tilde{\mu}(x_1, x_2).c : A_1 \wedge A_2 \vdash \Delta}$$

$$\frac{c_1 : (\Gamma, x_1 : A_1 \vdash \Delta) \qquad c_2 : (\Gamma, x_2 : A_2 \vdash \Delta)}{\Gamma \,|\, \tilde{\mu}[inl(x_1).c_1|inr(x_2).c_2] : A_1 \vee A_2 \vdash \Delta}$$

(deactivation)

$$\frac{\Gamma \vdash v : A \,|\, \Delta}{\langle v \,|\, \alpha\rangle : (\Gamma \vdash \alpha : A, \Delta)} \qquad \frac{\Gamma \,|\, e : A \vdash \Delta}{\langle x \,|\, e\rangle : (\Gamma, x : A \vdash \Delta)}$$

Note that the activation rules are packaged in the introduction rules and in the cut rule. As for the underlying sequent calculus rules, we have made the following choices:

1. We have preferred *additive* formulations for the cut rule and for the right introduction of conjunction (to stay in tune with the tradition of typed λ-calculi) over a multiplicative one where the three occurrences of Γ would be resp. Γ_1, Γ_2, and (Γ_1, Γ_2) (idem for Δ). An important consequence of this choice is that contraction is a derived rule of our system, whence the name of *cut/contraction* rule above[2]:

$$\frac{\overline{\Gamma, A \vdash A, \Delta} \qquad \Gamma, A, A \vdash \Delta}{\Gamma, A \vdash \Delta} \qquad \frac{\Gamma \vdash A, A, \Delta \qquad \overline{\Gamma, A \vdash A, \Delta}}{\Gamma \vdash A, \Delta}$$

[2] In usual syntactic accounts of contraction, one says that if, say t denotes a proof of $\Gamma, x : A, y : A \vdash \Delta$, then $t[z/x, z/y]$ denotes a proof of $\Gamma, z : A \vdash \Delta$. Note that if this substitution is explicit, then we are back to an overloading of cut and contraction.

2. Still in the λ-calculus tradition, weakening is "transparent". If $c : \Gamma \vdash \Delta$ is well-typed, then $c : (\Gamma, \Gamma' \vdash \Delta, \Delta')$ is well-typed (idem v, e). (Also, we recall that all free variables of c are among the ones declared in Γ, Δ.)
3. More importantly, we have adopted *irreversible* rules for right introduction of disjunction. On the other hand, we have given a *reversible* rule for left introduction of conjunction: the premise is derivable from the conclusion. *This choice prepares the ground for the next section on focalisation.*[3]

The relation between our typed terms and LK proofs is as follows.
- Every typing proof induces a proof tree of LK (one erases variables naming assumptions and conclusions, terms, the distinction between the three kinds of sequents, and the application of the deactivation rules).
- If bound variables are explicitly typed (which we shall refrain from doing in the sequel), then every provable typing judgement, say $\Gamma \,|\, e : A \vdash \Delta$, has a unique typing proof, i.e. all information is in Γ, A, Δ, e.
- If Π is an LK proof tree of $(A_1, \ldots, A_m \vdash B_1, \ldots, B_n)$, and if names $x_1, \ldots, x_m$, $\alpha_1, \ldots, \alpha_n$ are provided, then there exists a unique command $c : (x_1 : A_1, \ldots, x_m : A_m \vdash \alpha_1 : B_1, \ldots, \alpha_n : B_n)$, whose (unique) typing proof gives back Π by erasing.

With this syntax, we can express the cut-elimination rules of LK as *rewriting rules*:
Logical rules (redexes of the form $\langle \mu\alpha.\langle v \,|\, \alpha\rangle \,|\, \tilde{\mu}x.\langle x \,|\, e\rangle\rangle$):

$\langle \mu\alpha.\langle (\tilde{\mu}x.c)^\bullet \,|\, \alpha\rangle \,|\, \tilde{\mu}y.\langle y \,|\, \tilde{\mu}\alpha^\bullet.d\rangle\rangle \rightarrow \langle \mu\alpha.d \,|\, \tilde{\mu}x.c\rangle$
(similar rules for conjunction and disjunction)

Commutative rules (going "up left", redexes of the form $\langle \mu\alpha.\langle v \,|\, \beta\rangle \,|\, \tilde{\mu}x.c\rangle$):

$\langle \mu\alpha.\langle (\tilde{\mu}y.c)^\bullet \,|\, \beta\rangle \,|\, \tilde{\mu}x.d\rangle \rightarrow \left\langle \mu\beta'.\langle (\tilde{\mu}y.\langle \mu\alpha.c \,|\, \tilde{\mu}x.d\rangle)^\bullet \,|\, \beta'\rangle \,\middle|\, \tilde{\mu}y.\langle y \,|\, \beta\rangle \right\rangle$ ($\neg$ right)
(similar rules with the other right introduction rules and with the left introduction rules)

$\left\langle \mu\alpha.\langle \mu\beta.\langle y \,|\, \beta\rangle \,|\, \tilde{\mu}y'.c\rangle \,\middle|\, \tilde{\mu}x.d\right\rangle \rightarrow \langle \mu\beta.\langle y \,|\, \beta\rangle \,|\, \tilde{\mu}y'.\langle \mu\alpha.c \,|\, \tilde{\mu}x.d\rangle\rangle$ (contraction right)

$\left\langle \mu\alpha.\langle \mu\beta'.c \,|\, \tilde{\mu}y.\langle y \,|\, \beta\rangle\rangle \,\middle|\, \tilde{\mu}x.d\right\rangle \rightarrow \langle \mu\beta'.\langle \mu\alpha.c \,|\, \tilde{\mu}x.d\rangle \,|\, \tilde{\mu}y.\langle y \,|\, \beta\rangle\rangle$ (contraction left)

$\left\langle \mu\alpha.\left\langle \mu\alpha'.c \,\middle|\, \tilde{\mu}x'.\langle x' \,|\, \alpha\rangle\right\rangle \,\middle|\, \tilde{\mu}x.d\right\rangle \rightarrow \left\langle \mu\alpha.\langle \mu\alpha'.c \,|\, \tilde{\mu}x.d\rangle \,\middle|\, \tilde{\mu}x.d\right\rangle$ (duplication)

$\langle \mu\alpha.\langle y \,|\, \beta\rangle \,|\, \tilde{\mu}x.d\rangle \rightarrow \langle y \,|\, \beta\rangle$ (erasing)

Commutative rules (going "up right", redexes of the form $\langle \mu\alpha.c \,|\, \tilde{\mu}x.\langle y \,|\, e\rangle\rangle$): similar.

The (only?) merit of this syntax is its tight fit with proof trees and traditional cut elimination defined as transformations of undecorated proof trees. If we accept to losen this, we arrive at the following more "atomic" syntax:

Commands	$c ::= \langle v \,|\, e\rangle \,\big|\, c[\sigma]$
Expressions	$v ::= x \,\big|\, \mu\alpha.c \,\big|\, e^\bullet \,\big|\, (v, v) \,\big|\, inl(v) \,\big|\, inr(v) \,\big|\, v[\sigma]$
Contexts	$e ::= \alpha \,\big|\, \tilde{\mu}x.c \,\big|\, \tilde{\mu}\alpha^\bullet.c \,\big|\, \tilde{\mu}(x_1, x_2).c \,\big|\, \tilde{\mu}[inl(x_1).c_1 \,|\, inr(x_2).c_2] \,\big|\, e[\sigma]$

where σ is a list $v_1/x_1, \ldots, v_m/x_m, e_1/\alpha_1, \ldots, e_n/\alpha_n$. In this syntax, activation becomes "first class", and two versions of the axiom are now present (x, α, which give back the axiom of the previous syntax by deactivation). The typing rules are as follows

[3] For the same reason, we have three connectives instead of just, say, $\vee$ and $\neg$, because in the focalised setting $\neg(\neg A \vee \neg B)$ is only equivalent to $A \wedge B$ at the level of *provavility*.

(we omit the rules for $\tilde{\mu}x.c$, $\tilde{\mu}\alpha^\bullet.c$, $\tilde{\mu}(x_1,x_2).c$, $\tilde{\mu}[inl(x_1).c_1|inr(x_2).c_2]$, which are unchanged):

$$\frac{}{\Gamma\,,\,x:A\vdash x:A\,|\,\Delta}\qquad\frac{}{\Gamma\,|\,\alpha:A\vdash\alpha:A\,,\,\Delta}\qquad\frac{\Gamma\vdash v:A\,|\,\Delta\qquad\Gamma\,|\,e:A\vdash\Delta}{\langle v\,|\,e\rangle:(\Gamma\vdash\Delta)}$$

$$\frac{c:(\Gamma\,,\,x:A\vdash\Delta)}{\Gamma\,|\,\tilde{\mu}x.c:A\vdash\Delta}\qquad\frac{c:(\Gamma\vdash\alpha:A\,,\,\Delta)}{\Gamma\vdash\mu\alpha.c:A\,|\,\Delta}$$

$$\frac{\Gamma\,|\,e:A\vdash\Delta}{\Gamma\vdash e^\bullet:\neg A\,|\,\Delta}\qquad\frac{\Gamma\vdash v_1:A_1\,|\,\Delta\qquad\Gamma\vdash v_2:A_2\,|\,\Delta}{\Gamma\vdash(v_1,v_2):A_1\wedge A_2\,|\,\Delta}$$

$$\frac{\Gamma\vdash v_1:A_1\,|\,\Delta}{\Gamma\vdash inl(v_1):A_1\vee A_2\,|\,\Delta}\qquad\frac{\Gamma\vdash v_2:A_2\,|\,\Delta}{\Gamma\vdash inr(v_2):A_1\vee A_2\,|\,\Delta}$$

$$\frac{\begin{array}{c}c:(\Gamma,x_1:A_1,\ldots,x_m:A_m\vdash\alpha_1:B_1,\ldots,\alpha_n:B_n)\\ \ldots\;\Gamma\vdash v_i:A_i\,|\,\Delta\Gamma\,|\,e_j:B_j\vdash\Delta\;\ldots\end{array}}{c[v_1/x_1,\ldots,v_m/x_m,e_1/\alpha_1,\ldots,e_n/\alpha_n]:(\Gamma\vdash\Delta)}\quad(\text{idem } v[\sigma],e[\sigma])$$

Note that we have now *explicit substitutions* $t[\sigma]$, which feature a form of (multi-)cut where the receiver t's active formula, if any, is not among the cut formulas, in contrast with the construct $\langle v\,|\,e\rangle$ where the cut formula is active on both sides.

It is still the case that, by erasing, a well-typed term of this new syntax induces a proof of LK, and that all proofs of LK are reached (although not injectively anymore), since all terms of the previous syntax are terms of the new syntax. The rewriting rules divide now in *three* groups:

$$\begin{array}{ll}
(\text{control}) & \langle\mu\alpha.c\,|\,e\rangle\to c[e/\alpha]\qquad\langle v\,|\,\tilde{\mu}x.c\rangle\to c[v/x]\\
(\text{logical}) & \langle e^\bullet\,|\,\tilde{\mu}\alpha^\bullet.c\rangle\to c[e/\alpha]\quad\langle(v_1,v_2)\,|\,\tilde{\mu}(x_1,x_2).c\rangle\to c[v_1/x_1,v_2/x_2]\\
 & \langle inl(v_1)\,|\,\tilde{\mu}[inl(x_1).c_1|inr(x_2).c_2]\rangle\to c_1[v_1/x_1]\quad(\text{idem } inr)\\
(\text{commutation}) & \langle v\,|\,e\rangle[\sigma]\to\langle v[\sigma]\,|\,e[\sigma]\rangle\\
 & x[\sigma]\to x\;\;(x\text{ not declared in }\sigma)\qquad x[v/x,\sigma]\to v\quad(\text{idem }\alpha[\sigma])\\
 & (\mu\alpha.c)[\sigma]\to\mu\alpha.(c[\sigma])\quad(\text{idem }(\tilde{\mu}x.c)[\sigma])\quad(\text{capture avoiding})\\
 & (\text{etc, no rule for composing substitutions})
\end{array}$$

The *control rules* mark the decision to launch a substitution (and, in this section, of the direction in which to go, see below). The *logical rules* provide the interesting cases of cut elimination, corresponding to cuts where the active formula has been just introduced on both sides. The *commutative cuts* are now accounted for "trivially" by means of the *explicit substitution machinery* that carries substitution progressively inside terms towards their variable occurrences. Summarising, by liberalising the syntax, we have gained considerably in readability of the cut elimination rules[4].

Remark 1. In the "atomic" syntax, contractions are transcribed as terms of the form $\langle v\,|\,\beta\rangle$ (resp. $\langle x\,|\,e\rangle$) where β (resp. x) occurs free in v (resp. e). If β (resp. x) does not occur free in v (resp. e), then the command expresses a simple deactivation.

[4] The precise relation with the previous rules is as follows: for all s_1, s_2 such that $s_1 \to s_2$ in the first system, there exists s such that $s_1 \to^* s$ and $s_2 \to^* s$ in the new system.

The problem with classical logic viewed as a computational system is its wild non confluence, as captured by Lafont's critical pair [6,4], for which the $\mu\tilde{\mu}$ kit offers a crisp formulation. For any c_1, c_2 both of type $(\Gamma \vdash \Delta)$, we have (with α, x fresh for c_1, c_2, respectively): $c_1 \;{}^*\!\!\leftarrow\; \langle \mu\alpha.c_1 \,|\, \tilde{\mu}x.c_2 \rangle \;\rightarrow^*\; c_2$. So, all proofs are identified... *Focalisation*, discussed in the next section, will guide us to solve this dilemma.

4 A Syntax for Focalised Classical Logic

We adapt the *focalisation discipline* (originally introduced by [2] in the setting of linear logic) to LK. A focalised proof search alternates between right and left phases:

- *Left phase*: Decompose (copies of) formulas on the left, in any order. Every decomposition of a negation on the left feeds the right part of the sequent. At any moment, one can change the phase from left to right.

- *Right phase*: Choose a formula A on the right, and *hereditarily* decompose a copy of it in all branches of the proof search. This *focusing* in any branch can only end with an axiom (which ends the proof search in that branch), or with a decomposition of a negation, which prompts a phase change back to the left. Etc...

Note the irreversible (or *positive, active*) character of the whole right phase, by the choice of A, by the choice of the left or right summand of a disjunction. One takes the risk of not being able to eventually end a proof search branch with an axiom. In contrast, all the choices on the left are reversible (or *negative, passive*). This strategy is not only complete (see below), it also guides us to design a disciplined logic whose behaviour will not collapse all the proofs.

To account for right focalisation, we introduce a fourth kind of judgement and a fourth syntactic category of terms: the *values*, typed as $(\Gamma \vdash V : A\,;\, \Delta)$ (the zone between the turnstyle and the semicolon is called the *stoup*, after [7]). We also make official the existence of two disjunctions (since the behaviours of the conjunction on the left and of the disjunction on the right are different) and two conjunctions, by renaming $\wedge, \vee, \neg$ as $\otimes, \oplus, \neg^+$, respectively. Of course, this choice of linear logic like notation is not fortuitous. Note however that the source of distinction is not based here on the use of resources like in the founding work on linear logic, which divides the line between *additive* and *multiplicative* connectives. In contrast, our motivating dividing line here is that between *irreversible* and *reversible* connectives, and hopefully this provides additional motivation for the two conjunctions and the two disjunctions. Our formulas are thus defined by the following syntax:

$$P ::= X \mid P \otimes P \mid P \oplus P \mid \neg^+ P$$

These formulas are called positive. We can define their De Morgan duals as follows:

$$\overline{P_1 \otimes P_2} = \overline{P_1} \parr \overline{P_2} \qquad \overline{P_1 \oplus P_2} = \overline{P_1} \& \overline{P_2} \qquad \overline{\neg^+ P} = \neg^- \overline{P}$$

These duals are *negative* formulas: $N ::= \overline{X} \mid N \parr N \mid N \& N \mid \neg^- N$. They restore the duality of connectives, and are implicit in the presentation that follows (think of P on the left as being a $\overline{P}$ in a unilateral sequent $\vdash \overline{\Gamma}, \Delta$).

$$\frac{}{\Gamma\,,\,x:P\vdash x:P\,;\,\Delta}\qquad\frac{}{\Gamma\,|\,\alpha:P\vdash\alpha:P\,,\,\Delta}\qquad\frac{\Gamma\vdash v:P\,|\,\Delta\qquad\Gamma\,|\,e:P\vdash\Delta}{\langle v\,|\,e\rangle:(\Gamma\vdash\Delta)}$$

$$\frac{c:(\Gamma\,,\,x:P\vdash\Delta)}{\Gamma\,|\,\tilde{\mu}x.c:P\vdash\Delta}\qquad\frac{c:(\Gamma\vdash\alpha:P\,,\,\Delta)}{\Gamma\vdash\mu\alpha.c:P\,|\,\Delta}\qquad\frac{\Gamma\vdash V:P\,;\,\Delta}{\Gamma\vdash V^{\diamond}:P\,|\,\Delta}$$

$$\frac{\Gamma\,|\,e:P\vdash\Delta}{\Gamma\vdash e^{\bullet}:\neg^{+}P\,;\,\Delta}\qquad\frac{\Gamma\vdash V_1:P_1\,;\,\Delta\qquad\Gamma\vdash V_2:P_2\,;\,\Delta}{\Gamma\vdash(V_1,V_2):P_1\otimes P_2\,;\,\Delta}\qquad\frac{\Gamma\vdash V_1:P_1\,;\,\Delta}{\Gamma\vdash inl(V_1):P_1\oplus P_2\,;\,\Delta}$$

$$\frac{c:(\Gamma\vdash\alpha:P,\Delta)}{\Gamma\,|\,\tilde{\mu}\alpha^{\bullet}.c:\neg^{+}P\vdash\Delta}\qquad\frac{c:(\Gamma,x_1:P_1,x_2:P_2\vdash\Delta)}{\Gamma\,|\,\tilde{\mu}(x_1,x_2).c:P_1\otimes P_2\vdash\Delta}$$
$$\frac{c_1:(\Gamma,x_1:P_1\vdash\Delta)\qquad c_2:(\Gamma,x_2:P_2\vdash\Delta)}{\Gamma\,|\,\tilde{\mu}[inl(x_1).c_1|inr(x_2).c_2]:P_1\oplus P_2\vdash\Delta}$$

$$\frac{c:(\Gamma\,\ldots,q:P,\ldots\vdash\Delta,\ldots,\alpha:Q,\ldots)\qquad\ldots\quad\Gamma\vdash V:P\,;\,\Delta\quad\ldots\quad\Gamma\,|\,e:Q\vdash\Delta\quad\ldots}{c[\ldots,V/q,\ldots,e/\alpha]:(\Gamma\vdash\Delta)}\qquad(\text{idem } v[\sigma],V[\sigma],e[\sigma])$$

Fig. 1. System LKQ

We are now ready to give the syntax of our calculus, which is a variant of the one given by the second author in [19][5].

Commands	$c ::= \langle v\,|\,e\rangle \mid c[\sigma]$
Expressions	$v ::= V^{\diamond} \mid \mu\alpha.c \mid v[\sigma]$
Values	$V ::= x \mid (V,V) \mid inl(V) \mid inr(V) \mid e^{\bullet} \mid V[\sigma]$
Contexts	$e ::= \alpha \mid \tilde{\mu}x.c \mid \tilde{\mu}\alpha^{\bullet}.c \mid \tilde{\mu}(x_1,x_2).c \mid \tilde{\mu}[inl(x_1).c_1|inr(x_2).c_2] \mid e[\sigma]$

The typing rules are given in Figure 1. Henceforth, we shall refer to the calculus of this section (syntax + rewriting rules) as L_{foc}, and to the typing system as LKQ (after [4]). Here are examples of proof terms in LKQ.

Example 1. $(\vdash\ (\tilde{\mu}(x,\alpha^{\bullet}).\langle x^{\diamond}\,|\,\alpha\rangle)^{\bullet}\ :\ \neg^{+}(P\otimes\neg^{+}P)\,;)$, where $\tilde{\mu}(x,\alpha^{\bullet}).c$ is an abbreviation for $\tilde{\mu}(x,y).\langle y^{\diamond}\,|\,\tilde{\mu}\alpha^{\bullet}.c\rangle$.
$\langle inr((\tilde{\mu}x.\langle inl(x)^{\diamond}\,|\,\alpha\rangle)^{\bullet})^{\diamond}\,|\,\alpha\rangle : (\vdash\alpha:P\oplus\neg^{+}P)$.
$(\,|\,\tilde{\mu}(x_2,x_1).\langle(x_1,x_2)^{\diamond}\,|\,\alpha\rangle : P_2\otimes P_1\vdash\alpha:P_1\otimes P_2)$.

Proposition 1. *If $\Gamma\vdash\Delta$ is provable in* LK, *then it is provable in* LKQ.

[5] The main differences with the system presented in [19] is that we have here an explicit syntax of values, with an associated form of typing judgement, while focalisation is dealt with at the level of the reduction semantics in [19]. Also, the present system is bilateral but limited to positive formulas on both sides, it thus corresponds to the positive fragment of the bilateral version of L_{foc} as presented in [19][long version, Appendix A].

(control)	$\langle \mu\alpha.c \,\vert\, e\rangle \to c[e/\alpha]$	$\langle V^\diamond \,\vert\, \tilde\mu x.c\rangle \to c[V/x]$
(logical)	$\langle (e^\bullet)^\diamond \,\vert\, \tilde\mu\alpha^\bullet.c\rangle \to c[e/\alpha]$	$\langle (V_1,V_2)^\diamond \,\vert\, \tilde\mu(x_1,x_2).c\rangle \to c[V_1/x_1, V_2/x_2]$
	$\langle \mathit{inl}(V_1)^\diamond \,\vert\, \tilde\mu[\mathit{inl}(x_1).c_1 \vert \mathit{inr}(x_2).c_2]\rangle \to c_1[V_1/x_1]$	(idem inr)
(commutation)	$\langle v \,\vert\, e\rangle[\sigma] \to \langle v[\sigma] \,\vert\, e[\sigma]\rangle$ etc...	

Fig. 2. Cut eliminition in L_{foc}

PROOF. We translate the syntax given in section 3 into the focalised one. All cases are obvious except for the introduction of $\otimes$ and $\oplus$ on the right. We define $(\mu\alpha_1.c_1, \mu\alpha_2.c_2)$ as $(\Gamma \vdash \mu\alpha.\left\langle \mu\alpha_2.c_2 \,\middle\vert\, \tilde\mu x_2.\langle \mu\alpha_1.c_1 \,\vert\, \tilde\mu x_1.\langle (x_1,x_2)^\diamond \,\vert\, \alpha\rangle\rangle\right\rangle : P_1 \otimes P_2 \,\vert\, \Delta)$. □

We make two observations on the translation involved in the proof of Proposition 1.

Remark 2. The translation *introduces cuts*: in particular, a cut-free proof is translated to a proof with cuts. It also *fixes an order of evaluation*: one should read the translation of right and introduction as a protocol prescribing the evaluation of the second element of a pair and then of the first (the pair is thus in particular *strict*, as observed independently in [27] and [19]). An equally reasonable choice would have been to permute the two $\tilde\mu$s: that would have encoded a left-to-right order of evaluation. This non-determinism of the translation has been known ever since Girard's seminal work [7].

We move on to cut elimination, which (cf. Section 3) is expressed by means of three sets of rewriting rules, given in Figure 2. Note that we now have only one way to reduce $\langle \mu\alpha.c_1 \,\vert\, \tilde\mu x.c_2\rangle$ (no more critical pair). As already stressed in Section 3), the commutation rules are the usual rules defining (capture-avoiding) substitution. The overall operational semantics features call-by-value by the fact that variables x receive values, and features also call-by-name (through symmetry, see the logic LKT in Section 5) by the fact that continuation variables α receive contexts.

The reduction system presented in Figure 2 is *confluent*, as it is an orthogonal system in the sense of higher-order rewriting systems (left-linear rules, no critical pairs) [21].

Remark 3. About μ: we note that $\mu\beta.c$ is used only in a command $\langle \mu\beta.c \,\vert\, e\rangle$, and in such a context it can be expressed as $\langle (e^\bullet)^\diamond \,\vert\, \tilde\mu\beta^\bullet.c\rangle$, which indeed reduces to $c[e/\beta]$. However, using such an encoding would mean to shift from a direct to an indirect style for terms of the form $\mu\beta.c$.

Proposition 2. *Cut-elimination holds in* LKQ.

PROOF. This is an easy consequence of the following three properties:

1) *Subject reduction.* This is checked as usual rule by rule.

2) *Weak normalisation.* As for LK, or for simply typed λ-calculus.

3) *Characterisation of normal forms.* A command in normal form has one of the following shapes (all contractions):

$$\langle V^\diamond \,\vert\, \alpha\rangle \quad \langle x^\diamond \,\vert\, \tilde\mu\alpha^\bullet.c\rangle \quad \langle x^\diamond \,\vert\, \tilde\mu(x_1,x_2).c\rangle \quad \langle x^\diamond \,\vert\, \tilde\mu[\mathit{inl}(x_1).c_1 \vert \mathit{inr}(x_2).c_2]\rangle$$ □

Corollary 1. *Every sequent $\Gamma \vdash \Delta$ that is provable in* LK *admits a (cut-free) proof respecting the focalised discipline.*

PROOF. Let π be a proof of $\Gamma \vdash \Delta$. By Propositions 1 and 2, one obtains a term denoting a focalised, cut-free proof of $\Gamma \vdash \Delta$. □

We can add η-equivalences (or expansion rules, when read from right to left) to the system, as follows (where all mentioned variables are fresh for the mentioned terms):

$$\begin{array}{ll} \mu\alpha.\langle v \,|\, \alpha\rangle = v & \tilde{\mu}(x_1,x_2).\langle (x_1,x_2)^\diamond \,|\, e\rangle = e \\ \tilde{\mu}x.\langle x^\diamond \,|\, e\rangle = e & \tilde{\mu}[inl(x_1).\langle inl(x_1)^\diamond \,|\, e\rangle | inr(x_2).\langle inr(x_2)^\diamond \,|\, e\rangle] = e \\ & \tilde{\mu}\alpha^\bullet\langle(\alpha^\bullet)^\diamond \,|\, e\rangle = e \end{array}$$

The rules on the left column allow us to cancel a deactivation followed by an activation (the control rules do the job for the sequence in the reverse order), while the rules in the right column express the reversibility of the negative rules.

We end the section with a lemma that will be useful in Section 6.

Lemma 1. – *If $\Gamma, x : \neg^+ P \,|\, e : Q \vdash \Delta$, then $\Gamma \,|\, e\{\alpha^\bullet/x\} : Q \vdash \alpha : P, \Delta$.*
– *If $\Gamma, x : P_1 \otimes P_2 \,|\, e : Q \vdash \Delta$, then $\Gamma, x_1 : P_1, x_2 : P_2 \,|\, e\{(x_1,x_2)/x\} : Q \vdash \Delta$.*
– *If $\Gamma, x : P_1 \oplus P_2 \,|\, e : Q \vdash \Delta$, then $\Gamma, x_1 : P_1 \,|\, e\{inl(x_1)/x\} : Q \vdash \Delta$ and $\Gamma, x_2 : P_2 \,|\, e\{inr(x_2)/x\} : Q \vdash \Delta$.*
(and similarly for c, V, v).

5 Encodings

Encoding CBV $\lambda(\mu)$-calculus into LKQ. We are now in a position to hook up with the material of Section 2. We can encode the call-by-value λ-calculus, by defining the following derived CBV implication and terms:

$$P \rightarrow^v Q = \neg^+(P \otimes \neg^+ Q)$$

$$\lambda x.v = ((\tilde{\mu}(x,\alpha^\bullet).\langle v \,|\, \alpha\rangle)^\bullet)^\diamond \qquad v_1 v_2 = \mu\alpha.\langle v_2 \,\big|\, \tilde{\mu}x.\langle v_1 \,|\, ((x,\alpha^\bullet)^\diamond)^\blacklozenge\rangle\rangle$$

where $\tilde{\mu}(x,\alpha^\bullet).c$ is the abbreviation used in Example 1 and where $V^\blacklozenge$ stands for $\tilde{\mu}\alpha^\bullet.\langle V^\diamond \,|\, \alpha\rangle$. The translation extends to (call-by-value) $\lambda\mu$-calculus [22], and factors though $\overline{\lambda}\mu\tilde{\mu}_Q$-calculus (cf. Section 2), defining $V \cdot e$ as $(V, e^\bullet)^\blacklozenge$. The translation makes also sense in the untyped setting, as the following example shows.

Example 2. Let $\Delta = \lambda x.xx$. We have $[\![\Delta\Delta]\!]^+_{\mathrm{v}} = \mu\gamma.c$, and $c \rightarrow^* c$, with

$$c = \langle (e^\bullet)^\diamond \,\big|\, \tilde{\mu}z.\langle (e^\bullet)^\diamond \,|\, (z,\gamma^\bullet)^\blacklozenge\rangle\rangle \quad \text{and} \quad e = \tilde{\mu}(x,\alpha^\bullet).\langle x^\diamond \,\big|\, \tilde{\mu}y.\langle x^\diamond \,|\, (y,\alpha^\bullet)^\blacklozenge\rangle\rangle$$

Encoding CBN $\lambda(\mu)$-calculus. What about CBN? We can translate it to LKQ, but at the price of translating terms to contexts, which is a violence to our goal of giving an intuitive semantics to the first abstract machine presented in Section 2. But keeping the *same* term language, we can type sequents of the form $(\ldots, \alpha : N, \ldots \vdash \ldots, x : N, \ldots)$, giving rise to a dual logic LKT, renaming the metavariables for expressions, values, and contexts as e (now contexts), E (now *covalues*, also called applicative contexts in [3]),

Translation of formulas:

$$X_{cps} = X \qquad (\neg^+ P)_{cps} = R^{P_{cps}}$$
$$(P \otimes Q)_{cps} = (P_{cps}) \times (Q_{cps}) \quad P \oplus Q_{cps} = P_{cps} + Q_{cps}$$

Translation of terms:

$$\langle v \,|\, e\rangle_{cps} = (v_{cps})(e_{cps}) \qquad (V^{\diamond})_{cps} = \lambda k.k(V_{cps}) \qquad (\mu\alpha.c)_{cps} = \lambda k_\alpha.(c_{cps}) = \tilde{\mu}\alpha^{\bullet}.c_{cps}$$
$$x_{cps} = x \quad (V_1, V_2)_{cps} = ((V_1)_{cps}, (V_2)_{cps}) \quad inl(V_1)_{cps} = inl((V_1)_{cps}) \quad (e^{\bullet})_{cps} = e_{cps}$$
$$\alpha_{cps} = k_\alpha \qquad (\tilde{\mu}x.c)_{cps} = \lambda x.(c_{cps}) \qquad (\tilde{\mu}(x_1, x_2).c)_{cps} = \lambda z.(c_{cps}[fst(z)/x_1, snd(z)/x_2])$$
$$(\tilde{\mu}[inl(x_1).c_1 | inr(x_2).c_2])_{cps} = \lambda z.case\ z\ [inl(x_1) \mapsto (c_1)_{cps}, inr(x_2) \mapsto (c_2)_{cps}]$$

Fig. 3. Translation of LKQ into the λ-calculus / NJ

and v (now expressions). For example the rules for left introduction of & and of right introduction for ⅋ are as follows:

$$\frac{\Gamma\,;\, E_1 : N_1 \vdash \Delta}{\Gamma\,;\, inl(E_1) : N_1 \& N_2 \vdash \Delta} \quad \frac{\Gamma\,;\, E_2 : N_2 \vdash \Delta}{\Gamma\,;\, inr(E_2) : N_1 \& N_2 \vdash \Delta} \quad \frac{c : (\Gamma \vdash x_1 : N_1\,,\, x_2 : N_2\,,\, \Delta)}{\Gamma \vdash \tilde{\mu}(x_1, x_2).c : N_1 ⅋ N_2 \,|\, \Delta}$$

In what follows, it will be handier (and closer to the tradition of CBN $\lambda\mu$-calculus) to use $\tilde{x}$ (resp. $\tilde{\alpha}$) instead of a negative variable α (resp. continuation variable x).

We would have arrived to this logic naturally if we had chosen in Section 3 to present LK with a reversible disjunction on the right and an irreversible conjunction on the left, and in Section 4 to present a focalisation discipline with focusing on formulas on the left. In LKT we can define the following derived CBN implication and terms:

$$M \rightarrow^n N = (\neg^- M) ⅋ N$$
$$\lambda x.v = \tilde{\mu}(\tilde{x}^{\bullet}, \tilde{\alpha}).\langle v \,|\, \tilde{\alpha}^{\diamond}\rangle \qquad v_1 v_2 = \mu\tilde{\alpha}.\langle v_1 \,|\, (v_2^{\bullet}, \tilde{\alpha})\rangle$$

The translation extends to $\lambda\mu$-calculus [23] and factors though the $\overline{\lambda}\mu\tilde{\mu}_T$-calculus of [3], defining $v \cdot E$ as $(v^{\bullet}, E)$. Note that the covalues involved in executing call-by-name λ-calculus are just *stacks* of expressions (cf. Section 2).

Translating LKQ into NJ. Figure 3 presents a translation from LKQ to intuitionistic natural deduction NJ, or, via Curry-Howard, to λ-calculus extended with products and sums. In the translation, R is a fixed target formula (cf. Section 2). We translate $(\neg^+ \_)$ as "_ implies R" (cf. [12,14]). We write B^A for function types / intuitionistic implications. The rules of $\mathsf{L_{foc}}$ are simulated by β-reductions. One may think of the source $\mathsf{L_{foc}}$ terms as a description of the target ones "in direct style" (cf. [5]).

Proposition 3. *Let* $\Gamma_{cps} = \{x : P_{cps} \mid x : P \in \Gamma\}$, $R^{\Delta_{cps}} = \{k_\alpha : R^{P_{cps}} \mid \alpha : P \in \Delta\}$. *We have:*

$$C : (\Gamma \vdash \Delta) \;\Rightarrow \Gamma_{cps}\,,\, R^{\Delta_{cps}} \vdash C_{cps} : R$$
$$\Gamma \vdash V : P\,;\, \Delta \Rightarrow \Gamma_{cps}\,,\, R^{\Delta_{cps}} \vdash V_{cps} : P_{cps}$$
$$\Gamma \vdash v : P \,|\, \Delta \;\Rightarrow \Gamma_{cps}\,,\, R^{\Delta_{cps}} \vdash v_{cps} : R^{R^{P_{cps}}}$$
$$\Gamma \,|\, e : P \vdash \Delta \;\Rightarrow \Gamma_{cps}\,,\, R^{\Delta_{cps}} \vdash e_{cps} : R^{P_{cps}}$$

Moreover, the translation preserves reduction: if $t \rightarrow t'$, *then* $t_{cps} \rightarrow^* (t')_{cps}$.

6 A Synthetic System

In this section we pursue two related goals.

1. We want to account for the full (or strong) focalisation (cf. [25]), which consists in removing the use of contractions in the negative phases and carrying these phases maximally, up to having only atoms on the left of the sequent. The positive phases are made also "more maximal" by allowing the use of the axiom only on positive atoms X. This is of interest in a proof search perspective, since the stronger discipline further reduces the search space.
2. We would like our syntax to quotient proofs over the order of decomposition of negative formulas. The use of structured pattern-matching (cf. Example 1) is relevant, as we can describe the construction of a proof of $(\Gamma, x : (P_1 \otimes P_2) \otimes (P_3 \otimes P_4) \vdash \Delta)$ out of a proof of $c : (\Gamma, x_1 : P_1, x_2 : P_2, x_3 : P_3, x_4 : P_4 \vdash \Delta)$ "synthetically", by writing $\langle x^\diamond \,|\, \tilde{\mu}((x_1, x_2), (x_3, x_4)).c\rangle$, where $\tilde{\mu}((x_1, x_2), (x_3, x_4)).c$ stands for an abbreviation of either of the following two commands:

$$\left\langle x^\diamond \,\middle|\, \tilde{\mu}(y, z).\left\langle y^\diamond \,\middle|\, \tilde{\mu}(x_1, x_2).\langle z^\diamond \,|\, \tilde{\mu}(x_3, x_4).c\rangle\right\rangle\right\rangle$$
$$\left\langle x^\diamond \,\middle|\, \tilde{\mu}(y, z).\left\langle z^\diamond \,\middle|\, \tilde{\mu}(x_3, x_4).\langle y^\diamond \,|\, \tilde{\mu}(x_1, x_2).c\rangle\right\rangle\right\rangle$$

The two goals are connected, since applying strong focalisation will forbid the formation of these two terms (because y, z are values appearing with non atomic types), keeping the synthetic form only... provided we make it first class.

We shall proceed in *two steps*. The first, intermediate one, consists in introducing first-class *counterpatterns* and will serve goal 1 but not quite goal 2:

Simple commands $c ::= \langle v \,|\, e\rangle$	Commands $C ::= c \,\big|\, [C \;{}^{q,q}\; C]$
Expressions $v ::= V^\diamond \,\big|\, \mu\alpha.C$	Values $V ::= x \,\big|\, (V, V) \,\big|\, inl(V) \,\big|\, inr(V) \,\big|\, e^\bullet$
Contexts $\boxed{e ::= \alpha \,\big|\, \tilde{\mu}q.C}$	Counterpatterns $\boxed{q ::= x \,\big|\, \alpha^\bullet \,\big|\, (q, q) \,\big|\, [q, q]}$

The counterpatterns are to be thought of as constructs that match patterns (see below).

In this syntax, we have gained a unique $\tilde{\mu}$ binder, but the price to pay is that now commands are trees of copairings $[\_ \;{}^{q_1,q_2}\; \_]$ whose leaves are simple commands.

The typing discipline is restricted with respect to that of Figure 1 (and adapted to the setting with explicit counterpatterns). Let $\Xi = x_1 : X_1, \ldots, x_n : X_n$ denote a left context consisting of *atomic formulas only*. The rules are as follows:

$$\frac{}{\Xi\,,\, x : X \vdash x : X \,;\, \Delta} \qquad \frac{C : (\Xi\,,\, q : P \vdash \Delta)}{\Xi \,|\, \tilde{\mu}q.C : P \vdash \Delta} \qquad \frac{C : (\Xi \vdash \alpha : P\,,\, \Delta)}{\Xi \vdash \mu\alpha.C : P \,|\, \Delta}$$

$$\frac{C : (\Gamma \vdash \alpha : P\,,\, \Delta)}{C : (\Gamma\,,\, \alpha^\bullet : \neg^+ P \vdash \Delta)} \qquad \frac{C : (\Gamma\,,\, q_1 : P_1\,,\, q_2 : P_2 \vdash \Delta)}{C : (\Gamma\,,\, (q_1, q_2) : P_1 \otimes P_2 \vdash \Delta)}$$

$$\frac{C_1 : (\Gamma\,,\, q_1 : P_1 \vdash \Delta) C_2 : (\Gamma\,,\, q_2 : P_2 \vdash \Delta)}{[C_1 \;{}^{q_1,q_2}\; C_2] : (\Gamma\,,\, [q_1, q_2] : P_1 \oplus P_2 \vdash \Delta)}$$

(all the other rules as in Figure 1, with Ξ in place of Γ)

Our aim now (*second step*) is to get rid of the tree structure of a command. Indeed, if $c_{ij} : (\Gamma, x_i : P_i, x_j : P_j \vdash_S \Delta)$ ($i = 1, 2, j = 3, 4$), we want to identify

$$[[c_{13} \; {}^{x_3,x_4} \; c_{14}] \; {}^{x_1,x_2} \; [c_{23} \; {}^{x_3,x_4} \; c_{24}]] \text{ and } [[c_{13} \; {}^{x_1,x_2} \; c_{23}] \; {}^{x_3,x_4} \; [c_{14} \; {}^{x_1,x_2} \; c_{24}]] \,.$$

To this effect, we need a last ingredient. We introduce a syntax of *patterns*, and we redefine the syntax of values, as follows:

$$\boxed{\mathcal{V} ::= x \mid e^{\bullet} \quad V ::= p \, \langle \mathcal{V}_i / i \mid i \in p \rangle \qquad p ::= x \mid \alpha^{\bullet} \mid (p, p) \mid inl(p) \mid inr(p)}$$

where $i \in p$ is defined by:

$$\frac{}{x \in x} \quad \frac{}{\alpha^{\bullet} \in \alpha^{\bullet}} \quad \frac{i \in p_1}{i \in (p_1, p_2)} \quad \frac{i \in p_2}{i \in (p_1, p_2)} \quad \frac{i \in p_1}{i \in inl(p_1)} \quad \frac{i \in p_2}{i \in inr(p_2)}$$

Moreover, $\mathcal{V}_i$ must be of the form y (resp. $e^{\bullet}$) if $i = x$ (resp. $i = \alpha^{\bullet}$).

Patterns are required to be linear, as well as the counterpatterns, for which the definition of "linear" is adjusted in the case $[q_1, q_2]$, in which a variable can occur (but recursively linearly so) in both q_1 and q_2.

We can now rephrase the logical reduction rules in terms of pattern/counterpattern interaction (whence the terminology), resulting in the following packaging of rules:

$$\frac{V = p \, \langle \ldots y/x, \ldots, e^{\bullet}/\alpha^{\bullet}, \ldots \rangle \qquad C[p/q] \rightarrow^{*} c}{\langle V^{\diamond} \mid \tilde{\mu} q.C \rangle \rightarrow c\{\ldots, y/x, \ldots, e/\alpha, \ldots\}}$$

where $c\{\sigma\}$ is the usual, implicit substitution, and where c (see the next proposition) is the normal form of $C[p/q]$ with respect to the following set of rules:

$$\begin{array}{ll} C[(p_1, p_2)/(q_1, q_2), \sigma] \rightarrow C[p_1/q_1, p_2/q_2, \sigma] & C[\beta^{\bullet}/\alpha^{\bullet}, \sigma] \rightarrow C[\beta/\alpha, \sigma] \\ [C_1 \; {}^{q_1,q_2} \; C_2][inl(p_1)/[q_1, q_2], \sigma] \rightarrow C_1[p_1/q_1, \sigma] & \text{(idem } inr\text{)} \end{array}$$

Logically, this means that we now consider each formula as made of blocks of *synthetic* connectives.

Example 3

– Patterns for $P = X \otimes (Y \oplus \neg^{+} Q)$. Focusing on the right yields two possible proof searches:

$$\frac{\Gamma \vdash x'\{\mathcal{V}_{x'}\} : X \,;\, \Delta \quad \Gamma \vdash y'\{\mathcal{V}_{y'}\} : Y \,;\, \Delta}{\Gamma \vdash (x', inl(y'))\{\mathcal{V}_{x'}, \mathcal{V}_{y'}\} : X \otimes (Y \oplus \neg^{+} Q) \,;\, \Delta}$$

$$\frac{\Gamma \vdash x'\{\mathcal{V}_{x'}\} : X \,;\, \Delta \quad \Gamma \vdash \alpha'^{\bullet}\{\mathcal{V}_{\alpha'^{\bullet}}\} : \neg^{+} Q \,;\, \Delta}{\Gamma \vdash (x', inr(\alpha'^{\bullet}))\{\mathcal{V}_{x'}, \mathcal{V}_{\alpha'^{\bullet}}\} : X \otimes (Y \oplus \neg^{+} Q) \,;\, \Delta}$$

– Counterpattern for $P = X \otimes (Y \oplus \neg^{+} Q)$. The counterpattern describes the tree structure of P:

$$\frac{c_1 : (\Gamma \,,\, x : X \,,\, y : Y \vdash \Delta) \qquad c_2 : (\Gamma \,,\, x : X \,,\, \alpha^{\bullet} : \neg^{+} Q \vdash \Delta)}{[c_1 \; {}^{y, \alpha^{\bullet}} \; c_2] : (\Gamma \,,\, (x, [y, \alpha^{\bullet}]) : X \otimes (Y \oplus \neg^{+} Q) \vdash \Delta)}$$

$$c ::= \langle v \,|\, e\rangle \qquad v ::= V^{\diamond} \;\big|\; \mu\alpha.c$$
$$V ::= p\,\langle \mathcal{V}_i/i \mid i \in p\rangle \qquad \mathcal{V} ::= x \;\big|\; e^{\bullet} \qquad p ::= x \;\big|\; \alpha^{\bullet} \;\big|\; (p,p) \;\big|\; inl(p) \;\big|\; inr(p)$$
$$e ::= \alpha \;\big|\; \tilde{\mu}q.\{p \mapsto c_p \mid q \perp p\} \qquad q ::= x \;\big|\; \alpha^{\bullet} \;\big|\; (q,q) \;\big|\; [q,q]$$

$$(\tilde{\mu}^{+})\ \langle (p\,\langle \ldots, y/x, \ldots, e^{\bullet}/\alpha^{\bullet} \ldots\rangle)^{\diamond} \,|\, \tilde{\mu}q.\{p \mapsto c_p \mid q \perp p\}\rangle \rightarrow c_p\,\{\ldots, y/x, \ldots, e/\alpha, \ldots\rangle\}$$
$$(\mu)\quad \langle \mu\alpha.c \,|\, e\rangle \rightarrow c\{e/\alpha\}$$

Typing rules: the old ones for $\alpha, x, e^{\bullet}, c$, plus the following ones:

$$\frac{\ldots \quad \Gamma \vdash \mathcal{V}_i : P_i \,;\, \Delta \quad ((i : P_i) \in \Gamma(p, P)) \quad \ldots}{\Gamma \vdash p\,\langle \mathcal{V}_i/i \mid i \in p\rangle : P \,;\, \Delta}$$

$$\frac{\ldots \quad c_p : (\Gamma\,,\, \Gamma(p,P) \vdash \Delta) \quad (q \perp p) \quad \ldots}{\Gamma \,|\, \tilde{\mu}q.\{p \mapsto c_p \mid q \perp p\} \vdash \Delta}$$

where $\Gamma(p,P)$ must be successfully defined as follows:

$$\Gamma(x, X) = (x : X) \qquad \Gamma(\alpha^{\bullet}, \neg^{+}P) = (\alpha^{\bullet} : \neg^{+}P)$$
$$\Gamma((p_1,p_2), P_1 \otimes P_2) = \Gamma(p_1, P_1)\,,\Gamma(p_2, P_2) \quad \Gamma(inl(p_1), P_1 \oplus P_2) = \Gamma(p_1, P_1) \text{ (idem } inr)$$

Fig. 4. The syntax and reduction semantics of $\mathsf{L}_{\text{synth}}$

We observe that the leaves of the decomposition are in one-to-one correspondence with the patterns p for the (irreversible) decomposition of P on the right:

$$[c_1 \;{}^{y,\alpha^{\bullet}}\; c_2][p_1/q] = c_1\{x'/x, y'/y\} \qquad [c_1 \;{}^{y,\alpha^{\bullet}}\; c_2][p_2/q] = c_2\{x'/x, \alpha'/\alpha\}$$

where $q = (x, [y, \alpha^{\bullet}])$, $p_1 = (x', inl(yk'))$, $p_2 = (x', inr(\alpha'^{\bullet}))$.

This correspondence is general. We define two predicates $c \in C$ and $q \perp p$ ("q is orthogonal to p") as follows:

$$\frac{}{c \in c} \qquad \frac{c \in C_1}{c \in [C_1 \;{}^{q_1,q_2}\; C_2]} \qquad \frac{c \in C_2}{c \in [C_1 \;{}^{q_1,q_2}\; C_2]}$$

$$\frac{}{x \perp x} \qquad \frac{}{\alpha^{\bullet} \perp \alpha^{\bullet}} \qquad \frac{q_1 \perp p_1 \quad q_2 \perp p_2}{(q_1,q_2) \perp (p_1,p_2)} \qquad \frac{q_1 \perp p_1}{[q_1,q_2] \perp inl(p_1)} \qquad \frac{q_2 \perp p_2}{[q_1,q_2] \perp inr(p_2)}$$

We can now state the correspondence result.

Proposition 4. *Let* $C : (\Xi\,,\, q : P \vdash \Delta)$ *(as in the assumption of the typing rule for* $\tilde{\mu}q.C$*), and let* p *be such that* q *is orthogonal to* p*. Then the normal form* c *of* $C[p/q]$ *is a simple command, and the mapping* $p \mapsto c$ *(*q, C *fixed) from* $\{p \mid q \perp p\}$ *to* $\{c \mid c \in C\}$ *is one-to-one and onto.*

Thanks to this correspondence, we can quotient over the "bureaucracy" of commands, and we arrive at the calculus described in Figure 4, together with its typing rules, which we call *synthetic system* L, or $\mathsf{L}_{\text{synth}}$. The $\tilde{\mu}$ construct of $\mathsf{L}_{\text{synth}}$ is closely related to Zeilberger's higher-order abstract approach to focalisation in [27]: indeed we can view $\{p \mapsto c \mid q \perp p\}$ as a function from patterns to commands. We actually prefer to see here a *finite* record whoses fields are the p's orthogonal to q. There are only two reduction rules in $\mathsf{L}_{\text{synth}}$. the μ-rule now expressed with implicit substitution and the $\tilde{\mu}^+$-rule, which combines two familiar operations: select a field p (like in object-oriented programming), and substitute (like in functional programming). The next proposition relates $\mathsf{L}_{\text{synth}}$ to L_{foc}.

Proposition 5. *The typing system of* L_{synth} *is complete with respect to* LKQ.

PROOF. The completeness of $\mathsf{L}_{\text{synth}}$ with respect to the intermediate system above is an easy consequence of Proposition 4. In order to prove the completeness of the intermediate system, we define the following rewriting relation between sets of sequents:

$$\begin{array}{l}(\Gamma, x : \neg^+ P \vdash \Delta), \mathbf{S} \rightsquigarrow (\Gamma \vdash \alpha : P, \Delta), \mathbf{S}\\ (\Gamma, x : P_1 \otimes P_2 \vdash \Delta), \mathbf{S} \rightsquigarrow (\Gamma, x_1 : P_1, x_2 : P_2 \vdash \Delta), \mathbf{S}\\ (\Gamma, x : P_1 \oplus P_2 \vdash \Delta), \mathbf{S} \rightsquigarrow (\Gamma, x_1 : P_1 \vdash \Delta), (\Gamma, x_2 : P_2 \vdash \Delta), \mathbf{S}\end{array}$$

(where α, x_1, x_2 are fresh). One proves the following properties together:

1) if $c : (x_1 : P_1, \ldots, x_m : P_m \vdash \Delta)$, then there exist $q_1, \ldots, q_m$ and C such that $C : (q_1 : P_1, \ldots, q_m : P_m \vdash_S \Delta)$,
2) if $\Xi \mid e : P \vdash \Delta$, then there exists e' such that $\Xi \mid e' : P \vdash_S \Delta$ (and similarly for expressions v),

where $\vdash_S$ (resp. $\vdash$) refers to the intermediate system (resp. to L_{foc}). The proof of 1) goes as follows. Using Lemma 1 and induction, we get simple commands c_i proving all the sequents in the normal form of $(x_1 : P_1, \ldots, x_m : P_m \vdash \Delta)$ w.r.t. the above rewriting rules. One can then assemble the c_i's to form a command C as in the statement. □

Putting together Propositions 1 and 5, we have proved that $\mathsf{L}_{\text{synth}}$ is complete with respect to LK for provability.

Remark 4. In the multiplicative case (no C, $inl(V)$, $inr(V)$, $[q_1, q_2]$), there is a unique p such that $q \perp p$, namely q, and the syntax boils down to:

$$\mathcal{V} ::= x \mid e^{\bullet} \quad V ::= p\,\langle \mathcal{V}_i / i \mid i \in p\rangle \quad v ::= x \mid \tilde{\mu}q.\{c\} \quad c = \langle V^{\diamond} \mid \alpha\rangle$$

Compare with *Böhm trees*: $M ::= \overbrace{\lambda \boldsymbol{x}.\underbrace{P}_{c}}^{e} \qquad P ::= \underbrace{y\,\overbrace{M_1}^{\mathcal{V}} \ldots \overbrace{M_n}^{\mathcal{V}}}_{V}.$

7 Conclusion

We believe that Curien-Herbelin's syntactic kit, which we could call *system* L for short, provides us with a robust infrastructure for proof-theoretical investigations, and for applications in formal studies in operational semantics. Thus, the work presented here is faithful to the spirit of Herbelin's Habilitation Thesis [11], where he advocated an incremental approach to connectives, starting from a pure control kernel.

The good fit between abstract machines and our syntax $\mathsf{L}_{\mathrm{foc}}$ makes it a good candidate for being used as an intermediate language appropriate to reason about the correctness of abstract machines (see also [18]). In this spirit, in order to account for languages with mixed call-by-value / call-by-name features, one may give a truly bilateral presentation of $\mathsf{L}_{\mathrm{foc}}$ that freely mixes positive and negative formulas like in Girard's LC[7].[6] Such a system is presented in the long version of [19].

We wish to thank R. Harper, H. Herbelin, and O. Laurent for helpful discussions.

References

1. Abadi, M., Cardelli, L., Curien, P.-L., Lévy, J.-J.: Explicit Substitutions. Journal of Functional Programming 1(4) (1992)
2. Andreoli, J.-M.: Logic programming with focusing proofs in linear logic. Journal of Logic and Computation 2(3), 297–347 (1992)
3. Curien, P.-L., Herbelin, H.: The duality of computation. In: Proc. Int. Conf. on Functional Programming 2000 (2000)
4. Danos, V., Joinet, J.-B., Schellinx, H.: A new deconstructive logic: linear logic. Journal of Symbolic Logic 62(3) (1997)
5. Danvy, O.: Back to direct style. Science of Computer Programming 22(3), 183–195 (1994)
6. Girard, J.-Y., Lafont, Y., Taylor, P.: Proofs and Types. Cambridge University Press, Cambridge (1989)
7. Girard, J.-Y.: A new constructive logic: classical logic. Mathematical Structures in Computer Science 1, 255–296 (1991)
8. Girard, J.-Y.: Locus solum: from the rules of logic to the logic of rules. Mathematical Structures in Computer Science 11(3), 301–506 (2001)
9. Griffin, T.: A formulae-as-types notion of control. In: Proc. Principles of Programming Languages 1990 (1990)
10. Herbelin, H.: Séquents qu'on calcule, Thèse de Doctorat, Université Paris 7 (1995), `http://pauillac.inria.fr/~herbelin`
11. Herbelin, H.: C'est maintenant qu'on calcule, au cœur de la dualité, Mémoire d'habilitation (2005) (available from cited url)
12. Krivine, J.-L.: Lambda-calcul, types et modèles, Masson (1991)
13. Krivine, J.-L.: A call-by-name lambda-calculus machine. Higher Order and Symbolic Computation 20, 199–207 (2007)
14. Lafont, Y., Reus, B., Streicher, T.: Continuation Semantics or Expressing Implication by Negation. Technical Report (1993)
15. Landin, P.: The mechanical evaluation of expressions. Computer Journal 6, 308–320 (1964)
16. Laurent, O.: Etude de la polarisation en logique. Thèse de Doctorat, Univ. Aix-Marseille II (2002)
17. Laurent, O., Quatrini, M., Tortora de Falco, L.: Polarised and focalised linear and classical proofs. Ann. of Pure and Appl. Logic 134(2-3), 217–264 (2005)
18. Levy, P.B.: Call-by-push-value. In: A functional/imperative synthesis, Semantic Structures in Computation. Springer, Heidelberg (2004)
19. Munch-Maccagnoni, G.: Focalisation and classical realisability. In: Grädel, E., Kahle, R. (eds.) CSL 2009. LNCS, vol. 5771, pp. 409–423. Springer, Heidelberg (2009), `http://perso.ens-lyon.fr/guillaume.munch/articles`

[6] See also [20] for an early analysis of the computational meaning of LC from a programming language perspective.

20. Murthy, C.: A computational analysis of Girard's translation and LC. In: Proc. LICS 1992 (1992)
21. Nipkow, T.: Orthogonal higher-order rewriting systems are confluent. In: Bezem, M., Groote, J.F. (eds.) TLCA 1993. LNCS, vol. 664, pp. 306–317. Springer, Heidelberg (1993)
22. Ong, L., Stewart, C.: A Curry-Howard foundation for functional computation with control. In: Proc. POPL '97 (1997)
23. Parigot, M.: $\lambda\mu$-calculus: An algorithmic interpretation of classical natural deduction. In: Voronkov, A. (ed.) LPAR 1992. LNCS, vol. 624, pp. 190–201. Springer, Heidelberg (1992)
24. Plotkin, G.: Call-by-name, call-by-value and the lambda-calculus. TCS 1, 125–159 (1975)
25. Quatrini, M., Tortora de Falco, L.: Polarisation des preuves classiques et renversement. C.R.A.S.. 323(I), 113–116 (1996)
26. Wadler, P.: Call-by-value is dual to call-by-name. In: Proc. ICFP 2003 (2003)
27. Zeilberger, N.: On the unity of duality. Ann. of Pure and Appl. Logic 153(1), 66–96 (2008)

Polarized Resolution Modulo

Gilles Dowek

École polytechnique and INRIA
LIX, École polytechnique, 91128 Palaiseau Cedex, France
gilles.dowek@polytechnique.edu
http://www.lix.polytechnique.fr/~dowek

Abstract. We present a restriction of Resolution modulo where the rewrite rules are such that clauses rewrite to clauses, so that the reduct of a clause needs not be further transformed into clause form. Restricting Resolution modulo in this way requires to extend it in another and distinguish the rules that apply to negative and positive atomic propositions. This method can be seen as a restriction of Equational resolution that mixes clause selection and literal selection restrictions. Unlike many restrictions of Resolution, it is not an instance of Ordered resolution.

1 Introduction

Deduction modulo is an extension of first-order predicate logic where axioms, for instance $P \Leftrightarrow (Q \Rightarrow R)$, are replaced by rewrite rules, for instance $P \longrightarrow (Q \Rightarrow R)$. These rules define an equivalence relation and, in a proof, a proposition can be replaced by an equivalent one at any time.

A motivation for introducing Deduction modulo was its applications to automated theorem proving. Together with Thérèse Hardin and Claude Kirchner, we have defined a proof search method called *Extended Narrowing and Resolution*, or *Resolution modulo*, that extends first-order Resolution to handle such rewrite rules [8]. The term rewrite rules define an equivalence relation on terms that is used by the unification algorithm, but the proposition rewrite rules, such as $P \longrightarrow (Q \Rightarrow R)$, are used, in a different way, to directly rewrite, or more generally narrow, the clauses. For instance, with the rewrite rule above, the clause P, S narrows to $Q \Rightarrow R, S$.

The proof-search method obtained this way is complete provided the theory defined by the rewrite rules has the cut elimination property. Moreover this completeness theorem has a converse: if Resolution modulo is complete, then the theory has the cut elimination property [9]. More generally, whether the theory has the cut elimination property or not, the method proves exactly the propositions that have a cut free proof.

Resolution modulo is more efficient than Resolution used with axioms. For instance, a naive search for a Resolution proof of a contradiction with the axiom $\forall x\ (P(x) \Leftrightarrow P(f(x)))$ generates an infinite search space. But attempting to prove a contradiction with Resolution modulo the rule $P(x) \longrightarrow P(f(x))$ generates an empty search space. Besides this trivial example, Simple type theory can be

C.S. Calude and V. Sassone (Eds.): TCS 2010, IFIP AICT 323, pp. 182–196, 2010.

expressed in Deduction modulo and applying Resolution modulo to this theory yields a step by step simulation of Higher-order resolution [1,10], that generates an empty search space when attempting to prove a contradiction in this theory.

Yet, a problem with Resolution modulo is that narrowing the clause P, S yields the set of propositions $Q \Rightarrow R, S$ that is not a clause, and this set needs to be further transformed into clause form: $\neg Q, R, S$. In the general case, this transformation includes skolemization. For instance, with the rule $P(x) \longrightarrow \forall y\ Q(x,y)$, the clause $P(X), S$ narrows to $Q(X,Y), S$ but the clause $\neg P(X), S$ narrows to $\neg Q(X, f(X)), S$ where f is a new Skolem symbol. This dynamic skolemization is an unpleasant feature of Resolution modulo that is cumbersome to implement and that complicates the completeness proof.

To address this problem, we restrict, in this paper, Resolution modulo to *clausal* rewrite systems, defined in such as way that a clause always narrows to a clause. However, restricting Resolution modulo this way requires to extend it in another. Indeed, the rule $P \longrightarrow (Q \Rightarrow R)$ must be replaced by the rule $P \longrightarrow (\neg Q \vee R)$ when applied to the literal P, but it must be replaced by the rules $P \longrightarrow \neg Q$ and $P \longrightarrow \neg\neg R$ when applied to the literal $\neg P$. Thus, negative and positive occurrences of atomic propositions must be rewritten in a different way, like in the so-called *Polarized deduction modulo* [5], hence the name *Polarized resolution modulo* for the method. Like Resolution modulo, Polarized resolution modulo proves a proposition if and only if this proposition has a cut free proof. Thus, it is complete if and only if the theory defined by the rewrite rules has the cut elimination property.

Another advantage of Polarized resolution modulo over the original formulation is that the **Extended Narrowing** rule can be seen as a particular case of the **Resolution** rule with extra clauses added to the problem. Indeed, instead of using the rewrite rule $P \longrightarrow (\neg Q \vee R)$ to transform the clause P, S into $\neg Q, R, S$, we may as well add an extra clause $\underline{\neg P}, \neg Q, R$ and derive $\neg Q, R, S$ with the **Resolution** rule from P, S and this new clause. However, the use of this new clause is restricted in such a way that the resolved literal in this clause must always be $\neg P$. We shall call such a literal *selected* and a clause with an selected literal a *one-way* clause. A further restriction is that the **Resolution** rule cannot be applied to two one-way clauses.

Thus, Polarized resolution modulo appears to be a restriction of Equational resolution, that combines two types of restrictions used in resolution based proof methods: clause selection restrictions like in the *Set of support* method [14] and in *Semantic resolution* [13] and literal selection restrictions like in *Ordered resolution* [2], preserving completeness, provided the theory defined by the rewrite rules has the cut elimination property. Yet, it is more restricted than each of these methods. In particular, together with Guillaume Burel [4], we have proved that, unlike many other restrictions of Resolution, it is not an instance of Ordered Resolution. Indeed, Polarized resolution modulo fails in finite time when attempting to prove a contradiction in Simple type theory. Thus, its completeness implies the consistency of Simple type theory, and, from Gödel's second incompleteness theorem, the completeness of this method cannot be proved in Simple type theory, while the completeness of all instances of Ordered resolution can.

This also simplifies the implementation of the method and unlike Resolution modulo, that has never been fully implemented, there is an implementation of Polarized resolution modulo, that gives very promising first results [3], in particular for Simple type theory.

2 Polarized Deduction Modulo

2.1 Polarized Deduction Modulo

Definition 1 (Polarized rewrite system). *A* polarized rewrite system *is a triple $\mathcal{R} = \langle \mathcal{E}, \mathcal{R}_-, \mathcal{R}_+ \rangle$ where $\mathcal{E}$ is a set of equations between terms, $\mathcal{R}_-$ and $\mathcal{R}_+$ are sets of rewrite rules whose left hand sides are atomic propositions and right hand sides are arbitrary propositions. The rules of $\mathcal{R}_-$ are called* negative *rules and those of $\mathcal{R}_+$ are called* positive *rules.*

Definition 2 (Polarized rewriting). *Let $\mathcal{R} = \langle \mathcal{E}, \mathcal{R}_-, \mathcal{R}_+ \rangle$ be a polarized rewrite system. We define the equivalence relation $=_\mathcal{E}$ as the congruence on terms generated by the equations of $\mathcal{E}$. We then define the one step negative and positive rewriting relations $\longrightarrow_-$ and $\longrightarrow_+$ as follows.*

- *If $t_i =_\mathcal{E} u$ then both $P(t_1, \ldots, t_i, \ldots, t_n) \longrightarrow_- P(t_1, \ldots, u, \ldots, t_n)$ and $P(t_1, \ldots, t_i, \ldots, t_n) \longrightarrow_+ P(t_1, \ldots, u, \ldots, t_n)$.*
- *If $P \longrightarrow A$ is a rule of $\mathcal{R}_s$ and σ is a substitution then $\sigma P \longrightarrow_s \sigma A$, where s is either $-$ or $+$.*
- *If $A \longrightarrow_{\bar{s}} A'$ then $\neg A \longrightarrow_s \neg A'$, where $\bar{\cdot}$ swaps $-$ and $+$.*
- *If ($A \longrightarrow_s A'$ and $B = B'$) or ($A = A'$ and $B \longrightarrow_s B'$), then $A \wedge B \longrightarrow_s A' \wedge B'$ and $A \vee B \longrightarrow_s A' \vee B'$.*
- *If ($A \longrightarrow_{\bar{s}} A'$ and $B = B'$) or ($A = A'$ and $B \longrightarrow_s B'$), then $A \Rightarrow B \longrightarrow_s A' \Rightarrow B'$.*
- *If $A \longrightarrow_s A'$ then $\forall x\ A \longrightarrow_s \forall x\ A'$ and $\exists x\ A \longrightarrow_s \exists x\ A'$.*

We define the sequent one step term rewriting relation $\longrightarrow$ as follows.

- *If $A \longrightarrow_- A'$ then $(\Gamma, A \vdash \Delta) \longrightarrow (\Gamma, A' \vdash \Delta)$.*
- *If $A \longrightarrow_+ A'$ then $(\Gamma \vdash A, \Delta) \longrightarrow (\Gamma \vdash A', \Delta)$.*

As usual, if R is any binary relation, we write R^* for its reflexive-transitive closure. The rules of *Polarized sequent calculus modulo* are those of Figure 1. Proof checking is decidable when the relations $\longrightarrow_-^*$ and $\longrightarrow_+^*$ are. The usual, non polarized, Deduction modulo can be recovered by taking $\mathcal{R}_- = \mathcal{R}_+$ and predicate logic by taking $\mathcal{E} = \mathcal{R}_- = \mathcal{R}_+ = \varnothing$.

The following propositions are proved by induction over proof structure.

Proposition 1. *If $(\Gamma \vdash \Delta) \longrightarrow^* (\Gamma' \vdash \Delta')$ and $\Gamma' \vdash \Delta'$ has a cut free proof modulo $\mathcal{R}$ then $\Gamma \vdash \Delta$ has a cut free proof modulo $\mathcal{R}$ of the same size.*

Proposition 2. *Assume that the language contains a closed term and that $\Gamma \vdash \Delta$ is a closed sequent. Then, if $\Gamma \vdash \Delta$ has a cut free proof using neither the left rule of the existential quantifier, nor the right rule of the universal quantifier, it has a cut free proof where all the sequents are closed.*

$$\frac{}{A \vdash B} \text{ axiom if } A \longrightarrow^*_- P, B \longrightarrow^*_+ P \text{ and } P \text{ atomic}$$

$$\frac{\Gamma, B \vdash \Delta \quad \Gamma \vdash C, \Delta}{\Gamma \vdash \Delta} \text{ cut if } A \longrightarrow^*_- B, A \longrightarrow^*_+ C$$

$$\frac{\Gamma, B, C \vdash \Delta}{\Gamma, A \vdash \Delta} \text{ contr-left if } A \longrightarrow^*_- B, A \longrightarrow^*_- C$$

$$\frac{\Gamma \vdash B, C, \Delta}{\Gamma \vdash A, \Delta} \text{ contr-right if } A \longrightarrow^*_+ B, A \longrightarrow^*_+ C$$

$$\frac{\Gamma \vdash \Delta}{\Gamma, A \vdash \Delta} \text{ weak-left}$$

$$\frac{\Gamma \vdash \Delta}{\Gamma \vdash A, \Delta} \text{ weak-right}$$

$$\frac{}{\Gamma \vdash A, \Delta} \top\text{-right if } A \longrightarrow^*_+ \top$$

$$\frac{}{\Gamma, A \vdash \Delta} \bot\text{-left if } A \longrightarrow^*_- \bot$$

$$\frac{\Gamma \vdash B, \Delta}{\Gamma, A \vdash \Delta} \neg\text{-left if } A \longrightarrow^*_- \neg B$$

$$\frac{\Gamma, B \vdash \Delta}{\Gamma \vdash A, \Delta} \neg\text{-right if } A \longrightarrow^*_+ \neg B$$

$$\frac{\Gamma, B, C \vdash \Delta}{\Gamma, A \vdash \Delta} \wedge\text{-left if } A \longrightarrow^*_- (B \wedge C)$$

$$\frac{\Gamma \vdash B, \Delta \quad \Gamma \vdash C, \Delta}{\Gamma \vdash A, \Delta} \wedge\text{-right if } A \longrightarrow^*_+ (B \wedge C)$$

$$\frac{\Gamma, B \vdash \Delta \quad \Gamma, C \vdash \Delta}{\Gamma, A \vdash \Delta} \vee\text{-left if } A \longrightarrow^*_- (B \vee C)$$

$$\frac{\Gamma \vdash B, C, \Delta}{\Gamma \vdash A, \Delta} \vee\text{-right if } A \longrightarrow^*_+ (B \vee C)$$

$$\frac{\Gamma \vdash B, \Delta \quad \Gamma, C \vdash \Delta}{\Gamma, A \vdash \Delta} \Rightarrow\text{-left if } A \longrightarrow^*_- (B \Rightarrow C)$$

$$\frac{\Gamma, B \vdash C, \Delta}{\Gamma \vdash A, \Delta} \Rightarrow\text{-right if } A \longrightarrow^*_+ (B \Rightarrow C)$$

$$\frac{\Gamma, C \vdash \Delta}{\Gamma, A \vdash \Delta} \langle x, B, t\rangle \ \forall\text{-left if } A \longrightarrow^*_- \forall x\ B,\ (t/x)B \longrightarrow^*_- C$$

$$\frac{\Gamma \vdash B, \Delta}{\Gamma \vdash A, \Delta} \langle x, B\rangle \ \forall\text{-right if } A \longrightarrow^*_+ \forall x\ B,\ x \notin FV(\Gamma\Delta)$$

$$\frac{\Gamma, B \vdash \Delta}{\Gamma, A \vdash \Delta} \langle x, B\rangle \ \exists\text{-left if } A \longrightarrow^*_- \exists x\ B,\ x \notin FV(\Gamma\Delta)$$

$$\frac{\Gamma \vdash C, \Delta}{\Gamma \vdash A, \Delta} \langle x, B, t\rangle \ \exists\text{-right if } A \longrightarrow^*_+ \exists x\ B,\ (t/x)B \longrightarrow^*_+ C$$

Fig. 1. Polarized sequent calculus modulo

2.2 Compatibility

We want to show that rewrite rules build in axioms, *i.e.* that for each rewrite system $\mathcal{R}$, there is a set of axioms $\mathcal{T}$ such that $\Gamma \vdash \Delta$ is provable modulo $\mathcal{R}$ if and only if there exists a finite subset $\mathcal{T}'$ of $\mathcal{T}$ such that $\Gamma, \mathcal{T}' \vdash \Delta$ is provable in predicate logic. As we sometimes want to transform some, but not all, rewrite rules into axioms, we shall transform the rewrite system $\mathcal{R}$ into a pair formed with a weaker rewrite system $\mathcal{R}'$ and a set of axioms $\mathcal{T}$.

Definition 3 (Compatibility). *Let $\mathcal{R}$ and $\mathcal{R}'$ be polarized rewrite systems and $\mathcal{T}$ be a set of axioms. The system $\mathcal{R}$ is* compatible *with the pair $\langle \mathcal{R}', \mathcal{T} \rangle$ when*

1. *if $A \longrightarrow_{-}^{*} B$ in $\mathcal{R}'$ then $A \longrightarrow_{-}^{*} B$ in $\mathcal{R}$ and if $A \longrightarrow_{+}^{*} B$ in $\mathcal{R}'$ then $A \longrightarrow_{+}^{*} B$ in $\mathcal{R}$,*
2. *if $A \in \mathcal{T}$, then $\vdash A$ is provable modulo $\mathcal{R}$,*
3. *if $A \longrightarrow_{-}^{*} B$ in $\mathcal{R}$, then there exists a finite subset $\mathcal{T}'$ of $\mathcal{T}$ such that $\mathcal{T}' \vdash A \Rightarrow B$ is provable modulo $\mathcal{R}'$,*
4. *if $A \longrightarrow_{+}^{*} B$ in $\mathcal{R}$, then there exists a finite subset $\mathcal{T}'$ of $\mathcal{T}$ such that $\mathcal{T}' \vdash B \Rightarrow A$ is provable modulo $\mathcal{R}'$.*

Proposition 3 (Equivalence). *Let $\mathcal{R}$ be a polarized rewrite system and $\langle \mathcal{R}', \mathcal{T} \rangle$ be a pair compatible with $\mathcal{R}$, then the sequent $\Gamma \vdash \Delta$ is provable modulo $\mathcal{R}$, if and only if there exists a finite subset $\mathcal{T}'$ of $\mathcal{T}$ such that the sequent $\Gamma, \mathcal{T}' \vdash \Delta$ is provable modulo $\mathcal{R}'$.*

Proof. If $\Gamma, \mathcal{T}' \vdash \Delta$ is provable modulo $\mathcal{R}'$, it is provable modulo $\mathcal{R}$ and each A of $\mathcal{T}'$ is provable modulo $\mathcal{R}$. We conclude with the cut rule. The converse is a simple induction over proof structure.

Two particular cases are useful: $\mathcal{R}' = \varnothing$ *i.e.* all the rewrite rules are transformed into axioms, and $\mathcal{R}' = \mathcal{E}$, *i.e.* only proposition rewrite rules are transformed into axioms.

Proposition 4. *For all polarized rewrite systems $\mathcal{R}$, there exists a set of axioms $\mathcal{T}$ such that $\mathcal{R}$ and $\langle \varnothing, \mathcal{T} \rangle$ are compatible.*

Proof. Take the universal closures of all the propositions $A \Rightarrow B$ such that $A \longrightarrow_{-}^{*} B$ or $B \longrightarrow_{+}^{*} A$.

Proposition 5. *For all polarized rewrite systems $\mathcal{R} = \langle \mathcal{E}, \mathcal{R}_{-}, \mathcal{R}_{+} \rangle$, there exists a set of axioms $\mathcal{T}$ such that $\mathcal{R}$ and $\langle \mathcal{E}, \mathcal{T} \rangle$ are compatible.*

Proof. Take for each rule $P \longrightarrow_{-} A$ of $\mathcal{R}_{-}$ the universal closure of $P \Rightarrow A$ and for each rule $P \longrightarrow_{+} A$ of $\mathcal{R}_{+}$ the universal closure of $A \Rightarrow P$.

2.3 Clausal Rewrite Systems

Definition 4 (Literal, Clausal proposition). *A proposition is a* literal *if it is either atomic or the negation of an atomic proposition. A proposition is* clausal *if it is $\bot$ or of the form $\forall x_1 \ldots \forall x_p \ (L_1 \vee \ldots \vee L_n)$ where $L_1, \ldots, L_n$ are literals and $x_1, \ldots, x_p$ variables.*

Definition 5 (Clausal rewrite system). *A rewrite system is* clausal *if negative rules rewrite atomic propositions to clausal propositions and positive rules atomic propositions to negations of clausal propositions.*

For instance, the rewrite system $\mathcal{R}$ formed with the negative rule $P \longrightarrow (\neg Q \vee R)$ and the positive rules $P \longrightarrow \neg Q$ and $P \longrightarrow \neg\neg R$ is clausal. This rewrite system is compatible with the axiom $P \Leftrightarrow (Q \Rightarrow R)$, in the same way the rule $P \longrightarrow (Q \Rightarrow R)$ is in usual Deduction modulo.

Example 1. A presentation of Simple type theory in Deduction modulo has been given in [7]. To adapt it to Polarized deduction modulo, we just need to duplicate each rule, but this polarized rewrite system is not clausal. An equivalent one, that is clausal has been given in [6]. The sorts of this system are simple types built from two base types ι and o. The language contains

- for each pair of sorts, a constant $K_{T,U}$ of sort $T \to U \to T$,
- for each triple of sorts, a constant $S_{T,U,V}$ of sort $(T \to U \to V) \to (T \to U) \to T \to V$,
- a constant $\dot{\vee}$ of sort $o \to o \to o$,
- a constant $\dot{\neg}$ of sort $o \to o$,
- for each sort, a constant $\dot{\forall}_T$ of sort $(T \to o) \to o$,
- for each pair of sorts, a function symbol $\alpha_{T,U}$ of rank $\langle T \to U, T, U \rangle$,
- for each sort T, a Skolem symbol H_T of sort $(T \to o) \to T$,
- a predicate symbol ε of rank $\langle o \rangle$.

As usual, we write $(t\ u)$ for $\alpha_{T,U}(t,u)$ and $(t\ u_1\ \dots\ u_n)$ for $(\dots(t\ u_1)\dots u_n)$. The rewrite rules are

$$(K_{T,U}\ x\ y) =_{\mathcal{E}} x$$

$$(S_{T,U,V}\ x\ y\ z) =_{\mathcal{E}} (x\ z\ (y\ z))$$

$$\begin{array}{rlrl}
\varepsilon(x\ \dot{\vee}\ y) \longrightarrow_- (\varepsilon(x) \vee \varepsilon(y)) & & \varepsilon(x\ \dot{\vee}\ y) \longrightarrow_+ \neg\neg\varepsilon(x) & \\
& & \varepsilon(x\ \dot{\vee}\ y) \longrightarrow_+ \neg\neg\varepsilon(y) & \\
\varepsilon(\dot{\neg}\ x) \longrightarrow_- \neg\varepsilon(x) & & \varepsilon(\dot{\neg}\ x) \longrightarrow_+ \neg\varepsilon(x) & \\
\varepsilon(\dot{\forall}_T\ x) \longrightarrow_- \forall y\ \varepsilon(x\ y) & & \varepsilon(\dot{\forall}_T\ x) \longrightarrow_+ \neg\neg\varepsilon(x\ H_T(x)) &
\end{array}$$

This theory does not have the cut elimination property as the sequent $\varepsilon(x\ H_T(x)) \vdash \forall y\ \varepsilon(x\ y)$ has a proof with a cut (on $\varepsilon(\dot{\forall}_T\ x)$) but no cut free proofs. Yet, as proved in [6], for sequents not containing the symbols H_T, cut free provability in this theory characterizes exactly provability in Simple type theory.

The fact that there is an infinite number of objects of type ι can be expressed by the rules

$$(Pred\ (Succ\ x)) =_{\mathcal{E}} x$$

$$\varepsilon(Null\ 0) \longrightarrow_+ \neg\bot$$

$$\varepsilon(Null\ (Succ\ x)) \longrightarrow_- \bot$$

The first expresses that the function *Succ* of type $\iota \to \iota$ has a left inverse *Pred*, *i.e.* that it is injective. The two others that 0 is not in its image, *i.e.* that it is not surjective.

3 Polarized Resolution Modulo

Definition 6 (Clause, Constraint, Unifier, Constrained clause). *A* clause *is a finite set of literals. A* constraint *is a pair of terms or of atomic propositions, written* $t = u$. *A* unifier *of a constraint* $t = u$ *is a substitution* θ *such that* $\theta t =_{\mathcal{E}} \theta u$. *A* constrained clause *is a pair* $U[\mathcal{C}]$ *such that* U *is a clause and* $\mathcal{C}$ *is a finite set of constraints.*

The empty clause is written $\Box$. If U is a clause and L is a literal, we write U, L for the clause $U \cup \{L\}$. If $A = \forall x_1 \ldots \forall x_p\ (L_1 \vee \ldots \vee L_n)$ is a clausal proposition, we write $|A|$ for the clause $\{L_1, \ldots, L_n\}$. By convention, $|\bot| = \Box$. If ψ is a constrained clause and Φ a set of constrained clauses, a *Φ-renaming* of ψ is a renaming of ψ with variables that do not occur in Φ.

Definition 7 (One-way clause, Selected literal). *To each polarized rewrite system, we associate a set of clauses called the* one-way clauses *of* $\mathcal{R}$. *These clauses have a privileged literal called the* selected *literal. For each negative rule* $P \longrightarrow \forall x_1 \ldots \forall x_p\ (L_1 \vee \ldots \vee L_n)$, *we take the clause* $\underline{\neg P}, L_1, \ldots, L_n$ *and, for each positive rule* $P \longrightarrow \neg \forall x_1 \ldots \forall x_p\ (L_1 \vee \ldots \vee L_n)$, *we take the clause* $\underline{P}, L_1, \ldots, L_n$ *where the selected literal is the underlined one.*

Definition 8 (Polarized resolution modulo). *Let* Φ *be a set of constrained clauses, we write* $\Phi \mapsto_{\mathcal{R}} \psi$ *if the constrained clause* ψ *can be derived from the constrained clauses of* Φ *using finitely many applications of the* **Resolution** *and* **Extended Narrowing** *rules described in Figure 2. This means that there exists a derivation of the clause* ψ *under the assumptions* Φ, i.e. *a sequence* $\psi_1, \ldots, \psi_n$ *such that either* $n = 0$ *and* ψ *is an element of* Φ *or* $n \geq 1$, $\psi_n = \psi$ *and each* ψ_i *is derived with a rule of Figure 2 from renamings of clauses of the set* $\Phi \cup \{\psi_1, \ldots, \psi_{i-1}\}$.

When $\mathcal{R}_- = \mathcal{R}_+ = \varnothing$, Polarized resolution modulo boils down to Plotkin's Equational resolution [12,11]: the **Extended Narrowing** rule never applies, and the only difference with first-order Resolution is that unification is replaced by equational unification modulo $\mathcal{E}$.

As discussed in the introduction, the **Extended Narrowing** rule can be seen as an instance of the **Resolution** rule where, from an ordinary clause $(U, P)[\mathcal{C}]$ and a one-way clause $V, \underline{\neg Q}$, we derive the clause $(U \cup V)[\mathcal{C} \cup \{P = Q\}]$. Thus instead of having the **Extended Narrowing** rule, we could add the one-way clauses to the set of clauses to be refuted and restrict Equational resolution in such a way that the **Resolution** rule cannot be applied to two one-way clauses and can be applied to a one-way clause and another clause only if the resolved literal in the one-way clause is the selected one. Yet, we prefer to distinguish this **Extended Narrowing** rule for better clarity.

$$\frac{(U, P_1, \ldots, P_n)[\mathcal{C}_1] \quad (V, \neg Q_1, \ldots, \neg Q_p)[\mathcal{C}_2]}{(U \cup V)[\mathcal{C}_1 \cup \mathcal{C}_2 \cup \{P_1 = \ldots = P_n = Q_1 = \ldots = Q_p\}]} \ \textbf{Resolution}$$

$$\frac{(U, P)[\mathcal{C}]}{(U \cup V)[\mathcal{C} \cup \{P = Q\}]} \text{ if } V, \underline{\neg Q} \text{ one-way clause of } \mathcal{R} \ \textbf{Extended Narrowing}$$

$$\frac{(U, \neg P)[\mathcal{C}]}{(U \cup V)[\mathcal{C} \cup \{P = Q\}]} \text{ if } V, \underline{Q} \text{ one-way clause of } \mathcal{R} \ \textbf{Extended Narrowing}$$

Fig. 2. Polarized resolution modulo

Example 2. Using the rewrite system presented in Example 1, we get the one way clauses

$$\begin{array}{cc}
\underline{\neg\varepsilon(x \mathbin{\dot\vee} y)}, \varepsilon(x), \varepsilon(y) & \underline{\varepsilon(x \mathbin{\dot\vee} y)}, \neg\varepsilon(x) \\
 & \underline{\varepsilon(x \mathbin{\dot\vee} y)}, \neg\varepsilon(y) \\
\underline{\neg\varepsilon(\dot\neg\ x)}, \neg\varepsilon(x) & \underline{\varepsilon(\dot\neg\ x)}, \varepsilon(x) \\
\underline{\neg\varepsilon(\dot\forall_T\ x)}, \varepsilon(x\ y) & \underline{\varepsilon(\dot\forall_T\ x)}, \neg\varepsilon(x\ H_T(x))
\end{array}$$

As we shall prove, Polarized resolution modulo with these one-way clauses is a complete method for Simple type theory, and attempting to prove a contradiction in this theory with this method yields an empty search space.

An alternative to this method is to transform the rules of $\mathcal{R}_-$ and $\mathcal{R}_+$ into axioms, with Proposition 3 and 5, add the clause form of these axioms to the set of clauses to be refuted, and use Equational resolution modulo $\mathcal{E}$. We obtain this way the same set of clauses, except that they are not one-way clauses:

$$\begin{array}{cc}
\neg\varepsilon(x \mathbin{\dot\vee} y), \varepsilon(x), \varepsilon(y) & \varepsilon(x \mathbin{\dot\vee} y), \neg\varepsilon(x) \\
 & \varepsilon(x \mathbin{\dot\vee} y), \neg\varepsilon(y) \\
\neg\varepsilon(\dot\neg\ x), \neg\varepsilon(x) & \varepsilon(\dot\neg\ x), \varepsilon(x) \\
\neg\varepsilon(\dot\forall_T\ x), \varepsilon(x\ y) & \varepsilon(\dot\forall_T\ x), \neg\varepsilon(x\ H_T(x))
\end{array}$$

equational resolution, modulo SK, with these clauses is a complete proof search method for Simple type theory, but attempting to prove a contradiction in this theory with this method yields an infinite search space.

4 Soundness and Completeness

We now want to prove that Polarized resolution modulo is sound and complete, *i.e.* that if $A_1, \ldots, A_n$ are closed clausal propositions, then $|A_1|[\varnothing], \ldots, |A_n|[\varnothing] \mapsto_{\mathcal{R}} \Box[\mathcal{C}]$ for $\mathcal{C}$ unifiable if and only if the sequent $A_1, \ldots, A_n \vdash$ has a cut free proof modulo $\mathcal{R}$. As a corollary, Polarized resolution modulo is complete if and only if the theory defined by the rewrite rules has the cut elimination property.

As usual we introduce an intermediate system that we prove sound and complete and then lift the result to Polarized resolution modulo.

Definition 9 (Polarized extended identical resolution). *Let $\mathcal{R}$ be a polarized rewrite system and K a set of clauses, we write $K \hookrightarrow_{\mathcal{R}} U$ if the clause U can be derived from the clauses of K using finitely many applications of the*

$$\frac{U}{(t/x)U} \textbf{ Instantiation}$$

$$\frac{U}{U'} \text{ if } U =_{\mathcal{E}} U' \textbf{ Conversion}$$

$$\frac{U, P}{U \cup V} \text{ if } P \longrightarrow_{-} A,\ V = |A| \textbf{ Reduction}$$

$$\frac{U, \neg P}{U \cup V} \text{ if } P \longrightarrow_{+} \neg A,\ V = |A| \textbf{ Reduction}$$

$$\frac{U, P \quad U', \neg P}{U \cup U'} \textbf{ Identical Resolution}$$

Fig. 3. Polarized extended identical resolution (PEIR)

Polarized extended identical resolution *(PEIR) rules described in Figure 3. This means that there exists a derivation of the clause U under the assumptions K,* i.e. *a sequence $U_1, \dots, U_n$ such that either $n = 0$ and U is an element of K or $n \geq 1$, $U_n = U$ and each U_i is derived with a rule of Figure 3 from clauses of the set $K \cup \{U_1, \dots, U_{i-1}\}$.*

Like [9], we prove directly the soundness of the PEIR method with respect to the cut free sequent calculus.

We write $\overline{\forall} A$ for the universal closure of A.

Proposition 6. *Let $A_1, \dots, A_n, B_1, \dots, B_n$ be clausal propositions such that $|A_1| = |B_1|, \dots, |A_n| = |B_n|$. If $\Gamma, A_1, \dots, A_n \vdash \Delta$ has a cut free proof, then so does $\Gamma, B_1, \dots, B_n \vdash \Delta$.*

Proof. We first prove that $\Gamma, C \vee D \vdash \Delta$ has a cut free proof if and only if $\Gamma, C \vdash \Delta$ and $\Gamma, D \vdash \Delta$ do. The result follows by a simple induction on proofs.

Definition 10 (Partial instance). *A* partial instance *of a proposition A is a reduct for $\longrightarrow_{-}^{*}$ of a proposition of the form $\forall x_1 \ \dots \ \forall x_n \ (\sigma A)$ for some variables $x_1, \dots, x_n$ and substitution σ. The instance is* strict *if $n > 0$.*

Proposition 7. *Let A and B be two propositions and $C_1, \dots, C_n$ be partial instances of $A \vee B$. If the sequent $\Gamma, C_1, \dots, C_n \vdash \Delta$ has a cut free proof modulo $\mathcal{R}$, then so does $\Gamma, \overline{\forall}(A \vee P), \overline{\forall}(B \vee \neg P) \vdash \Delta$.*

Proof. By induction on the structure of the proof of the sequent $\Gamma, C_1, \dots, C_n \vdash \Delta$. If the last rule is a rule on a proposition of Γ or Δ, a contraction rule, a weakening rule, or the left rule of the universal quantifier, we just apply the induction hypothesis. If it is the left rule of the disjunction, say to $C_1 = A' \vee B'$, then we have cut free proofs of $\Gamma, A', C_2, \dots, C_n \vdash \Delta$ and $\Gamma, B', C_2, \dots, C_n \vdash \Delta$, with $\sigma A \longrightarrow_{-}^{*} A'$ and $\sigma B \longrightarrow_{-}^{*} B'$. By induction hypothesis, we get cut free proofs of the sequents $\Gamma, A', \overline{\forall}(A \vee P), \overline{\forall}(B \vee \neg P) \vdash \Delta$ and $\Gamma, B', \overline{\forall}(A \vee P), \overline{\forall}(B \vee \neg P) \vdash \Delta$ and we build a cut free proof of $\Gamma, \overline{\forall}(A \vee P), \overline{\forall}(B \vee \neg P) \vdash \Delta$.

Proposition 8. *Let A and B be two propositions and $C_1, \dots, C_n$ be partial instances of $A \vee B$. Let P be a proposition such that $P \longrightarrow_-^* \forall x_1 \dots \forall x_p\ B$ or $P \longrightarrow_-^* \neg\neg\forall x_1 \dots \forall x_p\ B$ where $x_1, \dots, x_p$ are variables not occurring free in A. If the sequent $\Gamma, C_1, \dots, C_n \vdash \Delta$ has a cut free proof modulo $\mathcal{R}$, then so does $\Gamma, \overline{\forall}(A \vee P) \vdash \Delta$.*

Proof. By induction on the structure of the proof of the sequent $\Gamma, C_1, \dots, C_n \vdash \Delta$. If the last rule is a rule on a proposition of Γ or Δ, a contraction rule, a weakening rule, or the left rule of the universal quantifier, we just apply the induction hypothesis. If it is the left rule of the disjunction, say to $C_1 = A' \vee B'$, then we have cut free proofs of $\Gamma, A', C_2, \dots, C_n \vdash \Delta$ and $\Gamma, B', C_2, \dots, C_n \vdash \Delta$, with $\sigma A \longrightarrow_-^* A'$ and $\sigma B \longrightarrow_-^* B'$. By induction hypothesis, we get cut free proofs of $\Gamma, A', \overline{\forall}(A \vee P) \vdash \Delta$ and $\Gamma, B', \overline{\forall}(A \vee P) \vdash \Delta$, and we build a cut free proof of $\Gamma, \overline{\forall}(A \vee P) \vdash \Delta$.

Proposition 9. *Let A be a proposition and $C_1, \dots, C_n$ be strict partial instances of $(t/x)A$. If the sequent $\Gamma, C_1, \dots, C_n \vdash \Delta$ has a cut free proof modulo $\mathcal{R}$, then so does $\Gamma, \overline{\forall}A \vdash \Delta$.*

Proof. By induction on the structure of the proof of $\Gamma, C_1, \dots, C_n \vdash \Delta$. If the last rule is a rule on a proposition of Γ or Δ, a contraction rule, a weakening rule, or the left rule of the universal quantifier producing a strict partial instance of $(t/x)A$, we just apply the induction hypothesis. If it is the left rule of the universal quantifier, say to C_1, producing a reduct A' of $\sigma(t/x)A$, then we have a cut free proof of $\Gamma, A', C_2, \dots, C_n \vdash \Delta$ and by induction hypothesis we get a cut free proof of $\Gamma, A', \overline{\forall}A \vdash \Delta$ and we build a cut free proof of $\Gamma, \overline{\forall}A \vdash \Delta$.

Proposition 10 (PEIR Soundness). *Let $A_1, \dots, A_n$ be closed clausal propositions. If $|A_1|, \dots, |A_n| \hookrightarrow_{\mathcal{R}} \Box$, then $A_1, \dots, A_n \vdash$ has a cut free proof modulo $\mathcal{R}$.*

Proof. By induction on the structure the derivation $|A_1|, \dots, |A_n| \hookrightarrow_{\mathcal{R}} \Box$. If the derivation is empty, then one of the clauses $|A_i|$ is $\Box$. Thus, the proposition A_i is $\bot$ and $A_1, \dots, A_n \vdash$ has a cut free proof modulo $\mathcal{R}$. Otherwise, the derivation of $|A_1|, \dots, |A_n| \hookrightarrow_{\mathcal{R}} \Box$ starts by producing a clause U and there is a shorter derivation of $|A_1|, \dots, |A_n|, U \hookrightarrow_{\mathcal{R}} \Box$. Let A' be a closed clausal proposition such that $U = |A'|$, by induction hypothesis, we have a cut free proof of $A_1, \dots, A_n, A' \vdash$. We consider four cases, according to the rule used to derive U.

- If this rule is the **Identical Resolution** rule, then there are two propositions, say A_1 and A_2, such that $|A_1|$ contains a literal P and $|A_2|$ a literal $\neg P$. Using Proposition 6, we can consider that $A_1 = \overline{\forall}(A_1' \vee P)$, $A_2 = \overline{\forall}(A_2' \vee \neg P)$ and $A' = \overline{\forall}(A_1' \vee A_2')$. The proposition A' is a partial instance of $A_1' \vee A_2'$, thus, by Proposition 7, we get a cut free proof of the sequent $A_1, \dots, A_n, A_1, A_2 \vdash$ and, with a contraction, one of $A_1, \dots, A_n \vdash$.
- If this rule is the **Reduction** rule, then there is a proposition, say A_1, such that $A_1 = \overline{\forall}(A_1' \vee P)$ with $P \longrightarrow_-^* \forall x_1 \dots \forall x_p\ B$ or $P \longrightarrow_-^* \neg\neg\forall x_1 \dots \forall x_p\ B$

where B is a disjunction of literals, and $A' = \overline{\forall}(A'_1 \vee B)$. The proposition A' is a partial instance of $A'_1 \vee B$, thus, by Proposition 8, we get a cut free proof of the sequent $A_1, \ldots, A_n, A_1 \vdash$ and, with a contraction, one of $A_1, \ldots, A_n \vdash$.
- If this rule is the **Conversion** rule, then there is a proposition, say A_1 that is $\mathcal{E}$-equivalent to A'. We have $A_1 \longrightarrow^*_- A'$. By Proposition 1, we get a cut free proof of the sequent $A_1, \ldots, A_n, A_1 \vdash$ and, with a contraction, one of $A_1, \ldots, A_n \vdash$.
- If this rule is the **Instantiation** rule, then there is a proposition, say A_1, such that $A_1 = \overline{\forall} B$ and $A' = \overline{\forall}(t/x)B$. If the proposition A' is a strict partial instance of $(t/x)B$, then, by Proposition 9, we get a cut free proof of the sequent $A_1, \ldots, A_n, A_1 \vdash$ and, with a contraction, one of $A_1, \ldots, A_n \vdash$. Otherwise, $A' = (t/x)B$, and we build a cut free proof of $A_1, \ldots, A_n \vdash$.

We now prove the completeness of the PEIR method.

Proposition 11 (Interpolation). *Let P be an atomic proposition and A be a non atomic one. If $P \longrightarrow^*_- A$, then there exists an atomic proposition P' and a non atomic clausal proposition A' such that $P \longrightarrow^*_- P' \longrightarrow_- A' \longrightarrow^*_- A$. If $P \longrightarrow^*_+ A$, then there exists an atomic proposition P' and a clausal proposition A_1 such that $P \longrightarrow^*_+ P' \longrightarrow_+ \neg A_1 \longrightarrow^*_+ A$.*

Proof. Consider a reduction sequence, $P = B_0, \ldots, B_n = A$ from P to A and let P' be the last atomic proposition in this sequence. As A is not atomic, P' is not the last proposition of the sequence, let A' be the next proposition in the sequence. We have $P \longrightarrow^*_- P' \longrightarrow_- A' \longrightarrow^*_- A$. As P' reduces to A' in one step, A' is clausal proposition in the first case and it is the negation of a clausal proposition in the second.

Proposition 12. *Let K be a set of clauses and U and V two clauses. If $K, U \hookrightarrow_{\mathcal{R}} \Box$ and $K, V \hookrightarrow_{\mathcal{R}} \Box$ then $K, (U \cup V) \hookrightarrow_{\mathcal{R}} \Box$.*

Proof. By induction on the structure of the derivation of $K, U \hookrightarrow_{\mathcal{R}} \Box$, there exists a derivation of $K, (U \cup V) \hookrightarrow_{\mathcal{R}} \Box$ or a derivation of $K, (U \cup V) \hookrightarrow_{\mathcal{R}} V$. In the first case we are done, in the second, we use $K, V \hookrightarrow_{\mathcal{R}} \Box$ to conclude.

Proposition 13 (PEIR Completeness). *Let $A_1, \ldots, A_n$ be closed clausal propositions and $P_1, \ldots, P_m$ be closed atomic propositions. If $A_1, \ldots, A_n \vdash P_1, \ldots, P_m$ has a cut free proof then $|A_1|, \ldots, |A_n|, \neg P_1, \ldots, \neg P_m \hookrightarrow_{\mathcal{R}} \Box$.*

Proof. By Proposition 2, the sequent $A_1, \ldots, A_n \vdash P_1, \ldots, P_m$ has a closed cut free proof. By induction on the size of this proof.

- If the last rule is an axiom, then $n = m = 1$, $A_1 \longrightarrow^*_- Q$ and $P_1 \longrightarrow^*_+ Q$ for an atomic proposition Q. Thus, A_1 is atomic, $|A_1| = A_1$ and, using the **Reduction**, **Conversion** and **Identical Resolution** rules, we get $|A_1|, \ldots, |A_n|, \neg P_1, \ldots, \neg P_m \hookrightarrow_{\mathcal{R}} \Box$.
- If the last rule is the left contraction rule, then one of the propositions, say A_1, reduces to propositions B and C and $B, C, A_2, \ldots, A_n \vdash P_1, \ldots, P_m$

has a smaller cut free proof. By Proposition 1, $A_1, A_1, A_2, \ldots, A_n \vdash P_1, \ldots, P_m$ has a cut free proof of the same size. Thus, by induction hypothesis, $|A_1|, |A_2|, \ldots, |A_n|, \neg P_1, \ldots, \neg P_m \hookrightarrow_{\mathcal{R}} \Box$.

- If the last rule is the right contraction rule, the argument is the same.
- If the last rule is the left weakening rule, then one of the propositions, say A_1, is erased and the sequent $A_2, \ldots, A_n \vdash P_1, \ldots, P_m$ has a smaller cut free proof. By induction hypothesis, $|A_2|, \ldots, |A_n|, \neg P_1, \ldots, \neg P_m \hookrightarrow_{\mathcal{R}} \Box$ and thus $|A_1|, |A_2|, \ldots, |A_n|, \neg P_1, \ldots, \neg P_m \hookrightarrow_{\mathcal{R}} \Box$.
- If the last rule is the right weakening rule, the argument is the same.
- If the last rule is the left rule of the disjunction, then one of the propositions, say A_1, reduces to a disjunction $B \vee C$ and $B, A_2, \ldots, A_n \vdash P_1, \ldots, P_m$ and $C, A_2, \ldots, A_n \vdash P_1, \ldots, P_m$ have smaller cut free proofs. Thus, A_1 is either a disjunction $B' \vee C'$ or an atomic proposition, in which case $|A_1| = A_1$, and, by Proposition 11, there exists an atomic proposition A' and a clausal proposition $B' \vee C'$ such that $A_1 \longrightarrow_{-}^{*} A' \longrightarrow_{-} B' \vee C' \longrightarrow_{-}^{*} B \vee C$. In both cases, we have $B' \longrightarrow_{-}^{*} B$ and $C' \longrightarrow_{-}^{*} C$, by Proposition 1, $B', A_2, \ldots, A_n \vdash P_1, \ldots, P_m$ and $C', A_2, \ldots, A_n \vdash P_1, \ldots, P_m$ have cut free proofs of the same size, by induction hypothesis, $|B'|, |A_2|, \ldots, |A_n|, \neg P_1, \ldots, \neg P_m \hookrightarrow_{\mathcal{R}} \Box$ and $|C'|, |A_2|, \ldots, |A_n|, \neg P_1, \ldots, \neg P_m \hookrightarrow_{\mathcal{R}} \Box$ and by Proposition 12, $|B' \vee C'|, |A_2|, \ldots, |A_n|, \neg P_1, \ldots, \neg P_m \hookrightarrow_{\mathcal{R}} \Box$. In the first case, we have $A_1 = B' \vee C'$ and we are done. In the second, we have $A_1 \longrightarrow_{-}^{*} A' \longrightarrow_{-} B' \vee C'$, thus, with the **Conversion** and **Reduction** rules, $|A_1|, |A_2|, \ldots, |A_n|, \neg P_1, \ldots, \neg P_m \hookrightarrow_{\mathcal{R}} \Box$.
- If the last rule is the left rule of the negation, then one of the propositions, say A_1, reduces to a negation $\neg B$ and $A_2, \ldots, A_n \vdash B, P_1, \ldots, P_m$ has a smaller cut free proof. Thus, A_1 is either a negation $\neg B'$ or an atomic proposition, in which case $|A_1| = A_1$, and, by Proposition 11, there exists an atomic proposition A' and a clausal proposition $\neg B'$ such that $A_1 \longrightarrow_{-}^{*} A' \longrightarrow_{-} \neg B' \longrightarrow_{-}^{*} \neg B$. In both cases, we have $B' \longrightarrow_{+}^{*} B$, by Proposition 1, $A_2, \ldots, A_n \vdash B', P_1, \ldots, P_m$ has a cut free proof of the same size, and, by induction hypothesis, $|A_2|, \ldots, |A_n|, \neg B', \neg P_1, \ldots, \neg P_m \hookrightarrow_{\mathcal{R}} \Box$. In the first case, we have $A_1 = \neg B'$ and we are done. In the second, we have $A_1 \longrightarrow_{-}^{*} A' \longrightarrow_{-} \neg B'$, thus, with the **Conversion** and **Reduction** rules, $|A_1|, |A_2|, \ldots, |A_n|, \neg P_1, \ldots, \neg P_m \hookrightarrow_{\mathcal{R}} \Box$.
- If the last rule is the left rule of the universal quantifier, then one of the propositions, say A_1, reduces to a universal proposition $\forall x\ B$ and $(t/x)B, A_2, \ldots, A_n \vdash P_1, \ldots, P_m$ has a smaller cut free proof. Thus, A_1 is either a universal proposition $\forall x\ B'$ or an atomic proposition, in which case $|A_1| = A_1$, and, by Proposition 11, there exists an atomic proposition A' and a clausal proposition $\forall x\ B'$ such that $A_1 \longrightarrow_{-}^{*} A' \longrightarrow_{-} \forall x\ B' \longrightarrow_{-}^{*} \forall x\ B$. In both cases, we have $(t/x)B' \longrightarrow_{-}^{*} (t/x)B$, by Proposition 1, $(t/x)B', A_2, \ldots, A_n \vdash P_1, \ldots, P_m$ has a cut free proof of the same size, by induction hypothesis, $|(t/x)B'|, |A_2|, \ldots, |A_n|, \neg P_1, \ldots, \neg P_m \hookrightarrow_{\mathcal{R}} \Box$ and with the **Instantiation** rule, $|\forall x\ B'|, |A_2|, \ldots, |A_n|, \neg P_1, \ldots, \neg P_m \hookrightarrow_{\mathcal{R}} \Box$. In the first case, we have $A_1 = \forall x\ B'$ and we are done. In the second, we have

$A_1 \longrightarrow_-^* A' \longrightarrow_- \forall x\ B'$, thus, with the **Conversion** and **Reduction** rules, $|A_1|, |A_2|, \ldots, |A_n|, \neg P_1, \ldots, \neg P_m \hookrightarrow_{\mathcal{R}} \Box$.

- If the last rule is the right rule of the negation, then one of the propositions, say P_1, reduces to a negation $\neg B$ and $B, A_1, \ldots, A_n \vdash P_2, \ldots, P_m$ has a smaller cut free proof. By Proposition 11, there exists an atomic proposition P' and a clausal proposition B' such that $P_1 \longrightarrow_+^* P' \longrightarrow_+ \neg B' \longrightarrow_+^* \neg B$. Thus $B' \longrightarrow_-^* B$, by Proposition 1, $B', A_1, \ldots, A_n \vdash P_2, \ldots, P_m$ has a cut free proof of the same size, and, by induction hypothesis, $|B'|, |A_1|, \ldots, |A_n|, \neg P_2, \ldots, \neg P_m \hookrightarrow_{\mathcal{R}} \Box$. We have $P_1 \longrightarrow_+^* P' \longrightarrow_+ \neg B'$, thus, with the **Conversion** and **Reduction** rules, $|A_1|, |A_2|, \ldots, |A_n|, \neg P_1, \ldots, \neg P_m \hookrightarrow_{\mathcal{R}} \Box$.

We now lift the soundness and completeness results from the PEIR method to Polarized resolution modulo.

Definition 11 (Instance). *An* instance *of a constrained clause $U[\mathcal{C}]$ is a clause θU where θ is a unifier of $\mathcal{C}$.*

Proposition 14. *If the constrained clause ψ is derived with the* **Resolution** *rule from the renamings of two constrained clauses ϕ_1 and ϕ_2, then any instance of ψ is derived in the PEIR system from instances of ϕ_1 and ϕ_2.*

Proof. Let $(V_1, P_1, \ldots, P_n)[\mathcal{C}_1]$ and $(V_2, \neg Q_1, \ldots, \neg Q_p)[\mathcal{C}_2]$ be the renamings of ϕ_1 and ϕ_2 used to derive ψ. Then, $\psi = (V_1 \cup V_2)[\mathcal{C}_1 \cup \mathcal{C}_2 \cup \{P_1 = \ldots = P_n = Q_1 = \ldots = Q_p\}]$. Any instance of ψ has the form $\theta(V_1 \cup V_2)$ for some unifier θ of $\mathcal{C}_1 \cup \mathcal{C}_2 \cup \{P_1 = \ldots = P_n = Q_1 = \ldots = Q_m\}$. The substitution θ is a unifier of $\mathcal{C}_1$, thus $\theta(V_1, P_1, \ldots, P_n)$ is an instance of $(V_1, P_1, \ldots, P_n)[\mathcal{C}_1]$, hence it is also an instance of ϕ_1. In the same way and $\theta(V_2, \neg Q_1, \ldots, \neg Q_p)$ is an instance of ϕ_2. And $\theta(V_1 \cup V_2)$ is derived from these two clauses with the **Conversion** and **Identical Resolution** rules.

Proposition 15. *If the constrained clause ψ is derived with the* **Extended Narrowing** *rule from the renaming of a constrained clause ϕ, then any instance of ψ is derived in the PEIR system from an instance of ϕ.*

Proof. If the **Extended Narrowing** rule applied is the negative one, then let $(V_1, P)[\mathcal{C}]$ be the renaming of ϕ and $V_2, \neg Q$ be the renaming of the one-way clause of $\mathcal{R}$ used to derive ψ. We have $\psi = (V_1 \cup V_2)[\mathcal{C} \cup \{P = Q\}]$. Any instance of ψ has the form $\theta(V_1 \cup V_2)$ for some unifier θ of $\mathcal{C} \cup \{P = Q\}$. The substitution θ is a unifier of $\mathcal{C}$, thus $\theta(V_1, P)$ is an instance of $(V_1, P)[\mathcal{C}]$ hence it is also an instance of ϕ. There exists a proposition A such that $\theta Q \longrightarrow A$ and $|A| = \theta V_2$, thus $\theta(V_1 \cup V_2)$ is derived from this clause with the **Conversion** and **Reduction** rules. We proceed in the same way for the positive **Extended Narrowing** rule.

Proposition 16 (Soundness). *Let $U_1, \ldots U_n$ be clauses. If $U_1[\varnothing], \ldots, U_n[\varnothing]$ $\mapsto_{\mathcal{R}} \Box[\mathcal{C}]$ where $\mathcal{C}$ is a unifiable set of constraints. Then, $U_1, \ldots, U_n \hookrightarrow_{\mathcal{R}} \Box$.*

Proof. Let $K = \{U_1, \ldots U_n\}$ and $\Phi = \{U_1[\varnothing], \ldots, U_n[\varnothing]\}$. With a simple induction on the structure of derivations and using Propositions 14 and 15, we get that if ψ is a constrained clause such that $\Phi \mapsto_{\mathcal{R}} \psi$ and U is an instance of ψ, then there exists a set L of instances of clauses of Φ such that $L \hookrightarrow_{\mathcal{R}} U$. Then, as $\mathcal{C}$ is unifiable, the clause $\Box$ is an instance of $\Box[\mathcal{C}]$, thus there exists a set L of instances of clauses of Φ, such that $L \hookrightarrow_{\mathcal{R}} \Box$. As each element of L can be obtained from a clause of K with the **Instantiation** rule, we get $K \hookrightarrow_{\mathcal{R}} \Box$.

Proposition 17. *If the clause V is derived with the* **Identical Resolution** *rule from clauses U_1 and U_2, $\mathcal{E}$-equivalent to instances of constrained clauses ϕ_1 and ϕ_2, then V is $\mathcal{E}$-equivalent to an instance of a constrained clause derived in Polarized resolution modulo from renamings of ϕ_1 and ϕ_2.*

Proof. As the **Identical Resolution** rule applies to U_1 and U_2 we have $U_1 = (U'_1, P)$ and $U_2 = (U'_2, \neg P)$, and $V = U'_1 \cup U'_2$. Consider two renamings $W_1[\mathcal{C}_1]$ and $W_2[\mathcal{C}_2]$ of ϕ_1 and ϕ_2. The clauses U_1 and U_2 are instance of $W_1[\mathcal{C}_1]$ and $W_2[\mathcal{C}_2]$, thus there exist two domain-disjoint unifiers θ_1 and θ_2 of $\mathcal{C}_1$ and $\mathcal{C}_2$, such that $\theta_1 W_1 =_{\mathcal{E}} (U'_1, P)$ and $\theta_2 W_2 =_{\mathcal{E}} (U'_2, \neg P)$. The substitution $\theta = \theta_1 \cup \theta_2$ is a unifier of $\mathcal{C}_1 \cup \mathcal{C}_2$ and we have $\theta W_1 =_{\mathcal{E}} (U'_1, P)$ and $\theta W_2 =_{\mathcal{E}} (U'_2, \neg P)$. Thus, the clause W_1 has the form $W'_1, P_1, \ldots, P_n$ and the clause W_2 has the form $W'_2, \neg Q_1, \ldots, \neg Q_p$ with $\theta W'_1 =_{\mathcal{E}} U'_1$, $\theta W'_2 =_{\mathcal{E}} U'_2$, $\theta P_i =_{\mathcal{E}} P$ and $\theta Q_j =_{\mathcal{E}} P$. The **Resolution** rule applies to $W_1[\mathcal{C}_1]$ and $W_2[\mathcal{C}_2]$ and derives the constrained clause $\psi = (W'_1 \cup W'_2)[\mathcal{C}_1 \cup \mathcal{C}_2 \cup \{P_1 = \ldots = P_n = Q_1 = \ldots = Q_p\}]$. The substitution θ is a unifier of the constraints of this clause and $V = U'_1 \cup U'_2 =_{\mathcal{E}} \theta(W'_1 \cup W'_2)$. Thus V is $\mathcal{E}$-equivalent to an instance of ψ.

Proposition 18. *If the clause V is derived with the* **Reduction** *rule from a clause U, $\mathcal{E}$-equivalent to an instance of a constrained clause ϕ, then V is $\mathcal{E}$-equivalent to an instance of a constrained clause derived in Polarized resolution modulo from a renaming of ϕ.*

Proof. If the **Reduction** rule applied is negative, we have $U = (U', P)$, and there is a negative rule $Q \longrightarrow A$ in $\mathcal{R}$ and a substitution σ such that $P = \sigma Q$, $V = U' \cup |\sigma A|$. Taking the variables bound in A out of the domain of σ, we have $|\sigma A| = \sigma |A|$. Let $Z = |A|$. The clause $(Z, \underline{\neg Q})$ is a one-way clause of $\mathcal{R}$, $P = \sigma Q$ and $V = U' \cup \sigma Z$. Consider a renaming $W[\mathcal{C}]$ of ϕ with fresh variables. There exists a unifier θ_0 of $\mathcal{C}$ such that $\theta_0 W =_{\mathcal{E}} (U', P)$. Thus, the clause W has the form $W', P'_1, \ldots, P'_n$ and $\theta_0 W' =_{\mathcal{E}} U'$ and $\theta_0 P'_i =_{\mathcal{E}} P$. Let $(Z_1, \underline{\neg Q_1}), \ldots, (Z_n, \underline{\neg Q_n})$ be n renamings of the one-way clause $(Z, \underline{\neg Q})$ and $\theta_1, \ldots, \theta_n$ be domain-disjoint substitutions such that $\theta_i Q_i = \sigma Q$ and $\theta_i Z_i = \sigma Z$. Let $\theta = \theta_0 \cup \theta_1 \cup \ldots \cup \theta_n$, θ is a unifier of $\mathcal{C}$, $\theta W' =_{\mathcal{E}} U'$, $\theta P'_i =_{\mathcal{E}} P$, $\theta Q_i = \sigma Q = P$ and $\theta Z_i = \sigma Z$. Applying the **Extended Narrowing** rule n times to $W[\mathcal{C}]$ yields the constrained clause $\psi = (W' \cup Z_1 \cup \ldots \cup Z_n)[\mathcal{C} \cup \{P_1 = Q_1, \ldots, P_n = Q_n\}]$. The substitution θ is a unifier of the constraints of ψ and $V = U' \cup \sigma Z =_{\mathcal{E}} \theta(W' \cup Z_1 \cup \ldots \cup Z_n)$. We proceed in the same way for the positive **Reduction** rule.

Proposition 19 (Completeness). *Let $U_1, \ldots, U_n$ be clauses. If $U_1, \ldots, U_n \hookrightarrow_{\mathcal{R}} \Box$ then $U_1[\varnothing], \ldots, U_n[\varnothing] \mapsto_{\mathcal{R}} \Box[\mathcal{C}]$, where $\mathcal{C}$ is a unifiable set of constraints.*

Proof. Let $K = \{U_1, \ldots, U_n\}$ and $\Phi = \{U_1[\varnothing], \ldots, U_n[\varnothing]\}$. With a simple induction on the structure of derivations and with Propositions 17 and 18, we prove that if $K \hookrightarrow_{\mathcal{R}} U$ then there exists a constrained clause ψ such that $\Phi \mapsto_{\mathcal{R}} \psi$ and U is $\mathcal{E}$-equivalent to an instance of ψ. Then, if $K \hookrightarrow_{\mathcal{R}} \square$ then there exists a constrained clause ψ such that $\Phi \mapsto_{\mathcal{R}} \psi$ and $\square$ is $\mathcal{E}$-equivalent to an instance of ψ. Thus $\psi = \square[\mathcal{C}]$ where $\mathcal{C}$ is a unifiable set of constraints.

Theorem 1. *Let $A_1, \ldots, A_n$ be closed clausal propositions. Then $|A_1|[\varnothing], \ldots, |A_n|[\varnothing] \mapsto_{\mathcal{R}} \square[\mathcal{C}]$ for $\mathcal{C}$ unifiable if and only if $A_1, \ldots, A_n \vdash$ has a cut free proof modulo $\mathcal{R}$.*

Proof. From Propositions 10, 13, 16, and 19.

References

1. Andrews, P.B.: Resolution in type theory. The Journal of Symbolic Logic 36, 414–432 (1971)
2. Bachmair, L., Ganzinger, H.: Resolution Theorem Proving. In: Robinson, J.A., Voronkov, A. (eds.) Handbook of Automated Reasoning. Elsevier, Amsterdam (2001)
3. Burel, G.: Embedding Deduction Modulo into a Prover, manuscript available on the web page of the author (2010)
4. Burel, G., Dowek, G.: How can we prove that a proof search method is not an instance of another? In: Fourth International Workshop on Logical Frameworks and Meta-Languages: Theory and Practice. ACM International Conference Proceeding Series (2009)
5. Dowek, G.: What is a theory? In: Alt, H., Ferreira, A. (eds.) STACS 2002. LNCS, vol. 2285, pp. 50–64. Springer, Heidelberg (2002)
6. Dowek, G.: Simple Type Theory as a clausal theory. Manuscript available on the web page of the author (2010)
7. Dowek, G., Hardin, T., Kirchner, C.: HOL-lambda-sigma: an intentional first-order expression of higher-order logic. Mathematical Structures in Computer Science 11, 1–25 (2001)
8. Dowek, G., Hardin, T., Kirchner, C.: Theorem proving modulo. Journal of Automated Reasoning 31(1), 33–72 (2003)
9. Hermant, O.: Resolution is cut-free. Journal of Automated Reasoning 44(3), 245–276 (2010)
10. Huet, G.: A mechanisation of Type Theory. In: Third International Joint Conference on Artificial Intelligence, pp. 139–146 (1973)
11. Peterson, G., Stickel, M.E.: Complete sets of reductions for some equational theories. Journal of the ACM 28, 233–264 (1981)
12. Plotkin, G.: Building-in equational theories. Machine Intelligence 7, 73–90 (1972)
13. Slagle, J.R.: Automatic theorem proving with renamable and semantic resolution. J. ACM 14, 687–697 (1967)
14. Wos, L., Robinson, G.A., Carson, D.F.: Efficiency and completeness of the set of support strategy in theorem proving. J. ACM 12, 536–541 (1965)

A Logic on Subobjects and Recognizability

H.J. Sander Bruggink and Barbara König

Universität Duisburg-Essen, Germany
{sander.bruggink,barbara_koenig}@uni-due.de

Abstract. We introduce a simple logic that allows to quantify over the subobjects of a categorical object. We subsequently show that, for the category of graphs, this logic is equally expressive as second-order monadic graph logic (MSOGL). Furthermore we show that for the more general setting of hereditary pushout categories, a class of categories closely related to adhesive categories, we can recover Courcelle's result that every MSOGL-expressible property is recognizable. This is done by giving an inductive translation of formulas of our logic into so-called automaton functors which accept recognizable languages of cospans.

1 Introduction

Regular languages have been studied extensively in computer science and have a large number of applications, such as model checking [3] and termination analysis [10]. The notions of regularity and finite automata can be straightforwardly generalized to trees and tree automata, opening the possibility to define regular tree languages and exploit the convenient closure properties that these languages enjoy. In recent years, the success of regular languages has sparked interest in obtaining a similar notion for other classes of object, in particular graphs. Courcelle has focused on the notion of recognizability – which is equivalent to regularity in the case of word languages – in an algebra of graphs with interfaces. It turns out that recognizable graph languages in this setting can be characterized by locally finite congruences. Bozapalidis and Kalampakas explored a similar characterization based on magmoids [4]. The authors of this paper defined automaton functors to investigate recognizability in a more category theoretic setting [6].

A common disadvantage of the approaches above, is that it is in general not possible to describe a recognizable graph language in a finite way, because the size of the interface of a graph is in principle unbounded. Several solutions for this problem have been developed, such as monadic second-order graph logic [7] and graph automata [5]. In both cases, the class of languages described is a proper subclass of the class of all recognizable graph languages.

In this paper, we develop a logic, similar to monadic second-order graph logic, which describes properties of objects in a category. We show that – under some assumptions on the underlying category – every language describable by the logic is recognizable (the converse does not hold) and that in the category of graphs our logic has the same expressive power as Courcelle's monadic second-order graph logic. This work extends the work of Courcelle in two aspects: First, we generalize the monadic second-order graph logic of Courcelle to arbitrary categories. Second, we prove, for hereditary pushout categories in which for each

C.S. Calude and V. Sassone (Eds.): TCS 2010, IFIP AICT 323, pp. 197–212, 2010.

composable pair of arrows there exist finitely many pushout complements (up to isomorphism), that each language described by a logic formula is recognizable. We do this by giving an inductive construction (on the structure of the formula), which is more convenient in practice than the construction given by Courcelle in [7]. However, another inductive construction has recently been developed independently from our work [9].

The paper is organized as follows: In §2 we give preliminary definitions and fix notation. In §3 we present the syntax and semantics of the logic on subobjects. We continue in §4 to compare the logic to monadic second-order graph logic, and show that, in the category of hypergraphs, the expressive power of our logic and monadic second-order logic are the same. Finally, in §5, we show, by constructing automaton functors from logic formulas, that all languages definable by the logic on subobjects are recognizable, and in §6 an example of the translation is given.

2 Preliminaries

We assume a basic familiarity with category theory. In the following we fix a category **C**. For a morphism $f\colon A \to B$ we denote by $dom(f) = A$ the domain and by $cod(f) = B$ the codomain of f. When f and g are (composable) morphisms, we write $f \mathbin{;} g$ for the morphism f postcomposed with g, that is $f \mathbin{;} g = g \circ f$.

Let $f\colon A \rightarrowtail T$ and $g\colon B \rightarrowtail T$ be monos with the same codomain T. We write $f \sqsubseteq g$ if there exists an arrow $h\colon A \to B$ (which is necessarily unique) such that $h \mathbin{;} f = g$. The subobject lattice $Sub(T)$ of an object T is formed by isomorphism classes of monos with codomain T, where $\sqsubseteq$ forms the inclusion order. (In practice, we will take unique representatives of the isomorphism classes.)

In the second half of this paper, we will restrict our attention to so-called *hereditary pushout categories* (HPCs) [13], which are related to the well-known adhesive categories [15]. Most adhesive categories are also HPC, including all topoi. In particular, the categories **Set** of sets and **Graph** of hypergraphs (see page 199) are HPC. A category **C** is a HPC if

1. **C** has pushouts along monos;
2. **C** has all pullbacks;
3. given a cube diagram as shown on the right, where a, b and c are monos, the bottom face is a pushout and the back faces are pullbacks, we have that the top face is a pushout if and only if the front faces are pullbacks and d is a mono.

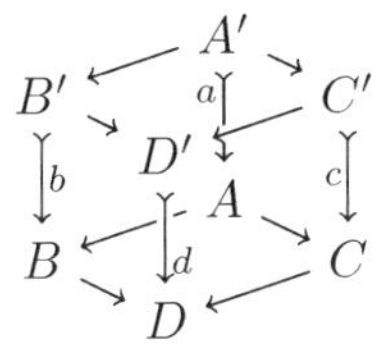

Different from adhesive categories the vertical arrows in the cube must be mono, instead of one of the arrows in the lower square.

In [6], the authors of the present paper defined recognizable languages of arrows by means of *finite automaton functors*[1] (compare also with a similar notion introduced by Griffing [11]). Let **Rel** be the category which has sets as objects and relations between sets as arrows.

[1] What we call *finite automaton functor* here, is simply called *automaton functor* in [6].

Definition 2.1 (Recognizability). *Let* **C** *be a category. An* automaton functor *is a functor* $\mathcal{A}\colon \mathbf{C} \to \mathbf{Rel}$ *which maps each object* X *of* **C** *is to a set* $\mathcal{A}(X)$ *(called the set of* states *of* X*) and each arrow* $f\colon X \to Y$ *to a relation* $\mathcal{A}(f) \subseteq \mathcal{A}(X) \times \mathcal{A}(Y)$*. Additionally, each state set* $\mathcal{A}(X)$ *contains a distinguished set of* start states *and a distinguished set of* final states *as subsets.*

An automaton functor is finite *if every set in the image of* $\mathcal{A}$ *is finite, and* deterministic *if every relation* $\mathcal{A}(f)$ *is functional and every state set contains exactly one initial state.*

Let J, K *be two* **C***-objects. The* (J, K)-language $L_{J,K}(\mathcal{A})$ *(of arrows from* J *to* K*) is defined as follows:* $f\colon J \to K$ *is contained in* $L_{J,K}(\mathcal{A})$ *if and only if* $\mathcal{A}(f)$ *relates a start state of* $\mathcal{A}(J)$ *to a final state of* $\mathcal{A}(K)$*.*

A language $L_{J,K}$ *of arrows from* J *to* K *is* recognizable in **C** *if it is the* (J, K)*-language of a finite automaton functor* $\mathcal{A}\colon \mathbf{C} \to \mathbf{Rel}$.

This notion of recognizable language is a generalization of finite automata for word languages. If we take **C** as a one-object category with all words as arrows (the free monoid of the alphabet), then a finite automaton is isomorphic to an automaton functor (mapping the single object to the state set of the automaton and each arrow to its respective transition relation).

The intuition behind the definition is to have a mapping into a (finite) domain that respects compositionality and identities, that is, which is a functor. The functor property ensures that decomposing the arrow in different ways does not affect acceptance in any way. This is different from the case of words where there is essentially only one way to decompose a word into atomic components.

Let **C** be a category with pushouts. A cospan $c\colon D \xrightarrow{c_L} E \xleftarrow{c_R} F$ is a pair of **C**-arrows with the same codomain. Here, D and F are the domain (or *inner interface*) and codomain (or *outer interface*) of the cospan c, respectively. The identity cospan for an object E is the cospan consisting of twice the identity arrow of E. Let $c\colon D \xrightarrow{c_L} E \xleftarrow{c_R} F$ and $d\colon F \xrightarrow{d_L} G \xleftarrow{d_R} H$ be cospans (where the codomain of c equals the domain of d). The composition of c and d is obtained by taking the pushout of c_R and d_L.

A *semi-abstract cospan* is an equivalence class of cospans, where we take the middle object of the cospan up to isomorphism. (In practice, we will choose unique representatives from each isomorphism class.)

Now, the category *Cospan*(**C**) is defined as the category which has the objects of **C** as objects, and semi-abstract cospans as arrows. In [6] we have shown that Courcelle's notion of recognizable graph language [7,8] coincides with our notion of recognizability in the category of cospans of graphs when we consider cospans of the form $\emptyset \to G \leftarrow \emptyset$.

For the comparison with the monadic second-order logic of Courcelle, and for most examples, we introduce a category of hypergraphs (just called *graphs* in the following). Fix a signature Σ of labels, each element A of which has an arity $ar(A)$. A graph is a tuple $G = \langle V_G, E_G, att_G, lab_G\rangle$, consisting of a set V_G of vertices (or nodes), a set E_G of edges, an attachment function $att_G\colon E_G \to V_G^*$ and a labeling function $lab_G\colon E_G \to \Sigma$, such that for each $e \in E_G$ it holds that

$|att_G(e)| = ar(lab(e))$. (Here, A^* is the set of finite sequences over A, and $|\boldsymbol{a}|$ denotes the length of a sequence $\boldsymbol{a}$.) A graph is *discrete* if it has no edges. A graph morphism is a structure preserving map between graphs. The category **Graph** is the category of finite graphs and graph morphisms.

We define the following "special" graphs and morphisms: The graph Dis_k is the discrete graph with node set $\{1, \ldots, k\}$. Furthermore, for each $A \in \Sigma$, we define the graph E_A, consisting of a single A-labelled edge and adjacent (pairwise unequal) nodes, and the morphisms $e^i_A \colon Dis_1 \to E_A$ mapping the single node in Dis_1 to the node connected to the i-th port of the single edge $e \in E_A$ (that is, to the ith node of $att_{E_A}(e)$). Furthermore, we define Epi_A to be the set of epimorphisms with domain E_A, up to isomorphism (in the case of **Graph** this set is finite).

For the examples, we will usually consider unlabeled, directed (multi)graphs, i.e. we take take $\Sigma = \{\star\}$, with $ar(\star) = 2$. We define $E = E_\star$ to be the graph consisting of a single (directed) edge connecting two nodes, and morphisms $src = e^0_\star$ and $tgt = e^1_\star$, mapping the node of Dis_1 to the source and the target of the edge in E, respectively.

3 A Logic on Subobjects

In this section we introduce the syntax and semantics of the logic for a fixed category **C**. The logic will be used to describe properties of objects of **C**.

Syntax. Let Var be a (countably infinite) set of variables. A variable typing is a partial map $\tau \colon Var \rightharpoonup Obj(\mathbf{C}) \cup \{\Omega\}$. There are two kinds of variables: *first-order variables* of sort T (where T is an arbitrary object of **C**), representing subobjects of fixed structure, and *second-order variables* of sort Ω, representing arbitrary subobjects.[2] Unless otherwise indicated, first-order variables are denoted by lowercase letters (x, y, z) and second-order variables by capitals (X, Y, Z).

Subobject *expressions* are generated by the grammar $e := X \mid f \,;\, x$, where X is of sort Ω, x is of sort T and $f \colon T' \rightarrowtail T$ is a mono. We then say that the expression $f \,;\, x$ is of sort T'. (Intuitively f restricts the graph denoted by x to a subgraph T'.) Variables of sort Ω cannot be precomposed with monos.

The set $Form(\tau)$ of formulas typed by τ is specified by the following grammar:

$$Form(\tau) := e_1 \sqsubseteq e_2 \mid Form(\tau) \wedge Form(\tau) \mid \neg Form(\tau) \mid \\ (\exists X \colon \Omega)\, Form(\tau[X \mapsto \Omega]) \mid (\exists x \colon T)\, Form(\tau[x \mapsto T]).^3$$

[2] Later, in the comparison with MSOGL, it will become clearer why these types of variables are called first-order and second-order, respectively.

[3] Let $f \colon A \to B$ be a function and let a, b be two elements, which are not necessarily contained in A or B. Then $f[a \mapsto b] \colon A \cup \{a\} \to B \cup \{b\}$ denotes the function defined as follows:

$$f[a \mapsto b](a') = \begin{cases} b & \text{if } a' = a \\ f(a') & \text{otherwise} \end{cases}$$

Note that in a formula of the form $e_1 \sqsubseteq e_2$ the two expressions can have arbitrary sorts. The set of free variables of a formula φ, denoted $FV(\varphi)$ is defined as usual. We also define the abbreviation $(x = y) \equiv (x \sqsubseteq y \wedge y \sqsubseteq x)$. Furthermore, we use the usual abbreviations for falsity ($\bot$), disjunction ($\vee$), implication ($\rightarrow$) and universal quantification ($\forall$).
Note that we do not define syntax for defining the morphism f and the object T in expressions and formulas of the form $f \,⨟\, x$ and $(\exists \varphi \colon T)$. The exact syntax needed for this depends on the category, and falls outside the scope of this paper.

Semantics. Let φ be formula typed by variable typing τ and B a **C**-object. A B-valuation η for φ is a function which assigns:

- to each $x \in FV(\varphi)$, with $\tau(x) = T$ (where $T \neq \Omega$), a mono $v_x \colon T \rightarrowtail B$; and
- to each $X \in FV(\varphi)$, with $\tau(X) = \Omega$, a mono $v_X \colon V \rightarrowtail B$ (where V is arbitrary).

Now we can define the semantics of formulas of the logic. Let φ be a subobject formula typed by τ and let B be a **C**-object. We say that $B, \eta \models \varphi$, for some B-valuation η, whenever:

- $B, \eta \models X \sqsubseteq Y$ if $\eta(X) \sqsubseteq \eta(Y)$.
- $B, \eta \models f \,⨟\, x \sqsubseteq g \,⨟\, y$ if $f \,;\, \eta(x) \sqsubseteq g \,;\, \eta(y)$.
- $B, \eta \models f \,⨟\, x \sqsubseteq Y$ if $f \,;\, \eta(x) \sqsubseteq \eta(Y)$.
- $B, \eta \models X \sqsubseteq g \,⨟\, y$ if $\eta(X) \sqsubseteq g \,;\, \eta(y)$.
- $B, \eta \models \varphi_1 \wedge \varphi_2$ if $B, \eta \models \varphi_1$ and $B, \eta \models \varphi_2$.
- $B, \eta \models \neg\varphi$ if $B, \eta \not\models \varphi$.
- $B, \eta \models (\exists x \colon T)\, \varphi$ if there is a mono $v \colon T \rightarrowtail D$ such that $B, \eta[x \mapsto v] \models \varphi$.
  $B, \eta \models (\exists X \colon \Omega)\, \varphi$ if there is a mono $v \colon V \rightarrowtail D$ such that $B, \eta[X \mapsto v] \models \varphi$.

Furthermore, for a closed formula φ, we write $B \models \varphi$ whenever $B, \eta \models \varphi$ for the empty valuation η. Note that this definition works for any category. However the results of §5 (translation of formulas into automaton functors) will only be valid for hereditary pushout categories (which satisfy some additional conditions).

Examples. In an arbitrary category **C** we can define the following formula:

- The join of two expressions:
  $(e = e_1 \sqcup e_2) := e_1 \sqsubseteq e \wedge e_2 \sqsubseteq e \wedge (\forall X \colon \Omega) \big((e_1 \sqsubseteq X \wedge e_2 \sqsubseteq X) \rightarrow e \sqsubseteq X\big)$.

In the next examples we will use the category of unlabeled directed graphs, as presented on page 200.

- The subgraph X is closed under reachability:
  $RC(X \colon \Omega) := (\forall y \colon E)\,(src \,⨟\, y \sqsubseteq X \rightarrow tgt \,⨟\, y \sqsubseteq X)$
- There exists a path from node x to node y (every reachability closed subgraph containing x also contains y):
  $Path(x, y \colon Dis_1) := (\forall Z \colon \Omega) \big((id \,⨟\, x \sqsubseteq Z \wedge RC(Z)) \rightarrow id \,⨟\, y \sqsubseteq Z\big)$.

4 Comparison to Monadic Second-Order Graph Logic

Consider the category **Graph** as presented on page 199. We show that for this category the logic on subobjects has the same expressive power as monadic second-order graph logic [8,7]. We do this by defining translations from monadic second-order logic to the logic on subobjects and vice versa, and proving that a graph satisfies a formula if and only if it satisfies the translation of the formula.

4.1 Monadic Second-Order Graph Logic

First we define monadic second-order graph logic (MSOGL), mainly in order to fix notation and terminology. This logic is one of the most important specification logics for graphs. Especially, Courcelle's theorem says that every graph property definable in MSOGL is decidable in linear time on (finite) graphs of bounded tree-width.

The MSOGL is a sorted second-order logic with four kinds of variables: first-order node variables (range over nodes), first-order edge variables (range over edges), second-order node variables (range over sets of nodes) and second-order edge variables (range over sets of edges). As a notational convention, first-order variables will be denoted by lowercase letters (x, y, z) and second-order variables by capitals (X, Y, Z). The syntax of MSOGL is given by the following grammar:

$$\begin{aligned}\varphi := \varphi_1 \wedge \varphi_2 \mid \neg\varphi \mid (\exists X : V)\,\varphi \mid (\exists X : E)\,\varphi \mid (\exists x \colon v)\,\varphi \mid (\exists x \colon e)\,\varphi \mid \\ x = y \mid x \in X \mid \mathit{edge}_A(x, y_1, \dots, y_{ar(A)}),\end{aligned}$$

where typing must be respected, that is, in formulas of the form $x = y$ both variables have the same type and in formulas of the form $x \in X$ it holds that x is a first-order node (edge) variable and X a second-order node (edge) variable. Formulas of the form $\mathit{edge}_A(x, y_1, \dots, y_{ar(A)})$ denote that the edge x has label A and is adjacent to the nodes $y_1, \dots, y_n$.

A graph $G = \langle V_G, E_G, \mathit{att}_G, \mathit{lab}_G\rangle$ satisfies a formula φ, written $G \models \varphi$, if there exists a valuation θ, mapping first-order variables to nodes and edges of G and second-order variables to sets of nodes and sets of edges of G, such that $G, \theta \models \varphi$, where:

- $G, \theta \models x = y$ if $\theta(x) = \theta(y)$ and $G, \theta \models x \in X$ if $\theta(x) \in \theta(X)$.
- $G, \theta \models \mathit{edge}_A(x, y_1, \dots, y_n)$ if $\mathit{lab}_G(\theta(x)) = A$ and $\mathit{att}_G(\theta(x)) = \theta(y_1) \dots \theta(y_n)$.
- $G, \theta \models \varphi_1 \wedge \varphi_2$ if $G, \theta \models \varphi_1$ and $G, \theta \models \varphi_2$.
- $G, \theta \models \neg\varphi$ if $G, \theta \not\models \varphi$.
- $G, \theta \models (\exists x \colon v)\,\varphi$ if there is a $v' \in V_G$ such that $G, \theta[x \mapsto v'] \models \varphi$.
- $G, \theta \models (\exists x \colon e)\,\varphi$ if there is a $e' \in E_G$ such that $G, \theta[x \mapsto e'] \models \varphi$.
- $G, \theta \models (\exists X : V)\,\varphi$ if there is a $V \subseteq V_G$ such that $G, \theta[X \mapsto V] \models \varphi$.
- $G, \theta \models (\exists X : E)\,\varphi$ if there is a $E \subseteq E_G$ such that $G, \theta[X \mapsto E] \models \varphi$.

In [7] an extension to monadic second-order logic is presented which also considers cardinality constraints of the form $\mathit{card}_{n,p}(X)$, expressing that the set represented by X contains n elements modulo p, which are omitted here for simplicity. It is currently not entirely clear to us how to integrate a similar predicate into the logic on subobjects in a natural way.

4.2 From Monadic Second-Order Logic to the Logic on Subobjects

We define a translation $[\![\cdot]\!]_{\mathrm{S}}$ from formulas of MSOGL to formulas of the logic on subobjects. For this, we define an edge typing as a map ζ from first-order edge variables (labelled with A) to epimorphisms (with domain E_A). We define the translation function $[\![\varphi]\!]_{\mathrm{S}} = [\![\varphi]\!]_{\mathrm{S}}^{\emptyset}$ where, for an edge typing ζ, $[\![\varphi]\!]_{\mathrm{S}}^{\zeta}$ is inductively defined as follows:

$$
\begin{aligned}
[\![\neg\varphi]\!]_{\mathrm{S}}^{\zeta} &:= \neg[\![\varphi]\!]_{\mathrm{S}}^{\zeta} & [\![x = y]\!]_{\mathrm{S}}^{\zeta} &:= x = y \\
[\![\varphi \wedge \psi]\!]_{\mathrm{S}}^{\zeta} &:= [\![\varphi]\!]_{\mathrm{S}}^{\zeta} \wedge [\![\psi]\!]_{\mathrm{S}}^{\zeta} & [\![x \in X]\!]_{\mathrm{S}}^{\zeta} &:= x \sqsubseteq X \\
[\![(\exists X\colon V)\,\varphi]\!]_{\mathrm{S}}^{\zeta} &:= (\exists X\colon \Omega)\,[\![\varphi]\!]_{\mathrm{S}}^{\zeta} & [\![(\exists x\colon v)\,\varphi]\!]_{\mathrm{S}}^{\zeta} &:= (\exists x\colon \mathit{Dis}_1)\,[\![\varphi]\!]_{\mathrm{S}}^{\zeta} \\
[\![(\exists X\colon E)\,\varphi]\!]_{\mathrm{S}}^{\zeta} &:= (\exists X\colon \Omega)\,[\![\varphi]\!]_{\mathrm{S}}^{\zeta} & [\![(\exists x\colon e)\,\varphi]\!]_{\mathrm{S}}^{\zeta} &:= \bigvee_{A \in \zeta}\ \bigvee_{f \in \mathit{Epi}_A} (\exists x\colon \mathit{cod}(f))\,[\![\varphi]\!]_{\mathrm{S}}^{\zeta[x \mapsto f]}
\end{aligned}
$$

$$
[\![\mathit{edge}_A(x, y_1, \ldots, y_n)]\!]_{\mathrm{S}}^{\zeta} := \begin{cases} \bigwedge_{1 \le i \le ar(A)} (e_A^i \,;\, \zeta(x)) \,\fatsemi\, x = y_i & \text{if } \mathit{dom}(\zeta(x)) = E_A \\ \bot & \text{otherwise.} \end{cases}
$$

Proposition 4.1. *Let G be a graph, and φ a closed formula of monadic second order logic. Then $G \models_{\mathrm{M}} \varphi$ if and only if $G \models [\![\varphi]\!]_{\mathrm{S}}$.*

4.3 From the Logic on Subobjects to Monadic Second-Order Logic

We define a translation $[\![\cdot]\!]_{\mathrm{M}}$ from formulas of our logic to formulas of MSOGL. The main difference between the two logics is that in our logic, we can quantify over arbitrary subobjects, while in MSOGL we can only quantify over nodes, edges, sets of nodes and sets of edges. Thus, a single quantification in the logic on subobjects will in general correspond to more than one quantification in MSOGL. In order to make sure that the multiple variables in an MSOGL-formula evaluate to a possible subobject, we need to express the following two "consistency properties" as MSOGL-formulas (the exact definitions of both formulas is left as an exercise to the reader):

- Let T be a graph and $f\colon X \to (V_T \cup E_T)$ a bijection between first-order variables and nodes and edges of T. The formula $\mathit{struct}_f(T)$ expresses that the nodes and edges assigned to the variables in the codomain of f build a graph isomorphic to T.
- Let X_V be a second-order node variable and X_E a second-order edge variable. The formula $\mathit{cons}(X_E, X_V)$ expresses that all nodes adjacent to an edge in X_E must be in X_V.

A *variable mapping* ξ is a function which maps:

- each free first-order variable x of type T in the formula over subobjects to a bijection from a subset of first-order node and edge variables in the MSOGL-formula to the nodes and edges of T, and

- each free second-order variable X of the source formula to a pair of a second-order node and a second-order edge variable in the target formula.

Now, we define $[\![\varphi]\!]_{\mathrm{M}} = [\![\varphi]\!]_{\mathrm{M}}^{\emptyset}$, where $[\![\varphi]\!]_{\mathrm{M}}^{\xi}$, parametrized by a variable mapping ξ, is inductively defined as follows:

$$[\![\neg\varphi]\!]_{\mathrm{M}}^{\xi} := \neg[\![\varphi]\!]_{\mathrm{M}}^{\xi}$$

$$[\![\varphi \wedge \psi]\!]_{\mathrm{M}}^{\xi} := [\![\varphi]\!]_{\mathrm{M}}^{\xi} \wedge [\![\psi]\!]_{\mathrm{M}}^{\xi}$$

$$[\![(\exists X\colon \Omega)\, \varphi]\!]_{\mathrm{M}}^{\xi} := (\exists X_E\colon E)\,(\exists X_V\colon V)\, \mathit{cons}(X_E, X_V) \wedge [\![\varphi]\!]_{\mathrm{M}}^{\xi[X \mapsto \langle X_E, X_V\rangle]}$$
where X_E and X_V are fresh variables.

$$[\![(\exists x\colon T)\, \varphi]\!]_{\mathrm{M}}^{\xi} := (\exists x_1, \dots, x_m\colon e)\,(\exists y_1, \dots, y_n\colon v)\, \mathit{struct}_{\xi'(x)}(T) \wedge [\![\varphi]\!]_{\mathrm{M}}^{\xi'}$$
where T is a graph with m edges $(e_1, \dots, e_m)$ and n nodes $(v_1, \dots, v_n)$, the x_i and y_i are fresh variables, and

$$\xi' := \xi[x \mapsto \{x_1 \mapsto e_1, \dots, x_m \mapsto e_m, y_1 \mapsto v_1, \dots, y_n \mapsto v_n\}].$$

$$[\![X \sqsubseteq Y]\!]_{\mathrm{M}}^{\xi} := (\forall x\colon e)\big(x \in X_E \to x \in Y_E\big) \wedge (\forall x\colon v)\big(x \in X_V \to x \in Y_V\big)$$
where $(X_E, X_V) := \xi(X)$ and $(Y_E, Y_V) := \xi(Y)$.

$$[\![f \mathbin{;} x \sqsubseteq X]\!]_{\mathrm{M}}^{\xi} := x_1 \in X_E \wedge \dots \wedge x_m \in X_E \wedge y_1 \in X_V \wedge \dots \wedge y_n \in X_V$$
where $(X_E, X_V) := \xi(X)$,
$\{x_1, \dots, x_m\} := \{u \mid \exists e\colon \langle u, f(e)\rangle \in \xi(x)\}$ and
$\{y_1, \dots, y_n\} := \{w \mid \exists v\colon \langle w, f(v)\rangle \in \xi(x)\}$.

$$[\![X \sqsubseteq f \mathbin{;} x]\!]_{\mathrm{M}}^{\xi} := (\forall x'\colon e)\big(x' \in X_E \to (x' = x_1 \vee \dots \vee x' = x_m)\big) \wedge (\forall y'\colon v)\big(y' \in X_V \to (y' = y_1 \vee \dots \vee y' = y_n)\big)$$
where $(X_E, X_V) := \xi(X)$,
$\{x_1, \dots, x_m\} := \{u \mid \exists e\colon \langle u, f(e)\rangle \in \xi(x)\}$ and
$\{y_1, \dots, y_n\} := \{w \mid \exists v\colon \langle w, f(v)\rangle \in \xi(x)\}$.

$$[\![f \mathbin{;} x \sqsubseteq g \mathbin{;} x']\!]_{\mathrm{M}}^{\xi} := (x_1 = x'_1 \vee \dots \vee x_1 = x'_p) \wedge \dots \wedge (x_m = x'_1 \vee \dots \vee x_m = x'_p) \wedge (y_1 = y'_1 \vee \dots \vee y_1 = y'_q) \wedge \dots \wedge (y_n = y'_1 \vee \dots \vee y_n = y'_q)$$
where $\{x_1, \dots, x_m\} := \{u \mid \exists e\colon \langle u, f(e)\rangle \in \xi(x)\}$,
$\{y_1, \dots, y_n\} := \{w \mid \exists v\colon \langle w, f(v)\rangle \in \xi(x)\}$,
$\{x'_1, \dots, x'_p\} := \{u \mid \exists e\colon \langle u, f(e)\rangle \in \xi(x')\}$ and
$\{y'_1, \dots, y'_q\} := \{w \mid \exists v\colon \langle w, f(v)\rangle \in \xi(x')\}$.

Proposition 4.2. *Let G be a graph, and φ a closed formula of the logic on subobjects. Then $G \models \varphi$ if and only if $G \models_{\mathrm{M}} [\![\varphi]\!]_{\mathrm{M}}$.*

5 Logic and Recognizability

In this section we prove a generalization of Courcelle's result which says that every language definable in monadic second-order graph logic is recognizable [7,8]: we show that every language of objects of a hereditary pushout category definable by our logic is recognizable in the sense described in [6], by giving an encoding of a formula into an automaton functor. The resulting automaton functor is finite if the category enjoys the property that each composable pair of arrows has finitely many pushout complements (up to isomorphism). In order to be able to use structural induction on the logical formula, we need objects which keep track of the free variables. To this end we introduce a category of objects with valuations.

We fix a hereditary pushout category **C** with an initial object 0.[4]

Definition 5.1 (Object with valuation). *Let τ be a variable typing. An object with valuation (short:* V-object*) of type τ is a triple $D = \langle \mathrm{B}^D, \eta^D, \sigma^D \rangle$, where*

- B^D *(the* base object*) is a* **C***-object;*
- η^D *maps each variable x for which $\tau(x)$ is defined to a mono $\eta^D(x)\colon V_x^D \rightarrowtail \mathrm{B}^D$ (the* valuation morphism*); and*
- σ^D *maps each variable x for which $\tau(x)$ is defined and $\tau(x) \neq \Omega$ to an arrow $\sigma^D(x)\colon V_x^D \to \tau(x)$ (the* typing morphism*).*

We say that D is well-typed *whenever all arrows $\sigma^D(x)$ are identities.*

Let τ be defined only on the variables $x_1, \dots, x_n$ and $Y_1, \dots, Y_m$, with $\tau(x_i) = T_i$ and $\tau(Y_j) = \Omega$ (for $1 \le i \le n$ and $1 \le j \le m$). Then a V-object of type τ is a diagram as shown on the right (where $t_i = \sigma^D(x_i)$, $v_i = \eta^D(x_i)$ and $w_j = \eta^D(Y_j)$). Note that if D is well-typed (all typing morphisms are identities), η^D corresponds exactly to a valuation (see §3). For the translation we need to allow typing morphisms which are not identities, however, because some objects of the category may not contain the type in its entirety.

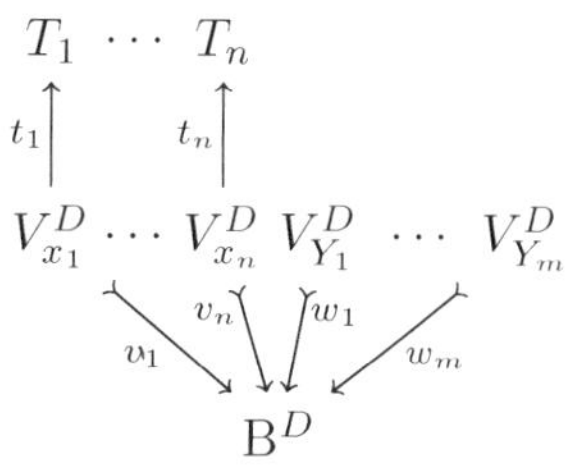

We introduce the following operators for diagram extension and restriction. Let $D = \langle \mathrm{B}^D, \eta^D, \sigma^D \rangle$ be a V-object of type τ. By $drop_x(D)$ we denote the V-object of type $\tau|_{Var\setminus\{x\}}$ from which the morphisms and objects associated to x have been dropped. Furthermore, let $v\colon V \rightarrowtail \mathrm{B}^D$ and $t\colon V \rightarrowtail T$ be given. Then $add_y^v(D) = \langle \mathrm{B}^D, \eta^D[y \mapsto v], \sigma^D \rangle$ denotes the V-object of type $\tau[y \mapsto \Omega]$, which is obtained by adding the arrow v (indexed by y) to D. Similarly, $add_y^{v,t}(D) = \langle \mathrm{B}^D, \eta^D[y \mapsto v], \sigma^D[y \mapsto t] \rangle$ denotes the V-object of type $\tau[y \mapsto T]$ which is obtained by adding the arrows v and t (indexed by y).

We consider the following category of objects with vertical interfaces, some of which might be typed.

Definition 5.2 (Category of objects with valuations). *Let τ be a variable typing. We define the category $\mathbf{V}_\tau^{\mathbf{C}}$ (or simply $\mathbf{V}_\tau$) as follows.*

The objects of $\mathbf{V}_\tau^{\mathbf{C}}$ are the objects with valuation of type τ (see Def. 5.1). An arrow $p\colon D \to E$ of $\mathbf{V}_\tau^{\mathbf{C}}$ consists of **C***-arrows $\alpha^p\colon \mathrm{B}^D \to \mathrm{B}^E$ and $\nu_x^p\colon \eta^D(x) \to$*

[4] We require an initial object since we want to convert an arbitrary object A into the corresponding cospan $0 \to A \leftarrow 0$. Then the automaton functor recognizes such cospans by "starting" and "ending" with the initial object.

$\eta^E(x)$ (for each $x \in Var$ such that $\tau(x)$ is defined) such that the square below is a pullback and the triangle commutes (whenever $\tau(x) \neq \Omega$):

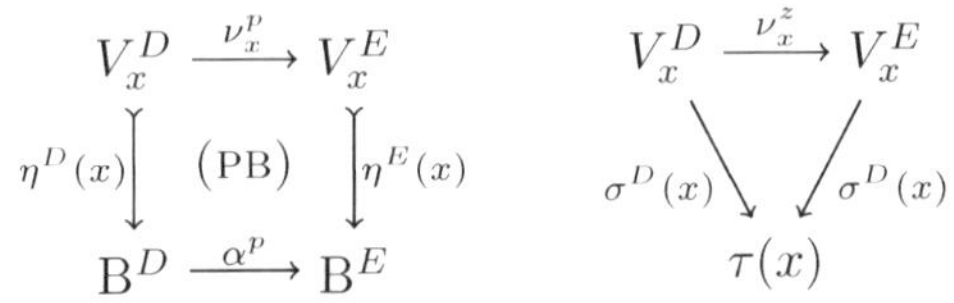

The two diagrams above specify the following: the valuation morphisms of D can be obtained from the valuation morphisms of E by taking a pullback (if α^p is mono this is simply some form of restriction). Furthermore the typing morphisms must be consistent.

We will consider (semi-abstract) cospans over $\mathbf{V}_\tau^\mathbf{C}$, i.e., we will work with the category *Cospan*($\mathbf{V}_\tau^\mathbf{C}$). Note that due to Property 3 on page 198 pushouts in $\mathbf{V}_\tau^\mathbf{C}$ – and hence cospan composition in *Cospan*($\mathbf{V}_\tau^\mathbf{C}$) – can be computed componentwise by taking pushouts of all the component morphisms and obtaining the morphisms of the resulting diagram as mediating morphisms. In the initial object 0 all objects (apart from the $\tau(x)$) are the initial objects of $\mathbf{C}$. We extend the operation $drop_x$ to $\mathbf{V}_\tau^\mathbf{C}$-cospans in the straightforward way.

Given a $\mathbf{V}_\tau$-object $D = \langle \mathrm{B}^D, \eta^D, \sigma^D \rangle$ and a variable x such that $\tau(x)$ is defined, we define the *selection morphism* sel_x^D (in the case that $\tau(x) \neq \Omega$ parametrized by a morphism $f\colon V_x^D \to \tau(x)$) as follows:

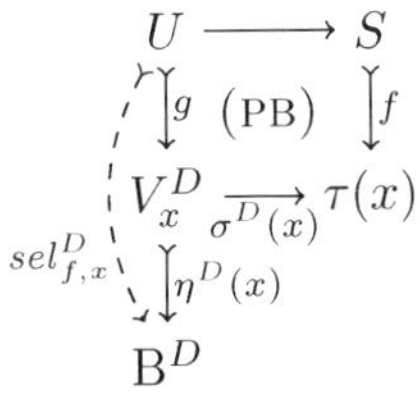

– Suppose $\tau(x) \neq \Omega$. Let $f\colon S \rightarrowtail \tau(x)$. We take the pullback of $\sigma^D(x)$ and f, and obtain an object U and arrows $U \to S$ and $g\colon U \to V_x^D$ (see the diagram on the right). Now we take $sel_{f,x}^D := g \,;\, v_x^D$.
– Suppose $\tau(x) = \Omega$. Then we simply take $sel_x^D := \eta^D(x)$.

We extend the definition of selection morphism to expressions of subobject logic in the obvious way, i.e. $sel_{f⨟x}^D := sel_{f,x}^D$.

We will now present an inductive encoding that takes a formula $\varphi \in Form(\tau)$ and translates it into an automaton functor $\mathcal{A}_\tau^\varphi$ (or simply $\mathcal{A}$) for the category *Cospan*($\mathbf{V}_\tau^\mathbf{C}$). The definition is divided into four subcases: *atomic formulas*, *boolean operations*, *first-order quantification* and *second-order quantification*.

Atomic formulas: Suppose $\varphi \equiv e_1 \sqsubseteq e_2$. Since the variables contained in e_1, e_2 are free and hence the corresponding vertical interfaces are present, it is enough to just check inclusion of those interfaces. This information is recorded in just one state $\star$ and we produce the empty relation whenever inclusion fails.

Formally, we define the automaton functor $\mathcal{A}_\tau^\varphi$ as follows. To each object D, $\mathcal{A}_\tau^\varphi$ assigns the one-element set $\{\star\}$ if $sel_{e_1}^D \sqsubseteq sel_{e_2}^D$ (where $\star$ is the initial as well as the final state), and the empty set otherwise.

For a cospan $c\colon D \,{-}l{\to}\, E \,{\leftarrow}r{-}\, F$ we define $\mathcal{A}_\tau^\varphi(c) = \mathcal{C}(l) \,;\, \mathcal{C}(r)^{-1}$, where, for a $\mathbf{V}_\tau$-arrow $p\colon D_1 \to D_2$, we define

$$\mathcal{C}(p) := \begin{cases} id_{\{\star\}} & \text{if } sel_{e_1}^{D_2} \sqsubseteq sel_{e_2}^{D_2} \\ \emptyset & \text{otherwise.} \end{cases}$$

Here, $id_{\{\star\}}$ refers to the identity relation on $\{\star\}$ and $\emptyset$ to the empty relation. Note that the empty relation is the identity relation on the empty set, i.e. $id_\emptyset = \emptyset$.

Boolean operations: Suppose $\varphi \equiv \varphi_1 \wedge \varphi_2$ or $\varphi \equiv \neg\varphi$. In this case compute the automaton functors for the subformulas and apply the standard techniques for intersection or complement to the automaton functors (due to a result of [6] these operations can be performed on all automaton functors, independent of the category). In the latter case (negation/complement) it is necessary to first construct the equivalent deterministic automaton functor.

Second-order quantification: Since the second-order quantification case is much simpler than the first-order case, we present it first. Suppose $\varphi \equiv (\exists X : \Omega)$ φ'. Let $\mathcal{A}' := \mathcal{A}_{\tau'}^{\varphi'}$, where $\tau' = \tau[X \mapsto \Omega]$, be the automaton functor constructed for φ'.

The domain of the automaton functor for the subformula φ' is a category of objects with an additional vertical interface. The automaton functor for φ works in the following way: non-deterministically, a satisfying assignment for X is chosen and then it behaves like the automaton functor for φ'.

The automaton functor $\mathcal{A}$ for φ is formally defined as follows:

$$\mathcal{A}(D) = \bigcup_{v \in Sub(\mathrm{B}^D)} \mathcal{A}'(add_X^v(D)) \times \{v\},$$

where $v \subset Sub(\mathrm{B}^D)$ means that v ranges over representatives of isomorphism classes of monos into B^D. To a cospan $c\colon D \overset{l}{\rightarrow} E \overset{r}{\leftarrow} F$ we assign the following relation $\mathcal{A}(c) \subseteq \mathcal{A}(D) \times \mathcal{A}(F)$: $\langle q, v^D \rangle$ is in relation with $\langle q', v^F \rangle$ whenever there exists a cospan

$$c'\colon add_X^{v^D}(D) \to E' \leftarrow add_X^{v^F}(F)$$

of type τ' such that $drop_X(c') = c$ and $\langle q, q' \rangle \in \mathcal{A}'(c')$.

Finally, a state $\langle q, v \rangle$ is initial (final) if and only if q is initial (final).

First-order quantification: Suppose $\varphi \equiv (\exists x\colon T)\, \varphi'$. Let $\mathcal{A}' := \mathcal{A}_{\tau'}^{\varphi'}$, where $\tau' = \tau[x \mapsto T]$, be the automaton functor constructed for φ'.

As in the case of second-order quantification, we non-deterministically choose a satisfying assignment for x. This time, however, we have to track how much of the sought after subobject (T) has already been recognized (see explanation below).

We define the new automaton functor $\mathcal{A}_\tau^\varphi$ as follows:

$$\mathcal{A}_\tau^\varphi(D) = \bigcup_{\substack{(v\colon V \to \mathrm{B}^D) \in Sub(\mathrm{B}^D),\\ (t\colon V \to T)}} \mathcal{A}'(add_x^{v,t}(D)) \times \{\langle v, t_1, t_2 \rangle \mid t = t_1; t_2, \text{POC exists}\},$$

where, by "POC exists" we mean that there exists arrows s_1, s_2 such that $t_1; t_2 = s_1; s_2$ and the four arrows form a pushout. In the cases of v and the decomposition $t_1 ; t_2$ we actually take representatives of the respective isomorphism classes.

To a cospan $c\colon D \stackrel{l}{\rightarrow} E \stackrel{r}{\leftarrow} F$ we assign the following relation $\mathcal{A}_\tau^\varphi(c) \subseteq \mathcal{A}_\tau^\varphi(D) \times \mathcal{A}_\tau^\varphi(F)$: $\langle q, v^D, t_1^D, t_2^D\rangle$ is in relation with $\langle q', v^F, t_1^F, t_2^F\rangle$ whenever c can be extended to a cospan

$$c'\colon add_x^{v^D,(t_1^D;t_2^D)}(D) \xrightarrow{l'} add_x^{v^E,t^E}(E) \xleftarrow{r'} add_x^{v^F,(t_1^F;t_2^F)}(F),$$

satisfying the following conditions:

- $\langle q, q'\rangle \in \mathcal{A}'(c')$ *and*
- we have the commuting diagram below (on the left), where $\overline{V}^F$ is the pushout object of t_1^D and $\nu^{l'}$.

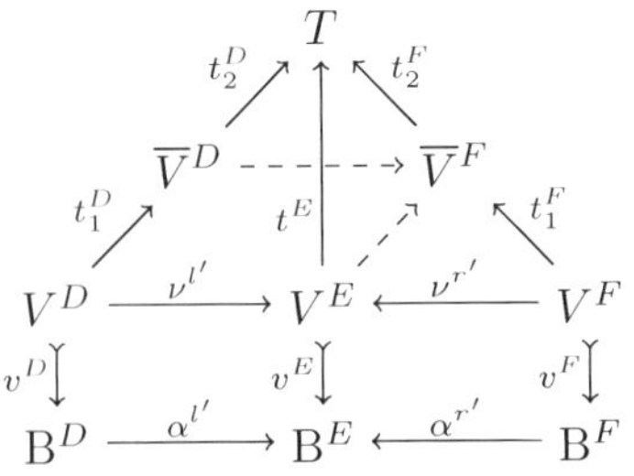

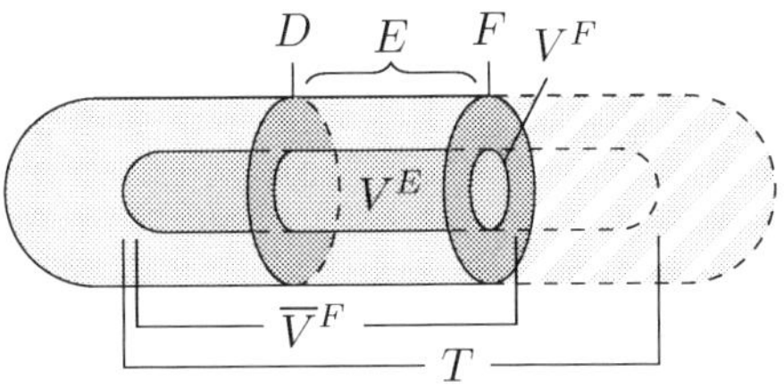

A state $\langle q, v, t_1, t_2\rangle$ is initial if and only if q is initial and t_1 is an identity. It is final if and only if q is final and the arrow t_2 is an identity.

The intuition behind the diagram above is the following: we are tracking an object of type T, while we are reading the "complete" object step by step. The vertical interface V^F (with mono v^F) denotes the part of the outer interface that corresponds to this object. On the other hand $\overline{V}^F$ (with mapping t_2^F into the type T) tells which part of the object we have already seen. Finally t_1^F relates the part which is currently in the (outer) interface to the part we have already seen (see image above, on the right). Similar explanations can be given for v^D, t_1^D and t_2^D. Finally, $\overline{V}^F$ is obtained from $\overline{V}^D$ by gluing those (new) parts of the tracked object that have been seen in the current cospan, namely V^E. (Additional intuition is provided by the example in §6).

Proposition 5.3. $\mathcal{A}_\tau^\varphi$, *constructed for a formula φ and a typing τ as described above, is a functor, that is, it preserves identities and composition.*

Theorem 5.4. *Let φ be a formula, let τ be a typing and let $D = \langle \mathrm{B}^D, \eta^D, \sigma^D\rangle$ be a well-typed V-object of type τ. Then $\mathrm{B}^D, \eta^D \models \varphi$ if and only if D is contained in the $(0,0)$-language of $\mathcal{A}_\tau^\varphi$, that is, if there exists an initial state i_0 and a final state f_0 with $\langle i_0, f_0\rangle \in \mathcal{A}_\tau^\varphi(c)$, where c is the unique cospan of the form $0 \rightarrow D \leftarrow 0$.*

Finiteness. Note that so far we did not impose any restrictions on the finiteness of the state sets. For this we first require that the objects in our category are finite in the sense that they contain only finitely many subobjects. In the case of graphs that would be the finite graphs and in the case of sets the finite sets.

However, in addition we need another requirement: in the encoding of first-order quantification we split a given arrow t into $t = t_1; t_2$ such that all pushout complements for this split exist. In order to guarantee finiteness it is hence also necessary that a given arrow t only admits finitely many such splits up to isomorphism.

It is currently not clear to us how subobject finiteness is related to the condition of having finitely many pushout complement splits. Clearly the latter property implies the former, but the other direction is unclear. In any case, the category **Graph** satisfies both requirements.

6 Detailed Example

As an example, we consider (in the category of cospans of unlabeled directed graphs) the translation into an automaton functor of the formula

$$\neg RC(X) \equiv (\exists y\colon E)\big(src \mathbin{⨾} y \sqsubseteq X \wedge \neg(tgt \mathbin{⨾} y \sqsubseteq X)\big),$$

which expresses that the subgraph X is not closed under reachability.

The automaton functor for the atomic formula $\varphi_2 := tgt \mathbin{⨾} y \sqsubseteq X$ maps each graph, in which the target of edge y does not lie in X, to the empty set, and all other graphs to the state set $\{\star\}$. It maps a cospan to $id_{\{\star\}}$ if the above also holds for the middle object of the cospan. The automaton functor of the other atomic formula, $\varphi_1 := src \mathbin{⨾} y \sqsubseteq X$, is built analogously.

To calculate the negation of φ_2, we must first make its automaton functor deterministic by means of the powerset construction (see [6]). Graphs are now mapped to either the state set $\{\emptyset, \{\star\}\}$ (where $\{\star\}$ is initial as well as final) or the state set $\{\emptyset\}$ (no initial or final states), and cospans are mapped accordingly. After the negation, final and non-final states are swapped.

To construct the automaton functor for $\varphi_1 \wedge \neg\varphi_2$, we use a Cartesian product construction. In the rest of the example, we will restrict our attention to an object D' with $\mathcal{A}^{\varphi_1}(D') = \{\star\}$ and $\mathcal{A}^{\neg\varphi_2}(D') = \{\emptyset, \{\star\}\}$. For this object D' we have that $\mathcal{A}^{\varphi_1 \wedge \neg\varphi_2}(D') = \{\langle\{\star\}, \emptyset\rangle, \langle\{\star\}, \{\star\}\rangle\}$ where $\langle\{\star\}, \{\star\}\rangle$ is the initial and $\langle\{\star\}, \emptyset\rangle$ the final state. By reaching the final state we record that both the source node of the edge assigned to y is contained in X and the target node is not contained in X.

Finally, we build an automaton functor $\mathcal{A}$ for $\varphi \equiv (\exists y\colon E)(\varphi_1 \wedge \neg\varphi_2)$. Recall that $E = \circ\!\!\rightarrow\!\!\circ$. We obtain a V-object $D = drop_y(D')$. Assume it has base object $\mathrm{B}^D = Dis_2 = \circ \quad \circ$, a two-node discrete graph. States of the new automaton functor consist of arbitrary monos $v\colon V \rightarrowtail \mathrm{B}^D$, allowed decompositions t_1, t_2 of arbitrary typing morphisms $t\colon V \to E$, and the states of D extended with v, t_1, t_2. Let us list the possible decompositions of the typing morphism for all $2^2 = 4$ possible v into B^D:

- For $v\colon \emptyset \rightarrowtail \mathrm{B}^D$, there is a single typing morphism, and two possible decompositions, given by the two legs of the pushout diagram on the right. The top leg expresses the situation where no part of the sought after subobject has been encountered yet, whereas the bottom leg expresses the situation that the entire sought after subobject was already encountered.

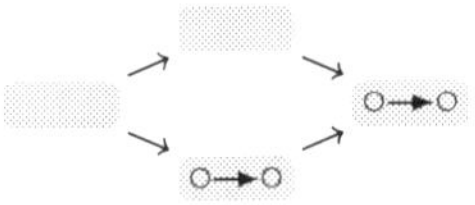

- For $v =$ 1○ ↣ 1○ ○, there are two possible typing morphisms (mapping the node to the source and the target of the edge, respectively), with two decompositions each. For $v =$ ○2 ↣ ○ ○2, four decompositions are obtained analogously.[5]
- Let $v = id_{\mathrm{B}^D}$. There are four possible typing morphisms. For $t =$ 1○ ○2 → 1○→○2 there are two allowed decompositions, which can be read from the diagram on the right. For $t =$ 1○ ○2 → 1,2○→○ the allowed decompositions can be read from the pushout diagrams below. Since two decompositions occur twice, there are four decompositions in total.

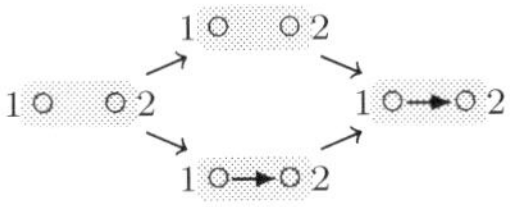

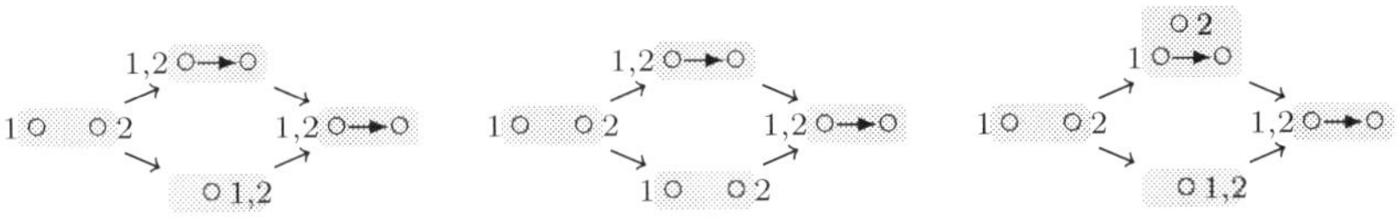

For $t =$ 1○ ○2 → 2○→○1 and $t =$ 1○ ○2 → ○→○1,2 we symmetrically obtain five decompositions.

As an example, consider the decomposition 1○ ○2 → 1○→○ ○2 → 1,2○→○ (the top right in the three diagrams above). This decomposition expresses that both nodes of B^D are part of the sought after graph (as source node), but still need to be merged.

Suppose that for all possible v, t, the object D extended with v, t has the state set above (2 states). The new automaton functor then has $2 \cdot 20 = 40$ states. Accepting states are the ones which contain an accepting state of the automaton functor for the subterm, and in which the second part of the decomposition (t_2) is an isomorphism (that is, a subgraph isomorphic to E was found).

The automaton functor works as follows: given a cospan $c\colon D \xrightarrow{c_{\mathrm{L}}} E \xleftarrow{c_{\mathrm{R}}} F$, it non-deterministically chooses what parts of the new information (the parts of E not in the range of c_{L}) belong to the sought-after type E, and then works the same as the automaton functor constructed for the subformula.

7 Conclusion and Further Research

We have introduced a logic on subobjects and shown how it is related to monadic second-order graph logic. Although we are working in a categorical setting our choice was to focus on a classical logic, quantifying over sets of subobjects,

[5] The numbers beside the nodes indicate which nodes are mapped to which.

and not a categorical logic where the universe is replaced by an object [14,16]. With our current understanding it is not clear to us how to obtain a similar correspondence of MSOGL with a categorical logic. For instance, our predicates on subobjects can not directly be interpreted as subobjects of a product object, as would be customary for subobject logic. Although our logic falls out of scope of known categorical logics, we still believe that its intimate connection to MSOGL and recognizability makes it an interesting logic to study.

Furthermore it would be interesting to study which kind of equivalences on objects are induced by the logics in various categories (also in **Set**). Another interesting question is to consider in greater detail the relation to the graph predicates of [17] which are equivalent to first-order graph logic.

Note that although here we focused exclusively on graphs as examples, the greater generality of the logic allows us to easily talk about all kinds of "graph-like" structures, such as hierarchical graphs, graphs with scopes, attributed graphs or graphs with higher-order edges.

We also introduced a procedure for translating formulas of our logic inductively into automaton functors, which are automata for accepting cospans in hereditary pushout categories, a class of categories which includes all topoi. That is, we have shown how to convert specifications into algorithms, albeit in a fairly abstract setting. Other methods for converting MSOGL-formulas into recognizable languages which are known to us [7,12] do not follow such an inductive strategy, but directly specify state sets by forming equivalence classes of logical formulas. We hope that such an inductive method can help in practice in order to generate and use automaton functors. In implementations, we can construct the automaton functor only for a restricted set of "atomic" cospans from which all cospans can be generated by composition. We are especially interested in applications in verification such as invariant checking [1,2] and termination analysis. Despite the inductive approach the state sets of automata can still become fairly large, as is already evident from the detailed example in §6. Our current approach to solve this problem is to represent automaton functors (which are basically relations) via binary decision diagrams. Initial experiments have been quite encouraging.

Finally, decomposing a graph into atomic cospans is basically equivalent to the path decomposition of a graph and checking whether a graph is contained in the language is hence linear-time for graphs of bounded pathwidth. For efficiency reasons it would be more suitable to consider generalizations of tree automata that can handle tree decompositions of graphs, as it is similarly done in the work by Courcelle. While we think that this should be feasible in principle, we did not choose to follow this path here since it would have added additional complexity to the encoding into automaton functors. In the implementation we will restrict ourselves to discrete interfaces and, out of necessity, to graphs of bounded pathwidth or treewidth in order to work with finitely many state sets.

Acknowledgements. We are grateful to Tobias Heindel for his suggestions and his help with the categorical foundations. Furthermore we would like to thank Paolo Baldan and Andrea Corradini for stimulating discussions on this research topic.

References

1. Blume, C.: Graphsprachen für die Spezifikation von Invarianten bei verteilten und dynamischen Systemen. Master's thesis, Universität Duisburg-Essen (November 2008)
2. Blume, C., Sander Bruggink, H.J., König, B.: Recognizable graph languages for checking invariants. In: Proc. of GT-VMT '10 (Workshop on Graph Transformation and Visual Modeling Techniques), Electronic Communications of the EASST (2010)
3. Bouajjani, A., Jonsson, B., Nilsson, M., Touili, T.: Regular model checking. In: Emerson, E.A., Sistla, A.P. (eds.) CAV 2000. LNCS, vol. 1855, pp. 403–418. Springer, Heidelberg (2000)
4. Bozapalidis, S., Kalampakas, A.: Recognizability of graph and pattern languages. Acta Informatica 42(8/9), 553–581 (2006)
5. Bozapalidis, S., Kalampakas, A.: Graph automata. Theoretical Computer Science 393, 147–165 (2008)
6. Bruggink, H.J.S., König, B.: On the recognizability of arrow and graph languages. In: Ehrig, H., Heckel, R., Rozenberg, G., Taentzer, G. (eds.) ICGT 2008. LNCS, vol. 5214, pp. 336–350. Springer, Heidelberg (2008)
7. Courcelle, B.: The monadic second-order logic of graphs I. Recognizable sets of finite graphs. Information and Computation 85, 12–75 (1990)
8. Courcelle, B.: The expression of graph properties and graph transformations in monadic second-order logic. In: Rozenberg, G. (ed.) Handbook of Graph Grammars and Computing by Graph Transformation, ch. 5, Foundations, vol. 1, World Scientific, Singapore (1997)
9. Courcelle, B., Durand, I.: Verifying monadic second order graph properties with tree automata. In: European Lisp Symposium (May 2010)
10. Geser, A., Hofbauer, D., Waldmann, J.: Match-bounded string rewriting systems. Applicable Algebra in Engineering, Communication and Computing 15(3-4), 149–171 (2004)
11. Griffing, G.: Composition-representative subsets. Theory and Applications of Categories 11(19), 420–437 (2003)
12. Grohe, M.: Logic, graphs and algorithms. In: Flum, J., Grädel, E., Wilke, T. (eds.) Logic and Automata – History and Perspectives. Amsterdam University Press (2007)
13. Heindel, T.: A category theoretical approach to the concurrent semantics of rewriting. PhD thesis, Universität Duisburg–Essen (September 2009), `http://www.ti.inf.uni-due.de/people/heindel/diss.pdf`
14. Jacobs, B.: Categorical Logic and Type Theory. Studies in Logic and the Foundation of Mathematics, vol. 141. Elsevier, Amsterdam (1999)
15. Lack, S., Sobociński, P.: Adhesive and quasiadhesive categories. RAIRO – Theoretical Informatics and Applications 39(3) (2005)
16. Pitts, A.M.: Categorical logic. In: Abramsky, S., Gabbay, D.M., Maibaum, T.S.E. (eds.) Handbook of Logic in Computer Science V. Oxford University Press, Oxford (2001)
17. Rensink, A.: Representing first-order logic using graphs. In: Ehrig, H., Engels, G., Parisi-Presicce, F., Rozenberg, G. (eds.) ICGT 2004. LNCS, vol. 3256, pp. 319–335. Springer, Heidelberg (2004)

Terminating Tableaux for $\mathcal{SOQ}$ with Number Restrictions on Transitive Roles*

Mark Kaminski and Gert Smolka

Saarland University, Saarbrücken, Germany

Abstract. We show that the description logic $\mathcal{SOQ}$ with number restrictions on transitive roles is decidable by a terminating tableau calculus. The language decided by the calculus includes the universal role, which allows us to internalize TBox axioms. Termination of the system is achieved through pattern-based blocking.

1 Introduction

Number restrictions on roles are an expressive feature of description logics that allows to impose counting constraints on the number of objects that are related via a certain role. Qualified number restrictions [6] correspond to graded modalities [4,3,5] in modal logics. Transitive roles are prominently used in description logics for representing parthood relationships [21].

Efficient tableau algorithms are available for a wide range of description logics, including logics that contain both transitive roles and number restrictions, such as $\mathcal{SIN}$ [11], $\mathcal{SHIF}$ [8,13], $\mathcal{SHIQ}$ [12], $\mathcal{SHOQ}$ [9], $\mathcal{SHOIQ}$ [10], and $\mathcal{SROIQ}$ [7]. In all cases, however, the language is restricted to contain no number restrictions on *complex roles*, e.g., on transitive roles, or roles containing transitive subroles. Although desirable for applications [19], number restrictions on complex roles lead to undecidability for logics extending $\mathcal{SHIN}$ [13]. In the absence of inverse roles ($\mathcal{I}$), however, the limitation of number restrictions to simple roles can be significantly relaxed [19]. In particular, the result in [19] implies the decidability of $\mathcal{SQ}$ extended by number restrictions on transitive roles. Obtained via a small model theorem, this decidability result does not yield practical decision procedures. Nor does it imply the decidability of extensions of $\mathcal{SQ}$ with nominals.

We consider the logic $\mathcal{SOQ}$ with number restrictions on transitive roles, and call it $\mathcal{SOQ}^+$. As indicated by its name, $\mathcal{SOQ}^+$ extends the basic description logic $\mathcal{ALC}$ [23] by primitive transitive roles ($\mathcal{S}$), nominals ($\mathcal{O}$), and qualified number restrictions ($\mathcal{Q}$), where we allow such restrictions on transitive roles (+). We show that reasoning in $\mathcal{SOQ}^+$ is decidable by giving a terminating tableau calculus for concept satisfiability in $\mathcal{SOQ}^+$ extended by the universal role. Having the universal role in the language allows us to internalize terminological axioms, reducing reasoning with respect to TBoxes to concept satisfiability [1,22].

* A preliminary version of this work appeared in [17].

C.S. Calude and V. Sassone (Eds.): TCS 2010, IFIP AICT 323, pp. 213–228, 2010.

For termination, our calculus employs *pattern-based blocking*. Pattern-based blocking is introduced in [15,16] for converse-free hybrid logic with global modalities. In [14], the technique is extended to graded logics subsuming $\mathcal{SOQ}$ and $\mathcal{SHOQ}$. To provide a complete treatment of number restrictions on transitive roles, we extend pattern-based blocking further, incorporating ideas [25,2] used in tableau systems for propositional dynamic logic and propositional μ-calculus.

2 Preliminaries

Following [15,16,14], our formal presentation is based on simple type theory. Notationally, our presentation is based on modal syntax, but can easily be translated to the traditional DL notation [22]. We start with two base types B and I. The interpretation of B is fixed and consists of the two truth values. The interpretation of I is a nonempty set whose elements are called *individuals*. Given two types σ and τ, the *functional type* $\sigma\tau$ is interpreted as the set of all total functions from the interpretation of σ to that of τ. We write $\sigma_1\sigma_2\sigma_3$ for $\sigma_1(\sigma_2\sigma_3)$.

We employ three kinds of variables: *Nominals* x, y, z of type I (we assume there are infinitely many nominals), *propositional variables* p, q of type IB, and *role variables* r of type IIB. Since the language in question contains no role expressions other than role variables, we call role variables *roles* for short. We use the logical constants $\bot, \top : \mathrm{B}$, $\neg : \mathrm{BB}$, $\vee, \wedge, \rightarrow : \mathrm{BBB}$, $\doteq : \mathrm{IIB}$, $\exists, \forall : (\mathrm{IB})\mathrm{B}$. Terms are defined as usual. We write st for applications, $\lambda x.s$ for abstractions, and $s_1s_2s_3$ for $(s_1s_2)s_3$. We also use infix notation, e.g., $s \wedge t$ for $(\wedge)st$.

Terms of type B are called *formulas*. We employ some common notational conventions: $\exists x.s$ for $\exists(\lambda x.s)$, $\forall x.s$ for $\forall(\lambda x.s)$, and $x \dot{\neq} y$ for $\neg(x \doteq y)$.

Let us write $\exists X.s$ for $\exists x_1 \ldots x_n.s$ if $|X| = n$ and $X = \{x_1, \ldots, x_n\}$. Also, given a set X of nominals, we use the following abbreviation:

$$DX := \bigwedge_{\substack{x,y \in X \\ x \neq y}} x \dot{\neq} y$$

We use the following constants, which we call *modal operators*.

$$\begin{array}{rrcl}
\dot{\neg} : (\mathrm{IB})\mathrm{IB} & \dot{\neg} p & = & \lambda x.\neg px \\
\dot{\wedge} : (\mathrm{IB})(\mathrm{IB})\mathrm{IB} & p \mathbin{\dot{\wedge}} q & = & \lambda x.\, px \wedge qx \\
\dot{\vee} : (\mathrm{IB})(\mathrm{IB})\mathrm{IB} & p \mathbin{\dot{\vee}} q & = & \lambda x.\, px \vee qx \\
\langle \text{-} \rangle_n : (\mathrm{IIB})(\mathrm{IB})\mathrm{IB} & \langle r \rangle_n p & = & \lambda x.\exists Y.\, DY \wedge (\bigwedge_{y \in Y} rxy \wedge py) \\
[\text{-}]_n : (\mathrm{IIB})(\mathrm{IB})\mathrm{IB} & [r]_n p & = & \lambda x.\forall Y.\, (\bigwedge_{y \in Y} rxy) \wedge DY \rightarrow \bigvee_{y \in Y} py \\
E_n : (\mathrm{IB})\mathrm{IB} & E_n p & = & \lambda x.\exists Y.\, DY \wedge \bigwedge_{y \in Y} py \\
A_n : (\mathrm{IB})\mathrm{IB} & A_n p & = & \lambda x.\forall Y.\, DY \rightarrow \bigvee_{y \in Y} py \\
\dot{_} : \mathrm{IIB} & \dot{x} & = & \lambda y.x \doteq y \\
T : (\mathrm{IIB})\mathrm{B} & Tr & = & \forall xyz.rxy \wedge ryz \rightarrow rxz
\end{array}$$

where $n \geq 0$ and $|Y| = n + 1$ in all equations

To the right of each constant is an equation defining its semantics. Formulas of the form $[r]_n tx$ are called *box formulas* or *boxes*, and formulas $\langle r\rangle_n tx$ are called *diamond formulas* or *diamonds*. The semantics of boxes and diamonds is defined following [3,5]. Intuitively, it can be described as follows:

- $\langle r\rangle_n p$: There are at least $n+1$ r-successors satisfying p.
- $[r]_n p$: All r-successors but possibly n exceptions satisfy p.

Our language does not contain a dedicated symbol for the universal role. Instead, we use graded *global modalities* E_n and A_n, which are semantically equivalent to qualified number restrictions on the universal role. So, for instance, $E_1 p$ holds if there are at least two distinct states satisfying p. Formulas of the form Tr are called *transitivity assertions*. We assume the application of modal operators to have a higher precedence than regular functional application. So, for instance, we write $\dot\neg\langle r\rangle_2 \dot y \mathbin{\dot\vee} p\ x$ for $((\dot\neg(\langle r\rangle_2(\dot y)))\mathbin{\dot\vee} p)x$.

A *modal interpretation* $\mathfrak{M}$ is an interpretation of simple type theory that interprets B as the set $\{0,1\}$, $\bot$ as 0 (i.e., false), $\top$ as 1 (i.e., true), maps I to a non-empty set, gives the logical constants $\neg$, $\wedge$, $\vee$, $\rightarrow$, $\exists$, $\forall$, $\doteq$ their usual meaning, and satisfies the equations defining the modal operators $\dot\neg$, $\dot\wedge$, $\dot\vee$, $\langle\text{-}\rangle_n$, $[\text{-}]_n$, E, A, $\dot{\ }$ and T. If $\mathfrak{M}t = 1$, we say that $\mathfrak{M}$ *satisfies* t. A formula is called *satisfiable* if it has a satisfying modal interpretation.

3 Branches

For the sake of simplicity, we will define our tableau calculus $\mathcal{T}$ on negation normal *modal expressions*, i.e., terms of the form:

$$t \ ::= \ p \mid \dot\neg p \mid \dot x \mid \dot\neg\dot x \mid t \mathbin{\dot\wedge} t \mid t \mathbin{\dot\vee} t \mid \langle r\rangle_n t \mid [r]_n t \mid E_n t \mid A_n t$$

A *branch* Γ is a finite set of formulas s of the form

$$s \ ::= \ tx \mid rxy \mid Tr \mid x\dot=y \mid x\dot{\neq}y \mid \bot \mid \alpha{:}[r]_n tx$$

where t is a negation normal modal expression. The new form $\alpha{:}[r]_n tx$ serves algorithmic purposes. The *label* α of such *label introductions* is taken from a countably infinite set of labels. Formulas of the form rxy are called *edges*. We use the formula $\bot$ to explicitly mark unsatisfiable branches. We call a branch Γ *closed* if $\bot \in \Gamma$. Otherwise, Γ is called *open*. An interpretation $\mathfrak{M}$ satisfies a branch Γ if $\mathfrak{M}$ satisfies all *proper* formulas on Γ, i.e., all formulas except for label introductions. Given a finite set of input formulas (i.e., a branch) Γ_0, our tableau calculus decides if Γ_0 is satisfiable. We call Γ_0 the *initial branch*. The initial branch must contain no edges or label introductions. This restriction is inessential for the expressiveness of the language since label introductions are semantically irrelevant, and edges rxy can equivalently be expressed as $\langle r\rangle_0 \dot y x$.

Let Γ be a branch. With $\sim_\Gamma$ we denote the least equivalence relation $\sim$ on nominals such that $x \sim y$ for every equation $x\dot=y \in \Gamma$. We define the *equational closure* $\tilde\Gamma$ of a branch Γ as

$$\begin{aligned}\tilde{\Gamma} \;:=\; & \Gamma \cup \{tx \mid t \text{ modal expression and } \exists x' : x' \sim_\Gamma x \text{ and } tx' \in \Gamma\} \\ & \cup \{rxy \mid \exists x', y' : x' \sim_\Gamma x \text{ and } y' \sim_\Gamma y \text{ and } rx'y' \in \Gamma\}.\end{aligned}$$

4 Evidence and Pre-evidence

The proof of model existence for our calculus $\mathcal{T}$ proceeds in three stages. Applied to a satisfiable initial branch, the rules of $\mathcal{T}$ (defined in Sect. 5) construct a *quasi-evident* branch (defined in Sect. 6). We show that every quasi-evident branch can be extended to a *pre-evident* branch, which, in turn, can be extended to an *evident* branch. For evident branches, we show model existence.

We write $D_\Gamma X$ as an abbreviation for $\forall x, y \in X : x \neq y \implies x \dot{\neq} y \in \Gamma$. A branch Γ is called *evident* if it satisfies all of the following *evidence conditions*:

$$\begin{aligned}
(t_1 \dot{\wedge} t_2)x \in \Gamma &\implies t_1x \in \tilde{\Gamma} \text{ and } t_2x \in \tilde{\Gamma} \\
(t_1 \dot{\vee} t_2)x \in \Gamma &\implies t_1x \in \tilde{\Gamma} \text{ or } t_2x \in \tilde{\Gamma} \\
\langle r \rangle_n tx \in \Gamma &\implies \exists Y\colon\ |Y| = n+1 \text{ and } D_\Gamma Y \text{ and } \{rxy, ty \mid y \in Y\} \subseteq \tilde{\Gamma} \\
[r]_n tx \in \Gamma &\implies |\{y \mid rxy \in \tilde{\Gamma},\ ty \notin \tilde{\Gamma}\}/_{\sim_\Gamma}| \leq n \\
E_n tx \in \Gamma &\implies \exists Y\colon\ |Y| = n+1 \text{ and } D_\Gamma Y \text{ and } \{ty \mid y \in Y\} \subseteq \tilde{\Gamma} \\
A_n tx \in \Gamma &\implies |\{y \mid ty \notin \tilde{\Gamma}\}/_{\sim_\Gamma}| \leq n \\
\dot{x}y \in \Gamma &\implies x \sim_\Gamma y \\
\dot{\neg}\dot{x}y \in \Gamma &\implies x \not\sim_\Gamma y \\
x \dot{\neq} y \in \Gamma &\implies x \not\sim_\Gamma y \\
\dot{\neg}px \in \Gamma &\implies px \notin \tilde{\Gamma} \\
Tr \in \Gamma &\implies \forall x, y, z :\ rxy \in \tilde{\Gamma} \text{ and } ryz \in \tilde{\Gamma} \implies rxz \in \tilde{\Gamma}
\end{aligned}$$

A formula s is called *evident on* Γ if Γ satisfies the right-hand side of the evidence condition corresponding to s. For instance, $(t_1 \dot{\wedge} t_2)x$ is evident on Γ if and only if $\{t_1x, t_2x\} \subseteq \tilde{\Gamma}$.

We will now show that evident branches are satisfiable. Given a term t, we write $\mathcal{N}t$ for the set of nominals that occur in t. The notation is extended to sets of terms in the natural way: $\mathcal{N}\Gamma := \bigcup\{\mathcal{N}t \mid t \in \Gamma\}$.

Given a branch Γ, we construct the interpretation $\mathfrak{M}^\Gamma$ by taking as the domain of S the nominals on Γ, and interpreting propositional variables and roles as the smallest sets that are consistent with the respective assertions on Γ. To satisfy the equality constraints on Γ, all nominals that are equivalent modulo $\sim_\Gamma$ are mapped to the same fixed representative.

Let Γ be a branch and let $x_0 \in \mathcal{N}\Gamma$. Let ρ be a function from finite sets of nominals to nominals such that $\rho X \in X$ whenever X is nonempty. We define the interpretation $\mathfrak{M}^\Gamma$ as follows:

$$\mathfrak{M}^\Gamma \mathrm{S} := \mathcal{N}\Gamma$$
$$\mathfrak{M}^\Gamma x := \text{if } x \in \mathcal{N}\Gamma \text{ then } \rho\{y \in \mathcal{N}\Gamma \mid y \sim_\Gamma x\} \text{ else } x_0$$
$$\mathfrak{M}^\Gamma p := \{x \in \mathcal{N}\Gamma \mid px \in \tilde{\Gamma}\}$$
$$\mathfrak{M}^\Gamma r := \{(x, y) \in (\mathcal{N}\Gamma)^2 \mid rxy \in \tilde{\Gamma}\}$$

Note that in the last two lines of the definition, we interpret the set notation as a convenient description for the respective characteristic functions.

Theorem 4.1 (Model Existence). *If Γ is an evident branch, then $\mathfrak{M}^\Gamma$ satisfies Γ.*

Proof. Let Γ be an evident branch. For every $s \in \Gamma$, we show that $\mathfrak{M}^\Gamma$ satisfies s by induction on s. The details are straightforward. □

To simplify the treatment of transitivity, we introduce the notion of pre-evidence. We define the relation $\rhd_\Gamma^r$ as the least relation such that:

$$rxy \in \tilde{\Gamma} \implies x \rhd_\Gamma^r y$$
$$x \rhd_\Gamma^r y \text{ and } y \rhd_\Gamma^r z \text{ and } Tr \in \Gamma \implies x \rhd_\Gamma^r z$$

We write $x \trianglerighteq_\Gamma^r y$ iff $x \sim_\Gamma y$ or $x \rhd_\Gamma^r y$.

The *pre-evidence conditions* are obtained from the evidence conditions by omitting the condition for transitivity assertions and replacing the condition for boxes as follows:

$$[r]_n tx \in \Gamma \implies |\{y \mid x \rhd_\Gamma^r y \text{ and } ty \notin \tilde{\Gamma}\}/_{\sim_\Gamma}| \leq n$$

Pre-evidence of individual formulas is defined analogously to the corresponding evidence condition. Note that for all formulas but boxes and transitivity assertions, the notions of evidence and pre-evidence coincide.

We now show that every pre-evident branch can be extended to an evident branch. Let the *evidence closure* $\hat{\Gamma}$ of a branch Γ be defined as $\Gamma \cup \{rxy \mid x \rhd_\Gamma^r y\}$.

Proposition 4.1. $rxy \in \hat{\Gamma} \iff rxy \in \tilde{\hat{\Gamma}} \iff x \rhd_\Gamma^r y$

Theorem 4.2 (Evidence Completion). *Γ pre-evident $\implies$ $\hat{\Gamma}$ evident*

Proof. Since $\hat{\Gamma}$ differs from Γ only in that $\hat{\Gamma}$ may contain more edges, and Γ is pre-evident, $\hat{\Gamma}$ satisfies all of the evidence conditions but possibly the ones for boxes and transitivity assertions. The evidence condition for transitivity assertions holds in $\hat{\Gamma}$ by Proposition 4.1 since $\rhd_\Gamma^r$ is transitively closed for every r such that $Tr \in \Gamma$. The condition for boxes is immediate by Proposition 4.1. □

5 Tableau Rules

The tableau rules of our calculus $\mathcal{T}$ are defined in Fig. 1. In the rules, we write $\exists x \in X : \Gamma(x)$ for $\Gamma(x_1) \mid \ldots \mid \Gamma(x_n)$, where $X = \{x_1, \ldots, x_n\}$ and $\Gamma(x)$ is

$$\mathcal{R}_{\dot\wedge}\ \frac{(s \mathbin{\dot\wedge} t)x}{sx,\ tx} \qquad\qquad \mathcal{R}_{\dot\vee}\ \frac{(s \mathbin{\dot\vee} t)x}{sx \mid tx}$$

$$\mathcal{R}_{\Diamond}\ \frac{\langle r\rangle_n tx}{\forall y \in Y\colon\ rxy,\ ty,\ \forall z \in Y,\ y \neq z\colon\ y \dot{\neq} z}\ \begin{array}{l} Y \text{ fresh},\ |Y| = n+1, \\ \langle r\rangle_n tx \text{ not quasi-evident on } \Gamma \end{array}$$

$$\mathcal{R}_{\Box}\ \frac{[r]_n tx}{\exists y, z \in Y,\ y \neq z\colon\ y \dot{=} z \mid \exists y \in Y\colon\ ty}\ Y \subseteq \{y \mid x \rhd^r_\Gamma y\},\ |Y| = |Y/_{\sim_\Gamma}| = n+1$$

$$\mathcal{R}_{T}\ \frac{Tr,\ rxy}{\alpha{:}[r]_n tx}\ \alpha \text{ fresh},\ [r]_n tx \in \tilde{\Gamma},\ [r]_n tx \text{ not subsumed on } \Gamma$$

$$\mathcal{R}_{E}\ \frac{E_n tx}{\forall y \in Y\colon\ ty,\ \forall z \in Y,\ y \neq z\colon\ y \dot{\neq} z}\ Y \text{ fresh},\ |Y| = n+1,\ E_n tx \text{ not evident on } \Gamma$$

$$\mathcal{R}_{A}\ \frac{A_n tx}{\exists y, z \in Y,\ y \neq z\colon\ y \dot{=} z \mid \exists y \in Y\colon\ ty}\ Y \subseteq \mathcal{N}\Gamma,\ |Y| = |Y/_{\sim_\Gamma}| = n+1$$

$$\mathcal{R}_{N}\ \frac{\dot{x}y}{x \dot{=} y} \qquad \mathcal{R}_{\bar{N}}\ \frac{\dot\neg \dot{x}y}{x \dot{\neq} y} \qquad \mathcal{R}^{\perp}_{\dot\neg}\ \frac{\dot\neg px}{\perp}\ px \in \tilde{\Gamma} \qquad \mathcal{R}^{\perp}_{\dot\neq}\ \frac{x \dot{\neq} y}{\perp}\ x \sim_\Gamma y$$

Γ is the branch to which a rule is applied. "Y fresh" stands for $Y \cap \mathcal{N}\Gamma = \emptyset$.
"α fresh" stands for $\nexists t, x : \alpha{:}tx \in \Gamma$

Fig. 1. Tableau rules for $\mathcal{T}$

a set of formulas parametrized by x. In case $X = \emptyset$, the notation translates to $\perp$. Dually, we write $\forall x \in X\colon \Gamma(x)$ for $\Gamma(x_1), \ldots, \Gamma(x_n)$ ($X = \{x_1, \ldots, x_n\}$). If $X = \emptyset$, the notation stands for the empty set of formulas.

The side condition of $\mathcal{R}_\Diamond$ uses the notion of quasi-evidence, which we will introduce in Sect. 6. For now, assume the rule is formulated with the restriction "$\langle r\rangle_n tx$ not evident on Γ".

A box formula $[r]_n tx$ is *subsumed* on Γ if there is a nominal y and a label α such that $y \unrhd^r_\Gamma x$ and $\alpha{:}[r]_n ty \in \Gamma$. The rule $\mathcal{R}_T$ is constrained to be applicable only to boxes that are not subsumed on Γ. This ensures, in particular, that $\mathcal{R}_T$ is applied at most once to each individual box formula on the branch.

A branch Δ is called a *proper extension* of a branch Γ if $\Delta \supseteq \Gamma$ and $\tilde{\Delta} \supsetneq \tilde{\Gamma}$. Note that if Δ is a proper extension of Γ, then in particular it holds $\Delta \supsetneq \Gamma$. The converse does not hold: Let $\Gamma := \{\dot{x}y,\ x \dot{=} z,\ z \dot{=} y\}$ and $\Delta := \Gamma \cup \{x \dot{=} y\}$. Then $\Delta \supsetneq \Gamma$ but Δ is not a proper extension of Γ. We implicitly restrict the applicability of the tableau rules so that a rule $\mathcal{R}$ is only applicable to a formula $s \in \Gamma$ if all of the alternative branches $\Delta_1, \ldots, \Delta_n$ resulting from this application are proper extensions of Γ.

Proposition 5.1 (Soundness). *Let $\Delta_1, \ldots, \Delta_n$ be the branches obtained from a branch Γ by a rule of $\mathcal{T}$. Then Γ is satisfiable if and only if there is some $i \in \{1, \ldots, n\}$ such that Δ_i is satisfiable.*

6 Blocking Conditions and Quasi-evidence

The restrictions on the applicability of the tableau rules given by the pre-evidence conditions are not sufficient for termination. Consider $\Gamma_0 := \{A_0\langle r\rangle_0 px\}$. An application of $\mathcal{R}_A$ to Γ_0 yields $\Gamma_1 := \Gamma_0 \cup \{\langle r\rangle_0 px\}$, which can be extended by $\mathcal{R}_\Diamond$ to $\Gamma_2 := \Gamma_1 \cup \{rxy, py\}$. Now $\mathcal{R}_A$ is applicable again and yields $\Gamma_3 := \Gamma_2 \cup \{\langle r\rangle_0 py\}$, which in turn can be extended by $\mathcal{R}_\Diamond$, and so ad infinitum.

To obtain a terminating calculus, we restrict the rule $\mathcal{R}_\Diamond$ by weakening the notion of pre-evidence for diamond formulas. The weaker notion, called quasi-evidence, is then used in the side condition of $\mathcal{R}_\Diamond$ in place of pre-evidence. Quasi-evidence must be weak enough to guarantee termination but strong enough to preserve completeness.

The *edge graph* of a branch Γ is a labelled graph with the nodes $\mathcal{N}\Gamma$ and edges $\{(x, y) \mid \exists r : \; rxy \in \Gamma\}$, where a node x is labelled with all expressions t such that $tx \in \Gamma$, and an edge (x, y) is labelled with all roles r such that $rxy \in \Gamma$. A branch can always be represented graphically through its edge graph.

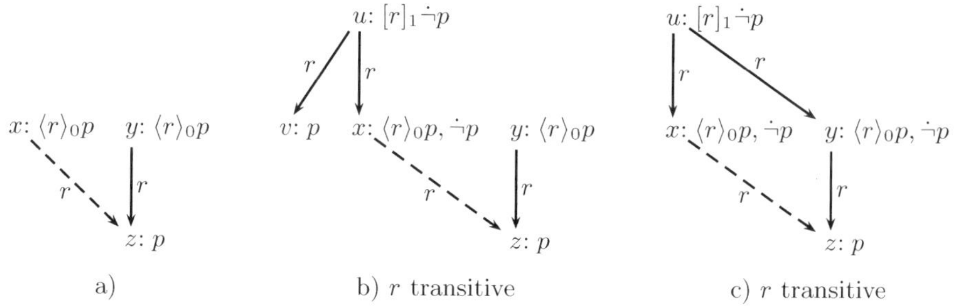

Fig. 2. Number restrictions and transitivity

In [14], the notion of quasi-evidence is based on the following observation. Let Γ be a branch and x, y be nominals such that: (1) *x has no r-successor on Γ*, i.e., there is no z such that $rxz \in \tilde{\Gamma}$, (2) for every r-diamond or r-box $tx \in \tilde{\Gamma}$, it holds $ty \in \tilde{\Gamma}$, and (3) all r-diamonds and r-boxes $sy \in \tilde{\Gamma}$ are evident on Γ. Then all r-diamonds and r-boxes $sx \in \tilde{\Gamma}$ can be made evident by extending Γ with $\{rxz \mid ryz \in \tilde{\Gamma}\}$. As an example, consider the edge graph in Fig. 2(a). There, the formula $\langle r\rangle_0 px$ can be made evident by adding the edge rxz (represented by the dashed arrow) to the branch. In the presence of transitivity, extending a branch Γ by an edge rxz may destroy the evidence of r-boxes tu such that $u \rhd^r_\Gamma x$ (Fig. 2(b)). Note, however, that adding an edge rxz cannot destroy the evidence of a box tu such that $u \rhd^r_\Gamma x$ if we already have $u \rhd^r_\Gamma z$ (Fig. 2(c)).

To deal with non-local constraints introduced by number restrictions on transitive roles, we refine the notion of a pattern and the quasi-evidence conditions from [14]. When blocking a nominal x we have to make sure not to violate any graded boxes at the predecessors of x. To track the relevant boxes we tag them with labels.

Given a role r, an *r-pattern* is a set consisting of modal expressions of the form μt, where $\mu \in \{\langle r\rangle_n, [r]_n \mid n \in \mathbb{N}\}$, and labels α, such that, for some n, t, x: $\alpha{:}[r]_n tx \in \Gamma$ (although not required by the definition, in all cases where patterns play a role for termination they will contain at least one diamond). We define:

$$x{:}_\Gamma\alpha \iff \exists r, n, t, y:\ \alpha{:}[r]_n ty \in \Gamma \text{ and } y \rhd^r_\Gamma x$$

We write $P^r_\Gamma x$ for the largest r-pattern P such that $P \subseteq \{\mu t \mid \mu tx \in \tilde{\Gamma}\} \cup \{\alpha \mid x{:}_\Gamma\alpha\}$. We call $P^r_\Gamma x$ the r-pattern of x on Γ. Looking back at Fig. 2 (b), we have $P^r_\Gamma x = \{\langle r\rangle_0 p\}$, $P^r_\Gamma u = \{[r]_1 \dot{\neg} p\}$, and $P^{r'}_\Gamma x = \emptyset$ for all $r' \neq r$. An r-pattern P is *expanded on* Γ if there are nominals x, y such that $rxy \in \Gamma$ and $P \subseteq P^r_\Gamma x$. In this case, we say that the nominal x *expands* P *on* Γ.

A diamond $\langle r\rangle_n sx \in \Gamma$ is *quasi-evident on* Γ if it is either evident on Γ or x has no r-successor on Γ and $P^r_\Gamma x$ is expanded on Γ. The rule $\mathcal{R}_\Diamond$ can only be applied to diamonds that are not quasi-evident. Note that whenever $\langle r\rangle_n sx \in \Gamma$ is quasi-evident but not evident (on Γ), there is a nominal y that expands $P^r_\Gamma x$.

The *quasi-evidence conditions* are obtained from the pre-evidence conditions by replacing the condition for diamond formulas and adding a condition for transitivity assertions and label introductions as follows:

$$\langle r\rangle_n tx \in \Gamma \implies \langle r\rangle_n tx \text{ is quasi-evident on } \Gamma$$
$$Tr \in \Gamma \implies \forall n, t, x\colon\ [r]_n tx \in \tilde{\Gamma} \implies \exists z, \alpha\colon\ z \unrhd^r_\Gamma x \text{ and } \alpha{:}[r]_n tz \in \Gamma$$
$$\alpha{:}[r]_n tx \in \Gamma \implies [r]_n tx \in \tilde{\Gamma} \text{ and } \exists y\colon rxy \in \Gamma \text{ and } \forall s, z\colon \alpha{:}sz \in \Gamma \implies s = [r]_n t$$

Proposition 6.1. *If Γ satisfies the quasi-evidence condition for label introductions and $\alpha{:}[r]_n tx \in \Gamma$, then for all y, $x \rhd^r_\Gamma y \iff y{:}_\Gamma\alpha$.*

Lemma 6.1. *Let Γ be a branch. Let $\{[r]_n tx, [r]_n ty\} \subseteq \tilde{\Gamma}$ such that $Tr \in \Gamma$ and $x \unrhd^r_\Gamma y$. Then:* $[r]_n tx$ is pre-evident on $\Gamma \implies [r]_n ty$ is pre-evident on Γ.

Proof. Let Γ be a branch such that $\{[r]_n tx, [r]_n ty\} \subseteq \tilde{\Gamma}$, $Tr \in \Gamma$ and $x \unrhd^r_\Gamma y$. Because $\rhd^r_\Gamma$ is transitively closed, we have $x \rhd^r_\Gamma z$ whenever $y \rhd^r_\Gamma z$. The claim follows. □

Lemma 6.2. *Let Γ be a quasi-evident branch. Let $\langle r\rangle_n sx \in \Gamma$ be not evident on Γ, y be a nominal that expands $P^r_\Gamma x$ on Γ, and $\Delta := \Gamma \cup \{rxz \mid ryz \in \tilde{\Gamma}\}$. Then:*

1. *$\forall z:\ rxz \in \tilde{\Delta} \iff ryz \in \tilde{\Gamma}$ and $x \rhd^r_\Delta z \iff y \rhd^r_\Gamma z$,*
2. *$\forall m, t:\ \langle r\rangle_m t \in P^r_\Gamma x \implies \langle r\rangle_m tx$ is evident on Δ,*
3. *$\langle r\rangle_n sx$ is evident on Δ,*
4. *$\forall r', m, t, z:\ \langle r'\rangle_m tz$ is evident on $\Gamma \implies \langle r'\rangle_m tz$ is evident on Δ,*
5. *Δ is quasi-evident.*

Proof. We begin with (1). Let z be a nominal. We only show $rxz \in \tilde{\Delta} \Leftrightarrow ryz \in \tilde{\Gamma}$. The other claim follows by induction on the construction of $\rhd^r_\Gamma$ and $\rhd^r_\Delta$. By construction, it holds $ryz \in \tilde{\Gamma} \Rightarrow rxz \in \Delta$. The converse implication holds by the fact that $\langle r\rangle_n sx$ is quasi-evident but not evident on Γ, meaning that x has no r-successor on Γ. It remains to show: $rxz \in \Delta \Leftrightarrow rxz \in \tilde{\Delta}$. The direction from left to right is obvious. For the other direction, assume $rxz \in \tilde{\Delta}$. Then there are x', z' such that $x' \sim_\Gamma x$, $z' \sim_\Gamma z$, and $rx'z' \in \Delta$. Since x has no r-successor on Γ, neither does x'. Hence, since $rx'z' \in \Delta - \Gamma$, we must have $x' = x$, and so $rxz' \in \Delta$. But then $ryz' \in \tilde{\Gamma}$, and consequently, $ryz \in \tilde{\Gamma}$. The claim follows by the definition of Δ.

Now to (2). Let $\langle r \rangle_m t \in P^r_\Gamma x$. Since $P^r_\Gamma y \supseteq P^r_\Gamma x$, in particular it holds $\langle r \rangle_m ty \in \tilde{\Gamma}$, i.e., there is some $y' \sim_\Gamma y$ such that $\langle r \rangle_m ty' \in \Gamma$. By (1), it suffices to show that $\langle r \rangle_m ty$ is evident on Γ. This is the case since $\langle r \rangle_m ty'$ is quasi-evident on Γ (as Γ is quasi-evident) and y' has an r-successor on Γ (as y has one on Γ).

Claim (3) immediately follows from (2), and (4) is obvious as the evidence of diamonds on a branch cannot be destroyed by adding edges.

Now to (5). Note that the quasi-evidence condition for transitivity assertions holds in Δ as $\trianglerighteq^r_\Gamma \subseteq \trianglerighteq^r_\Delta$. The quasi-evidence of diamonds $\langle r \rangle_m tx \in \Delta$ holds by (2). So, the only conditions that might in principle be violated in Δ are:

a) the pre-evidence condition for boxes $[r]_m tx \in \tilde{\Delta}$ and
b) the pre-evidence condition for boxes $[r]_m tz \in \Delta$ such that $z \triangleright^r_\Delta x$, if $Tr \in \Gamma$.

For (a), it holds $[r]_m ty \in \tilde{\Gamma}$ as $P^r_\Gamma y \supseteq P^r_\Gamma x = P^r_\Delta x$. Hence by (1) it suffices to show that $[r]_m ty$ is pre-evident on Γ, which is the case since Γ is quasi-evident. For (b), by the quasi-evidence condition for transitivity assertions, there is a nominal u and a label α such that $u \trianglerighteq^r_\Gamma z$ and $\alpha{:}[r]_m tu \in \Gamma$. Since $Tr \in \Gamma$, $u \trianglerighteq^r_\Gamma z$ and $z \triangleright^r_\Delta x$, it holds $u \triangleright^r_\Gamma x$. Then $x{:}_\Gamma\alpha$ and, by the quasi-evidence condition for label introductions, $[r]_m tu \in \tilde{\Gamma}$. By Lemma 6.1, it suffices to show that $[r]_m tu$ is pre-evident on Δ. Since $P^r_\Gamma y \supseteq P^r_\Gamma x$, we have $y{:}_\Gamma\alpha$ and hence $u \triangleright^r_\Gamma y$ (Proposition 6.1). So, by (1), $x \triangleright^r_\Delta v$ implies $u \triangleright^r_\Gamma v$ for all nominals v, and consequently, $\forall v:\ u \triangleright^r_\Delta v \Leftrightarrow u \triangleright^r_\Gamma v$. The claim follows since $[r]_m tu$ is pre-evident on Γ. □

For an illustration of Lemma 6.2, let the edge graph in Fig. 2(a) (without the dashed arrow) represent Γ. Then $\langle r \rangle_0 px$ is quasi-evident but not evident on Γ, and y expands $P^r_\Gamma x$. The graph with the dashed arrow added corresponds to the branch Δ in the lemma. The five claims for Γ and Δ are easy to verify.

Theorem 6.1 (Pre-evidence Completion). *For every quasi-evident branch Γ there is a pre-evident branch Δ such that $\Gamma \subseteq \Delta$.*

Proof. For every branch Γ, we define: $\varphi\Gamma := |\{\langle r \rangle_n sx \mid \langle r \rangle_n sx \in \Gamma \text{ and } \langle r \rangle_n sx \text{ is not evident on } \Gamma\}|$. Let Γ be quasi-evident. We proceed by induction on $\varphi\Gamma$. If $\varphi\Gamma = 0$, then Γ is pre-evident and we are done. Otherwise, there is a diamond $\langle r \rangle_n sx \in \Gamma$ that is not pre-evident on Γ. Let y be a nominal that expands $P^r_\Gamma x$ on Γ, and let $\Gamma' := \Gamma \cup \{rxz \mid ryz \in \tilde{\Gamma}\}$. By Lemma 6.2(3-5), Γ' is quasi-evident and $\varphi\Gamma' < \varphi\Gamma$. So, by the inductive hypothesis, there is some pre-evident branch Δ such that $\Delta \supseteq \Gamma' \supseteq \Gamma$. □

We write $\Gamma \xrightarrow{\mathcal{R}} \Delta$ to denote that Δ is obtained from Γ by a single application of the rule $\mathcal{R}$. We write $\Gamma \rightarrow \Delta$ if there is some $\mathcal{R}$ such that $\Gamma \xrightarrow{\mathcal{R}} \Delta$. A branch is called *maximal* if it cannot be extended by any tableau rule.

Lemma 6.3. *Let Γ be a branch that is obtained from an initial branch. Then Γ satisfies the quasi-evidence condition for label introductions.*

Proof. Let $\Gamma_0 \to \ldots \to \Gamma_n$ be a derivation such that Γ_0 is an initial branch and $\Gamma_n = \Gamma$. The claim is shown by induction on n. Note that the claim is trivial for $n = 0$ since initial branches must contain no edges or label introductions. □

In conjunction with Theorems 4.1, 4.2 and 6.1, the following theorem shows that open maximal branches are satisfiable. Taken together with the termination argument in Section 7, this establishes the completeness of our calculus.

Theorem 6.2 (Quasi-evidence). *Every open and maximal branch obtained in $\mathcal{T}$ from an initial branch is quasi-evident.*

Proof. Let Γ be an open and maximal branch obtained from an initial branch. We show that every $s \in \Gamma$ that is not of the form px, rxy or $x \dot{=} y$ is either pre-evident or quasi-evident on Γ by induction on the size of s. Quasi-evidence for label introductions follows by Lemma 6.3. □

7 Termination

We will now show that every tableau derivation is finite. Since the tableau rules are all finitely branching, by König's lemma it suffices to show that the construction of every individual branch terminates. Since rule application always produces proper extensions of branches, it then suffices to show that the size (i.e., cardinality) of an individual branch is bounded. First, we show that the size of a branch Γ is bounded by a function in the number of nominals on Γ. Then, we show that this number itself is bounded, completing the termination proof.

We write $\mathcal{S}\Gamma$ for the set of all modal expressions occurring on Γ, possibly as subterms of other expressions, and $\mathrm{Rel}\,\Gamma$ for the set of all roles that occur on Γ. Crucial for the termination argument is the fact the tableau rules cannot introduce any modal expressions that do not already occur on the initial branch.

Proposition 7.1. *If Γ, Δ are branches such that Δ is obtained from Γ by any rule of $\mathcal{T}$, then $\mathcal{S}\Delta = \mathcal{S}\Gamma$.*

For every pair of nominals x, y and every role r, a branch Γ may contain an edge rxy, an equation $x \dot{=} y$ or a disequation $x \dot{\neq} y$. For every expression $s \in \mathcal{S}\Gamma$, Γ may contain a formula sx. The tableau rules can introduce at most one formula $\alpha{:}[r]_n tx$ for each box expression $[r]_n t$ and each nominal x. Finally, a branch may contain $\bot$. So, since the initial branch Γ_0 contains no formulas of the form $\alpha{:}tx$, the size of Γ derived from Γ_0 is bounded by $|\mathrm{Rel}\,\Gamma| \cdot |\mathcal{N}\Gamma|^2 + 2|\mathcal{N}\Gamma|^2 + 2|\mathcal{S}\Gamma| \cdot |\mathcal{N}\Gamma| + 1$. By Proposition 7.1, we know that $|\mathcal{S}\Gamma|$ and $|\mathrm{Rel}\,\Gamma|$ depend only on Γ_0.

By the above, it suffices to show that $|\mathcal{N}\Gamma|$ is bounded in the sum of the sizes of the input formulas (of which there are only finitely many). We do so by giving a bound on the number of applications of $\mathcal{R}_\Diamond$ and $\mathcal{R}_E$ that can occur in the derivation of a branch, which suffices since the two rules are the only ones that can introduce new nominals.

For $\mathcal{R}_E$, we do so by defining $\psi_E\Gamma := \{E_n s \in \mathcal{S}\Gamma \mid \exists x \in \mathcal{N}\Gamma : \; E_n sx$ is not evident on $\Gamma\}$ and showing that $|\psi_E\Gamma|$ decreases with every application of $\mathcal{R}_E$ (and is non-increasing otherwise, which is obvious).

Proposition 7.2. $\Gamma \overset{\mathcal{R}_E}{\to} \Delta \implies |\psi_E\Gamma| > |\psi_E\Delta|$

The proof proceeds analogously to the corresponding arguments in [15,16].

Now we show that $\mathcal{R}_\Diamond$ can be applied only finitely often. Since $\mathrm{Rel}\,\Gamma$ is bounded, it suffices to show that $\mathcal{R}_\Diamond$ can be applied only finitely often for each role. Since $\mathcal{R}_\Diamond$ is only applicable to diamonds that are not quasi-evident, we have:

Proposition 7.3. *If $\mathcal{R}_\Diamond$ is applicable to a formula $\langle r\rangle_n sx \in \Gamma$, then either*

1. *x has an r-successor on Γ, or*
2. *$P^r_\Gamma x$ is not expanded on Γ.*

Since $\Gamma \to \Delta$ implies $\tilde{\Gamma} \subseteq \tilde{\Delta}$, it holds:

Proposition 7.4. *Let $s \in \Gamma$ be a diamond formula and $\Gamma \to \Delta$.*

1. *If s is evident on Γ, then s is evident on Δ.*
2. *If Δ is obtained from Γ by applying $\mathcal{R}_\Diamond$ to s, then s is evident on Δ.*

Proposition 7.5. *Let $\Gamma \to \Delta$, $x \in \mathcal{N}\Gamma$, and P be an r-pattern.*

1. *$P^r_\Gamma x \subseteq P^r_\Delta x$.*
2. *If P is expanded on Γ, then P is expanded on Δ.*

In the case of [14], the bound on the number of applications of $\mathcal{R}_\Diamond$ for each role r can be given as $|\mathrm{Pat}^r\Gamma_0|$ where Γ_0 is the initial branch and $\mathrm{Pat}^r\Gamma := \mathcal{P}(\{\langle r\rangle_n s \mid \langle r\rangle_n s \in \mathcal{S}\Gamma\} \cup \{[r]_n s \mid [r]_n s \in \mathcal{S}\Gamma\})$. The present situation is more complex since now patterns may contain labels in addition to modal expressions. Unlike $\mathcal{S}\Gamma$, the set of labels on the branch may grow during tableau construction. Still, we can bound the number of applications of $\mathcal{R}_\Diamond$ for every given set of labels.

A rule $\mathcal{R}$ is said to be applied to a nominal $x \in \mathcal{N}\Gamma$ if $\mathcal{R}$ is applied to a formula $tx \in \Gamma$. Given a pattern P, we define $\mathcal{A}P := \{\alpha \mid \alpha \in P\}$. Let $N^{\Gamma_0}_{\langle r\rangle}$ be the number of distinct r-diamonds occurring on Γ_0: $N^{\Gamma_0}_{\langle r\rangle} := |\{\langle r\rangle_k t \mid \langle r\rangle_k t \in \mathcal{S}\Gamma_0\}|$. Let Δ be obtained from Γ by applying $\mathcal{R}_\Diamond$ to a formula $\langle r\rangle_n sx \in \Gamma$ such that $P^r_\Gamma x$ is not expanded on Γ. Clearly, $P^r_\Delta x$ must be expanded on Δ. Hence, let us call such an application of $\mathcal{R}_\Diamond$ *pattern-expanding*.

Lemma 7.1. *Let Γ_0 be an initial branch and $\Gamma_0 \to \Gamma_1 \to \ldots$ a derivation. Let r be a role, A a set of labels, and*

$$I^r_A := \{i \mid \exists x : \Gamma_{i+1} \text{ is obtained from } \Gamma_i \text{ by applying } \mathcal{R}_\Diamond \text{ to } x \text{ and } \mathcal{A}(P^r_{\Gamma_i}x) = A\}$$

Then $|I^r_A| \leq 2^{|A|} \cdot |\mathrm{Pat}^r\Gamma_0| \cdot N^{\Gamma_0}_{\langle r\rangle}$.

Proof. Let $\Gamma_0 \to \Gamma_1 \to \dots$ be a derivation, r a role and A a set of labels. We begin with two observations:

1. For every set B of labels, there are at most $|\mathrm{Pat}^r\Gamma_0|$ distinct patterns P such that $\mathcal{A}P = B$. Hence, by Proposition 7.5 (2), for every B there are at most $|\mathrm{Pat}^r\Gamma_0|$ pattern-expanding applications of $\mathcal{R}_\Diamond$ in the entire derivation, i.e., at most $|\mathrm{Pat}^r\Gamma_0|$ indices $i \in I^r_B$ such that the application of $\mathcal{R}_\Diamond$ to Γ_i is pattern-expanding. Let us denote the set of such indices by J^r_B.

2. By Propositions 7.4 and 7.5 (2), every pattern-expanding application of $\mathcal{R}_\Diamond$ to a nominal x is followed by at most $N^{\Gamma_0}_{\langle r\rangle} - 1$ applications of $\mathcal{R}_\Diamond$ to nominals that are equivalent to x at the time of the respective application (clearly, none of these following applications is pattern-expanding).

By definition, every index in I^r_A corresponds to an application of $\mathcal{R}_\Diamond$. Let $i \in I^r_A$ and let x be the nominal to which $\mathcal{R}_\Diamond$ is applied on Γ_i. By Proposition 7.3, either the application is pattern-expanding or x already has a successor on Γ_i. In the latter case, the application must be preceded by a pattern-expanding application of $\mathcal{R}_\Diamond$ to some nominal y that is equivalent to x ($x \sim_{\Gamma_i} y$). As for the index j corresponding to this preceding application, by Proposition 7.5 (1), we must have $j \in J^r_B$ for some $B \subseteq A$. By the above two observations, we obtain:

$$
\begin{aligned}
|I^r_A| &\le |J^r_A| + \sum_{B \subseteq A} |J^r_B| \cdot (N^{\Gamma_0}_{\langle r\rangle} - 1) \\
&\le |\mathrm{Pat}^r\Gamma_0| + 2^{|A|} \cdot |\mathrm{Pat}^r\Gamma_0| \cdot (N^{\Gamma_0}_{\langle r\rangle} - 1) \le 2^{|A|} \cdot |\mathrm{Pat}^r\Gamma_0| \cdot N^{\Gamma_0}_{\langle r\rangle}
\end{aligned}
$$
□

A set of labels A is called a *pattern space* for a role r on a branch Γ if there is some $x \in \mathcal{N}\Gamma$ such that $\mathcal{A}(P^r_\Gamma x) = A$. By Lemma 7.1, it suffices to show that for each role r, the number of pattern spaces created in a derivation is bounded.

Lemma 7.2. *Let Γ_0 be an initial branch, r a role and A a set of labels. There is a function $f : \mathbb{N} \to \mathbb{N}$ such that, for every derivation $\Gamma_0 \to \Gamma_1 \to \dots$:*

$$|\{x \mid \exists i, y :\ i \ge 0 \text{ and } \mathcal{A}(P^r_{\Gamma_i} x) = A \text{ and } rxy \in \Gamma_i\}| \le f(|A|)$$

Proof. Let r and $\Gamma_0 \to \Gamma_1 \to \dots$ be as required. Let $X_A := \{x \mid \exists i, y :\ i \ge 0$ and $\mathcal{A}(P^r_{\Gamma_i} x) = A$ and $rxy \in \Gamma_i\}$. We proceed by induction on $n := |A|$. For every $x \in X_A$, let i_x be the least i such that

1. $\mathcal{A}(P^r_{\Gamma_i} x) = A$, and
2. for some y, $rxy \in \Gamma_i$.

Since Γ_0 is an initial branch, it contains no edges, and so $i_x \ge 1$. No single rule application can make 1 and 2 true at the same time. Hence, for every $x \in X_A$ exactly one of the following is true:

Case $\mathcal{A}(P^r_{\Gamma_{i_x - 1}} x) \subsetneq A$. Then there is some y such that $rxy \in \Gamma_{i_x - 1}$. So, $x \in X_B$ for some proper subset B of A. Clearly, this case is only possible if $|A| > 0$.

Case $\nexists y :\ rxy \in \Gamma_{i_x - 1}$. Then $\mathcal{A}(P^r_{\Gamma_{i_x - 1}} x) = A$. So, $i_x - 1$ belongs to the set I^r_A from Lemma 7.1. This is the only case possible if $|A| = 0$.

By the above, f can be defined as follows:

$$f0 := |\mathrm{Pat}^r \Gamma_0| \cdot N_{\langle r \rangle}^{\Gamma_0}$$

$$fn := 2^n \cdot |\mathrm{Pat}^r \Gamma_0| \cdot N_{\langle r \rangle}^{\Gamma_0} + \sum_{k=0}^{n-1} \binom{n}{k} \cdot fk \qquad \text{if } n > 0$$

□

We define the *level* of an r-pattern P on Γ as:

$$L_\Gamma P := |\{[r]_m t \in \mathcal{S}\Gamma \mid \exists \alpha, y : \ \alpha \in P \text{ and } \alpha{:}[r]_m ty \in \Gamma\}|$$

A label α is said to be *generated at level* n in a derivation $\Gamma_0 \to \Gamma_1 \to \dots$ if there is some $i \geq 0$ such that α is generated by an application of $\mathcal{R}_T$ extending Γ_i by a formula $\alpha{:}[r]_m tx$, and $L_{\Gamma_i}(P_{\Gamma_i}^r x) = n$.

Lemma 7.3. *Let $\Gamma_0 \to \Gamma_1 \to \dots$ be a derivation where Γ_0 is initial and $Tr \in \Gamma_0$. Let $x \in \mathcal{N}\Gamma_i$. Then every label $\alpha \in P_{\Gamma_i}^r x$ is generated at level strictly less than $L_{\Gamma_i}(P_{\Gamma_i}^r x)$.*

Proof. Assume, by contradiction, Γ_i, r, and x are all as required and there is some $\alpha \in P_{\Gamma_i}^r x$ such that α is generated at level $m \geq L_{\Gamma_i}(P_{\Gamma_i}^r x)$. Then there is some $j < i$ such that α is generated by an application of $\mathcal{R}_T$ to some $ryz \in \Gamma_j$ such that $y \rhd_{\Gamma_i}^r x$ and $L_{\Gamma_j}(P_{\Gamma_j}^r y) = m$. Then $\mathcal{A}(P_{\Gamma_j}^r y) \cup \{\alpha\} \subseteq \mathcal{A}(P_{\Gamma_k}^r x')$ and hence (by the applicability restriction on $\mathcal{R}_T$) $L_{\Gamma_k}(P_{\Gamma_k}^r x') > m$ holds for all $k \geq j+1$ and all x' such that $y \rhd_{\Gamma_k}^r x'$. Consequently, $L_{\Gamma_i}(P_{\Gamma_i}^r x) > m \geq L_{\Gamma_i}(P_{\Gamma_i}^r x)$. Contradiction □

By Lemma 7.3, the number of pattern spaces with level n (i.e., pattern spaces whose patterns have level n) is bounded from above by 2^m, where m is the number of labels generated at levels less than n. Clearly, the level of r-patterns in a derivation from Γ_0 is bounded by the number $N_{[r]}^{\Gamma_0}$ of distinct r-boxes occurring on Γ_0 ($N_{[r]}^{\Gamma_0} := |\{[r]_k t \mid [r]_k t \in \mathcal{S}\Gamma_0\}|$). Also, by the applicability restriction on $\mathcal{R}_T$ (non-subsumption), no labels can be generated at level $N_{[r]}^{\Gamma_0}$. Hence, in order to show that the number of pattern spaces created during a derivation is bounded, it suffices to bound the number of labels generated at all levels less than $N_{[r]}^{\Gamma_0}$. A label α is called *r-label* (in a derivation $\Gamma_0 \to \Gamma_1 \to \dots$) if there are i, n, t, x such that $\alpha{:}[r]_n tx \in \Gamma_i$.

Lemma 7.4. *Let Γ_0 be an initial branch and $Tr \in \Gamma_0$. There is a function $f : \mathbb{N} \to \mathbb{N}$ such that, for every derivation $\Gamma_0 \to \Gamma_1 \to \dots$ and $0 \leq n < N_{[r]}^{\Gamma_0}$: $|\{\alpha \mid \exists m < n : \ \alpha$ is an r-label generated at level $m\}| \leq fn$.*

Proof. We define f by induction on n. Let $A_m := \{\alpha \mid \exists k < m : \ \alpha$ is an r-label generated at level $k\}$. Clearly, $A_0 = \emptyset$. A new label can only be generated by an application of $\mathcal{R}_T$. Therefore, by the applicability condition of $\mathcal{R}_T$:

$$|A_n| \leq N_{[r]}^{\Gamma_0} \cdot |\{x \mid \exists i, y : \ i \geq 0 \text{ and } L_{\Gamma_i}(P_{\Gamma_i}^r x) \leq n-1 \text{ and } rxy \in \Gamma_i\}|$$

By Lemma 7.3, for all $n > 0$:

$$|A_n| \leq N_{[r]}^{\Gamma_0} \cdot |\bigcup_{B \subseteq A_{n-1}} \{x \mid \exists i, y : \ i \geq 0 \text{ and } \mathcal{A}(P_{\Gamma_i}^r x) = B \text{ and } rxy \in \Gamma_i\}|$$

Then, by Lemma 7.2, there is a function g such that, for all $n > 0$:

$$|A_n| \leq N_{[r]}^{\Gamma_0} \cdot \sum_{k=0}^{|A_{n-1}|} \binom{|A_{n-1}|}{k} \cdot gk \leq N_{[r]}^{\Gamma_0} \cdot 2^{|A_{n-1}|} \cdot g(|A_{n-1}|)$$

Hence, we can define $f0 := 0$ and, for $n > 0$, $fn := N_{[r]}^{\Gamma_0} \cdot 2^{f(n-1)} \cdot g(f(n-1))$ □

By Lemma 7.1, for every role r the number of applications of $\mathcal{R}_\Diamond$ is bounded by $\sum_{A \in \Phi} 2^{|A|} \cdot |\text{Pat}^r \Gamma_0| \cdot N_{\langle r \rangle}^{\Gamma_0}$ where $\Phi := \{A \mid \exists i \geq 0 \colon A$ is a pattern space for r on $\Gamma_i\}$. Using Lemma 7.3, this bound can be approximated from above by $|\text{Pat}^r \Gamma_0| \cdot N_{\langle r \rangle}^{\Gamma_0} \cdot N_{[r]}^{\Gamma_0} \cdot (2^{2f(N_{[r]}^{\Gamma_0})})$ where f is the function from Lemma 7.4. Since we have only finitely many roles, together with Proposition 7.2, this gives us a bound on $|\mathcal{N}\Gamma|$ that we need for termination. Since f is clearly non-elementary in its argument, the bound is non-elementary.

8 Conclusion

To account for non-local constraints introduced by number restrictions on transitive roles, the notion of patterns from [14] needs to be extended. The extension is semantically intuitive and allows for a simple proof of model existence. As it comes to termination, the reasoning in [14] needs to be refined considerably.

The termination proof establishes a non-elementary complexity bound for the associated decision procedure. Presently, we do not know if this bound is tight. The NExpTime completeness result for (nominal-free) graded modal logic over transitive frames by Kazakov and Pratt-Hartmann [18] gives us a lower bound for the complexity of $\mathcal{SOQ}^+$ and hence of the decision procedure ([19] provides no complexity bounds). Despite the potentially high worst-case complexity of our procedure, we believe it to be well-suited for efficient implementation. In fact, on problems that do not contain number restrictions on transitive roles, the complexity of the procedure matches the NExpTime bound of [14], which is even lower than the 2-NExpTime bound established for practically successful procedures of [8,13,12,9,10].

Schröder and Pattinson [24] show concept satisfiability decidable in the presence of role hierarchies and number restrictions on transitive roles, provided the semantics is restricted to tree-like roles. They argue that the resulting logic, $\mathcal{PHQ}$, may be better suited for modeling parthood relations than the established logics extending $\mathcal{SH}$. We believe that our current approach for $\mathcal{SOQ}^+$ may be adapted to obtain an efficient tableau calculus for $\mathcal{PHQ}$.

Acknowledgment. We are grateful to our reviewers for their detailed and constructive comments.

References

1. Baader, F.: Augmenting concept languages by transitive closure of roles: An alternative to terminological cycles. In: Mylopoulos, Reiter (eds.) [20], pp. 446–451
2. De Giacomo, G., Massacci, F.: Combining deduction and model checking into tableaux and algorithms for converse-PDL. Inf. Comput. 162(1–2), 117–137 (2000)
3. Fattorosi-Barnaba, M., De Caro, F.: Graded modalities I. Stud. Log. 44(2), 197–221 (1985)
4. Fine, K.: In so many possible worlds. Notre Dame J. Form. Log. 13(4), 516–520 (1972)
5. van der Hoek, W., de Rijke, M.: Counting objects. J. Log. Comput. 5(3), 325–345 (1995)
6. Hollunder, B., Baader, F.: Qualifying number restrictions in concept languages. In: Allen, J., Fikes, R., Sandewall, E. (eds.) KR'91, pp. 335–346. Morgan Kaufmann, San Francisco (1991)
7. Horrocks, I., Kutz, O., Sattler, U.: The even more irresistible $\mathcal{SROIQ}$. In: Doherty, P., Mylopoulos, J., Welty, C.A. (eds.) KR 2006, pp. 57–67. AAAI Press, Menlo Park (2006)
8. Horrocks, I., Sattler, U.: A description logic with transitive and inverse roles and role hierarchies. J. Log. Comput. 9(3), 385–410 (1999)
9. Horrocks, I., Sattler, U.: Ontology reasoning in the $\mathcal{SHOQ}$(D) description logic. In: Nebel, B. (ed.) IJCAI 2001, pp. 199–204. Morgan Kaufmann, San Francisco (2001)
10. Horrocks, I., Sattler, U.: A tableau decision procedure for $\mathcal{SHOIQ}$. J. Autom. Reasoning 39(3), 249–276 (2007)
11. Horrocks, I., Sattler, U., Tobies, S.: A PSPACE-algorithm for deciding $\mathcal{ALCNI}_{R^+}$-satisfiability. Technical Report LTCS-98-08, RWTH Aachen, Germany (1998)
12. Horrocks, I., Sattler, U., Tobies, S.: Practical reasoning for expressive description logics. In: Ganzinger, H., McAllester, D., Voronkov, A. (eds.) LPAR 1999. LNCS, vol. 1705, pp. 161–180. Springer, Heidelberg (1999)
13. Horrocks, I., Sattler, U., Tobies, S.: Practical reasoning for very expressive description logics. L. J. IGPL 8(3), 239–263 (2000)
14. Kaminski, M., Schneider, S., Smolka, G.: Terminating tableaux for graded hybrid logic with global modalities and role hierarchies. In: Giese, M., Waaler, A. (eds.) TABLEAUX 2009. LNCS, vol. 5607, pp. 235–249. Springer, Heidelberg (2009)
15. Kaminski, M., Smolka, G.: Hybrid tableaux for the difference modality. In: Areces, C., Demri, S. (eds.) M4M-5. ENTCS, vol. 231, pp. 241–257. Elsevier, Amsterdam (2009)
16. Kaminski, M., Smolka, G.: Terminating tableau systems for hybrid logic with difference and converse. J. Log. Lang. Inf. 18(4), 437–464 (2009)
17. Kaminski, M., Smolka, G.: Terminating tableaux for $\mathcal{SOQ}$ with number restrictions on transitive roles. In: Grau, B.C., Horrocks, I., Motik, B., Sattler, U. (eds.) DL 2009. CEUR Workshop Proceedings, vol. 477 (2009)
18. Kazakov, Y., Pratt-Hartmann, I.: A note on the complexity of the satisfiability problem for graded modal logics. In: LICS 2009, pp. 407–416. IEEE Computer Society, Los Alamitos (2009)
19. Kazakov, Y., Sattler, U., Zolin, E.: How many legs do I have? Non-simple roles in number restrictions revisited. In: Dershowitz, N., Voronkov, A. (eds.) LPAR 2007. LNCS (LNAI), vol. 4790, pp. 303–317. Springer, Heidelberg (2007)

20. Mylopoulos, J., Reiter, R. (eds.): IJCAI'91. Morgan Kaufmann, San Francisco (1991)
21. Sattler, U.: Description logics for the representation of aggregated objects. In: Horn, W. (ed.) ECAI 2000, pp. 239–243. IOS Press, Amsterdam (2000)
22. Schild, K.: A correspondence theory for terminological logics: Preliminary report. In: Mylopoulos, Reiter (eds.) [20], pp. 466–471
23. Schmidt-Schauß, M., Smolka, G.: Attributive concept descriptions with compliments. Artif. Intell. 48(1), 1–26 (1991)
24. Schöder, L., Pattinson, D.: How many toes do I have? Parthood and number restrictions in description logics. In: Brewka, G., Lang, J. (eds.) KR 2008, pp. 307–317. AAAI Press, Menlo Park (2008)
25. Stirling, C., Walker, D.: Local model checking in the modal mu-calculus. Theor. Comput. Sci. 89(1), 161–177 (1991)

Proof System for Applied Pi Calculus

Jia Liu[1,2,⋆] and Huimin Lin[1]

[1] State Key Laboratory of Computer Science
Institute of Software, Chinese Academy of Sciences
[2] Graduate University, Chinese Academy of Sciences
{jliu,lhm}@ios.ac.cn

Abstract. A symbolic-style proof system is presented to reason about observational equivalence for applied pi-calculus. The proofs of the soundness and completeness of the system rely on a recently developed theory of symbolic bisimulation for applied pi-calculus. The completeness result of the proof system is restricted to the finite fragment of applied pi-calculus which admits finite partition, and it is demonstrated that this fragment covers an important subset of applied pi-calculus which is practically useful for analyzing security protocols.

1 Introduction

The applied pi-calculus is a descendant of the pi-calculus designed for cryptographic applications. It extends pi-calculus with value-passing, primitive function symbols and equational theory. To capture the knowledge exposed by processes to the environment, *active substitutions* are employed. For example, let $A = \nu k.(a(x).\ \mathit{if}\ \ dec(x,k) = m\ \mathit{then}\ \overline{a}\ \mathit{else}\ \overline{c} \mid \{enc(m,k)/y\})$. Process A contains an active substitution $\{enc(m,k)/y\}$, where $enc(m,k)$ denotes a ciphertext obtained by encrypting the plaintext m by the secret key k and y can be regarded as an alias of the ciphertext. The secret key k in process A is restricted since we do not wish k to be visible to the environment, while the ciphertext can be accessed through the alias y. To model the shared-key cryptography, we use the equation $dec(enc(w_1, w_2), w_2) = w_1$ to decrypt the ciphertext. Thus the equality test $dec(x,k) = m$ can be satisfied when x takes the value represented by y, leading to the following transitions in concrete semantics:

$$\begin{aligned} A &\xrightarrow{a(y)} \nu k.(\ \mathit{if}\ \ dec(y,k) = m\ \mathit{then}\ \overline{a}\ \mathit{else}\ \overline{c} \mid \{enc(m,k)/y\}) \\ &\equiv\ \ \nu k.(\ \mathit{if}\ \ dec(enc(m,k),k) = m\ \mathit{then}\ \overline{a}\ \mathit{else}\ \overline{c} \mid \{enc(m,k)/y\}) \\ &\xrightarrow{\tau}\ \ \nu k.(\overline{a} \mid \{enc(m,k)/y\}) \end{aligned}$$

Security protocols are modeled as processes in the applied pi calculus and security properties such as anonymity, privacy and strong secrecy can be expressed as indistinguishability properties from the view of attackers, formalized by the

⋆ This work is supported by the National Natural Science Foundation of China (Grants No.60721061 and No.60833001).

C.S. Calude and V. Sassone (Eds.): TCS 2010, IFIP AICT 323, pp. 229–243, 2010.

notion of *observational equivalence*. Two processes are observationally equivalent if they cannot be distinguished in any context. A context models an active attacker which can intercept and forge messages. The universal quantification over contexts makes observational equivalence difficult to check, hence an alternative notion of *labeled bisimilarity* is introduced in [1] which relies on direct comparison of labeled transitions rather than contexts. However, in labeled transitional semantics, an input prefix may give rise to infinitely many branches, as in $a(x).P \xrightarrow{a(M)} P\{M/x\}$, for *every* term M, which hinders computer-assisted verification. To hurdle this problem, *symbolic bisimulations* have recently been advocated for the applied pi-calculus [9] and [15], and the later is shown exactly captures observational equivalence. The aim of this paper is to formulate a proof system to reason about observational equivalence, based on the symbolic bisimulation theory of [15].

The statements of our proof system are of the form $(\mathcal{D}, \Phi) \rhd A = B$ where $(\mathcal{D}, \Phi)$ is a *constraint* consisting of a trail $\mathcal{D}$ and a formula Φ. The proof system consists of *axioms* and *inference rules*. Different from the previous works [10,16,3,12,14], the basic entities of the proof system are *agents* of the form $\nu\widetilde{n}.(P \mid \sigma)$, where σ is a collection of active substitutions, rather than process P. The reasoning crosses through the frame and directly applies to the process part, as in the rule

$$\textbf{Tau} \quad \frac{(\mathcal{D}, \Phi) \rhd \nu\widetilde{n}.(P \mid \sigma) = \nu\widetilde{m}.(Q \mid \theta)}{(\mathcal{D}, \Phi) \rhd \nu\widetilde{n}.(\tau.P \mid \sigma) = \nu\widetilde{m}.(\tau.Q \mid \theta)}.$$

This is because the equality tests in P should be evaluated with the knowledge represented by the "frame" $\nu\widetilde{n}.\sigma$. For example, we can derive $(\emptyset, \mathit{true}) \rhd \nu s.(a(x).[x = s]\overline{b}\langle c\rangle \mid \{s/y\}) = \nu k.(a(x).[\mathit{dec}(x,k) = m]\overline{b}\langle c\rangle \mid \{\mathit{enc}(m,k)/y\})$; However, we cannot derive $(\emptyset, \mathit{true}) \rhd a(x).[x = s]\overline{b}\langle c\rangle = a(x).[\mathit{dec}(x,k) = m]\overline{b}\langle c\rangle$, because the equality tests $[x = s]$ and $[\mathit{dec}(x,k) = m]$ cannot be satisfied at the same time without the knowledge exposed by the frames $\nu s.\{s/y\}$ and $\nu k.\{\mathit{enc}(m,k)/y\}$.

The proof system is for agent equivalence and has to inevitably rely on some form of reasoning about the underlying equational theories on terms (which are parameters to applied pi-calculus). We have decided to factor out reasoning on terms from the proof system, using "semantical judgments" of the form $\Phi \models_{\mathcal{D}} \Psi$, as can be seen in the following rule:

$$\textbf{Partition} \quad \frac{(\mathcal{D}, \Phi_i) \rhd A = B,\ i = 1,2,\ \ \Phi \models_{\mathcal{D}} \Phi_1 \vee \Phi_2}{(\mathcal{D}, \Phi) \rhd A = B}.$$

The rule states that, if we can infer $(\mathcal{D}, \Phi_1) \rhd A = B$ and $(\mathcal{D}, \Phi_2) \rhd A = B$ in the proof system, and we know, by some means, that Φ semantically implies $\Phi_1 \vee \Phi_2$ under $\mathcal{D}$, then we can derive $(\mathcal{D}, \Phi) \rhd A = B$. One may think of such semantical judgments as questions about the term domain, to be answered by an "oracle". In practice they can be resolved by invoking some decision procedures, like the one in [2] for instance, or appealing to a separate proof system specially designed for the underlying equational theories.

Our proof system is sound in general while complete on a class of finite processes on which finite partition on constraint systems always suffices. We will show that this class of processes covers an important fragment of the applied pi-calculus termed *simple processes*, which has been used for describing and analyzing security protocols.

Due to space limitation proofs are sketched. For a complete and rigorous treatment please refer to the full version of this paper, available at `http://lcs.ios.ac.cn/~jliu`.

2 Applied Pi Calculus

Applied pi-calculus [1] is an extension of pi-calculus with value-passing, primitive functions and equational theory. We assume two disjoint, infinite sets $\mathcal{N}$ and $\mathcal{V}$ of names and variables, respectively. An implicit sort system, including a *base sort* and a *channel sort*, splits $\mathcal{N}$ (resp. $\mathcal{V}$) into base sort $\mathcal{N}_b$ (resp. $\mathcal{V}_b$) and channel sort $\mathcal{N}_{ch}$ (resp. $\mathcal{V}_{ch}$). Unless otherwise stated, we will use a, b, c to range over channel names, s, k over base names, and m, n over names of either sort; we will also use x, y, z to range over variables, and u, v, w over either names or variables. Function symbols, such as f, enc, dec etc., are required to take arguments and produce results of base sort only. Terms, ranged over by M, N, are builded up from names and variables by function applications. We shall write $var(M)$ and $name(M)$ for variables and names respectively in M. *Extended processes* are created by extending *plain processes* with *active substitutions* of the form $\{M/x\}$ which is required to be defined on base sort only.

$$
\begin{array}{llcll}
P_r, Q_r, R_r ::= & \text{plain processes} & \qquad & A_r, B_r, C_r ::= & \text{extended processes} \\
 & 0 & & & P_r \\
 & P_r \mid Q_r & & & A_r \mid B_r \\
 & !P_r & & & \nu n.A_r \\
 & \nu n.P_r & & & \nu x.A_r \\
 & \text{if } M = N \text{ then } P_r \text{ then } Q_r & & & \{M/x\} \\
 & u(x).P_r & & & \\
 & \overline{u}\langle N\rangle.P_r & & &
\end{array}
$$

In an extended process, there is at most one substitution for each variable and exactly one when the variable is restricted. Substitutions are sort-respecting partial mappings of finite domains. Substitutions of terms for variables, ranged over by σ, θ, are always required to be cycle-free. The domain and range of σ are denoted $dom(\sigma)$ and $ran(\sigma)$, respectively. $Z\sigma$ is the result of applying σ to Z. The null process 0 is identified with the empty substitution. A substitution $\theta = \{M_1/x_1, \cdots, M_n/x_n\}$ will be identified with the parallel composition $\{M_1/x_1\} \mid \cdots \mid \{M_n/x_n\}$, and $\theta\sigma$ is defined as $\{M_1\sigma/x_1, \cdots, M_n\sigma/x_n\}$. A substitution σ is *idempotent* if $dom(\sigma) \cap var(ran(\sigma)) = \emptyset$. We shall write σ^* for the result of iterating σ until reaching idempotence, and use ϱ to denote one-to-one renaming of names and variables. To avoid confusion, we write $\varrho(Z)$ for the application of ϱ to Z, and $\varrho(\theta)$ means $\{\varrho(M_1)/\varrho(x_1), \cdots, \varrho(M_n)/\varrho(x_n)\}$.

We shall write $fn(A_r)$, $bn(A_r)$, $fv(A_r)$ and $bv(A_r)$ for the sets of free and bound names, free and bound variables, respectively, of A_r. A_r is *closed* if every variable in A_r is either bound or defined by an active substitution.

Terms are equipped with an equational theory $=_E$ that is an equivalence relation closed under substitutions of terms for variables, one-to-one renamings, and term contexts.

Observational equivalence $\approx$ [1] is a contextual equivalence relation on closed extended processes such that $A_r \approx B_r$ implies $C[A_r] \approx C[B_r]$ for any context C. Contexts model active attackers who can intercept and forge messages. Thus observational equivalence captures security properties in the presence of attackers, such as anonymity and privacy. Since the universal quantification over contexts makes $\approx$ difficult to verify, an alternative characterisation, namely *labeled bisimilarity*, is introduced in [1] which relies on direct comparison of labeled transitions rather than contexts. To overcome the problem of infinite branching caused by input transitions in labeled bisimulation, *symbolic bisimulations* are proposed in [9] and [15], and the notion of symbolic bisimulation presented in the later has been shown to be sound and complete w.r.t. $\approx$. We shall briefly review the symbolic semantics of [15] in next section.

3 Symbolic Semantics

Language. For technical reasons, symbolic semantics [15] is built up on top of "intermediate processes", originally proposed in [9], which is a sufficient subset of extended processes. For the purpose of axiomatisation we extend the language of [15] with summation.

$$
\begin{array}{rcll}
S, T & ::= & true \mid M = N \mid \neg S \mid S \wedge T & \\
\pi & ::= & \tau \mid u(x) \mid \overline{u}\langle M\rangle & \text{prefix} \\
P, Q, R & ::= & 0 \mid S\pi.P \mid P + Q \mid P \mid Q \mid !P_r & \text{plain agents} \\
F, G, H & ::= & P \mid \{M/x\} \mid F \mid G & \text{framed agents} \\
A, B, C & ::= & F \mid \nu n.A \mid A + B & \text{agents}
\end{array}
$$

Here $S\pi.P$ is one-armed conditional, and the two-armed conditional operator "*if* $M = N$ *then* P *else* Q" of [1] and [15] can be defined as "$(M = N)\tau.P + \neg(M = N)\tau.Q$". We abbreviate $true\,\pi.P$ to $\pi.P$ and $\neg(M = N)$ to $M \neq N$. The domain of a framed agent F, denoted by $dom(F)$, is the set of variables x for which F contains a substitution $\{M/x\}$. Each framed agent F is required to be *applied*, that is, every variable in $dom(F)$ occurs only once in F. For example, $\overline{a}\langle k\rangle \mid \{k/x\}$ is applied but $\overline{a}\langle x\rangle \mid \{k/x\}$ is not.

The choice operator $+$ does not appear in the original applied pi-calculus. We introduce it here in order to axiomatize parallel composition, as in the case of CCS and pi-calculus. Thus the operator merely serves as a vehicle to achieve a complete axiomatization, not intended to be used by the users. Since $+$ is only used when a parallel composition is expanded, it is reasonable to required $dom(A) = dom(B)$ in a summation $A+B$, and $dom(A+B)$ is defined as $dom(A)$. For an agent A, we define the *frame* $\varphi(A)$ *of* A as follows:

$$\varphi(0) = \varphi(S\pi.P) = 0 \quad \varphi(\{M/x\}) = \{M/x\} \quad \varphi(A \mid B) = \varphi(A) \cup \varphi(B)$$
$$\varphi(A + B) = \begin{cases} 0 & \text{if } \varphi(A) = 0 \text{ or } \varphi(B) = 0 \\ \varphi(A) + \varphi(B) & \text{otherwise} \end{cases}$$
$$\varphi(\nu n.A) = \sum_{i \in I} \nu n.\nu \widetilde{m}_i.\sigma_i \text{ where } \varphi(A) = \sum_{i \in I} \nu \widetilde{m}_i.\sigma_i$$

Constraints. A *constraint* $(\mathcal{D}, \Phi)$ is a pair where $\mathcal{D}$ is a *trail* and Φ a *formula.* A trail abstractly represents the ability of the attackers to deduce messages from a given set of messages. We shall use $\mathcal{D}, \mathcal{E}, \mathcal{F}$ to range over trails.

Formally, a *trail* is a set of the form $\{x_1 : U_1, \cdots, x_\ell : U_\ell\}$ where x_i are variables and U_i are finite sets of channel names and base variables, satisfying:

1. $x_1, \cdots, x_\ell$ are pairwise-distinct and do not appear in any U_j, $1 \leq j \leq \ell$;
2. for each $1 \leq i < \ell$, $name(U_i) \supseteq name(U_{i+1})$ and $var(U_i) \subseteq var(U_{i+1})$.

For a trail $\mathcal{D} = \{x_i : U_i\}_{i \in I}$, let $dom(\mathcal{D}) = \{x_i\}_{i \in I}$ and $fnv(\mathcal{D}) = dom(\mathcal{D}) \cup \bigcup_{i \in I} U_i$. Let A be an agent with $\varphi(A) = \sum_{j \in J} \nu \widetilde{n}_j.\sigma_j$. $\mathcal{D}$ is *compatible with* A if the following conditions are satisfied:

1. $dom(\mathcal{D}) \cap dom(A) = \emptyset$,
2. $var(\bigcup_{i \in I} U_i) \subseteq dom(A)$, $fv(A) \subseteq dom(A) \cup dom(\mathcal{D})$, and
3. for any $x_i : U_i$ and $y \in U_i$ with $i \in I$, $x_i \notin var(y\sigma_j)$ for every $j \in J$.

Intuitively, the variables x_i in $\mathcal{D}$ are input variables. The corresponding U_i records all the variables that *can* be used by x_i and the names that *cannot* be used by x_i, at the moment when the input action of x_i fires.

A substitution θ *respects* $\mathcal{D}$ if

1. $dom(\theta) = dom(\mathcal{D})$,
2. for any $i \in I$, $var(x_i\theta) \subseteq U_i$ and $name(x_i\,\theta) \cap U_i = \emptyset$.

Example 1. Let $A = \overline{c}\langle x \rangle \mid \{h(y)/w_1, g(y,z)/w_2\}$ and $\mathcal{D} = \{x : \{c\}, y : \emptyset, z : \{w_1\}\}$. Then $\mathcal{D}$ is a trail which is compatible with A. The substitution $\{a/x, h(k)/y, f(k, w_1)/z\}$ respects $\mathcal{D}$, while $\{c/x, h(k)/y, f(w_2)/z\}$ does not (because c cannot be used by x, and w_2 cannot be used by z).

Formulas are specified by the following grammar:

$$\Phi, \ \Psi \quad ::= S \quad | \quad \sigma \blacktriangleright \Phi \quad | \quad \Phi \wedge \Psi \quad | \quad \neg\Phi \quad | \quad \mathrm{H}n.\Phi$$

S is a formula as defined in the previous page. In $\sigma \blacktriangleright \Phi$, σ is an idempotent substitution that represents the environmental knowledge accumulated so far to define some variables occurring in Φ. $\mathrm{H}n.\Phi$ hides n in Φ and n is binding. We shall identify α-convertible formulas. We write *false* for $\neg$*true*, $\Phi \vee \Psi$ for $\neg(\neg\Phi \wedge \neg\Psi)$, $\Phi \Rightarrow \Psi$ for $\neg\Phi \vee \Psi$, and $\Phi \Leftrightarrow \Psi$ for $(\Phi \Rightarrow \Psi) \wedge (\Psi \Rightarrow \Phi)$.

The satisfiability relation $\models$ is defined between idempotent substitutions and formulas as follows, where the standard clauses for negation and conjunction are omitted:

$$\begin{array}{lll} \theta \models M = N & \textit{if} & M\theta =_{E} N\theta \\ \theta \models \sigma \blacktriangleright \Phi & \textit{if} & \theta\sigma \text{ is cycle-free and } (\theta\sigma)^* \models \Phi \\ \theta \models \mathrm{H}n.\Phi & \textit{if} & \exists m \notin fn(\mathrm{H}n.\,\Phi) \cup name(\theta) \text{ such that } \theta \models \{m/n\}\Phi \end{array}$$

We write $\Phi \models_{\mathcal{D}} \Psi$ to mean: $\theta \models \Phi$ implies $\theta \models \Psi$ for any θ respecting $\mathcal{D}$.

Definition 1 (Partition). *A collection of formulas Σ is a* partition of Φ under *$\mathcal{D}$ if for any θ respecting $\mathcal{D}$ it holds that $\theta \models \Phi$ implies $\theta \models \Psi$ for some $\Psi \in \Sigma$.*

Example 2. Let $\mathcal{D} = \{x : \{y\}\}$, $\Phi = \mathrm{H}s.(\{enc(m,s)/y\} \blacktriangleright dec(x,s) = m)$ and $\Psi = \mathrm{H}k.(\{k/y\} \blacktriangleright x = k)$, with the equation $dec(enc(w_1, w_2), w_2) =_E w_1$. Then we have $\{y/x\} \models \Phi$ because $\{enc(m,s)/x\} \models dec(x,s) = m$. Similarly $\{y/x\} \models \Psi$. Moreover we can deduce that $(x = y) \models_{\mathcal{D}} \Phi \wedge \Psi$.

Symbolic Semantics. Symbolic semantics will be defined modulo *symbolic structural equivalence* $\equiv_s$, which is defined by the AC properties of $|$ with neutral 0 and the AC properties of $+$, such as $(\overline{a}\langle b\rangle \mid 0) + \overline{c}\langle k\rangle \equiv_s \overline{c}\langle k\rangle + \overline{a}\langle b\rangle$.

Symbolic actions are of the form $\tau, u(x), \overline{u}\langle v\rangle$ or $\nu w.\overline{u}\langle w\rangle$, where $u, v \in \mathcal{N}_{ch} \cup \mathcal{V}_{ch}$ and $w \in \mathcal{N}_{ch} \cup \mathcal{V}_b$. For two symbolic actions α and β with the same bound objects, we use $[\alpha = \beta]$ to denote the formula obtained by comparison of their subjects and free objects; for instance $[\overline{u}\langle w\rangle = \overline{v}\langle w'\rangle]$ denotes $(u = v) \wedge (w = w')$ and $[u(x) = v(x)]$ denotes $u = v$.

Symbolic transition relations, $\{ \xrightarrow{\Phi,\alpha} \mid \Phi$ a formula, α a symbolic action$\}$, are defined on agents by the following typical rules:

$$S\, u(x).P \xrightarrow{S,\ u(x)} P \qquad\qquad S\,\overline{u}\langle v\rangle.P \xrightarrow{S,\overline{u}\langle v\rangle} P$$

$$S\overline{u}\langle M\rangle.P \xrightarrow{S,\nu x.\overline{u}\langle x\rangle} P \mid \{M/x\} \quad x \in \mathcal{V}_b,\ x \notin fv(S\overline{u}\langle M\rangle.P) \qquad\qquad !P_r \xrightarrow{true,\tau} \nu\widetilde{m}.(P \mid !P_r) \quad \Gamma(P_r) = \nu\widetilde{m}.P$$

$$\frac{A \xrightarrow{\Phi,\alpha} A' \quad n \notin name(\alpha)}{\nu n.A \xrightarrow{\mathrm{H}n.\Phi,\alpha} \nu n.A'} \qquad \frac{A \xrightarrow{\Phi,\overline{u}\langle c\rangle} A' \quad u \neq c}{\nu c.A \xrightarrow{\mathrm{H}c.\Phi,\nu c.\overline{u}\langle c\rangle} A'} \qquad \frac{A \xrightarrow{\Phi,\alpha} A'}{A + B \xrightarrow{\Phi,\alpha} A'}$$

$$\frac{A \xrightarrow{\Psi,\alpha} \nu\widetilde{n}.F \quad bv(\alpha) \cap fv(B) = \{\widetilde{n}\} \cap fn(B) = \emptyset}{A \mid B \xrightarrow{\Phi,\alpha} \nu\widetilde{n}.(F \mid B)} \qquad \begin{array}{l}\Phi = (\sigma \cup \varphi(B)) \blacktriangleright S \\ \text{if } \Psi = \sigma \blacktriangleright S,\ dom(B) \cap dom(\sigma) = \emptyset\end{array}$$

Example 3. Let $P = [x = s]\overline{b}\langle c\rangle$. Then $\nu c\, s.(a(x).P \mid \{s/y\}) \xrightarrow{\mathrm{H}c,\ s.(\{s/y\} \blacktriangleright true), a(x)} \nu c\, s.(P \mid \{s/y\})$ and $\nu c\, s.(P \mid \{s/y\}) \xrightarrow{\mathrm{H}c\ s.(\{s/y\} \blacktriangleright x = s), \nu c.\overline{b}\langle c\rangle} \nu s.\{s/y\}$.

After each symbolic transition, we need to update the relevant trail. Let $\mathcal{D} = \{x_i : U_i\}_{i \in I}$ be compatible with A, and $A \xrightarrow{\Phi,\alpha} A'$ with $bnv(\alpha) \cap fnv(\mathcal{D}) = \emptyset$, then the result of $\mathcal{D}$ updated by this transition is defined thus:

$$\mathcal{X}(\alpha, dom(A), \mathcal{D}) \triangleq \begin{cases} \mathcal{D} \cup \{x : dom(A)\} & \alpha \text{ is } u(x) \\ \{x_i : (U_i \cup \{c\})\}_{i \in I} & \alpha \text{ is } \nu c.\overline{u}\langle c\rangle \\ \mathcal{D} & \text{otherwise} \end{cases}$$

It can be shown that $\mathcal{X}(\alpha, dom(A), \mathcal{D})$ is also a trail and compatible with A' [15]. Intuitively, it records the current abstract knowledge (i.e. $dom(A)$) on input and prevents the prior input variables from using the fresh name (i.e. c) yielded by the opening of channel name.

Example 4. For the symbolic transitions in Example 3, we have $\mathcal{X}(a(x), \{y\}, \emptyset) = \{x : \{y\}\}$ and $\mathcal{X}(\nu c.\overline{b}\langle c\rangle, \{y\}, \{x : \{y\}\}) = \{x : \{y, c\}\}$.

$\Gamma(0) = 0 \quad \Gamma(\{M/x\}) = \{M/x\} \quad \Gamma(u(x).P_r) = \nu\widetilde{n}.u(x).P$, where $\Gamma(P_r) = \nu\widetilde{n}.P$
$\Gamma(!P_r) = !P_r \quad \Gamma(\nu n.A_r) = \nu n.\Gamma(A_r) \quad \Gamma(\overline{u}\langle N\rangle.P_r) = \nu\widetilde{n}.\overline{u}\langle N\rangle.P$, where $\Gamma(P_r) = \nu\widetilde{n}.P$
$\Gamma(\nu x.A_r) = \Gamma(A_r)_{\setminus x} \quad \Gamma(\mathit{if}\ M = N\ \mathit{then}\ P_r\ \mathit{else}\ Q_r) = \nu\widetilde{n}.\nu\widetilde{m}.\mathit{if}\ M = N\ \mathit{then}\ P\ \mathit{else}\ Q$
where $\Gamma(P_r) = \nu\widetilde{n}.P, \Gamma(Q_r) = \nu\widetilde{m}.Q$
$\Gamma(A_r \mid B_r) = \nu\widetilde{n}.\nu\widetilde{m}.(F \mid G)(\varphi(F) \cup \varphi(G))^*$, where $\Gamma(A_r) = \nu\widetilde{n}.F, \Gamma(B_r) = \nu\widetilde{m}.G$
where $\Gamma(A_r)_{\setminus x}$ is obtained by replacing $\{M/x\}$ in $\Gamma(A_r)$ to 0

Fig. 1. Transformation Γ

Weak symbolic transitions $\overset{\Phi,\gamma}{\Longrightarrow}$ (γ is α or ϵ) are generated by absorbing τ transitions as usual. We write $\overset{\Phi,\widehat{\alpha}}{\Longrightarrow}$ to mean $\overset{\Phi,\alpha}{\Longrightarrow}$ if α is not τ and $\overset{\Phi,\epsilon}{\Longrightarrow}$ otherwise.

To capture observational equivalence in applied pi-calculus we also need a means to compare the environmental knowledge exposed by agents:

Definition 2 (Symbolic Static Equivalence). *Let A, B be agents with $\varphi(A) = \sum_{i\in I} \nu\widetilde{n}_i.\sigma_i$ and $\varphi(B) = \sum_{j\in J} \nu\widetilde{m}_j.\theta_j$. We write $A \sim^{(\mathcal{D},\Phi)} B$ if*

1. *$\mathcal{D}$ is compatible with A and B*
2. *$dom(A) = dom(B)$*
3. *for some fresh $x, y \in \mathcal{V}_b$, it holds that $\Phi \models_{\mathcal{E}} (\bigvee_{i\in I} \Phi_i) \Leftrightarrow (\bigvee_{j\in J} \Psi_j)$, where $\Phi_i = \mathrm{H}\widetilde{n}_i.(\sigma_i \blacktriangleright x = y), \Psi_j = \mathrm{H}\widetilde{m}_j.(\theta_j \blacktriangleright x = y), i \in I, j \in J$ and $\mathcal{E} = \mathcal{D} \cup \{x : dom(A)\} \cup \{y : dom(B)\}$.*

Definition 3 (Symbolic Bisimilarity). *$\{\approx^{(\mathcal{D},\Phi)} \mid (\mathcal{D}, \Phi)$ a constraint$\}$ is the largest family of symmetric relations on agents such that whenever $A \approx^{(\mathcal{D},\Phi)} B$ then*

1. *$A \sim^{(\mathcal{D},\Phi)} B$*
2. *if $A \xrightarrow{\Phi_1,\alpha} A'$ with $bnv(\alpha) \cap fnv(A, B, \Phi, \mathcal{D}) = \emptyset$, let $\mathcal{F} = \mathcal{X}(\alpha, dom(A), \mathcal{D})$, then there is a partition Σ of $\Phi \wedge \Phi_1$ under $\mathcal{F}$, such that for any $\Psi \in \Sigma$ there are Φ_2, β, B_1 satisfying $B \overset{\Phi_2,\widehat{\beta}}{\Longrightarrow} B_1$, $\Psi \models_{\mathcal{E}} [\alpha = \beta] \wedge \Phi_2$ and $A_1 \approx^{(\mathcal{E},\Psi)} B_1$.*

To relate symbolic bisimulation to observational equivalence, which is defined on extended processes in the previous section, we employ the function Γ, as defined in Fig. 1, to turn extended processes into an agent, by pulling name binders to the top level, applying active substitutions and eliminating variable restrictions. For example, $\Gamma(\nu x.(\overline{a}\langle x\rangle.\nu n.\overline{a}\langle n\rangle \mid \nu k.\{k/x\})) = \nu n.\nu k.(\overline{a}\langle k\rangle.\overline{a}\langle n\rangle \mid 0)$. The soundness and completeness of symbolic bisimulation w.r.t. observational equivalence was shown in [15]:

Theorem 1. *Let A_r, B_r be closed extended processes. Then $A_r \approx B_r$ iff $\Gamma(A_r) \approx^{(\emptyset,\,true)} \Gamma(B_r)$.*

This result was shown in [15] for the applied pi calculus without choice operator $+$. As explained before, the choice operator is used in the current work only for the sake of axiomatization. When starting from a $+$-free agent, the semantic constructions defined so far do not introduce this operator. Hence the theorem also holds here.

4 Proof System

This section is devoted to presenting a proof system for symbolic bisimulation and proving its soundness and completeness. The following discussion is confined to the finite fragment of the calculi, namely the fragment which does not contain replications. Our proof system can be viewed as a general extension of the previous works [10,16,3,12,14]

The statements of the proof system are of the form $(\mathcal{D}, \Phi) \rhd A = B$. The proof system consists of axioms and inference rules. The axioms are shown in Fig. 2. Apart from those familiar axioms from CCS and pi-calculus, we have **Es** to distribute active substitutions over summation.

The inference rules are presented in Fig. 3. Different from the proof systems for value-passing CCS [12] or pi-calculus [3,14], the basic entities are of the form $\nu\widetilde{n}.(P \mid \sigma)$, where P is a plain process, rather than just P. The main reason is that the evaluation of the equality tests occurred in P may depend on the knowledge exposed by frame $\nu\widetilde{n}.\sigma$. This will be further explained later. In **Par**, the side conditions ensure that the trail $\mathcal{E}$ is compatible with the agents in the derived equation $(\mathcal{E}, \Phi) \rhd A \mid C = B \mid C$. Rule **Frame** relates frames which are symbolically static equivalent, namely they expose the same knowledge to the environment. The equation $x = y$ in formula $\Phi_i = \mathrm{H}\widetilde{n}.(\sigma_i \rhd x = y)$ abstractly represents the set of tests $\{\, M = N \mid var(M, N) \subseteq dom(\sigma_i)\,\}$. Φ_i holds means these tests can be satisfied under the knowledge exposed by $\nu\widetilde{n}_i.\sigma_i$. When $\bigvee \Phi_i$ is equavelant to $\bigvee \Psi_j$, the frames $\sum_i \nu\widetilde{n}_i.\sigma_i$ and $\sum_j \nu\widetilde{m}_j.\theta_j$ expose the same knowledge. In **Outt**, the active substitutions $\{M/y\}$ and $\{N/x\}$ in the premise are eliminated when output prefixes are introduced. This reflects the fact that active substitutions are generated by output transitions: $S\overline{u}\langle M\rangle.P \xrightarrow{S,\nu x.\overline{u}\langle x\rangle} P \mid \{M/x\}$. The rule **Partition** permits a case analysis on formula Φ.

The proof system is designed to reason about agent equivalence and has to inevitably rely on some form of reasoning on the underlying equational theories on terms, which are taken as parameters to the applied pi-calculus. We have decided to factor out reasoning on terms and substitutions from the proof system, using "semantical judgments" of the form $\Phi \models_{\mathcal{D}} \Psi$, as can be seen in **Frame**, **Input**, **Outt**, **Outch**, and **Partition**. One may think of these as questions about the term domain, to be answered by an "oracle". In practice they can be resolved by invoking some decision procedures, as the one in [2] for instance, or appealing to a separate proof system specially designed for the underlying equational theories. The following lemma is easy to prove (using **Guard**):

Lemma 1. *Assume $\mathcal{D}$ is compatible with $\nu\widetilde{n}.(S\pi.P \mid o)$.*

1. *If $\Phi \models_{\mathcal{D}} \mathrm{H}\widetilde{n}.(\sigma \blacktriangleright S)$ then $\vdash (\mathcal{D}, \Phi) \rhd \nu\widetilde{n}.(S\pi.P \mid \sigma) = \nu\widetilde{n}.(\pi.P \mid \sigma)$.*
2. *If $\Phi \wedge \mathrm{H}\widetilde{n}.(\sigma \blacktriangleright S) \models_{\mathcal{D}} false$ then $\vdash (\mathcal{D}, \Phi) \rhd \nu\widetilde{n}.(S\pi.P \mid \sigma) = \nu\widetilde{n}.\sigma$.*

Example 5. Assuming $dec(enc(w_1, w_2), w_2) =_E w_1$, let us prove:

$$(\emptyset, true) \rhd \nu s.\overline{a}\langle s\rangle.a(x).[x = s]\overline{b}\langle c\rangle$$
$$= \nu k.\overline{a}\langle enc(m, k)\rangle.a(x).[dec(x, k) = m]\overline{b}\langle c\rangle.$$

By OUTT, it suffices to derive

$$(\emptyset, true) \rhd \nu s.(a(x).[x = s]\overline{b}\langle c\rangle \mid \{s/y\}) \\ = \nu k.(a(x).[dec(x,k) = m]\overline{b}\langle c\rangle \mid \{enc(m,k)/y\})$$

Invoking INPUT and PARTITION leads to the following two statements:
$(\mathcal{D}, x = y) \rhd \nu s.([x = s]\overline{b}\langle c\rangle \mid \{s/y\}) = \nu k.([dec(x,k) = m]\overline{b}\langle c\rangle \mid \{enc(m,k)/y\})$
$(\mathcal{D}, x \neq y) \rhd \nu s.([x = s]\overline{b}\langle c\rangle \mid \{s/y\}) = \nu k.([dec(x,k) = m]\overline{b}\langle c\rangle \mid \{enc(m,k)/y\})$
where $\mathcal{D} = \{x : \{y\}\}$.

We continue with the first one and the other is similar. From Example 2, we know that $(x = y) \models_{\mathcal{D}} \text{H}s.(\{s/y\} \blacktriangleright x = s) \wedge \text{H}k.(\{enc(m,k)/y\} \blacktriangleright dec(x,k) = m)$, hence by Lemma 1 this statement can be reduced to

$$(\mathcal{D}, x = y) \rhd \nu s.(\overline{b}\langle c\rangle \mid \{s/y\}) = \nu k.(\overline{b}\langle c\rangle \mid \{enc(m,k)/y\}).$$

Applying OUTCH, we are left to show that

$$(\mathcal{D}, x = y) \rhd \nu s.\{s/y\} = \nu k.\{enc(m,k)/y\}.$$

By FRAME, this leads to the "semantical judgement" $(x = y) \models_{\mathcal{D}} \text{H}s.(\{s/y\} \blacktriangleright z_1 = z_2) \Leftrightarrow \text{H}k.(\{enc(m,k)/y\} \blacktriangleright z_1 = z_2)$, which can be easily verified by the algorithm developed in [2], for instance.

As shown in this example, we can derive $(\emptyset, true) \rhd \nu s.(a(x).[x = s]\overline{b}\langle c\rangle \mid \{s/y\}) = \nu k.(a(x).[dec(x,k) = m]\overline{b}\langle c\rangle \mid \{enc(m,k)/y\})$; However, we cannot derive $(\emptyset, true) \rhd a(x).[x = s]\overline{b}\langle c\rangle = a(x).[dec(x,k) = m]\overline{b}\langle c\rangle$, because the equality tests $[x = s]$ and $[dec(x,k) = m]$ cannot be satisfied at the same time without the knowledge exposed by the frames $\nu s.\{s/y\}$ and $\nu k.\{enc(m,k)/y\}$. This explains why the basic entities of the proof system are agents of the form $\nu\widetilde{n}.(P \mid \sigma)$, which are plain processes equipped with frames, not just plain processes.

Since weak bisimilarity is not preserved by summation, we need to introduce a refined equivalence which takes care of initial τ moves. The equivalence is defined on top of weak bisimilarity as follows:

Definition 4 (Symbolic Congruence). *$\{\cong^{(\mathcal{D},\Phi)} \mid (\mathcal{D},\Phi)$ a constraint$\}$ is the largest family of symmetric relations between agents and whenever $A \cong^{(\mathcal{D},\Phi)} B$,*

1. *$A \sim^{(\mathcal{D},\Phi)} B$*
2. *if $A \xrightarrow{\Phi_1,\alpha} A'$ with $bnv(\alpha) \cap fnv(A, B, \Phi, \mathcal{D}) = \emptyset$, let $\mathcal{E} = \mathcal{X}(\alpha, dom(A), \mathcal{D})$, then there is a partition Σ of $\Phi \wedge \Phi_1$ under $\mathcal{E}$, such that for any $\Psi \in \Sigma$ there are Φ_2, β, B_1 satisfying $B \stackrel{\Phi_2,\beta}{\Longrightarrow} B_1$, $\Psi \models_{\mathcal{E}} [\alpha = \beta] \wedge \Phi_2$ and $A_1 \approx^{(\mathcal{E},\Psi)} B_1$.*

Theorem 2 (Soundness). *If $\vdash (\mathcal{D},\Phi) \rhd A = B$ then $A \cong^{(\mathcal{D},\Phi)} B$.*

Soundness ensures correctness of the proof system. It is easy to see that $\cong^{(\mathcal{D},\Phi)} \subseteq \approx^{(\mathcal{D},\Phi)}$. Combining with Theorem 1, we know that the proof system is sound w.r.t observational equivalence.

Now we turn to completeness. Since the rule **Partition** can only be used finitely many times in a proof, to capture $A \cong^{(\mathcal{D},\Phi)} B$ by purely syntactical inferencing requires the partitions in Def. 3 and Def. 4 must be finite. It has been shown that in the case of value-passing CCS and pi-calculus, such finite partitions always exist for processes whose symbolic transition graphs are finite

P1	$A = A \mid 0$	**S1**	$A + 0 = A$
P2	$A \mid B = B \mid A$	**S2**	$A + A = A$
P3	$(A \mid B) \mid C = A \mid (B \mid C)$	**S3**	$A + B = B + A$
		S4	$(A + B) + C = A + (B + C)$
R1	$\nu n.A = A$ if $n \notin fn(A)$	**T1**	$\pi.\tau.P = \pi.P$
R2	$\nu n.\nu m.A = \nu m.\nu n.A$	**T2**	$P + \tau.P = \tau.P$
R3	$\nu n.(S\pi.P \mid \sigma) = \nu n.\sigma$ if $n \in sub(\pi)$	**T3**	$\pi.(P + \tau.Q) + \pi.Q = \pi.(P + \tau.Q)$
Er	$\nu n.(A + B) = \nu n.A + \nu n.B$	**Es**	$(A + B) \mid \sigma = (A \mid \sigma) + (B \mid \sigma)$

Ep Let $P = \sum_{i \in I} S_i\pi_i.P_i$ and $Q = \sum_{j \in J} T_j\pi'_j.Q_j$ with $bnv(\pi_i) \cap fnv(Q) = bnv(\pi'_j) \cap fnv(P) = \emptyset$.

$$P \mid Q = \sum_{i \in I} S_i\pi_i.(P_i \mid Q) + \sum_{j \in J} T_j\pi'_j.(P \mid Q_j) + \sum_{\pi_i \ opp \ \pi'_j} S_i \wedge T_j \wedge (u_i = v_j)\tau.R_{ij}$$

where π_i *opp* π'_j and R_{ij} are defined as follows

1. $\pi_i = u_i(x)$, $\pi'_j = \overline{v}_j\langle M\rangle$ with M, x the same sort; then $R_{ij} = P_i\{M/x\} \mid Q_j$
2. The converse of the above clause;

where subject of prefix π is $sub(\tau) = \emptyset$ and $sub(u(x)) = sub(\overline{u}\langle M\rangle) = \{u\}$.

Fig. 2. The Axioms

[11,14]. However, the situation is less clear in the applied pi-calculus, since here we have to consider not only dynamic behaviors of processes but also static equivalence of knowledge, i.e. $\sim^{(\mathcal{D},\Phi)}$, which depends on the expressiveness of the constraint systems [11,4,13]. Let us say that a class of agents *admit finite partition* if symbolic equivalences on them can be established when the phrase "there exists a partition Σ" is replaced by "there exists a finite partition Σ" in Def. 3 and Def. 4. The completeness of the proof system holds on agents that admit finite partition. In next section we will demonstrate that a widely used fragment of applied pi-calculus admits finite partition, hence this restriction is acceptable in practical applications. In what follows all agents are assumed to admit finite partition.

The following lemma "lifts" $\approx^{(\mathcal{D},\Phi)}$ to $\cong^{(\mathcal{D},\Phi)}$:

Lemma 2 (Lifting). *$\nu\widetilde{n}.(P \mid \sigma) \approx^{(\mathcal{D},\Phi)} \nu\widetilde{m}.(Q \mid \theta)$ iff there exists a finite partition Σ of Φ under $\mathcal{D}$ such that for any $\Psi \in \Sigma$ we have either $\nu\widetilde{n}.(P \mid \sigma) \cong^{(\mathcal{D},\Psi)} \nu\widetilde{m}.(\tau.Q \mid \theta)$, or $\nu\widetilde{n}.(\tau.P \mid \sigma) \cong^{(\mathcal{D},\Psi)} \nu\widetilde{m}.(Q \mid \theta)$, or $\nu\widetilde{n}.(P \mid \sigma) \cong^{(\mathcal{D},\Psi)} \nu\widetilde{m}.(Q \mid \theta)$.*

Definition 5 (Normal Forms)

- *Agent A is in* head normal form *if $A = \sum_i \nu\widetilde{n}_i.(P_i \mid \sigma_i)$ with each $P_i = S_i\pi_i.Q_i$ or 0 and $sub(\pi_i) \cap \{\widetilde{n}_i\} = \emptyset$.*
- *A head normal form A is a* full normal form *if $A \overset{\Phi_1,\epsilon}{\Longrightarrow} \xrightarrow{\Phi_2,\alpha} A'$ implies $A \xrightarrow{\Phi,\alpha} A'$ with $(\Phi_1 \wedge \Phi_2) \Leftrightarrow \Phi$.*

The *height* of an agent A, $|A|$, is defined inductively thus: $|0| = |\{M/x\}| = 0$, $|S\pi.P| = |P| + 1$, $|A \mid B| = |A| + |B|$, $|A + B| = \max(|A|, |B|)$ and

Axiom $$\frac{}{(\mathcal{D}, true) \rhd A = B}$$ $A = B$ is an axiom and $\mathcal{D}$ is compatible with A, B

Equiv $$\frac{(\mathcal{D}, \Phi) \rhd A = B}{(\mathcal{D}, \Phi) \rhd B = A} \qquad \frac{(\mathcal{D}, \Phi) \rhd A = B,\ B = C}{(\mathcal{D}, \Phi) \rhd A = C}$$

Par $$\frac{(\mathcal{D}, true) \rhd A = B}{(\mathcal{E}, true) \rhd A \mid C = B \mid C}$$
$\mathcal{E} = \{x_i : U_i\}_i$ is compatible with $A \mid C$ and $B \mid C$
$\mathcal{D} = \{x_i : (U_i - dom(C))\}_i$

Frame $$\frac{\Phi \models_{\mathcal{E}} (\bigvee_i \Phi_i) \Leftrightarrow (\bigvee_j \Psi_j)}{(\mathcal{D}, \Phi) \rhd \sum_i \nu\widetilde{n}_i.\sigma_i = \sum_j \nu\widetilde{m}_j.\theta_j}$$
$\mathcal{D}$ is compatible with each σ_i and θ_j
$dom(\sigma_i) = dom(\theta_j)$, $\Phi_i = \mathrm{H}\widetilde{n}_i.(\sigma_i \blacktriangleright (x = y))$, $\Psi_j = \mathrm{H}\widetilde{m}_j.(\theta_j \blacktriangleright (x = y))$
$\mathcal{E} = \mathcal{D} \cup \{\, x : dom(\sigma_i),\ y : dom(\sigma_i) \,\}$ for some fresh $x, y \in \mathcal{V}_b$.

Tau $$\frac{(\mathcal{D}, \Phi) \rhd \nu\widetilde{n}.(P \mid \sigma) = \nu\widetilde{m}.(Q \mid \theta)}{(\mathcal{D}, \Phi) \rhd \nu\widetilde{n}.(\tau.P \mid \sigma) = \nu\widetilde{m}.(\tau.Q \mid \theta)}$$

Input $$\frac{(\mathcal{E}, \Phi) \rhd \sum_i \nu\widetilde{n}_i.(\tau.P_i \mid \sigma_i) = \sum_j \nu\widetilde{m}_j.(\tau.Q_j \mid \theta_j),\ \ \Phi \models_{\mathcal{D}} \bigwedge_{i,j} u_i = v_j}{(\mathcal{D}, \Phi) \rhd \sum_i \nu\widetilde{n}_i.(u_i(x).P_i \mid \sigma_i) = \sum_j \nu\widetilde{m}_j.(v_j(x).Q_j \mid \theta_j)}$$
$\mathcal{E} = \mathcal{D} \uplus \{x : dom(\sigma_i)\}$, $x \notin fv(\mathcal{D}, \Phi, \{\sigma_i, \theta_j\}_{i,j})$
$var(\{u_i, v_j\}_{i,j}) \subseteq dom(\mathcal{D})$, $name(\{u_i, v_j\}_{i,j}) \cap \{\widetilde{n}_i, \widetilde{m}_j\}_{i,j} = \emptyset$

Guard $$\frac{(\mathcal{D}, \Phi \wedge \mathrm{H}\widetilde{n}.(\sigma \blacktriangleright S)) \rhd \nu\widetilde{n}.(\pi.P \mid \sigma) = A,\ \ (\mathcal{D}, \Phi \wedge \mathrm{H}\widetilde{n}.(\sigma \blacktriangleright \neg S)) \rhd \nu\widetilde{n}.\sigma = A}{(\mathcal{D}, \Phi) \rhd \nu\widetilde{n}.(S\pi.P \mid \sigma) = A}$$
$var(S) \subseteq dom(\mathcal{D})$

Outt $$\frac{(\mathcal{D}, \Phi) \rhd \nu\widetilde{n}.(P \mid \sigma \mid \{M/y\}) = \nu\widetilde{m}.(Q \mid \theta \mid \{N/y\}),\ \ \Phi \models_{\mathcal{D}} u = v}{(\mathcal{D}, \Phi) \rhd \nu\widetilde{n}.(\overline{u}\langle M\rangle.P \mid \sigma) = \nu\widetilde{m}.(\overline{v}\langle N\rangle.Q \mid \theta)}$$
$var(u, v) \subseteq dom(\mathcal{D})$, $name(u, v) \cap \{\widetilde{n}, \widetilde{m}\} = \emptyset$ and $y \notin fv(\mathcal{D}, \Phi)$

Outch $$\frac{(\mathcal{D}, \Phi) \rhd \nu\widetilde{n}.(P \mid \sigma) = \nu\widetilde{m}.(Q \mid \theta),\ \ \Phi \models_{\mathcal{D}} [\overline{u}\langle w\rangle = \overline{v}\langle w'\rangle]}{(\mathcal{D}, \Phi) \rhd \nu\widetilde{n}.(\overline{u}\langle w\rangle.P \mid \sigma) = \nu\widetilde{m}.(\overline{v}\langle w'\rangle.Q \mid \theta)}$$
$var(\overline{u}\langle w\rangle, \overline{v}\langle w'\rangle) \subseteq dom(\mathcal{D})$, $name(\overline{u}\langle w\rangle, \overline{v}\langle w'\rangle) \cap \{\widetilde{n}, \widetilde{m}\} = \emptyset$

Sum $$\frac{(\mathcal{D}, \Phi) \rhd A_i = B_i,\ i = 1, 2}{(\mathcal{D}, \Phi) \rhd A_1 + A_2 = B_1 + B_2}$$

Res $$\frac{(\mathcal{D}, \Phi) \rhd A = B}{(\mathcal{E}, \mathrm{H}n.\Phi) \rhd \nu n.A = \nu n.B}$$
$n \notin fn(\Phi)$ if $n \notin name(\mathcal{D})$
$\mathcal{E} = \{x_i : (U_i - \{n\})\}_i$ if $\mathcal{D} = \{x_i : U_i\}_i$

Partition $$\frac{(\mathcal{D}, \Phi_i) \rhd A = B,\ i = 1, 2,\ \ \Phi \models_{\mathcal{D}} \Phi_1 \vee \Phi_2}{(\mathcal{D}, \Phi) \rhd A = B}$$

Absurd $$\frac{}{(\mathcal{D}, false) \rhd A = B}$$ $\mathcal{D}$ is compatible with A, B

Fig. 3. The Inference Rules

$|\nu n.A| = |A|$. Every agent can be rewritten to head normal form and full normal form without increasing its height, as stated in the lemma below.

Lemma 3. *For any agent A, there is a head/full normal form B such that, for any $\mathcal{D}$ compatible with A,*

1. $\vdash (\mathcal{D}, true) \rhd A = B$, $|B| \leq |A|$, $fnv(B) \subseteq fnv(A)$ *and* $dom(B) = dom(A)$
2. *if* $A = \nu\widetilde{n}.F$ *then* B *has the form* $\sum_{i\in I} \nu\widetilde{n}.(S_i\pi_i.P_i \mid \varphi(F))$.

For example, let $A = \nu s.[((\overline{a}\langle s\rangle \mid a(x)) + \tau.\overline{a}\langle c\rangle) \mid \{s/y\}]$. Then we can deduce a full normal form for A by the following sequence:

$$\begin{aligned}(\emptyset, true) \rhd A &= \nu s.((\overline{a}\langle s\rangle.a(x) + a(x).\overline{a}\langle s\rangle + \tau + \tau.\overline{a}\langle c\rangle) \mid \{s/y\}) && \textbf{Ep}\\ &= \nu s.((\overline{a}\langle s\rangle.a(x) + a(x).\overline{a}\langle s\rangle + \tau + \tau.\overline{a}\langle c\rangle + \overline{a}\langle c\rangle) \mid \{s/y\}) && \textbf{T2}\\ &= \nu s.(\overline{a}\langle s\rangle.a(x) \mid \{s/y\}) + \nu s.(a(x).\overline{a}\langle s\rangle \mid \{s/y\})\\ &\quad + \nu s.(\tau \mid \{s/y\}) + \nu s.(\tau.\overline{a}\langle c\rangle \mid \{s/y\}) + \nu s.(\overline{a}\langle c\rangle \mid \{s/y\}) && \textbf{Er}, \textbf{Es}\end{aligned}$$

Theorem 3 (Completeness). *If $A \cong^{(\mathcal{D},\Phi)} B$ then $\vdash (\mathcal{D}, \Phi) \rhd A = B$.*

Proof. The proof proceeds by induction on the joint height $|A| + |B|$. By Lemma 3, we rewrite A and B to full normal form $\sum_{i\in I} \nu\widetilde{n}_i.(\widehat{P}_i \mid \sigma_i)$ and $\sum_{j\in J} \nu\widetilde{m}_j.(\widehat{Q}_i \mid \theta_j)$ respectively, where $\widehat{P}_i = S_i\pi_i.P_i$ or 0 and $\widehat{Q}_j = T_j\pi'_j.Q_j$ or 0. We group the summands of A according to type γ of π_i and write A_γ for the result. It suffices to show that $(\mathcal{D}, \Phi) \rhd A_\gamma + B = B$ and $(\mathcal{D}, \Phi) \rhd B_\gamma + A = A$ for each γ.

We only sketch the proof for the case $\gamma = \tau$. Assume $A_\tau = \sum_i \nu\widetilde{n}_i.(S_i\tau.P_i \mid \sigma_i)$ and $B_\tau = \sum_j \nu\widetilde{m}_j.(T_j\tau.Q_j \mid \theta_j)$. Then $A \xrightarrow{\Phi_i,\tau} A_i \equiv_s \nu\widetilde{n}_i.(P_i \mid \sigma_i)$ where $\Phi_i = \mathrm{H}\widetilde{n}_i.(\sigma_i \blacktriangleright S_i)$. Since $A \cong^{(\mathcal{D},\Phi)} B$, there is a finite partition Σ of $\Phi \wedge \Phi_i$ under $\mathcal{D}$, and for each $\Psi \in \Sigma$, there exist $B \xrightarrow{\Psi_j,\tau} B_j \equiv_s \nu\widetilde{m}_j.(Q_j \mid \theta_j)$, such that $\Psi \models_{\mathcal{D}} \Psi_j$ and $A_i \approx^{(\mathcal{D},\Psi)} B_j$. By Theorem 2, induction hypothesis, **T2** and **Partition**, we can derive $(\mathcal{D}, \Psi) \rhd \nu\widetilde{n}_i.(\tau.P_i \mid \sigma_i) = \nu\widetilde{m}_j.(\tau.Q_j \mid \theta_j)$. By Lemma 1.*1*, we have $(\mathcal{D}, \Psi) \rhd \nu\widetilde{n}_i.(S_i\tau.P_i \mid \sigma_i) = \nu\widetilde{m}_j.(T_j\tau.Q_j \mid \theta_j)$, and hence $(\mathcal{D}, \Psi) \rhd \nu\widetilde{n}_i.(S_i\tau.P_i \mid \sigma_i) + B = \nu\widetilde{m}_j.(T_j\tau.Q_j \mid \theta_j) + B = B$. By **Partition**, we obtain $(\mathcal{D}, \Phi \wedge \Phi_i) \rhd \nu\widetilde{n}_i.(S_i\tau.P_i \mid \sigma_i) + B = B$. By Lemma 1.*2*, we have $(\mathcal{D}, \Phi \wedge \neg\Phi_i) \rhd \nu\widetilde{n}_i.(S_i\tau.P_i \mid \sigma_i) = \nu\widetilde{n}_i.\sigma_i$ since we can deduce that $\neg\Phi_i \wedge \mathrm{H}\widetilde{n}.(\sigma_i \blacktriangleright S_i) \models_{\mathcal{D}}$ *false*. Adding B to both sides we have $(\mathcal{D}, \Phi \wedge \neg\Phi_i) \rhd \nu\widetilde{n}_i.(S_i\tau.P_i \mid \sigma_i) + B = B$. By **Partition** again, $(\mathcal{D}, \Phi) \rhd \nu\widetilde{n}_i.(S_i\tau.P_i \mid \sigma_i) + B = B$. Finally, by **Sum** we obtain $(\mathcal{D}, \Phi) \rhd A_\tau + B = B$. Similarly we can derive $(\mathcal{D}, \Phi) \rhd B_\tau + A = A$.

For any extended processes A_r, it is easy to see that $\Gamma(A_r) \equiv_s \nu\widetilde{n}.(P \mid \sigma)$ for some $\widetilde{n}, P, \sigma$. The following theorem is a direct corollary of Theorem 1, 2 and 3, using Lemma 2 and axiom **T1**.

Theorem 4. *Let A_r, B_r be closed extended processes and $\Gamma(A_r) \equiv_s \nu\widetilde{n}.(P \mid \sigma)$ and $\Gamma(B_r) \equiv_s \nu\widetilde{m}.(Q \mid \theta)$. Then $A_r \approx B_r$ iff $\vdash (\emptyset, true) \rhd \nu\widetilde{n}.(\tau.P \mid \sigma) = \nu\widetilde{m}.(\tau.Q \mid \theta)$.*

Thus our proof system is sound and complete w.r.t. observational equivalence for finite extended processes which admit finite partition.

5 Finiteness of Partition

In practice we do not always need full applied pi-calculus for describing and analyzing security protocols. For example, as argued in [7,8], it is generally assumed that all communications are controlled by the attacker thus private channels between processes are not accurate. We shall show in this section that a useful fragment of the applied pi-calculus, called "simple processes" [7,8], admit finite partition. Simple processes are built up from "basic processes". A basic process represents a session of protocol role which knows exactly what to do next. Simple processes are used to analyze security protocols whose roles have a deterministic behavior, such as the protocols in [6]. For simple processes without ELSE branch nor replications, it is shown in [8] that symbolic trace equivalence coincides with observational equivalence. In comparison, we use symbolic bisimilarity to fully capture observational equivalence, and we will show that finite partitions are sufficient for simple processes, even in the presence of ELSE branch and replications.

The sets of *basic processes* $\mathcal{B}(c, U)$ with $c \in \mathcal{N}_{ch}$ and finite $U \subset \mathcal{V}_b$ are the least sets of processes such that

1. $0 \in \mathcal{B}(c, U)$
2. if $B \in \mathcal{B}(c, U)$, $var(M) \subseteq U$ and $name(M) \subset \mathcal{N}_b$ then $\overline{c}\langle M\rangle.B \in \mathcal{B}(c, U)$
3. if $B_1, B_2 \in \mathcal{B}(c, U)$, $var(M, N) \subseteq U$ and $name(M, N) \subset \mathcal{N}_b$, then $\mathit{if}\ M = N\ \mathit{then}\ B_1\ \mathit{else}\ B_2 \in \mathcal{B}(c, U)$
4. if $B \in \mathcal{B}(c, U \uplus \{x\})$ and $x \in \mathcal{V}_b$, then $c(x).B \in \mathcal{B}(c, U)$.

Let us abbreviate $A_1 \mid A_2 \mid \cdots \mid A_m$ to $\prod_{i\in I} A_i$. Then *simple processes* are those of the form

$$\nu\widetilde{n}.(\prod_{i\in I} \nu\widetilde{n}_i.(B_i \mid \sigma_i) \mid \prod_{j\in J} !(\nu c_j, \widetilde{m}_j).\overline{b}_j\langle c_j\rangle.B'_j)$$

where $B_i \in \mathcal{B}(a_i, \emptyset)$, $B'_j \in \mathcal{B}(c_j, \emptyset)$; a_i, b_j with $i \in I, j \in J$ are pairwise-distinct channel names. As argued in [8], the pairwise-distinct channel names for each basic process correspond to the fact that the attacker is able to schedule the messages and know which process the message comes from (*e.g.* via IP addresses).

To cater simple processes, in symbolic semantics it is adequate to consider *simple agents* of the form

$$A \equiv_s \nu\widetilde{n}.(\prod_{i\in I} B_i \mid \prod_{j\in J} !(\nu c_j, \widetilde{m}_j).\overline{b}_j\langle c_j\rangle.B'_j \mid \sigma)$$

where $B_i \in \mathcal{B}(a_i, U_i)$, $B'_j \in \mathcal{B}(c_j, \emptyset)$; U_i with $i \in I$ are pairwise-distinct and σ is idempotent with $dom(\sigma) \cap \bigcup_{i\in I} U_i = \emptyset$; a_i, b_j with $i \in I, j \in J$ are pairwise-distinct channel names. In what follows we shall use A to range over simple agents.

For simple agents we do not have to use the rule $!P_r \xrightarrow{true,\tau} \nu\widetilde{m}.(P \mid !P_r)$, where $\Gamma(P_r) = \nu\widetilde{m}.P$, to expand replications since replications in simple agents are always guarded by bound output. Instead, we can use the following simpler rule (conflicts on $\widetilde{m}$ can be avoided by α-conversion):

$$!(\nu c, \widetilde{m}).\overline{b}\langle c\rangle.B \xrightarrow{true,\nu c.\overline{b}\langle c\rangle} \nu\widetilde{m}.(B \mid !(\nu c, \widetilde{m}).\overline{b}\langle c\rangle.B).$$

We still use $\approx^{(\mathcal{D},\Phi)}$ to denote the symbolic bisimilarity in the resulting symbolic semantics. Note that the definition of simple agents is closed under $\xrightarrow{\Phi,\alpha}$.

Theorem 5. *For simple agents A and B, $A \approx^{(\mathcal{D},\Phi)} B$ can be established when the phrase "there exists a partition Σ" is replaced by "there exists a finite partition Σ" in Definition 3.*

Proof. To show finite partition always suffices, assume $A \approx^{(\mathcal{D},\Phi)} B$ and $A \xrightarrow{\Phi_1,\alpha} A_1$. Let $\Sigma_\alpha = \{\, \Phi \wedge \Phi_1 \wedge \Psi_1 \mid B \overset{\Psi_1,\widehat{\alpha}}{\Longrightarrow} B_1 \overset{\mathcal{T}}{\not\rightarrow} \}$, where $B_1 \overset{\mathcal{T}}{\not\rightarrow}$ denotes that there is no Ψ', B_1' such that $B_1 \xrightarrow{\Psi',\tau} B_1'$. We can verify that Σ_α is a finite partition of $\Phi \wedge \Phi_1$ under $\mathcal{E}$, and $A_1 \approx^{(\mathcal{E},\Phi\wedge\Phi_1\wedge\Psi_1)} B_1$.

Thus, by Theorem 4, our proof system is sound and complete for observational equivalence on finite fragment of simple processes.

6 Conclusions

We have presented a proof system for observational equivalence in the applied pi-calculus, and shown its soundness and completeness. The completeness result is obtained via a recently developed theory of symbolic bisimulation which exactly captures observational equivalence. This is the first inference system for the applied pi calculus which makes it possible to reason on security properties by syntactic manipulations.

As the applied pi-calculus is parameterized on equational theories for cryptographic operations while our proof system mainly concerns with behavioural properties of processes, "static" reasoning about cryptographic operations has been factored out from the proof system, as "semantic judgements" of the form $\Phi \models_{\mathcal{D}} \Psi$. The verification of $\Phi \models_{\mathcal{D}} \Psi$ is a second order E-unification problem. The reasoning about some special class of the problem is discussed in [2], where sound and complete transformation rules are proposed to handle the constraint systems without negation for convergent equational theories, and a decision procedure for convergent subterm theories. The ongoing work of [5] mainly dedicates to finding a simpler decision algorithm than [2] for a larger class of equational theories in the presence of negation.

Our completeness result is confined to finite processes which admit finite partition. This contrasts to the proof systems for value-passing CCS and pi-calculus, where finite partitions are sufficient for finite processes. The expressiveness of formulas is highly relevant in this regard. The formula language in this paper includes two operators $\sigma \blacktriangleright \Phi$ and $\mathrm{H}n.\Phi$, which are mainly needed for symbolic output transitions: $\nu k.(\mathit{if}\ x = k\ \mathit{then}\ P\ \mathit{else}\ Q \mid \{k/y\}) \xrightarrow{\mathrm{H}k.(\{k/y\}\blacktriangleright x=k),\mathit{true}} P$. When an agent tries to match a symbolic transition from the other, the choices on the branches are closely dependent on symbolic static equivalence. It is still unclear whether the expressiveness of the formulas is sufficient to guarantee finite partitions for symbolic static equivalence, or how to extend the formula language if not.

References

1. Abadi, M., Fournet, C.: Mobile values, new names, and secure communication. In: POPL, pp. 104–115 (2001)
2. Baudet, M.: Deciding security of protocols against off-line guessing attacks. In: CCS '05: Proceedings of the 12th ACM conference on Computer and communications security, pp. 16–25. ACM, New York (2005)
3. Boreale, M., De Nicola, R.: A symbolic semantics for the pi-calculus (extended abstract). In: Jonsson, B., Parrow, J. (eds.) CONCUR 1994. LNCS, vol. 836, pp. 299–314. Springer, Heidelberg (1994)
4. Borgström, J.: A complete symbolic bisimilarity for an extended spi calculus. Electron. Notes Theor. Comput. Sci. 242(3) (2009)
5. Cheval, V., Comon-Lundh, H., Delaune, S.: A decision procedure for proving observational equivalence. In: Boreale, M., Kremer, S. (eds.) Preliminary Proceedings of the 7th International Workshop on Security Issues in Coordination Models, Languages and Systems (SecCo'09), Bologna, Italy (October 2009)
6. Clark, J., Jacob, J.: A survey of authentication protocol literature (1997), `http://www.cs.york.ac.uk/~jac/papers/drareviewps.ps`
7. Comon-Lundh, H., Cortier, V.: Computational soundness of observational equivalence. In: CCS '08: Proceedings of the 15th ACM Conference on Computer and Communications Security, pp. 109–118. ACM, New York (2008)
8. Cortier, V., Delaune, S.: A method for proving observational equivalence. In: Proceedings of the 22nd IEEE Computer Security Foundations Symposium (CSF'09), Port Jefferson, NY, USA, July 2009, pp. 266–276. IEEE Computer Society Press, Los Alamitos (2009)
9. Delaune, S., Kremer, S., Ryan, M.D.: Symbolic bisimulation for the applied pi calculus. In: FSTTCS, pp. 133–145 (2007)
10. Hennessy, M.: A proof system for communicating processes with value-passing (extended abstract). In: Veni Madhavan, C.E. (ed.) FSTTCS 1989. LNCS, vol. 405, pp. 325–339. Springer, Heidelberg (1989)
11. Hennessy, M., Lin, H.: Symbolic bisimulations. Theor. Comput. Sci. 138(2), 353–389 (1995)
12. Hennessy, M., Lin, H.: Proof systems for message-passing process algebras. Formal Asp. Comput. 8(4), 379–407 (1996)
13. Johansson, M., Victor, B., Parrow, J.: A fully abstract symbolic semantics for psi-calculi. Accepted for SOS'09 (2009)
14. Lin, H.: Complete inference systems for weak bisimulation equivalences in the pi-calculus. Inf. Comput. 180(1), 1–29 (2003)
15. Liu, J., Lin, H.: A complete symbolic bisimulation for full applied pi calculus. In: van Leeuwen, J., Muscholl, A., Peleg, D., Pokorný, J., Rumpe, B. (eds.) SOFSEM 2010. LNCS, vol. 5901, pp. 552–563. Springer, Heidelberg (2010)
16. Parrow, J., Sangiorgi, D.: Algebraic theories for name-passing calculi. Information and Computation 120, 174–197 (1994)

Concurrent Pattern Calculus

Thomas Given-Wilson[1], Daniele Gorla[2], and Barry Jay[1]

[1] Centre for Quantum Computation and Intelligent Systems & School of Software, University of Technology, Sydney
[2] Dip. di Informatica, Univ. di Roma "La Sapienza"

Abstract. Concurrent pattern calculus drives interaction between processes by unifying patterns, just as sequential pattern calculus drives computation by matching a pattern against a data structure. By generalising from pattern matching to unification, interaction becomes symmetrical, with information flowing in both directions. This provides a natural language for describing any form of exchange or trade. Many popular process calculi can be encoded in concurrent pattern calculus.

1 Introduction

The π-calculus [13] holds a pivotal position among process calculi as it is the simplest that is able to support computation as represented by λ-calculus [1]. However, *pattern calculus* [11,9] supports even more computations than λ-calculus since pattern-matching functions are commonly intensional with respect to their arguments [10]. For example, the pattern $x\ y$ can decompose any data structure in (static) pattern calculus by matching against the internal structure. Hence it is natural to wonder what a concurrent pattern calculus might look like. In fact it turns out rather well.

This paper adapts the pattern matching mechanism of the pure pattern calculus [11,9] to a concurrent process language that supports the standard constructs of parallel composition, name restriction and replication. This yields a *concurrent pattern calculus* (CPC) where the usual prefixes for input and output can be combined into patterns; their *unification* triggers a two-way, or symmetric, flow of information, as represented by the sole interaction rule

$$(p \to P \mid q \to Q) \quad \longmapsto \quad \sigma P \mid \rho Q$$

where σ and ρ are the substitutions on names resulting from the unification of p and q.

Its support for structure and symmetry of interaction makes its pattern matching more expressive than several representative approaches in the literature. For example, checking equality of channel names, as in π-calculus [13], can be viewed as a trivial form of pattern matching. This can be generalised to match tuples of names, as in polyadic π-calculus [12], fusion calculus [15] and Linda [4]. Spi calculus [6] has an even richer collection of patterns, for equality of terms, pairs of terms, numbers (zero and successors) and encryptions.

C.S. Calude and V. Sassone (Eds.): TCS 2010, IFIP AICT 323, pp. 244–258, 2010.

More formally, π-calculus, Spi calculus and Linda can all be encoded into CPC but CPC cannot be encoded in any of them. Although the patterns of fusion calculus are relatively simple, the peculiarities of name fusion ensure that there are no encodings of fusion calculus into CPC or conversely, of CPC into fusion calculus.

A natural objection to CPC is that the unification is too complex to be an atomic operation. In particular, any limit to the size of communicated messages could be violated by some match. Also, one cannot, in practice, implement a simultaneous exchange of information, so that pattern unification must be implemented in terms of simpler primitives.

This objection is similar to those made against λ-calculus, whose substitution is not atomic either. Even more, the pattern matching of Linda suffers from the same problems (it cannot be implemented as an atomic action), but there are many existing programming environments based on it (e.g. [14,16]). Really it is a question of deciding how granular one wishes to be. CPC may prove to be a convenient specification language since, if symmetry between processes is to be taken seriously, there must always be some give and take, some exchange of information. This is most obvious in the world of trade, where negotiation is paramount, and the mechanics of settlement are secondary.

To this end, our major example supports a simple negotiation. Buyer and seller must *discover* their compatibility in an open environment, establish trust (through a third party) and then communicate privately.

The structure of the paper is as follows. Section 2 introduces symmetric matching through a concurrent pattern calculus. Section 3 develops a share trading example. Section 4 formalises the relation of CPC to other process calculi. Section 5 concludes and considers future work. Most proofs are omitted from this paper but can be found on-line [5].

2 Concurrent Pattern Calculus

This section presents a *concurrent pattern calculus* (CPC) that uses symmetric pattern matching as the basis of communication. Both symmetry and pattern matching appear in existing models of concurrency, but in more limited ways. For example, π-calculus requires a sender and receiver to share a channel, so that the presence of the channel is symmetric but information flow is in one direction only. Fusion calculus achieves symmetry by fusing names together but has no intensional patterns. On the other hand, Spi calculus has intensional patterns, e.g. for natural numbers, and can check equality of terms (i.e. patterns), but does not perform matching in general, or support much symmetry.

The expressiveness of CPC comes from extending the traditional names to a class of *patterns* and unifying them (symmetrically) rather than matching them (asymmetrically). This supports equality testing and bi-directional input and output in a single step. Although the increased expressive power makes it harder to protect private information, this can be managed by allowing some names (and patterns) to be protected, in the sense that they can be matched but not shared.

2.1 Syntax

The CPC has two syntactic classes, the *patterns* (meta-variables $p, p_1, q, q_1, \ldots$) and the *processes* (meta-variables $P, P', P_1, Q, Q', Q_1 \ldots$).

The patterns have the following forms

$$\begin{array}{llll} \textit{Patterns} & p ::= & x & \text{variable name} \\ & & \ulcorner x \urcorner & \text{protected name} \\ & & \lambda x & \text{binding name} \\ & & p \bullet p & \text{compound.} \end{array}$$

Variable names x are available for equality, output and substitution. Protected names $\ulcorner x \urcorner$ are only available for equality and substitution. Binding names λx are available for input only. A compound combines two patterns into a single one.

Given a pattern p the sets of: *variables names*, denoted $\mathsf{vn}(p)$; *protected names*, denoted $\mathsf{pn}(p)$; and *binding names*, denoted $\mathsf{bn}(p)$, are as expected with the union being taken for compounds. The *free names* of a pattern p, written $\mathsf{fn}(p)$, is the union of the variable names and protected names of p. A pattern is *well formed* if each binding name appears exactly once. All patterns appearing in the rest of the paper are assumed to be well formed.

As the protected names serve to test for equality and the binding names represent input, neither should be able to be communicated to another process. Thus, a pattern is *communicable* if it contains no protected or binding names.

Protection can be extended to a communicable pattern p by defining

$$\ulcorner x \urcorner = \ulcorner x \urcorner \qquad\qquad \ulcorner p \bullet q \urcorner = \ulcorner p \urcorner \bullet \ulcorner q \urcorner \, .$$

A *substitution* σ (also denoted $\sigma_1, \rho, \rho_1, \ldots$) is defined as a partial function from names to communicable patterns. These are applied to patterns in the obvious manner on the understanding that

$$\sigma \ulcorner x \urcorner = \ulcorner \sigma x \urcorner \quad \text{if } x \text{ is in the domain of } \sigma.$$

The *symmetric matching* or *unification* $\{p \| q\}$ of two patterns p and q attempts to unify p and q by generating substitutions upon their binding names. When defined, the result is some pair of substitutions whose domains are the binding names of p and of q. The rules to generate the substitutions are:

$$\begin{array}{rll} \left.\begin{array}{r} \{x \| x\} \\ \{x \| \ulcorner x \urcorner\} \\ \{\ulcorner x \urcorner \| x\} \\ \{\ulcorner x \urcorner \| \ulcorner x \urcorner\} \end{array}\right\} & = \mathsf{Some}\ (\{\}, \{\}) & \\ \{\lambda x \| q\} & = \mathsf{Some}\ (\{q/x\}, \{\}) & \text{if } q \text{ is communicable} \\ \{p \| \lambda x\} & = \mathsf{Some}\ (\{\}, \{p/x\}) & \text{if } p \text{ is communicable} \\ \{p_1 \bullet p_2 \| q_1 \bullet q_2\} & = \mathsf{Some}\ ((\sigma_1 \cup \sigma_2), (\rho_1 \cup \rho_2)) & \left\{\begin{array}{l} \{p_1 \| q_1\} = \mathsf{Some}\ (\sigma_1, \rho_1) \\ \{p_2 \| q_2\} = \mathsf{Some}\ (\sigma_2, \rho_2) \end{array}\right. \\ \{p \| q\} & = \text{undefined} & \text{otherwise.} \end{array}$$

A name matches against itself when both instances are either variable or protected. That a protected name $\ulcorner x \urcorner$ unifies with the variable name x means that a process that protects a name may communicate with one that does not. A binding name λx binds any communicable pattern p by generating a substitution $\{p/x\}$. If both patterns are compounds and there is some matching for their respective components, then take the union of the substitutions. Otherwise the patterns cannot be unified and the matching is undefined.

Lemma 1. *If the unification of patterns p and q is defined then any protected name of p is a free name of q.*

The processes of CPC are given by

$$\begin{array}{llll} \textit{Processes} & P ::= & \mathbf{0} & \text{zero} \\ & & P|P & \text{parallel composition} \\ & & !P & \text{replication} \\ & & (\nu x)P & \text{restriction} \\ & & p \to P & \text{case.} \end{array}$$

The zero, parallel composition, replication and restriction are all familiar. The traditional input and output primitives are replaced by the case $p \to P$ that has a pattern p and a *body* P. The pattern of a case may be considered as a form of prefix, as commonly used for input or output.

The free names of processes, denoted $\mathsf{fn}(P)$, are defined as usual for all the traditional primitives and

$$\mathsf{fn}(p \to P) \quad = \quad \mathsf{fn}(p) \cup (\mathsf{fn}(P) \backslash \mathsf{bn}(p))$$

where the binding names of the pattern bind their free occurrences in the body.

The general *structural equivalence relation* $\equiv$ is defined just as in π-calculus [12], with α-conversion defined in the usual manner.

The application of a substitution to a process is defined in the usual manner, to avoid name capture.

2.2 Operational Semantics

CPC has one *interaction rule* given by

$$(p \to P \mid q \to Q) \quad \longmapsto \quad (\sigma P) \mid (\rho Q) \qquad \text{if } \{p \| q\} = \mathsf{Some}\ (\sigma, \rho).$$

It states that if the unification of two patterns p and q is defined and generates $\mathsf{Some}\ (\sigma, \rho)$, then apply the substitutions σ and ρ to the bodies P and Q, respectively. If the matching of p and q is undefined then no interaction occurs. The interaction rule is then closed under parallel composition, restriction and structural equivalence in the usual manner. The reflexive, transitive closure of $\longmapsto$ is denoted $\Longmapsto$. The examples and theorems developed later in the paper rely on control of interaction, as now defined.

Definition 1. *The processes P and Q* do not interact *if, whenever $P|Q \Longmapsto R$, then there are processes P' and Q' such that $P \Longmapsto P'$, $Q \Longmapsto Q'$ and $R \equiv P'|Q'$.*

Lemma 2. *A process of the form $p \rightarrow P$ with a protected name n in the pattern can only interact with a process Q containing n among its the free names.*

3 Trade

This section uses the example of share trading to explore the potential of CPC. The scenario is that two potential traders, a buyer and a seller, wish to engage in trade. To complete a transaction the traders need to progress through two stages: *discovering* each other and *exchanging* information. Both traders begin with a pattern for their desired transaction. The discovery phase can be characterised as a pattern-unification problem, where traders' patterns are used to find a compatible partner. The exchange phase occurs when a buyer and seller have agreed upon a transaction. Now each trader wishes to exchange information in a single interaction, preventing any incomplete trades from occurring.

The rest of this section explores three solutions to completing a transaction. The first demonstrates discovery, the second introduces a registrar to validate traders, the third extends the second with protected names to ensure privacy.

Solution 1. Consider two traders, a buyer and a seller. The buyer Buy_1 with bank account b and desired shares s can be given by

$$\mathsf{Buy}_1 = s \bullet \lambda m \rightarrow m \bullet b \bullet \lambda x \rightarrow B(x) \ .$$

The first pattern $s \bullet \lambda m$ is used to match with a compatible seller using share information s, and to input a name m to be used as a channel to exchange bank account information b for share certificates bound to x. The transaction successfully concludes with $B(x)$.

The seller Sell_1 with share certificates c and desired share sale s is given by

$$\mathsf{Sell}_1 = (\nu n) s \bullet n \rightarrow n \bullet \lambda y \bullet c \rightarrow S(y) \ .$$

The seller creates a channel name n and then tries to find a buyer for the shares described in s, offering n to the buyer to continue the transaction. The channel is then used to exchange billing information, bound to y, for the share certificates c. The seller then concludes with the successfully completed transaction as $S(y)$.

The discovery phase succeeds when the traders are place in a parallel composition and discover each other by matching on s

$$\begin{aligned} \mathsf{Buy}_1|\mathsf{Sell}_1 \;&\equiv\; (\nu n)(s \bullet \lambda m \rightarrow m \bullet b \bullet \lambda x \rightarrow B(x) \mid s \bullet n \rightarrow n \bullet \lambda y \bullet c \rightarrow S(y)) \\ &\longmapsto (\nu n)(n \bullet b \bullet \lambda x \rightarrow B(x) \mid n \bullet \lambda y \bullet c \rightarrow S(y)) \ . \end{aligned}$$

The next phase is to exchange billing information for share certificates, as in

$$(\nu n)(n \bullet b \bullet \lambda x \rightarrow B(x) \mid n \bullet \lambda y \bullet c \rightarrow S(y)) \longmapsto (\nu n)(B(c) \mid S(b)).$$

The transaction concludes with the buyer having the share certificates c and the seller having the billing account b.

This solution allows the traders to discover each other and exchange information atomically to complete a transaction. However, there is no way to determine if a process is a trustworthy trader.

Solution 2. Now add a registrar that keeps track of registered traders. Traders offer their identity to potential partners and the registrar confirms if the identity belongs to a valid trader. The buyer is now

$$\mathsf{Buy}_2 = s \bullet i_B \bullet \lambda j \to n_B \bullet j \bullet \lambda m \to m \bullet b \bullet \lambda x \to B(x) .$$

The first pattern now swaps the buyer's identity i_B for the seller's, bound to j. The buyer then consults the registrar using the identifier n_B to validate j, if valid the exchange continues as before.

Now define the seller symmetrically by

$$\mathsf{Sell}_2 = s \bullet \lambda j \bullet i_S \to n_S \bullet j \bullet \lambda m \to m \bullet \lambda y \bullet c \to S(y) .$$

Also define the registrar Reg_2 with identifiers n_B and n_S to communicate with the buyer and seller, respectively, by

$$\mathsf{Reg}_2 = (\nu n)(n_B \bullet \ulcorner i_S \urcorner \bullet n \to \mathbf{0} \mid n_S \bullet \ulcorner i_B \urcorner \bullet n \to \mathbf{0}) .$$

The registrar creates a new identifier n to provide to traders who have been validated; then it makes the identifier available to known traders who attempt to validate another known trader. Although rather simple, the registrar can easily be extended to support a multitude of traders.

Running these processes in parallel yields the following interaction

$$\begin{aligned}
&\mathsf{Buy}_2 \mid \mathsf{Sell}_2 \mid \mathsf{Reg}_2 \\
\equiv\ &(\nu n)(s \bullet i_B \bullet \lambda j \to n_B \bullet j \bullet \lambda m \to m \bullet b \bullet \lambda x \to B(x) \mid n_B \bullet \ulcorner i_S \urcorner \bullet n \to \mathbf{0} \\
&\qquad \mid s \bullet \lambda j \bullet i_S \to n_S \bullet j \bullet \lambda m \to m \bullet \lambda y \bullet c \to S(y) \mid n_S \bullet \ulcorner i_B \urcorner \bullet n \to \mathbf{0}) \\
\longmapsto\ &(\nu n)(n_B \bullet i_S \bullet \lambda m \to m \bullet b \bullet \lambda x \to B(x) \mid n_B \bullet \ulcorner i_S \urcorner \bullet n \to \mathbf{0} \\
&\qquad \mid n_S \bullet i_B \bullet \lambda m \to m \bullet \lambda y \bullet c \to S(y) \mid n_S \bullet \ulcorner i_B \urcorner \bullet n \to \mathbf{0}) .
\end{aligned}$$

The share information s allows the buyer and seller to discover each other and swap identities i_B and i_S. The next two interactions involve the buyer and seller validating each other's identity and inputting the identifier to complete the transaction

$$\begin{aligned}
&(\nu n)(n_B \bullet i_S \bullet \lambda m \to m \bullet b \bullet \lambda x \to B(x) \mid n_B \bullet \ulcorner i_S \urcorner \bullet n \to \mathbf{0} \\
&\qquad \mid n_S \bullet i_B \bullet \lambda m \to m \bullet \lambda y \bullet c \to S(y) \mid n_S \bullet \ulcorner i_B \urcorner \bullet n \to \mathbf{0}) \\
\longmapsto\ &(\nu n)(n \bullet b \bullet \lambda x \to B(x) \\
&\qquad \mid n_S \bullet i_B \bullet \lambda m \to m \bullet \lambda y \bullet c \to S(y) \mid n_S \bullet \ulcorner i_B \urcorner \bullet n \to \mathbf{0}) \\
\longmapsto\ &(\nu n)(n \bullet b \bullet \lambda x \to B(x) \mid n \bullet \lambda y \bullet c \to S(y)) .
\end{aligned}$$

Now that the traders have validated each other, they can continue with the exchange step from before

$$(\nu n)(n \bullet b \bullet \lambda x \to B(x) \mid n \bullet \lambda y \bullet c \to S(y)) \quad \longmapsto \quad (\nu n)(B(c) \mid S(b)) \;.$$

The traders exchange information and successfully complete with $B(c)$ and $S(b)$.

Although this solution satisfies the desire to validate that traders are legitimate, the freedom of matching allows for malicious processes to interfere. Consider the promiscuous process Prom given by

$$\mathsf{Prom} = \lambda z_1 \bullet \lambda z_2 \bullet a \to P(z_1, z_2) \;.$$

This process is willing to match any other process that will swap two pieces of information for some arbitrary name a. Such a process could interfere with the traders trying to complete the exchange phase of a transaction. For example,

$$\begin{aligned} &(\nu n)(n \bullet b \bullet \lambda x \to B(x) \mid n \bullet \lambda y \bullet c \to S(y)) \mid \mathsf{Prom} \\ \longmapsto\ &(\nu n)(B(a) \mid n \bullet \lambda y \bullet c \to S(y) \mid P(n, b)) \end{aligned}$$

where the promiscuous process has stolen the identifier n and the bank account information b. The unfortunate buyer is left with some useless information a and the seller is waiting to complete the transaction.

Solution 3. The vulnerability of Solution 2 can be repaired by using protected names. The buyer, seller and registrar can be repaired to

$$\begin{aligned} \mathsf{Buy}_3 &= s \bullet i_B \bullet \lambda j \to \ulcorner n_B \urcorner \bullet j \bullet \lambda m \to \ulcorner m \urcorner \bullet b \bullet \lambda x \to B(x) \\ \mathsf{Sell}_3 &= s \bullet \lambda j \bullet i_S \to \ulcorner n_S \urcorner \bullet j \bullet \lambda m \to \ulcorner m \urcorner \bullet \lambda y \bullet c \to S(y) \\ \mathsf{Reg}_3 &= (\nu n)(\ulcorner n_B \urcorner \bullet \ulcorner i_S \urcorner \bullet n \to \mathbf{0} \mid \ulcorner n_S \urcorner \bullet \ulcorner i_B \urcorner \bullet n \to \mathbf{0}) \;. \end{aligned}$$

Now all communication between the buyer, seller and registrar use protected identifiers: $\ulcorner n_B \urcorner, \ulcorner n_S \urcorner$ and $\ulcorner m \urcorner$. Thus, all that remains is to ensure appropriate restrictions:

$$(\nu n_B)(\nu n_S)(\mathsf{Buy}_3 \mid \mathsf{Sell}_3 \mid \mathsf{Reg}_3) \;.$$

Therefore, other processes can only interact with the traders during the discovery phase, which will not lead to a successful transaction. The registrar will only interact with the traders as all the registrar's patterns have protected names known only to the registrar and a trader (Lemma 2).

The solution could be extended further: although the share information is treated as a variable name in the example, it could be represented as a compound structure with a company code, number of shares and price per share, e.g. $\mathsf{ABC} \bullet 100 \bullet \$0.38$. This format allows discovery based on partial share information, for example: specify a company code and price, but not the number of shares $\mathsf{ABC} \bullet \lambda v \bullet \$0.38$; or specify only the price and accept any company or number of shares $\lambda u \bullet \lambda v \bullet \$0.38$. The seller could also offer similarly partial share information, although this may be a very risky business strategy! Observe that either trader can protect any component of the pattern if they wish to ensure that the other party exactly meets that criterion.

Another possibility is to allow for some checking of the integrity of the patterns being communicated. Given some standard language for the representation of data, such as XML, this could be checked by the matching. For example, a valid bank account may be required to have an account number and account name. Thus, a pattern to input only valid bank accounts, binding the account number to u, the name to v and using standardised tags accountnumber and accountname, could be $(\ulcorner \mathsf{accountnumber} \urcorner \bullet \lambda u) \bullet (\ulcorner \mathsf{accountname} \urcorner \bullet \lambda v)$. Thus, any pattern that successfully matches must be identically structured and tagged. Indeed, this could be developed further to account for XML and web services such as in `PiDuce` [3].

4 Comparison with Other Process Calculi

This section exploits the techniques developed in [7,8] to formally asses the expressive power of CPC w.r.t. π-calculus, Linda, Fusion and Spi calculus. After briefly recalling these models and some basic material from [8], the relation to CPC is formalised. First, let each model, including CPC, be augmented with a reserved process '$\surd$', used to signal successful termination.

4.1 Some Process Calculi

π-calculus [13,12]. The π-calculus processes given by the following grammar:

$$P ::= \mathbf{0} \mid \surd \mid \overline{a}\langle b\rangle.P \mid a(x).P \mid (\nu n)P \mid P|Q \mid !P$$

and the only reduction rule is

$$\overline{a}\langle b\rangle.P \mid a(x).Q \quad \longmapsto \quad P \mid Q\{b/x\} \ .$$

Linda [4]. Consider an instance of Linda formulated to follow CPC's syntax.

Processes are defined as:

$$P ::= \mathbf{0} \mid \surd \mid \langle b_1, \ldots, b_k\rangle \mid (t_1, \ldots, t_k).P \mid (\nu n)P \mid P|Q \mid !P$$

where b ranges over names and t denotes a template field, defined by:

$$t ::= \lambda x \quad \mid \quad \ulcorner b \urcorner \ .$$

Assume that input variables occurring in templates are all distinct. This assumption rules out template $(\lambda x, \lambda x)$, but accepts $(\lambda x, \ulcorner b \urcorner, \ulcorner b \urcorner)$. Templates are used to implement Linda's pattern matching, defined as follows:

$$\textsc{Match}(\ ;\ ) = \{\} \qquad \textsc{Match}(\ulcorner b \urcorner; b) = \{\} \qquad \textsc{Match}(\lambda x; b) = \{b/x\}$$

$$\frac{\textsc{Match}(t; b) = \sigma_1 \qquad \textsc{Match}(\widetilde{t}; \widetilde{b}) = \sigma_2}{\textsc{Match}(t, \widetilde{t}\,;\, b, \widetilde{b}) = \sigma_1 \uplus \sigma_2}$$

where $\widetilde{e}$ denotes a (possibly empty) sequence of entities of kind e (names or template fields, in our case) and '$\uplus$' denotes the union of partial functions with disjoint domains. The interaction rule is given by:

$$\langle \widetilde{b} \rangle \mid (\widetilde{t}).P \longmapsto \sigma P \qquad \text{if } \textsc{Match}(\widetilde{t}; \widetilde{b}) = \sigma \, .$$

The reduction relation is obtained by closing this interaction rule by parallel, restriction and the same structural equivalence relation defined for CPC.

Fusion [15]. Following the the presentation in [17], processes are defined as:

$$P ::= \mathbf{0} \mid P|P \mid (\nu x)P \mid !P \mid \overline{u}\langle \widetilde{x} \rangle.P \mid u(\widetilde{x}).P \, .$$

The interaction rule for Fusion is

$$(\nu \widetilde{u})(\overline{u}\langle \widetilde{x} \rangle.P \mid u(\widetilde{y}).Q \mid R) \longmapsto \sigma P \mid \sigma Q \mid \sigma R \;\; \begin{array}{l} \text{with } \mathsf{dom}(\sigma) \cup \mathsf{ran}(\sigma) \subseteq \{\widetilde{x}, \widetilde{y}\} \\ \text{and } \widetilde{u} = \mathsf{dom}(\sigma) \setminus \mathsf{ran}(\sigma) \text{ and} \\ \sigma(v) = \sigma(w) \text{ iff } (v, w) \in E(\widetilde{x} = \widetilde{y}) \end{array}$$

where $E(\widetilde{x} = \widetilde{y})$ is the least equivalence relation on names generated by the equalities $\widetilde{x} = \widetilde{y}$ (that is defined whenever $|\widetilde{x}| = |\widetilde{y}|$). Fusion's reduction relation is obtained by closing the interaction axiom under parallel, restriction and the structural equivalence as for CPC.

Spi calculus [6]. This language is unusual as names are now generalised to *terms* of the form

$$M, N \quad ::= \quad n \quad | \quad x \quad | \quad (M, N) \quad | \quad 0 \quad | \quad suc(M) \quad | \quad \{M\}_N$$

They are rather similar to the patterns of CPC in that they may have internal structure. Of particular interest are the pair, successor and encryption that may be bound to a name and then decomposed later by an intensional reduction.

Concerning the operational semantics, we consider a slightly modified version of Spi calculus where interaction is generalised to

$$\overline{M}\langle N \rangle.P \mid M(x).Q \quad \longmapsto \quad P \mid \{N/x\}Q$$

where M is any term of the Spi calculus.

4.2 Valid Encodings and Their Properties

An *encoding* of a language $\mathcal{L}_1$ into another language $\mathcal{L}_2$ is a pair $([\![\cdot]\!], \varphi_{[\![\,]\!]})$ where $[\![\cdot]\!]$ translates every $\mathcal{L}_1$-process into an $\mathcal{L}_2$-process and $\varphi_{[\![\,]\!]}$ maps every source name into a k-tuple of (target) names, for $k > 0$. The translation $[\![\cdot]\!]$ turns every source term into a target term; in doing this, the translation may fix some names to play a precise rôle or it may translate a single name into a tuple of names. This can be obtained by exploiting $\varphi_{[\![\,]\!]}$ (details in [8]).

Now consider only encodings that satisfy the following properties, that are justified and discussed at length in [8]. Let a *k-ary context* $\mathcal{C}(\_{1}; \ldots; \_{k})$ be a term where k occurrences of $\mathbf{0}$ are linearly replaced by the holes $\{-_1; \dots; -_k\}$ (every hole must occur once and only once). Moreover, denote with $\longmapsto_i$ and $\Longmapsto_i$ the relations $\longmapsto$ and $\Longmapsto$ in language $\mathcal{L}_i$; denote with $\longmapsto_i^\omega$ an infinite sequence of reductions in $\mathcal{L}_i$. Moreover, we let $\simeq_i$ denote the reference behavioural equivalence for language $\mathcal{L}_i$. Also, let $P \Downarrow_i$ mean that there exists P' such that $P \Longmapsto_i P'$ and $P' \equiv P'' \mid \surd$, for some P''. Finally, to simplify reading, let S range over processes of the source language (viz., $\mathcal{L}_1$) and T range over processes of the target language (viz., $\mathcal{L}_2$).

Definition 2 (Valid Encoding). *An encoding* $(\llbracket \cdot \rrbracket, \varphi_{\llbracket\,\rrbracket})$ *is* valid *if it satisfies the following five properties:*

1. Compositionality: *for every k-ary operator* op *of $\mathcal{L}_1$ and for every subset of names N, there exists a k-ary context $\mathcal{C}^N_{\mathsf{op}}(-_1; \dots; -_k)$ such that, for all $S_1, \dots, S_k$ with $\mathsf{fn}(S_1, \dots, S_k) = N$, it holds that $\llbracket \mathsf{op}(S_1, \dots, S_k) \rrbracket = \mathcal{C}^N_{\mathsf{op}}(\llbracket S_1 \rrbracket; \dots; \llbracket S_k \rrbracket)$.*
2. Name invariance: *for every S and name substitution σ, it holds that*
$$\llbracket \sigma S \rrbracket \begin{cases} = \sigma' \llbracket S \rrbracket & \text{if } \sigma \text{ is injective} \\ \simeq_2 \sigma' \llbracket S \rrbracket & \text{otherwise} \end{cases}$$
where σ' is such that $\varphi_{\llbracket\,\rrbracket}(\sigma(a)) = \sigma'(\varphi_{\llbracket\,\rrbracket}(a))$ for every name a.
3. Operational correspondence:
   – *for all $S \Longmapsto_1 S'$, it holds that $\llbracket S \rrbracket \Longmapsto_2 \simeq_2 \llbracket S' \rrbracket$;*
   – *for all $\llbracket S \rrbracket \Longmapsto_2 T$, there exists S' such that $S \Longmapsto_1 S'$ and $T \Longmapsto_2 \simeq_2 \llbracket S' \rrbracket$.*
4. Divergence reflection: *for every S such that $\llbracket S \rrbracket \longmapsto_2^\omega$, it holds that $S \longmapsto_1^\omega$.*
5. Success sensitiveness: *for every S, it holds that $S \Downarrow_1$ if and only if $\llbracket S \rrbracket \Downarrow_2$.*

[8] contains some results concerning valid encodings. In particular, it shows some proof-techniques for showing separation results, i.e. for proving that no valid encoding can exist between a pair of languages $\mathcal{L}_1$ and $\mathcal{L}_2$ satisfying certain conditions. Here, these languages will be limited to CPC and those introduced in Section 4.1. Further, the valid encodings considered will be assumed to be *semi-homomorphic*, i.e. where the interpretation of parallel composition is via a context of the form $(\nu\widetilde{n})(-_1 \mid -_2 \mid R)$, for some $\widetilde{n}$ and R that only depend on the free names of the translated processes.

Proposition 1 (from [8]). *Let $\llbracket \cdot \rrbracket$ be a valid encoding; then, $S \not\longmapsto_1$ implies that $\llbracket S \rrbracket \not\longmapsto_2$.*

Theorem 1 (from [8]). *Assume that there exists S such that $S \not\longmapsto_1$, $S \not\Downarrow_1$ and $S \mid S \Downarrow_1$; moreover, assume that every T that does not reduce is such that $T \mid T \not\longmapsto_2$. Then, there cannot exist any semi-homomorphic valid encoding of $\mathcal{L}_1$ into $\mathcal{L}_2$.*

To state the following proof-technique, define the *matching degree* of a language $\mathcal{L}$, written $\textsc{Md}(\mathcal{L})$, as the least upper bound on the number of names that must be matched to yield a reduction in $\mathcal{L}$.

Theorem 2 (from [8]). *If $\textsc{Md}(\mathcal{L}_1) > \textsc{Md}(\mathcal{L}_2)$, then there exists no valid encoding of $\mathcal{L}_1$ into $\mathcal{L}_2$.*

4.3 CPC vs. π-Calculus and Linda

A hierarchy of process calculi with different communication primitives is obtained in [7] by combining four features: synchronism (synchronous vs asynchronous), arity (monadic vs polyadic data exchange), communication medium (channels vs shared dataspaces), and the presence of a form of pattern matching (that checks the arity of the tuple of names and equality of some specific names). This hierarchy is built upon a very similar notion of encoding to that presented in Definition 2 and, in particular, it is proved that Linda [4] (called $L_{\text{A,P,D,PM}}$ in [7]) is more expressive than monadic/polyadic π-calculus [13,12] (called $L_{\text{S,M,C,NO}}$ and $L_{\text{S,P,C,NO}}$, respectively, in [7]). Thus, it suffices to show that CPC is more expressive than $L_{\text{A,P,D,PM}}$ (this is the language called Linda in Section 4.1).

First notice that CPC cannot be encoded into $L_{\text{A,P,D,PM}}$: this is a corollary of Theorem 1. Indeed, consider the self-matching CPC process $x \rightarrow \surd$: alone it cannot reduce and cannot report success but, reports success in parallel with itself. On the contrary, it is easy to prove that every $L_{\text{A,P,D,PM}}$-process that reduces if put in parallel with itself is such that it reduces in isolation.

The next step is to show a valid encoding of $L_{\text{A,P,D,PM}}$ into CPC. The encoding is a homomorphism w.r.t. to all operators, with the only two following exceptions:

$$[\![\langle \widetilde{b} \rangle]\!] \stackrel{\text{def}}{=} \mathsf{pat\text{–}d}(\widetilde{b}) \rightarrow \mathbf{0} \qquad\qquad [\![(\widetilde{t}).P]\!] \stackrel{\text{def}}{=} \mathsf{pat\text{–}t}(\widetilde{t}) \rightarrow [\![P]\!]$$

Functions $\mathsf{pat\text{–}d}(\cdot)$ and $\mathsf{pat\text{–}t}(\cdot)$ are used to translate data and templates into CPC patterns; they are defined as follows:

$$\begin{array}{lll} \mathsf{pat\text{–}d}(\,) \stackrel{\text{def}}{=} \lambda x & \mathsf{pat\text{–}d}(b,\widetilde{b}) \stackrel{\text{def}}{=} \lambda x \bullet b \bullet \mathsf{pat\text{–}d}(\widetilde{b}) & \text{for } x \notin \mathsf{bn}(\mathsf{pat\text{–}d}(\widetilde{b})) \\ \mathsf{pat\text{–}t}(\,) \stackrel{\text{def}}{=} \mathsf{in} & \mathsf{pat\text{–}t}(t,\widetilde{t}) \stackrel{\text{def}}{=} \mathsf{in} \bullet t \bullet \mathsf{pat\text{–}t}(\widetilde{t}) & \end{array}$$

where in is any name (a symbolic name is used for clarity but no result relies upon this). Moreover, the function $\mathsf{pat\text{–}d}(\cdot)$ associates a bound variable to every name in the sequence; this fact ensures that a pattern that translates a datum and a pattern that translates a template match only if they have the same length (this is a feature of $L_{\text{A,P,D,PM}}$'s pattern matching but not of CPC's). It is worth noting that the simpler translation $[\![\langle b_1, \ldots, b_n \rangle]\!] \stackrel{\text{def}}{=} b_1 \bullet \ldots \bullet b_n \rightarrow \mathbf{0}$ would not work: the $L_{\text{A,P,D,PM}}$-process $\langle b \rangle \mid \langle b \rangle$ does not reduce, whereas such an encoding $(b \rightarrow \mathbf{0} \mid b \rightarrow \mathbf{0})$ does. This fact would contradict Proposition 1.

Next is to prove that this encoding is valid. This is an easy corollary of the following lemma, stating a strict correspondence between $L_{\text{A,P,D,PM}}$'s pattern matching and CPC's one (on patterns arising from the translation).

Lemma 3. $\text{M}\textsc{atch}(\widetilde{t};\widetilde{b}) = \sigma$ *if and only if* $\{\mathsf{pat\text{–}t}(\widetilde{t}) \| \mathsf{pat\text{–}d}(\widetilde{b})\} = \mathsf{Some}(\sigma, \{\mathsf{in}/x_0, \ldots, \mathsf{in}/x_n\})$*, where* $\{x_0, \ldots, x_n\} = \mathsf{bn}(\mathsf{pat\text{–}d}(\widetilde{b}))$ *and* σ *maps names to names.*

4.4 CPC vs. Fusion

Fusion calculus and CPC are unrelated in that there exists no valid encoding from one into the other. The impossibility for a valid encoding of CPC into Fusion is ensured by Theorem 2: the matching degree of Fusion is 1 (only the channel name is checked for equality in any interaction); by contrast, the matching degree of CPC is ∞, since any number of name equalities can be checked atomically in a single CPC interaction. The converse separation result is ensured by the following theorem.

Theorem 3. *There exists no valid encoding of Fusion into CPC.*

Proof:(Sketch) The idea is to show that any interaction in Fusion can be rendered only by having: (1) two parallel processes performing an input and an output on the same channel, and (2) a restriction enclosing them to allow application of name fusions. Thus, to yield a reduction three entities have to mutually cooperate; this ternary interaction cannot be rendered in CPC, and this can be used to prove that no valid encoding can exist (see the technical report [5] for full details). □

4.5 CPC vs. Spi

That CPC cannot be encoded into Spi calculus is a corollary of Theorem 1 and identical to the technique used in Section 4.3. The self-matching CPC process $x \rightarrow \surd$ cannot be encoded into Spi.

The remainder of this section develops an encoding of Spi calculus into CPC. The terms can be encoded as patterns using the reserved names pair, encr, 0 and suc by

$$
\begin{array}{ll}
[\![n]\!] \stackrel{\text{def}}{=} n & [\![(M,N)]\!] \stackrel{\text{def}}{=} \mathsf{pair} \bullet [\![M]\!] \bullet [\![N]\!] \\
[\![x]\!] \stackrel{\text{def}}{=} x & [\![\{M\}_N]\!] \stackrel{\text{def}}{=} \mathsf{encr} \bullet [\![M]\!] \bullet [\![N]\!] \\
[\![0]\!] \stackrel{\text{def}}{=} 0 & [\![suc(M)]\!] \stackrel{\text{def}}{=} \mathsf{suc} \bullet [\![M]\!] \,.
\end{array}
$$

The tagging is used for safety, as otherwise there are potential pathologies in the translation: without tags, the representation of a natural number could be confused with a pair or an encryption.

The processes of the Spi calculus are

$$
\begin{aligned}
P, Q ::= \;& 0 \mid P|Q \mid !P \mid (\nu m)P \mid M(x).P \mid \overline{M}\langle N\rangle.P \\
& \mid [M \ is \ N]P \mid let\ (x,y) = M \ in \ P \\
& \mid case\ M\ of\ \{x\}_N : P \mid case\ M\ of\ 0 : P\ suc(x) : Q \,.
\end{aligned}
$$

The nil process, parallel composition, replication and restriction are all familiar. The input $M(x).P$ and output $\overline{M}\langle N\rangle.P$ are generalised to allow terms in the place of channel names and output arguments. The match $[M\ is\ N]P$ determines equality of M and N. The splitting $let\ (x,y) = M\ in\ P$ decomposes pairs. The decryption case $case\ M\ of\ \{x\}_N : P$ decrypts M binding the encrypted message to x. The integer case *case* M *of* $0 : P$ *suc*$(x) : Q$ branches according to the number. Note that the last four can all get stuck if M is an incompatible term. Further, the last three are intensional, i.e. they depend on the internal structure of M.

The encoding of the familiar forms are homomorphic as expected. The input and output both encode as cases:

$$[\![M(x).P]\!] \stackrel{\text{def}}{=} \mathsf{in} \bullet \ulcorner [\![M]\!] \urcorner \bullet \lambda x \to [\![P]\!]$$
$$[\![\overline{M}\langle N\rangle.P]\!] \stackrel{\text{def}}{=} \lambda x \bullet \ulcorner [\![M]\!] \urcorner \bullet ([\![N]\!]) \to [\![P]\!] \qquad x \notin \mathsf{fn}([\![P]\!], [\![M]\!], [\![N]\!])\ .$$

The reserved name in (input) and fresh name x (output) are used to ensure that encoded inputs will only match with encoded outputs. Observe that in both processes forms $[\![M]\!]$ contains no binding names, and so is communicable.

The four remaining process forms all require pattern matching and so translate to cases in parallel. In each encoding a fresh name n is used to prevent interaction with other processes, see Lemma 2. As in the Spi calculus, the encodings will reduce only after a successful matching and will be stuck otherwise. The encodings are

$$[\![[M\ is\ N]P]\!] \stackrel{\text{def}}{=} (\nu n)(\ulcorner n \urcorner \bullet [\![M]\!] \to [\![P]\!] \mid \ulcorner n \urcorner \bullet [\![N]\!] \to \mathbf{0})$$
$$[\![let\ (x,y) = M\ in\ P]\!] \stackrel{\text{def}}{=} (\nu n)(\ulcorner n \urcorner \bullet (\mathsf{pair} \bullet \lambda x \bullet \lambda y) \to [\![P]\!]$$
$$\mid \ulcorner n \urcorner \bullet [\![M]\!] \to \mathbf{0})$$
$$[\![case\ M\ of\ \{x\}_N : P]\!] \stackrel{\text{def}}{=} (\nu n)(\ulcorner n \urcorner \bullet (\mathsf{encr} \bullet \lambda x \bullet [\![N]\!]) \to [\![P]\!]$$
$$\mid \ulcorner n \urcorner \bullet [\![M]\!] \to \mathbf{0})$$
$$[\![case\ M\ of\ 0 : P\ suc(x) : Q]\!] \stackrel{\text{def}}{=} (\nu n)(\ulcorner n \urcorner \bullet 0 \to [\![P]\!]$$
$$\mid \ulcorner n \urcorner \bullet (\mathsf{suc} \bullet \lambda x) \to [\![Q]\!]$$
$$\mid \ulcorner n \urcorner \bullet [\![M]\!] \to \mathbf{0})\ .$$

The match $[M\ is\ N]P$ only reduces to P if $M = N$, thus the encoding creates two patterns using $[\![M]\!]$ and $[\![N]\!]$ with one reducing to $[\![P]\!]$. The pair splitting *let* $(x,y) = M$ *in* P encoding creates a case with a pattern that matches a tagged pair and binds the components to x and y in $[\![P]\!]$. This is put in parallel with another case that has $[\![M]\!]$ in the pattern. The decryption case *case* M *of* $\{x\}_N$: P checks whether M is a message encoded with key $[\![N]\!]$ and retrieves the value encrypted by binding it to x in the continuation. Lastly the integer case *case* M *of* $0 : P$ *suc*$(x) : Q$ translation creates a case for each of the zero and the successor possibilities. These cases match the tag and the reserved names 0, reducing to $[\![P]\!]$, or suc and binding x in $[\![Q]\!]$. The term to be compared M is as in the others.

Theorem 4. *The encoding of Spi calculus into CPC is valid.*

To conclude, notice that the criteria for a valid encoding does not imply full abstraction of the encoding (actually, they were defined in [7,8] as an alternative to full abstraction). This means that the encoding of equivalent Spi calculus processes can be distinguished by contexts in CPC that do not result from the encoding of any Spi calculus context. Indeed, while this encoding allows Spi calculus to be modelled in CPC, it does *not* entail that cryptography can be properly rendered. Consider the pattern $\mathsf{encr} \bullet \lambda x \bullet \lambda y$ that could match the encoding of an encrypted term to bind the message and key, so that CPC can break any encryption! One solution is to simply add this encryption to CPC, a topic for future work.

5 Conclusions and Future Work

The concurrent pattern calculus uses patterns to represent input, output and tests for equality, whose interaction is driven by unification that allows a two-way flow of information. This symmetric information exchange provides a concise model of trade in the information age. This is illustrated by the example of traders who can discover each other in the open and then close the deal in private.

CPC supports valid encodings of many popular concurrent calculi such as π-calculus, Spi calculus and Linda as its patterns describe more structures. However, these three calculi do not support valid encodings of CPC because, among other things, they are insufficiently symmetric. On the other hand, while fusion calculus is completely symmetric, it has an incompatible approach to interaction.

Future work may proceed in several directions. Just as pattern calculus expands upon the expressive power of sequential programming, CPC expands the expressive power of concurrent programming. The consequences of this remain to be developed. Possibilities applications include web services based upon symmetric information exchange. As first step is to implement the calculus, perhaps by augmenting the programming language **bondi** [2] that was built to implement pattern calculus.

Concurrent pattern calculus supports a generous class of patterns whose interaction is fully symmetric. The implications of this increased expressive power are worthy of further investigation.

Acknowledgements. Thanks to Eugenio Moggi and the reviewers for their helpful comments on drafts of this paper.

References

1. Barendregt, H.P.: The Lambda Calculus. Its Syntax and Semantics. Studies in Logic and the Foundations of Mathematics. Elsevier Science Publishers B.V., Amsterdam (1985)
2. bondi programming language, `http://www-staff.it.uts.edu.au/~cbj/bondi`
3. Brown, A.L., Laneve, C., Meredith, L.G.: Piduce: A process calculus with native XML datatypes. In: Bravetti, M., Kloul, L., Zavattaro, G. (eds.) EPEW/WS-EM 2005. LNCS, vol. 3670, pp. 18–34. Springer, Heidelberg (2005)

4. Gelernter, D.: Generative communication in LINDA. ACM Transactions on Programming Languages and Systems 7(1), 80–112 (1985)
5. Given-Wilson, T., Gorla, D., Jay, B.: Concurrent pattern calculus, long version (2010), http://www.progsoc.uts.edu.au/~sanguinev/files/cpc-long.pdf
6. Gordon, A., Abadi, M.: A calculus for cryptographic protocols: The spi calculus. In: 4th ACM Conference on Computer and Communications Security, pp. 36–47 (1997)
7. Gorla, D.: Comparing communication primitives via their relative expressive power. Information and Computation 206(8), 931–952 (2008)
8. Gorla, D.: Towards a unified approach to encodability and separation results for process calculi. In: van Breugel, F., Chechik, M. (eds.) CONCUR 2008. LNCS, vol. 5201, pp. 492–507. Springer, Heidelberg (2008)
9. Jay, B.: Pattern Calculus: Computing with Functions and Data Structures. Springer, Heidelberg (2009)
10. Jay, B., Given-Wilson, T.: A combinatory account of internal structure (2010), http://www-staff.it.uts.edu.au/~cbj/Publications/factorisation.pdf
11. Jay, B., Kesner, D.: First-class patterns. Journal of Functional Programming 19(2), 34pages (2009)
12. Milner, R.: The polyadic π-calculus: A tutorial. In: Bauer, F.L., Brauer, W., Schwichtenberg, H. (eds.) Logic and Algebra of Specification. NATO ASI., vol. 94. Springer, Heidelberg (1993)
13. Milner, R., Parrow, J., Walker, D.: A calculus of mobile processes, part I/II. Information and Computation 100, 1–77 (1992)
14. Nicola, R.D., Ferrari, G., Pugliese, R.: KLAIM: A kernel language for agents interaction and mobility. IEEE Transactions on Software Engineering 24(5), 315–330 (1998)
15. Parrow, J., Victor, B.: The fusion calculus: Expressiveness and symmetry in mobile processes. In: Proc. of LICS, pp. 176–185. IEEE Computer Society, Los Alamitos (1998)
16. Picco, G., Murphy, A., Roman, G.-C.: LIME: Linda Meets Mobility. In: Garlan, D. (ed.) Proc. of the 21st Int. Conference on Software Engineering (ICSE'99), pp. 368–377. ACM Press, New York (1999)
17. Wischik, L., Gardner, P.: Explicit fusions. Theor. Comput. Sci. 340(3), 606–630 (2005)

Initial Segment Complexities of Randomness Notions

Rupert Hölzl[1,⋆], Thorsten Kräling[1], Frank Stephan[2,⋆⋆], and Guohua Wu[3]

[1] Institut für Informatik, Universität Heidelberg,
INF 294, 69120 Heidelberg, Germany
hoelzl@math.uni-heidelberg.de, kraeling@informatik.uni-heidelberg.de
[2] Department of Mathematics, National University of Singapore,
2 Science Drive 2, Singapore 117543, Singapore
fstephan@comp.nus.edu.sg
[3] Division of Mathematical Sciences, School of Physical and Mathematical Sciences,
College of Science, Nanyang Technological University, Singapore
guohua@ntu.edu.sg

Abstract. Schnorr famously proved that Martin-Löf-randomness of a sequence A can be characterised via the complexity of A's initial segments. Nies, Stephan and Terwijn as well as independently Miller showed that Kolmogorov randomness coincides with Martin-Löf randomness relative to the halting problem K; that is, a set A is Martin-Löf random relative to K iff there is no function f such that for all m and all $n > f(m)$ it holds that $C(A(0)A(1)\ldots A(n)) \leq n - m$.

In the present work it is shown that characterisations of this style can also be given for other randomness criteria like strongly random, Kurtz random relative to K, PA-incomplete Martin-Löf random and strongly Kurtz random; here one does not just quantify over all functions f but over functions f of a specific form. For example, A is Martin-Löf random and PA-incomplete iff there is no A-recursive function f such that for all m and all $n > f(m)$ it holds that $C(A(0)A(1)\ldots A(n)) \leq n - m$. The characterisation for strong randomness relates to functions which are the concatenation of an A-recursive function executed after a K-recursive function; this solves an open problem of Nies.

In addition to this, characterisations of a similar style are also given for Demuth randomness and Schnorr randomness relative to K. Although the unrelativised versions of Kurtz randomness and Schnorr randomness do not admit such a characterisation in terms of plain Kolmogorov complexity, Bienvenu and Merkle gave one in terms of Kolmogorov complexity defined by computable machines.

1 Introduction

Kolmogorov complexity [9,13] aims to describe when a set is random in an algorithmic way. Here randomness means that no type of patterns can be exploited by

⋆ R. Hölzl is supported by DFG grant ME 1806/3-1.

⋆⋆ F. Stephan is supported in part by the NUS grants R146-000-114-112 and R252-000-308-112.

C.S. Calude and V. Sassone (Eds.): TCS 2010, IFIP AICT 323, pp. 259–270, 2010.

an algorithm in order to generate initial segments of the characteristic function from shorter programs. Randomness notions have been formalised by Martin-Löf [10], Schnorr [18] and others. A special emphasis was put on describing randomness of a set A in terms of the complexity of the initial segments $A(0)A(1)\dots A(n)$. The first important result in that direction was that Schnorr [19] proved that a set A is Martin-Löf random if and only if for almost all n the prefix free Kolmogorov complexity $H(A(0)A(1)\dots A(n))$ of the $(n+1)$-th initial segment is at least n. It is easy to see that the counterpart of this characterisation is that a set A is *not Martin-Löf random* iff there is an A-recursive function f such that $H(A(0)A(1)\dots A(f(m))) \leq f(m) - m$ for all m. In other words, one can find — relative to A — points to witness the non-randomness effectively. It should be noted that the function f has to be taken relative to A and not relative to some fixed oracle B independent of A as the sets 2-generic relative to B are not Martin-Löf random but would not admit a B-recursive function f witnessing the non-randomness in the way just mentioned.

The scope of the present paper is to study the notions of randomness beyond Martin-Löf randomness. These are the relativised versions "Kurtz random relative to K", "Schnorr random relative to K" and "Kolmogorov random" which coincides with "Martin-Löf random relative to K" where K is the halting problem or any other creative set. In addition, the two independently defined notions of "Demuth random" and "strongly random" are considered. Strong randomness is by some authors considered to be the next counterpart of Kurtz randomness, although it is not the relativised version; therefore they call Kurtz random also "weakly random" and strongly random also "weakly 2-random" [13]. Strong randomness [8,17] has various nice characterisations, in particular the following: A is strongly random iff A is Martin-Löf random and forms a minimal pair with K with respect to Turing reducibility [4, Footnote 2]. For these notions, in order to quantify the degree of non-randomness of a sequence, one studies from which value $f(m)$ onwards all initial segments can be compressed by m bits. That is, one looks at functions f such that $C(A(0)A(1)\dots A(n)) \leq n - m$ for all $n > f(m)$; here f might also be an upper bound of the least possible point with this property as one might want to have that f is in a certain Turing degree. This idea is quite natural as Kolmogorov random is just the notion of randomness which is defined by the absence of any such f and which coincides with Martin-Löf random relative to K.

The main results of this article will be that other randomness notions can be characterised in similar ways. The characterisations of these notions will differ in how the function f can be computed (e.g., relative to which oracles) and whether the compressibility condition holds for infinitely many or for all m. Note that due to finite modifications of f it would be equivalent to postulate the condition for all m or for almost all m. Several proofs make use of this fact.

Although the unrelativised versions of Kurtz randomness and Schnorr randomness do not admit such a characterisation in terms of plain Kolmogorov complexity, Bienvenu and Merkle [1] gave one in terms of Kolmogorov complexity defined by computable machines. There is a close connection between the plain Kolmogorov complexity C and prefix-free Kolmogorov complexity H. This is formalised in the following remark and this connection helps to establish many bounds obtained for C also for H.

Remark 1. If $C(x) \leq |x| - 1 - 3m$ with a minimal plain code x^* for x, and if n^* and m^* are minimal *prefix-free* codes for $n := |x|$ and m, respectively, then some prefix-free machine can use $n^* m^* 0^k 1 x^*$ as a prefix-free code for x, where k is chosen such that $|0^k 1 x^*| = n - 3m$.

It easily follows that there is a constant c such that whenever a set A and a function f satisfy that $C(A(0)A(1)\dots A(n)) \leq n - 3m$ for all m and all $n > f(m)$, then A and f also satisfy that for all $m > c$ and all $n > f(m)$ it holds that $H(A(0)A(1)\dots A(n)) \leq n + H(n) - m$.

We will also use the following theorem.

Theorem 2 (Chaitin's Counting Theorem [3]). *There is a constant c such that for all n and m it holds that*

$$|\{\sigma : |\sigma| = n + 1 \wedge H(\sigma) \leq n + H(n) - m\}| \leq 2^{n-m+c}.$$

For the scientific background of this paper, the reader is referred to the usual textbooks on recursion theory [15,16,20] and algorithmic randomness [2,9,13].

2 Characterising Strong Randomness

Nies [13, Problem 3.6.23] asks whether one can characterise strong randomness via the growth of the initial segment complexity. In the present paper, an answer will be provided, but for that answer the growth-rate depends also on the Turing degree of the set A for which it is asked whether it is strongly random. After the characterisation in Theorem 5, it will be shown in two further results that there is no obvious way to simplify the characterisation.

Remark 3. An open r.e. class V_e consists of sets A such that for each member $A \in V_e$ it is verified in some finite time s that A belongs to V_e; let $V_{e,s}$ be the class of all A such that it is verified in time s that A belongs to V_e. Now the notion is chosen such that whenever $A \in V_{e,s}$ and $B(m) = A(m)$ for all $m \leq s$ then $B \in V_{e,s}$ as well. An open r.e. class V_e is called finitely generated iff there is a step-number s such that $V_{e,s} = V_e$.

Furthermore, in the following, let C be the plain and H be the prefix-free Kolmogorov complexity. K denotes the halting problem. f_s is then the s-th approximation of a K-recursive function f, the mapping $x, s \mapsto f_s(x)$ is recursive in both inputs. The following notion was originally introduced by Kurtz [8] and is one of the central notions of this paper.

Definition 4 (Kurtz [8]). A set A is called *strongly random* iff there is no uniform sequence $V_0, V_1, V_2, \dots$ of open r.e. classes such that $\mu(V_e) \to 0$ for $e \to \infty$ and $A \in \bigcap_e V_e$.

The next result gives a characterisation of strong randomness in the desired form.

Theorem 5. *The following are equivalent for a set A.*
(a) A is not strongly random.
(b) There is an A-recursive function f and a K-recursive function g such that for all m and all $n \geq f(g(m))$ it holds that $C(A(0)A(1)\ldots A(n)) \leq n - m$.
(c) There is an A-recursive function f and a K-recursive function g such that for all m and all $n \geq f(g(m))$ it holds that $H(A(0)A(1)\ldots A(n)) \leq n + H(n) - m$.

Proof. $(a) \Rightarrow (b)$: Let $V_0, V_1, V_2, \ldots$ be the test which witnesses that A is not strongly random. Now let $h(m)$ be the first index e with $\mu(V_e) \leq 2^{-2m-1}$ and let $h_0, h_1, h_2, \ldots$ be a recursive approximation to h; this approximation is from below, as one can define that $h_0(m) = 0$ and

$$h_{s+1}(m) = \begin{cases} h_s(m) & \text{if } \mu(V_{h_s(m),s}) \leq 2^{-2m-1}; \\ h_s(m) + 1 & \text{otherwise.} \end{cases}$$

Now let $g(m) = \langle m, s\rangle$ for the first s such that $h_s(m) = h(m)$. Next define the A-recursive function f which assigns to $\langle m, s\rangle$ the first encountered $\ell > s + m$ satisfying

$$A(0)A(1)\ldots A(\ell) \cdot \{0,1\}^\infty \subseteq V_{h_s(m)}.$$

Now one defines a plain machine M such that, for all m, n with $n \geq 2m + 1$ and all $x \in \{0,1\}^{n-1-2m}$, $M(1^m 0x)$ is the x-th string y of length n for which it is verified in time n that $y \cdot \{0,1\}^\infty \subseteq V_{h_n(m)}$; for small n there might be too many of these strings y and then only the first 2^{n-1-2m} of them are in the range of M; but for $n \geq f(g(m))$ it holds that $h_n(m) = h(m)$ and that therefore by the choice of $V_{h(m)}$ there are at most 2^{n-1-2m} of these strings and each of them occurs in the range of M. One of these strings is the prefix of length n of A. Hence, there is a constant c such that for the function $m \mapsto f(g(m + c))$ and every n greater than the value of this function it holds that

$$C(A(0)A(1)\ldots A(n)) \leq n - m.$$

$(b) \Rightarrow (c)$: This follows from Remark 1 and a substitution of g by $\tilde{g}(m) := g(3m)$.

$(c) \Rightarrow (a)$: It follows from Chaitin's Counting Theorem 2 that if ℓ is sufficiently large, then for all n there are at most $2^{n-m+\ell}$ strings σ of length $n + 1$ with $H(\sigma) \leq n + H(n) - m$. Let $g \leq_T K$ and $f = \varphi_e^A$ be the functions from condition (c). Without loss of generality fix them such that g is recursively approximable from below by $g_0, g_1, g_2, \ldots$ and that f is monotone. Now define $V_{\langle m,n,s\rangle}$ as the class of all sets B satisfying one of the following conditions:

1. $\exists t > s[g_t(m) \neq g_s(m)$ or $H_t(n) \neq H_s(n)]$;
2. $\varphi_e^B(g_s(m)) \downarrow > n$;
3. $H(B(0)B(1)\ldots B(n)) \leq n + H_s(n) - m$.

Note that the first condition ensures that *all* sets are enumerated into those classes $V_{\langle n,m,s\rangle}$ where the parameters are not chosen adequately.

The set A is in every class $V_{\langle m,n,s\rangle}$ as whenever the first condition and the second condition do not put A into $V_{\langle m,n,s\rangle}$ then $g_s(m) = g(m)$ and $H_s(n) = H(n)$ and $\varphi_e^A(g(m)) \leq n$ and therefore $H(A(0)A(1)\dots A(n)) \leq n + H(n) - m$. Furthermore, one can for every m choose the n so large compared to m and the s so large compared to m, n that $g_t(m) = g(m)$ and $H_t(m) = H(m)$ for all $t \geq s$ and $\varphi_e^B(g(m)) \geq n$ only for a class of B of measure below 2^{-m}. It follows then that $\mu(V_{\langle m,n,s\rangle})$ is at most $2^{-m} + 2^{\ell-m}$ as the first condition of putting oracles B into $V_{\langle m,n,s\rangle}$ does not apply, the second condition contributes a class of oracles with measure 2^{-m} and the third condition contributes a class of oracles with measure $2^{\ell-m}$. As ℓ is a constant, one can come as close to measure 0 as desired by starting off with a sufficiently large m and then choosing n in dependence of m and s in dependence on m, n as indicated.

From this sequence of the $V_{\langle m,n,s\rangle}$, one can construct a new sequence of the form $e \mapsto \bigcap_{n\leq e, m\leq e, s\leq e} V_{\langle m,n,s\rangle}$ which satisfies that the measures of the members tend to 0 and that each member contains the set A as an element. Hence this sequence witnesses that A is not strongly random. □

Note that in the above construction the machine M can be chosen such that its domain is recursive, that is, M can be chosen as a decidable machine.

The above conditions (b) and (c) contain a function which is a concatenation of an A-recursive and a K-recursive function. One might ask whether this condition could be simplified by taking only a K-recursive or only an $(A \oplus K)$-recursive function. The answer is "no" as these two choices will give rise to other randomness notions as shown in the next two results.

Theorem 6. *The following are equivalent for every set A:*
(a) A is not Martin-Löf random relative to K;
(b) There is $f \leq_T A \oplus K$ such that $\forall m\, \forall n > f(m)\ [C(A(0)A(1)\dots A(n)) \leq n - m]$;
(c) There is $f \leq_T A \oplus K$ such that $\forall m\, \forall n > f(m)\ [H(A(0)A(1)\dots A(n)) \leq n + H(n) - m]$.

Proof. If A is Martin-Löf random relative to K then the two conditions (b) and (c) cannot be satisfied for any function f by known results [11,12,14]. So assume that (a) holds.

Let U^K be a prefix-free universal machine relative to the oracle K and $x, s \mapsto U_s(x)$ be a recursive approximation to this machine such that every U_s is prefix-free. Now there is an $A \oplus K$-recursive function which produces for every m a number $f(m)$ such that there exists z with $|z| + 2m < |U^K(z)| \leq f(m)$, $U^K(z)$ is a prefix of A and $U_s(z) \downarrow = U^K(z)$ for all $s \geq f(m)$.

Now one can construct a plain machine $\tilde{U}$ which sends every input of the form xy with $x \in \mathrm{dom}(U_{|xy|})$ to $U_{|xy|}(x) \cdot y$ and which is undefined on inputs which cannot be brought into this form; note that because of prefix-freeness for each input u the splitting into xy is unique or does not exist. Now for all m there is a z as above. If $U^K(z) = A(0)A(1)\dots A(k)$, then it follows that

$\tilde{U}(zA(k+1)A(k+2)\dots A(n)) = U_{n+1}(z)\cdot A(k+1)\dots A(n) = A(0)A(1)\dots A(n)$ and hence $C(A(0)A(1)\dots A(n)) \leq (k-2m)+(n-k)+O(1) \leq n-m$ for almost all m and all $n > f(m)$. Note that we can modify f for finitely many m such that f satisfies the condition (b). Remark 1 establishes that (c) follows from (b). □

The next result characterises Kurtz randomness relative to K.

Definition 7. A set A is called *Kurtz-random* iff it is contained in every r.e. class of Lebesgue measure 1.

Theorem 8. *The following are equivalent for every set A:*
(a) A is not Kurtz random relative to K;
(b) There is a sequence of finitely generated r.e. open classes such that each class contains A and the infimum of their measures is 0;
(c) There is a K-recursive function f such that for all m and all $n > f(m)$ it holds that $C(A(0)A(1)\dots A(n)) \leq n-m$;
(d) There is a K-recursive function f such that for all m and all $n > f(m)$ it holds that $H(A(0)A(1)\dots A(n)) \leq n+H(n)-m$.

Proof. $(a) \Rightarrow (b)$: By definition, A is covered by a K-recursive Kurtz-test. According to Bienvenu and Merkle [1, Definition 7] a (K-recursive) Kurtz-test is given by a recursive (K-recursive) function f which determines for each m a finite set $D_{f(m)}$ of strings such that for all m, A has a prefix in $D_{f(m)}$ and the measure of the class of all sets B with a prefix in $D_{f(m)}$ is at most 2^{-m}. For the given K-recursive Kurtz test, let $f_0, f_1, f_2, \dots$ be a recursive approximation of the corresponding function f. Now let $V_{\langle m,s\rangle} = \{B : B$ has a prefix in $D_{f_t(m)}$ for some $t \geq s\}$. It is clear that every $V_{\langle m,s\rangle}$ contains A as a prefix of A is in almost all $D_{f_t(m)}$. Furthermore, as the f_t converge, the union of all $D_{f_t(m)}$ with $t \geq s$ is finite and contains only finitely many strings; that is, the r.e. class generated by it is finitely generated. Furthermore, for every m and every sufficiently large s, $f_t(m) = f(m)$ for all $t \geq s$ and hence $V_{m,s}$ has at most measure 2^{-m}.

$(b) \Rightarrow (c)$: Let $V_0, V_1, V_2, \dots$ be a given sequence of finitely generated r.e. open classes as in condition (b). Let $V_{e,s}$ be the class of all B for which is verified in time s that they belong to V_e; by choice there is for every e an s with $V_{e,s} = V_e$. For every m let $g_s(m)$ be the smallest number e such that $\mu(V_{e,s}) < 2^{-3m-1}$.

This function $g_s(m)$ is always defined as it is bounded by the index $g(m)$ of the first class whose measure is strictly below 2^{-3m-1}. Now let $f(m)$ be the first step s such that $g_s(m) = g(m)$ and $V_{g_s(m),s} = V_{g(m)}$, that is, all sets which are put into $V_{g(m)}$ are already enumerated into it. Observe that $g_t(m) = g(m)$ for all $t \geq f(m)$. Now let $M(1^m0x)$ be the x-th string y of length $n+1$ found in $V_{g_n(m)}$ where $n = 3m+|x|$. Note that $A(0)A(1)\dots A(n)$ is in the range of M whenever $n > f(m)$. As the corresponding 1^m0x has the length $(n+1)-2m$, it follows that $C(A(0)A(1)\dots A(n)) \leq n-2m+O(1) \leq n-m$ for almost all m and all $n > f(m)$. Hence, by a suitable finite modification of f one obtains condition (c).

$(c) \Rightarrow (d)$: This follows from Remark 1 and a substitution of f by $\tilde{f}(m) := f(3m)$.

$(d) \Rightarrow (a)$: Again, by the Counting Theorem 2 there is a constant c such that for every n, m there are at most 2^{n-m+c} strings σ of length $n+1$ with $H(\sigma) \leq n + H(n) - m$. Furthermore let f be given as in condition (d); in particular $H(A(0)A(1)\dots A(f(m)))$ is at most $f(m) + H(f(m)) - m$. The measure of the class of the sets B with the same property is at most 2^{-m-1+c}. It follows that the mapping of m to the class of all B with $H(B(0)B(1)\dots B(f(m+c))) \leq f(m+c) + H(f(m+c)) - m$ is a Kurtz test relative to K. □

Let A be given such that every A-recursive function is majorised by a K-recursive one. Then the above characterisations show that A is strongly random iff A is Kurtz random relative to K. But this coincidence does not hold in general as 2-generic sets are Kurtz random relative to K but not strongly random. It should also be noted that there is no oracle B such that every set A which is not strongly random satisfies that there is an B-recursive function f with $C(A(0)A(1)\dots A(n)) \leq n - m$ for all m and all $n > f(m)$. Hence the condition in Theorem 5 cannot be replaced by a class of functions which is independent of the set A analyzed. It should be noted that the characterisation of "Schnorr random relative to K" is quite similar to that one of "Kurtz random relative to K".

Theorem 9. *The following are equivalent for a set A:*
(a) A is not Schnorr random relative to K;
(b) There is a K-recursive function f such that for infinitely many m and all $n > f(m)$ it holds that $C(A(0)A(1)\dots A(n)) \leq n - m$;
(c) There is a K-recursive function f such that for infinitely many m and all $n > f(m)$ it holds that $H(A(0)A(1)\dots A(n)) \leq n + H(n) - m$.

Proof. $(a) \Rightarrow (b)$: Downey and Griffiths [5] showed that a set A is not Schnorr random iff there is a recursive sequence of strings $\sigma_0, \sigma_1, \sigma_2, \dots$ such that infinitely many of these strings are prefixes of A and $\sum_j 2^{-|\sigma_j|}$ is a finite rational number; without loss of generality let the sum be 1. This characterisation can be relativised to K by taking the sequence to be K-recursive. Now one can choose a K-recursive sequence $n_0, n_1, \dots$ of indices such that for each m it holds that $\sum_{\ell \geq n_m} 2^{-|\sigma_\ell|} \leq 2^{-3m}$; this n_m can be found as the first number with $\sum_{\ell < n_m} 2^{-|\sigma_\ell|} > 1 - 2^{-3m}$. Note that the measure of each subsum $\sum_{\ell = n_m, n_m+1, \dots, n_{m+1}} 2^{-|\sigma_\ell|}$ is also bounded by 2^{-3m}. Now one can define a plain machine M such that $M(1^m 0 \tau)$ is the τ-th string of length $|\tau| + 3m$ which extends one of the finitely many strings $\sigma^t_{n_m}, \sigma^t_{n_m+1}, \dots, \sigma^t_{n_{m+1}}$, where $t = |\tau| + 3m$ and σ^s_n is the value of σ_n after s steps in some recursive approximation of the sequence. When approximating n_m, n_{m+1} and the strings $\sigma_{n_m}, \sigma_{n_m+1}, \dots, \sigma_{n_{m+1}}$, there is a K-recursive function f such that $f(m)$ is an upper bound on the time which is necessary to converge to the correct values; furthermore, one can choose $f(m)$ to be also an upper bound on $|\sigma_\ell| + 3m$ for each of these strings. It follows that for each string η of length at least $f(m)$ there is a string τ of length $|\eta| - 3m$ such that $M(1^m 0 \tau) = \eta$; hence the plain Kolmogorov complexity of all of these strings η is at most $|\eta| + c - 2m$ for some constant c. As there are infinitely many m such that one of the σ_ℓ with $n_m \leq \ell \leq n_{m+1}$ is a prefix of A, it follows that there are infinitely many m such that for all $n \geq f(m)$ it holds that $C(A(0)A(1)\ldots A(n)) \leq n - m$.

$(b) \Rightarrow (c)$: This follows from Remark 1 and a substitution of f by $\tilde{f}(m) := f(3m)$.

$(c) \Rightarrow (a)$: Let $S_m^{c'} := \{B : H(B(0)\ldots B(f(m+c'))) \leq f(m+c')+H(m+c')-m\}$. The Counting Theorem 2 yields a c' such that $(S_m^{c'})_{m\in\omega}$ can be enlarged to a total Solovay test (as defined by Downey and Griffiths [5]) relative to K. This test covers A, so A is not Schnorr random relative to K. □

3 Characterising Demuth Randomness

Demuth has defined in the context of analysis a randomness notion which was formalised as follows in the framework of algorithmic randomness [13, Definition 3.6.24].

Definition 10. In the following let $V_0, V_1, V_2, \ldots$ be an acceptable numbering of all r.e. open classes. Now one says that a set A is Demuth random iff there is no ω-r.e. function f such that $\mu(V_{f(m)}) \leq 2^{-m}$ for all m and $A \in V_{f(m)}$ for infinitely many m.

Theorem 11. *The following are equivalent for a set A:*
(a) A is not Demuth random;
(b) There exist ω-r.e. functions g and h such that $A \in V_{g(m),h(m)}$ for infinitely many m and $\mu(V_{g(m),h(m)}) \leq 2^{-m}$ for all m;
(c) There exists an ω-r.e. function k such that for infinitely many m and all $n \geq k(m)$ it holds that $C(A(0)A(1)\ldots A(n)) \leq n - m$;
(d) There exists an ω-r.e. function $\tilde{k}$ such that for infinitely many m and all $n \geq \tilde{k}(m)$ it holds that $H(A(0)A(1)\ldots A(n)) \leq n + H(n) - m$.

Proof. $(a) \Rightarrow (b)$: Let f be the ω-r.e. function witnessing that A is not Demuth random. Now define a function $\tilde{h}(e,m)$ such that $\tilde{h}(e,m)$ is the maximum step $s > 0$ for which there is $\ell \in \{1, 2, \ldots, 2^m - 1\}$ with $\mu(V_{e,s-1}) \leq \ell \cdot 2^{-m} < \mu(V_{e,s})$; if no such step exists then $\tilde{h}(e,m) = 0$ and $V_{e,0} = \emptyset$. Note that $\mu(V_e) - \mu(V_{e,\tilde{h}(e,m)}) \leq 2^{-m}$. Given $f, \tilde{h}$, consider a function g such that

$$V_{g(m)} = \bigcup_{\ell=0,1,\ldots,m,m+1} (V_{f(\ell),\tilde{h}(f(\ell),2m+4-\ell)} - V_{f(\ell),\tilde{h}(f(\ell),2m+2-\ell)})$$

and the function h defined by

$$h(m) = \max\{\tilde{h}(f(\ell), 2m+4-\ell) : \ell \in \{0, 1, \ldots, m, m+1\}\}.$$

Without loss of generality we may assume $V_{g(m)} = V_{g(m),h(m)}$. Furthermore,

$$\begin{aligned}\mu(V_{f(\ell),\tilde{h}(f(\ell),2m+4-\ell)} - V_{f(\ell),\tilde{h}(f(\ell),2m+2-\ell)}) &\leq \mu(V_{f(\ell)} - V_{f(\ell),\tilde{h}(f(\ell),2m+2-\ell)}) \\ &\leq 2^{\ell-2m-2}\end{aligned}$$

and therefore $\mu(V_{g(m)}) \leq 2^{-m-1} + 2^{-m-2} + \ldots + 2^{-2m-2} \leq 2^{-m}$. It remains to show that g and h are ω-r.e. and that $A \in V_{g(m)} = V_{g(m),h(m)}$. As f and $\tilde{h}$ are both ω-r.e. and $\tilde{h}(e,m)$ makes at most 2^m mind changes, the functions g and h are also ω-r.e. functions. Now consider any i. Then there is $j > i+1$ such that $A \in V_{f(j)}$. It follows that there is an $m \geq j-1$ such that $A \in V_{f(j),\tilde{h}(f(j),2m+4-j)} - V_{f(j),\tilde{h}(f(j),2m+2-j)}$; the reason is that $\mu(V_f(j)) \leq 2^{-j}$ and thus $\tilde{h}(f(j), 2m+2-j) = 0$ for $m \leq j-1$. Now $V_{g(m)}$ contains A and $m > i$. Hence there are infinitely many m with $A \in V_{g(m),h(m)}$. So (b) holds.

$(b) \Rightarrow (c)$: Let g, h be given as required in (b) and assume that $g_s(m) \neq g_{s+1}(m) \vee h_s(m) \neq h_{s+1}(m)$ implies that $h_{s+1}(m) \geq s+1$. Otherwise one can without loss of generality modify g and h accordingly while preserving (b). Now let $M(1^m0x)$ be the x-th string found in $\{0,1\}^s$ such that $s = |x| + 3m$ and $M(1^m0x) \cdot \{0,1\}^\infty \subseteq V_{g_s(3m),s} \cup V_{g_s(3m+1),s} \cup V_{g_s(3m+2),s}$. For infinitely many m and all $n > \max\{h(3m), h(3m+1), h(3m+2)\}$ it holds that $A(0)A(1)\ldots A(n) \cdot \{0,1\}^\infty \subseteq V_{g(3m)} \cup V_{g(3m+1)} \cup V_{g(3m+2)}$. For such m, n there are only 2^{n+1-3m} strings of length n qualifying for the search condition, hence there is an x of length $n+1-3m$ such that $M(1^m0x) = A(0)A(1)\ldots A(n)$ and — if m is furthermore large enough — $C(A(0)A(1)\ldots A(n)) \leq n - m$. Hence one can choose k to be a finite variant of the ω-r.e. function $m \mapsto \max\{h(3m), h(3m+1), h(3m+2)\} + 1$ in order to satisfy condition (c).

$(c) \Rightarrow (d)$: This follows from Remark 1 by choosing $\tilde{k}(m) := k(3m)$.

$(d) \Rightarrow (a)$: Let $\tilde{k}$ be as in condition (d). There is a function f defining the class $V_{f(m)} = \{B : H(B(0)B(1)\ldots B(\tilde{k}(2m))) \leq \tilde{k}(2m) + H(\tilde{k}(2m)) - 2m\}$.

Note that $V_{f(m)}$ has at most measure 2^{-m} for almost all m and we can assume that $V_{f(m)}$ contains A for infinitely many m (otherwise we can replace $\tilde{k}$ by the function $n \mapsto \tilde{k}(n+1)$). Furthermore, there is a recursive function which maps each triple (m, a, b) to an index for the class $\{B : H(B(0)B(1)\ldots B(a)) \leq a + b - 2m\}$ and therefore maps $(m, \tilde{k}(2m), H(\tilde{k}(2m)))$ to $f(m)$. There is a recursive function $\hat{k}$ such that the approximation of $\tilde{k}(m)$ makes at most $\hat{k}(m)$ mind changes. As one can code m and the number of mind changes in order to get $\tilde{k}(m)$, for almost all m, the value $H(\tilde{k}(m))$ is at most $\hat{k}(m)+m$ and once the value $\tilde{k}(m)$ has stabilised, $H(\tilde{k}(m))$ can be approximated from above with $\hat{k}(m) + m$ many mind changes. It follows that the mapping $m \mapsto (\tilde{k}(2m), H(\tilde{k}(2m)))$ is ω-r.e. with the number of mind changes bounded by $(\hat{k}(2m) + 2m)^2$ for almost all m. Hence the function f can be taken to be ω-r.e. as well. Then, after a finite modification which preserves f to be ω-r.e., one has that not only for almost all m but indeed for all m the measure of $V_{f(m)}$ is bounded by 2^{-m}. So A is not Demuth random. □

4 Characterising Turing-Incomplete Martin-Löf Random Sets

Recall that a set A is PA-complete iff there is an A-recursive consistent and complete extension of Peano Arithmetic. This condition is equivalent to saying that every partial-recursive $\{0,1\}$-valued function has a total A-recursive extension. Stephan [21] showed that a Martin-Löf random set is Turing above K iff it is PA-complete. This showed that the Martin-Löf random sets fall into two classes: those above K which coincide with the PA-complete ones and those not above K which coincide with the PA-incomplete ones. The next result shows that the PA-incomplete Martin-Löf random sets have a natural characterisation in terms of initial segment complexity. Note that all Demuth random and all strongly random sets are PA-incomplete. On the other hand, there are Martin-Löf random sets which are PA-complete like Chaitin's Ω. Gács [6] and Kučera [7] showed that every $\mathbf{a} \geq_T K$ contains a Martin-Löf random set and those are PA-complete.

Theorem 12. *The following statements are equivalent for a set A:*
(a) A is PA-complete or A is not Martin-Löf random;
(b) $A \geq_T K$ or A is not Martin-Löf random;
(c) There is an A-recursive function f such that $C(A(0)A(1)\ldots A(n)) \leq n - m$ for all m and all $n > f(m)$;
(d) There is an A-recursive function f such that $H(A(0)A(1)\ldots A(n)) \leq n + H(n) - m$ for all m and all $n > f(m)$.

Proof. $(a) \Leftrightarrow (b)$ is already known [21] and $(c) \Rightarrow (d)$ follows from Remark 1.

$(b) \Rightarrow (c)$: If A is not Martin-Löf random, the construction of f is straightforward, using the fact that A has $2m$-compressible prefixes for each m.

If $K \leq_T A$, then if A were Martin-Löf random relative to K, K would be a base for ML-randomness. By [13, Theorem 5.1.22] we would have $K \in \text{Low(MLR)}$, a contradiction. So A is not Martin-Löf random relative to K and by Theorem 6 there is an $A \oplus K$-recursive function f with

$$\forall m\, \forall n > f(m)\ [C(A(0)A(1)\ldots A(n)) \leq n - m].$$

By assumption, this function f is also A-recursive and satisfies the claim.

$(d) \Rightarrow (b)$: Assume that $A \not\geq_T K$ as otherwise there is nothing to prove. Let f be as in condition (d) and let U be the universal prefix-free machine that defines H. The function $m \mapsto f(2m)$ is A-recursive and does not majorise the function

$$g\colon m \mapsto \max\{U(\tau) : \tau \in \text{dom}(U) \cap \{0,1\}^m\},$$

since $A \not\geq_T K$ and only oracles Turing above K can compute functions which majorise g. Hence there are infinitely many m where the largest value $U(\tau)$ for $\tau \in \text{dom}(U) \cap \{0,1\}^m$ is beyond $f(2m)$. By assumption on f and τ,

$$H(A(0)A(1)\ldots A(U(\tau))) \leq U(\tau) + H(U(\tau)) - 2m \leq U(\tau) + |\tau| - 2m = U(\tau) - m.$$

This shows that A is not Martin-Löf random. □

Stephan and Wu [22] called a set A strongly Kurtz random iff there is no recursive function f such that $H(A(0)A(1)\ldots A(f(m))) \leq f(m) - m$ for all m. Applying similar methods as above this can be generalized as follows.

Theorem 13. *The following are equivalent for a set A:*
(a) A is not strongly Kurtz-random;
(b) There is a recursive function g such that $C(A(0)A(1)\dots A(n)) \leq n - m$ for all m and all $n > g(m)$;
(c) There is a recursive function h such that $H(A(0)A(1)\dots A(n)) \leq n + H(n) - m$ for all m and all $n > h(m)$.

5 Conclusion and Future Work

The overall idea of this article is to measure the degree of randomness of a set A by analyzing the function

$$R^A(m) = \min\{k \in \mathbb{N} \cup \{\infty\} : \forall n\, [k < n < \infty \Rightarrow C(A(0)A(1)\dots A(n)) \leq n - m]\}.$$

Note that $R^A(m) \leq R^A(m+1)$ for all m and that A is Kolmogorov random iff R^A assumes the value ∞ on some inputs. One can now reformulate the main results of the paper in terms of the function R^A. For example, A is strongly random iff there are no $f \leq_T A$ and no $g \leq_T K$ such that the concatenation $n \mapsto f(g(n))$ dominates R^A. Here f dominates g iff $f(m) \geq g(m)$ for almost all $m \in \mathbb{N}$. The other results in this article can be formulated analogously in an obvious way.

When looking at R^A, one could define a new reducibility as follows.

Definition 14. A set A is said to be Kurtz-Kolmogorov-reducible to B ($A \leq_{KK} B$) if there is a recursive function f and a constant c such that for all $m \in \mathbb{N}$ it holds that $R^A(m) \leq f(R^B(m + c))$. Here, f is extended to $\mathbb{N} \cup \{\infty\}$ by letting $f(\infty) = \infty$, where the conventions $\infty \leq \infty$ and $\infty \not\leq n$ hold for all $n \in \mathbb{N}$.

Note that this definition is invariant under recursive permutations g, so if $B = \{g(n) : n \in A\}$ then $A \equiv_{KK} B$. Also, it holds that all sets A, B satisfy $A \oplus B \leq_{KK} A$. This meets the intuition that a sequence can become more random but not less random by omitting half of the bits.

Besides this, it can be seen that the following classes are closed upward under KK-reducibility (that is, whenever A is in the class and $A \leq_{KK} B$ then also B is in the class): the class of all Kolmogorov random sets (as it consists of the greatest KK-degree); the class of all strongly Kurtz random sets (as it consists of all degrees except the least one); the class of all Demuth random sets; the class of all sets which are Kurtz random relative to K; the class of all sets which are Schnorr random relative to K.

The reason is that for all of these classes, the randomness notion is defined by comparing the growth rate of R^A with that of a certain list of functions which do not depend on A.

Somehow, for the classes $\{A : A$ is strongly random$\}$ and $\{A : A$ is Martin-Löf random and $A \not\geq_T K\}$, A becomes involved and the upward closure is no longer guaranteed. Indeed, it would be interesting to know whether the role of A could be replaced by something else, so that one or both of the mentioned classes would be closed upward with respect to KK-reducibility. Another topic for study could be the properties of KK-reducibility and its interactions with other reducibilities.

Acknowledgements. The authors want to thank Laurent Bienvenu and Wolfgang Merkle for fruitful discussions and ideas used in this paper.

References

1. Bienvenu, L., Merkle, W.: Reconciling Data Compression and Kolmogorov Complexity. In: Arge, L., Cachin, C., Jurdziński, T., Tarlecki, A. (eds.) ICALP 2007. LNCS, vol. 4596, pp. 643–654. Springer, Heidelberg (2007)
2. Calude, C.S.: Information and Randomness. In: An Algorithmic Perspective, 2nd edn., Springer, Heidelberg (2002)
3. Chaitin, G.J.: A theory of program size formally identical to information theory. Journal of the ACM 22, 329–340 (1975)
4. Downey, R., Nies, A., Weber, R., Yu, L.: Lowness and Π_2^0 Nullsets. Journal of Symbolic Logic 71, 1044–1052 (2006)
5. Downey, R., Griffiths, E.: On Schnorr randomness. Journal of Symbolic Logic 69, 533–554 (2004)
6. Gács, P.: Every sequence is reducible to a random one. Information and Control 70, 186–192 (1986)
7. Kučera, A.: Measure, Π_1^0-classes and complete extensions of PA. In: PPSN 1996. LNM, vol. 1141, pp. 245–259. Springer, Heidelberg (1985)
8. Kurtz, S.A.: Randomness and genericity in the degrees of unsolvatibility. PhD dissertation, University of Illinois at Urbana-Champaign (1981)
9. Li, M., Vitányi, P.: An Introduction to Kolmogorov Complexity and Its Applications, 3rd edn. Springer, Heidelberg (2008)
10. Martin-Löf, P.: The definition of random sequences. Information and Control 9, 602–619 (1966)
11. Miller, J.S.: Every 2-random real is Kolmogorov random. Journal of Symbolic Logic 69, 907–913 (2004)
12. Miller, J.S.: The K-degrees, low for K degrees and weakly low for K oracles. Notre Dame Journal of Formal Logic (to appear)
13. Nies, A.: Computability and Randomness. Oxford Science Publications (2009)
14. Nies, A., Stephan, F., Terwijn, S.A.: Randomness, relativization and Turing degrees. Journal of Symbolic Logic 70, 515–535 (2005)
15. Odifreddi, P.: Classical Recursion Theory I. North-Holland, Amsterdam (1989)
16. Odifreddi, P.: Classical Recursion Theory II. Elsevier, Amsterdam (1999)
17. Osherson, D., Weinstein, S.: Recognizing the strong random reals. The Review of Symbolic Logic 1, 56–63 (2008)
18. Williams, H.C. (ed.): CRYPTO 1985. LNCS, vol. 218. Springer, Heidelberg (1971)
19. Schnorr, C.-P.: Process complexity and effective random tests. Journal of Computer and System Sciences 7, 376–388 (1973)
20. Soare, R.I.: Recursively Enumerable Sets and Degrees. Springer, Heidelberg (1987)
21. Stephan, F.: Martin-Löf Random and PA-complete Sets. In: Proceedings of ASL Logic Colloquium 2002. ASL Lecture Notes in Logic, vol. 27, pp. 342–348 (2006)
22. Stephan, F., Wu, G.: Presentations of K-Trivial Reals and Kolmogorov Complexity. In: Cooper, S.B., Löwe, B., Torenvliet, L. (eds.) CiE 2005. LNCS, vol. 3526, pp. 461–469. Springer, Heidelberg (2005)

Topologies Refining the Cantor Topology on X^ω

Sibylle Schwarz[1] and Ludwig Staiger[2]

[1] Fachgruppe Informatik, Westsächsische Hochschule Zwickau
sibylle.schwarz@fh-zwickau.de
[2] Institut für Informatik, Martin-Luther-Universität Halle-Wittenberg
staiger@informatik.uni-halle.de

Abstract. The space of one-sided infinite words plays a crucial rôle in several parts of Theoretical Computer Science. Usually, it is convenient to regard this space as a metric space, the Cantor-space. It turned out that for several purposes topologies other than the one of the Cantor-space are useful, e.g. for studying fragments of first-order logic over infinite words or for a topological characterisation of random infinite words.

It is shown that both of these topologies refine the topology of the Cantor-space. Moreover, from common features of these topologies we extract properties which characterise a large class of topologies. It turns out that, for this general class of topologies, the corresponding closure and interior operators respect the shift operations and also, to some respect, the definability of sets of infinite words by finite automata.

The space of one-sided infinite words plays a crucial rôle in several parts of Theoretical Computer Science (see [7,20] and the surveys [6,13,17,18]). Usually, it is convenient to regard this space as a topological space provided with the CANTOR topology. This topology can be also considered as the natural continuation of the left topology of the prefix relation on the space of finite words; for a survey see [2].

It turned out that for several purposes other topologies on the space of infinite words are also useful [9,12], e.g. for investigations in first-order logic [3], to characterise the set of random infinite words [1] or the set of disjunctive infinite words [15] and to describe the converging behaviour of not necessarily hyperbolic iterative function systems [5,14].

Most of these papers use topologies on the space of infinite words which are certain refinements of the CANTOR topology showing a certain kind of shift invariance. The aim of this paper is to give a unified treatment of those topologies and to investigate their relations to CANTOR topology.

Special attention is paid to subsets of the space of infinite words definable by finite automata. It turns out that several of the refinements of the CANTOR topology under consideration behave well with respect to finite automata, that is, the corresponding closure and interior operators preserve at least one of the classes of finite-state or regular ω-languages.

C.S. Calude and V. Sassone (Eds.): TCS 2010, IFIP AICT 323, pp. 271–285, 2010.

1 Notation and Preliminaries

We introduce the notation used throughout the paper. By $\mathbb{N} = \{0, 1, 2, \ldots\}$ we denote the set of natural numbers. Let X be a finite alphabet of cardinality $|X| = r \geq 2$. By X^* we denote the set (monoid) of words on X, including the *empty word* e, and X^ω is the set of infinite sequences (ω-words) over X. For $w \in X^*$ and $\eta \in X^* \cup X^\omega$ let $w \cdot \eta$ be their *concatenation*. This concatenation product extends in an obvious way to subsets $W \subseteq X^*$ and $P \subseteq X^* \cup X^\omega$. For a language W let $W^* := \bigcup_{i \in \mathbb{N}} W^i$ be the *submonoid* of X^* generated by W, and by $W^\omega := \{w_1 \cdots w_i \cdots : w_i \in W \setminus \{e\}\}$ we denote the set of infinite strings formed by concatenating words in W. Furthermore $|w|$ is the *length* of the word $w \in X^*$ and $\mathbf{pref}(P)$ is the set of all finite prefixes of strings in $P \subseteq X^* \cup X^\omega$. We shall abbreviate $w \in \mathbf{pref}(\eta)$ ($\eta \in X^* \cup X^\omega$) by $w \sqsubseteq \eta$. A language $V \subseteq X^*$ is called a *prefix-free* provided for arbitrary $w, v \in V$ the relation $w \sqsubseteq v$ implies $w = v$.

Further we denote by $P/w := \{\eta : w \cdot \eta \in P\}$ the *left derivative* or *state* of the set $P \subseteq X^* \cup X^\omega$ generated by the word w. We refer to P as *finite-state* provided the set of states $\{P/w : w \in X^*\}$ is finite. It is well-known that a language $W \subseteq X^*$ is finite state if and only if it is accepted by a finite automaton, that is, it is a regular language.[1]

In the case of ω-languages *regular ω-languages*, that is, ω-languages accepted by finite automata, are the finite unions of sets of the form $W \cdot V^\omega$, where W and V are regular languages (cf. e.g. [13]). In particular, every regular ω-language is finite-state, but, as it was observed in [19], not every finite-state ω-language is regular (cf. also [11]).

It is well-known that the families of regular or finite-state ω-languages are closed under Boolean operations [7,20,6,13,17,18] or [11].

1.1 Topological Spaces in General

A topological space is a pair $(\mathcal{X}, \mathcal{O})$ where $\mathcal{X}$ is a non-empty set and $\mathcal{O} \subseteq 2^{\mathcal{X}}$ is a family of subsets of $\mathcal{X}$ which is closed under arbitrary union and under finite intersection. The family $\mathcal{O}$ is usually called the family of *open* subsets of the space $\mathcal{X}$. Their complements are referred to as *closed* sets of the space $\mathcal{X}$.

As usually, a set $\mathbb{B} \subseteq \mathcal{O}$ is a *base* for a topology $(\mathcal{X}, \mathcal{O})$ on $\mathcal{X}$ provided every set $M \in \mathcal{O}$ is the (possibly empty) union of sets from $\mathbb{B}$. Thus it does no harm if one considers bases containing $\emptyset$. It is well-known that a family of subsets $\mathbb{B}$ of a set $\mathcal{T}$ which is closed under finite intersection generates in this way a topology on $\mathcal{T}$.

Kuratowski observed that topological spaces can be likewise defined using closure or interior operators. A topological *interior* operator $\mathcal{J}$ is a mapping $\mathcal{J} : 2^{\mathcal{X}} \to 2^{\mathcal{X}}$ satisfying the following relations. It assigns to a subset $M \subseteq \mathcal{X}$ the largest open set contained in M.

[1] Observe that the relation $\sim_P$ defined by $w \sim_P v$ iff $P/w = P/v$ is the Nerode right congruence of P.

$$\begin{aligned}\mathcal{J}\mathcal{X} &= \mathcal{X}\\ \mathcal{J}\mathcal{J}M &= \mathcal{J}M \subseteq M \text{ , and}\\ \mathcal{J}(M_1 \cap M_2) &= \mathcal{J}M_1 \cap \mathcal{J}M_2\end{aligned} \tag{1}$$

The interior operator $\mathcal{J}$ mapping each subset $M \subseteq \mathcal{X}$ to the largest open set contained in M can be described as follows.

$$\mathcal{J}(M) := \bigcup \{B : B \subseteq M \wedge B \in \mathbb{B}\} \tag{2}$$

Using the complementary (duality) relation between open and closed sets one defines the *closure* (smallest closed set containing) of M as follows.

$$\mathcal{C}M := \mathcal{X} \setminus \mathcal{J}(\mathcal{X} \setminus M) \tag{3}$$

Then the following holds.

$$\begin{aligned}\mathcal{C}\emptyset &= \emptyset\\ \mathcal{C}\mathcal{C}M &= \mathcal{C}M \supseteq M\\ \mathcal{C}(M_1 \cup M_2) &= \mathcal{C}M_1 \cup \mathcal{C}M_2\end{aligned} \tag{4}$$

As usual, in a topological space, we denote the classes of countable unions of closed sets as $\mathbf{F}_\sigma$ and of countable intersections of open sets as $\mathbf{G}_\delta$.

1.2 The Cantor-Space: Basic Properties

In this section we list some properties of the Cantor-space (see [7,13,17,20]).

We consider the space of infinite words (ω-words) X^ω as a metric space with metric ρ defined as follows

$$\rho(\xi,\eta) := \begin{cases} 0, & \text{if } \xi = \eta \text{ , and}\\ \sup\{|X|^{-|w|} : w \in \mathbf{pref}(\xi) \cap \mathbf{pref}(\eta)\} & \text{if } \xi \neq \eta \,. \end{cases} \tag{5}$$

This space (X^ω, ρ) can be also considered as a topological space with base $\mathbb{B}_C := \{w \cdot X^\omega : w \in X^*\} \cup \{\emptyset\}$.[2]

Then the following is well-known.

Property 1

1. Open sets in Cantor-space (X^ω, ρ) are of the form $W \cdot X^\omega$ where $W \subseteq X^*$.
2. A subset $E \subseteq X^\omega$ is open and closed (clopen) if and only if $E = W \cdot X^\omega$ where $W \subseteq X^*$ is finite.
3. A subset $F \subseteq X^\omega$ is closed if and only if $F = \{\xi : \mathbf{pref}(\xi) \subseteq \mathbf{pref}(F)\}$.
4. $\mathcal{C}(F) := \{\xi : \xi \in X^\omega \wedge \mathbf{pref}(\xi) \subseteq \mathbf{pref}(F)\} = \bigcap_{n\in\mathbb{N}} (\mathbf{pref}(F) \cap X^n) \cdot X^\omega$ is the closure of F.
5. If F is a finite-state ω-language then $\mathcal{C}(F)$ and $\mathcal{J}(F)$ are regular ω-languages.

[2] It is sometimes convenient to include the empty set into a base. Here $\mathbb{B}_C$ becomes a Boolean algebra.

Moreover, the CANTOR-space (X^ω, ρ) is a compact space, that is, for every family of open sets $(E_i)_{i\in I}$ such that $\bigcup_{i\in I} E_i = X^\omega$ there is a finite sub-family $(E_i)_{i\in I'}$ satisfying $\bigcup_{i\in I'} E_i = X^\omega$. This property is in some sense characteristic for the CANTOR topology on X^ω. In particular, no topology refining CANTOR topology and having at least one isolated point[3] is compact.

Lemma 1. *Let $(X^\omega, \mathcal{O})$ be a topology such that $\{W \cdot X^\omega : W \subseteq X^*\} \subseteq \mathcal{O}$ and there is a $\xi \in X^\omega$ satisfying $\{\xi\} \in \mathcal{O}$. Then the space $(X^\omega, \mathcal{O})$ is not compact.*

Proof. It suffices to give an infinite family $(E_i)_{i\in\mathbb{N}}$ of pairwise disjoint open sets with $\bigcup_{i\in\mathbb{N}} E_i = X^\omega$.

Let $U := (\mathbf{pref}(\xi) \cdot X) \setminus \mathbf{pref}(\xi)$. Then the sets $w \cdot X^\omega$, $w \in U$, are pairwise disjoint and satisfy $\xi \notin w \cdot X^\omega$. It is now easy to see that $X^\omega = \{\xi\} \cup \bigcup_{w\in U} w \cdot X^\omega$.

1.3 Regular ω-Languages

As a last part of this section we mention some facts on regular ω-languages known from the literature, e.g. [7,13,17,20].

The first one shows the importance of ultimately periodic ω-words. Denote by $\mathsf{Ult} := \{w \cdot v^\omega : w, v \in X^* \setminus \{e\}\}$ the set of ultimately periodic ω-words.

Lemma 2 (Büchi). *The class of regular ω-languages is a Boolean algebra.*

Every non-empty regular ω-language contains an ultimately periodic ω-word, and regular ω-languages $E, F \subseteq X^\omega$ coincide if only $E \cap \mathsf{Ult} = F \cap \mathsf{Ult}$.

The next one gives a connection between accepting devices and topology.

Theorem 1 (Landweber). *An ω-language F is accepted by a deterministic* BÜCHI *automaton if and only if F is regular and a $\mathbf{G}_\delta$-set.*

And, finally, we obtain a topological sufficient condition when finite-state ω-languages are regular.

Theorem 2 ([11]). *Every finite-state ω-language in the class $\mathbf{F}_\sigma \cap \mathbf{G}_\delta$ is already regular.*

2 Topologies Refining the CANTOR Topology

In this section we consider some general principles pursued in this paper of the refinement of the CANTOR topology. Most of the following topologies are defined by introducing a suitable base for the topology. In the sequel, we will often require that our bases $\mathbb{B} \subseteq 2^{X^\omega}$ in the space X^ω satisfy the following condition.

Definition 1. *We will refer to a base $\mathbb{B}$ for a topology $\mathcal{T}$ on X^ω as* shift-invariant *provided*

$$\forall F \forall w \forall v (F \in \mathbb{B} \wedge w \in X^* \wedge v \in \mathbf{pref}(F) \rightarrow w \cdot F, F/v \in \mathbb{B}) . \tag{6}$$

[3] A point $\xi \in X^\omega$ is called *isolated* if $\{\xi\}$ is an open set.

The property in Definition 1 is, in particular, satisfied for the base $\mathbb{B}_C$. It is now easy to see that for shift-invariant bases the following holds true.

Topologies on the space of finite words satisfying the same condition as in Eq. (6) were investigated in [8].

Property 2. 1. If $\mathbb{B}$ is a shift invariant base for a topology on X^ω then $\forall w(w \in X^* \to \forall E(E \in \mathbb{B} \leftrightarrow w \cdot E \in \mathbb{B}))$.
2. If $\mathbb{B}$ is a base for a topology on X^ω satisfying $X^\omega \in \mathbb{B}$ and $\forall w(w \in X^* \to \forall E(E \in \mathbb{B} \leftrightarrow w \cdot E \in \mathbb{B}))$ then $\mathbb{B}$ is shift-invariant.
3. A topology $\mathcal{T}$ on X^ω has a shift-invariant base if and only if $\forall w\big(w \in X^* \to \forall E(E \text{ is open in } \mathcal{T} \leftrightarrow w \cdot E \text{ is open in } \mathcal{T})\big)$.

The proof of Property 2.3 uses the obvious fact that the set of all open sets is itself a base for the topology.

Moreover, Property 2.3 shows that all topologies on X^ω having a shift-invariant base refine the Cantor topology. The converse is not true as we shall see in Section 4.3.

Next we are going to describe the interior operator in topologies on X^ω having a shift-invariant base. To this end we call a subset $M_\mathbb{B} \subseteq \mathbb{B}$ of a base a *shift generator* of $\mathbb{B}$ provided $\mathbb{B} \setminus \{\emptyset\} \subseteq \{w \cdot E : w \in X^* \wedge E \in M_\mathbb{B}\}$. In particular, if $\mathbb{B}$ is shift invariant, $\mathbb{B}$ itself and $\mathbb{B} \setminus \{\emptyset\}$ are shift generators of $\mathbb{B}$. For the Cantor topology, for instance, $M_{\mathbb{B}_C} = \{X^\omega\}$ is a minimal shift generator of $\mathbb{B}_C$.

Now, the interior operator can be described using a suitably chosen shift generator $M_\mathbb{B}$ and the following construction. Let $E, F \subseteq X^\omega$. We set

$$L(F; E) := \{w : w \in X^* \wedge F/w \supseteq E\} . \tag{7}$$

Lemma 3. *Let $\mathbb{B}$ be a shift-invariant base, and let $M_\mathbb{B} \subseteq \mathbb{B}$ be a shift generator of $\mathbb{B}$. If $\mathcal{J}$ is the corresponding interior operator then*

$$\mathcal{J}(F) = \bigcup\nolimits_{E \in M_\mathbb{B}} L(F; E) \cdot E$$

for every $F \subseteq X^\omega$.

Proof. Since $\mathcal{J}(F)$ is open, it is a union of base sets. In view of the special property of our base there are a family of sets $E_j \in M_j$ and a family of words $w_j \in X^*$ such that $\mathcal{J}(F) = \bigcup_{j \in J} w_j \cdot E_j$. Thus $F/w_j \supseteq E_j$ for $j \in J$, that is, $w_j \in L(F; E_j)$. Now, the assertion follows with $\bigcup_{j \in J} w_j \cdot E_j = \bigcup_{j \in J} L(F; E_j) \cdot E_j$.

It should be mentioned that the languages $L(F; E)$ have a simple structure, if only F has a simple structure.

Lemma 4. *If $F \subseteq X^\omega$ is finite-state then $L(F; E)$ is a regular language.*

Proof. It suffices to prove the identity

$$L(F/v; E) = L(F; E)/v . \tag{8}$$

Indeed, we have $w \in L(F/v; E)$ if and only if $F/(v \cdot w) \supseteq E$ which, in turn, is equivalent to $v \cdot w \in L(F; E)$, that is, $w \in L(F; E)/v$.

The subsequent lemma shows that for shift-invariant topologies on X^ω the closure and the interior operator are stable with respect to the derivative.

Lemma 5. *If $\mathbb{B}$ is a shift-invariant base then $\mathcal{J}_\mathbb{B}(F)/v = \mathcal{J}_\mathbb{B}(F/v)$ and $\mathcal{C}_\mathbb{B}(F)/v = \mathcal{C}_\mathbb{B}(F/v)$ for all $F \subseteq X^\omega$ and $v \in X^*$.*

Proof. Let $M_\mathbb{B}$ be a shift generator for $\mathbb{B}$. Then, in view of Eq. (8),

$$\begin{aligned}\mathcal{J}_\mathbb{B}(F)/v &= \big(\textstyle\bigcup_{E\in M_\mathbb{B}} L(F;E)\cdot E\big)/v \\ &= \textstyle\bigcup_{E\in M_\mathbb{B}} \big(L(F;E)/v\big)\cdot E \cup \bigcup_{E\in M_\mathbb{B}} \bigcup_{\substack{v'\cdot v''=v \\ v'\in L(F;E)}} E/v''\,.\end{aligned}$$

Thus it remains to show that $E'/v'' \subseteq \bigcup_{E\in M_\mathbb{B}}\big(L(F;E)/v\big)\cdot E$ whenever $E' \in M_\mathbb{B}$ and $v = v' \cdot v''$ with $v' \in L(F;E)$. In the case the latter conditions are satisfied we have $F/v' \supseteq E'$ which implies $F/v \supseteq E'/v''$.

In view of Eq. (6) $E'/v'' \in \mathbb{B}$ for $E' \in \mathbb{B}$. Consequently, there are $u \in X^*$ and an $E'' \in M_\mathbb{B}$ such that $E'/v'' = u \cdot E''$. From $F/v \supseteq E'/v'' = u \cdot E''$ follows $(F/v)/u \supseteq E''$, that is, $u \in L(F/v;E'') = L(F;E'')/v$. The proof is concluded by the now obvious observation $E'/v'' = u \cdot E'' \subseteq \big(L(F;E'')/v\big)\cdot E''$.

The proof for $\mathcal{C}_\mathbb{B}$ follows from the identity $X^\omega \setminus E/w = (X^\omega \setminus E)/w$ and Eq. (3).

As a consequence of Lemma 5 we obtain

Corollary 1. *If $\mathbb{B}$ is a shift-invariant base for a topology on X^ω then $\mathcal{J}_\mathbb{B}(v\cdot F) = v\cdot\mathcal{J}_\mathbb{B}(F)$ and $\mathcal{C}_\mathbb{B}(v\cdot F) = v\cdot\mathcal{C}_\mathbb{B}(F)$ for all $F \subseteq X^\omega$ and $v \in X^*$.*

Proof. First observe that in view of Property 2.3 the topology $\mathcal{T}_\mathbb{B}$ generated by the shift-invariant base $\mathbb{B}$ refines the Cantor topology on X^ω, hence every set $v\cdot X^\omega$ is also open and closed in $\mathcal{T}_\mathbb{B}$. Consequently, $\mathcal{J}_\mathbb{B}(v\cdot F) \subseteq \mathcal{C}_\mathbb{B}(v\cdot F) \subseteq v\cdot X^\omega$.

Now according to Lemma 5 the identities $\mathcal{J}_\mathbb{B}(F) = \mathcal{J}_\mathbb{B}((v\cdot F)/v) = \mathcal{J}_\mathbb{B}(v\cdot F)/v$ hold. This yields $v\cdot\mathcal{J}_\mathbb{B}(F) = \mathcal{J}_\mathbb{B}(v\cdot F)\cap v\cdot X^\omega$ and the assertion follows with $\mathcal{J}_\mathbb{B}(v\cdot F) \subseteq v\cdot X^\omega$. The proof for $\mathcal{C}_\mathbb{B}$ is the same.

The following is a consequence of the Lemmata 3, 4 and 5.

Corollary 2. *Let a base $\mathbb{B}$ for a topology on X^ω be shift-invariant and let $F \subseteq X^\omega$ be a finite-state ω-language.*

1. *Then $\mathcal{J}_\mathbb{B}(F)$ and $\mathcal{C}_\mathbb{B}(F)$ are finite-state ω-languages.*
2. *If moreover, there is a finite shift generator $M_\mathbb{B}$ of $\mathbb{B}$ consisting solely of regular ω-languages then $\mathcal{J}_\mathbb{B}(F)$ and $\mathcal{C}_\mathbb{B}(F)$ are even regular ω-languages.*

Proof. The classes of finite-state and regular ω-languages are both closed under Boolean operations. Thus the first assertion follows from Lemma 5.

For proving the assertion on the regularity of the ω-languages $\mathcal{J}_\mathbb{B}(F)$ and $\mathcal{C}_\mathbb{B}(F)$ we observe that the strong assumption on $M_\mathbb{B}$ and Lemmata 3 and 4 yield $\mathcal{J}_\mathbb{B}(F) = \bigcup_{E\in M_\mathbb{B}} L(F;E)\cdot E$ where the union is finite and $L(F;E) \subseteq X^*$ and $E \subseteq X^\omega$ are regular. Thus $\mathcal{J}_\mathbb{B}(F)$ is also regular. The assertion for $\mathcal{C}_\mathbb{B}(F)$ now follows from Eq. (3).

3 Topologies Related to Finite Automata

In this section we consider four shift-invariant topologies refining CANTOR topology. These topologies are closely related to finite automata. The first topology is the smallest topology having all regular ω-languages which are also closed in CANTOR topology as open sets. This topology is remarkable because here all ω-languages accepted by deterministic BÜCHI-automata are closed.

The subsequent two topologies are derived from Diekert's and Kufleitner's [3] alphabetic topology which is useful for investigations in restricted first-order theories for infinite words.

Finally, for the sake of completeness we add the topology having all regular ω-languages as open (and closed) sets.

Every of the four considered topologies has an infinite set of isolated points. Thus in view of Lemma 1 none of them is a compact topology on X^ω.

3.1 The Automatic Topology

Definition 2. *The* automatic topology $\mathcal{T}_A$ *on* X^ω *is defined by the base*

$$\mathbb{B}_A := \{F : F \subseteq X^\omega \wedge F \textit{ is a regular } \omega\textit{-language closed in } \text{CANTOR}\textit{-space}\}.$$

It should be remarked that the sets (open balls) $w \cdot X^\omega$ are regular and closed in CANTOR-space. Moreover, the properties of regular ω-languages show that $\mathbb{B}_A$ is shift-invariant. Thus the base $\mathbb{B}_A$ contains $\mathbb{B}_C$, and the automatic topology refines the CANTOR topology.

$\mathcal{T}_A$ has the following properties:

Property 3

1. If $F \subseteq X^\omega$ is open (closed) in CANTOR topology $\mathcal{T}_C$ then F is open (closed) in $\mathcal{T}_A$.
2. Every non-empty set open in $\mathcal{T}_A$ contains an ultimately periodic ω-word.
3. The set Ult of ultimately periodic ω-words is the set $\mathbb{I}_A$ of all isolated points in $\mathcal{T}_A$.

Proof. 1. and 2. are obvious.

3. Every ω-language $\{w \cdot v^\omega\} = w \cdot \{v\}^\omega$ is regular and closed in CANTOR-space, and if $\{\xi\}$ is regular then ξ is an ultimately periodic ω-word.

The following theorem characterises the closure and the interior operators for the automatic topology. Here the second identity resembles the identity in Property 1.4.

Theorem 3

$$\mathcal{J}_A(F) = \bigcup\nolimits_{E \in \mathbb{B}_A \setminus \{\emptyset\}} L(F;E) \cdot E \tag{9}$$

$$\mathcal{C}_A(F) = \bigcap \{W \cdot X^\omega : F \subseteq W \cdot X^\omega \wedge W \textit{ is regular}\} \tag{10}$$

Proof. The assertion of Eq.(9) is Lemma 3.

To prove Eq.(10) observe that, for regular $W \subseteq X^*$, the set $W \cdot X^\omega$ is closed in $\mathcal{T}_A$. Thus the inclusion "$\subseteq$" is obvious.

Let, conversely, $\xi \notin \mathcal{C}_A(F)$. Then there is a set $F' \in \mathbb{B}_A$ such that $\xi \in F'$ and $F \cap F' = \emptyset$. F' is a regular ω-language closed in $\mathcal{T}_C$. Thus $X^\omega \setminus F' = W' \cdot X^\omega$ for some regular language $W' \subseteq X^*$. Consequently, $\xi \notin W' \cdot X^* \supseteq \bigcap\{W \cdot X^\omega : F \subseteq W \cdot X^\omega \wedge W \text{ is regular}\}$.

The next lemma describes sets open in $\mathcal{T}_A$. As usual, a set is called *nowhere dense* if its closure does not contain a non-empty open subset.

Lemma 6. *A set $F \subseteq X^\omega$ is open in $\mathcal{T}_A$ if and only if*

$$F = W \cdot X^\omega \cup \bigcup\nolimits_{i \in \mathbb{N}} F_i$$

where the sets F_i are regular, closed and nowhere dense in CANTOR-*space.*

Proof. If, in CANTOR-space, $F \subseteq X^\omega$ is closed then $F = V_F \cdot X^\omega \cup F'$ where $V_F = \{v : v \cdot X^\omega \subseteq F\}$ and F' is nowhere dense and closed. If, moreover, F is a regular ω-language then $V_F \subseteq X^*$ is a regular language and, consequently, $F' = F \setminus V_F \cdot X^\omega$ is a regular ω-language.

If E is open in $\mathcal{T}_A$ then E, as a union of base sets, has the form $E = W' \cdot X^\omega \cup \bigcup_{i \in \mathbb{N}} F_i$ where the F_i are regular ω-languages closed in CANTOR-space.

Now, from the preceding consideration we obtain the required form $E = (W' \cup \bigcup_{i \in \mathbb{N}} V_{F_i}) \cdot X^\omega \cup \bigcup_{i \in \mathbb{N}} F_i'$.

As an immediate consequence we obtain the following.

Corollary 3. *Every set open in $\mathcal{T}_A$ is an $\mathbf{F}_\sigma$-set in* CANTOR-*space, and every set closed in $\mathcal{T}_A$ is a $\mathbf{G}_\delta$-set in* CANTOR-*space.*

The converse of Corollary 3 is not true in general.

Example 1. Let $\eta \notin \mathsf{Ult}$ and consider the countable ω-language $F := \{0^n \cdot 1 \cdot \eta : n \in \mathbb{N}\}$.

Then, in CANTOR-space, $F = (\{0\}^\omega \cup F) \cap 0^* \cdot 1 \cdot \{0,1\}^\omega$ is the intersection of a closed set with an open set, hence, simultaneously an $\mathbf{F}_\sigma$-set and a $\mathbf{G}_\delta$-set. As F does not contain any ultimately periodic ω-word, it cannot be open in $\mathcal{T}_A$. Thus $X^\omega \setminus F$ is not closed in $\mathcal{T}_A$.

Consequently, $0 \cdot F \cup 1 \cdot (X^\omega \setminus F)$ is a set being neither open nor closed in $\mathcal{T}_A$ but being simultaneously an $\mathbf{F}_\sigma$-set and a $\mathbf{G}_\delta$-set in CANTOR-space. □

For regular ω-languages, however, we have the following. Here the second item shows a difference to the CANTOR topology.

Proposition 1. *1. Let $F \subseteq X^\omega$ be a regular ω-language. Then F is an $\mathbf{F}_\sigma$-set in* CANTOR-*space if and only if F is open in $\mathcal{T}_A$, and F is a $\mathbf{G}_\delta$-set in* CANTOR-*space if and only if F is closed in $\mathcal{T}_A$.*

2. There are clopen sets in $\mathcal{T}_A$ which are not regular.

Proof. 1. In CANTOR-space, every regular ω-language F being an $\mathbf{F}_\sigma$-set is a countable union of closed regular ω-languages (see [16]).

2. The ω-language $F_\Box := \bigcup_{n\in\mathbb{N}} 0^{n^2} \cdot 1 \cdot X^\omega$ and its complement $X^\omega \setminus F_\Box = \{0^\omega\} \cup \bigcup_{n \text{ is not a square}} 0^n \cdot 1 \cdot X^\omega$ partition the whole space $X^\omega = \{0,1\}^\omega$ into two non-regular ω-languages open in $\mathcal{T}_A$.

3.2 Finite-State and Regular ω-Languages

In this section we investigate whether finite-state and regular ω-languages are preserved by $\mathcal{J}_A$ and $\mathcal{C}_A$.

The first simple result is a consequence of Corollary 2.

Proposition 2. *If $F \subseteq X^\omega$ is finite-state the also $\mathcal{J}_A(F)$ and $\mathcal{C}_A(F)$ are finite-state ω-languages.*

It is, however, not true that the interior or the closure of finite-state ω-languages are regular. To this end we consider the set Ult of all ultimately periodic ω-words.

Example 2. The set $\mathsf{Ult} \subseteq X^\omega$ is the set of all isolated points of the topology $\mathcal{T}_A$ hence open. Thus $\mathcal{J}_A(\mathsf{Ult}) = \mathsf{Ult}$.

Moreover $\mathsf{Ult}/w = \mathsf{Ult}$ for all $w \in X^*$, that is, Ult is a one-state ω-language, but Ult is not regular. If we consider, for $a, b \in X$, $a \neq b$, the ω-language $F = a \cdot \mathsf{Ult} \cup b \cdot (X^\omega \setminus \mathsf{Ult})$ then F is finite-state and we obtain $\mathcal{J}_A(F) = a \cdot \mathsf{Ult}$ and $\mathcal{C}_A(F) = a \cdot X^\omega \cup b \cdot (X^\omega \setminus \mathsf{Ult})$. So neither, $\mathcal{J}_A(F)$ nor $\mathcal{C}_A(F)$ are regular ω-languages. □

A still more striking difference to CANTOR topology (see Property 1.5) is the fact that the closure (and also the interior) of a regular ω-language need not be regular again.

Example 3. We use the fact (Lemma 2) that two regular ω-languages E, F already coincide if only $E \cap \mathsf{Ult} = F \cap \mathsf{Ult}$ and consider $\mathcal{C}_A(\{0,1\}^* \cdot 0^\omega)$.

Utilising Eq. (10) we get $\mathcal{C}_A(\{0,1\}^* \cdot 0^\omega) \subseteq \bigcap_{k\in\mathbb{N}} \{0,1\}^* \cdot 0^k \cdot \{0,1\}^\omega$. Consequently, $\mathcal{C}_A(\{0,1\}^* \cdot 0^\omega) \cap \mathsf{Ult} = \{0,1\}^* \cdot 0^\omega$.

If, now, $\mathcal{C}_A(\{0,1\}^* \cdot 0^\omega)$ were a regular ω-language, the identity $\mathcal{C}_A(\{0,1\}^* \cdot 0^\omega) = \{0,1\}^* \cdot 0^\omega$ would follow. This implies, according to Corollary 3 that $\{0,1\}^* \cdot 0^\omega$ is a $\mathbf{G}_\delta$-set in CANTOR-space which is not true. □

3.3 The Alphabetic Topologies

We start with the alphabetic topology which was introduced in [3]. Then we consider a variant of the alphabetic topology. We define both topologies by their respective bases.

Definition 3. *The* alphabetic topology *is defined by the base*

$$\mathbb{B}_\alpha := \{w \cdot A^\omega : w \in X^* \wedge A \subseteq X\}.$$

All base sets are regular and closed, so the generated topology $\mathcal{T}_\alpha$ is coarser than the automatic topology $\mathcal{T}_A$.

For the next definition we fix the following notation (cf. [3]). For $A \subseteq X$ the ω-language A^{im} is the set of all ω-words $\xi \in X^\omega$ where exactly the letters in A occur infinitely often. In particular, $A^{\mathrm{im}} = X^* \cdot A^{\mathrm{im}}$.

Definition 4. *The* strong alphabetic topology *is defined by the base*
$$\mathbb{B}_s := \{w \cdot (A^\omega \cap A^{\mathrm{im}}) : w \in X^* \wedge A \subseteq X\}.$$

The ω-languages in this base $\mathbb{B}_s$ are regular ω-languages and $\mathbf{G}_\delta$-sets in CANTOR-space but, for $|A| \geq 2$, no $\mathbf{F}_\sigma$-sets in CANTOR-space. Thus they are closed but not open in the automatic topology. This shows that the strong alphabetic topology $\mathcal{T}_s$ does not coincide with $\mathcal{T}_A$.

For both alphabetic topologies suitable finite shift generators M_α and M_s for the bases $\mathbb{B}_\alpha$ and $\mathbb{B}_s$, respectively, can be chosen in the following way:

$$M_\alpha := \{A^\omega : A \subseteq X\} \text{ and } M_s := \{A^\omega \cap A^{\mathrm{im}} : A \subseteq X\}$$

This yields the following property of the corresponding interior operators.

Proposition 3. $\mathcal{J}_\alpha(F) = \bigcup_{A\subseteq X} L(F; A^\omega) \cdot A^\omega$
$$\mathcal{J}_s(F) = \bigcup_{A\subseteq X} L(F; A^\omega \cap A^{\mathrm{im}}) \cdot (A^\omega \cap A^{\mathrm{im}})$$

With Corollary 2 we obtain the following.

Corollary 4. *If $F \subseteq X^\omega$ is finite-state then $\mathcal{J}_\alpha(F)$, $\mathcal{C}_\alpha(F)$, $\mathcal{J}_s(F)$ and $\mathcal{C}_s(F)$ are regular ω-languages.*

Proof. Here it suffices to observe that the shift generators $M_\alpha := \{A^\omega : \emptyset \neq A \subseteq X\}$ and $M_s := \{A^\omega \cap A^{\mathrm{im}} : \emptyset \neq A \subseteq X\}$ fulfil the assumption of Corollary 2.

Corollary 4 and Example 3 show that neither of the topologies $\mathcal{T}_\alpha$ and $\mathcal{T}_s$ coincides with the automatic topology $\mathcal{T}_A$.

This latter fact could be also obtained by considering the set of isolated points $\mathbb{I}_\alpha$ and $\mathbb{I}_s$ of the topologies $\mathcal{T}_\alpha$ and $\mathcal{T}_s$, respectively. Since for every isolated point ξ the singleton $\{\xi\}$ has to be an element of every base of the topology, we obtain the identity
$$\mathbb{I}_\alpha = \mathbb{I}_s = \{w \cdot a^\omega : w \in X^* \wedge a \in X\}. \tag{11}$$

3.4 The Büchi Topology and the Hierarchy of Topologies

For the sake of completeness we introduce still another topology which we call Büchi topology because its base consists of all regular ω-languages.

Definition 5. *The* Büchi topology *is defined by the base*
$$\mathbb{B}_B := \{F : F \subseteq X^w \wedge F \textit{ is a regular } \omega\textit{-language}\}.$$

Here, trivially, closure and interior of regular ω-languages are again regular.

What concerns closure and interior of regular ω-langueges consider the set F defined in Example 2. One easily verifies that $\mathcal{J}_B(F) = \mathcal{J}_A(F)$ and $\mathcal{C}_B(F) = \mathcal{C}_A(F)$.

So F is an example of a finite-state ω-language having non-regular interior and closure also with respect to $\mathcal{T}_B$. Thus, no base for the BÜCHI topology has a subset fulfilling the assumption of Corollary 2.2.

Arguing in the same way as for $\mathcal{T}_\alpha$ and $\mathcal{T}_s$ we obtain that the set of isolated points of the Büchi topology is $\mathbb{I}_B = \mathsf{Ult}$.

Next we show that the following inclusion relation holds for the topologies considered so far. All inclusions are proper and other ones than the indicated do not exist.

$$\begin{array}{ccc} & \mathcal{T}_B & \\ \nearrow & & \nwarrow \\ \mathcal{T}_A & & \mathcal{T}_s \\ \nwarrow & & \nearrow \\ & \mathcal{T}_\alpha & \\ & \uparrow & \\ & \mathcal{T}_C & \end{array}$$

First, the obvious inclusions $\mathbb{B}_B \supseteq \mathbb{B}_A \supseteq \mathbb{B}_\alpha \supseteq \mathbb{B}_C$ and $\mathbb{B}_B \supseteq \mathbb{B}_s$ imply the inclusions except for $\mathcal{T}_s \supseteq \mathcal{T}_\alpha$. This latter follows from the fact that in virtue of the identity

$$w \cdot A^\omega = \bigcup_{B \subseteq A} \bigcup_{v \in A^*} (w \cdot v \cdot B^\omega \cap B^{\mathrm{im}}) \tag{12}$$

every base set of $\mathcal{T}_\alpha$ is open in $\mathcal{T}_s$.

To show the properness of the inclusions, we observe that the set of isolated points of the above topologies satisfy $\mathbb{I}_C = \emptyset$, $\mathbb{I}_\alpha = \mathbb{I}_s = \{w \cdot a^\omega : w \in X^* \wedge a \in X\}$ and $\mathbb{I}_A = \mathbb{I}_B = \mathsf{Ult}$. Thus $\mathcal{T}_\alpha \neq \mathcal{T}_C$ and $\mathcal{T}_A \not\subseteq \mathcal{T}_s$.

The converse relation $\mathcal{T}_s \not\subseteq \mathcal{T}_A$ follows from the above mentioned fact that the sets $A^\omega \cap A^{\mathrm{im}}$ for $2 \leq |A|$ are open in $\mathcal{T}_s$ but, since they are regular ω-languages not being $\mathbf{F}_\sigma$-sets in CANTOR-space, according to Proposition 1 not open in $\mathcal{T}_A$.

3.5 Metrisability

In this part we show that all the above topologies are metrisable. To this end we observe that for every topology, the sets contained in the above introduced bases are not only open but also closed. For $\mathcal{T}_C$ this is known, for $\mathcal{T}_\alpha$ and $\mathcal{T}_A$ the base sets are even closed in CANTOR-space. For $\mathcal{T}_B$ this follows because $\mathbb{B}_B$ is closed under complementation. Finally, the identity

$$X^\omega \setminus (w \cdot A^\omega \cap A^{\mathrm{im}}) = \bigcup_{\substack{v \neq w \\ |v| = |w|}} v \cdot X^\omega \cup \bigcup_{B \neq A} B^{\mathrm{im}} \tag{13}$$

shows that $\mathbb{B}_s$ consists of sets closed in $\mathcal{T}_s$.

To show the metrisability of all spaces we refer to Theorem 4.2.9 of [4] which states the following.

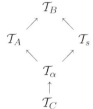

Theorem 4. *Let $\mathcal{X}$ be a topological space with a countable base. Then $\mathcal{X}$ is metrisable if and only if $\mathcal{X}$ is a regular topological space.*

A topological space $\mathcal{X}$ is called *regular* if every finite set is closed and for every point $p \in \mathcal{X}$ and every closed set $M \subseteq \mathcal{X}$, $p \notin M$, there are disjoint open sets O_1, O_2 such that $p \in O_1$ and $M \subseteq O_2$. In particular, this condition is satisfied if every finite subset of $\mathcal{X}$ is closed and $\mathcal{X}$ has a base consisting of closed sets.

Thus we obtain our result.

Theorem 5. *Each of the topologies $\mathcal{T}_C$, $\mathcal{T}_\alpha$, $\mathcal{T}_A$, $\mathcal{T}_s$ and $\mathcal{T}_B$ is metrisable.*

4 Topologies Obtained by Adding Isolated Points

All topologies $\mathcal{T}_A$, $\mathcal{T}_B$, $\mathcal{T}_s$ and $\mathcal{T}_\alpha$ on X^ω considered so far have isolated points. In particular, all their isolated points belong to the set of ultimately periodic ω-words Ult. In this section we are going to investigate in more detail topologies on X^ω which are obtained from Cantor topology by adding all elements of a certain fixed set $\mathbb{I} \subseteq X^\omega$ as isolated points to the base $\mathbb{B}_C$.

Definition 6. *Let $\mathbb{I} \subseteq X^\omega$. Define $\mathcal{T}_\mathbb{I}$ as the topology $(X^\omega, \mathcal{O}_\mathbb{I})$ generated by the base $\mathbb{B}_\mathbb{I} := \mathbb{B}_C \cup \{\{\xi\} : \xi \in \mathbb{I}\}$.*

4.1 General Properties

First we characterise the closure $\mathcal{C}_\mathbb{I}$ in the space $(X^\omega, \mathcal{O}_\mathbb{I})$. To this end observe that $\xi \notin \mathcal{C}_\mathbb{I}(F)$ if and only if there is a base set $E \in \mathbb{B}_\mathbb{I}$ such that $\xi \in E$ and $E \cap F = \emptyset$. This yields the following.

$$X^\omega \setminus \mathcal{C}_\mathbb{I}(F) = \bigcup\{w \cdot X^\omega : w \cdot X^\omega \cap F = \emptyset\} \cup (\mathbb{I} \setminus F) \tag{14}$$

By complementation, we obtain the following connection to the closure in Cantor-space, $\mathcal{C}(F) = \{\xi : \mathbf{pref}(\xi) \subseteq \mathbf{pref}(F)\}$.

$$\begin{aligned} \mathcal{C}_\mathbb{I}(F) &= \mathcal{C}(F) \cap ((X^\omega \setminus \mathbb{I}) \cup F) \\ &= F \cup (\mathcal{C}(F) \setminus \mathbb{I}) \end{aligned} \tag{15}$$

An immediate consequence of Eq. (15) is the following.

Corollary 5. *If $F \supseteq X^\omega \setminus \mathbb{I}$ then F is closed in $\mathcal{T}_\mathbb{I}$.*

We call a point $\xi \in X^\omega$ an *accumulation point* of a set $F \subseteq X^\omega$ with respect to a topology $\mathcal{T} = (X^\omega, \mathcal{O})$ provided every open set E containing ξ contains a point of $F \setminus \{\xi\}$. This is equivalent to the requirement that every base set (in any base for $(X^\omega, \mathcal{O})$) E containing ξ contains a point of $F \setminus \{\xi\}$.

Theorem 6. *In the space $(X^\omega, \mathcal{O}_\mathbb{I})$ the set $X^\omega \setminus \mathbb{I}$ is the set of accumulation points of the whole space.*

Proof. Let M be the set of accumulation points of the whole space. Then, obviously, $M \cap \mathbb{I} = \emptyset$.

Conversely, if $\xi \notin \mathbb{I}$ then every base set containing ξ is of the form $w \cdot X^\omega$, thus contains infinitely many points of X^ω.

Next we turn to metrisability of the topologies. Since our spaces $(X^\omega, \mathcal{O}_\mathbb{I})$ do not necessarily have a countable base, we cannot conclude metrisability as in Theorem 5.

Therefore we use the HANAI-MORITA-STONE-Theorem (cf. [4, Theorem 4.47])

Theorem 7 (Hanai,Morita,Stone). *Let $\mathcal{M}_1 = (M_1, \mathcal{O}_1), \mathcal{M}_2 = (M_2, \mathcal{O}_2)$ be topological spaces. If $\mathcal{M}_1$ is metrisable and there is a surjective mapping $\Psi : M_1 \to M_2$ such that $\Psi(M)$ is closed whenever $M \subseteq M_1$ is closed then the following are equivalent.*

1. *$\mathcal{M}_2$ is metrisable, and*
2. *$\mathcal{M}_2$ has a base $\mathbb{B}$ such that for every $m \in \mathcal{M}_2$ the set $\mathbb{B}_m := \{B : B \in \mathbb{B} \wedge m \in B\}$ is countable.*[4]

It is now obvious that every topological space $(X^\omega, \mathcal{O}_\mathbb{I})$ satisfies the Condition 2 of Theorem 7. In fact, for $\xi \in X^\omega$ it holds $\mathbb{B}_{\mathbb{I},\xi} = \{w \cdot X^\omega : w \sqsubset \xi\} \cup \{\xi\}$ or $\mathbb{B}_{\mathbb{I},\xi} = \{w \cdot X^\omega : w \sqsubset \xi\}$ according to whether $\xi \in \mathbb{I}$ or not.

If we use as Ψ the identity mapping from CANTOR-space $(X^\omega, \mathcal{O}_C)$ to $(X^\omega, \mathcal{O}_\mathbb{I})$ then Ψ trivially satisfies the hypothesis of the HANAI-MORITA-STONE-Theorem and we obtain the following.

Theorem 8. *Let $\mathbb{I} \subseteq X^\omega$. Then the topology $\mathcal{T}_\mathbb{I} = (X^\omega, \mathcal{O}_\mathbb{I})$ is metrisable.*

4.2 U-δ-Topology

In this section we show that the topology $\mathcal{T}_\mathbb{I}$ admits a nice metrisation resembling Eq. (5) provided the set $\mathbb{I}$ is an $\mathbf{F}_\sigma$-set in CANTOR-space.

Let $U \subseteq X^*$ be a fixed language and define $U^\delta := \{\xi : \xi \in X^\omega \wedge |\mathbf{pref}(\xi) \cap U| = \aleph_0\}$. Then the following holds true.

Lemma 7. *A subset $F \subseteq X^\omega$ is a $\mathbf{G}_\delta$-set in* CANTOR*-space if and only if there is a $U \subseteq X^*$ such that $F = U^\delta$.*

Next, following [12], using the language U we introduce a topology on X^ω.

Definition 7 (U-δ-topology). *The* U-δ-topology *of X^ω is the metric topology generated by the following metric*

$$\rho_U(\xi, \eta) := \begin{cases} 0\,, & \text{if } \xi = \eta\,,\text{ and} \\ |X|^{-|\mathbf{pref}(\xi) \cap \mathbf{pref}(\eta) \cap U|}\,, & \text{otherwise.} \end{cases}$$

This topology has the following properties (see [12,14,15]). Denote by $\mathcal{C}_U$ the topological closure induced by the metric ρ_U.

[4] $\mathcal{M}_2$ is second countable.

Proposition 4

1. *In the* U-δ-*topology of* X^ω *every point in* $\mathbb{I}_U := X^\omega \setminus U^\delta$ *is an isolated point.*
2. $\mathcal{C}_U(F) = \mathcal{C}(F) \cap (U^\delta \cup F) = F \cup (\mathcal{C}(F) \cap U^\delta)$

Now Proposition 4.2 in connection with Eq. (15) shows that, for $\mathbb{I} := X^\omega \setminus U^\delta$ the U-δ-topology of X^ω coincides with $\mathcal{T}_\mathbb{I}$.

Next we consider the set of isolated point s of the topologies $\mathcal{T}_\alpha$, $\mathcal{T}_s$, $\mathcal{T}_A$ and $\mathcal{T}_B$. Recall that $\mathbb{I}_\alpha = \mathbb{I}_s = \bigcup_{a\in X} X^* \cdot a^\omega$ and $\mathbb{I}_A = \mathbb{I}_B = \mathsf{Ult}$. Both sets are $\mathbf{F}_\sigma$-sets in Cantor space. Thus the following holds true.

Proposition 5. *One can construct languages* U_α *and* U_A *such that the set of isolated points of the* U_α-δ-*topology of* X^ω *is* $\mathbb{I}_\alpha = \bigcup_{a\in X} X^* \cdot a^\omega$, *and the set of isolated points of the* U_A-δ-*topology of* X^ω *is* $\mathbb{I}_A = \mathsf{Ult}$.

For the case $\mathbb{I} = \bigcup_{a\in X} X^* \cdot a^\omega$ one obtains a regular language U_α.

Corollary 6. *It holds* $\mathbb{I}_\alpha = X^\omega \setminus \left(\bigcup_{a,b\in X, a\neq b} X^* \cdot ab\right)^\delta$.

4.3 Shift-Invariance

Finally, we derive a necessary and sufficient condition when a topology $\mathcal{T}_\mathbb{I}$ has a shift-invariant base. To this end we use the results of Section 2.

Lemma 8. *A topology* $\mathcal{T}_\mathbb{I}$ *has a shift-invariant base if and only if* $\mathbb{I} = \mathbb{I}/w$ *for all* $w \in X^*$.

Proof. For every isolated point $\xi \in \mathbb{I}$ the set $\{\xi\}$ is open in $\mathcal{T}_\mathbb{I}$. Thus according to Lemma 5 and Corollary 1 also $\{\xi\}/w$ and $\{w \cdot \xi\}$ are open. This shows the required identity.

Conversely, if $\mathbb{I} = \mathbb{I}/w$ for all $w \in X^*$ then, obviously, the base $\mathbb{B}_C \cup \{\{\xi\} : \xi \in \mathbb{I}\}$ is shift-invariant.

Having this necessary and sufficient condition one easily verifies that adding isolated points may result in non-shift-invariant refinements of Cantor topology.

References

1. Calude, C.S., Marcus, S., Staiger, L.: A topological characterization of random sequences. Inform. Process. Lett. 88, 245–250 (2003)
2. Calude, C.S., Jürgensen, H., Staiger, L.: Topology on words. Theoret. Comput. Sci. 410, 2323–2335 (2009)
3. Diekert, V., Kufleitner, M.: Fragments of first-order logic over infinite words. In: Albers, S., Marion, J.-Y. (eds.) Proceedings of STACS 2009, Freiburg, Germany, February 26-28, pp. 325–336 (2009); Online proceedings at DROPS and HAL
4. Engelking, R.: General Topology. Państwowe wydawnictwo naukowe, Warszawa (1977)
5. Fernau, H., Staiger, L.: Iterated function systems and control languages. Inform. and Comput. 168, 125–143 (2001)

6. Hoogeboom, H.J., Rozenberg, G.: Infinitary languages: Basic theory and applications to concurrent systems. In: de Bakker, J.W., de Roever, W.-P., Rozenberg, G. (eds.) Current Trends in Concurrency. LNCS, vol. 224, pp. 266–342. Springer, Heidelberg (1986)
7. Perrin, D., Pin, J.-E.: Infinite Words. Elsevier, Amsterdam (2004)
8. Prodinger, H.: Topologies on free monoids induced by closure operators of a special type. RAIRO Inform. Théor. Appl. 14(2), 225–237 (1980)
9. Redziejowski, R.R.: Infinite word languages and continuous mappings. Theoret. Comput. Sci. 43(1), 59–79 (1986)
10. Rozenberg, G., Salomaa, A. (eds.): Handbook of formal languages. Springer, Berlin (1997)
11. Staiger, L.: Finite-State ω-Languages. J. Comput. Syst. Sci. 27(3), 434–448 (1983)
12. Staiger, L.: Sequential Mappings of ω-Languages. ITA 21(2), 147–173 (1987)
13. Staiger, L.: ω-languages. In: [10], vol. 3, pp. 339–387
14. Staiger, L.: Weighted Finite Automata and Metrics in Cantor Space. Journal of Automata, Languages and Combinatorics 8(2), 353–360 (2003)
15. Staiger, L.: Topologies for the Set of Disjunctive ω-words. Acta Cybern. 17(1), 43–51 (2005)
16. Staiger, L., Wagner, K.: Automatentheoretische und automatenfreie Charakterisierungen topologischer Klassen regulärer Folgenmengen. Elektronische Informationsverarbeitung und Kybernetik·10(7), 379–392 (1974)
17. Thomas, W.: Automata on Infinite Objects. In: Van Leeuwen, J. (ed.) Handbook of Theoretical Computer Science, vol. B, pp. 133–191. Elsevier, Amsterdam (1990)
18. Thomas, W.: Languages, automata, and logic. In: [10], vol. 3, pp. 389–455
19. Trakhtenbrot, B.A.: Finite automata and monadic second order logic. Sibirsk. Mat. Ž 3, 103–131 (1962) (Russian); English translation: AMS Transl. 59, 23–55
20. Trakhtenbrot, B.A., Barzdin, Y.M.: Finite Automata, Behaviour and Synthesis Nauka Publishers, Moscow (1970) (Russian); English translation: North Holland, Amsterdam (1973)

On Symbolic Representations of Maximum Matchings and (Un)directed Graphs

Beate Bollig

LS2 Informatik, TU Dortmund,
44221 Dortmund, Germany

Abstract. The maximum matching problem is one of the most fundamental algorithmic graph problems and OBDDs are one of the most common dynamic data structures for Boolean functions. Since in some applications graphs become larger and larger, a research branch has emerged which is concerned with the theoretical design and analysis of so-called symbolic algorithms for classical graph problems on OBDD-represented graph instances. Typically problems get harder when their input is represented symbolically, nevertheless not many concrete non-trivial lower bounds are known. Here, it is shown that symbolic OBDD-based algorithms for the maximum matching problem need exponential space (with respect to the OBDD size of the input graph). Furthermore, it is shown that OBDD-representations for undirected graphs can be exponentially larger than OBDD-representations for their directed counterparts and vice versa.

Keywords: Computational complexity, lower bounds, maximum matching, ordered binary decision diagrams, symbolic algorithms.

1 Introduction

Since modern applications require huge graphs, explicit representations by adjacency matrices or adjacency lists may cause conflicts with memory limitations and even polynomial time algorithms seem to be not applicable any more. As time and space resources do not suffice to consider individual vertices, one way out seems to be to deal with sets of vertices and edges represented by their characteristic functions. Ordered binary decision diagrams, denoted OBDDs, introduced by Bryant in 1986 [6], are well suited for the representation and manipulation of Boolean functions, therefore, a research branch has emerged which is concerned with the theoretical design and analysis of so-called symbolic algorithms for classical graph problems on OBDD-represented graph instances (see, e.g., [11,12], [13], [18,19], [21], [23,24], and [28]). Symbolic algorithms have to solve problems on a given graph instance by efficient functional operations offered by the OBDD data structure.

Representing graphs with regularities by means of data structures smaller than adjacency matrices or adjacency lists seems to be a natural idea. But problems typically get harder when their input is represented implicitly. For circuit representations this has been shown in [1,10,20]. These results do not directly carry

C.S. Calude and V. Sassone (Eds.): TCS 2010, IFIP AICT 323, pp. 286–300, 2010.

over to problems on OBDD-represented inputs since there are Boolean functions like some output bits of integer multiplication whose OBDD complexity is exponentially larger than its circuit size [2,7]. In [8] it has been shown that even the very basic problem of deciding whether two vertices s and t are connected in a directed graph G, the so-called graph accessibility problem GAP, is PSPACE-complete on OBDD-represented graphs. Nevertheless, OBDD-based algorithms are successful in many applications and despite the hardness results there are not many concrete non-trivial lower bounds known for the complexity of problems on OBDD-represented graph instances. In [23] exponential lower bounds on the space complexity of OBDD-based algorithms for the single-source shortest paths problem, the maximum flow problem, and a restricted class of algorithms for the reachability problem have been presented. Recently, the last result has been generalized and an exponential lower bound on the space complexity of all OBDD-based algorithms for reachability analysis has been shown in [3]. The results are not very astonishing but the proofs present worst-case examples which could be helpful to realize why OBDD-based algorithms are successful in many applications by characterizing the special cases that can be handled efficiently and the cases that are difficult to process. In this paper one aim is to present concrete exponential lower bounds and not only existence proofs that there have to be objects of large size or that exponential blow-ups may happen for various problems.

Due to the problem's rich area of applications the maximum matching problem has received a considerable amount of attention for explicit graph representations. Answering an open question posed by Sawitzki (page 186, table 7.4.1 in [22]), we prove that OBDD-based representations of maximum matchings can be exponentially larger than the OBDD representation of the input graph. Using simple counting arguments it can be shown that there exists a complete bipartite graph whose OBDD complexity is small and for which there exists a maximum matching whose OBDD complexity is large. In order to present concrete proofs we present such a graph and a corresponding maximum matching. Searching for advantageous properties of real-world instances that cause an essentially better behavior than in the worst-case, the complexity of graph problems with respect to structured properties of input and/or output OBDDs is interesting. In [21] and [28] symbolic algorithms for maximum flow in 0-1 networks and topological sorting have been presented which have polylogarithmic running time with respect to the number of vertices of a given grid graph. These results rely on the very structured input graph and on restrictions on the width of occuring OBDDs during the computation. Our first result on the size of maximum (perfect) matchings shows that constant input OBDD width is not sufficient to guarantee polynomial space complexity for the maximum matching problem. Afterwards we present a graph whose edge set can be represented by OBDDs of small size but for which the implicit representation of its unique maximum matching needs exponential OBDD size.

By simple counting arguments it is easy to see that almost all graphs on N vertices cannot be represented by OBDDs of polylogarithmic size with respect to N. On the other hand, it is quite obvious that very simple structured graphs, e.g., grid graphs, have a small OBDD representation. Therefore, in [18,19] the question has been investigated whether succinct OBDD representations can be found for significant graph classes. In this paper we consider whether undirected graphs can be exponentially larger than their so-called directed counterparts and vice versa. Our results can be summarized as follows.

Theorem 1. *Symbolic* OBDD*-based algorithms for the maximum matching problem need exponential space with respect to the size of the implicit representation of the input graph.*

Theorem 2. *There exists a directed graph G_d and a corresponding undirected graph G_u, obtained from G_d by changing the directed edges into undirected ones, such that the symbolic* OBDD *representation of G_u is exponentially larger than the* OBDD *representation of G_d.*

The paper is organized as follows. In Section 2 we define some notation and present some basics concerning OBDDs, symbolic graph representations, and the maximum matching problem. Section 3 contains the proof of Theorem 1. Finally, in Section 4 Theorem 2 is shown and we discuss why the result is not as obvious as it seems to be at first glance. For a slightly more general model than OBDDs the representation size for the corresponding undirected counterparts of directed graphs can only be by a factor of 2 larger than the size for the directed graph. Furthermore, we will look at an undirected graph G_U and a corresponding directed graph G_D, obtained from G_U by changing each undirected edges into one directed edge, such that the symbolic OBDD representation of G_D is exponentially larger than the OBDD representation of G_U.

2 Preliminaries

In order to make the paper self-contained we briefly recall the main notions we are dealing with in this paper.

2.1 Ordered Binary Decision Diagrams

When working with Boolean functions as in circuit verification, synthesis, and model checking, ordered binary decision diagrams are one of the most often used data structures that support efficiently all fundamental operations on Boolean functions, like binary operators, quantifications or satisfiability tests. (For a history of results on binary decision diagrams see, e.g., the monograph of Wegener [27]).

Definition 1. *Let $X_n = \{x_1, \ldots, x_n\}$ be a set of Boolean variables. A variable ordering π on X_n is a permutation on $\{1, \ldots, n\}$ leading to the ordered list $x_{\pi(1)}, \ldots, x_{\pi(n)}$ of the variables.*

In the following a variable ordering π is sometimes identified with the corresponding ordering $x_{\pi(1)}, \ldots, x_{\pi(n)}$ of the variables if the meaning is clear from the context.

Definition 2. *A π-*OBDD *on X_n is a directed acyclic graph $G = (V, E)$ whose sinks are labeled by Boolean constants and whose non-sink (or decision) nodes are labeled by Boolean variables from X_n. Each decision node has two outgoing edges one labeled by 0 and the other by 1. The edges between decision nodes have to respect the variable ordering π, i.e., if an edge leads from an x_i-node to an x_j-node, then $\pi^{-1}(i) \leq \pi^{-1}(j)$ (x_i precedes x_j in $x_{\pi(1)}, \ldots, x_{\pi(n)}$). Each node v represents a Boolean function $f_v \in B_n$, i.e., $f_v : \{0,1\}^n \rightarrow \{0,1\}$, defined in the following way. In order to evaluate $f_v(b)$, $b \in \{0,1\}^n$, start at v. After reaching an x_i-node choose the outgoing edge with label b_i until a sink is reached. The label of this sink defines $f_v(b)$. The width of a π-*OBDD *is the maximum number of nodes labeled by the same variable. The size of a π-*OBDD *G is equal to the number of its nodes and the π-*OBDD *size of a function f is the size of the minimal π-*OBDD *representing f.*

It is well known that the size of an OBDD representing a function f that depends essentially on n Boolean variables (a function g depends essentially on a Boolean variable z if $g_{|z=0} \neq g_{|z=1}$) may be different for different variable orderings and may vary between linear and exponential size with respect to n.

Definition 3. *The* OBDD *size or* OBDD *complexity of f is the minimum of all π-*OBDD*(f).*

The size of the reduced π-OBDD representing f is described by the following structure theorem [25].

Theorem 3. *The number of $x_{\pi(i)}$-nodes of the minimal π-*OBDD *for f is the number s_i of different subfunctions $f_{|x_{\pi(1)}=a_1,\ldots,x_{\pi(i-1)}=a_{i-1}}$, $a_1, \ldots, a_{i-1} \in \{0,1\}$, that essentially depend on $x_{\pi(i)}$.*

Theorem 3 implies the following simple observation which is helpful in order to prove lower bounds. Given an arbitrary variable ordering π the number of nodes labeled by a variable x in the reduced π-OBDD representing a given function f is not smaller than the number of x-nodes in a reduced π-OBDD representing any subfunction of f.

Partitioned binary decision diagrams, denoted PBDDs, have been introduced in [14] as a generalized OBDD model allowing a restricted use of nondeterminism and different variable orderings. They are restricted enough such that most of the essential operations can be performed efficiently and they allow polynomial-size representations for more Boolean functions than OBDDs.

Definition 4. *A k-*PBDD *consists of k* OBDD*s whose variable orderings may be different. The output value for an input b is defined as 1 iff at least one of the* OBDD*s computes 1 on b. A* PBDD *is a k-*PBDD *for some k. The size of a k-*PBDD *is the sum of the sizes of the k* OBDD*s.*

2.2 Symbolic OBDD-Based Graph Representations and the Maximum Matching Problem

In the following for $z = (z_{n-1}, \dots, z_0) \in \{0,1\}^n$ let $|z| := \sum_{i=0}^{n-1} z_i 2^i$. Let $G = (V, E)$ be a graph with N vertices $v_0, \dots v_{N-1}$. The edge set E can be represented by an OBDD for its characteristic function, where

$$\mathcal{X}_E(x, y) = 1 \Leftrightarrow (|x|, |y| < N) \wedge (v_{|x|}, v_{|y|}) \in E, x, y \in \{0,1\}^n \text{ and } n = \lceil \log N \rceil.$$

Undirected edges are represented by symmetric directed ones. In the rest of the paper we assume that N is a power of 2 since it has no bearing on the essence of our results. OBDD-represented graphs on N vertices are typically only defined on $\log N$ Boolean variables in comparison to other implicit graph representations where at least $c \log N$ bits for some constant $c > 1$ are allowed [16,26]. One of the reasons is that the number of variables of intermediate OBDDs during a symbolic algorithms can be seen as a performance parameter. Multiplying the number of variables on which an OBDD depends by a constant c enlarge the worst-case size asymptotically from S to S^c. (See, e.g., [9] for the importance to keep the number of variables as low as possible.)

A matching in an undirected graph $G = (V, E)$ is a subset $M \subseteq E$ such that no two edges of M are adjacent. A matching M is maximum if there exists no matching $M' \subseteq E$ such that $|M'| > |M|$, where $|S|$ denotes the cardinality of a set S. A perfect matching is a matching of cardinality $|V|/2$. In the symbolic setting the maximum (perfect) matching problem is the following one. Given an OBDD for the characteristic function of the edge set of an undirected input graph G, the output is an OBDD that represents the characteristic function of a maximum (perfect) matching in G. A graph $G = (V, E)$ is bipartite, if V can be partitioned into two disjoint nonempty sets U and W, such that for all edges $(u, w) \in E$ it holds $u \in U$ and $w \in W$ or vice versa.

3 The Maximum Matching Problem on OBDD-Represented Graphs

In this section we prove Theorem 1 and demonstrate that an exponential blow-up from input to output size for the maximum matching problem is possible in the symbolic setting.

Our proof structure is the following one. First, we define an input graph G for the maximum matching problem. It is not difficult to see that the size of the corresponding OBDD representation for the characteristic function of its edge set is polynomial with respect to the number of Boolean variables. Afterwards we prove that there exists a maximum matching in G represented by its edge set for which the corresponding characteristic function has exponential OBDD complexity. Therefore, every OBDD-based algorithm solving the maximum matching problem need exponential space with respect to its input length. We start with a very simple input graph and show that there exists a maximum matching whose OBDD complexity is exponentially larger than the OBDD complexity of the input graph. The investigated maximum matching is also a perfect matching. Afterwards we present an example where the maximum matching is unique but not a perfect matching because the input graph contains many isolated vertices. Now, we make our ideas more precise.

1) The definition of the input graph G:

Our input graph $G = (V, E)$ is a complete bipartite graph on 2^{n^2+1} vertices. The vertex set V is partitioned into two nonempty sets U and W of equal size such that there exists no edge incident to two vertices in U respectively W. The Boolean encoding of a vertex $v \in V$ consists of $n^2 + 1$ Boolean variables $z, x_{11}, \dots, x_{nn}$, the variable z indicates whether v is in U $(z = 0)$ or in W $(z = 1)$. The x-variables can be seen as a Boolean matrix of dimension $n \times n$.

2) The polynomial upper bound on the OBDD size for the characteristic function of the edge set of G:

G can be represented by an OBDD of size 5. The characteristic function $\mathcal{X}_E$ of E is defined on the variables $((z^1, x^1_{11}, \dots, x^1_{nn}), (z^2, x^2_{11}, \dots, x^2_{nn}))$. The function value is 1 iff $z^1 \oplus z^2 = 1$.

3) A maximum matching in G and an exponential lower bound on the OBDD size for its characteristic function:

It remains to show that there exists a maximum matching in G defined by the characteristic function of its edge set whose OBDD complexity is exponential. Note, that our aim is to present a constructive and not only an existence proof. A vertex v in G has the property $\mathcal{P}$ iff the x-variables of its Boolean encoding correspond to a Boolean matrix that contains exactly one 1-entry in each row and in each column. Now, we are ready to define a maximum matching in G whose OBDD complexity is exponential. The crucial idea for the definition of a perfect matching with large OBDD size is the following. Vertices with property $\mathcal{P}$ are matched to vertices with property $\mathcal{P}$ and vertices without $\mathcal{P}$ to vertices without property $\mathcal{P}$. To be more precise, let $z^u, x^u_{11}, \dots, x^u_{nn}$ be the variables of the Boolean encoding of a vertex $u \in U$ and $z^w, x^w_{11}, \dots, x^w_{nn}$ those of a vertex $w \in W$. The vertices u and w are matched if both have the property $\mathcal{P}$ and $x^u_{ij} = x^w_{ji}$ for all $i, j \in \{1, \dots, n\}$ or if both have not the property $\mathcal{P}$ and $x^u_{ij} = x^w_{ij}$ for all $i, j \in \{1, \dots, n\}$. Obviously, this is a complete definition of a perfect matching in G. Let $\mathcal{X}_M$ be the characteristic function of this edge set. Next, we prove that the OBDD complexity of $\mathcal{X}_M$ is exponential. In [15,17] exponential lower bounds on the size of so-called nondeterministic read-once branching programs (a more general OBDD model) representing the Boolean function PERM_n, the test, whether a Boolean matrix contains exactly one 1-entry in each row and in each column, are presented. In the following we consider an arbitrary OBDD for a carefully chosen subfunction of $\mathcal{X}_M$ and we investigate several paths from the source of the OBDD to the 1-sink. Here, for the choice of the considered paths and for the estimation of the number of different chosen subpaths some of the ideas presented in [15,17] are used but because of the different definition of our investigated function we have to add some ideas.

Let G_M be an OBDD on the variables $((z', x_{11}, \ldots, x_{nn}), (z'', y_{11}, \ldots, y_{nn}))$ for the representation of $\mathcal{X}_M$ and G'_M be the OBDD obtained from G_M by replacing the variables x_{23}, y_{32} by 1 and x_{32}, y_{23} by 0. The reason for these replacements is that all 1-inputs for the subfunction of $\mathcal{X}_M$ represented by G'_M correspond to edges between vertices in the input graph G with property $\mathcal{P}$. As a result it is a little bit easier to argue that G'_M and therefore G_M need an exponential number of nodes. Furthermore, we set z' to 1 and z'' to 0. This is not crucial for our lower bound proof but convenient to keep our proof as simple as possible.

Our aim is to show that there is an exponential number of nodes in the OBDD G'_M. For the ease of notations we assume w.l.o.g. that n is an even number. We investigate the paths in G'_M from the source to the 1-sink called accepting paths. There are $2n-2$ 1-edges, i.e., variables set to 1, on these paths and the number of these paths is $(n-2)(n-2)!$. Now, we separate each accepting path p into its initial part p_u and into the remaining part p_ℓ to the 1-sink. Here, we have to use a different cut as considered in [15,17]. A pair (x_{ij}, y_{ji}), $i, j \in \{1, \ldots, n\}$, is called (x, y)-pair. We define a cut through all accepting paths after for exactly $n/2-2$ (x, y)-pairs there exists at least one variable set to 1 for the first time. Let R_{p_u} (C_{p_u}) be the set of indices i for which a variable x_{i*} or y_{*i} (x_{*i} or y_{i*}) is set to 1 on p_u. If $n/2-1$ *rows* and *columns* are fixed, there are $(n/2-1)!$ possibilities to map the indices of the rows to the indices of the columns. Each initial part of an accepting path can be continued by at most $(n/2)!$ subpath to the 1-sink. Therefore, there is a set P of different initial paths from the source to the cut, $|P| \geq \binom{n-1}{n/2-1}$, such that for two different paths p'_u and p''_u in P we know that $R_{p'_u} \neq R_{p''_u}$ or $C_{p'_u} \neq C_{p''_u}$. Due to our choice of the considered paths, there are extensions p'_ℓ of p'_u and p''_ℓ of p''_u which lead to the 1-sink. Since $R_{p'_u} \neq R_{p''_u}$ or $C_{p'_u} \neq C_{p''_u}$, p'_u concatenate with p''_ℓ cannot correspond to a Boolean encoding, where in each row and in each column is exactly one 1-entry, and therefore, cannot be an accepting path. Here, we make use of the fact that we investigate a subfunction of $\mathcal{X}_M$ whose 1-inputs correspond to edges between vertices with property $\mathcal{P}$ in the input graph. Therefore, the paths in P cannot lead to the same node in G'_M and the size of the set P is a lower bound on the size of G'_M. Using Stirling's formula we obtain a lower bound of $\Omega(n^{-1/2}2^n)$ and we are done.

Summarizing, we have shown that the maximum matching problem may cause exponential space requirements on OBDD-represented graphs by generating instances with an exponential gap between the input and the output OBDD size. On the other hand, there exists a perfect matching in G whose OBDD complexity is linear. Therefore, the representation sizes for maximum matchings in a graph can be quite different. Now, we show that an exponential gap between input and output size is also possible if the maximum matching is unique. In this way we demonstrate that every symbolic OBDD-based algorithm for the maximum matching problem need exponential space. We start with the definition of a function which is well known in the BDD literature.

Definition 5. *The hidden weighted bit function* $\mathrm{HWB}_n : \{0,1\}^n \rightarrow \{0,1\}$ *computes the bit* b_{sum} *on the input* $b = (b_1, \ldots, b_n)$*, where* $sum := \sum_{i=1}^{n} b_i$ *and* $b_0 := 0$.

Bryant [7] has introduced this function as a very simple version of storage access where each variable is control and data variable. He has also already shown that the OBDD complexity of HWB_n is $\Omega(2^{(1/5-\epsilon)n})$ which has been slightly improved up to $\Omega(2^{n/5})$ in [5].

1) The definition of the input graph G_n:

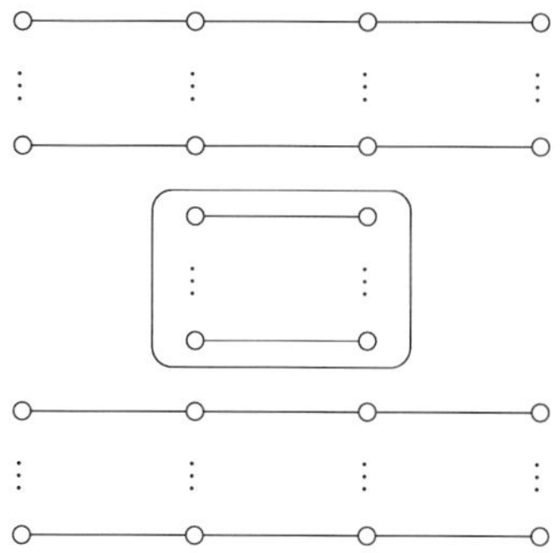

Fig. 1. The input graph G_n and the set of hidden difficult edges

The graph $G_n = (V, E)$ consists of 2^{2n+2} vertices v_{i_1,i_2,i_3}, $i_1 \in \{0, \ldots, 3\}$, $i_2, i_3 \in \{0, \ldots, 2^n - 1\}$. Let $b^i = (b^i_0, \ldots, b^i_{n-1})$ be the binary representation of an integer $i \in \{0, \ldots, 2^n - 1\}$. There exists an edge between a vertex v_{i_1,i_2,i_3} and a vertex v_{j_1,j_2,j_3} if one of the following requirements is fulfilled:

- $i_1 = 0, i_2 = 2^k$, $\sum_{\ell=0}^{n-1} b^{i_3}_\ell = k$ and $b^{i_3}_{k-1} = 1$,
  $j_1 = 1, j_2 = 0$, and $j_3 = i_3$, or
- $i_1 = 2, i_2 = 0$, $\sum_{\ell=0}^{n-1} b^{i_3}_\ell = k$ and $b^{i_3}_{k-1} = 1$,
  $j_1 = 3, j_2 = 2^k$, and $j_3 = i_3$, or
- $i_1 = 1, i_2 = 0$, $j_1 = 2, j_2 = 0$, and $j_3 = i_3$.

Figure 1 shows the structure of the input graph G_n, where isolated vertices are missing. Obviously, the maximum matching in G_n is unique (see Figure 2). The important property of G_n is that an edge from a vertex v_{1,i_2,i_3} to a vertex v_{2,j_2,j_3} belongs to the maximum matching iff $i_2 = j_2 = 0$, $i_3 = j_3$, and the binary representation of i_3 respectively j_3 corresponds to an input that belongs to $\mathrm{HWB}_n^{-1}(0)$. The characteristic function of this edge set is a difficult function but in our input graph this edge set is in some sense hidden (see Figure 1) such that the characteristic function of the edge set of the input graph can be represented by OBDDs of small size.

2) The polynomial upper bound on the OBDD size of $\mathcal{X}_E$:

Let $x^1_0, x^1_1, x^2_0, \ldots, x^2_{n-1}, x^3_0, \ldots, x^3_{n-1}$ be the variables of the Boolean encoding of a vertex v_{i_1,i_2,i_3}, where x^1_0, x^2_0, and x^3_0 denote the least significant bits, the x^1-variables represent i_1, the x^2-variables i_2, and the x^3-variables i_3. The

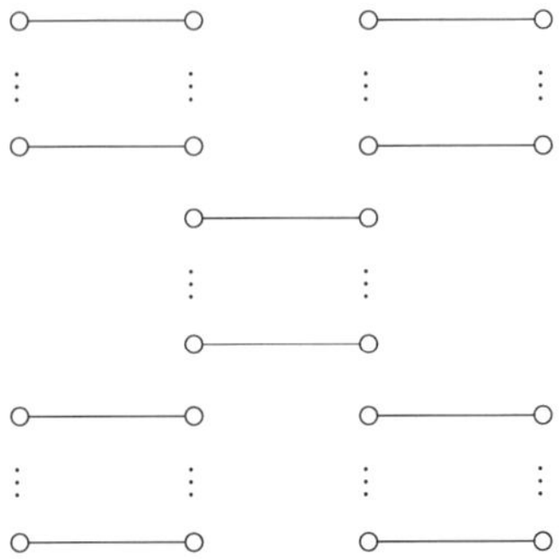

Fig. 2. The unique maximum matching in G_n

characteristic function $\mathcal{X}_E$ of the edge set depends on $2(2n+2)$ Boolean variables $((x_0^1, x_1^1, x_0^2, \ldots, x_{n-1}^2, x_0^3, \ldots, x_{n-1}^3), (y_0^1, y_1^1, y_0^2, \ldots, y_{n-1}^2, y_0^3, \ldots, y_{n-1}^3))$.

Our aim is to prove that $\mathcal{X}_E$ can be represented by OBDDs of size $O(n^2)$ according to the variable ordering

$$x_0^1, y_0^1, x_1^1, y_1^1, x_0^2, y_0^2, \ldots, x_{n-1}^2, y_{n-1}^2, x_0^3, y_0^3, \ldots, x_{n-1}^3, y_{n-1}^3.$$

There are three different disjoint edge sets, from $v_{0,\cdot,\cdot}$- to $v_{1,\cdot,\cdot}$-, from $v_{1,\cdot,\cdot}$- to $v_{2,\cdot,\cdot}$-, and from $v_{2,\cdot,\cdot}$- to $v_{3,\cdot,\cdot}$-vertices. We prove that each of them can be represented by OBDDs of small size. Since the different edge sets can be identified by the assignments to the x^1- and y^1-variables which are tested at the beginning of the OBDD, it suffices to add the OBDD sizes in order to obtain an upper bound on the OBDD complexity of $\mathcal{X}_E$.

If $x_0^1 = x_1^1 = 0$, $y_0^1 = 0$, and $y_1^1 = 1$, it is checked whether $y_0^2 = \ldots = y_{n-1}^2 = 0$, and there exists exactly one x^2-variable set to 1. If $|x^2| = 2^i$, the number of x^3-variables is counted. The function value is 1 if $\sum_{\ell=0}^{n-1} x_\ell^3 = i$, $x_{i-1}^3 = 1$, and $y_\ell^3 = x_\ell^3$, $0 \leq \ell \leq n-1$. Since we only have to distinguish n different values for $|x^2|$, this can be done by an OBDD of width $O(n)$.

If $x_0^1 = 0$, $x_1^1 = 1$, $y_0^1 = y_1^1 = 0$, the roles of the x- and y-variables are exchanged. The cases $x_0^1 = 1$, $x_1^1 = 0$, $y_0^1 = y_1^1 = 1$, and $x_0^1 = x_1^1 = 1$, $y_0^1 = 0$, $y_1^1 = 1$ are similar.

If $x_0^1 = 1$, $x_1^1 = 0$, $y_0^1 = 0$, $y_1^1 = 1$, or $x_0^1 = 0$, $x_1^1 = 1$, $y_0^1 = 1$, $y_1^1 = 0$, it is checked whether $|x^2| = |y^2| = 0$ and $|x^3| = |y^3|$. This can be done by an OBDD of constant width.

Altogether, we have seen that $\mathcal{X}_E$ can be represented by an OBDD of size $O(n^2)$.

3) The exponential lower bound on the OBDD size for the characteristic function of the maximum matching $\mathcal{X}_M$ in G_n:

Due to our definition of G_n the maximum matching contains an edge from a vertex v_{1,i_2,i_3} to a vertex v_{2,j_2,j_3} if $i_2 = j_2 = 0$, $i_3 = j_3$, and the binary representation of i_3 respectively j_3 corresponds to an input that belongs to $\text{HWB}_n^{-1}(0)$.

Our aim is to adapt the ideas for the exponential lower bound on the OBDD size of HWB_n presented in [7]. Therefore, we consider the subfunction of $\mathcal{X}_M$, where $x_0^1 = 1$, $x_1^1 = 0$, $y_0^1 = 0$, $y_1^1 = 1$, and the x^2- and y^2-variables are replaced by 0. In the following we assume that n is a multiple of 10 because it has no bearing on the essence of the proof. Let π be an arbitrary but fixed variable ordering. A pair (x_ℓ^3, y_ℓ^3) is called (x, y)-pair and x_ℓ^3 a partner of y_ℓ^3 and vice versa. Now, we define a cut in the variable ordering after for the first time for exactly $(6/10)n$ (x, y)-pairs there exist at least one variable. T contains the variables before the cut according to π and B the remaining variables. Let P_H be the set of all pairs (x_i^3, y_i^3), $i \in \{(5/10)n + 1, \ldots, (9/10)n\}$, and P_L be the set of all pairs (x_j^3, y_j^3), $j \in \{(1/10)n + 1, \ldots, (5/10)n\}$. Obviously, T contains at least for $(2/10)n$ pairs in P_H or at least for $(2/10)n$ pairs in P_L at least one variable. W.l.o.g. we assume that T contains at least for $(2/10)n$ pairs in P_L at least one variable. In the following we only consider assignments where variables that belong to the same (x, y)-pair are replaced by the same constant. We consider all assignments to the variables in T where exactly $(1/10)n$ pairs in P_L are replaced by 1, all other variables in T are set to 0. There are at least $\binom{(2/10)n}{(1/10)n} = \Omega(n^{-1/2}2^{n/5})$ different assignments. Using Theorem 3 it is sufficient to prove that these assignments lead to different subfunctions. For this reason we consider two different assignments b and b' to the variables in T. Let $(x_{\ell-1}^3, y_{\ell-1}^3)$ be an (x, y)-pair for which at least one variable is replaced differently in b and b'. W.l.o.g. $x_{\ell-1}^3$ is set to 0 in b and to 1 in b'. Now, we consider the following assignment b_r to the variables in B. The variables for which there is a partner in T are replaced by the assignment to the partner according to b. The remaining variables are replaced in such a way that there are exactly $\ell - (1/10)n$ pairs that are set to 1. This can be done because there are $(4/10)n$ pairs for which both variables are in B and $\ell \leq (5/10)n$. Obviously, the function value of the subfunction induced by b on b_r is 1. The function value for the subfunction induced by b' on b_r is 0 because either $|x^3| \neq |y^3|$ or $x^3 \in \text{HWB}_n^{-1}(1)$.

Altogether, we have shown that the OBDD complexity of $\mathcal{X}_M$ is at least $\Omega(n^{-1/2}2^{n/5})$.

4 Exponential Blow-Ups for the OBDD-Complexity of Directed and Undirected Graphs

In this section we prove Theorem 2 and consider the OBDD size of directed and undirected graphs.

Definition 6. *An undirected graph $G_u = (V, E_u)$ is called the counterpart of a directed graph $G_d = (V, E_d)$ iff for all edges $(u, w) \in E_d$ the edge (u, w) is in E_u. An asymmetric directed graph $G_D = (V, E_D)$ is called a counterpart of an undirected graph $G_U = (V, E_U)$ if for all edges $(u, w) \in E_U$ the edge (w, u) is not in E_D but $(u, w) \in E_D$ or vice versa.*

In order to prove Theorem 2, we investigate the following directed bipartite graph $G_d = (V, E_d)$ defined on 2^{n^2+1} vertices. V is partitioned into the sets U

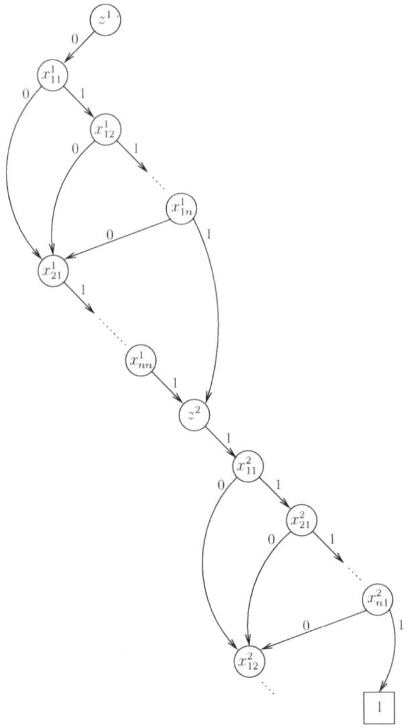

Fig. 3. An OBDD for $\mathcal{X}_{E_d}$. Missing edges are leading to the 0-sink.

and W of equal size. The Boolean encoding of a vertex $v \in V$ consists of $n^2 + 1$ Boolean variables $z, x_{11}, \ldots, x_{nn}$, where the variable z indicates whether $v \in U$ ($z = 0$) or in W ($z = 1$). The x-variables can be seen as a Boolean matrix X of dimension $n \times n$. There exists an edge from a node $u \in U$ to a node $w \in W$ if there exists a row that consists only of 1-entries in the Boolean encoding X of u and a column that contains only 1-entries in the Boolean encoding according to the x-variables of w. Next, we prove that G_d can be represented by OBDDs of linear size with respect to the number of Boolean variables but the undirected counterpart G_u needs exponential size. The characteristic function of the edge set of G_d is defined on the variables $(z^1, x^1_{11}, \ldots, x^1_{nn}), (z^2, x^2_{11}, \ldots, x^2_{nn})$. Our aim is to prove that $\mathcal{X}_{E_d}$ can be represented by OBDDs of size $O(n^2)$ and constant width according to the variable ordering

$$z^1, x^1_{11}, x^1_{12}, \ldots, x^1_{nn}, z^2, x^2_{11}, x^2_{21}, \ldots, x^2_{nn},$$

i.e., the first x-variables are tested in a row-wise manner, variables that belong to the same row are tested one after another, and the last x-variables are tested in a column-wise manner. Applying Theorem 3 is is sufficient to prove that there are only a constant number of different subfunctions obtained by replacements of the first i variables for all $i \in \{1, \ldots, 2n^2 + 2\}$ with respect to the considered variable ordering. If z^1 is 1, the function value is 0 because there are no edges from a vertex $w \in W$ to a vertex $u \in U$. If z^1 is 0, the x^1-variables are tested row-wise and it is checked whether there exists a row that consists only of 1-entries. This can be done by an OBDD of width 1. If the test is negative, the function value is 0. If the test is positive, the variable z^2 is tested. The function value is 0, if z^2 is 0, because there are no edges between vertices in U. Afterwards the x^2-variables are tested column-wise and the function value is 1 iff there exists a column that contains only 1-entries. This can also be done by an OBDD of width 1. Figure 3 shows an OBDD for $\mathcal{X}_{E_d}$.

For the lower bound proof on the OBDD size for the characteristic function of the undirected counterpart G_u let π be an arbitrary but fixed variable ordering. We define a cut in π where for the first time $n/2-1$ rows or $n/2-1$ columns have a tested x^1- or x^2-variable. X_U contains the x-variables before the cut in π, X_L the remaining x-variables.

Case 1: There are $n/2-1$ rows for which an x^1-variable or $n/2-1$ columns for which an x^2-variable is in X_U.

W.l.o.g. we assume that there are $n/2-1$ rows for which an x^1-variable is in X_U. First, we set z^1 to 0 and z^2 to 1. The x^2-variables are replaced by constants in the following way:

- the variables $x^2_{11}, x^2_{21}, \ldots, x^2_{n1}$ are set to 1,
- the remaining x^2-variables are set to 0.

As a result we obtain a subfunction of $\mathcal{X}_{E_u}$ whose function value is 1 iff the Boolean matrix defined by $x^1_{11}, \ldots, x^1_{nn}$ contains a row that consists only of 1-entries. Now, we prove that a π-OBDD for this subfunction needs exponential size. We set the x^1-variables tested first in the first $n/2-1$ rows with respect to π to all possible assignments. Variables in X_U that belong to the same row are set to the same constant. Next, we prove that two different assignments b and b' of these $2^{n/2-1}$ partial assignments lead to different subfunctions. For this reason we consider the following assignment b_r to the remaining x^1-variables in X_L. Let ℓ be a row for which the x^1-variables in b are set to 1 and in b' to 0 (or vice versa). W.l.o.g. we assume that the $x_{\ell\cdot}$-variables in b are set to 1 and in b' to 0. In b_r the $x^1_{\ell\cdot}$ -variables are set to 1, the remaining x^1-variables are set to 0. There exist $x^1_{\ell\cdot}$-variables in X_L because otherwise there are n rows that have a variable in X_U. The function value of the considered subfunction obtained by b respectively b' for b_r is 1 respectively 0, therefore the induced subfunctions are different and we are done.

Case 2: There are $n/2-1$ columns for which an x^1-variable or $n/2-1$ rows for which an x^2-variable is in X_U.

By replacing the variables z^1 by 1 and z^2 by 0 the case is similar to the first one and we are done.

One might think that our result is not very astonishing because the orientation of an edge can store some kind of information and without this information the representation size may enlarge. Nevertheless, if the characteristic function $\mathcal{X}_{E_d}$

of a directed graph $G_d = (V, E_d)$ is represented by a circuit, the representation size for the undirected counterpart can only enlarge by a factor of 2. In the following we show that the same holds for 2-PBDDs which are slightly more general than OBDDs. Let E_d^R be the set of edges obtained by replacing each directed edge $(u, v) \in E_d$ by the directed edge (v, u). Let G_{E_d} be an OBDD for the characteristic function $\mathcal{X}_{E_d}$ which is defined on x- and y-variables. The PBDD consists of two OBDDs according to different variable orderings. The first part represents the edges in E_d and is equal to G_{E_d}, the second part represents $\mathcal{X}_{E_d}^R$. For the second part of the 2-PBDD we change the variable ordering of G_{E_d} by renaming the x-and the y-variables, i.e., nodes labeled by x_i are now y_i-nodes and vice versa (for all indices). Obviously, the second part of the 2-PBDD has the same size as G_{E_d} and represents $\mathcal{X}_{E_d}^R$. Altogether, our result on the OBDD size of directed graphs and their undirected counterparts is not as obvious as it seems to be.

In the design and analysis of symbolic graph algorithms OBDDs are often ordered according to so-called interleaved variable orderings, where x- and y-variables of the same significance (or with the same indices) are tested consecutively (see, e.g., [21] and [28]). This seems to be reasonable, since the characteristic function of an undirected graph is symmetric. If a directed graph $G_d = (V, E_d)$ can be represented symbolically by an OBDD G_{E_d} of small size according to an interleaved variable ordering, its undirected counterpart $G_u = (V, E_u)$ can also be represented symbolically by an OBDD of small size. To be more precise, if S is the size of G_{E_d}, the OBDD size of $\mathcal{X}_{E_u}$ is bounded above by $O(S^2)$. The reason is the following one. If we modify a π-OBDD for a function f into a π'-OBDD for f, where π' can be obtained from π by only exchanging the position of neighbored variables, the size of the π'-OBDD can only be by a factor of 3 larger than the size of the π-OBDD (see Theorem 4 in [4]). Afterwards an OBDD for $\mathcal{X}_{E_u}$ can be obtained by applying an $\vee$-synthesis on the OBDDs for $\mathcal{X}_{E_d}$ and $\mathcal{X}_{E_d^R}$ because now the OBDDs are ordered with respect to the same variable ordering. Using the well-known results on the worst-case complexity of the synthesis-operation (see, e.g., [6]), the OBDD size for $\mathcal{X}_{E_u}$ can be bounded above by the product of the OBDD sizes for $\mathcal{X}_{E_d}$ and $\mathcal{X}_{E_d^R}$.

In the rest of this section we show that also between undirected graphs and their directed counterparts an exponential blow-up in the representation size is possible. Again, we consider the complete undirected bipartite graph $G_U = (V, E_U)$ defined in Section 3. For each undirected edge in E_U we have two possibilities to choose the orientation. Using a simple counting argument, it is easy to see that there exists a directed counterpart of G_U whose OBDD complexity is exponential. Finally, we present a concrete directed counterpart of G_U whose OBDD size is exponential. The graph is defined in the following way. There exists an edge from $u \in U$ to a vertex $w \in W$ iff the x-variables of the Boolean encoding of u correspond to a Boolean matrix that contains exactly one 1-entry in each row and in each column. If we replace z^1 by 0 and the variables $z^2, x_{11}^2, \ldots, x_{nn}^2$ by 1, we obtain the function PERM$_n$. As already mentioned in Section 3 the OBDD size of PERM$_n$ is $\Omega(n^{-1/2}2^n)$. Therefore, we are done.

Concluding Remarks

Symbolic graph algorithms on OBDD-based representations are implicitly parallel, since vertices or edges are treated simultaneously if they share their OBDD representations. Sawitzki [24] has shown that a problem is in the complexity class NC, which contains the problems that can be solved efficiently in parallel, if it can be solved with a polylogarithmic number of OBDD-operations with respect to the number of the vertices in a given graph. It is an open problem whether the maximum matching problem is in NC. Nevertheless, we have seen that symbolic algorithms for this problem need exponential space (with respect to the number of Boolean variables). Since in the complete bipartite graph presented in Section 3 there exists a maximum matching of linear OBDD size (a node in U in matched to a node in W if the x-variables in the Boolean encoding are equal) and a maximum matching whose representation size is exponential even for a more general model than OBDDs called nondeterministic read-once branching programs, we have seen that the representation sizes for maximum matchings in an input graph can be quite different.

Acknowledgment

The author would like to thank the anonymous referees for their helpful comments.

References

1. Balcázar, J.L., Lozano, A.: The complexity of graph problems for succinctly represented graphs. In: Nagl, M. (ed.) WG 1989. LNCS, vol. 411, pp. 277–285. Springer, Heidelberg (1990)
2. Bollig, B.: On the OBDD complexity of the most significant bit of integer multiplication. In: Agrawal, M., Du, D.-Z., Duan, Z., Li, A. (eds.) TAMC 2008. LNCS, vol. 4978, pp. 306–317. Springer, Heidelberg (2008)
3. Bollig, B.: Symbolic OBDD-based reachability analysis needs exponential space. In: van Leeuwen, J., Muscholl, A., Peleg, D., Pokorný, J., Rumpe, B. (eds.) SOFSEM 2010. LNCS, vol. 5901, pp. 224–234. Springer, Heidelberg (2010)
4. Bollig, B., Löbbing, M., Wegener, I.: On the effect of local changes in the variable ordering of ordered decision diagrams. Information Processing Letters 59, 233–239 (1996)
5. Bollig, B., Löbbing, M., Sauerhoff, M., Wegener, I.: On the complexity of the hidden weighted bit function for various BDD models. Theoretical Informatics and Applications 33, 103–115 (1999)
6. Bryant, R.E.: Graph-based algorithms for Boolean function manipulation. IEEE Trans. on Computers 35, 677–691 (1986)
7. Bryant, R.E.: On the complexity of VLSI implementations and graph representations of Boolean functions with application to integer multiplication. IEEE Trans. on Computers 40, 205–213 (1991)

8. Feigenbaum, J., Kannan, S., Vardi, M.V., Viswanathan, M.: Complexity of problems on graphs represented as OBDDs. In: Meinel, C., Morvan, M. (eds.) STACS 1998. LNCS, vol. 1373, pp. 216–226. Springer, Heidelberg (1998)
9. Fisler, K., Vardi, M.Y.: Bisimulation, minimization, and symbolic model checking. Formal Methods in System Design 21(1), 39–78 (2002)
10. Galperin, H., Wigderson, A.: Succinct representations of graphs. Information and Control 56, 183–198 (1983)
11. Gentilini, R., Piazza, C., Policriti, A.: Computing strongly connected components in a linear number of symbolic steps. In: Proc. of SODA, pp. 573–582. ACM Press, New York (2003)
12. Gentilini, R., Piazza, C., Policriti, A.: Symbolic graphs: linear solutions to connectivity related problems. Algorithmica 50, 120–158 (2008)
13. Hachtel, G.D., Somenzi, F.: A symbolic algorithm for maximum flow in $0-1$ networks. Formal Methods in System Design 10, 207–219 (1997)
14. Jain, J., Bitner, J., Fussell, D.S., Abraham, J.A.: Functional partitioning for verification and related problems. In: Brown MIT VLSI Conference, pp. 210–226 (1992)
15. Jukna, S.: The effect of null-chains on the complexity of contact schemes. In: Csirik, J.A., Demetrovics, J., Gecseg, F. (eds.) FCT 1989. LNCS, vol. 380, pp. 246–256. Springer, Heidelberg (1989)
16. Kannan, S., Naor, M., Rudich, S.: Implicit representations of graphs. SIAM Journal on Discrete Mathematics 5, 596–603 (1992)
17. Krause, M., Meinel, C., Waack, S.: Separating the eraser Turing machine classes L_e, NL_e, co-NL_e and P_e. Theoretical Computer Science 86, 267–270 (1991)
18. Meer, K., Rautenbach, D.: On the OBDD size for graphs of bounded tree- and clique-width. Discrete Mathematics 309(4), 843–851 (2009)
19. Nunkesser, R., Woelfel, P.: Representation of graphs by OBDDs. Discrete Applied Mathematics 157(2), 247–261 (2009)
20. Papadimitriou, C.H., Yannakakis, M.: A note on succinct representations of graphs. Information and Control 71, 181–185 (1986)
21. Sawitzki, D.: Implicit flow maximization by iterative squaring. In: Van Emde Boas, P., Pokorný, J., Bieliková, M., Štuller, J. (eds.) SOFSEM 2004. LNCS, vol. 2932, pp. 301–313. Springer, Heidelberg (2004)
22. Sawitzki, D.: Algorithmik und Komplexität OBDD-repräsentierter Graphen. PhD thesis, University of Dortmund (2006) (in German)
23. Sawitzki, D.: Exponential lower bounds on the space complexity of OBDD-based graph algorithms. In: Correa, J.R., Hevia, A., Kiwi, M. (eds.) LATIN 2006. LNCS, vol. 3887, pp. 781–792. Springer, Heidelberg (2006)
24. Sawitzki, D.: The complexity of problems on implicitly represented inputs. In: Wiedermann, J., Tel, G., Pokorný, J., Bieliková, M., Štuller, J. (eds.) SOFSEM 2006. LNCS, vol. 3831, pp. 471–482. Springer, Heidelberg (2006)
25. Sieling, D., Wegener, I.: NC-algorithms for operations on binary decision diagrams. Parallel Processing Letters 48, 139–144 (1993)
26. Talamo, M., Vocca, P.: Representing graphs implicitly using almost optimal space. Discrete Applied Mathematics 108, 193–210 (2001)
27. Wegener, I.: Branching Programs and Binary Decision Diagrams - Theory and Applications. SIAM Monographs on Discrete Mathematics and Applications (2000)
28. Woelfel, P.: Symbolic topological sorting with OBDDs. Journal of Discrete Algorithms 4(1), 51–71 (2006)

Traceable Sets

Rupert Hölzl and Wolfgang Merkle*

Institut für Informatik,
Ruprecht-Karls-Universität,
Heidelberg, Germany
{hoelzl,merkle}@math.uni-heidelberg.de

Abstract. We investigate systematically into the various possible notions of traceable sets and the relations they bear to each other and to other notions such as diagonally noncomputable sets or complex and autocomplex sets. We review known notions and results that appear in the literature in different contexts, put them into perspective and provide simplified or at least more direct proofs. In addition, we introduce notions of traceability and complexity such as infinitely often versions of jump traceability and of complexity, and derive results about these notions that partially can be viewed as a natural completion of the previously known results. Finally, we give a result about polynomial-time bounded notions of traceability and complexity that shows that in principle the equivalences derived so far can be transferred to the time-bounded setting.

1 Introduction and Overview

The various notions of a traceable set have received quite a lot of attention in the area of algorithmic randomness. On the one hand, traceability naturally comes up in connection with lowness notions, as it is exemplified in the work of Terwijn and Zambella [12] on Schnorr randomness and, more recently, the attempts to characterize lowness for Martin-Löf randomness and the equivalent notion of K-triviality by an appropriate version of jump traceability [1,3]. On the other hand, traceability has been shown [9] to interact informatively with classical notions from computability theory such as diagonally noncomputable sets and with notions such as autocomplex that are defined in terms of Kolmogorov complexity of initial segments of sets.

In this article, we investigate into notions of traceability from a systematic point of view. We review standard notions of traceability and some basic results known on them, giving simplified or at least more direct proofs than in the current literature, which in particular are meant to provide an intuitive picture of why the stated relations hold. One of our aims is to give a unified view of notions and results that appear in the literature, and for example we argue that a recent results on anticomplex sets by Franklin et al. [5] can be seen as a variant of results on the relations between notions of complexity and i.o. traceability [9].

* The first and the second author are supported and partially supported, respectively, by DFG grant ME 1806/3-1.

C.S. Calude and V. Sassone (Eds.): TCS 2010, IFIP AICT 323, pp. 301–315, 2010.

We also introduce new notions of traceability such as infinitely often versions of jump traceability and derive an interesting collapse result. Finally, we give a result about polynomial-time bounded notions of traceability and complexity that shows that in principle the equivalences derived so far can be transferred to the time-bounded setting.

Notation. In the sequel, set refers to a subset of the natural numbers $\mathbb{N}$ and functions and partial functions map natural numbers to natural numbers, unless explicitly specified differently. We let $\mathrm{W}_0, \mathrm{W}_1, \ldots$ be the standard acceptable numbering of all computably enumerable (c.e.) sets, i.e., W_e is the domain of the e-th partial computable function φ_e. Let C and K denote the plain and prefix-free versions of Kolmogorov complexity [4,10]. Let $\leq^+$ denote the relation less than or equal to up to an additive constant, and $\geq^+$ is defined likewise.

2 Traceability

The various traceability notions considered in the sequel are either well-known or have at least been considered implicitly in the literature, except for, to the best of our knowledge, the infinitely often versions of jump traceable and strongly jump traceable introduced in Definition 9 below.

Definition 1. *A* trace *is a sequence* $(T_n)_n$ *of sets. A trace* $(T_n)_n$ is a trace for *a partial function* f *if* $f(n) \in T_n$ *holds for all* n *such that* $f(n)$ *is defined. A trace* $(T_n)_n$ *is an* i.o. trace for *a partial function* f *if there are infinitely many* n *such that* $f(n) \in T_n$.

We will also say, for short, that a trace traces or i.o. traces a partial function f, in case the trace is a trace or an i.o. trace, respectively, for f. For the traces $(T_n)_n$ considered in the sequel, the sets T_n will always be finite.

Definition 2. *For a function* h*, a trace* $(T_n)_n$ *is* h-bounded, *if* $|T_n| \leq h(n)$ *holds for all* n.

A trace $(T_n)_n$ *is* computably enumerable (c.e.) *if there is a computable function* g *such that* T_n *is equal to* $\mathrm{W}_{g(n)}$ *for all* n*. A trace* $(T_n)_n$ *is* computable *if there is a computable function* g *such that* T_n *is equal to* $\mathrm{D}_{g(n)}$ *for all* n*, where* D_e *is the finite set with canonical index* e.

Definition 3. *An* order *is a nondecreasing and unbounded function. A set* A *is* c.e. traceable *iff there is a computable order* h *such that all functions* $f \leq_{\mathrm{T}} A$ *are traced by an* h*-bounded c.e. trace* $(T_n)_n$*. A set* A *is* c.e. i.o. traceable *iff there is a computable order* h *such that all functions* $f \leq_{\mathrm{T}} A$ *are i.o. traced by an* h*-bounded c.e. trace* $(T_n)_n$.

The concepts of computably traceable *and of* computably i.o. traceable *are defined similarly where in addition the traces are required to be computable instead of being merely c.e.*

For all the concepts introduced above, there are variants where Turing reducibility is replaced by weak truth-table or truth-table reducibility, e.g., we say a set A *is* i.o. wtt-traceable *iff there is a computable order* h *such that all functions* $f \leq_{\mathrm{wtt}} A$ *are i.o. traced by an* h*-bounded c.e. trace* $(T_n)_n$.

Remark 4. Stephan [11] made the interesting observation that a set is c.e. traceable if and only if there is a computable function h such that every $f \leq_T A$ satisfies $\mathrm{C}(f(n)) < h(n)$ for almost all n. This characterization has the advantage that it works without defining traces and just uses classical concepts. The disadvantage of this style of characterization is that for other traceability concepts it yields more complicated equivalences; for example the case of computable traceability would require the use of Kolmogorov complexity defined over total machines.

Terwijn and Zambella [12] observed that the notions of computable and c.e. traceability remain the same if one requires in their respective definitions the existence of h-bounded traces not just for a single but for all computable orders h. The corresponding argument extends directly to the notions c.e. and computably wtt-traceable, as well as c.e. and computably tt-traceable, but also to the infinitely often versions of these notions, as is shown in the following remark. For the notion of i.o. c.e. traceable this also follows by Theorem 10 below, and, what is more, by Corollaries 21 and 23 for some notions even the existence of 1-bounded traces of the considered type is equivalent.

Remark 5. A set A is c.e. i.o. traceable if and only if for all computable orders h all functions $f \leq_{\mathrm{T}} A$ are i.o. traced by an h-bounded c.e. trace $(T_n)_n$, and a similar statement holds for the notion computably i.o. traceable, as well as for variants of these notions defined in terms of weak truth-table or truth-table reducibility in place of Turing reducibility.

The proof uses the same technique as the proof [12] for the analogous everywhere version of the statement. Let us assume we have i.o. traces bounded by a computable order g and let us construct a i.o. trace $(S_n)_n$ for some function $f \leq_T A$ bounded by some given computable order h.

Let $\hat{g}(n)$ be the least number k such that $h(k) \geq g(n)$. This is computable and well-defined. Therefore the mapping $\hat{f}$ defined by $i \mapsto (f(0), \ldots, f(\hat{g}(i+1)))$ is Turing-reducible to A and therefore has a trace $(T_i)_i$ with bound g.

Let $\hat{g}^{-1}$ be the discrete inverse of $\hat{g}$, that is, for a given k, $\hat{g}^{-1}(k)$ is the largest number n such that $g(n) \leq h(k)$. Then define $(S_n)_n$ by

$$S_n := \{\pi_n(x) \colon x \in T_{\hat{g}^{-1}(n)}\}$$

where π_n is the projection to the n-th coordinate.

Then S_n has at most $g(\hat{g}^{-1}(n)) \leq h(n)$ entries. For infinitely many i, T_i is right; that is, it contains some correct $\hat{g}(i+1)$-tuple $(f(0), \ldots, f(\hat{g}(i+1)))$. This tuple then contains (among other) the correct information about the values of all $f(n)$ with n such that $\hat{g}^{-1}(n) = i$. So S_n will be a correct trace for $f(n)$ for all such n. □

The following theorem is attributed to Kjos-Hanssen et al. [9] by Downey and Hirschfeldt [4], however, the assertion of the theorem does not even implicitly appear in the published versions of the corresponding article [9], nor does its proof. Since the proof presented by Downey and Hirschfeldt is via a chain of equivalent statements, we consider it useful and instructive to give a direct argument here. Among the various equivalent definitions for the notion high, we will work with the one according to which a set A is high iff A computes a function that dominates every computable function.

Theorem 6. *The following statements are equivalent.*

(i) The set A is computably i.o. traceable.
(ii) The set A is c.e. i.o. traceable and nonhigh.

Proof. (i) implies (ii): Any computably i.o. traceable set A is *a fortiori* c.e. i.o. traceable, and is also nonhigh because given an A-computable function g we obtain a computable function f such that $g(n) \leq f(n)$ for infinitely many n by letting $f(n) = 1 + \max T_n$ where $(T_n)_n$ is a computable trace for g.

(ii) implies (i): Let us assume we have a i.o. trace $(T_n)_n$ of a function $\ell \leq_T A$. Define the function g such that on argument n one starts to enumerate in parallel the traces T_m for all $m \geq n$ and A-computably recognizes when for the first time for some m_n the correct value $\ell(m_n)$ is enumerated into T_{m_n}, then letting $g(n)$ be the number of computational steps of the enumeration of T_{m_n} that are required to enumerate $\ell(m_n)$. In this situation, let us say that n has found m_n. Since g is computable in A and A is nonhigh, there is a computable function f that at infinitely many places is larger than g, where in addition we can assume that f is nondecreasing.

We can now get a computable trace $(\widetilde{T}_n)_n$ for ℓ that is correct at infinitely many places as follows: simply let $\widetilde{T}_n$ contain all elements that are enumerated into T_n in at most $f(n)$ steps.

This trace is correct infinitely often. Indeed, *any* n finds *some* m_n, and among the corresponding pairs (n, m_n) there are infinitely many where we have

$$g(n) \leq f(n) \leq f(m_n),$$

i.e., for these pairs $f(m_n)$ exceeds the number of steps needed to enumerate $\ell(m_n)$ into T_{m_n}, so for these pairs the the correct value $\ell(m_n)$ will be a member of $\widetilde{T}_{m_n}$.

Finally observe that in the construction the set $\widetilde{T}_n$ is always contained in T_n, hence any uniform bound h for the c.e. traces of the functions computable in A will also be a uniform bound for the corresponding computable traces. □

We review the concepts of jump traceable and strongly jump traceable, which can be seen as stricter versions of the notion of c.e. traceable where not only the total but also all partial functions computable in a given set must be traced.

Definition 7. *A set A set is* jump traceable *iff there is a computable order h such that for all functions partially computable in A there is an h-bounded c.e. trace. A set A is* strongly jump-traceable *iff for all computable orders h it holds that for all functions partially computable in A there is an h-bounded c.e. trace.*

Remark 8. It is easier for our purposes to work with the given definition. Alternatively, jump traceability can be defined by requiring that the diagonal jump function is traceable. For more details, see Downey and Hirschfeldt [4].

It is well-known that the class of strongly jump-traceable sets is a proper subclass of the jump-traceable sets, in fact, the two classes are proper sub- and superclasses, respectively, of the class of K-trivial sets [1,3]. However, for the infinitely often versions of these two notions we get an interesting collapse of traceability notions.

Definition 9. *A set A is* i.o. jump-traceable *iff there is a computable order h such that for all functions partially computable in A that have an infinite domain there is an h-bounded c.e. i.o. trace.*

A set A is strongly i.o. jump-traceable *iff for all computable orders h it holds that for all all functions f partially computable in A that have an infinite domain there is an h-bounded c.e. i.o. trace.*

Theorem 10. *The following statements are equivalent.*

(i) The set A is strongly i.o. jump-traceable.
(ii) The set A is i.o. jump-traceable.
(iii) The set A is c.e. i.o. traceable.

Proof. By definition, (i) implies (ii) and (ii) implies (iii), so it suffices to show that not strongly i.o. jump traceable implies not c.e. i.o. traceable. So let A be a set that computes a partial function f that for some computable order h_0 cannot be i.o. traced by any h_0-bounded c.e. trace. We show that for any given computable order h there is an A-computable function that cannot be i.o. traced by any h-bounded c.e. trace. Fix an appropriate effective enumeration $(T_n^0)_n, (T_n^1)_n, \ldots$ of all h-bounded c.e. traces, e.g., let T_n^e be the subset of the n-th row of W_e that contains the first $h(n)$ elements that are enumerated into this row. Furthermore, let S_n be the union of all T_i^e where $i < n$ and $e < n$ and observe that this way the cardinality of S_n is at most $c(n) = n^2 h(n)$. For all n, let T_n be equal to S_m where m is maximum such that $c(m) \leq h_0(n)$ and call the trace $(T_n)_n$ the universal h_0-bounded trace, which by construction is indeed h_0-bounded, hence does not i.o. trace f. Hence for almost all m such that $f(m)$ is defined, we have $f(m) \notin T_m$. So we obtain an A-computable function as required by mapping n to a value of the form $f(m)$ such that this value is defined and $c(n) \leq h_0(m)$. □

In order to render the statement of results in Section 5 and 6 more intuitive, we introduce the following alternate notation for notions of not being traceable.

Definition 11. *A set* avoids c.e. traces *if the set is not c.e. i.o. traceable and the set* i.o. avoids c.e. traces *if it is not c.e. traceable. Similarly, a set* tt-avoids c.e. traces *if the set is not c.e. i.o. tt-traceable, and further notions such as c.e. wtt-avoiding computable traces are defined in the same manner.*

3 Autocomplex and Complex Sets

The notions of complexity and autocomplexity were first defined in an article by Kanovich [8], where he showed that autocomplex sets are Turing complete and complex sets are wtt-complete for the class of c.e. sets.

Definition 12. *A set A is* complex *if there is a computable order h such that for all n, it holds that $C(A \restriction n) \geq h(n)$.*

A set A is called autocomplex if there is an A-computable order h such that for all n, it holds that $C(A \restriction n) \geq h(n)$.

We omit the straightforward proof of the following known fact [4,9]. Note that by the standard proof of Proposition 13 it is immediate that all the functions g that occur in the proposition can be assumed to be order functions.

Proposition 13. *A set A is complex if and only if there is a computable function g such that for all n, we have $C(A \restriction g(n)) \geq n$ if and only if there is a function $g \leq_{\mathrm{tt}} A$ such that for all n, we have $C(g(n)) \geq n$ if and only if there is a function $g \leq_{\mathrm{wtt}} A$ such that for all n, we have $C(g(n)) \geq n$.*

A set A is autocomplex if and only if there is an A-computable function g such that for all n, we have $C(A \restriction g(n)) \geq n$ if and only if there is an A-computable function g such that for all n, we have $C(g(n)) \geq n$.

In Section 6, we will see that it is interesting to consider variants of the notions autocomplex and complex where the condition $C(A \restriction g(n)) \geq n$ is not required for all but just for infinitely many n. In connection with the following definition, note that the notion of *not* being i.o. complex has been introduced by Franklin et al. [5] under the name of anticomplex.

Definition 14. *A set A is* i.o. complex *iff there is a computable order g such that for infinitely many n, we have $\mathrm{C}(A \restriction g(n)) \geq n$.*

A set A is i.o. autocomplex *iff there is an A-computable order g such that for infinitely many n, we have $\mathrm{C}(A \restriction g(n)) \geq n$.*

The equivalent characterizations of complex suggest different ways to define i.o. complex (and similar remarks can be made for the notion i.o. autocomplex). However, it would neither be equivalent nor even make sense to define i.o. complexity by requiring that there is some computable order h such that for infinitely many n it holds that $\mathrm{C}(A \restriction n) \geq h(n)$, because for small h such as the map $n \mapsto \log\log n$ this inequality is satisfied for infinitely many initial segments of any set A, simply because a code for $A \restriction n$ is always also a code for n. In Section 8, we will see that equivalent definitions in this style are still possible by considering specific variants of Kolmogorov complexity. Furthermore, the two following propositions show that in the defining condition $\mathrm{C}(A \restriction g(n)) \geq n$ of i.o. autocomplexity and i.o. complexity the lower bound n can equivalently be replaced by a wide range of lower bounds in case g may depend on this bound.

Proposition 15. *The following assertions are equivalent.*

(i) The set A is i.o. autocomplex.

(ii) There is a computable order h and an A-computable function g such that there are infinitely many n where $\mathrm{C}(A \restriction g(n)) \geq \mathrm{C}(n) + h(n)$.
(iii) For every A-computable order h there is an A-computable function g such that there are infinitely many n where $\mathrm{C}(A \restriction g(n)) \geq h(n)$.

Proof. It is immediate that (i) implies (ii) and that (iii) implies (i). For a proof of the remaining implication from (ii) to (iii), fix h and g that satisfy (ii), and let h_A be any A-computable order. Let $m_0 = 0$ and for all $n > 0$ let

$$m_n = \min\{m \colon m_{n-1} < m \text{ and } 3h_A(n) \leq h(m)\} \quad \text{and} \quad I_n = [m_n, m_{n+1}) .$$

For all n, let $\widetilde{g}(n)$ an appropriate representation of the pair of the restriction of g to I_n and the initial segment of A of length $\max_{j \in I_n} g(j)$, and observe that the function $\widetilde{g}$ is A-computable. By assumption on g and by construction, there are infinitely many j such that for the index n where $j \in I_n$, we have

$$\mathrm{C}(A \restriction g(j)) \geq \mathrm{C}(j) + h(j) \geq \mathrm{C}(j) + h(m_n) \geq \mathrm{C}(j) + 3h_A(n) .$$

For each such j and n, it holds that $\mathrm{C}(\widetilde{g}(n)) \geq h_A(n)$, because otherwise $A \restriction g(j)$ could be described by a word of length $\mathrm{C}(j) + 2h_A(n) + \mathrm{O}(1)$. □

The following variant of Proposition 15 can be shown by an almost literally identical proof, which we omit.

Proposition 16. *The following assertions are equivalent.*

(i) The set A is i.o. complex.
(ii) There is a computable order h and a computable function g such that there are infinitely many n where $\mathrm{C}(A \restriction g(n)) \geq \mathrm{C}(n) + h(n)$.
(iii) For every computable order h there is a computable function g such that there are infinitely many n where $\mathrm{C}(A \restriction g(n)) \geq h(n)$.

4 Diagonally Noncomputable Sets

Definition 17. *A set A is* diagonally noncomputable (DNC) *if there is a function $f \leq_{\mathrm{T}} A$ such that $f(n)$ differs from $\varphi_n(n)$ whenever the latter value is defined. With an appropriate coding scheme for finite sequences of natural numbers understood, a set A is* strongly diagonally noncomputable (SDNC) *if there is a function $f \leq_{\mathrm{T}} A$ such that when z is a code for the sequence $e_1, x_1, \ldots, e_m, x_m$, then $f(z)$ differs for $i = 1, \ldots, m$ from $\varphi_{e_i}(x_i)$ whenever this value is defined.*

The notions of wtt-DNC, wtt-SDNC, tt-DNC, *and* tt-SDNC *are defined likewise, where in the above definitions $f \leq_{\mathrm{T}} A$ is replaced by $f \leq_{\mathrm{wtt}} A$ and $f \leq_{\mathrm{tt}} A$, respectively.*

Note that if we can compute a function f such that for given n the value $f(n)$ differs from $\varphi_n(n)$, we can also compute a function g such that for given e, x the value $g(e, x)$ differs from $\varphi_e(x)$, because by the s-m-n theorem one can effectively find an index i such that $\varphi_e(x)$ and $\varphi_i(i)$ are either both undefined or both defined and have the same value. By a result of Jokusch [7], indeed even the notions of DNC and SDNC coincide.

Theorem 18. *A set A is DNC if and only if A is SDNC.*

Proof. By definition, it suffices to show that DNC implies SDNC. If A is DNC, one obtains an A-computable function f as required as follows. By fixing uniformly effective and uniformly effectively invertible bijections between $\mathbb{N}$ and $\mathbb{N}^m$, for any m, natural numbers can be uniquely identified with m-tuples of natural numbers. Then given a sequence $e_1, x_1, \ldots, e_m, x_m$ with code z, let $f(z)$ be equal to the m-tuple $(y_1, \ldots, y_m)$, where y_i differs from the i-th component of $\varphi_{e_i}(x_i)$, whenever this value is defined. □

The following infinitely often versions of the notion DNC is due to Kjos Hanssen et al. [9]. Note that there are computable functions g such that $g(e)$ differs from $\varphi_e(e)$ for infinitely many e, hence in order to get interesting infinitely often versions of the various variants of the concept of DNC, one has to require more than just to be able to compute a function that differs from the partial diagonal function at infinitely many places.

Definition 19. *For a function g, let $E_g = \{e\colon g(e) = \varphi_e(e)\}$ be the* (diagonal) equality set *of g. A set A is* i.o. DNC *if for all computable functions z there is a function $g \leq_{\mathrm{T}} A$ such that there are infinitely many n where*

$$|E_g \cap \{0, \ldots, z(n) - 1\}| \leq n\ .$$

The concepts of i.o. tt-DNC *and* i.o. wtt-DNC *are defined likewise, where in the definition $g \leq_{\mathrm{T}} A$ is replaced by $g \leq_{\mathrm{tt}} A$ and $g \leq_{\mathrm{wtt}} A$, respectively.*

By definition, a set A is DNC if and only if there is an A-computable function such that E_g is empty, and consequently any set that is DNC is also i.o. DNC. More precisely, if a set A is DNC, then it satisfies the definition of i.o. DNC by a function $g \leq_{\mathrm{T}} A$ that does not depend on z. It can be shown that the latter also holds true for a set that is i.o. DNC and high, and that a DNC set A is high if and only if there is a single function $g \leq_{\mathrm{T}} A$ that works for all z such that in addition E_g is infinite.

5 Equivalences of the Almost Everwhere Notions

The following theorem is due to Kjos-Hanssen, Merkle and Stephan [9, Theorems 2.3 and 2.7]. The proof of their result given here is somewhat more direct, furthermore, their short but slightly technical proof of the implication from DNC to autocomplex is replaced by a simplified argument due to Khodyrev and Shen, who rediscovered the known equivalence of DNC and SDNC and observed that SDNC easily implies autocomplex. The equivalence results of this and the following sections are formulated in terms of avoidance as introduced in Definition 11 in order to render these results more intuitive.

Theorem 20. *The following assertions are equivalent.*

(i) The set A is autocomplex.

(ii) The set A is DNC.
(iii) The set A avoids c.e. traces.

Proof. First, assume that A is autocomplex. Then there is an A-computable function g such that for all n, we have $\mathrm{C}(g(n)) \geq n$. So $g(n)$ differs from $\varphi_n(n)$ for almost all n, because the latter value, if defined, has plain complexity of $\log n$ up to an additive constant, and consequently, A is DNC. Similarly, the set A is not c.e. i.o. traceable, i.e., avoids c.e. traces, because otherwise the function g had an n-bounded c.e. trace by Remark 5, which implied $\mathrm{C}(g(n)) \leq^+ 2\log n$.

Next assume that A is DNC and hence SDNC. Then A is autocomplex because in order to obtain for given n a value $g(n)$ where $\mathrm{C}(g(n)) \geq n$, it suffices to obtain a value that differs from all the values $\varphi_e(p)$ where the latter value is defined, p has length at most n, and e is an index for the universal machine used in the definition of the plain complexity C.

Finally, assume that the set A avoids c.e. traces, i.e., is not c.e. i.o. traceable. In order to see that A is DNC, let the diagonal trace $(T_n)_n$ be defined by $T(n) = \{\varphi_e(e)\}$. By assumption, there is an A-computable function g that is not i.o. traced by the diagonal trace, hence $g(e)$ differs from $\varphi_e(e)$, whenever the latter value is defined. □

Corollary 21. *A set A is c.e. i.o. traceable if and only if every A-computable function has a 1-bounded c.e. i.o. trace.*

Proof. It suffices to show the implication from left to right. By the proof of the implication from (iii) to (ii) in Theorem 20, if there is an A-computable function that has no 1-bounded c.e. i.o. trace, then this function witnesses that A is DNC, hence, by the same theorem, A is not i.o. c.e. traceable. □

The following variant of Theorem 20 is again due to Kjos-Hanssen et al. [9]. The proofs of Theorem 22 and its corollary are omitted because they are almost literally the same as for Theorem 22 and Corollary 21 when using the characterizations of the notion complex from Proposition 13 and showing separately the equivalences for truth-table and weak truth-table reducibility.

Theorem 22. *The following assertions are equivalent.*

(i) The set A is complex.
(ii) The set A is tt-DNC.
(iii) The set A tt-avoids c.e. traces.

The three assertions remain equivalent if one replaces in the two last assertions truth-table reducibility by weak truth-table reducibility.

Corollary 23. *The following assertions are all equivalent to A not being complex.*

(i) The set A is c.e. i.o. tt-traceable.
(ii) Every function $f \leq_{\mathrm{tt}} A$ *has a 1-bounded c.e. i.o. trace.*
(iii) The set A is c.e. i.o. wtt-traceable.
(iv) Every function $f \leq_{\mathrm{wtt}} A$ *has a 1-bounded c.e. i.o. trace.*

6 Equivalence of the Infinitely Often Notions

In Section 5 we have seen equivalences between first, notions of complexity and autocomplexity, second, computing diagonally noncomputable functions, and third, notions of avoiding c.e. traces. The corresponding proofs were rather direct and functions g as required in the definitions of these three notions where obtained place by place in the sense that, for example, a function value $g(n)$ that has a certain complexity is obtained by considering a value $g(n)$ that is not contained in a component T_n of an appropriate trace and vice versa. Accordingly, by identical or similar arguments, we obtain infinitely often versions of these equivalence results where now, for example, for all n such that the value $g(n)$ has high complexity the value $g(n)$ avoids a corresponding set T_n and vice versa.

The two following theorems are infinitely often versions of Theorems 20 and 22. The equivalence of assertions (i) and (iii) in Theorem 25 for the case of weak truth-table reducibility is due to Franklin et al. [5].

Theorem 24. *The following assertions are equivalent.*

(i) The set A is i.o autocomplex.
(ii) The set A is i.o. DNC.
(iii) The set A i.o. avoids c.e. traces.

Proof. We first show that (i) and (iii) are equivalent, which follows by essentially the same arguments as the equivalence of being autocomplex and being DNC stated in Theorem 20. If A is i.o. autocomplex, then there is an A-computable function g such that for infinitely many n it holds that $\mathrm{C}(g(n)) \geq n$, and such a function g cannot have a c.e. trace that, e.g., is n-bounded, hence A is not c.e. traceable, i.e., A i.o. avoids c.e. traces. Conversely, if A i.o. avoids c.e. traces, there is an A-computable function g that has no 2^n-bounded c.e. trace, hence in particular, there are infinitely many n such that there is no word w of length strictly less than n such that $g(n) = U(w)$, where U is the universal machine used in the definition of C, and consequently A is i.o. autocomplex.

In order to show that (i) implies (ii), assume that A is i.o. autocomplex. Fix any computable function z and let $m_0, m_1, \ldots$ be a strictly increasing computable sequence of natural numbers such that for all i, we have $z(m_i) < m_{i+1}$. This way the natural numbers are partitioned into consecutive intervals $I_i = [m_i, m_{i+1})$. By Proposition 15, choose some A-computable function g_0 such that there are infinitely many n such that $\mathrm{C}(g_0(n)) \geq \max I_n$. For all n and all j in I_n, let $g(j) = g_0(n)$. Then g is A-computable and there are infinitely many n where for all j in I_n we have

$$\mathrm{C}(\varphi_j(j)) \leq^+ \log j < j \leq \max I_n \leq \mathrm{C}(g_0(n)) = \mathrm{C}(g(j)) ,$$

i.e., the set E_g has an empty intersection with I_n and thus contains at most $m_n = \min I_n$ numbers that are less than or equal to $z(m_n) \leq \max I_n$.

In order to demonstrate that (ii) implies (iii), we show the contrapositive, so assume that A does not i.o. avoid c.e. traces, i.e., that A is c.e. traceable. Fix some appropriate effective way of coding finite sequences of natural numbers of arbitrary length by single natural numbers. Let $(T^0_\ell)_{\ell\in\mathbb{N}}, (T^1_\ell)_{\ell\in\mathbb{N}}, \ldots$ be an appropriate effective enumeration of all c.e. traces. Let s be a computable function such that for all i and j the partial computable function $\varphi_{s(i,j)}$ on input y is computed by enumerating the numbers $c_0, c_1, \ldots$ in T^i_y until c_j is reached, where c_j is then considered as a code for a finite sequence of the form $g(0), g(1), \ldots, g(\ell)$ and in case $y \leq \ell$ the output is $g(y)$.

Next define a computable function z where for all n the value $z(n)$ is chosen so large that for all $i < n$ and $j < n$ there are at least $n+1$ mutually distinct indices $e \leq z(n)$ such that the partial function φ_e is the same as $\varphi_{s(i,j)}$. Then given any function $g \leq_T A$, let $\widetilde{g}(n)$ be a code for the finite sequence $g(0), \ldots g(z(n))$. By assumption on A, for $h\colon n \mapsto n$ there is an index i such that the c.e. trace $(T^i_\ell)_{\ell\in\mathbb{N}}$ is h-bounded and traces the function $\widetilde{g}$. For given n, let j be minimum such that $\widetilde{g}(n) = c_j$, where $c_0, c_1, \ldots$ are the numbers that are enumerated into T^i_n. Then for all sufficiently large n, there are at least $n+1$ places $e \leq z(n)$ such that

$$\varphi_e(e) = \varphi_{s(i,j)}(e) = g(e),$$

and since g was an arbitrary A-computable function and z does not depend on g, the set A is not i.o. DNC. □

Theorem 25. *The following assertions are equivalent.*

(i) The set A is i.o. complex.
(ii) The set A is i.o. tt-DNC.
(iii) The set A i.o. tt-avoids c.e. traces.

The three assertions remain equivalent if one replaces in the two last assertions truth-table reducibility by weak truth-table reducibility.

7 Computable Traces and Total Machines

We have seen above that traceability notions defined in terms of c.e. traces can be characterized by concepts such as autocomplexity that relate to the plain Kolmogorov complexity of the initial segments of a set. We will see now that these characterizations can be extended to traceability notions defined in terms of computable traces if one considers the complexity of initial segments with respect to total machines.

Remark 26. Bienvenu and Merkle [2] have defined the notion of decidable machines, that is, machines whose domain is decidable. Obviously, every total machine is decidable, and every decidable machine can be easily converted into a total machine by first deciding whether a string is in the domain and then executing the machine as normal if that is the case, and outputting a constant otherwise.

Definition 27. *A set A is* totally complex *iff there is a computable function g such that for all total machines M and almost all n, we have $\mathrm{C}_M(A \upharpoonright g(n)) \geq n$. A set A is* totally i.o. complex *iff there is a computable function g such that for all total machines M there are infinitely many n where $\mathrm{C}_M(A \upharpoonright g(n)) \geq n$.*

Theorem 28 can be obtained from a result of Kjos-Hanssen et al. [9, Theorem 5.1] and Theorem 6. We omit the proof of Theorem 28 and give instead the very similar proof of its infinitely often version Theorem 29. In connection with the latter theorem, note that Franklin and Stephan [6] considered computably tt-traceable sets, that is, sets that do not i.o. tt-avoid computable traces, and showed that these sets are exactly the Schnorr-trivial sets.

Theorem 28. *A set A is totally complex if and only if A tt-avoids computable traces.*

Theorem 29. *A set A is totally i.o. complex if and only if A i.o. tt-avoids computable traces.*

Proof. First assume that A is not totally i.o. complex, i.e., for any computable function g there is a total machine M such that for almost all n, we have $C_M(A \upharpoonright g(n)) \leq n$. Fix any function $f \leq_{\mathrm{tt}} A$ and some tt-reduction witnessing this fact, which has use bound $u(n)$. By assumption on A, there is a total machine M such that for almost all n, we have $C_M(A \upharpoonright u(n)) \leq n$. In order to obtain a computable trace $(T_n)_n$ for f that is bounded by the function $n \mapsto 2^{n+1}$, execute all codes of length up to n on M, view the outputs as initial segments of oracles, and let T_n contain all values that one obtains by simulating the fixed tt-reduction for computing f at place n with any of these oracles. Then $f(n)$ is contained in T_n for almost all n. Since the bound 2^{n+1} on the size of the sets T_n does not depend on f, the set A is computably tt-traceable.

Next assume that A does not i.o. tt-avoid computable traces, i.e., that A is is computably tt-traceable, and recall that by the discussion preceding Remark 5 we can assume that any function wtt-reducible to A has a computable trace that is n-bounded. Given a computable function g, we need to show that there is a total machine M such that for almost all n, we have $C_M(A \upharpoonright g(n)) \leq n$. We can assume that the function $n \mapsto A \upharpoonright g(n)$ has a computable trace $(T_n)_n$ where T_n has size at most n. Let M be the machine, which on input (n, i) outputs the i-th element of T_n, if this element exists, and outputs some constant otherwise. Since the set T_n has size at most n and its canonical index can be computed from n, M is total and satisfies $C_M(A \upharpoonright g(n)) \leq 2 \log n \leq n$ for almost all n. □

8 Characterizing i.o. Complex and i.o. Autocomplex via Lower Bounds on the Complexity of Initial Segments

When introducing the notions of i.o. complex and i.o. autocomplex, we have argued that it does not make sense to define these notions by requiring for the set A under consideration that for a computable or A-computable order, respectively, infinitely often the order provides a lower bound for the plain Kolmogorov complexity of an initial segment of A, and the reason for this was simply that by choosing a small enough order this condition would be trivially satisfied by all sets. We will argue in this section, however, that equivalent definitions in terms of lower bounds for the complexity of initial segments can be given if plain Kolmogorov complexity C is replaced by appropriate variants, e.g., by uniform or monotonic complexity (see Li and Vitányi [10] for a more detailed account of these notions). Due to space considerations, we will restrict attention to the concept of i.o. autocomplex.

Definition 30. *Let U be the universal Turing machine used to define plain Kolmogorov complexity* C.

The length-conditioned complexity $\mathrm{C}(w \mid n)$ *of w is the length of the shortest program p such that U on input $(p, |w|)$ will output w.*

The uniform complexity $\mathrm{C}(w; n)$ *of w is the length of the shortest program p such that for all $i \leq |w|$, U on input (p, i) will output the first i bits of w, while U may do anything on inputs (p, i) with $|w| < i$.*

The monotonic complexity $\mathrm{C}_{\mathrm{mon}}(w)$ *is the length of the shortest program p such that U on input p will output some extension of w.*

From these definitions, the following chain of inequalities is immediate,

$$\mathrm{C}(w \mid n) \leq^{+} \mathrm{C}(w; n) \leq^{+} \mathrm{C}_{\mathrm{mon}}(w) \leq^{+} \mathrm{C}(w) \,. \tag{1}$$

Definition 31. *A set A is* length-conditionedly i.o. autocomplex *iff there is an A-computable order h such that for infinitely many n, we have $h(n) \leq \mathrm{C}(A \upharpoonright n \mid n)$.*

A set A is uniformly i.o. autocomplex *iff there is an A-computable order h such that for infinitely many n, we have $h(n) \leq \mathrm{C}(A \upharpoonright n; n)$.*

A set A is monotonically i.o. autocomplex *iff there is an A-computable order h such that for infinitely many n, we have $h(n) \leq \mathrm{C}_{\mathrm{mon}}(A \upharpoonright n)$.*

In connection with the following theorem, recall that the first, and hence also the second and third assertion are equivalent to A not being c.e. traceable. We omit the proof of the following theorem due to space considerations.

Theorem 32. *The following assertions are equivalent.*

(i) The set A is i.o. autocomplex.
(ii) The set A is monotonically i.o. autocomplex.
(iii) The set A is uniformly i.o. autocomplex.

These three equivalent assertions are all implied by

(iv) The set A is length-conditionedly i.o. autocomplex.

9 Time Bounded Traceability and Complexity

In this last section, we will show that for appropriately chosen notions of complexity and traceability, the relations between these two notions can be transferred to the time-bounded setting, more precisely, to a setting of polynomial time bounds.

Definition 33. *For $t \in \mathbb{N}$, let $C^t(x) := \min\{|\sigma| : U(\sigma) = x$ in at most t steps$\}$.*

Consider a coding of finite sets of natural numbers where the code of a set D consists of the concatenation of the binary expansion of elements of D in the natural order, where all the bits in the binary expansions are doubled and the binary expansions are separated from each other by the word 01. In the sequel, we will identify a finite set D with its code. Instead of looking at the Kolmogorov complexity of initial segments we will examine the Kolmogorov complexity of strings $A \upharpoonright D$ where D is a finite subset of $\mathbb{N}$. This will be defined in the straightforward way.

Definition 34. *A set A is* i.o. poly-complex *iff there is a computable order h such that for all polynomials p there are infinitely many sets D where we have for $t = p(|D| + |\max D|)$ that $\mathrm{C}^t(A \upharpoonright D \mid D) \geq h(\max D)$.*

Definition 35. *A set A is polynomial-time tt-traceable iff for all computable orders h, we have that for every function $f \leq^{\mathbf{P}}_{\mathrm{tt}} A$ there is an h-bounded trace $(T_n)_n$ such that for given n, the list of elements of T_n can be computed (or, say, printed) in time polynomial in the length of n.*

Theorem 36. *The following statements are equivalent.*

(i) A is not i.o. poly-complex.
(ii) A is polynomial-time tt-traceable.

Proof. (i) implies (ii): Let h be the desired trace bound, where we can assume $h(n) \leq n$ by switching to a delayed version of h, and let $f \leq^{\mathbf{P}}_{\mathrm{tt}} A$ be the function to be traced. Let q be the polynomial time bound of some fixed tt-reduction from f to A, and let $D(n)$ be the query set of this reduction at place n, where we can assume that $D(n)$ always contains n.

Now the mapping $g\colon n \mapsto \lfloor \log h(n) \rfloor$ is surely a computable order, so we know by assumption that for some p and almost all n we have for $t = p(|D(n)| + |\max D(n)|)$ that $\mathrm{C}^t(A \upharpoonright D(n) \mid D(n)) < g(n)$. Since t and $g(n)$ are both polynomial in the length of n, polynomial time in the length of n suffices to run the universal machine on all programs p of length strictly less than $g(n)$ with conditioning $D(n)$ for at most t steps each, interpreting the outputs obtained this way as oracles and to simulate the given reduction at place n with all of these oracles in order to obtain at most $h(n) \leq 2^{g(n)} - 1$ values that are put into the set T_n.

(ii) implies (i): We have to show for a given computable order h that there is a polynomial p such that for almost all finite sets D it holds for $t = p(|D| + |\max D|)$ that $\mathrm{C}^t(A \upharpoonright D \mid D) < h(\max D)$. Let f be the function which maps n to $A \upharpoonright D$, for all n that are a code for some finite set D, and let $f(n) = 0$ in case n is not such a code. By definition of the coding, computing $f(n)$ from A requires at most $\log n$ queries to A of length at most $\log n$. So $f \leq^{\mathbf{P}}_{\mathrm{tt}} A$, say with polynomial time bound q.

Since the length of the code for a finite set D is effectively bounded in $\max D$, we can fix a computable order h' such that for any finite set D, we have $h'(|D|) \leq$

$h(\max D)$. By assumption on A, let $(T_n)_n$ be an h'-bounded trace for f with polynomial time bound, i.e., for any finite set D with code n the value $f(n) = A \upharpoonright D$ occurs among the at most $h'(n) \leq h(\max D)$ elements of T_n and $C^t(A \upharpoonright D \mid D) \leq h(\max D)$ with t polynomial in $|D| + |\max D|$, as desired. □

References

1. Barmpalias, G., Downey, R., Greenberg, N.: K-trivial degrees and the jump-traceability hierarchy. Proc. Amer. Math. Soc. 137(6), 2099–2109 (2009)
2. Bienvenu, L., Merkle, W.: Reconciling data compression and kolmogorov complexity. In: Arge, L., Cachin, C., Jurdziński, T., Tarlecki, A. (eds.) ICALP 2007. LNCS, vol. 4596, pp. 643–654. Springer, Heidelberg (2007)
3. Cholak, P., Downey, R., Greenberg, N.: Strong jump-traceability I: The computably enumerable case. Advances in Mathematics 217(5), 2045–2074 (2008)
4. Downey, R., Hirschfeldt, D.: Algorithmic Randomness. Springer (to appear)
5. Franklin, J., Greenberg, N., Stephan, F., Wu, G.: Anti-complexity, lowness and highness notions, and reducibilities with tiny use (2009) (manuscript)
6. Franklin, J., Stephan, F.: Schnorr trivial sets and truth-table reducibility. Journal of Symbolic Logic 75, 501–521 (2010)
7. Jockusch Jr., C.G.: Degrees of functions with no fixed points. In: Proceedings of the Eighth International Congress of Logic, Methodology and Philosophy of Science, Moscow, 1987. Stud. Logic Found. Math, vol. 126, pp. 191–201. North-Holland, Amsterdam (1989)
8. Kanovich, M.I.: On the complexity of enumeration and decision of predicates. Soviet Math. Dokl. 11, 17–20 (1970)
9. Kjos-Hanssen, B., Merkle, W., Stephan, F.: Kolmogorov complexity and the recursion theorem. Trans. Amer. Math. Soc. (in print)
10. Li, M., Vitányi, P.: An Introduction to Kolmogorov Complexity and Its Applications. Springer, Heidelberg (2008)
11. Stephan, F.: Private communication (April 2010)
12. Terwijn, S.A., Zambella, D.: Computational randomness and lowness. The Journal of Symbolic Logic 66(3), 1199–1205 (2001)

Approximating the Non-contiguous Multiple Organization Packing Problem

Marin Bougeret*[1], Pierre François Dutot[1], Klaus Jansen[2], Christina Otte[2], and Denis Trystram[1]

[1] Grenoble University
ZIRST 51, avenue Jean Kuntzmann
38330 Montbonnot Saint Martin, France
{bougeret,pfdutot,trystram}@imag.fr
[2] Department of Computer Science
Christian-Albrechts-University to Kiel
Christian-Albrechts-Platz 4, 24098 Kiel, Germany
{kj,cot}@informatik.uni-kiel.de

Abstract. We present in this paper a $5/2$-approximation algorithm for scheduling rigid jobs on multi-organizations. For a given set of n jobs, the goal is to construct a schedule for N organizations (composed each of m identical processors) minimizing the maximum completion time (makespan). This algorithm runs in $O(n(N + \log(n)) \log(np_{max}))$, where p_{max} is the maximum processing time of the jobs. It improves the best existing low cost approximation algorithms. Moreover, the proposed analysis can be extended to a more generic approach which suggests different job partitions that could lead to low cost approximation algorithms of ratio better than $5/2$.

1 Problem Statement

In this paper we consider the problem of scheduling rigid jobs on Multi-organizations. An organization is a set of m identical available processors. A job j must be executed on q_j processors (sometimes called the *degree of parallelism*) during p_j units of time. The q_j processors must be allocated on the same organization. The makespan of the schedule is defined as the maximum finishing time over all the jobs. Given a set of n jobs, the goal is to find a non-overlapping schedule of all the jobs on N organizations while minimizing the makespan.

This problem is closely related to strip packing problems. Indeed, if we add the constraint of using contiguous processors, then scheduling a job j on q_j contiguous processors during p_j units of time is equivalent to packing a rectangle of width q_j and height p_j.

* This work has been supported by DGA-CNRS.

C.S. Calude and V. Sassone (Eds.): TCS 2010, IFIP AICT 323, pp. 316–327, 2010.

Related works. Strip packing, rigid jobs scheduling and Multi-organizations scheduling problems are all strongly $\mathcal{NP}$-hard, and Zhuk [1] showed that there is no polynomial time approximation algorithm with absolute ratio better than 2 for strip packing.

For Strip Packing problem, Coffman et al. gave in [2] an overview about performance bounds for shelf-oriented algorithms as $NFDH$ (Next Fit Decreasing Height) and $FFDH$ (First Fit Decreasing Height). These algorithms have a approximation ratio of 3 and 2.7, respectively. Schiermeyer [3] and Steinberg [4] presented independently an algorithm for Strip Packing with absolute ratio 2. A further important result for the Strip Packing problem is an AFPTAS with additive constant $\mathcal{O}(1/\epsilon^2)$ of Kenyon and Rémila [5]. This constant was improved by Jansen and Solis-Oba, who presented in [6] an APTAS with additive constant 1. Concerning the multi-strip packing problem, there is a $2+\epsilon$ approximation in [7] whose algorithmic cost is doubly exponential in $\frac{1}{\epsilon}$. In [8] we gave a 2 approximation with a large algorithmic cost and an AFPTAS for this problem.

Let us now review the related work about rigid job scheduling. For one organization, the famous List Algorithm for scheduling with resource constraints of Garey and Graham [9] can be applied (when there is only one resource to share) to schedule rigid jobs, and is then a 2 approximation. The rigid job scheduling problem on multi-organization has been studied with an on-line setting in [10]. The authors achieved a ratio of 3 without release times (and 5 with release times). Notice that these results do not require the knowledge of the processing times of the jobs. Moreover, the organizations may have a different number of processors. The rigid job scheduling problem on multi-organizations has been extended in [11] for the case where the jobs are submitted to local queues on each cluster with the extra constraint that the initial local schedules must not be worsened. The authors provide a 3-approximation.

Generally, the results about rigid job scheduling cannot be adapted to the more constrained contiguous version. To the best of our best knowledge, there is still no (reasonable) α such that for any instance I, $Optc(I) \leq \alpha Optnc(I)$ (where $Optc$ denotes the contiguous optimal value and $Optnc$ the non-contiguous one). The authors of [12] show that $\alpha > 1$ by constructing a (rather) simple instance with 8 jobs and 4 machines.

Our contribution. In this paper, we present a $\frac{5}{2}$ approximation algorithm for the rigid job scheduling problem on multi-organizations that runs in $O(n(N+\log(n))\log(np_{max}))$, where p_{max} is the maximum processing time of the jobs. Moreover, we suggest how the approach used for the $5/2$-algorithm could extended to get approximation algorithms with better ratio and a low algorithmic cost.

Organization of the Paper. The preliminaries for the $5/2$-approximation are in Section 2. In Section 3.1 to 3.4 we describe how to construct a preallocation of the "big" jobs that fits in the targeted makespan. In Section 4 we show how to turn this preallocation into a compact schedule, and in Section 5 we analyze the complexity of the algorithm. The discussions on the approach are in Section 6.

2 Principle and Definitions

Let us now give some definitions that are used throughout the proofs and the description of the algorithm. We first extend the previous p_j and q_j notations to $Q(X)$ and $P(X)$ where X is a set of jobs. We also define the surface (sometimes also called the area) of a set of jobs as $S(X) = \Sigma_{j \in X} q_j p_j$. A *layer* is a set of jobs which are scheduled sequentially on the same organization. The length of a layer Lay is $P(Lay)$, the sum of the processing time of all the jobs in Lay. A *shelf* is a set of jobs which are scheduled on the same organization, and which start at the same time. Given a shelf sh, the value $Q(sh)$ is called the *height* of sh. What we call a *bin* can be seen as a reservation of a certain number of processors (generally m) during a certain amount of time. The algorithm will add some jobs to bins, and given a bin b, we denote by $Q(b)$ the value $\Sigma_{\{j \in b\}} q_j$. Given a sequence of bins seq, we denote by $Q(seq)$ the value $\Sigma_{b \in seq} Q(b)$. These notations are extended in the same way for P and S. In the whole paper, we consider that the sets of jobs used as parameters in the algorithms are modified after the calls.

Let us sketch how $5/2$ algorithm is constructed. Let OPT denote the value of an optimal solution. We target a $\frac{5}{2}$ ratio by both ensuring that, for each organization at least half of the processors are used at any time before the starting time of the last job, and that the small jobs (whose processing time is lower than $OPT/2$ and height lower than $m/2$) are scheduled at the end. Thus, if the makespan of the final schedule is due to a small job, it is lower than the processing time of the small job plus the starting time of this job, implying a makespan lower than $OPT/2 + 2OPT = 5OPT/2$. As the optimal value is not known, we use the well known dual approximation technique [13]. Let w denote the current guess of OPT. The schedule is built in three steps. In the first one we compute a preallocation π_0 of the "big" ($p_j > w/2$ or $q_j > m/2$) jobs. Then we apply a list algorithm which turns π_0 into a "compact" schedule π_1 (see Section 4). Finally, the final schedule π is constructed by adding to π_1 the small remaining jobs using again a list algorithm (see also Section 4).

Let us define the following sets:

- let $L_H = \{j | q_j > m/2\}$ be the set of high jobs
- let $L_{XL} = \{j | p_j > 3w/4\}$ be the set of extra long jobs
- let $L_L = \{j | 3w/4 \geq p_j > w/2\}$ be the set of long jobs
- let $L_B = (L_{XL} \bigcup L_L) \bigcap L_H$ be the set of huge jobs
- let $I' = L_H \bigcup L_{XL} \bigcup L_L$

We will prove that either we schedule I with a resulting makespan lower than $5w/2$, or $w < OPT$. Notice that for the sake of simplicity we did not add the "reject" instructions in the algorithm. Thus we consider in all the proof that $w \geq OPT$, and it is implicit that if one of the claimed properties is wrong during the execution, the considered w should be rejected. Notice that we only consider the w values such that $Q(L_{XL} \bigcup L_L) \leq Nm$ and $P(L_H) \leq Nw$.

We start by providing in Section 3 the three phase algorithm *Build_Prealloc* that builds the preallocation π_0 of the jobs of I'. We will denote by π_0^i the set of preallocated jobs in organization O_i. In phase 1 we preallocate the high jobs. In phase 2 and phase 3 we preallocate the long and extra long jobs by first packing shelves of jobs into bins, and then putting these bins into organizations. An example of a preallocation is depicted Figure 1.

3 Construction of the Preallocation

3.1 Phase 1

Let N_1 be the number of organizations used in phase 1. In phase 1, the jobs of L_H are packed in N_1 organizations. The $Create\_Layer(X, l)$ procedure creates a layer Lay of length at most l, using a Best Fit (according to the processing times) policy (BFP). Thus, $Create\_Layer(X, l)$ add at each step the longest job that fits. Thus, phase 1 calls for each organization (until L_H is empty) $Create\_Layer(L_H, {}^{5w}/2)$.

Let us introduce some notations. Let Lay_i denote the set of jobs scheduled in the layer created in organization O_i. Let L^1_{XL} and L^1_L denote the remaining jobs of L_{XL} and L_L after phase 1. Thus, for the moment we have $\pi^i_0 = Lay_i$ for all $i \leq N_1$.

Lemma 1 (phase 1). *If $\exists i_0 < N_1$ such that $P(\pi^{i_0}_0) \leq 2w$ then it is straightforward to pack all the jobs of I'. Otherwise, we get $\forall i \in \{1, \ldots, N_1 - 1\}$, $S(\pi^i_0) > wm$ and $N_1 \leq \lceil {}^N/2 \rceil$.*

Proof. First let us notice that phase 1 ends, as $P(L_H) \leq Nw$ and $P(\pi^i_0) > w$ for every organization where we do not run out of jobs to schedule. We first suppose that $\exists i_0 < N_1$ such that $P(\pi^{i_0}_0) \leq 2w$. In this case we just have to prove that it is straightforward to preallocate $L_{XL} \bigcup L_L$. We proceed by contradiction by supposing that we never ran out of jobs of $L_{XL} \bigcup L_L$. When the algorithm creates a layer for a organization i, we know due to the BFP order that it will pack at least two jobs of L_B, if L_B is not empty. The hypothesis implies that during the execution of phase 1, $L_H \setminus L_B$ was empty before L_B. Thus, for $i < N_1$, there is at least two jobs of L_B in π^i_0, meaning that $\forall i$ with $1 \leq i < N_1, Q((L_{XL} \bigcup L_L) \bigcap \pi^i_0) > m$.

Concerning the $N - N_1$ other organizations, we can create shelves of jobs of $L_L \bigcup L_{XL}$ using a best fit according to the height (BFH), implying that each shelf has a height of at least ${}^{2m}/3$ according to Lemma 2. Packing two shelves in each organization, we get $\forall i > N_1, Q((L_{XL} \bigcup L_L) \bigcap \pi^i_0) > {}^{4m}/3 > m$.

Finally, let us check what is scheduled in organization N_1. If two jobs of L_B are scheduled in this organization, then $Q((L_{XL} \bigcup L_L) \bigcap \pi^{N_1}_0) > m$. If one job of L_B is scheduled, then we create one shelf of jobs of $L_{XL} \bigcup L_L$, and $Q((L_{XL} \bigcup L_L) \bigcap \pi^{N_1}_0) > {}^m/2 + {}^{2m}/3$. If no huge job is scheduled in organization N_1, we pack as before two shelves of jobs of $L_{XL} \bigcup L_L$. Thus, if in every case we have $Q((L_{XL} \bigcup L_L) \bigcap \pi^{N_1}_0) > m$. Thus, we get $Q((L_{XL} \bigcup L_L)) > Nm$, which is impossible.

Let us prove the second part of the lemma. First notice that for any $i < N_1, S(\pi^i_0) > 2w{}^m/2 = mw$. Moreover, we have $2(N_1 - 1)w < \Sigma^{N_1}_{i=1} P(\pi^i_0) = P(L_H) \leq Nw$, implying $N_1 \leq \lceil {}^N/2 \rceil$. $\square$

Thus, we now assume until the end of the proof that we are in the second case of Lemma 1 where $\forall i \in \{1, \dots, N_1 - 1\}$, $S(\pi_0^i) > mw$ and $N_1 \leq \lceil N/2 \rceil$.

3.2 Phase 2

In phase 2 the jobs of $L_{XL}^1 \bigcup L_L^1$ are scheduled in organization N_1 by creating shelves according to what is already scheduled in organization N_1. We denote by L_{XL}^2 and L_L^2 the remaining jobs of L_{XL}^1 and L_L^1 after phase 2. Let us first define two procedures used for phase 2 and phase 3.

The procedure $Pack\_Shelf(X, b, f)$ creates a shelf sh using the Best Fit (according to the height) policy (BFH), and packs it into bin b. The f parameter represents the available height of b (meaning that b corresponds to f free processors during a certain amount of time), implying of course that $Q(sh) \leq f$. Thus $Pack\_Shelf(X, b, f)$ adds at each step the highest possible job of X that fits. We assume that the length of the bin is larger than p_j, for all $j \in X$.

The procedure $GreedyPack(X, seq)$ creates for each empty bin $b \in seq$ one shelf of jobs of X using $Pack\_Shelf(X, b, m)$. This procedure returns the last bin in which a shelf has been created. Let us now come back to the description of phase 2.

Depending on the set of jobs already scheduled in O_{N_1}, the $Create\_Padding()$ procedure creates n_{bin_L} empty bins of length $3w/4$ and $n_{bin_{XL}}$ empty bins of length w, which are added in organization O_{N_1}. Let us define for each case how many bins of each type are created by $Create\_Padding()$:

- If $P(Lay_{N_1}) \in]3w/2, 7w/4]$ then set $(n_{bin_L}, n_{bin_{XL}})$ to $(1, 0)$
- If $P(Lay_{N_1}) \in]w, 3w/2]$ then set $(n_{bin_L}, n_{bin_{XL}})$ to $(0, 1)$
- If $P(Lay_{N_1}) \in]3w/4, w]$ then
  if $Q(L_L^1) \geq 5/4$ then set $(n_{bin_L}, n_{bin_{XL}})$ to $(2, 0)$
  else set $(n_{bin_L}, n_{bin_{XL}})$ to $(0, 1)$
- If $P(Lay_{N_1}) \in]w/2, 3w/4]$ then set $(n_{bin_L}, n_{bin_{XL}})$ to $(1, 1)$
- If $P(Lay_{N_1}) \in [0, w/2]$ then set $(n_{bin_L}, n_{bin_{XL}})$ to $(0, 2)$

Let pad_L be a sequence of n_{bin_L} bins of length $3w/4$ and pad_{XL} be a sequence of $n_{bin_{XL}}$ bins of length w. $Create\_Padding()$ returns (pad_L, pad_{XL}). All in all, phase 2 can be described by the following procedure calls:

- Let $(pad_L, pad_{XL}) = Create\_Padding()$
- $GreedyPack(L_{XL}^1, pad_{XL})$
- $GreedyPack(L_L^1, pad_L)$
- $GreedyPack(L_L^1, pad_{XL})$

3.3 Phase 3

In phase 3 we first schedule the jobs of L_{XL}^2 using the $N_2 = N - N_1$ remaining organizations. Then, we schedule the jobs of L_L^2 using also this N_2 organizations. Finally, the possibly remaining jobs of L_L^2 are added to the last bin used for the

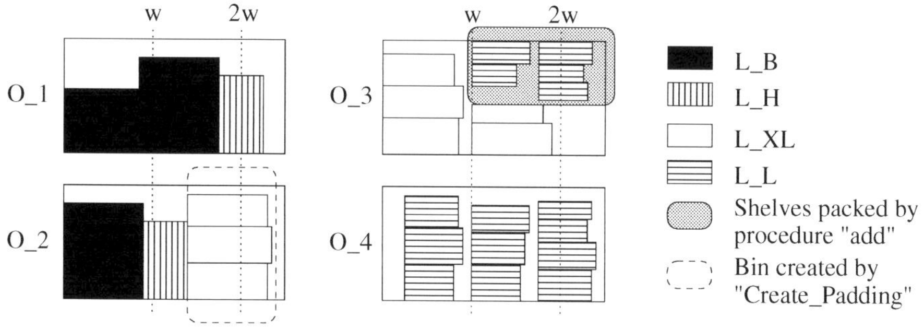

Fig. 1. An example of pre-allocation

extra long jobs. Therefore, let us define the $add(X, b)$ procedure. The $add(X, b)$ procedure packs one or two "small" shelves of jobs of X in the bin b (starting from the top of the bin for the sake of clarity). Notice that, as b will be the last bin used for extra long jobs, the available height (for the jobs of X) in b will be generally lower than m. Here is the description of $add(X, b)$:

- If the left side of b is at time w then let $l = 2$ else let $l = 1$
- Repeat l times the call $Pack\_Shelf(X, b, m - Q(b))$ and pack the created shelves in b.

An example of a call to the *add* procedure is given in Figure 1 for the case where $l = 2$.

We now define two sequences of bins seq_{XL} and seq_L, such that every bin of seq_{XL} (resp. seq_L) will (possibly) contains one shelf of jobs of L^2_{XL} (resp. L^2_L). Notice that a free organization can be seen as two bins of length w (and height m), three bins of length $3w/4$, or one bin of length w and two bins of length $3w/4$. Thus, seq_{XL} is composed of $2(N - N_1)$ bins $\left(b_1, \ldots, b_{2(N-N_1)}\right)$ of length w, considering that we created two bins in each of the organizations $\{O_{N_1+1}, \ldots O_N\}$, starting from O_{N_1+1}. This implies that for all $i \geq 1$, bins b_{2i-1} and b_{2i} are in O_{N_1+i}. The sequence seq_L is composed of $3(N - N_1)$ bins $\left(b'_1, \ldots, b'_{3(N-N_1)}\right)$ of length $3w/4$, considering that we created three bins in each of the organizations $\{O_{N_1+1}, \ldots O_N\}$, from O_N to O_{N_1+1}. This implies that for all $i \geq 1$, bins b'_{3i-2}, b'_{3i-1} and b'_{3i} are in O_{N-i+1}. Notice that these two sequences are not ordered in the same way.

All in all, phase 3 can be described by the following procedure calls:

- Let $last = GreedyPack(L^2_{XL}, seq_{XL})$
- $GreedyPack(L^2_L, seq_L)$
- $add(L^2_L, last)$

Let start the analysis of phase 3 with a remark about $Pack\_Shelf(X, b, f)$.

Lemma 2. *Let Sh denote the shelf created by $Pack\_Shelf(X, b, f)$. If we know that the k highest jobs of X fit in f, then $Q(Sh) > \frac{k}{k+1} f$.*

Proof. Let x be the cardinal of X. Let us assume that $q_i \geq q_{i+1}$ for $1 \leq i < x$. Let $i_0 \geq k+1$ be the first index such that job i_0 is not in Sh. Let $a = \Sigma_{i=1}^{i_0-1} q_i$. We have $Q(Sh) \geq a \geq (i_0 - 1)q_{i_0} > (i_0 - 1)(f - a)$ leading to $a > \frac{i_0-1}{i_0} f \geq \frac{k}{k+1} f$. □

Lemma 3 (phase 3). *If there remains an unscheduled job after phase 3, then* $S(L^2_{XL} \bigcup L^2_L) > (N_2 + {}^1/_8)mw$.

Proof. Let us first suppose that $L^2_{XL} \neq \emptyset$. Let $a_{XL} = 2(N - N_1)$ be the number of bins in seq_{XL}. After having filled the first $a_{XL} - 1$ bins (using a width of at least ${}^2/_3$ according to Lemma 2), the width of remaining jobs of L^2_{XL} is strictly larger than m. Thus we get $Q(L^2_{XL}) > {}^{2m}/_3(a_{XL} - 1) + m = {}^{4m}/_3 N_2 + {}^m/_3$ and $S(L^2_{XL}) > (N_2 + {}^1/_4)mw$.

We now suppose that $L^2_{XL} = \emptyset$. In every organization that contains two bins of jobs of L^2_{XL}, the total scheduled area is strictly larger than $2 \times {}^{2m}/_3 \times {}^{3w}/_4 = wm$. In every organization that contains three bins of jobs of L^2_L, the total scheduled area is strictly larger than $3 \times {}^{2m}/_3 \times {}^w/_2 = wm$. We have to consider two cases according to the position of the last bin $last$ (the left side of $last$ may be located at time 0 or w). Let i_0 be the index of the organization that contains $last$.

In the first case where the left side of $last$ is at time 0, two bins (of length ${}^{3w}/_4$ and height m) were created after the bin $last$ in organization O_{i_0}. Then, if the remaining jobs of L^2_L do not fit in $last$, the total area of the jobs scheduled in organization O_{i_0} is strictly larger than $(2{}^{2m}/_3 + m){}^w/_2 > {}^{7wm}/_6$. Then we just sum the area packed over all the organizations, and get the desired result.

In the second case where the left side of $last$ is at time w (as depicted in Figure 1), the only room in organization O_{i_0} to schedule jobs of L^2_L is in $last$. In organization O_{i_0}, the area of (extra long) jobs contained in the first bin is strictly larger than ${}^{wm}/_2$. The add procedure will create two shelves (one next to the other) of jobs of L^2_L in $last$.

Let $last'$ and L'_L be the set of jobs in $last$ and L^2_L respectively, just before the call of the add procedure. If $Q(last') > {}^m/_2$, and as the remaining jobs of L^2_L don't fit in $last$, we have that $Q(L'_L) > m - Q(last')'$. This implies $S(last' \bigcup L'_L) > {}^{3w}/_4 Q(last') + {}^w/_2(m - Q(last)') > {}^{5wm}/_8$. If $Q(last') \leq {}^m/_2$ (see Figure 1) then add creates a first shelf of jobs of L^2_L of height at least ${}^{(m-Q(last'))}/_2$, and then tries to pack the remaining jobs in the second shelf. Thus in this case, $S(last' \bigcup L'_L) > {}^{3w}/_4 Q(last') + {}^w/_2 \left(\frac{(m-Q(last'))}{2} + m - Q(last') \right) > {}^{3mw}/_4$. □

3.4 Main Algorithm

In this section we recall the overall algorithm that builds the preallocation, and we provide the main proof of the preallocation. Notice that we drop the L^i_L and L^i_{XL} notations for writing the algorithm as we consider that the sets of jobs (used as parameters in the procedures) are modified after the calls.

Theorem 1. *Build_Prealloc(I′) creates a preallocation* π_0 *of makespan lower than* ${}^{5w}/_2$.

Algorithm 1. ***Build_Prealloc(I')***

Phase 1 *[1] Let* $i = 0$
[2] Let $i = i + 1$, *and let* $Lay_i = Create\_Layer(L_H, {}^{5w}/_{2})$
Pack Lay_i *in organization* S_i *from time 0*
[3] Repeat step 3 until L_H *is empty*
Phase 2 *[4] Let* $(pad_L, pad_{XL}) = Create\_Padding()$
[5] Let $last = GreedyPack(L_{XL}, pad_{XL})$
[6] Call $GreedyPack(L_L, pad_L)$
[7] Call $GreedyPack(L_L, pad_{XL})$
Phase 3 *[8] Let* seq_{XL} *and* seq_L *be defined as described in Section 3.3*
[9] Let $last_2 = GreedyPack(L_{XL}, seq_{XL})$
[10] If $last_2$ *is not null, set last to* $last_2$
[11] Call $GreedyPack(L_L, seq_L)$
[12] Call $add(L_L, last)$

Proof. Remind that L^1_{XL} and L^1_L denote the remaining jobs of L_{XL} and L_L after Phase 1. The makespan of the preallocation is by construction lower than ${}^{5w}/_{2}$. We know that according to Lemma 1 phase 1 terminates and the area scheduled in the first $N_1 - 1$ organizations is greater than $(N_1 - 1)wm$. We proceed by contradiction by supposing that $L^1_{XL} \bigcup L^1_L$ is not empty after Phase 2 and Phase 3, and showing that $S(I') > Nmw$. We proceed by case analysis according to what is scheduled in O_{N_1}.

If $P(Lay_{N_1}) > \frac{7}{4}w$, then $S(Lay_{N_1}) > \frac{7}{8}mw$ and $CreatePadding$ doesn't create any bin. If L^1_{XL} and L^1_L are not completely scheduled by phase 3, then according to Lemma 3 we get $S(L^1_{XL} \bigcup L^1_L) > (N_2 + \frac{1}{8})mw$. Thus in this case we have $S(Lay_{N_1} \bigcup L^1_{XL} \bigcup L^1_L) > (N_2 + 1)mw$, implying $S(I') > Nmw$.

If $\frac{7}{4}w \geq P(Lay_{N_1}) > \frac{3}{2}w$, then $S(Lay_{N_1}) > \frac{3}{4}mw$ and $CreatePadding$ creates one bin of length $\frac{3}{4}w$. Recall that the jobs of L^1_L are first scheduled in pad_L. If $Q(pad_L)$ is larger than $\frac{m}{2}$, then $S(Lay_{N_1} \bigcup pad_L) > \frac{3}{4}mw + \frac{1}{4}mw = mw$. Thus, the total area packed in the first N_1 is strictly larger than N_1wm. Then, according to Lemma 3, $L^2_{XL} \bigcup L^2_L$ must fit in the N_2 remaining organizations. If $Q(pad_L) \leq \frac{m}{2}$, then the N_2 remaining organizations are available for L^1_{XL}. Thus, if $L^1_{XL} \neq \emptyset$ at the end, then $S(L^1_{XL}) > (N_2 + \frac{1}{4})mw$, and $S(Lay_{N_1} \bigcup L^1_{XL}) > (N_2 + 1)mw$.

If $\frac{3}{2}w \geq P(Lay_{N_1}) > w$, then $S(Lay_{N_1}) > \frac{1}{2}mw$ and $CreatePadding$ creates one bin of length w. If $Q(pad_{XL})$ is larger than $\frac{2m}{3}$ then $S(Lay_{N_1} \bigcup pad^1_{XL}) > mw$ and we conclude with Lemma 3. Otherwise, the N_2 remaining organizations are available for L^1_L. Moreover, remind that in this case the only bin in pad_{XL} will be used for jobs of L_L during the call of *add*. Then, if L^1_L does not fit, we have $Q(L^1_L \bigcup L^1_{XL}) > (2N_2 + 1)m$ and $S(Lay_{N_1} \bigcup L^1_L \bigcup L^1_{XL}) > \frac{mw}{2} + N_2wm + \frac{wm}{2} = (N_2 + 1)mw$.

If $w \geq P(Lay_{N_1}) > \frac{3}{4}w$, then $S(Lay_{N_1}) > \frac{3}{8}mw$ and two cases are possible according to the value of $Q(L^1_L)$. If $Q(L^1_L) \geq \frac{5m}{4}$, $CreatePadding$ creates two bins of length $\frac{3}{4}w$. Then, $S(Lay_{N_1} \bigcup pad_L) > (\frac{3}{8} + \frac{5}{8})mw$ and we conclude with Lemma 3. Otherwise, if $Q(L^1_L) < \frac{5m}{4}$, $CreatePadding$ creates one bin pad_{XL} of length w. If $Q(pad_{XL})$ (after the call line 5) is larger than $\frac{2m}{3}$ then

$S(Lay_{N_1} \bigcup pad^1_{XL}) > \frac{7}{8}mw$ and we conclude with Lemma 3. Otherwise, jobs of L^1_{XL} are all scheduled in pad_{XL}. As $N_2 \geq 1$, at least three bins are available for L^1_L, which is sufficient given that $Q(L^1_L) < \frac{5m}{4}$.

If $\frac{3}{4}w \geq P(Lay_{N_1}) > \frac{1}{2}w$, then $S(Lay_{N_1}) > \frac{1}{4}mw$ and $CreatePadding$ creates one bin of length w and one bin of length $\frac{3}{4}w$. If extra long jobs are not scheduled at the end of the algorithm, then $S(Lay_{N_1} \bigcup pad_{XL}) > \frac{3}{4}mw$. Since L^2_{XL} do not fit into N_2 free organizations, we have also $S(L^2_{XL}) > (N_2 + \frac{1}{4})mw$. Thus we conclude that the extra long jobs are successfully scheduled. Let us suppose now that the long jobs are not completely scheduled. If $Q(pad_{XL}) \geq \frac{5m}{9}$ then $S(Lay_{N_1} \bigcup pad_{XL} \bigcup pad_L) > (\frac{1}{4} + \frac{5}{12} + \frac{1}{3})mw = mw$. Otherwise, let L'_L denote the set of remaining jobs of L^1_L just before the call to *add*. The area scheduled in the N_2 last organizations is larger than the one scheduled in the optimal. If L'_L does not fit in pad_{XL} during the call to *add*, then $Q(L^1_{XL} + L'_L) > m$ and $S(Lay_{N_1} \bigcup pad_L \bigcup pad_{XL} \bigcup L'_L) > (\frac{1}{4} + \frac{1}{3} + \frac{1}{2})mw > mw$.

If $\frac{1}{2}w > P(Lay_{N_1})$, $CreatePadding$ creates two bins of length w. If $N_1 > 1$, then $S(\bigcup_{i=1}^{N_1} Lay_i) > S(\bigcup_{i=1}^{N_1-2} Lay_i) + \frac{5}{4}mw > (N_1 - 1)mw + \frac{1}{4}mw$ because the first job of Lay_{N_1} does not fit in the previous organization. Thus, if $Q(L^1_{XL}) > m$ then we have $S(\bigcup_{i=1}^{N_1} Lay_i \bigcup pad_{XL}) > N_1 mw$ and we conclude with Lemma 3. Otherwise, we have an empty bin in the sequence pad_{XL} and N_2 free organizations available for L^1_L. Let L'_L be L^1_L before the call to *add*. If *add* does not schedule L'_L in *last* then $Q(L^1_{XL}) + Q(L'_L) > m$ and $S(\bigcup_{i=1}^{N_1} Lay_i \bigcup L^1_{XL} \bigcup L'_L) > (N1 - \frac{3}{4} + \frac{1}{3} + \frac{1}{2})mw > N_1 mw$. If $N_1 \leq 1$ then we have two bins of length w in each of the N organizations, which is of course sufficient to pack $L^1_{XL} \bigcup L^1_L$. $\square$

4 From the Preallocation to the Final Schedule

From now on, we suppose that the preallocation π_0 is built. For each organization O_i, π_0 indicates first a (possibly empty) sequence of high jobs $j^i_1, \ldots, j^i_{x_i}$ that have to be scheduled sequentially from time 0. Then, π_0 contains an ordered sequence of shelves $Sh^i_1, \ldots, Sh^i_{x'_i}$. Moreover, the makespan of π_0 is by construction less than $5w/2$.

Definition 1. *Let $u_i(t)$ be the utilization of organization O_i at time t, i.e. $u_i(t)$ is the sum of all the q_j for any job j which scheduled on organization i at time t. A schedule is $1/2$ compact if and only if for every organization O_i there exists a time t_i such that for all $t \leq t_i, u_i(t) \geq m/2$ and u_i restricted to $t > t_i$ is not increasing.*

Let us now describe the algorithm LS_{π_0} which turns π_0 into a $1/2$ compact schedule π_1 of I'. We first define the procedure *Add_Asap*(X, O_i) which scans organization O_i from time 0, and for every time t starts any possible job(s) in X that fit(s) at time t. The LS_{π_0} works as follows: for every organization O_i, pack first sequentially the high jobs j^i_x for $1 \leq x \leq x_i$ and then call *Add_Asap*(Sh_x, O_i) for $1 \leq x \leq x'_i$.

Lemma 4. *The makespan of π_1 is lower than the one of π_0, and π_1 is $1/2$ compact.*

Proof. Let σ_i be a schedule in a (single) organization O_i (of makespan C_i), let X be a set of jobs and let σ_i' be the schedule (of makespan C_i') produced by *Add_Asap*(X, O_i). If σ_i is $1/2$ compact and if forall $j \in X, q_j \leq m/2$, then σ_i' is $1/2$ compact. The proof is straightforward by induction on the cardinality of X. Moreover, if $\sum_X q_j \leq m$, then $C_i' \leq C_i + max_X p_j$ because in the worst case all the jobs of X only start at time C_i. Using these two properties, we prove the lemma for every organization O_i by induction on the number of call(s) to *Add_Asap*(Sh_x, O_i). □

Remark 1. Notice that in Lemma 4 we do not take care of the particular structure which occurs when *add* creates two shelves of jobs of L_L as depicted Figure 1. However, it is easy to see that the proof can be adapted.

Now that π_1 is built, we add the small remaining jobs $(I \backslash I')$ using a list algorithm that scans all the organizations from time 0 and schedules as soon as possible any non scheduled job. Let π denote the obtained schedule.

Theorem 2. *The makespan of π is lower than $5w/2$.*

Proof. The proof is by induction on the cardinal of $I \setminus I'$. At the beginning, π_1 is $1/2$ compact, as proved in Lemma 4. Each time a job j is scheduled by the list algorithm, the obtained packing remains $1/2$ compact because $q_j \leq \frac{m}{2}$. Thus it is clear that π is $1/2$ compact.

Let us assume that the makespan of π is due to a job $j \in I \setminus I'$ that starts at time s. As π is $1/2$ compact, this implies that when scheduling job j we had $t_i \geq s$ for any organization i. Thus, we have $S(I) > \sum_{i=1}^{N} \frac{t_i}{2} \geq N\frac{s}{2}$, implying that $s < 2w$, and thus that the makespan of π is lower than $5w/2$. □

5 Complexity

Phase 1 can be implemented in $O(Nn + n\log(n))$. Indeed, we first sort the high jobs in non increasing order of their processing times. Then, each layer can be created in $O(n)$. Phase 2 and phase 3 can also be implemented in $O(Nn + n\log(n))$ by sorting the long (and extra long) jobs in non increasing order of their required processors. Thus π_0 is constructed in $O(Nn + n\log(n))$.

The LS_{π_0} algorithm can be implemented in $O(n\log(n))$. Instead of scanning time by time and organization by organization, this algorithm can be implemented by maintaining a list that contains the set of "currently" scheduled jobs. The list contains 3-tuples (j, t, i) indicating that job j (scheduled on organization i) finishes at time t. Thus, instead of scanning every time from 0 it is sufficient to maintain sorted this list according to the t values (in non decreasing order), and to only consider at every step the first element of the list. Then, it takes $O(\log(n))$ to find a job j_0 in the appropriate shelf that fits at time t, because a shelf can be created as a sorted array. It also takes $O(\log(n))$ to insert the new event corresponding to the end of j_0 in the list.

The last step, which turns π_1 into the final schedule can also be implemented in $O(n\log(n))$ using a similar global list of events. Notice that for any organization O_i, there exists a t_i such that before t_i the utilization is an arbitrary function strictly larger than $m/2$, and after t_i a non increasing after. Scheduling a small job before t_i would require additional data structure to handle the complex shape. Thus we do not schedule any small job before t_i as it is not necessary for achieving the $5/2$ ratio. Therefore, we only add those events that happen after t_i when initializing the global list for this step. To summarize, for this step we only need to sort the small jobs in non increasing order of their required number of processors, and then apply the same global list algorithm.

The binary search on w to find the smallest w which is not rejected can be done in $O(\log(np_{max}))$ as all the processing times can be assumed to be integers. Thus the overall complexity of the $5w/2$ approximation is in $O(\log(np_{max})n(N+\log(n)))$.

6 Toward Better Approximation Ratios

In this paper we provided a low cost $5/2$-approximation algorithm using a new approach. We discuss in this section how the proposed approach can be used for reaching better approximation bounds. The approach can be summarized in the two following main steps. The first one consists in constructing a $1/2$ compact schedule π_1 of the big jobs I' by creating a pre-allocation π_0 and "compressing" it. Then, the remaining small jobs $(I \setminus I')$ are added to π_1 in a second step using the classical list scheduling algorithm LS.

We would like to recall the arguments that make our second step easy to analyze, and see what could be some other promising partitions. In our partition, the second step guaranties a makespan lower than $5w/2$ because:

- adding a job j with $q_j \leq m/2$ to a $1/2$ compact schedule with LS produces another $1/2$ compact schedule,
- if the makespan is due to a small job j_0 that starts at time s_0, then $s_0 \leq 2w$ (since the schedule is $1/2$ compact), leading to a makespan lower than $s_0 + p_{j_0} \leq 5w/2$.

Let us now propose other partitions that could be considered. We could define $I' = \{j | q_j > \alpha m_i \text{ or } p_j > \beta w\}$ with appropriate values $0 < \alpha < 1$ and $0 < \beta < 1$. Then, the previous steps become:

1. construct a pre-allocation π_0 of I' (for instance based on shelves and layers) and make sure that, when compressed using LS_{π_0}, the obtained schedule π_1 is $1-\alpha$ compact (meaning that for every organization, the utilization is greater than $1-\alpha$, and then it is non-increasing),
2. add the small remaining jobs $(I \setminus I')$ using LS.

Thus, the makespan of jobs added in the second step would be bounded by $b = (\frac{1}{1-\alpha} + \beta)w$, implying that the makespan of the pre-allocation should also be bounded by b.

For example, we can target a 7/3 ratio by only studying how to pre-allocate $I' = \{j|q_j > \frac{m_i}{2}$ or $p_j > \frac{w}{3}\}$, or a ratio 2 by studying how to pre-allocate $I' = \{j|q_j > \frac{m_i}{3}$ or $p_j > \frac{w}{2}\}$. Obviously, if the preallocation is built using again shelves and layers, the difficulty will probably arise when merging the different types of jobs (high, extra long or long ones for example), and will may be only need to handle more particular cases.

Let us remark that this technique will not be easy to apply with (contiguous) rectangles, since the property of 1/2 compactness becomes hard to guarantee.

References

1. Zhuk, S.: Approximate algorithms to pack rectangles into several strips. Discrete Mathematics and Applications 16(1), 73–85 (2006)
2. Coffman Jr., E., Garey, M., Johnson, D., Tarjan, R.: Performance bounds for level-oriented two-dimensional packing algorithms. SIAM J. Comput. 9, 808 (1980)
3. Schiermeyer, I.: Reverse-fit: A 2-optimal algorithm for packing rectangles. In: van Leeuwen, J. (ed.) ESA 1994. LNCS, vol. 855, pp. 290–299. Springer, Heidelberg (1994)
4. Steinberg, A.: A strip-packing algorithm with absolute performance bound 2. SIAM Journal on Computing 26, 401 (1997)
5. Kenyon, C., Rémila, E.: A near-optimal solution to a two-dimensional cutting stock problem. Mathematics of Operations Research, 645–656 (2000)
6. Jansen, K., Solis-Oba, R.: New approximability results for 2-dimensional packing problems. In: Kučera, L., Kučera, A. (eds.) MFCS 2007. LNCS, vol. 4708, p. 103. Springer, Heidelberg (2007)
7. Ye, D., Han, X., Zhang, G.: On-Line Multiple-Strip Packing. In: Proceedings of the 3rd International Conference on Combinatorial Optimization and Applications, p. 165. Springer, Heidelberg (2009)
8. Bougeret, M., Dutot, P.-F., Jansen, K., Otte, C., Trystram, D.: Approximation algorithms for multiple strip packing. In: Bampis, E., Jansen, K. (eds.) Approximation and Online Algorithms. LNCS, vol. 5893, pp. 37–48. Springer, Heidelberg (2010)
9. Garey, M., Graham, R.: Bounds for multiprocessor scheduling with resource constraints. SIAM J. Comput. 4(2), 187–200 (1975)
10. Schwiegelshohn, U., Tchernykh, A., Yahyapour, R.: Online scheduling in grids. In: Proceedings of IPDPS, pp. 1–10 (2008)
11. Dutot, P.-F., Pascual, F., Rzadca, K., Trystram, D.: Approximation algorithms for the multi-organization scheduling problem. IEEE Transactions on Parallel and Distributed Systems, TPDS (2010) (submitted)
12. Dutot, P.-F., Mounié, G., Trystram, D.: Scheduling Parallel Tasks: Approximation Algorithms. In: Handbook of Scheduling. CRC Press, Boca Raton (2004)
13. Hochbaum, D.S., Shmoys, D.B.: A polynomial approximation scheme for scheduling on uniform processors: Using the dual approximation approach. SIAM J. Comput. 17(3), 539–551 (1988)

Improving the Competitive Ratios of the Seat Reservation Problem

Shuichi Miyazaki[1] and Kazuya Okamoto[2]

[1] Academic Center for Computing and Media Studies, Kyoto University
shuichi@media.kyoto-u.ac.jp
[2] Department of Medical Informatics, Kyoto University Hospital
kazuya@kuhp.kyoto-u.ac.jp

Abstract. In the seat reservation problem, there are k stations, s_1 through s_k, and one train with n seats departing from the station s_1 and arriving at the station s_k. Each passenger orders a ticket from station s_i to station s_j $(1 \le i < j \le k)$ by specifying i and j. The task of an online algorithm is to assign one of n seats to each passenger online, i.e., without knowing future requests. The purpose of the problem is to maximize the total price of the sold tickets. There are two models, the unit price problem and the proportional price problem, depending on the pricing policy of tickets. In this paper, we improve upper and lower bounds on the competitive ratios for both models: For the unit price problem, we give an upper bound of $\frac{4}{k-2\sqrt{k-1}+4}$, which improves the previous bound of $\frac{8}{k+5}$. We also give an upper bound of $\frac{2}{k-2\sqrt{k-1}+2}$ for the competitive ratio of Worst-Fit algorithm, which improves the previous bound of $\frac{4}{k-1}$. For the proportional price problem, we give upper and lower bounds of $\frac{3+\sqrt{13}}{k-1+\sqrt{13}} (\simeq \frac{6.6}{k+2.6})$ and $\frac{2}{k-1}$, respectively, on the competitive ratio, which improves the previous bounds of $\frac{4+2\sqrt{13}}{k+3+2\sqrt{13}} (\simeq \frac{11.2}{k+10.2})$ and $\frac{1}{k-1}$, respectively.

1 Introduction

The *seat reservation problem*, first introduced by Boyar and Larsen [4], is the following online problem. There are k stations s_1 through s_k, and one train with n seats numbered 1 through n. The train departs from the station s_1 and is destined for the station s_k. An input is a sequence of requests, where each request specifies an interval of the form $[i, j)$ $(1 \le i < j \le k)$, meaning that the current passenger wants to buy a ticket from station s_i to station s_j. The task of an online algorithm is to select which seat to assign to this passenger (if there are more than one available seats), without knowing future requests. In this problem, we consider only *fair* algorithms, i.e., if there is a seat available for the current passenger, it cannot reject her request. The purpose of the problem is to maximize the income, i.e., the sum of the prices of the sold tickets.

There are two models, *the unit price problem* and *the proportional price problem*, depending on the pricing policy of tickets. In the unit price problem, all

C.S. Calude and V. Sassone (Eds.): TCS 2010, IFIP AICT 323, pp. 328–339, 2010.

tickets have the same price of 1. In the proportional price problem, the price of a ticket is proportional to the distance traveled, i.e., the price of a ticket from s_i to s_j is $j - i$.

The performance of an online algorithm is evaluated by the *competitive analysis*. Let ALG be an online algorithm and σ be an input sequence. Let OPT be an optimal offline algorithm, namely, it optimally works after knowing the complete information of σ. Also, let $p_{ALG}(\sigma)$ and $p_{OPT}(\sigma)$ be the income obtained by ALG and OPT, respectively, for σ. If $p_{ALG}(\sigma) \geq r \cdot p_{OPT}(\sigma) - d$ for any input σ, where d is a constant independent of σ, we say that ALG is r-competitive[1].

Boyar and Larsen [4] studied the competitive ratios for both the unit price and the proportional price models. In particular, they studied three natural algorithms, *First-Fit*, *Best-Fit*, and *Worst-Fit*. First-Fit assigns each request to the available seat with the smallest number. Best-Fit assigns a request to a seat such that the empty space containing the current request interval is minimized (ties are broken arbitrarily). For example, suppose that there are eight stations and three seats, and that the current configuration is like Fig. 1, where shaded areas are assigned. Suppose that the next request is for the interval $[4, 6)$. We cannot assign it to seat 1. The empty space of seat 2 (seat 3, resp.) containing this interval is from s_2 to s_6 (from s_4 to s_7, resp.) and is of size 4 (3, resp.). So, Best-Fit selects seat 3 for this request. Conversely, Worst-Fit assigns a request to a seat such that the empty space containing the current request interval is maximized (again, ties are broken arbitrarily). In an example of Fig 1, if Worst-Fit receives a request for $[4, 6)$, then it assigns it to seat 2. Table 1, taken from [6], summarizes the best known results on the competitive ratios.

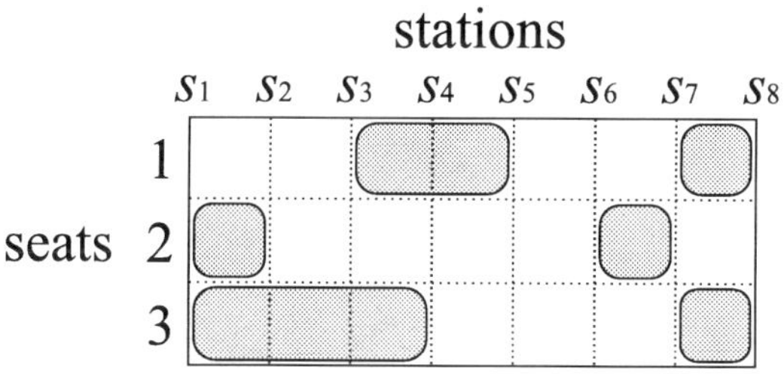

Fig. 1. An example configuration of assignment

Our Contributions. In this paper, we improve both upper and lower bounds on the competitive ratios. Our results are summarized in Table 2, where results obtained in this paper are highlighted in boldface. For the unit price problem, we improve an upper bound from $\frac{8}{k+5}$ to $\frac{4}{k-2\sqrt{k-1}+4}$. To improve a lower bound, we can see from Table 1 that it is hopeless to try to sophisticate the analysis for First-Fit or Best-Fit because an almost tight upper bound is already known for these algorithms, but there is some room for Worst-Fit. However, we show that

[1] There is an alternative definition such that competitive ratios are always at least 1. But here we use this definition following the previous seat reservation papers.

Table 1. Upper and lower bounds on the competitive ratios

	Unit Price	Proportional Price
Any deterministic algorithm	$r \leq \frac{8}{k+5}$	$r \leq \frac{4+2\sqrt{13}}{k+3+2\sqrt{13}} (\simeq \frac{11.2}{k+10.2})$
Worst-Fit	$\frac{2}{k} \leq r \leq \frac{4}{k+1}$	$r = \frac{1}{k-1}$
First-Fit/Best-Fit	$\frac{2}{k} \leq r \leq \frac{2-\frac{1}{k-1}}{k-1}$	$\frac{1}{k-1} \leq r \leq \frac{4}{k+2}$

Table 2. New results (results obtained in this paper are highlighted in boldface)

	Unit Price	Proportional Price
Any deterministic algorithm	$r \leq \boldsymbol{\frac{4}{k-2\sqrt{k-1}+4}}$	$r \leq \boldsymbol{\frac{3+\sqrt{13}}{k-1+\sqrt{13}}} (\simeq \boldsymbol{\frac{6.6}{k+2.6}})$
Worst-Fit	$\frac{2}{k} \leq r \leq \boldsymbol{\frac{2}{k-2\sqrt{k-1}+2}}$	$r = \frac{1}{k-1}$
First-Fit/Best-Fit	$\frac{2}{k} \leq r \leq \frac{2-\frac{1}{k-1}}{k-1}$	$\boldsymbol{\frac{2}{k-1}} \leq r \leq \frac{4}{k+2}$

Worst-Fit is also hopeless by improving its upper bound from $\frac{4}{k-1}$ to $\frac{2}{k-2\sqrt{k-1}+2}$. For the proportional price problem, we improve both upper and lower bounds. We improve an upper bound from $\frac{4+2\sqrt{13}}{k+3+2\sqrt{13}} (\simeq \frac{11.2}{k+10.2})$ to $\frac{3+\sqrt{13}}{k-1+\sqrt{13}} (\simeq \frac{6.6}{k+2.6})$. For a lower bound, we show that First-Fit and Best-Fit achieve the competitive ratio of $\frac{2}{k-1}$, which improves the previous bound of $\frac{1}{k-1}$. As a result, we improve the lower bound of the problem itself also. Note that previous lower bounds were obtained by using only the fact that algorithms are fair, and hence such bounds hold for any fair online algorithms. In contrast, the result in this paper is obtained by considering properties that are specific to First-Fit and Best-Fit.

Related Results. Besides the competitive analysis, Boyar and Larsen [4] analyzed the problem using the *accommodating ratio*, which takes not all the possible input sequences but only *accommodating sequences* into account. An accommodating sequence is a sequence for which an optimal offline algorithm can accommodate all the requests. They gave upper and lower bounds of $\frac{8k-9}{10k-15}$ and $\frac{1}{2}$, respectively, on the accommodating ratio for the unit price problem [4]. Later, Bach et al. [1] gave the matching upper bound of $\frac{1}{2}$.

There are some results on randomized algorithms. Boyar and Larsen [4] gave an upper bound of $\frac{8k-9}{10k-15}$ on the accommodating ratio for the unit price problem in the oblivious adversary model. Furthermore, Bach et al. [1] improved both upper and lower bounds for this problem and gave a matching bound of $\frac{7}{9}$.

Boyar, Larsen, and Nielsen [5] generalized the accommodating ratio. They introduced a variable $\alpha (\geq 1)$ and allowed α-*sequences* as possible input sequences. An α-sequence is a sequence for which an optimal offline algorithm can accommodate all the requests using αn seats. Then, they gave upper and lower bounds on the generalized accommodating ratio for the unit price problem. Boyar et al. [2] extended the above performance guarantees to more general ones for $\alpha(\leq 1)$ and gave several upper and lower bounds of First-Fit, Worst-Fit, and other online algorithms.

Boyar and Medvedev [6] used the *relative worst order ratio* to compare the performance of online algorithms (without using optimal offline algorithms). They showed that for both the unit price and the proportional price problems, First-Fit and Best-Fit are better than Worst-Fit.

Boyar, Krarup, and Nielsen [3] proposed a variant that allows x seat changes for each request, i.e., one ticket can be divided into at most $x + 1$ tickets for sub-intervals. They obtained several upper and lower bounds on the competitive and accommodating ratios.

Kohrt and Larsen [7] proposed a problem that lies in between the offline and online models. The task of an algorithm is not to assign a seat to a request but only to decide whether the request can be accepted or not (by arranging the previously accepted requests). They proposed an algorithm as well as an appropriate data structure, and proved that its running time is optimal.

2 The Unit Price Problem

For better understanding, we give a simple example for $k = 4$ and $n = 2$ (see Fig. 2). Consider the following input sequence $\sigma = (r_1, r_2, r_3, r_4, r_5)$, where r_1, r_2, r_3, r_4, and r_5 are requests for intervals $[1, 2)$, $[3, 4)$, $[1, 4)$, $[2, 4)$, and $[1, 2)$, respectively. Suppose that an online algorithm A assigns both r_1 and r_2 to seat 1. Then, it must assign r_3 to seat 2 because we only consider fair algorithms. So, it can accept neither r_4 nor r_5 and hence its income is 3. On the other hand, an optimal offline algorithm for σ assigns r_1 and r_2 into seats 1 and 2, respectively. It can then reject r_3 and accommodate both r_4 and r_5. So the income of this algorithm is 4.

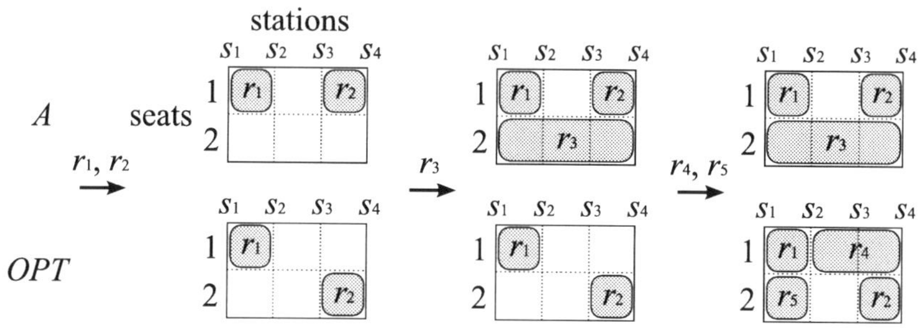

Fig. 2. An example of the unit price problem

2.1 An Upper Bound

We first improve a general upper bound.

Theorem 1. *No online algorithm for the unit price problem is more than* $\frac{4}{k-2\sqrt{k-1}+4}$*-competitive.*

Proof. Let A be an arbitrary online algorithm. Let m and c be arbitrary positive integers, and define $k = m^2 + 1$ be the number of stations and $n = 2cm$ be the number of seats. Our adversary first gives the request sequence σ_1 consisting of $2c$ requests for the interval $[1, 2)$, $2c$ requests for the interval $[2, 3)$, ..., $2c$ requests for the interval $[m, m + 1)$. All the requests in σ_1 must be assigned by algorithm A because A is a fair algorithm.

Let R be the set of seats to which A assigns requests for σ_1. We give a current assignment configuration in Fig. 3, in which seats are sorted appropriately: In region (i), at least one request is assigned for each seat. There may be or may not be assigned requests in region (ii). In region (iii), one request for the interval $[m, m + 1)$ is assigned for each seat. No request is assigned in region (iv).

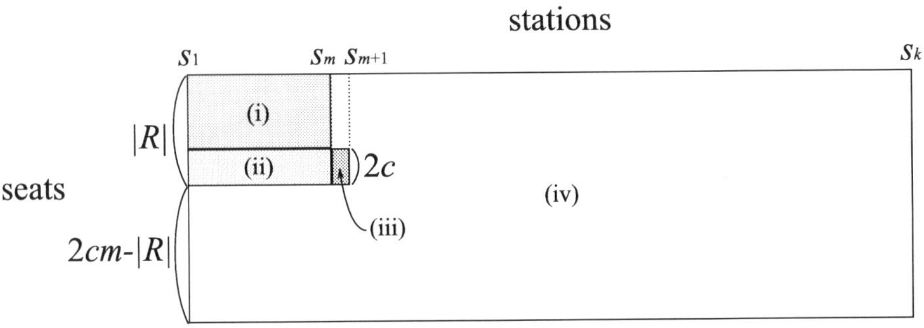

Fig. 3. Assignment configuration for σ_1 by algorithm A

The adversary selects subsequent sequences depending on the size of R. It executes Case (1) if $|R| < c(m + 1)$ and Case (2) otherwise.

Case (1): The adversary gives the following request sequences σ_2, σ_3, and σ_4 in this order: σ_2 consists of $2cm - |R|$ requests for the interval $[1, k)$. σ_3 consists of $|R| - 2c$ requests for the interval $[m, k)$. σ_4 consists of $2c$ requests for the interval $[m+1, k)$. It is easy to see that A accepts all the requests in σ_2, σ_3, and σ_4 because of the fairness, and hence after receiving σ_4, the whole region (iv) in Fig. 3 is filled with these requests. Finally, the adversary gives the sequence σ_5 consisting of $2cm-|R|$ requests for the interval $[m, m+1)$, $2cm-|R|$ requests for the interval $[m + 1, m + 2)$, ..., and $2cm - |R|$ requests for the interval $[k - 1, k)$, all of which are rejected by A. Thus, the income of A is $2cm + (2cm - |R|) + (|R| - 2c) + 2c$.

On the other hand, consider an algorithm which assigns each request of σ_1 to different seats. Then, it can reject all the requests in σ_2, and hence can accept all the requests in σ_3, σ_4, and σ_5. Thus, the income of the optimal offline algorithm is at least $2cm + (|R| - 2c) + 2c + (k - m)(2cm - |R|)$. Hence, the competitive ratio in this case is at most

$$\begin{aligned} & \frac{2cm + (2cm - |R|) + (|R| - 2c) + 2c}{2cm + (|R| - 2c) + 2c + (k - m)(2cm - |R|)} \\ = & \frac{4cm}{2cm + |R| + (k - m)(2cm - |R|)} \\ < & \frac{4}{k - 2\sqrt{k-1} + 4} \end{aligned}$$

because $|R| < c(m + 1)$.

Case (2): The adversary gives the request sequences σ_2, σ_2', σ_3, and σ_4 in this order, where σ_2, σ_3, and σ_4 are the same as before and σ_2' consists of $|R| - 2c$ requests for the interval $[1, m + 1)$. It is easy to see that A rejects all the requests in σ_2' but accepts all the requests in σ_2, σ_3, and σ_4. So, again, the whole region (iv) in Fig. 3 is filled with these requests. Finally, the adversary gives the sequence σ_5' consisting of $|R|-2c$ requests for the interval $[m+1, m+2)$, $|R| - 2c$ requests for the interval $[m + 2, m + 3)$, ..., and $|R| - 2c$ requests for the interval $[k - 1, k)$, all of which are rejected by A. Thus, the income of A is $2cm + (2cm - |R|) + (|R| - 2c) + 2c$.

On the other hand, consider an algorithm which assigns each request of σ_1 using First-Fit. Then, it accepts all the requests in σ_2, σ_2', σ_4, and σ_5', but rejects all the requests in σ_3. Thus, the income of an optimal offline algorithm is at least $2cm+(2cm-|R|)+(|R|-2c)+2c+(k-m-1)(|R|-2c)$. Hence, the competitive ratio in this case is at most

$$\begin{aligned} & \frac{2cm + (2cm - |R|) + (|R| - 2c) + 2c}{2cm + (2cm - |R|) + (|R| - 2c) + 2c + (k - m - 1)(|R| - 2c)} \\ = & \frac{4cm}{4cm + (k - m - 1)(|R| - 2c)} \\ \leq & \frac{4}{k - 2\sqrt{k-1} + 4} \end{aligned}$$

because $|R| \geq c(m + 1)$. □

2.2 An Upper Bound for Worst-Fit

Recall from Sec. 1 that Worst-Fit assigns each request to a seat such that the empty space containing the current request interval is maximized. As we have mentioned in Sec. 1, Worst-Fit has been a good candidate for improving a lower bound. But we rule out this possibility by giving an almost tight upper bound for it.

Theorem 2. *The competitive ratio of Worst-Fit for the unit price problem is at most* $\frac{2}{k-2\sqrt{k-1}+2}$.

Proof. As in the proof of Theorem 1, let m and c be arbitrary positive integers, and let $k = m^2 + 1$ and $n = 2cm$. First, we give the sequence σ_1 consisting of $2c$ requests for the interval $[1, 2)$, $2c$ requests for $[2, 3)$, ..., $2c$ requests for $[m, m+1)$. Worst-Fit assigns these $n = 2cm$ requests to different seats. Next, we give σ_2, σ_3, and σ_4 in this order where σ_2 consists of $2cm - 2c$ requests for the interval $[1, m+1)$, σ_3 consists of $2cm - 2c$ requests for the interval $[m, k)$, and σ_4 consists of $2c$ requests for the interval $[m+1, k)$. Worst-Fit rejects all the requests in σ_2 and accommodates all the requests in σ_3 and σ_4. So, after receiving σ_4, all the seats are full in the interval $[m + 1, k)$. Finally, we give σ_5 consisting of $2cm - 2c$ requests for $[m + 1, m + 2)$, $2cm - 2c$ requests for $[m + 2, m + 3)$, ..., $2cm - 2c$ requests for $[k - 1, k)$. Worst-Fit rejects all these requests. The income of Worst-Fit is then $2cm + (2cm - 2c) + 2c$.

On the other hand, consider an algorithm which assigns requests in σ_1 using First-Fit. Then it can accommodate all the requests in σ_2, and it rejects all the requests in σ_3. Hence, it can accept all the requests in σ_4 and σ_5, so the income of an optimal offline algorithm is at least $2cm+(2cm-2c)+2c+(k-m-1)(2cm-2c)$. Thus the competitive ratio is at most

$$\begin{aligned}
&\frac{2cm + (2cm - 2c) + 2c}{2cm + (2cm - 2c) + 2c + (k - m - 1)(2cm - 2c)} \\
&= \frac{4cm}{4cm + (k - m - 1)(2cm - 2c)} \\
&= \frac{2}{k - 2\sqrt{k - 1} + 2}.
\end{aligned}$$

□

3 The Proportional Price Problem

Recall that in the proportional price problem, the price of a ticket from s_i to s_j is $j - i$.

3.1 An Upper Bound

Theorem 3. *No online algorithm for the proportional price problem is more than* $\frac{3+\sqrt{13}}{k-1+\sqrt{13}}$*-competitive.*

Proof. Consider an arbitrary online algorithm A, and let k and $n(= 2m$ for a positive integer $m)$ be the numbers of stations and seats, respectively. The adversary first gives the sequence σ_1 consisting of m requests for the interval $[1, 2)$ and σ_2 consisting of m requests for the interval $[2, 3)$. Let R be the set of seats to which A assigns both requests of σ_1 and σ_2. The current configuration is given in Fig. 4, in which assigned areas are shaded.

The adversary selects subsequent sequences depending on the size of R. It executes Case (1) if $|R| < \frac{(\sqrt{13}-2)m}{3}$ and Case (2) otherwise.

Case (1): The adversary gives σ_3 and σ_4 in this order such that σ_3 consists of $|R|$ requests for the interval $[1, 3)$ and σ_4 consists of $m - |R|$ requests for the

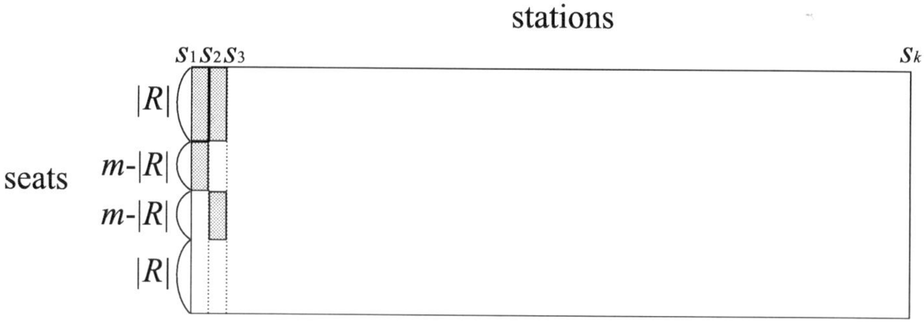

Fig. 4. Assignment configuration for σ_1 and σ_2 by algorithm A

interval $[1, k)$. A accepts all the requests in σ_3 but rejects all the requests in σ_4, so that its income is $2m + 2|R|$.

On the other hand, consider an algorithm which uses m seats to assign both requests of σ_1 and σ_2. Then, it can accomodate all the requests in σ_3 and σ_4 and hence the income of an optimal offline algorithm is at least $2m+2|R|+(k-1)(m-|R|)$. The competitive ratio is then at most

$$\begin{aligned} &\frac{2m+2|R|}{2m+2|R|+(k-1)(m-|R|)} \\ &< \frac{2+2\frac{\sqrt{13}-2}{3}}{2+2\frac{\sqrt{13}-2}{3}+(k-1)(1-\frac{\sqrt{13}-2}{3})} \\ &= \frac{3+\sqrt{13}}{k+2+\sqrt{13}} \end{aligned}$$

because $|R| < \frac{(\sqrt{13}-2)m}{3}$.

Case (2): The adversary gives σ_3, σ_4', and σ_5' in this order where σ_3 is the same as before, σ_4' consists of $m-|R|$ requests for the interval $[2, 3)$, and σ_5' consists of $|R|$ requests for the interval $[2, k)$. A accommodates all the requests of σ_3 and σ_4', but rejects all the requests of σ_5', so, its income is $2m + 2|R| + (m - |R|)$.

On the other hand, consider an algorithm which assigns requests of σ_1 and requests of σ_2 to different seats, i.e., each of $2m$ seats contains exactly one request. Then, it can reject all the requests of σ_3 and can accommodate all the requests of σ_4' and σ_5', and hence the income of an optimal offline algorithm is at least $2m + (m - |R|) + (k-2)|R|$. The competitive ratio is at most

$$\begin{aligned} &\frac{2m+2|R|+(m-|R|)}{2m+(m-|R|)+(k-2)|R|} \\ &\le \frac{3+\frac{\sqrt{13}-2}{3}}{3-\frac{\sqrt{13}-2}{3}+(k-2)\frac{\sqrt{13}-2}{3}} \end{aligned}$$

$$= \frac{3+\sqrt{13}}{k-1+\sqrt{13}}$$

because $|R| \geq \frac{(\sqrt{13}-2)m}{3}$. □

3.2 Lower Bounds for First-Fit and Best-Fit

Recall that First-Fit assigns each request to the available seat with the smallest number, and Best-Fit assigns a request to a seat such that the empty space containing the current request interval is minimized. We improve lower bounds on the competitive ratio for these algorithms, improving a general lower bound for the proportional price problem.

Theorem 4. *Both First-Fit and Best-Fit are* $\frac{2}{k-1}$*-competitive for the proportional price problem.*

Proof. We give a proof for First-Fit (denoted FF hereafter). The proof for Best-Fit is exactly the same. Consider an arbitrary input σ. If, for every seat, the total length of intervals assigned by FF is at least two, then we are done since FF earns at least $2n$ and an optimal offline algorithm OPT can earn at most $(k-1)n$ for an instance with k stations and n seats. If FF rejects no request in σ, then again we are done. Hence, we assume that there is a seat q to which only an interval of length 1, say $I = [i, i+1)$, is assigned. Let r be the request assigned to q by FF. We can see that no seat has a vacant space for I since if such a seat q' exists, assigned intervals of q and q' do not overlap, contradicting the definition of FF.

Let R_I be the set of requests for intervals containing I assigned by FF. By the above observation, $|R_I| = n$. Partition R_I into $R_I^{(1)}$ and $R_I^{(\geq 2)}$ so that $R_I^{(1)}$ is the set of requests for exactly the interval I, and $R_I^{(\geq 2)} = R_I \setminus R_I^{(1)}$ is the set of requests for intervals of length at least 2, containing I (see the upper figure of Fig. 5). Also, let $S^{(1)}$ and $S^{(\geq 2)}$ be the sets of seats to which requests in $R_I^{(1)}$ and $R_I^{(\geq 2)}$, respectively, are assigned. Note that $|S^{(1)}| = |R_I^{(1)}|$, $|S^{(\geq 2)}| = |R_I^{(\geq 2)}|$, and $|S^{(1)}| + |S^{(\geq 2)}| = n$.

Suppose that there is a request r' in $R_I^{(1)}$ that is rejected by OPT. Let R' be the set of requests for intervals containing I, accommodated by OPT. Since OPT is fair but rejected r', $|R'| = n$ and any request in R' precedes r'. Since the interval I is full for both OPT and FF, and since r' is accepted by FF but rejected by OPT, there is a request $r'' \in R'$ rejected by FF. Note that r'' precedes r' since $r'' \in R'$, but FF rejected r'' while it accepted r'. So, the interval requested by r'' must include an interval other than I, and when FF rejected r'', there must be a seat q'' in which the interval I was empty but some other intervals were assigned. If at this moment, FF has already received the request r and has assigned it to the seat q, then we can merge q and q'' without overlapping, contradicting the definition of FF. So, the request r has not been given to FF yet. But then q was empty for the whole interval at this moment, and FF could have assigned r'' to q, a contradiction. So, any request in $R_I^{(1)}$ is accepted by OPT.

Now, let S be the set of seats to which OPT assigns requests in $R_I^{(1)}$, and $R(S)$ be the set of requests assigned to S by OPT. Define $\overline{R} = R(S) \setminus R_I^{(1)}$ (see the lower figure of Fig. 5). Because FF is fair and the seat q (of FF) eventually contains only a request for the interval I, FF accommodates all the requests in $\overline{R}$. Also, since requests in $\overline{R}$ do not contain the interval I, $\overline{R}$, $R_I^{(1)}$, and $R_I^{(\geq 2)}$ are pairwise disjoint.

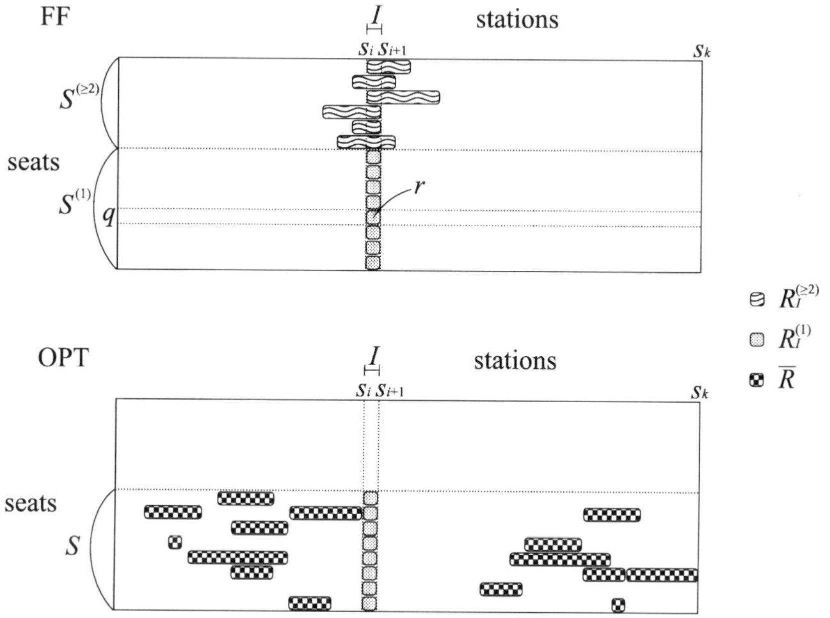

Fig. 5. Assignment configurations of FF and OPT for σ

For the set X of requests, let $p(X)$ be the total price of tickets for requests in X. Then, the income of FF is at least $p(R_I^{(1)}) + p(R_I^{(\geq 2)}) + p(\overline{R}) \geq |S^{(1)}| + 2|S^{(\geq 2)}| + p(\overline{R}) = |S| + 2(n - |S|) + p(\overline{R})$ because $|S^{(1)}| = |S|$ and $|S^{(1)}| + |S^{(\geq 2)}| = n$. On the other hand, the income of OPT is at most $(k-1)(n-|S|) + |S| + p(\overline{R})$. So, we have that

$$\frac{p_{FF}(\sigma)}{p_{OPT}(\sigma)} \geq \frac{2(n - |S|) + |S| + p(\overline{R})}{(k-1)(n - |S|) + |S| + p(\overline{R})} \geq \frac{2}{k-1},$$

which completes the proof. □

4 Concluding Remarks

In this paper, we narrowed the gap between upper and lower bounds on the competitive ratios for the seat reservation problem for both the unit price and the proportional price problems. An apparent future work is to further narrow the gaps for both models.

To obtain a better bound for the unit price problem, we need to develop other algorithms as we discussed in this paper. For the proportional price problem, there still remains a gap between upper and lower bounds for First-Fit and Best-Fit (see Table 2). Narrowing the gap for these algorithms is one of the next possible challenges. We finally give a short remark on this direction.

Let us generalize the problem to a *loop-line*, namely, $s_k = s_1$. So, there could be a request for an interval $[j, i)$ $(j > i)$, which means that the passenger is to get on the train at station s_j and go to station s_i by way of station s_k. (Strictly speaking, we must consider the number of *laps*. However, here we consider the case of only one lap, e.g., intervals $[2, 4)$ and $[5, 3)$ overlap. This definition may not be practical, but is meaningful for the analysis of First-Fit and Best-Fit, as one can see below.) For this setting, we can derive a matching bound of $\frac{2}{k-1}$ for First-Fit and Best-Fit. The upper bound will be proved below, and the lower bound can be derived from exactly the same way as Theorem 4 because the proof of Theorem 4 holds for the loop-line model also. This suggests that to improve the lower bound for First-Fit and Best-Fit, we need arguments that do not hold for the loop-line model.

Upper bound proofs for First-Fit and Best-Fit for loop-line model. We give a proof for First-Fit (FF). The proof for Best-Fit is exactly the same. Let k be the number of stations and $n = 2m$ be the number of seats. We give the following sequences to FF: σ_1 consisting of m requests for $[1, 2)$; σ_2 consisting of m requests for $[2, 3)$; σ_3 consisting of m requests for $[1, 3)$; σ_4 consisting of m requests for $[2, k)$; and σ_5 consisting of m requests for $[3, 2)$. It is not hard to see that FF accommodates all the requests in σ_1, σ_2, and σ_3, but rejects all the requests in σ_4 and σ_5. So, the income of FF is $4m$. On the other hand, an optimal offline algorithm assigns requests in σ_1 and requests in σ_2 to different seats. Then it can reject all the requests of σ_3, and can accept all the requests in σ_4 and σ_5, so its income is $2m(k - 1)$.

Acknowledgements

The authors would like to thank anonymous referees for their helpful comments. This work was supported by KAKENHI (19200001, 20700009 and 22700257).

References

1. Bach, E., Boyar, J., Epstein, L., Favrholdt, L.M., Jiang, T., Larsen, K.S., Lin, G.-H., Van Stee, R.: Tight bounds on the competitive ratio on accommodating sequences for the seat reservation problem. Journal of Scheduling 6(2), 131–147 (2003)

2. Boyar, J., Favrholdt, L.M., Larsen, K.S., Nielsen, M.N.: Extending the accommodating function. Acta Informatica 40(1), 3–35 (2003)
3. Boyar, J., Krarup, S., Nielsen, M.N.: Seat reservation allowing seat changes. Journal of Algorithms 52(2), 169–192 (2004)
4. Boyar, J., Larsen, K.S.: The seat reservation problem. Algorithmica 25(4), 403–417 (1999)
5. Boyar, J., Larsen, K.S., Nielsen, M.N.: The accommodating function: a generalization of the competitive ratio. SIAM Journal on Computing 31(1), 233–258 (2001)
6. Boyar, J., Medvedev, P.: The relative worst order ratio applied to seat reservation. ACM Transactions on Algorithms 4(4) (2008) Article No. 48
7. Kohrt, J.S., Larsen, K.S.: Online seat reservation via offline seating arrangements. International Journal of Foundations of Computer Science 16(2), 381–397 (2005)

A Semiring-Based Trace Semantics for Processes with Applications to Information Leakage Analysis

Michele Boreale[1], David Clark[2], and Daniele Gorla[3]

[1] Dipartimento di Sistemi e Informatica, Università di Firenze
[2] Department of Computer Science, King's College London
[3] Dipartimento di Informatica, "Sapienza" Università di Roma

Abstract. We propose a framework for reasoning about program security building on language-theoretic and coalgebraic concepts. The behaviour of a system is viewed as a mapping from traces of high (unobservable) events to low (observable) events: the less the degree of dependency of low events on high traces, the more secure the system. We take the abstract view that low events are drawn from a generic *semiring*, where they can be combined using product and sum operations; throughout the paper, we provide instances of this framework, obtained by concrete instantiations of the underlying semiring. We specify systems via a simple process calculus, whose semantics is given as the unique homomorphism from the calculus into the set of behaviours, i.e. *formal power series*, seen as a final coalgebra. We provide a compositional semantics for the calculus in terms of rational operators on formal power series and show that the final and the compositional semantics coincide.

1 Introduction

Security analysis of programs has traditionally been centered on a notion of *non-interference* [16]. Research has mostly been into a functional interpretation whereby a program is acceptable if low-confidentiality variables or actions do not depend on high-confidentiality ones. This approach has been developed in both imperative [24] and process algebraic [15] settings. Non-interference is now generally recognised as enforcing too strict a policy. For this reason, more flexible variants of this concept are often considered. In *declassification*, a program may be declared as acceptable if information can flow from *high* to *low* but only in prescribed ways [12,25]. In more recent years, attempts have been made to provide methods to *quantify* the amount of leaked information, mostly building on information-theoretic or probabilistic tools [13,14,9,6]. Then a program may be declared as acceptable if the information it leaks does not exceed a prescribed threshold.

In this paper, we propose a framework for reasoning about information leakage that builds on language-theoretic and coalgebraic concepts. The framework offers a unifying view of diverse facets of language security, such as those mentioned above, puts them in a more abstract perspective and possibly paves the way to their unification. It also elucidates interesting connections between language-based security, coalgebras and language theory.

C.S. Calude and V. Sassone (Eds.): TCS 2010, IFIP AICT 323, pp. 340–354, 2010.

Let us introduce a scenario that motivates our approach. Consider a discrete-time, nondeterministic system P. During the execution of P, certain events, such as updates of high-variables, are under the control of a secret scheduler and not directly observable from the outside. Some other events are observable, including updates of low variables, input/output actions, certain file accesses, and so on. These observable events are not directly controlled by the secret scheduler, and may obey nondeterministic or probabilistic laws. An attacker can perform observations upon the system only at prescribed times, e.g. only upon termination. Moreover, he can have the system re-execute as many times as he wishes: through these repeated executions, we assume the policy of the secret scheduler (high behaviour) remains fixed, while all the possibilities arising from the nondeterministic or probabilistic low behaviour of the system are observed. Through this process, the attacker collects a set of observations $o_1, o_2, \ldots$ and combines them into a global observation to make deductions about the non-observable events – in essence, about the choices of the secret scheduler. One can think of basically two ways the observations can be combined. The first one is a form of sequential composition, say $\star$, by which a sequence of consecutive observations, e.g. o_1, o_2, o_3, results into a combined observation, $o = o_1 \star o_2 \star o_3$. Note that, from the point of view of the attacker, only the final, combined observation o may be available, not the intermediate o_i – the $\star$ operation may not be actually available to him. The second operation, call it $+$, can be used to combine observations arising from the repeated executions of the system, e.g. $o_1 \star o_2$ and $o_3 \star o_4$, into a global observation $(o_1 \star o_2) + (o_3 \star o_4)$. This operation is therefore available to the attacker. In the end, to each sequence of unobservable events, say π, there corresponds a global observation o, thus defining a mapping from high traces to observations that we name $\mathcal{L}(P)$. This mapping can be deduced from P's specification, which must be assumed to be public. Hence, using $\mathcal{L}(P)$ and the global observation o, the attacker can learn information about the secret sequence π: at least, he can get to know that $\pi \in (\mathcal{L}(P))^{-1}(o)$.

To make a concrete case, consider a system P, informally specified as follows. Either of two unobservable events, h or h', is initially executed, the choice depending on the secret scheduler. Then, h leads to a state where the low-event l is always executed, while h' leads to a state where either of two branches is taken: in the first branch, l' and then l'' are executed, while in the second just l is executed. In any case, the system then terminates. The two branches are taken, respectively, with probability $\frac{3}{4}$ and $\frac{1}{4}$. In this case, the observations o are probability sub-distributions on low-traces, while $\star$ and $+$ are, respectively, the product and sum of sub-distributions (seen as weighted languages). The above specification hence yields $\mathcal{L}(P)(h) = [l \mapsto 1]$ and $\mathcal{L}(P)(h') = [l'l'' \mapsto \frac{3}{4}, l \mapsto \frac{1}{4}]$.

From the point of view of a designer that must assess the security of the system, the mapping $\mathcal{L}(P)$ is the central object of interest. For example, if $\mathcal{L}(P)$ is a constant, then the observed low-event does not depend on the secret sequence of high-events: the system is perfectly secure (see [26] for a similar notion of security, formulated in a synchronous setting, *Nondeducbility on Strategies*). If this is not the case, the designer might at least be interested in learning how many equivalence classes the domain $\mathcal{L}(P)$ is partitioned into (that is the number of pre-images $(\mathcal{L}(P))^{-1}(o)$, for o ranging over the observations): the fewer, the better. Also, he might want to perform quantitative measures, in case probabilistic behaviour is involved. In the example above, $\mathcal{L}(P)$ can be seen as a stochastic matrix whose rows and columns are indexed by high- and low-traces, respectively, and its capacity can be computed by standard techniques. Indeed, an information theorist might recognize in this example an instance of the noisy *Z-channel* having $\{h, h'\}$ and $\{l, l'l''\}$ as an input and an output alphabet, respectively.

In essence, it is crucial for the designer to be able to specify $\mathcal{L}(P)$, generate it and reason on it - e.g. prove that two system specifications generate the same behaviours - in a *compositional, syntax-driven* fashion. We face these issues and draw on language-theoretic concepts. We take the general view that observable events are elements of a *semiring* [18], $\mathbb{S}$, whose product and sum correspond to the $\star$ and $+$ operations mentioned above. A set of unobservable, high-events H is assumed. The security significant behaviour of the system, $\mathcal{L}(P)$, is then a mapping from H^* to $\mathbb{S}$, that is a *formal power series* (FPS) on H and $\mathbb{S}$ [18]. We provide a simple process calculus to specify systems, equipped with an operational semantics given in terms of Moore automata. Then, following [23], we characterize the semantic mapping $\mathcal{L}(\cdot)$ in terms of the unique homomorphism from this calculus into the set of formal power series seen as a final coalgebra. We next provide a compositional semantics of the calculus in terms of rational operators on FPS's, defined via *behavioural differential equations* (BDE's) [23]. We show that the final and the compositional semantics coincide. A consequence of this result is a Kleene theorem saying that, in our calculus, all and only the rational FPS's are definable. The benefits of the two semantics can be summed up as follows: the final semantics allows for reasoning – proving equivalences – on systems by co-induction, while the compositional semantics, and in particular the BDE's, can be used for step-wise, syntax-driven generation of the behaviours $\mathcal{L}(P)$, for any P. Throughout the paper, we provide instances of this framework obtained by concrete instantiations of the semiring $\mathbb{S}$, and examples that illustrate these ideas.

The rest of the paper is organized as follows: In Section 2 we provide background notions about semirings and formal power series and introduce a few concrete instances of them that are relevant to information leakage analysis. In Section 3 we give the syntax and operational semantics of the language. In Section 4 we describe the abstract semantics using finality and characterize the semantic mapping in terms of language equivalence. Following this, we provide a compositional semantics and show that the final and the compositional semantics coincide in Section 5. In Section 6, we provide two non-trivial examples illustrating the use of the compositional semantics and of the language as a modelling tool. To round off the paper, in Section 7 we briefly discuss an extension of the language with a simple form of parallel composition. Finally we offer some comparison with related work and directions for future research. All proofs have been confined to an extended version available online [8].

2 Semirings and Formal Power Series

Recall that a *semiring* $\mathbb{S}$ is a tuple $(S, +, \times, 0, 1)$ such that $(S, +, 0)$ is a commutative monoid, $(S, \times, 1)$ is a monoid, $\times$ distributes over $+$ both on the left and on the right, and 0 annihilates both on the left and on the right (i.e., $0 \times o = o \times 0 = 0$ for each $o \in S$). We let $o, o', ...$ range over S. Moreover, given $o_1, \ldots, o_n \in S$, we let $\sum_{i=1...n} o_i$ denote

$o_1 + \ldots + o_n$. A *semiring (endo)morphism* is a function $f : \mathbb{S} \to \mathbb{S}$ such that: $f(0) = 0$, $f(1) = 1$, and for each $o, o' \in \mathbb{S}$, $f(o + o') = f(o) + f(o')$ and $f(o \times o') = f(o) \times f(o')$.

The simplest possible semiring is $\mathbb{B}$, obtained by taking $S = \{0, 1\}$ and $+$ and $\times$ to be the sum and product of booleans, that is *or* and *and*. Other examples of semirings are the natural numbers $\mathbb{N}$ and the nonnegative reals $\mathbb{R}^+$. Every ring, hence every field, is of course a semiring. As an example of a non-commutative semiring, consider a finite and non-empty alphabet A; then, $\mathbb{L} = (2^{A^*}, \cup, \cdot, \emptyset, \{\epsilon\})$, with $\cup$ being language union, $\cdot$ being language concatenation and ϵ being the empty string, is the semiring of languages over A.

Fix a semiring $\mathbb{S} = (S, +, \times, 0, 1)$ and a finite, non-empty alphabet A. A *formal power series* (FPS) over A with coefficients in $\mathbb{S}$ is a function $\sigma : A^* \to \mathbb{S}$. The set of all such functions will be denoted by $\mathbb{F}_{A,\mathbb{S}}$, or simply by $\mathbb{F}$ when no ambiguity arises. Given $\sigma, \tau \in \mathbb{F}$, the sum $\sigma + \tau$ and convolution product $\sigma \times \tau$ are the FPS's defined in the expected manner, that is, by setting for each $w \in A^*$

$$(\sigma + \tau)(w) = \sigma(w) + \tau(w) \qquad (\sigma \times \tau)(w) = \sum_{u,v:uv=w} \sigma(u) \times \tau(v) \tag{1}$$

where, on the right-hand side $+$ ($\sum$) and $\times$ respectively denote sum and product in $\mathbb{S}$. Note that there is no harm in overloading the symbols $+$ and $\times$ as we do here. Indeed, $\mathbb{S}$ can be seen as a subset of $\mathbb{F}$ by identifying each $o \in \mathbb{S}$ with the FPS σ such that $\sigma(\epsilon) = o$ and $\sigma(w) = 0$ elsewhere. This identification is easily seen to preserve the meaning of $+$, $\times$, 0 and 1. It is readily checked that $(\mathbb{F}, +, \times, 0, 1)$ is in turn a (non-commutative) semiring.

Let us now fix a finite, non-empty alphabet L, ranged over by $l, l', \ldots$. In the rest of the paper, elements of L will usually be interpreted as observable, *low confidentiality actions*, as opposed to unobservable, high confidentiality actions, to be introduced in the next section. For the time being, however, there is no need to fix a specific interpretation of L. We let $\lambda, \lambda', \ldots$ range over L^*. The semiring $\mathbb{WL}$ of *weighted (low-)traces* is defined as $\mathbb{F}_{L,\mathbb{R}^+}$. That is, weighted (low-)traces are functions $o : L^* \to \mathbb{R}^+$, with operations of sum and product defined as in (1) above. The reason for our interest in this semiring is that it includes all functions $o : L^* \to [0, 1]$ such that $\sum_{\lambda \in L^*} o(\lambda) = 1$, that is, all *probability distributions* on low traces, as well as all functions o such that $\sum_{\lambda \in L^*} o(\lambda) \leq 1$, that is, all *probability sub-distributions*. Note that neither of these two sets forms a semiring, which explains why it is mathematically convenient to work with the larger set $\mathbb{WL}$. In what follows we shall sometimes take the freedom of writing down weighted (low-)traces as formal sums. For instance, $\frac{1}{3}ll' + \frac{2}{3}ll''$ denotes the element $o \in \mathbb{WL}$ such that: $o(\lambda) = \frac{1}{3}$ if $\lambda = ll'$, $o(\lambda) = \frac{2}{3}$ if $\lambda = ll''$ and $o(\lambda) = 0$ for any other $\lambda \in L^*$.

Let us give another instance of (noncommutative) semiring related to security analysis. Given any non-empty set V of program variables, a *store* is a partial function $m : V \to \mathbb{D}$, where $\mathbb{D}$ is some data-type. Let M be the set of all such stores. Each element of 2^M, the powerset of M, can be thought of as the result of the execution of a nondeterministic program. It is natural to endow 2^M with a semiring structure as follows. Let us denote by $m \star m'$ the sequential composition of two stores, defined thus: $(m \star m')(v) = m'(v)$ if $m'(v)$ is defined, $(m \star m')(v) = m(v)$ if $m(v)$ is defined and $m'(v)$ undefined, $(m \star m')(v)$ is undefined if neither of $m(v)$, $m'(v)$ are defined. In other words, $m \star m'$ describes the effect of running two programs one after another, the first producing

m and the second producing m'. Now consider $\mathbb{M} = (2^M, \cup, \star, \emptyset, \{\emptyset\})$, where: $\star$ is extended point-wise to 2^M (that is, given $I_1, I_2 \subseteq M$, $I_1 \star I_2 = \{m \star m' | m \in I_1, m' \in I_2\}$) and $\emptyset$ denotes the empty set, which is also the nowhere defined partial function. It is readily checked that $\mathbb{M}$ is a semiring.

3 A Process Calculus

Let us fix a finite, non-empty alphabet H, ranged over by $h, h', \ldots$. It is convenient to think of H as a set of unobservable, *high-confidentiality actions* (as opposed to the set L introduced in the preceding section; the two sets are assumed to be disjoint). We let $\pi, \pi', \ldots$ range over H^*. Let us fix a semiring $\mathbb{S}$. The set of all *processes* is given by the following syntax

$$P ::= o \mid h \mid P + P \mid P; P \mid P\langle f\rangle \mid P^*$$

where $o \in \mathbb{S}$, $h \in H$ and $f : \mathbb{S} \to \mathbb{S}$ is a semiring morphism. As usual, $+$, ; and $*$ denote nondeterministic choice, sequential composition and iteration, respectively; $P\langle f\rangle$ is a filtering operator that applies the filter f – a morphism on the semiring – to the observable events produced by P; the condition that f be a morphism appears to be quite natural, and yields a compositional way to compute filter applications. Given processes $P_1, \ldots, P_n$, we let $\sum_{i=1\ldots n} P_i$ denote $P_1 + \ldots + P_n$, where the summands are arranged in any arbitrary fixed order. By convention, we let this summation denote $0 \in \mathbb{S}$ when $n = 0$. In what follows, we shall not commit to any specific semiring, even though our reference instance is meant to be $\mathbb{WL}$. The set of all processes is denoted by $\mathcal{P}_{\mathbb{S}}$, or simply by $\mathcal{P}$ when there is no need to be specific about $\mathbb{S}$.

A *measure*, $\Delta : \mathcal{P}_{\mathbb{S}} \to \mathbb{S}$, is a map from processes to the semiring $\mathbb{S}$. Let $\mathcal{M}$ be the set of all measures. For any $P \in \mathcal{P}$, we let $\delta(P)$ denote the measure Δ s.t. $\Delta(Q) = 1$ if $Q = P$, $\Delta(Q) = 0$ otherwise; note that here $0, 1 \in \mathbb{S}$. It is useful to define operations of internal sum and scalar product for measures. For each P:

$$(\Delta + \Delta')(P) \triangleq \Delta(P) + \Delta'(P) \qquad (o \times \Delta)(P) \triangleq o \times \Delta(P) \tag{2}$$

where on the right hand side of the definitions the operations are those of the semiring $\mathbb{S}$. Such an overload of the symbols $+$ ($\sum$) and $\times$ is harmless, as any ambiguity is easily resolved by the context. With these operations, every measure can be written as $\Delta = \sum_{P\in\mathcal{P}} \Delta(P) \times \delta(P)$. A few syntactic operations on measures will be useful. Syntactic right-multiplication by a process: if $\Delta = \sum_{P\in\mathcal{P}} \Delta(P) \times \delta(P)$, then $\Delta; Q \triangleq \sum_{P\in\mathcal{P}} \Delta(P) \times \delta(P; Q)$. Syntactic left-multiplication, $Q; \Delta$, is defined similarly. Finally, syntactic filtering: with the same Δ as above, $\Delta\langle f\rangle \triangleq \sum_{P\in\mathcal{P}} f(\Delta(P)) \times \delta(P\langle f\rangle)$.

When describing the semantics, the following two notable measures will turn out to be useful. For every $P \in \mathcal{P}$:

$$0_{\mathcal{M}}(P) \triangleq 0 \qquad 1_{\mathcal{M}}(P) \triangleq \begin{cases} 1 & \text{if } P = 1 \\ 0 & \text{otherwise} \end{cases}$$

The operational semantics of $\mathcal{P}$ is given by a pair of functions $(\mathrm{w}, \longrightarrow)$. Here, for each P, $\mathrm{w}(P) \in \mathbb{S}$ is the *final weight* of P, corresponding to the observation that can be made upon P in the current state. A non-zero weight may be understood as indicating the possibility of immediate termination. Specifically, $w \in \mathcal{M}$ is a measure defined by induction on P as follows[1]:

$$\begin{array}{llll} \mathrm{w}(o) = o & \mathrm{w}(h) = 0 & \mathrm{w}(P_1;P_2) = \mathrm{w}(P_1) \times \mathrm{w}(P_2) & \\ \mathrm{w}(P\langle f\rangle) = f(\mathrm{w}(P)) & & \mathrm{w}(Q^*) = 1 & \text{if } \mathrm{w}(Q) = 0 \\ \mathrm{w}(P_1 + P_2) = \mathrm{w}(P_1) + \mathrm{w}(P_2) & & \mathrm{w}(Q^*) = 0 & \text{if } \mathrm{w}(Q) \neq 0 \end{array}$$

The function $\longrightarrow : (\mathcal{P} \times H) \rightarrow \mathcal{M}$, describes the effect of executing a high action and making a transition to a measure. As customary, $(P, h, \Delta) \in \longrightarrow$ will be written as $P \xrightarrow{h} \Delta$. The judgments defining $P \xrightarrow{h} \Delta$ are reported below, where we assume $h' \neq h$.

$$h \xrightarrow{h} 1_{\mathcal{M}} \qquad h' \xrightarrow{h} 0_{\mathcal{M}} \qquad o \xrightarrow{h} 0_{\mathcal{M}} \qquad \frac{P \xrightarrow{h} \Delta_1 \quad Q \xrightarrow{h} \Delta_2}{P + Q \xrightarrow{h} \Delta_1 + \Delta_2}$$

$$\frac{P \xrightarrow{h} \Delta_1 \quad Q \xrightarrow{h} \Delta_2}{P; Q \xrightarrow{h} (\Delta_1; Q) + (\mathrm{w}(P) \times \Delta_2)} \qquad \frac{P \xrightarrow{h} \Delta}{P\langle f\rangle \xrightarrow{h} \Delta\langle f\rangle} \qquad \frac{P \xrightarrow{h} \Delta}{P^* \xrightarrow{h} \Delta; P^*}$$

The rules should be self explanatory. In particular, the rule for sequential composition states that the h-derivative of $P; Q$ results from summing up h-derivatives originating from P, with Q as a sequel, and from Q; the latter contributes to the sum *only if* P may terminate immediately. The rule for filtering P with f applies the filter f to every element of the derivative of P. The rule for P^* is obvious if one thinks that Kleene's law, namely $P^* = 1 + P; P^*$, should remain valid in our setting.

The operational semantics $(\mathrm{w}, \longrightarrow)$ can be turned into a more traditional representation in terms of state-transition machines. Recall that a *weighted automaton* [18,23] is like a nondeterministic automaton, but both its arcs and its states are also labelled with *weights* taken from a semiring. Here, we define a weighted automaton where states are $\mathcal{P}$, the state labeling function is $\mathrm{w}(\cdot)$ and the transition relation $\longrightarrow \subseteq \mathcal{P} \times H \times \mathbb{S} \times \mathcal{P}$ is defined thus: $(P, h, o, P') \in \longrightarrow$, written $P \xrightarrow{h,o} P'$, whenever $P \xrightarrow{h} \Delta$ and $\Delta(P') = o \neq 0$. As an example, the weighted automaton for the process $Q = (o_2; h + o_3; h')^*$ is given here on the right, where the leftmost state corresponds to process Q and the rightmost one to $1; Q$. In the next section, we shall introduce an abstract semantics that equates automata with the same weighted language. It will turn out that the classical law $Q = 1; Q$ holds also in our setting; a possible application of such a law could be simplification of the previous automaton to one with just one state (the rightmost one).

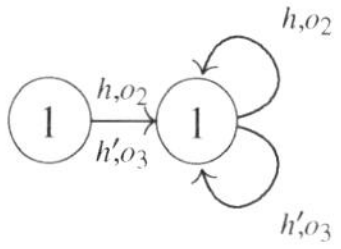

To conclude, let us fix $\mathbb{S} = \mathbb{WL}$ and give a specification in our language of the Z-channel mentioned in the Introduction. The input alphabet is $h, h' \in H$ and the output alphabet is $l, l'l'' \in L^*$; let $p \in [0, 1]$. Then

[1] Note that the semantics of Q^* is usually taken as undefined when $\mathrm{w}(Q) \neq 0$: the reason is evident if one tries to expand Q^* according to Kleene's law, namely $Q^* = 1 + Q; Q^*$. Here, for simplicity, in case $\mathrm{w}(Q) \neq 0$ we stipulate $\mathrm{w}(Q^*) = 0$, so as to avoid dealing with a partial semantic function.

$$Z = h; l + h'; pl'l'' + h'; (1 - p)l .$$

As we shall see, this turns out to be equivalent to $h; l + h'; (pl'l'' + (1 - p)l)$.

4 Abstract Semantics

We first describe the abstract semantics of $\mathcal{P}$ by finality and then characterize the semantic mapping in terms of (weighted) language equivalence.

We endow $\mathcal{P}$ with a Moore automaton structure[2] and then define its semantics coalgebraically, following [23,7]. Recall that a *Moore automaton* with inputs in a finite non-empty alphabet A and outputs in K is a triple (Q, δ, γ) where Q is a (not necessarily finite) set of states, $\delta : Q \times A \to Q$ is a transition function and $\gamma : Q \to K$ is an output function. Let us keep A and K fixed. Central to this treatment is the notion of bisimulation.

Definition 1 (bisimulation). *Given $M = (Q, \delta, o)$, a* bisimulation *is a binary relation $\mathcal{R} \subseteq Q \times Q$ such that, whenever $(q, q') \in \mathcal{R}$ then $\gamma(q) = \gamma(q')$ and $(\delta(q, a), \delta(q', a)) \in \mathcal{R}$, for every $a \in A$. We write $q \sim q'$ if there exists a bisimulation relating q and q'.*

The relation $\sim$ over Q is easily seen to be an equivalence relation and a bisimulation in turn. A *homomorphism* between two Moore automata M and M' is a function ϕ mapping the states of M to the states of M' such that, with an obvious symbology, for each $q \in Q$, $\gamma(q) = \gamma'(\phi(q))$ and, for each $a \in A$, $\phi(\delta(q, a)) = \delta'(\phi(q), a)$. The class of all Moore automata has a final object $\mathcal{F}$ that can be characterized in terms of FPS's. Specifically, we let $\mathcal{F}$ be the Moore automaton (Q, δ, γ) defined thus:

- $Q = \mathbb{F}_{A,K}$;
- $\delta(\sigma, a) = \sigma_a$, where $\sigma_a(w) = \sigma(aw)$, for each $w \in A^*$;
- $\gamma(\sigma) = \sigma(\epsilon)$.

Theorem 1 (Finality and Coinduction principle [23]). *$\mathcal{F}$ is final in the class of Moore automata with inputs in A and outputs in K. That is, for every such automaton M there exists a* unique *homomorphism $\phi : M \to \mathcal{F}$. Moreover, for every q and q' states of M, it holds that $q \sim q'$ if and only if $\phi(s) = \phi(s')$.*

We proceed now to endow $\mathcal{P}$ with a Moore automaton structure, with inputs in H and outputs in the semiring $\mathbb{S}$. Then, the above results will give us: (1) a notion of bisimulation, and (2) a canonical way of interpreting processes as FPS's, which is fully abstract w.r.t. bisimilarity. The construction goes as follows. We extend the weight function and transition relation to $\mathcal{M}$ by linearity. That is, if we let $\Delta_{P,h}$ be the unique measure such that $P \xrightarrow{h} \Delta_{P,h}$ (for each P, h and Δ), then we have:

- $\mathrm{w}(\Delta) \triangleq \sum_{P \in \mathcal{P}} \Delta(P) \times \mathrm{w}(P)$;
- $\Delta \overset{h}{\longmapsto} \Delta_h$, where $\Delta_h \triangleq \sum_{P \in \mathcal{P}} \Delta(P) \times \Delta_{P,h}$.

[2] To be precise, we are endowing $\mathcal{M}$ with a Moore automaton structure, i.e. we are considering Moore automata whose states are measures. With some abuse of terminology, we can consider states as processes, once we see a process P as the Dirac's measure $\delta(P)$.

Now, we let $\mathcal{A} \triangleq (\mathcal{M}, \delta, \mathrm{w})$, where $\delta(\Delta, h) = \Delta_h$: this is a Moore automaton with inputs in H and outputs in $\mathbb{S}$. Observe that $\mathcal{P}$ is naturally embedded in $\mathcal{M}$, once one identifies P with the measure $\delta(P)$. We now let $P \sim Q$ stand for $\delta(P) \sim \delta(Q)$. It is crucial for the compositionality of the semantics that bisimilarity over $\mathcal{P}$ be a congruence.

Theorem 2. *For every $P, Q, R \in \mathcal{P}$ such that $P \sim Q$ and for every semiring morphism $f : \mathbb{S} \to \mathbb{S}$, it holds that:*

$$(1)\ P + R \sim Q + R \qquad (2)\ P; R \sim Q; R \qquad (3)\ P\langle f\rangle \sim Q\langle f\rangle \qquad (4)\ P^* \sim Q^*$$

Let us denote by $\mathcal{L}$ the unique homomorphism from $\mathcal{A}$ to $\mathcal{F}$ given by Theorem 1; it is a function of type $\mathcal{M} \longrightarrow \mathbb{F}$, mapping every measure to a FPS. We want now to give a more explicit characterization of this homomorphism in terms of the operational semantics $(\mathrm{w}, \longrightarrow)$ of $\mathcal{P}$. To this purpose, we extend the notion of h-derivative of a state Δ, previously written Δ_h, to sequences of high actions $\pi \in H^*$ in the expected way: $\Delta_\epsilon \triangleq \Delta$ and $\Delta_{h\pi} \triangleq (\Delta_h)_\pi$.

Proposition 1. *For every Δ and π, $\mathcal{L}(\Delta)(\pi) = \mathrm{w}(\Delta_\pi)$, for every $\pi \in H^*$.*

To conclude, we can define the language generated by a process P, written $\mathcal{L}(P)$, as expected: $\mathcal{L}(P) \triangleq \mathcal{L}(\delta(P))$.

Let us now illustrate the semantics just introduced by a small, concrete example. Let us consider the Z-channel again, $Z = h; l + h'; pl'l'' + h'; (1-p)l$. The Moore automaton generated by $\delta(Z)$ (or, more formally, the portion of the infinite automaton $\mathcal{A}$ that is reachable from $\delta(Z)$) according to the operational rules is given by

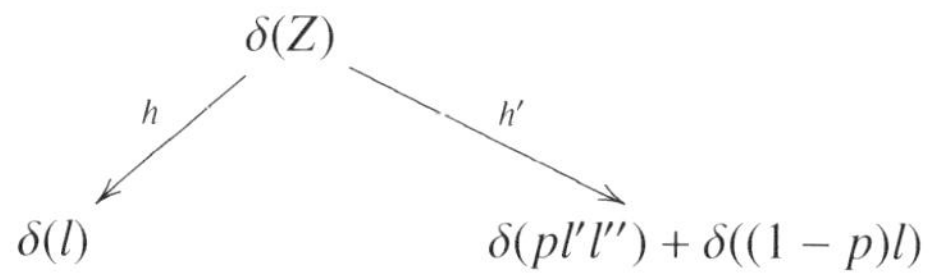

So $\mathrm{w}(\Delta_h) = l$, while $\mathrm{w}(\Delta_{h'}) = pl'l'' + (1-p)l$, as expected. The same result is obtained starting from $Z' = h; l + h'; (pl'l'' + (1-p)l)$; thus, $Z \sim Z'$.

5 A Compositional Construction

We want to provide now another, more informative way of describing the semantic mapping $\mathcal{L}$ discussed in Section 4. In particular, we want to introduce the analog of the process operators over $\mathbb{F}$ and then prove that $\mathcal{L}$ is compositional w.r.t. these process operators (see Corollary 1 below). We follow the approach in [23,7] and define operators on FPS's via *behavioural differential equations* (BDE's). Generally speaking, a BDE is a coinductive specification of a FPS, providing its initial value – $\sigma(\epsilon)$ – and the form of its derivatives σ_h, for every $h \in H$. Of course, one has in general to prove that the given equations have a unique solution. The advantage of this kind of definitions, over explicit but possibly more involved ones, is that they allow for coinductive, step-by-step

Table 1. Behavioural Differential Equations (BDE's)

Initial condition	Condition on derivatives
$o(\epsilon) \triangleq o$	$(o)_h \triangleq 0$
$h(\epsilon) \triangleq 0$	$(h)_{h'} \triangleq \begin{cases} 1 & \text{if } h = h' \\ 0 & \text{otherwise} \end{cases}$
$(\sigma + \sigma')(\epsilon) \triangleq \sigma(\epsilon) + \sigma'(\epsilon)$	$(\sigma + \sigma')_h \triangleq \sigma_h + \sigma'_h$
$(\sigma; \sigma')(\epsilon) \triangleq \sigma(\epsilon) \times \sigma'(\epsilon)$	$(\sigma; \sigma')_h \triangleq \sigma_h; \sigma' + \sigma(\epsilon) \times \sigma'_h$
$(\sigma\langle f\rangle)(\epsilon) \triangleq f(\sigma(\epsilon))$	$(\sigma\langle f\rangle)_h \triangleq (\sigma_h)\langle f\rangle$
$(\sigma^*)(\epsilon) \triangleq \begin{cases} 1 & \text{if } \sigma(\epsilon) = 0 \\ 0 & \text{otherwise} \end{cases}$	$(\sigma^*)_h \triangleq \sigma_h; \sigma^*$

reasoning on the FPS's they define. The BDE's defining the operators associated to the constructs of the language are given in Table 1. There, for every $\pi \in H^*$, we let

$$0_{\mathbb{F}}(\pi) \triangleq 0 \qquad\qquad 1_{\mathbb{F}}(\pi) \triangleq \begin{cases} 1 & \text{if } \pi = \epsilon \\ 0 & \text{otherwise} \end{cases}$$

Indeed, some of these BDE's give rise to operators well-known in the literature on rational series: $\sigma + \sigma'$ and $\sigma; \sigma'$ are, respectively, just the sum and convolution product defined by (1) – so another notation for $\sigma; \sigma'$ is just $\sigma \times \sigma'$, while σ^* is standard iteration (see e.g. [23]). The main result of this section is Corollary 1 below.

Theorem 3. *In $\mathbb{F}$, there exist unique constants 'o' and 'h' and operators '$+$', '$;$', '$\langle f\rangle$' and '*' that satisfy the BDE's in Table 1.*

Corollary 1 (compositionality). *In $\mathbb{F}$, the unique constants 'o' and 'h' and operators '$+$', '$;$', '$\langle f\rangle$' and '*' defined by the BDE's in Table 1 also satisfy the following equalities:*

$$\mathcal{L}(o) = o \qquad \mathcal{L}(h) = h \qquad \mathcal{L}(P + Q) = \mathcal{L}(P) + \mathcal{L}(Q)$$

$$\mathcal{L}(P\langle f\rangle) = (\mathcal{L}(P))\langle f\rangle \qquad \mathcal{L}(P; Q) = \mathcal{L}(P); \mathcal{L}(Q) \qquad \mathcal{L}(P^*) = (\mathcal{L}(P))^*$$

An obvious consequence of the above result is a Kleene theorem for our language. Recall that a FPS $\sigma \in \mathbb{F}$ is *rational* [18] if it can be inductively built starting from the FPS' o and h ($o \in \mathbb{S}, h \in H$) and using the sum, concatenation (sequential composition) and iteration operators defined above. The result entails that one can always eliminate $(\cdot)\langle f\rangle$, essentially by replacing each o occurring in the scope of $(\cdot)\langle f\rangle$ by $f(o)$.

Proposition 2 (a Kleene theorem). *Let σ be a FPS. Then σ is rational if and only if $\sigma = \mathcal{L}(P)$ for some process $P \in \mathcal{P}$.*

6 Examples

6.1 Modeling a "Single Bid" Auction

We model a scenario where each of a certain number of users (three, for simplicity) bids for an item at auction. Each user submits a single (secret) bid to a trusted central server that, in turn, decides the winner by choosing the user whose bid has the highest value. Let U_1, U_2, U_3 be the users; every user knows his bid and the outcome of the auction produced by the server; the problem is measuring the information that every user has about the other users' bids.

We choose a user, U_1, model his view of the auction and try to understand what inferences he can perform about other users' bids – that is, U_1 represents here the (passive) attacker. U_1's bid (a natural number between 1 and m) is an observable event modeled by actions $l_1, \ldots, l_m$; also the outcome of the auction (i.e., the index of the user that wins the auction) is an observable event modeled by actions l'_1, l'_2, l'_3. On the contrary, the bids of U_2 (taken from $\{1, \ldots, n\}$ and modeled by high actions $h_1, \ldots, h_n$) and of U_3 (taken from $\{1, \ldots, q\}$ and modeled by high actions $h'_1, \ldots, h'_q$) are unobservable events, from U_1's point of view. Let us fix the semiring as $\mathbb{S} = \mathbb{WL}$.

A simple way to model the auction is by the following process:

$$\sum_{j=1}^{n} h_j;\left(\sum_{k=1}^{q} h'_k;\left(\sum_{i=1}^{m}[l_i \mapsto \Pr(l_i)]; o_{i,j,k}\right)\right) \tag{3}$$

where $\Pr(l_i)$ denotes the probability of the event l_i and the element $o_{i,j,k} \in \mathbb{WL}$ determines who is the winner of the auction. The actual definition of $o_{i,j,k}$ depends on how we decide to resolve conflicts arising from different users submitting the same bid. A simple but crude way is to resolve the conflict deterministically, e.g. by choosing the user with lowest index:

$$o_{i,j,k} \triangleq \begin{cases} [l'_1 \mapsto 1] & \text{if } i \geq j \text{ and } i \geq k \\ [l'_2 \mapsto 1] & \text{if } j > i \text{ and } j \geq k \\ [l'_3 \mapsto 1] & \text{otherwise.} \end{cases} \tag{4}$$

A fairer way of choosing the winner is by letting

$$o_{i,j,k} \triangleq \left[l'_t \mapsto \frac{1}{|T_{i,j,k}|}\right]_{t \in T_{i,j,k}} \tag{5}$$

where $T_{i,j,k}$ is the set of user indexes (i.e., $T_{i,j,k} \subseteq \{1,2,3\}$) containing the indexes of the users who made the greatest bids among i, j, k. For example, if $i = j = k$, then $T_{i,j,k} = \{1,2,3\}$; if $i = j > k$, then $T_{i,j,k} = \{1,2\}$; if $i > j$ and $i > k$, then $T_{i,j,k} = \{1\}$; and so on.

We let P and Q be the process (3) that uses (4) and (5), respectively, as a definition of $o_{i,j,k}$.

Let us now describe the matrix $\mathcal{L}(P)$. By the BDE's (or the operational semantics), the only entries with non-zero values are $\mathcal{L}(P)(h_j h'_k)(l_i l'_t)$ for $i \in \{1, \ldots, m\}$, $j \in \{1, \ldots, n\}$, $k \in \{1, \ldots, q\}$ and t such that $o_{i,j,k} = [l'_t \mapsto 1]$; moreover, we have that $\mathcal{L}(P)(h_j h'_k)(l_i l'_t) = \Pr(l_i)$. Suppose now that an a priori probability distribution on high traces, $\Pr(\pi)$, reflecting the bidding behaviour of the users, is publicly known. U_1 can then perform some Bayesan inference about the bids of the other users: these inferences are of the form $\Pr(h_j h'_k \mid l_i l'_t)$; by noting that $\mathcal{L}(P)(h_j h'_k)(l_i l'_t)$ corresponds to $\Pr(l_i l'_t \mid h_j h'_k)$ and by elementary probability theory

$$\Pr(h_j h'_k \mid l_i l'_t) = \frac{\Pr(l_i l'_t \mid h_j h'_k) \cdot \Pr(h_j h'_k)}{\Pr(l_i l'_t)} = \frac{\Pr(l_i) \cdot \Pr(h_j h'_k)}{\Pr(l'_t \mid l_i) \cdot \Pr(l_i)} = \frac{\Pr(h_j h'_k)}{\Pr(l'_t \mid l_i)}.$$

To make a concrete case, let us assume that each user has only two possible bidding values; thus, $m = n = q = 2$. In this case, $\mathcal{L}(P)$ is

	$l_1l'_1$	$l_1l'_2$	$l_1l'_3$	$l_2l'_1$
$h_1h'_1$	$\Pr(l_1)$	0	0	$\Pr(l_2)$
$h_1h'_2$	0	0	$\Pr(l_1)$	$\Pr(l_2)$
$h_2h'_1$	0	$\Pr(l_1)$	0	$\Pr(l_2)$
$h_2h'_2$	0	$\Pr(l_1)$	0	$\Pr(l_2)$

Thus, $\Pr(h_1h'_1 \mid l_1l'_1) = 1$, since $\Pr(l'_1 \mid l_1) = \Pr(h_1h'_1)$: indeed, by (4), the only possibility for U_1 to be the winner if he has bid 1 is to have all the bids at 1. The case for $\Pr(h_1h'_2 \mid l_1l'_3)$ is similar. Let us consider now $\Pr(h_2h'_k \mid l_1l'_2)$, for any $k \in \{1, 2\}$; in this case, $\Pr(l'_2 \mid l_1) = \Pr(h_2)$ because, if U_1 has bid 1 and the winner is U_2, it must be that U_2's bid is 2, no matter of U_3's bid. Thus, $\Pr(h_2h'_k \mid l_1l'_2) = \Pr(h'_k)$, once we assume that the users bids are pairwise independent. Finally, let us consider $\Pr(h_jh'_k \mid l_2l'_1)$, for any j and k. In this case, U_1 will always win; thus, $\Pr(l'_1 \mid l_2) = \Pr(l_2)$ and, hence, $\Pr(h_jh'_k \mid l_2l'_1) = \frac{\Pr(h_jh'_k)}{\Pr(l_2)}$. To sum up:

1. if U_1 bids 1,
   (a) he can determine with certainty the other bids if the winner is himself or U_3: in the first case, the bids are 1 for everybody; in the second case, U_2 has bid 1 and U_3 has bid 2.
   (b) if the winner is U_2, his only uncertainty is on U_3's bid, since he knows that U_2 has bid 2.
2. if U_1 bids 2, he surely wins, but he cannot determine with certainty any other bid.

Let us now see how the matrix changes by passing from P to Q, and thus compare the two implementations of the auction system from the security point of view. The matrix for Q is:

	$l_1l'_1$	$l_1l'_2$	$l_1l'_3$	$l_2l'_1$	$l_2l'_2$	$l_2l'_3$
$h_1h'_1$	$\frac{\Pr(l_1)}{3}$	$\frac{\Pr(l_1)}{3}$	$\frac{\Pr(l_1)}{3}$	$\Pr(l_2)$	0	0
$h_1h'_2$	0	0	$\Pr(l_1)$	$\frac{\Pr(l_2)}{2}$	0	$\frac{\Pr(l_2)}{2}$
$h_2h'_1$	0	$\Pr(l_1)$	0	$\frac{\Pr(l_2)}{2}$	$\frac{\Pr(l_2)}{2}$	0
$h_2h'_2$	0	$\frac{\Pr(l_1)}{2}$	$\frac{\Pr(l_1)}{2}$	$\frac{\Pr(l_2)}{3}$	$\frac{\Pr(l_2)}{3}$	$\frac{\Pr(l_2)}{3}$

As expected, this system has more possible high-traces associated to the same low traces, that now are taken from a larger set. Therefore, in this second implementation of the auction system, U_1 can infer less information about the others' bids; in other words, Q is more secure than P. This statement can be made precise by saying that the capacity (see e.g. [9]) of $\mathcal{L}(Q)$ is less than the capacity of $\mathcal{L}(P)$.

We omit the detailed computation for lack of space. It is worth remarking that all the matrices shown can be calculated in a coinductive way via the BDE's presented in the previous section. Moreover, as discussed in [23], such calculations are mechanizable.

6.2 Imperative Computations

This section provides a different way of writing examples; indeed, instead of adopting a process algebraic flavour (like, e.g., in section 6.1), we adopt here a more imperative flavour, by exploiting the semiring of stores, $\mathbb{M}$, described in Section 2. We let $\mu, \mu', \ldots$ range over sets of stores, i.e. partial functions from a set of variables V to a data domain $\mathbb{D}$ that are both non-empty. Notationally, we write the singleton store $\{[x \mapsto v]\}$ as $[x = v]$.

The filter operator $(\cdot)\langle f \rangle$ can be used to express variable updates and conditionals mostly like in an imperative setting. Indeed, variable updates can be modelled by using elements of the semiring as process actions, like in e.g. $[x = 1]; P$. However, this feature only allows us to assign constants to variables. If we want to copy one variable into another, like in e.g. $x := y$, this trick does not work, and we have to use filters. For example, if $x, y \in V$, then the imperative program fragment $P; x := 0; y := x + 1; Q$ corresponds to the following term in the calculus

$$(P; [x = 0])\langle f_{y:=x+1} \rangle; Q$$

where $f_{y:=x+1} : \mathbb{M} \to \mathbb{M}$ is the morphism defined by

$$\begin{aligned} f_{y:=x+1}(\mu) \triangleq\ & \{m \star [y = m(x) + 1] \ :\ m \in \mu \text{ and } m(x) \text{ is defined}\} \\ & \cup \{m \in \mu \ :\ m(x) \text{ is not defined}\}\,. \end{aligned}$$

Similarly, the program fragment P; $\mathsf{if}\ (x \neq y)\ \mathsf{then}\ y := y + 1\ \mathsf{else}\ z := 1$ corresponds to the term

$$(\ P\langle f_{(x \neq y)} \rangle)\langle f_{y:=y+1} \rangle \ +\ (P\langle f_{(x=y)} \rangle\ )\ \langle f_{z:=1} \rangle\,.$$

Here the function $f_{(x \neq y)}$ filters out the stores not satisfying the condition $x \neq y$, that is

$$\begin{aligned} f_{(x \neq y)}(\mu) \triangleq\ & \{m \in \mu \mid m(x), m(y) \text{ are both defined and } m(x) \neq m(y)\} \\ & \cup \{m \in \mu \ :\ m(x) \text{ or } m(y) \text{ is not defined}\}\,. \end{aligned}$$

The other filtering functions are defined as expected.

We can use the above ingredients to model the non-interference scenario commonly employed when reasoning on imperative programs. Specifically, let us assume that the set of variables V is partitioned into low and high ones, viz. V_L and V_H. We shall need a filter $(\cdot)\langle f_L \rangle$ that hides from the attacker the high-part of stores and is defined to be $f_L(\mu) \triangleq \{m_{|V_L} \ :\ m \in \mu\}$. In a term like $P\langle f_L \rangle$, assignments to high variables, $[h = v]$, are not directly observable. Rather, in our modelling, it will be convenient to mark the occurrence of each such assignment with a distinct high event: the semantics $\mathcal{L}(P\langle f_L \rangle)$ then takes care of establishing the correct correspondence between sequences of such events and observed stores. As an example, the program fragment $h := 0; l := h$, where $h \in V_H$ and $l \in V_L$, is modelled as

$$Q =\ (\,(h_0; [h = 0])\langle f_{l:=h} \rangle\,)\,\langle f_L \rangle$$

and, as expected, $\mathcal{L}(Q)(h_0) = [l = 0]$.

In this setting, it is quite natural to model, for instance, a PIN checking scenario. A user chooses a 4-digit PIN and then stores it into a high variable h. The attacker chooses a guess for this PIN and stores it into a low variable l. This behaviour is modelled by

$$Choose \ \triangleq\ \left(\sum_{i \in \{0,\ldots,9999\}} h_i; [h = i] \right); \left(\sum_{j \in \{0,\ldots,9999\}} [l = j] \right)$$

The PIN-checker then checks h against l and stores the result of the comparison into the low variable r. The whole system is now modelled by:

$$Check \triangleq (\ Choose\langle f_{h=l}\rangle; [r = ok]\ +\ Choose\langle f_{h\neq l}\rangle; [r = no]\ )\ \langle f_L\rangle$$

where the filtering functions $f_{h=l}$ and $f_{h\neq l}$ are defined as expected. We could now generate the function $\mathcal{L}(Check)$ via the BDE's and check that it violates non-interference: indeed, $\mathcal{L}(Check)$ maps the trace h_i to the set of stores $\mu_i = \{[l = i, r = ok]\} \cup \{[l = j, r = no]\ :\ j \neq i\}$; therefore, for $i \neq j$, we have $\mu_i \neq \mu_j$. We could make the behaviour of the PIN checker more refined, by e.g. combining the two semirings considered in Section 2 and associate probabilities with the choice of the secret and the attacker's guess.

7 Parallelism

The interpretation of parallelism and synchronization is notoriously problematic when probability is involved. On the other hand, if we content ourselves with just weights – indeed in our calculus we never require weights to add up to 1 – parallelism becomes much easier, as studied e.g. by Hillston [17] and other authors doing stochastic process algebra. In fact, is technically easy to extend the language presented in Section 3 with operators that introduce some form of parallelism. The corresponding operational rules mimics those found in process calculi, e.g. CSP [7]. As a further simplification, in the following we shall confine ourselves to a pure interleaving operator, $||$. We set $\mathrm{w}(P||Q) = \mathrm{w}(P) \times \mathrm{w}(Q)$ and introduce the new operational rule

$$\frac{P \xrightarrow{h} \Delta \quad Q \xrightarrow{h} \Delta'}{P||Q \xrightarrow{h} (\Delta||Q) + (P||\Delta')}$$

where, as expected, $(\Delta||Q)$ is the measure that assigns the weight $\Delta(R)$ to any term of the form $R||Q$, and yields 0 elsewhere ($(P||\Delta')$ is defined symmetrically). In the final semantics, this corresponds to the *shuffle* operator on FPS defined by the following BDE: $(\sigma||\tau)(\epsilon) = \sigma(\epsilon) \times \tau(\epsilon)$ and $(\sigma||\tau)_h = (\sigma_h||\tau) + (\sigma||\tau_h)$, for $h \in H$.

As an example, assume $H = \{h, h'\}$ and $L = \{l, l'\}$ and consider $P \triangleq (h; o + h'; o')^*$, for distinct h, h' and o, o'. This process behaves as a noiseless channel that reveals to the attacker the sequence of actions $\pi \in H^*$ is performed by the secret scheduler. Assume now that two other processes work in parallel with P producing distinct observable effects associated with h and h', thus

$$S \triangleq P||(h; o')^*||(h'; o)^*\ .$$

The system S is a quasi-perfect scrambler, that only reveals the total length of the sequence π performed by the three processes. Indeed, assume for instance that $o = [l \mapsto \frac{1}{2}]$ and that $o' = [l' \mapsto \frac{1}{2}]$. Then, in the row π ($\in H^*$) of the matrix $\mathcal{L}(S)$, the probability is uniformly distributed on the low-traces of length k, $\{l, l'\}^k$, where $k = |\pi|$.

8 Concluding Remarks

In the last eight years there has been steady activity in developing concepts, definitions and analyses in the area of measuring information flows for different languages. Ultimately, these aim at being a means of enforcing quantity based security policies. A highly desirable outcome of this effort would be the automatic checking of enforcement via either model checking or program analysis. So far, the efforts have lead to some notable progress for simple imperative languages [14,22,21,4,11]. By contrast, progress for process algebras has been notably slower. One problem has been establishing appropriate concepts. Lowe's work [19] provided a starting point, developed in quite diverse directions by many authors [6,9,10,20,3,1]. Compared with these works, the present paper makes a conceptual, rather than technical, step, by introducing a general, flexible scheme for specifying and analysing regular behaviours of different kinds, of which quantitative ones are just one flavour.

Our study has connections to the work of Rutten and his collaborators on coalgebras. As mentioned throughout the paper, the coalgebraic treatment of streams and FPS's was introduced, in a syntax-free framework, in [23]. In a recent paper [5], they present a systematic way to generate languages of (generalised) regular expressions, and a sound and complete axiomatization thereof, for a wide variety of quantitative systems. There are two major differences between our work and theirs. First, they work with *branching*- rather than *linear*-time semantics: their final coalgebras are not FPS's, but more complicated objects with no natural interpretation in terms of traces, languages and security analysis. Second, they focus on axiomatizations rather than on compositional semantics in terms of rational operators and BDE's, as we do here.

Future developments of the present framework are exploring instantiations and interpretations of the semiring, as well as expanding the process language. Clearly the addition of a parallel operator with synchronization would be a significant enhancement, although it would lead us outside the realm of regular behaviours. So far this extension has presented non-trivial difficulties.

Acknowledgements. This work had the benefit of the support of a Royal Society joint international project between King's College, London and the Dipartimento di Informatica, Università "La Sapienza" di Roma. In addition, Clark was supported by the UK EPSRC project EP/C545605/1, Quantified Information Flow.

References

1. Aldini, A., Di Pierro, A.: A quantitative approach to noninterference for probabilistic systems. ENTC, vol. 99 (2004)
2. Askarov, A., Sabelfeld, A.: Tight enforcement of information-release policies for dynamic languages. In: Proc. of *IEEE CSF* (2009)
3. Backes, M.: Quantifying probabilistic information flow in computational reactive systems. In: di Vimercati, S.d.C., Syverson, P.F., Gollmann, D. (eds.) ESORICS 2005. LNCS, vol. 3679, pp. 336–354. Springer, Heidelberg (2005)
4. Backes, M., Kopf, B., Ribalchenko, A.: Automatic discovery and quantification of information leaks. In: IEEE Symposium on Security and Privacy (2009)

5. Bonchi, F., Bonsangue, M.M., Rutten, J.J.M.M., Silva, A.: Deriving syntax and axioms for quantitative regular behaviours. In: Bravetti, M., Zavattaro, G. (eds.) CONCUR 2009. LNCS, vol. 5710, pp. 146–162. Springer, Heidelberg (2009)
6. Boreale, M.: Quantifying information leakage in process calculi. Information and Computation 207(6), 699–725 (2009)
7. Boreale, M., Gadducci, F.: Processes as formal power series: A coinductive approach to denotational semantics. Theoretical Computer Science 360(1-3), 440–458 (2006)
8. Boreale, M., Clark, D., Gorla, D.: A Semiring-based Trace Semantics for Processes with Applications to Information Leakage Analysis. Extended version of the present paper, http://www.dsi.uniroma1.it/~gorla/papers
9. Chatzikokolakis, K., Palamidessi, C., Panangaden, P.: Anonymity protocols as noisy channels. In: Montanari, U., Sannella, D., Bruni, R. (eds.) TGC 2006. LNCS, vol. 4661, pp. 281–300. Springer, Heidelberg (2007)
10. Chatzikokolakis, K., Palamidessi, C., Panangaden, P.: On the bayes risk in information-hiding protocols. Journal of Computer Security 16(5), 531–571 (2008)
11. Chen, H., Malacaria, P.: Quantitative analysis of leakage for multi-threaded programs. In: Proc. of PLAS, pp. 31–40. ACM, New York (2007)
12. Chong, S., Myers, A.C.: Security policies for downgrading. In: Proc. of CCS, pp. 189–209. ACM, New York (2004)
13. Clark, D., Hunt, S., Malacaria, P.: Quantitative analysis of the leakage of confidential data. ENTCS, vol. 59 (2002)
14. Clark, D., Hunt, S., Malacaria, P.: A static analysis for quantifying information flow in a simple imperative language. Journal of Computer Security 15(3), 321–371 (2007)
15. Focardi, R., Gorrieri, R.: A classification of security properties for process algebras. Journal of Computer Security 3(1), 5–33 (1995)
16. Goguen, J., Meseguer, J.: Security policies and security models. In: IEEE Symposium on Security and Privacy, pp. 11–20 (1982)
17. Hillston, J.: A Compositional Approach to Performance Modelling. Cambridge University Press, Cambridge (1996)
18. Kuich, W., Salomaa, A.: Semirings, automata, languages. Theoretical Computer Science 5 (1986)
19. Lowe, G.: Quantifying information flow. In: Proc. of CSFW. IEEE, Los Alamitos (2002)
20. Mu, C.: Measuring information flow in reactive processes. In: Qing, S., Mitchell, C.J., Wang, G. (eds.) ICICS 2009. LNCS, vol. 5927, pp. 211–225. Springer, Heidelberg (2009)
21. Mu, C., Clark, D.: An abstraction quantifying information flow over probabilistic semantics. In: Proc. of QAPL. Elsevier, Amsterdam (2009)
22. Mu, C., Clark, D.: Quantitative analysis of secure information flow via probabilistic semantics. In: Proc. of ARES. IEEE, Los Alamitos (2009)
23. Rutten, J.J.M.M.: Behavioural differential equations: a coinductive calculus of streams, automata, and power series. Theoretical Computer Science 308(1-3), 1–53 (2003)
24. Sabelfeld, A., Myers, A.C.: Language-based information-flow security. IEEE Journal on Selelcted Areas in Communications 21(1) (2003)
25. Sabelfeld, A., Sands, D.: Dimensions and principles of declassification. In: Proc. of CSFW, pp. 255–269. IEEE, Los Alamitos (2005)
26. Wittbold, J.T., Johnson, D.M.: Information flow in nondeterministic systems. In: Proc. IEEE Symp. on Security and Privacy, pp. 144–161. IEEE, Los Alamitos (1990)

A Game-Theoretic Approach to Routing under Adversarial Conditions*

James Gross[1], Frank G. Radmacher[2], and Wolfgang Thomas[2]

[1] Mobile Network Performance Group, RWTH Aachen University
[2] Lehrstuhl für Informatik 7, RWTH Aachen University

Abstract. We present a game-theoretic framework for modeling and solving routing problems in dynamically changing networks. The model covers the aspects of reactivity and non-termination, and it is motivated by quality-of-service provisioning in cognitive radio networks where data transmissions are interfered by primary systems. More precisely, we propose an infinite two-player game where a routing agent has to deliver network packets to their destinations while an adversary produces demands by generating packets and blocking connections. We obtain results on the status of basic problems, by showing principal limitations to solvability of routing requirements and singling out cases with algorithmic solutions.

1 Introduction

An objection to research in theoretical computer science is often the simplicity of the models under consideration in relation to much more complex situations as they arise in practice. In the present paper we attempt to bridge this gap in a specific field of networking which draws much attention currently, namely routing problems over dynamically changing networks. This is motivated by a new system concept in the domain of wireless networking referred to as *cognitive radio* networks.

To illustrate this, consider a wireless communication network (referred to as *cognitive network* in the following) which consists of a certain set of nodes. For any pair of neighboring nodes, there are several radio channels that can be used to convey data packets from one node to the next one. The network is subject to some load, i.e., at different nodes data packets are created at different times which need to be forwarded to a particular destination. Packets are forwarded by a routing scheme, which can take different information into account (channel states, network load) and is therefore reactive. In such a network, dynamic changes of the connectivity between nodes can occur due to interference. Interference occurs if some (potentially malicious) device or multiple such devices start occupying radio channels that are used by the considered cognitive network. Such an action corrupts any data conveyed on that particular channel and blocks therefore the channel as the cognitive radio network can detect interference on radio channels prior to data transmission. The main envisioned application area of

* Work supported by the RWTH Aachen Research Cluster UMIC ("Ultra High-Speed Mobile Information and Communication") of the German Excellence Initiative, German Research Foundation grant DFG EXC 89.

C.S. Calude and V. Sassone (Eds.): TCS 2010, IFIP AICT 323, pp. 355–370, 2010.

such cognitive radio networks is the reuse of allocated radio channels owned by so called *primary systems*. It is well known that at any point in time the radio spectrum is heavily underutilized. Thus, "cognitive devices" that identify temporarily unused radio channels could solve the problem of underutilized radio spectrum (assuming that they vacate any used radio channels once a primary system starts transmitting data again).

An important question in such a network setting is if – and possibly under which conditions – a cognitive network can provide quality-of-service for transmission requests that it serves; for instance, does the system concept allow for a timely delivery of data packets, how much memory must be put into the nodes of the network to support such guarantees, how do routing schemes have to be designed etc. The key concept in this scenario is the routing of packets which is adversely affected by the way radio channels are interfered over time. As we are interested in worst-case system performance, this naturally leads to a dynamic network model with at least two decision instances: an entity performing the routing as well as an entity that causes interference. In this paper we are interested in theoretical limitations and possibilities of routing in such dynamic networks under various conditions which have implications for the technical design of a cognitive network.

To do so, we propose a game-theoretic model for routing under adversarial conditions. More precisely, we consider a structured scenario in which two adversarial agents perform actions in turn. The first agent, called demand agent, carries out actions that conflict quality-of-service provisioning in the cognitive network. As indicated, primary systems might block certain radio channels (edges) between nodes of the cognitive network, while new data packets are generated that have to be forwarded by the cognitive network to their destination. The other agent, called routing agent, sends packets from nodes to neighboring nodes, observing the fact that certain radio channels are blocked. We assume a time-slotted (discrete) mode of operation in which demand agent and routing agent do their actions in alternation. This results in an infinite system run that is also called "play", following game-theoretic terminology. Thus, our model includes the aspect of full reactivity (between demands and routing) and of non-termination. Different quality-of-service requirements to be guaranteed by the routing agent are condensed in "winning conditions" – a play that satisfies one such winning condition is considered won by routing agent, otherwise demand agent wins. A routing algorithm that leads to satisfaction of the given requirements under all possible behaviors of the demand agent is thus a winning strategy in this infinite game. Note that a winning strategy works fully adaptively over infinite time, even under radical changes of profiles of the demand player; it is thus a stronger kind of solution than standard routing schemes.

We introduce the model in more detail in the next section. Then we show results on principal limitations of algorithmic solutions. We show that for our model in general, it is algorithmically undecidable whether, given a network and some requirements, a solution (i.e. a winning strategy for routing agent) exists (Section 4). On the other hand we then show that, assuming specific technical requirements for our network model, the existence of a solution can be decided and that in the cases where a solutions exist routing schemes can be effectively constructed (Section 5).

The issue of routing in dynamic networks has been addressed previously in the context of of online algorithms and competitive analysis by Awerbruch, Mansour and

Shavit in [4]. In their work – and in a sequel of related ones [1,2,3] – the focus was on the design of online algorithms with the goal of balancing the load in the network to avoid congestion. Note that an online algorithm may be viewed as a strategy in a finite game (possibly of unbounded length), and its performance is measured relatively to a corresponding optimal offline algorithm. This view has two shortcomings. First, such a competitive analysis requires a reasonable comparison of the online algorithm with a corresponding offline algorithm. However, it is inappropriate for the analysis of problems where an online algorithm is only able to find a strict subset of the offline solutions. For example, routing problems can be analyzed via competitive analysis if the number of delivered packets (throughput) is the subject of interest. However, analyzing for which dynamic scenarios certain network properties as the delivery of all packets can be guaranteed (quality-of-service) is out of scope of the competitive analysis approach. The other shortcoming in our context is due to the fact that a network protocol or routing scheme should run without termination. As it is known from the theory of automatic verification (see e.g. [6]), several natural requirements, such as liveness and fairness conditions, can only be modeled faithfully when infinite system runs are considered rather than their approximations by finite runs of unbounded length.

Further related work on game-theoretic analysis of dynamic networks has been started in the studies of "sabotage games", which van Benthem introduced in [5]. There, a reachability problem over graphs is considered, where a "Runner" traverses a graph while a "Blocker" deletes an edges after each move. The theory of these games was developed by Löding and Rohde in [13,12,15,16] and also by others [11,8]. An enhanced non-terminating version of such games was studied in [14]. There, two players, "Constructor" and "Destructor" add resp. delete vertices/edges, and the problem of guaranteeing certain properties of the network graph (like connectivity) is addressed. However, all these approaches do not address the essential issue of simultaneous routing of many packets (which leads to a possibly infinite state space).

Let us finally mention some work on other, complementary aspects of cognitive radio networks. In [7] different solution concepts by equilibria are pursued. In [19] the construction of appropriate network architectures is addressed. Shiang and van der Schaar [17] consider a learning approach for constructing routing schemes adapted to the behavior of the network users.

2 Modeling Routing in Dynamic Networks via Games

We assume that the two agents acting in the network know the current network structure including all information about packets and blocked channels. So, in the present ideal setting we consider a game of perfect information. Moreover, the blocking of frequencies and the generation of packets are subject to certain constraints; these rules may depend on the whole network state. We allow only "deterministic" (rather than probabilistic) constraints; randomized packet generation and randomized frequency blocking [11] is not treated in the present paper.

The game and the game arena. A *dynamic network routing game* between two players, called demand agent and routing agent, is given by a tuple $\mathcal{G} = (G, C, W)$ where

G is the network graph, C a list of "constraints" for moves of demand agent, and W the requirement (winning condition) to be fulfilled by the routing agent. More precisely, the *network graph* or *connectivity graph* G is a graph of the form $G = (V, E)$ with finite vertex set V and a finite set E of multi-edges (network connections, where single edges correspond to frequencies). Formally, E is partitioned into sets E_a of single edges, where $a \in \Sigma$ for some index set Σ which denotes the set of available frequencies. We write $(u, v)_a$ for the edge (u, v) in E_a. For convenience we consider in the following all edges as undirected, i.e. $(u, v)_a \in E$ implies $(v, u)_a \in E$. (However, all results in this paper hold exactly in the same way for network graphs with directed edges.) C is a list of rules, called also *constraints*, i.e. conditions imposed on edge removal and packet generation. Finally, W is the *winning condition*, formally a set of infinite plays, and containing precisely those plays that are won by routing agent. We now explain in several stages the notion of play (or admissible system run consisting of network states).

Packets and blocked frequencies. A *packet* consists of a unique identifier from $\mathbb{N}$, its destination node, and a *timestamp*, which is the number of turns since its creation. Thus a packet is a triple $(id, u, k) \in \mathbb{N} \times V \times \mathbb{N}$, indicating that it has the identifier id, the destination u, and that it was generated k turns before the current moment. We define the *packet distribution* $\lambda\colon V \to 2^{\mathbb{N} \times V \times \mathbb{N}}$ by mapping each node to the set of packets which are currently stored at this node.

Network connections (edges) can be blocked (by demand agent, more precisely by the component of primary systems) for a certain number of turns. The current status of the edges is described by a *blocked links function* $bl\colon E \to \{0, 1, \ldots, m\}$ which says that edge e is blocked for the next $bl(e)$ turns. If $bl(e) = 0$, the edge e is not blocked. Communication between two nodes via the edge e is only possible if $bl(e) = 0$.

The maximal number of turns m that can be assigned to an edge for blocking is always given by the constraints C, which are described later. We denote the set of all possible functions bl for a game $\mathcal{G}$ (i.e. E and m are fixed) by $BL_{\mathcal{G}}$ or simply by BL when the context is clear.

Network states and plays. The positions or states of a dynamic network routing game $\mathcal{G}$ are called network states. A *network state* is a triple $(0/1, \lambda_i, bl_i)$ where 0 (resp. 1) indicates that routing agent (resp. demand agent) moves next, λ_i is a packet distribution, and bl_i is a blocked links function. We denote by $Q_{\mathcal{G}}$ the set of all network states in the game $\mathcal{G}$; note that $Q_{\mathcal{G}}$ can be infinite in general, since we do not impose an a priori bound on the number of packets in the network.

The initial network state is $(1, \lambda_0, bl_0)$ with $\lambda_0(u) = \emptyset$ and $bl_0(e) = 0$ for all $u \in V$, $e \in E$, i.e. no packets are in the network, no edges are blocked, and demand agent starts. The subsequent moves are chosen by routing agent and demand agent in alternation. A *turn* is defined as two consecutive movements: the first one by demand agent and the second one by routing agent; each of the player's moves we call a *half-turn*. In the i-th half-turn where i is even, demand agent moves and the network state $(1, \lambda_i, bl_i)$ is updated according to demand agent's action to $(0, \lambda_{i+1}, bl_{i+1})$. In the subsequent half-turn (where $i + 1$ is odd), routing agent acts and generates the network state $(1, \lambda_{i+2}, bl_{i+2})$. A detailed explanation of these updates follows. A *play* is an infinite sequence of network states that is generated in this way, i.e. a sequence $\rho = \rho_0\rho_1\rho_2\ldots \in Q_{\mathcal{G}}^{\omega}$ with $\rho_0 = (1, \lambda_0, bl_0)$.

Constraints and moves. When it is demand agent's half-turn, he generates new packets and blocks edges for a certain amount of turns. We restrict demand agent's movements that are possible in the game $\mathcal{G} = (G, C, W)$ by a list C of "constraints". An example of a constraint is the following:

$$\text{node } u \text{ has a packet } \wedge \neg \text{ edge } (u,v)_a \text{ is blocked } \longrightarrow \\ \text{block}_2((u,v)_a) \mid \text{block}_1((u,v)_a), \text{generate}(u,v') \ .$$

This constraint says that, when there exists a packet at node u and the edge $(u,v)_a$ is not blocked, then demand agent either must block the edge $(u,v)_a$ for the next two turns or he has to block the edge $(u,v)_a$ for one turn and generate a packet at node u with destination v'. If C is a list of more than one constraint, they are processed in their given order. Generally, a *constraint* C is a list of rules of the form

$$\text{Condition} \longrightarrow \text{Behavior} \ .$$

Here, the *condition* is a Boolean combination of statements of the following form:

1. edge $(u,v)_a$ is blocked
2. node u has a packet (possibly with destination d and/or timestamp t)

A constraint is called *weak* if all of its conditions only depend on blocked edges, i.e. every condition is a Boolean combination of statements of the first form. Weak constraints reflect the natural assumption that the possibility of demands (either channel blocking or packet generation) should be restricted by information on the currently blocked channels, but not on packets in the cognitive network.

The *behavior* is a disjunction (separated by "|") of conjunctions (separated by ",") of demands, i.e. instructions of the form (1) generate(u,d) and (2) block$_m((u,v)_a)$ The first says that demand agent must generate a packet at node u with destination d. The second says that demand agent has to block the edge $(u,v)_a$ for the next m turns. Notice that also an edge $(u,v)_a$ with $bl_i((u,v)_a) \neq 0$ can be blocked again; in this case $bl((u,v)_a)$ is updated to its new value k according to the rule block$_k(u,v)$.

In order to rule out some very exotic situations, the constraints always impose a uniform bound m on the number of turns for which an edge can be blocked and on the number of packets generated per turn. The blocked links function bl is then a function from E to $\{0,1,\ldots,m\}$ (if no "block" instruction exists in the constraints, we set $m := 0$). A bound for the maximal number of packets generated per turn can be defined by the number of all "generate" instructions in the constraints.

The semantics of the constraints is defined in the natural way: The list of constraints is processed in their given order, and whenever the condition (left hand side) is true (matches the current network state), demand agent has to choose exactly one of the conjunctions of the behavior (right hand side). Then all statements of the chosen conjunction are carried out.

On a more abstract level, the constraints can be seen as a function $C\colon Q_{\mathcal{G}} \to 2^{Q_{\mathcal{G}}}$ which assigns to each network state of demand player a set of possible successor network states that are described by the given list of constraints. Since in weak constraints only conditions of form 1 are used, these constraints depend on the blocked links only. So, on this abstract level, weak constraints can be seen as a function $C\colon BL_{\mathcal{G}} \to 2^{Q_{\mathcal{G}}}$ which assigns to each blocked links function a set of possible successor network states that are described by the given list of constraints.

When it is routing agent's half-turn, she can send packets to neighboring nodes. For each node $v \in V$ and each available frequency $a \in \Sigma$, at most one packet can be transmitted from node v via frequency a. Delivered packets, i.e. packets that reach their destination in this turn, are removed from the network. For all other packets the timestamp is increased by 1. After routing agent's half-turn the value of the blocked links function bl is decremented by one for every edge (if it is not already 0).

Strategies. In this paper we only consider deterministic strategies. A *strategy for demand agent* (resp. *routing agent*) is a function, here denoted by σ (resp. τ) that describes the decisions of the agents (possibly depending on the history of the play). Formally, a strategy for demand (resp. routing) agent is a (partial) function $\sigma\colon Q_{\mathcal{G}}^{+} \to Q_{\mathcal{G}}$ (resp. $\tau\colon Q_{\mathcal{G}}^{+} \to Q_{\mathcal{G}}$) that maps each possible play prefix $\rho_1 \cdots \rho_k$ to a new network state which is permitted by the before mentioned rules.

Winning conditions. The *winning condition* W (for routing agent) describes for each play $\rho \in Q_{\mathcal{G}}^{\omega}$ whether routing agent wins ρ. We consider the following fundamental winning conditions:

- DELIVERY. Routing agent wins a play ρ if in ρ each generated packet is eventually delivered.
- DELIVERY$_\ell$. Routing agent wins a play ρ if in ρ each packet is delivered within ℓ turns after it was generated.
- BOUNDEDNESS. Routing agent wins a play ρ if in ρ the number of packets in the network is bounded, i.e. there is a k such that the number of packets is always $\leq k$.

Demand agent wins a play if it is not won by routing agent. We say that demand agent (resp. routing routing) wins a game $\mathcal{G}$ if there exists a strategy σ (resp. τ) such that he (resp. she) wins every play $\rho \in Q_{\mathcal{G}}^{\omega}$ that is played according to this strategy.

Some basic problems. From the theory of infinite games it is known that in a very abstract view of winning conditions, there are winning conditions that do not allow a winning strategy for either player. Such games are called non-determined. All winning conditions in this paper are of a somewhat concrete and simple kind (called Borel conditions) that leads to games that are *determined*; so one of the two players has a winning strategy. So we do not not address the problem of determinacy in the sequel.

A *solution of a game* consists then of

1. the decision which of the two players wins
2. and then a presentation of a winning strategy for the winner.

We will first show that the first problem is undecidable for the winning conditions BOUNDEDNESS and DELIVERY. On the other hand, for DELIVERY$_\ell$ both problems 1 and 2 will be shown to be solvable. We will then present a variant where we restrict the constraints C to be weak; these games turn out to be solvable also for the DELIVERY winning condition.

3 Toy Example

Consider the tiny network G in Figure 1 with channels over $\Sigma = \{a, b\}$. We define the dynamic network routing game $\mathcal{G} = (G, C, W)$ where demand agent's constraints C are the following. In each turn, demand agent generates at node v_1 two packets with destination v_4. Also he blocks exactly one of the a-labeled edges for one turn; so, exactly one of these edges is blocked every turn. The constraints C are weak and can be formalized as follows:

$$\begin{aligned}
\text{true} &\longrightarrow \text{generate}(v_1, v_4),\ \text{generate}(v_1, v_4) \\
\text{true} &\longrightarrow \text{block}_1(v_1, v_2)_a \mid \text{block}_1(v_1, v_4)_a \mid \text{block}_1(v_2, v_3)_a \mid \text{block}_1(v_3, v_4)_a \ .
\end{aligned}$$

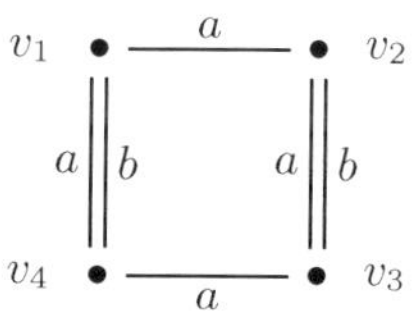

Fig. 1. A network graph of a dynamic network routing game

First, we analyze the game $\mathcal{G}$ for the DELIVERY winning condition. Routing agent wins the game with the strategy that she sends the packet with the highest timestamp at v_1 to v_4 via the b-labeled edge. This operation is always possible since demand agent cannot block the b-labeled edge in this game. With this strategy, the packet with the highest timestamp always reaches its destination in every turn. So, routing agent wins $\mathcal{G}$ for the DELIVERY winning condition.

Next, we discuss the game with the DELIVERY$_\ell$ winning condition. Routing agent does not win with the above strategy for the DELIVERY winning condition, because by playing this strategy more and more packets have to be kept at v_1. So, routing agent has to route packets via channel a either using the edge $(v_1, v_4)_a$ or the path $v_1v_2v_3v_4$. Now, consider that demand agent blocks the edge $(v_1, v_4)_a$; so, routing agent has to send a packet via the path $v_1v_2v_3v_4$. In this case, demand agent can keep this packet at the nodes v_2 and v_3 by deleting the edge $(v_1, v_2)_a$ if the packet is at v_2 (resp. the edge $(v_3, v_4)_a$ if the packet is at v_3). Such a packet will never be delivered. So, demand agent wins $\mathcal{G}$ with the DELIVERY$_\ell$ winning condition for every ℓ.

Surprisingly, routing agent can win the game for the BOUNDEDNESS winning condition. Her strategy is the following: In every turn routing agent delivers one of the generated packets at v_1 directly via the b-labeled edge. She also delivers the other generated packet via the a-labeled edge to v_4 if this edge is not blocked; otherwise, she sends this packet to v_2. Furthermore, routing agent sends packets at node v_2 always to v_3, and she sends packets at v_3 to v_4 whenever this is possible. It is easy to see that, by playing this strategy, each of the generated packets at v_1 is sent immediately to another node, and that the number of packets at node v_2 (resp. v_3) is at most 1 (resp. 2). So, the number of packets in the network is bounded.

4 Negative Results

Our first result shows that one has to assume a certain coarseness of the constraints in order to enable an algorithmic analysis of dynamic network routing games. For general (or exotic) constraints we obtain undecidability:

Theorem 4.1. *The following problem is undecidable: Given a network routing game with the* BOUNDEDNESS *winning condition, does routing agent have a winning strategy?*

Proof. We show this result by a reduction of the boundedness problem for 2-register machines to games with the BOUNDEDNESS winning condition. The boundedness problem for 2-register machines, which are Turing-complete, is known to be undecidable.

A *2-register machine* is a program which operations are the modification of two registers X_1, X_2; the allowed operations of these registers are the increment and decrement by 1, and the test whether a particular register is 0. Formally, a 2-register machine has the form $\mathcal{R} = I_1; I_2; \ldots; I_k$ where each I_j is one of the following instructions: $j\colon$ INC(X_i), i.e. increment register X_i by 1, $j\colon$ DEC(X_i), i.e. decrement X_i by 1 if $X_i > 0$, $j\colon$ IF $X_i = 0$ GOTO m, i.e. a conditional jump to instruction m, and $j\colon$ GOTO m, i.e. an unconditional jump to m (with $1 \leq m \leq k$). The last instruction stops the computation: $I_k = k\colon$ STOP.

We construct, given a 2-register machine $\mathcal{R} = I_1; I_2; \ldots; I_k$, a dynamic network routing game $\mathcal{G} = (G, C, \text{BOUNDEDNESS})$. The game arena $G = (V, E)$ has $|k| + 5$ vertices $V = \{v_1, \ldots, v_k, c_1, c_2, c_1', c_2', s\}$. Each of the vertices $v_1, \ldots, v_k$ corresponds to an instruction of the register machine. A packet starting on vertex v_1 with destination v_k will move according to the instructions of $\mathcal{R}$. The vertices c_1, c_2 represent the two counters (their values are given by the numbers of packets located at c_1, c_2), and in order to decrement a counter, the vertex s is used as destination for packets from c_1, c_2. The vertex c_1 (resp. c_2) is connected to s via the vertex c_1' (resp. c_2') and is used to force routing agent to decrement the number of packets in c_1 (resp. c_2). The construction only uses an edge relation over single edges; it is defined as follows:

$$\begin{aligned} E := &\{(v_j, v_{j+1}) \mid j\colon \text{IF } X_i = 0 \text{ GOTO } j', \text{ or } j\colon \text{INC } X_i, \text{ or } j\colon \text{DEC } X_i \in \mathcal{R}\} \\ &\cup \{(v_j, v_{j'}) \mid j\colon \text{ IF } X_i = 0 \text{ GOTO } j', \text{ or } j\colon \text{ GOTO } j' \in \mathcal{R}\} \\ &\cup \{(c_1, c_1'), (c_2, c_2'), (c_1', s), (c_2', s)\} \ . \end{aligned}$$

When there are no packets in the network – especially in the first turn – demand agent creates a packet with destination v_k at vertex v_1, which mimics the instruction pointer. The constraints ensure that exactly the edge between two vertices v_i and v_j is enabled when the packet is at v_i and the instruction which must be executed next in $\mathcal{R}$ corresponds to the vertex v_j. At the vertices c_1 and c_2 packets are generated according to the increment instructions, and the paths to the vertex s are enabled according to the decrement instructions. The vertices c'_1 and c'_2 allow that we can encode in the constraints a check whether routing agent really sends a packet towards s according to a decrement instruction. If the instruction pointer packet reaches its destination v_k, the game switches in a mode where all remaining packets in the network will be delivered.

With some work on the exact formulation of the constraints one can see, that with such a construction routing agent wins $\mathcal{G}$ iff the register machine $\mathcal{R}$ is bounded. □

Theorem 4.2. *The following problem is undecidable: Given a network routing game with the* DELIVERY *winning condition, does routing agent have a winning strategy?*

Proof. The argument is a one-to-one copy of the previous proof. Here we reduce the halting problem for 2-register machines to games with the DELIVERY winning condition. Namely, with the same construction as above, we see that if a 2-register machine reaches the stop instruction I_k, then all packets are delivered; so, routing agent wins. Conversely, if the 2-register machine does not reach the stop instruction I_k, at least the packet which mimics the instruction pointer does not reach its destination; so, demand agent wins. □

Note that the undecidability results above can be sharpened. They are still valid if we only consider single channel networks (using only one frequency) since only single edges are involved in the constructed network graphs.

The results can be also sharpened regarding the conditions used in the constraints. For the informally given description of the constraints, only statements of the form "edge e blocked" and "node u has a packet" are necessary. So, it is not necessary to check the destination or the timestamp of a packet in the network to obtain undecidability.

5 Positive Results

In this section we show first that dynamic network routing games with the DELIVERY$_\ell$ winning condition are solvable by a reduction to the so-called safety games. Then we show that dynamic network routing games with *weak* constraints are solvable even for the BOUNDEDNESS and the (unrestricted) DELIVERY winning condition.

5.1 Solving Games with the DELIVERY$_\ell$ Winning Condition

Before turning to dynamic network routing games with the DELIVERY$_\ell$ winning condition, we recall the fundamental notion of *safety game* from the theory of infinite games. In the case of network routing games, a *safety winning condition* for routing agent is given by a set A of "admissible network states". Routing agent wins a play $\rho = \rho_0\rho_1 \ldots$ if each network state ρ_i belongs to A. In other words, she has to avoid getting outside A at some point.

If the set of possible network states is finite, one can compute whether routing agent has a winning strategy (starting from the initial network state) in a safety game specified by the set A and, in this case, one can compute her winning strategy (a constructive proof can be found in [18,9]). We can now easily prove the following result:

Theorem 5.1. *Dynamic network routing games with the* DELIVERY$_\ell$ *winning condition, where* $\ell \in \mathbb{N}$, *are solvable (so that one can decide whether routing agent wins and in this case provide a winning strategy in terms of a suitable routing scheme).*

Proof. The idea is that the DELIVERY$_\ell$ winning condition ensures that the set of network states of the game $\mathcal{G} = (G, C, \text{DELIVERY}_\ell)$ can be assumed to be finite with a winning condition in the safety format, so that the remark above gives the desired solution.

It remains to be shown that it suffices to inspect only a finite subset of the network states. We can assume that the game is over when the timestamp of a packet exceeds ℓ (routing agent loses in this case). So, we can assume that it is sufficient to consider packet timestamps of at most $\ell + 1$. Also, the number of packets that can be generated in one turn is bounded by the constraints, say by a constant k. So, the total number of packets in the network is at most $(\ell + 1) \cdot k$. Since each packet gets the lowest available identifier when generated, the identifiers are also bounded by $(\ell+1)\cdot k$. So, in this case a packet distribution λ is a function from V to $2^{[(\ell+1)k] \times V \times [\ell+1]}$ where $[n] := \{0, \ldots, n\}$. The number of different functions of this form is finite. □

5.2 Solving Games under Weak Constraints

We exhibit another natural scenario under which the dynamic network routing game becomes solvable, even for the conditions BOUNDEDNESS and DELIVERY.

This scenario is given by a certain format of constraints of the demand player, taking into account the division of demands into those by the primary systems and the cognitive network. A natural assumption on the constraints is that the demand actions may depend on blocked frequencies (i.e. currently active demands of the primary systems) but not on information about packets that are currently in the cognitive network. This leads to the assumption that constraints depend on the information about blocked channels only.

We already defined these *weak constraints* in Section 2; they can be seen as a function $C\colon BL \rightarrow 2^{Q_\mathcal{G}}$ which assigns to each blocked links function a set of possible successor network states. We shall show, in contrast to the results of Section 4, the solvability of games with weak constraints. The central observation will be that – assuming weak constraints – inspecting only finitely many network states is sufficient to decide DELIVERY resp. BOUNDEDNESS. As a preparation we state some auxiliary propositions.

Remark 5.2. In a dynamic network routing game with weak constraints, consider a play ρ that is won by routing agent and results from demand agent playing according to a strategy σ and routing agent playing according to a strategy τ. If demand agent changes his strategy σ to σ' by leaving out the generation of some packets, he will also lose the resulting play, i.e. demand agent cannot improve his strategy in this way.

Remark 5.3. Consider a dynamic network routing game with weak constraints, a play ρ which is currently in a network state q_i with blocked links function bl_i. Let us assume that demand agent has a strategy to reach from q_i a network state q_j with blocked links function bl_j. Then, since the constraints do not depend on the packet distribution, demand agent has a strategy from q_i to reach a network state q'_j with same blocked links function bl_j within at most $|BL| - 1$ turns (note that $|BL|$ is always ≥ 1).

For the proofs in this section, we use the following terminology. We say that a packet (id, d, k) which is currently at vertex u (in a given network state) has the *type* (u, d). So, in a network with a vertex set V the packets have at most $|V|^2$ different types.

Further, for a given game, we denote with Δ_{out} the *maximal number of outgoing packets* that routing agent can send per node; formally, it is defined as

$$\Delta_{\text{out}} = \max_{u \in V}\{ \ |\{a \in \Sigma\}| \ : \ \text{it exists } v \in V \text{ such that } (u, v) \in E_a \ \} \ .$$

First we show solvability for the BOUNDEDNESS condition under weak constraints. For this winning condition we can give a uniform bound on the number of packets in the network (which is sufficient to achieve for routing agent).

Theorem 5.4. *Consider a network routing game $\mathcal{G}$ with weak constraints. Then, routing agent wins $\mathcal{G}$ with the* BOUNDEDNESS *winning condition iff she can guarantee in $\mathcal{G}$ that there exists at most $b := |BL| \cdot (\Delta_{out} + k)$ packets at each vertex where k is the maximal number of packets that can be generated per turn (given by the constraints).*

Proof. Clearly, if routing agent can guarantee the bound b for the number of packets at each vertex, she can guarantee the bound $|V| \cdot b$ for the total number of packets in the network; hence, she wins with the BOUNDEDNESS winning condition.

For the converse, we only sketch the proof. We assume that routing agent wins with the BOUNDEDNESS condition. Since demand agent's moves do not depend on the packet distribution, we can partition the network states $Q_{\mathcal{G}}$ in a set *Inf* for which demand agent has a strategy to visit a network state with the same blocked links function infinitely often and a set *Fin* which are network states whose blocked links function can occur at most once in a play. The sum of packets that can be generated in states in *Fin* in a play can be bounded by the constant $c := |BL| \cdot k$. For the states in *Inf* demand agent can revisit a network state with same blocked links function at least every $|BL|$ turns (see Remark 5.3). Since routing agent can send at most Δ_{out} packets to a neighboring node in each turn, routing agent can keep the number of packets at each vertex below $c + |BL| \cdot \Delta_{\text{out}}$ turns (with the c above); otherwise demand agent would have a strategy to generate an unbounded number of packets in the network (which would be a contradiction). □

With the previous theorem, we can easily reduce the game to a safety game with finite state space where routing agent has to ensure that there are at most b packets at each network node.

Corollary 5.5. *Dynamic network routing games with weak constraints and winning condition* BOUNDEDNESS *are solvable (so that one can decide whether routing agent wins and in this case provide a winning strategy in terms of a suitable routing scheme).*

Solving network routing games with DELIVERY winning condition under weak constraints requires a more involved proof. We start with some technical lemmata:

Lemma 5.6. *Given a game with weak constraints on a game arena* $(\{v_1, \ldots, v_k\}, E)$. *Assume demand agent can reach a network state with blocked links function bl where* v_l *stores at least* n_{lm} *packets with destination* v_m $(1 \leq l, m \leq k)$. *Let* $n := \sum_{l,m} n_{lm}$. *Then, demand agent can also reach such a state within* $|BL|^{n+1} \cdot (\Delta_{out})^n$ *turns; moreover it suffices to keep at most* $|BL|^n \cdot (\Delta_{out})^{n-1}$ *packets of each type for* $n > 0$ *(and* 0 *for* $n = 0$*), i.e. all other packets of each type may be discarded after each turn.*

Proof. We show the claim by induction over n. The case $n = 0$ is easy; demand agent has to reach a network state with blocked links function bl, which he can reach within $|BL| - 1$ turns according to Remark 5.3. For $n > 0$ demand agent has to generate at least n packets, say $P_1, \ldots, P_n$, and thereafter demand agent has to reach a network state q_j with $bl_j = bl$ such that the packets $P_1, \ldots, P_n$ (or equivalently n packets of the same types) remain at their vertices where there were generated. We distinguish two cases: In the first case, demand agent has a strategy to generate each packet P_i $(1 \leq i \leq n)$, say in a network state q_i, without visiting a network state with blocked links function bl_i twice, and after generating all n packets in this way he reaches a network state q_j with $bl_j = bl$ where the packets $P_1, \ldots, P_n$ still exist at their required vertices v_{lm}. This is the trivial case where demand agent can reach q_j within $(n+1) \cdot (|BL| - 1) \leq |BL|^{n+1} \cdot (\Delta_{\text{out}})^n$ turns (and it suffices to keep $(\Delta_{\text{out}} + 1) \cdot (n + 1) \cdot (|BL| - 1)$ packets of each type). In the second case, there exists a packet P_i (in $\{P_1, \ldots, P_n\}$) such that demand agent agent can reach the network state q_j only by revisiting a network state with blocked links function bl_i. We may assume due to our induction hypothesis that there is a strategy for demand agent to reach a network state q'_j with blocked links function bl within $x_{n-1} := |BL|^n \cdot (\Delta_{\text{out}})^{n-1}$ turns where at least the packets $P_1, \ldots, P_{i-1}, P_{i+1}, \ldots, P_n$ exist at their required vertices. Now, demand agent has a strategy to revisit a network state with blocked link function bl_i; hence, he can generate sufficiently many packets of the same type as P_i, so that at least one of these packets remains at its origin after taking the x_{n-1} turns for reaching a network state q_j with $bl_j = bl$. Since in the worst case routing agent can send at most Δ_{out} packets per node and turn, it is sufficient for demand agent to visit a network state with function bl_i at most $x_{n-1} \cdot \Delta_{\text{out}}$ times. For that demand agent needs at most $x_{n-1} \cdot \Delta_{\text{out}} \cdot (|BL| - 1)$ turns (due to Remark 5.3). Then, from this state, demand agent needs at most x_{n-1} turns to reach a network state q_j with $bl_j = bl$ and packets $P_1, \ldots, P_n$ at their required vertices v_{lm}. Overall, demand agent can reach q_j within $x_{n-1} \cdot \Delta_{\text{out}} \cdot (|BL| - 1) + x_{n-1} = |BL|^{n+1} \cdot (\Delta_{\text{out}})^n$ turns (and keeping $x_{n-1} = |BL|^n \cdot (\Delta_{\text{out}})^{n-1}$ packets of the same type at each vertex suffices). □

Lemma 5.7. *Given a network routing game with weak constraints on a game arena* $(\{v_1, \ldots, v_k\}, E)$, *and given a network state q with blocked links function bl where each vertex* v_l *stores* n_{lm} *packets with destination* v_m $(1 \leq l, m \leq k)$. *Assume that demand agent has a strategy such that from network state q routing agent cannot deliver one of the packets that are currently in the network. Then, from a network state* q' *with the same function bl where each vertex* v_l *stores only* $n'_{lm} = \min\{n_{lm}, |BL| \cdot \Delta_{out}\}$ *packets with destination* v_m *in the network, demand agent can also prevent the delivery of a packet.*

Proof. Towards a contradiction, we assume that demand agent has a strategy in q to prevent the delivery of at least one packet, but that routing agent has a winning strategy τ

in state q'. If demand agent can prevent the delivery of a packet forever, he can do so due to reaching a network state q_- with a certain blocked links function bl_- such that from q_- onwards a particular packet, say P_-, will never be delivered. Due to Remark 5.3 demand agent has a strategy σ to reach such a network state from q within $|BL| - 1$ turns. Also note it follows from Remark 5.2 that, if routing agent plays his winning strategy τ (which we assumed he has in q') in the network state q, he can guarantee that all of the n_{lm} packets of a type with $n_{lm} \leq |BL| \cdot \Delta_{\text{out}}$ will be delivered and that at least $|BL| \cdot \Delta_{\text{out}}$ of the packets with $n_{lm} > |BL| \cdot \Delta_{\text{out}}$ will be delivered. But since demand agent has a strategy in network state q to prevent the delivery of one of the packets, there is a type with $n_{lm} > |BL| \cdot \Delta_{\text{out}}$ such that one of the n_{lm} packets of this type will never be delivered if demand and routing agent play σ and τ from q. Since there are at least $|BL| \cdot \Delta_{\text{out}}$ many packets of this type in q' as well as in q, routing agent can deliver these packets at best in $\frac{|BL| \cdot \Delta_{\text{out}}}{\Delta_{\text{out}}} = |BL|$ turns. So, if the routing agent plays τ in q', there is still at least one of the n_{lm} packets of this type left at v_l after $|BL| - 1$ turns. But according to Remark 5.3 demand agent can reach from q' a state with function bl_- within $|BL| - 1$ turns; so, there is still one packet left that will never be delivered, which is a contradiction to our assumption that τ is a winning strategy in q'. □

For a game $\mathcal{G}$, we define the modified game $\mathcal{G}_{\restriction b}$ where at most b packets with the same destination are stored at each node. More precisely, for all vertices u and d, the following happen in $\mathcal{G}_{\restriction b}$ after each player's half-turn: While the number of packets at u with destination d is higher than b, the packet (id, d, t) at u with the highest id is deleted.

Theorem 5.8. *Consider a dynamic network routing game with weak constraints. Let $b := (|BL| \cdot \Delta_{out})^{|V|^2 \cdot |BL| \cdot \Delta_{out}}$. Then, routing agent wins $\mathcal{G}$ with the* DELIVERY *winning condition iff she wins $\mathcal{G}_{\restriction b}$ with the* DELIVERY *winning condition.*

Proof. Assume that routing agent wins $\mathcal{G}$. Towards a contradiction, we assume that demand agent wins $\mathcal{G}_{\restriction b}$, say with a strategy σ. We take demand agent's strategy σ for $\mathcal{G}$. Since the constraints C are independent from the packet distribution, routing agent must at least deliver all packets which would not be deleted by the additional rule in the modified game $\mathcal{G}_{\restriction b}$. Since routing agent cannot deliver all packets in $\mathcal{G}_{\restriction b}$, so in $\mathcal{G}$. Hence, demand agent wins $\mathcal{G}$ by playing σ, which is a contradiction to our assumption.

Conversely, assume that routing agent wins $\mathcal{G}_{\restriction b}$. Towards a contradiction, we assume that demand agent wins $\mathcal{G}$. Then demand agent has a strategy (for $\mathcal{G}$) to reach a network state q_- where he can guarantee that one of the packets will never be delivered. Due to Lemma 5.7 it suffices to keep at most $|BL| \cdot \Delta_{\text{out}}$ packets of each type from the network state q_- onwards. Since the number of different types is bounded by $|V|^2$, there have to be kept at most $n = |V|^2 \cdot |BL| \cdot \Delta_{\text{out}}$ packets in the network from q_- onwards. According to Lemma 5.6 demand agent has a strategy to reach q_- if only $|BL|^n \cdot (\Delta_{\text{out}})^{n-1} \leq b$ (and 0 in the case $n = 0$) packets of each type are kept in the network. So, demand agent also wins $\mathcal{G}_{\restriction b}$, which contradicts our assumption. □

So, for a network routing game $\mathcal{G}$ with weak constraints, deciding the restricted game $\mathcal{G}_{\restriction b}$ with bound b on the number of packets is sufficient for deciding the unbounded game $\mathcal{G}$. Although the number of network states of the restricted game is finite, it has not the safety game format as games with the DELIVERY_ℓ winning condition. With the following theorem, every restricted game with a DELIVERY winning condition can be turned into a game with DELIVERY_ℓ winning condition.

Theorem 5.9. *Given a restricted network routing game $\mathcal{G}_{\restriction b}$ with weak constraints, routing agent wins $\mathcal{G}_{\restriction b}$ with the DELIVERY_ℓ winning condition for $\ell = |BL|^2 \cdot |V|^2 \cdot b$ if and only if she wins $\mathcal{G}_{\restriction b}$ with the DELIVERY winning condition.*

Proof. Winning according to the DELIVERY_ℓ condition directly implies winning according to the DELIVERY condition. For the converse, we assume that routing agent wins the game $\mathcal{G}_{\restriction b}$ with the DELIVERY winning condition, say with a strategy τ. Since the the number of packets at each node is bounded by $|V| \cdot b$ (because there exist at most $|V|$ different destinations), we can assume that routing agent may delay sending a packet to a neighboring node due to other packets with a higher timestamp at least $|V| \cdot b$ times. Also, we can assume that routing agent has to wait at most $|BL| - 1$ turns until she sends one of the packets of a certain type at a certain node to a neighboring node. Otherwise a network state with the same blocked frequencies function would be reached twice in the meantime (see Remark 5.3), which would imply that there are no new possibilities for routing agent to route one of the packets towards its destination. Finally, we can assume by a similar argument that routing agent sends a packet to the same node at most $|BL| \cdot |V|$ times. Otherwise a packet would visit a node twice while also a network state with the same blocked frequencies function is reached (and this would imply that there are no new possibilities for routing agent to deliver this packet in the reached network state). Altogether, we can assume that routing agent can guarantee by playing his strategy τ for the game with the DELIVERY winning condition implies that each packet is delivered within at most $|V| \cdot b \cdot (|BL| - 1) \cdot |BL| \cdot |V|$ turns (which is less than $|BL|^2 \cdot |V|^2 \cdot b$ turns). Hence, by playing τ routing agent also wins the game $\mathcal{G}_{\restriction b}$ with the DELIVERY_ℓ winning condition. □

Now we have all ingredients to solve games with weak constraints. First we transform the game $\mathcal{G}$ in a restricted game $\mathcal{G}_{\restriction b}$ with a bound for the maximal number of packets at a node provided by Theorem 5.8. Then, the previous theorem give us a bound ℓ such that we can solve $\mathcal{G}_{\restriction b}$ with the DELIVERY_ℓ winning condition using Theorem 5.1. The bounds b and ℓ are computable and the reduction to a safety game allows the construction of a winning strategy for routing agent if one exists. We obtain the following result:

Corollary 5.10. *Dynamic network routing games with weak constraints and winning condition* DELIVERY *are solvable (so that one can decide whether routing agent wins and in this case provide a winning strategy in terms of a suitable routing scheme).*

6 Conclusion and Perspective

In this paper we introduced a game-theoretic framework for routing problems in a dynamic or adversarial environment that covers the aspects of reactivity and non-termination. We showed some principal results on the solvability of this problem in terms of routing procedures.

In these results, complexity issues and questions on optimization were suppressed. Under the very liberal assumptions on constraints as considered here, reasonable complexity bounds are not conceivable, both for computing a solution (if it exists at all) and for the mere description of the resulting routing scheme.

Let us mention some variants of the game and of possible solutions that allow a more efficient treatment or a refinement of solutions regarding efficiency. More uniformity can be introduced both into the network model and the format of routing algorithms. For example, one might assume that the possibilities of the primary systems for blocking a frequency are globally the same for all edges (and not dependent on any information of the cognitive network). Similarly, one can pursue the idea that the demands by primary systems are best described in a stochastic model and using identical (but stochastic) constraints for different nodes. Also the routing algorithms can be required to be more uniform.

In current work we address also refined solutions that include aspects of optimization. Only then it is possible to compare the performance of truly reactive routing algorithms with solutions in terms of online algorithms as discussed in the introduction. Rather than requiring delivery of packets "eventually" or "with fixed time bounds" it seems more reasonable to search for solutions that simply guarantee the "best possible" time intervals for delivery under the conditions of the considered network game. In [10] we developed a method to compute optimal strategies for a natural setting.

References

1. Afek, Y., Awerbuch, B., Gafni, E., Mansour, Y., Rosén, A., Shavit, N.: Slide – the key to polynomial end-to-end communication. Journal of Algorithms 22(1), 158–186 (1997)
2. Aiello, W., Ostrovsky, R., Kushilevitz, E., Rosén, A.: Dynamic routing on networks with fixed-size buffers. In: Proceedings of SODA, pp. 771–780 (2003)
3. Awerbuch, B., Brinkmann, A., Scheideler, C.: Anycasting in adversarial systems: Routing and admission control. In: Baeten, J.C.M., Lenstra, J.K., Parrow, J., Woeginger, G.J. (eds.) ICALP 2003. LNCS, vol. 2719, pp. 1153–1168. Springer, Heidelberg (2003)
4. Awerbuch, B., Mansour, Y., Shavit, N.: Polynomial end-to-end communication (extended abstract). In: Proceedings of FOCS, pp. 358–363. IEEE, Los Alamitos (1989)
5. van Benthem, J.: An essay on sabotage and obstruction. In: Hutter, D., Stephan, W. (eds.) Mechanizing Mathematical Reasoning. LNCS (LNAI), vol. 2605, pp. 268–276. Springer, Heidelberg (2005)
6. Clarke Jr., E.M., Grumberg, O., Peled, D.A.: Model Checking. MIT Press, Cambridge (1999)
7. Gao, L., Wang, X.: A game approach for multi-channel allocation in multi-hop wireless networks. In: Proceedings of MobiHoc, pp. 303–312. ACM, New York (2008)
8. Gierasimczuk, N., Kurzen, L., Velázquez-Quesada, F.R.: Learning and teaching as a game: A sabotage approach. In: He, X., Horty, J., Pacuit, E. (eds.) LORI 2009. LNCS, vol. 5834, pp. 119–132. Springer, Heidelberg (2009)
9. Grädel, E., Thomas, W., Wilke, T.: Automata, Logics, and Infinite Games. LNCS, vol. 2500. Springer, Heidelberg (2002)
10. Horn, F., Thomas, W., Wallmeier, N.: Optimal strategy synthesis in request-response games. In: Cha, S(S.), Choi, J.-Y., Kim, M., Lee, I., Viswanathan, M. (eds.) ATVA 2008. LNCS, vol. 5311, pp. 361–373. Springer, Heidelberg (2008)

11. Klein, D., Radmacher, F.G., Thomas, W.: The complexity of reachability in randomized sabotage games. In: Arbab, F., Sirjani, M. (eds.) Fundamentals of Software Engineering. LNCS, vol. 5961, pp. 162–177. Springer, Heidelberg (2010)
12. Löding, C., Rohde, P.: Model checking and satisfiability for sabotage modal logic. In: Pandya, P.K., Radhakrishnan, J. (eds.) FSTTCS 2003. LNCS, vol. 2914, pp. 302–313. Springer, Heidelberg (2003)
13. Löding, C., Rohde, P.: Solving the sabotage game is PSPACE-hard. In: Rovan, B., Vojtáš, P. (eds.) MFCS 2003. LNCS, vol. 2747, pp. 531–540. Springer, Heidelberg (2003)
14. Radmacher, F.G., Thomas, W.: A game theoretic approach to the analysis of dynamic networks. In: Proceedings of VerAS. Electronic Notes in Theoretical Computer Science, vol. 200(2), pp. 21–37. Elsevier, Amsterdam (2008)
15. Rohde, P.: Moving in a crumbling network: The balanced case. In: Marcinkowski, J., Tarlecki, A. (eds.) CSL 2004. LNCS, vol. 3210, pp. 310–324. Springer, Heidelberg (2004)
16. Rohde, P.: On Games and Logics over Dynamically Changing Structures. Ph.D. thesis, RWTH Aachen (2005)
17. Shiang, H.P., van der Schaar, M.: Distributed resource management in multihop cognitive radio networks for delay-sensitive transmission. IEEE Transactions on Vehicular Technology 58(2), 941–953 (2009)
18. Thomas, W.: On the synthesis of strategies in infinite games. In: Mayr, E.W., Puech, C. (eds.) STACS 1995. LNCS, vol. 900, pp. 1–13. Springer, Heidelberg (1995)
19. Xin, C., Ma, L., Shen, C.C.: A path-centric channel assignment framework for cognitive radio wireless networks. Mobile Networks and Applications 13(5), 463–476 (2008)

An Operational Model for Multiprocessors with Caches

Salil Joshi and Sanjiva Prasad

Indian Institute of Technology Delhi
salil.ssj@gmail.com,
sanjiva@cse.iitd.ac.in

Abstract. Modern multiprocessors are equipped with local caches, to enhance program performance. However, the presence of caches can lead to the violation of *sequential consistency* [7] assumptions regarding program order and write atomicity. With respect to such *relaxed memory models* [1], we provide an operational description of program execution (in the style of [4]) that accounts for cache effects. In particular, we provide an operational characterization of cache invalidation and update policies and an abstract characterization of cache consistency. The programming model consists of a simple imperative language extended with common synchronization primitives such as locks or barrier instructions. The main results show that by precluding certain data races or by placing certain synchronization constraints, sequentially consistent behavior can be obtained for multiprocessor execution even in the presence of local caches.

1 Introduction

While shared memory multiprocessor systems are becoming increasingly common today, writing correct concurrent programs for such systems remains a challenge. Program behavior is determined by a *memory model*. Programmers commonly assume a model of memory that is *sequentially consistent* [7], i.e., all memory accesses appear to occur atomically in some total order, and those issued by any given processor occur as specified by the program order.

One feature for improving performance, found in all modern processors, is a *cache*. The presence of caches in a *multiprocessor* system can lead to violations of program order and write atomicity assumptions [1]. The goal of this work is to understand the effect of caches on concurrent program execution with respect to a weaker memory model where these assumptions are relaxed [2], and to discover constraints under which sequentially consistent behavior is guaranteed.

We follow the approach of Boudol and Petri [4] in presenting an *operational* model of memory and describe the execution of programs written in a simple imperative language with respect to a sequentially consistent model ("the specification"), and then with respect to a relaxed model ("the implementation"). We then consider some *synchronization primitives* (called "safety nets" in [1]) supported by the model; these are instructions used to temporarily force program order or write atomicity in order to make the program behavior more manageable. In particular, we show that for *locks* a *well synchronizedness condition*

C.S. Calude and V. Sassone (Eds.): TCS 2010, IFIP AICT 323, pp. 371–385, 2010.

(equivalent to *data-race-freedom*), and for *barrier instructions*, a *multiple-race-free barrier condition*, are sufficient to ensure sequentially consistent behavior in an otherwise non-sequentially consistent system.

Technically, this is done by establishing precise correspondences (e.g., "bisimilarity") between the specification and implementation behaviors. The consequence of these results is that for programs satisfying these constraints (which are stated at the *specification* level), the programmer need only consider the more intuitive set of sequentially consistent executions rather than all possible executions, when reasoning about program behavior.

A novel contribution in this paper is an *abstract operational characterization* of a memory model, general enough to express multiprocessor memory with local caches as a particular instance, in terms of a small set of operational properties. The theorems are thus proven for any memory model exhibiting these properties. We believe that our implementation semantics closely resemble actual processor architectures (with caches). At the same time, the semantics abstract over processor specific details like cache replacement policies, cache consistency protocols etc. Thus our models (and hence our theorems) should hold for a wide variety of multiprocessor systems. We give an example of a *cache-based system* which exhibits the required properties, and which allows the following relaxations with respect to the classification of relaxed memory models in [1]:

1. **W** $\rightarrow$ **R**: Reordering of a write with a following read to a different variable.
2. **W** $\rightarrow$ **W**: Reordering of a write with a following write to a different variable.
3. **Read other's write early**: This violates write atomicity.
4. **Read own write early**: This violates both write atomicity and program order.

Our approach differs from that of Boudol and Petri [4] in several ways: (i) while they present a higher-order language with ML-style imperative features, dynamic thread creation and scoped locks, we prefer a simple imperative language that we believe has greater applicability; (ii) in addition to locks, we consider synchronization primitives such as barrier or fence instructions; (iii) while Boudol *et al* consider write buffers, we believe we consider a more general multiprocessor model with caches, while being able to deal with a variety of cache management policies (update, invalidation). Furthermore our operational characterization is presented in terms of abstract properties.

The rest of this paper is organised as follows. §2 presents the language and the specification semantics. The abstract characterization of the implementation semantics is given in §3 as a collection of properties on the operational relation. §4 introduces scoped locks as a synchronization primitive and shows sequential consistency can be ensured by data race freedom; similarly a barrier condition is shown to achieve this when using barrier instructions (§5). In §6, we present an intuitive model of caches which satisfies the abstract properties of §3.2. §7 concludes the paper with some directions for future work. Proofs of lemmas and theorems are omitted in this paper but can be found in [6].

2 The Language

We employ a simple imperative language, which will later be extended with two different synchronization primitives.

$$\begin{array}{lll} \langle e\rangle ::= \langle int\rangle & \langle b\rangle ::= \textbf{true} \mid \textbf{false} & \langle C\rangle ::= \langle var\rangle := \langle e\rangle \\ \quad\mid \langle e\rangle \oplus \langle e\rangle & \quad\mid \neg\langle b\rangle \mid \langle b\rangle \wedge \langle b\rangle & \quad\mid \langle C\rangle ; \langle C\rangle \\ \quad\mid \langle var\rangle & \quad\mid \langle e\rangle \le \langle e\rangle & \quad\mid \textbf{if } \langle b\rangle \textbf{ then } \langle C\rangle \textbf{ else } \langle C\rangle \\ & & \quad\mid \textbf{while } \langle b\rangle \textbf{ do } \langle C\rangle \end{array}$$

All variables are integer valued, boolean values are used only for tests and the $\oplus$ operator is any one of $+, *, \ldots$ We also have a runtime marker, (), which is 'returned' when a command is executed. It is used only to make the operational semantics easier to formulate.

2.1 Specification Semantics

A *configuration* $\mathbb{C}$ is a pair (S, P), where S is the *store* (main memory) that is shared across the system, and P is a list of *processes*. Each process runs on its own processor. The store is common to all, and is a simple mapping from variable names to integers. For convenience, we will use $\mathbb{C}.S$ and $\mathbb{C}.P$ to refer to the store and program respectively of a specific configuration $\mathbb{C}$.

Transitions involve reducing a *redex* in an *evaluation context* [10]. An evaluation context consists of a number i (indicating that the process P_i is being executed), and a one-hole context. We use $P_i[\boldsymbol{E}[]]$ to denote the hole $\boldsymbol{E}[]$ in the ith process in P.

The redexes and one-hole contexts ($\boldsymbol{E}[]$) are as follows:

$$\begin{array}{l} \langle bval\rangle ::= \textbf{true} \mid \textbf{false} \\ \langle redex\rangle ::= \langle int\rangle \oplus \langle int\rangle \\ \quad\mid \langle int\rangle \le \langle int\rangle \\ \quad\mid \neg\langle bval\rangle \mid \langle bval\rangle \wedge \langle bval\rangle \\ \quad\mid \langle var\rangle \mid \langle var\rangle := \langle int\rangle \\ \quad\mid \textbf{if } \langle bval\rangle \textbf{ then } \langle C\rangle \textbf{ else } \langle C\rangle \\ \quad\mid \textbf{while } \langle b\rangle \textbf{ do } \langle C\rangle \mid ();\langle C\rangle \end{array}$$

$$\begin{array}{l} \langle \boldsymbol{E}\rangle ::= [] \mid \boldsymbol{E} \oplus \langle e\rangle \mid \langle int\rangle \oplus \boldsymbol{E} \\ \quad\mid \boldsymbol{E} \le \langle e\rangle \mid \langle int\rangle \le \boldsymbol{E} \\ \quad\mid \neg\,\boldsymbol{E} \mid \boldsymbol{E} \wedge \langle b\rangle \mid \langle bval\rangle \wedge \boldsymbol{E} \\ \quad\mid \langle var\rangle := \boldsymbol{E} \mid \boldsymbol{E};\langle C\rangle \\ \quad\mid \textbf{if } \boldsymbol{E} \textbf{ then } \langle C\rangle \textbf{ else } \langle C\rangle \end{array}$$

The operational semantics are given in Figure 1. We have left out the obvious transitions such as those for the arithmetic and boolean operators.

Transitions are *decorated* as: $\xrightarrow{(a,i)}$. Here i is used to indicate that the transition is for process P_i, and a denotes the action being carried out. The possible actions are: τ (reduction which does not involve the store), $\mathtt{rd}_x^v$ (the value v is read from variable x) and $\mathtt{wr}_x^v$ (the value v is written to the variable x). For reads and writes we will use $\mathtt{rd}_x$ and $\mathtt{wr}_x$ when we do not care what value was read/written. Concurrent, conflicting transitions are said to form a race:

Definition 1. *In a sequence of transitions* $\mathbb{C}_0 \xrightarrow{(a_0,i_0)} \cdots \xrightarrow{(a_n,i_n)} \mathbb{C}_{n+1}$*, two transitions* $\xrightarrow{(a_j,i_j)}$ *and* $\xrightarrow{(a_k,i_k)}$ *are said to form a* race *if* $i_j \neq i_k$ *and* $a_j, a_k \in \{\mathtt{rd}_x, \mathtt{wr}_x\}$ *and at least one is* $\mathtt{wr}_x$.

$$(S, P_i[\boldsymbol{E}[x]]) \xrightarrow{(\mathtt{rd}^v_x, i)} (S, P_i[\boldsymbol{E}[v]]) \qquad \textit{where } S(x) = v$$
$$(S, P_i[\boldsymbol{E}[x{:=}v]]) \xrightarrow{(\mathtt{wr}^v_x, i)} (S[x \leftarrow v], P_i[\boldsymbol{E}[()]])$$
$$(S, P_i[\boldsymbol{E}[(); C]]) \xrightarrow{(\tau, i)} (S, P_i[\boldsymbol{E}[C]])$$
$$(S, P_i[\boldsymbol{E}[\textbf{if true then } C_t \textbf{ else } C_f]) \xrightarrow{(\tau, i)} (S, P_i[\boldsymbol{E}[C_t]])$$
$$(S, P_i[\boldsymbol{E}[\textbf{if false then } C_t \textbf{ else } C_f]) \xrightarrow{(\tau, i)} (S, P_i[\boldsymbol{E}[C_f]])$$
$$(S, P_i[\boldsymbol{E}[\textbf{while } b \textbf{ do } C]]) \xrightarrow{(\tau, i)} (S, P_i[\boldsymbol{E}[\textbf{if } b \textbf{ then } \{C; \textbf{ while } b \textbf{ do } C\} \textbf{ else } ()]])$$

Fig. 1. Specification Semantics

$$(M, P_i[\boldsymbol{E}[x]]) \xrightarrow{(\mathtt{rd}^v_x, i)} (M', P_i[\boldsymbol{E}[v]]) \qquad \textit{where } M_i[x] = (M', v)$$
$$(M, P_i[\boldsymbol{E}[x{:=}v]]) \xrightarrow{(\mathtt{wr}^v_x, i)} (M', P_i[\boldsymbol{E}[()]]) \qquad \textit{where } M_i[x \leftarrow v] = M'$$

Fig. 2. Implementation Semantics

Specification semantics correspond to a programmer's intuitive view of interleaving execution (i.e. a sequentially consistent memory model). Here, processes execute one at a time (conceptually) albeit in a non-deterministic order, program order is respected and writes are atomic. Storage features such as caches and write buffers can violate these guarantees in a multiprocessor setting [1].

3 Implementation Semantics

In the implementation semantics, we replace the store S with a more general abstraction for memory, denoted as M. Each processor has a different view of the memory; processor i sees the value of x as $M_i[x]$ and in general $M_i[x]$ and $M_j[x]$ need not be equal. We will use M to model a memory hierarchy where each processor has a local cache. Our semantic account abstracts from the internal structure of M. We place purely *operational* constraints on M in order to prove sequential consistency theorems and later show that common cache based architectures satisfy these constraints. Thus while our focus is on the effects of caches, the framework presented here is more general.

In Figure 2 we present the significant changes to the operational rules. We omit the rules of Figure 1 that do not involve memory.

Both $\mathtt{wr}^v_x$ and $\mathtt{rd}^v_x$ transitions access the memory, and potentially alter it. Writing a variable (denoted $M_i[x \leftarrow v]$) returns the modified memory M'. Reading a variable from memory (denoted $M_i[x]$) returns a pair (M', v) where v is the value read, and M' is the possibly modified memory (e.g. an altered cache). For convenience, we write $M_i[x].\mathit{val} = v$ when $M_i[x] = (M', v)$. The next section imposes some restrictions on the permissible changes in M'.

In addition, we have some more transitions called the 'system' transitions, denoted by $\rightarrow$. These are used by the system to manage the internal structure of the memory. We will use $\rightarrow$ moves later e.g. to model cache consistency and cache replacement protocols. These transitions can fire non-deterministically at any time. Moreover, the program does not constrain which system transitions can occur, or when. We abstractly characterize the system transitions in §3.2 by a series of properties which we use in the sequel. In particular the model described in §6 implements M as a cache based system satisfying these properties.

The transitions introduced in Figures 1 and 2 are now called 'program' transitions (since they fire as a direct result of some piece of code). We will use $\mathbb{C} \rightarrow_I^* \mathbb{C}'$ to denote that $\mathbb{C}'$ is reachable from $\mathbb{C}$ by the *implementation* semantics (program and system transitions), and similarly $\mathbb{C} \rightarrow_S^* \mathbb{C}''$ for the specification semantics. Note that we will use $\xrightarrow{*}$ to denote 0 or more *system* transitions, whereas $\rightarrow_I^*$ means 0 or more system and program transitions.

3.1 Coherence and Consistency

Let us call a configuration $\mathbb{C}$ "$\rightarrow$-normal" if it cannot make any $\rightarrow$ moves (i.e. system transitions). In order to relate implementation semantics to specification semantics, we need the following definition:

Definition 2. *An implementation configuration $\mathbb{C}_I$ is said to* reduce to *a specification configuration $\mathbb{C}_S$ (written $\mathbb{C}_I \Downarrow \mathbb{C}_S$) if $\exists \mathbb{C}'_I : \mathbb{C}_I \xrightarrow{*} \mathbb{C}'_I$, $\mathbb{C}'_I$ is $\rightarrow$-normal, and $\forall i \forall x\ \mathbb{C}'_I.M_i[x].val = \mathbb{C}_S.S[x]$. $\mathbb{C}_S$ is called a* reduct *of $\mathbb{C}_I$.*

In the next subsection we impose conditions that ensure the existence of reducts.

Definition 3. $\mathbb{C}$ *is* coherent for x *if* $\exists v : \forall \mathbb{C}_S : \mathbb{C} \Downarrow \mathbb{C}_S, \mathbb{C}_S.S(x) = v$.

A configuration is *coherent* if it is coherent for all x. It follows that a coherent configuration has a unique reduct. We use $\ulcorner\mathbb{C}\urcorner$ to refer to the unique reduct of a coherent configuration $\mathbb{C}$.

Definition 4. $\mathbb{C}$ *is* consistent for x *if (a) it is coherent for x, (b) $\forall i, j, \mathbb{C}.M_i[x].val = \mathbb{C}.M_j[x].val$, (c) $\forall \mathbb{C}_S, \mathbb{C} \Downarrow \mathbb{C}_S \Rightarrow \forall i, \mathbb{C}.M_i[x].val = \mathbb{C}_S.S(x)$ and (d) $\forall i, w$ if $\mathbb{C}'$ is the same as $\mathbb{C}$ except that $\mathbb{C}'.M = \mathbb{C}.M_i[x \leftarrow w]$, then $\mathbb{C}'$ is coherent for x.*

Condition (a) ensures that a consistent configuration is coherent, and (d) that it remains coherent after any single write. Thus there are no pending writes to x in a configuration that is consistent for x. Condition (b) ensures that all views of x coincide and (c) that it agrees on x with its reducts. $\mathbb{C}$ is *consistent* if it is consistent for all x. A consistent configurations is in some sense identifiable with its reduct.

3.2 Constraints on the Memory Model

We now present the properties that the memory structure and its system transitions should satisfy. The theorems in the following sections hold for any system which has these properties.

Property 1. *If $\mathbb{C} \rightarrow \mathbb{C}'$, then $\mathbb{C}.P = \mathbb{C}'.P$*

System transitions have no effect on the program.

Property 2. *An $\rightarrow$-normal configuration is consistent.*

Property 2 ensures that system transitions are adequate to ensure consistency. For example, it prevents pathological cache architectures where the contents of only one designated cache are copied to the rest. In this pathological system, in the absence of a cached entry in the designated cache, inconsistent $\rightarrow$-normal configurations are possible.

Property 3. *Every configuration reachable from a consistent configuration has at least one $\rightarrow$-normal configuration under $\xrightarrow{*}$.*

We restrict this condition to configurations reachable from a consistent configuration because we *always* begin with a consistent configuration in practice. The above two properties together mean that such a configuration has at least one reduct. They also imply that any such configuration can always become consistent, which is important for the synchronization primitives of the sequel.

Property 4. *Consider $\mathbb{C}_I \xrightarrow{*}\xrightarrow{(a,i)} \mathbb{C}'_I$. For any $\mathbb{C}'_S$ such that $\mathbb{C}'_I \Downarrow \mathbb{C}'_S$, $\exists \mathbb{C}_S$: $\mathbb{C}_I \Downarrow \mathbb{C}_S$ which is identical to $\mathbb{C}'_S$ except in the position of the redex in P_i, unless $\mathbb{C}'_S.S(x) = v$ and $a = wr^v_x$ in which case $\mathbb{C}_S$, $\mathbb{C}'_S$ may also differ on $S(x)$.*

Property 4 states that only writes may make a *fundamental* change in M, and only to a single variable. Reads are allowed to change M, but the change is superficial in this sense (and usually done solely for performance reasons).

Property 5. *If $\mathbb{C}$ is coherent (resp. consistent) for x and $\mathbb{C} \rightarrow \mathbb{C}'$, then $\mathbb{C}'$ is also coherent (resp. consistent) for x.*

Property 5 states that system transitions preserve coherence and consistency.

Property 6. *Let $\mathbb{C}$ be consistent for x and consider the sequence $\mathbb{C} \xrightarrow{*}\xrightarrow{(a_0,i_0)} \dots \xrightarrow{*}\xrightarrow{(a_n,i_n)} \mathbb{C}'$. If there is at most* one *processor i such that $(a_k, i_k) = (wr_x, i)$ in this sequence then $\mathbb{C}'$ is coherent for x.*

Property 6 says if there is no conflicting write then coherence is maintained.

Property 7. *If $\mathbb{C}$ is consistent, $\mathbb{C} \rightarrow^*_I \mathbb{C}'$ then for any i, if $\mathbb{C}'.M_i[x].val = v$ then either $\mathbb{C}.M_i[x].val = v$ or there is a wr^v_x on some processor in $\mathbb{C} \rightarrow^*_I \mathbb{C}'$.*

Property 7 states that a value is either set by some write or is preserved.

Property 8. *Let $\mathbb{C}$ be consistent for x, $\mathbb{C} \rightarrow^*_I \mathbb{C}_I \xrightarrow{(a,i)} \mathbb{C}'_I$, and $\mathbb{C}'_I \Downarrow \mathbb{C}'_S$. If $a \in \{wr^v_x, rd^v_x\}$ and $\mathbb{C}'_S.S(x) = w \neq v$ then there exists a transition (wr^w_x, j) with $j \neq i$ in $\mathbb{C} \rightarrow^*_I \mathbb{C}_I$.*

Property 8 means that the last write cannot be ignored and the last read cannot read the wrong value, *unless* they form a race with some earlier transition. System transitions must ensure that the effects of a write *can* propagate.

3.3 Derived Properties

The following lemmas can be derived from the above constraints.

Lemma 1. *If $\mathbb{C}$ is coherent for x, $\mathbb{C} \xrightarrow{(a,i)} \mathbb{C}'$ and $a \neq wr_x$ then $\mathbb{C}'$ is coherent for x.*

Any transition not involving a write on x will maintain coherence for x.

Lemma 2. *Let $\mathbb{C}$ be reachable from a consistent configuration. If $\mathbb{C}$ is consistent for x, $\mathbb{C} \rightarrow_I^* \mathbb{C}_I \xrightarrow{(a,i)} \mathbb{C}'_I$, $\mathbb{C}_I$ is coherent and $\mathbb{C}_I \Downarrow \mathbb{C}_S$, then $\exists \mathbb{C}'_s$ such that following diagram commutes:*

$$\begin{array}{ccc} \mathbb{C}_I & \xrightarrow{(a,i)} & \mathbb{C}'_I \\ \Downarrow & & \Downarrow \\ \mathbb{C}_S & \xrightarrow{(a,i)} & \mathbb{C}'_S \end{array}$$

where either a is not a memory access or if a accesses x then in $\mathbb{C} \rightarrow_I^* \mathbb{C}_I$ there is a wr_x transition only on i.

By Properties 2, 3, 4 and 8. This lemma means that a write-free sequence of transitions exactly implements the specification semantics.

The following is a useful special case of this lemma:

Lemma 3. *If $\mathbb{C}_I$ is a consistent configuration then $\exists \mathbb{C}'_S$ which makes the following diagram commutes:*

$$\begin{array}{ccc} \mathbb{C}_I & \xrightarrow{(a,i)} & \mathbb{C}'_I \\ \Downarrow & & \Downarrow \\ \ulcorner \mathbb{C}_I \urcorner & \xrightarrow{(a,i)} & \mathbb{C}'_S \end{array}$$

We are now ready to consider two synchronization primitives in turn, and give sufficient conditions for sequential consistency for each.

4 Locks

We extend our language with a *locking* construct, **with** l **do** $\langle C \rangle$ following the approach of [4].

$\langle C \rangle ::= \ldots \mid$ **with** l **do** $\langle C \rangle$ $\qquad$ $\langle \boldsymbol{E} \rangle ::= \ldots \mid$ **holding** l **do** $\langle \boldsymbol{E} \rangle$

$\langle redex \rangle ::= \ldots \mid$ **with** l **do** $\langle C \rangle \mid$ **holding** l **do** $()$

Additionally we have a construct **holding** l **do** $\langle C \rangle$ which is a *runtime* construct. It is used when a lock is held, and $\langle C \rangle$ is being executed. In the following subsection, we assume that the *initial* configuration we consider is written in the source language, and thus has no runtime constructs.

The configurations also change, becoming (S, L, P) (specification) and (M, L, P) (implementation) where L is the set of locks that are currently held. L remains

$$(S, L, P_i[\boldsymbol{E}[\textbf{with } l \textbf{ do } C]]) \xrightarrow{(\hat{1},i)} (S, L \cup \{l\}, P_i[\boldsymbol{E}[\textbf{holding } l \textbf{ do } C]]) \qquad \textit{where } l \notin L$$
$$(S, L, P_i[\boldsymbol{E}[\textbf{holding } l \textbf{ do}()]]) \xrightarrow{(\check{1},i)} (S, L - \{l\}, P_i[\boldsymbol{E}[()]])$$

Fig. 3. Locks: Specification Semantics

$$(M, L, P_i[\boldsymbol{E}[\textbf{with } l \textbf{ do } C]]) \xrightarrow{(\hat{1},i)} (M, L \cup \{l\}, P_i[\boldsymbol{E}[\textbf{holding } l \textbf{ do } C]]) \qquad \textit{where } l \notin L$$
$$(M, L, P_i[\boldsymbol{E}[\textbf{holding } l \textbf{ do } ()]]) \xrightarrow{(\check{1},i)} (M, L - \{l\}, P_i[\boldsymbol{E}[()]]) \quad \textit{configuration is consistent}$$

Fig. 4. Locks: Implementation Semantics

unaffected by all the transitions given so far, appearing unchanged on both sides. We introduce two new transitions for locking, with the decorations: $\hat{1}$ (acquire lock l) and $\check{1}$ (release lock l). The specification and implementation semantics for locks are given in Figures 3 and 4 respectively.

A lock l can only be acquired by a process if no other process holds l. Also, in the implementation semantics a lock can *only* be released when the configuration is consistent. Recall that Properties 2 and 3 ensure that this can happen.

4.1 Sequential Consistency

A sufficient condition to ensure sequential consistency even in the implementation semantics, is that the initial configuration must be Data Race Free (DRF):

Definition 5. *A consistent configuration* $\mathbb{C}$ *involves a* data race *if it has two redexes* $P_i[E[r]]$ *and* $P_j[E[r']]]$, $i \neq j$, r *and* r' *are both accesses to the same variable and at least one is a write.* $\mathbb{C}$ *is* data race free *(DRF) iff no configurations specification reachable from* $\ulcorner\mathbb{C}\urcorner$ *involve a data race.*

The following definition for *well synchronizedness* is often taken to be synonymous with DRF, and we treat it as such. Boudol and Petri's proof [4] of their equivalence applies to our model nearly unchanged since the proof is at the specification level, and our specification semantics are essentially the same as their 'strong' semantics. The full proof can be found in [6].

Definition 6. *A consistent configuration* $\mathbb{C}$ *is said to be* well-synchronized *(WS), iff in any valid sequence of specification transitions* $\ulcorner\mathbb{C}\urcorner = \mathbb{C}_0 \xrightarrow{(a_0,i_0)} \ldots \xrightarrow{(a_{n-1},i_{n-1})} \mathbb{C}_n$ *if there exists* n_1 *and* n_2 *(with* $n_1 < n_2$*) such that* (a_{n_1}, i_{n_1}) *and* (a_{n_2}, i_{n_2}) *form a race, then* $\exists n_3 : n_1 < n_3 < n_2 \wedge i_{n_3} = i_{n_1} \wedge a_{n_3} = \check{l}$.

For proofs, we will use this characterization rather than Definition 5. Informally, this property means that there must exist an unlocking operation between every pair of transitions forming a race (in every sequence of specification transitions). Note that we need only analyze sequentially consistent executions of a program in order to determine whether it is WS.

There is one last definition that is required in order to prove that the implementation and specification semantics coincide for WS programs.

Definition 7. *For any given consistent configuration* $\mathbb{C}$*, define* $R(\mathbb{C})$ *as:* $(\mathbb{C}_I, \mathbb{C}_S) \in R(\mathbb{C})$ *if and only if there exists a sequence of implementation transitions*

$$\mathbb{C} = \mathbb{C}_0 \xrightarrow{*}\xrightarrow{(a_0,i_0)} \mathbb{C}_1 \cdots \xrightarrow{*}\xrightarrow{(a_n,i_n)} \mathbb{C}_n = \mathbb{C}_I$$

such that

$$\overline{\mathbb{C}} = \mathbb{C}'_0 \xrightarrow{(a_0,i_0)} \mathbb{C}'_1 \cdots \xrightarrow{(a_n,i_n)} \mathbb{C}'_n = \mathbb{C}_S$$

is a valid sequence of specification transitions, with $\mathbb{C}_j \Downarrow \mathbb{C}'_j$ *for all* j*.*

We show that if $\mathbb{C}$ is WS then the relation $R(\mathbb{C})$ is a bisimulation (and thus the specification and implementation semantics are essentially the same).

In one direction, the simulation holds whether or not $\mathbb{C}$ is WS.

Theorem 1. *If* $(\mathbb{C}_I, \mathbb{C}_S) \in R(\mathbb{C})$ *and* $\mathbb{C}_S \xrightarrow{(a,i)} \overline{\mathbb{C}}_S$ *then there exists* $\overline{\mathbb{C}}_I$ *with* $\mathbb{C}_I \xrightarrow{*}\xrightarrow{(a,i)} \overline{\mathbb{C}}_I$ *such that* $(\overline{\mathbb{C}}_I, \overline{\mathbb{C}}_S) \in R(\mathbb{C})$*.*

The other direction also holds when the configuration is WS. Further, coherence is maintained.

Theorem 2. *If* $(\mathbb{C}_I, \mathbb{C}_S) \in R(\mathbb{C})$ *(with WS* $\mathbb{C}$*),* $\mathbb{C}_I$ *is coherent and* $\mathbb{C}_I \xrightarrow{*}\xrightarrow{(a,i)} \overline{\mathbb{C}}_I$ *then* $\overline{\mathbb{C}}_I$ *is coherent and there exists* $\overline{\mathbb{C}}_S$ *such that* $\mathbb{C}_S \xrightarrow{(a,i)} \overline{\mathbb{C}}_S$ *with* $(\overline{\mathbb{C}}_I, \overline{\mathbb{C}}_S) \in R(\mathbb{C})$*.*

5 Barriers

Barriers or fences are a common safety net in various processors with a relaxed memory model [1] and have also been used in other contexts [3]. Their role is to prevent instruction re-ordering across the barrier (hence the name). Unlike locks, they cannot entirely prevent data races but they can still guarantee sequential consistency (at least with the semantics that we present below).

We extend our language with a **bar** command, and a new expression for barred reads:

$$\langle e \rangle ::= \ldots \mid !\langle \mathit{var} \rangle \qquad \langle C \rangle ::= \ldots \mid \mathbf{bar} \qquad \langle \mathit{redex} \rangle ::= \ldots \mid \mathbf{bar} \mid !\langle \mathit{var} \rangle$$

The one-hole contexts remain unchanged. We introduce a barrier transition, decorated with `bar`. In the specification semantics, this is a no-op. In the implementation, it is a way of waiting for pending writes to complete. Figures 5 and 6 give the specification and implementation semantics respectively. The new read is only a way of introducing a barrier in the middle of an expression. The actual read is still handled by the usual $\mathtt{rd}_x^v$ actions.

Note that our barrier semantics enforces a *global* constraint. Hardware implementations today often provide barriers whose effects are in some way local to the current processor (e.g. x86 `mFence`) but as noted in [9], this is insufficient to ensure sequential consistency.

$$(S, P_i[\boldsymbol{E}[\mathbf{bar}]]) \xrightarrow{(\mathsf{bar},i)} (S, P_i[\boldsymbol{E}[()]]) \qquad \textit{i.e. do nothing}$$
$$(S, P_i[\boldsymbol{E}[!x]]) \xrightarrow{(\mathsf{bar},i)} (S, P_i[\boldsymbol{E}[x]]) \qquad \textit{i.e. do nothing}$$

Fig. 5. Barriers: Specification Semantics

$$(M, P_i[\boldsymbol{E}[\mathbf{bar}]]) \xrightarrow{(\mathsf{bar},i)} (M, P_i[\boldsymbol{E}[()]]) \qquad \textit{configuration is consistent}$$
$$(M, P_i[\boldsymbol{E}[!x]]) \xrightarrow{(\mathsf{bar},i)} (M, P_i[\boldsymbol{E}[x]]) \qquad \textit{configuration is consistent}$$

Fig. 6. Barriers: Implementation Semantics

5.1 Sequential Consistency

An important difference between this and the lock model is that in general, it is not possible to place `bars` in the program in a way that ensures that there is a `bar` between every pair of actions forming a race in every sequentially consistent execution. Instead, we achieve sequential consistency by preventing multiple races involving the *same* processor from appearing between a pair of `bars`.

Definition 8. *A sequence of transitions $\mathbb{C} \to_I^* \mathbb{C}'$ (resp. $\mathbb{C} \to_S^* \mathbb{C}'$) is called* multiple race free *iff for every k such that (a_k, i_k) forms a race with some transition in the sequence, if $\exists j : j \neq k \wedge i_j = i_k$ then (a_j, i_j) does not form a race with* any *transition in the sequence.*

Definition 9. *A consistent configuration $\mathbb{C}$ is said to satisfy the* barrier condition *iff in any valid sequence of specification transitions $\ulcorner\mathbb{C}\urcorner = \mathbb{C}_0 \xrightarrow{(a_0,i_0)} \mathbb{C}_1 \ldots \mathbb{C}_n \xrightarrow{(a_n,i_n)} \mathbb{C}_{n+1}$, if there are `bar` transitions at $\{k_1, k_2, \ldots, k_m\}$ then taking $k_0 = 0$ and $k_{m+1} = n+1$, each subsequence in $\{\mathbb{C}_{k_i} \to_S^* \mathbb{C}_{k_{i+1}} | 0 \leq i < n+1\}$ is multiple race free.*

As in the case for WS, we need only analyze sequentially consistent executions of a program to verify that it satisfies the barrier condition.

To prove the equivalence of the two semantics under this condition, we show that for every specification-reachable configuration there is an implementation-reachable configuration, and vice-versa. One direction is quite trivial, and the barrier condition is not required:

Theorem 3. *For any consistent configuration $\mathbb{C}$, for every specification configuration $\ulcorner\mathbb{C}\urcorner \to_S^* \mathbb{C}_S$, there exists an implementation configuration $\mathbb{C}_I$ such that $\mathbb{C} \to_I^* \mathbb{C}_I$ and $\mathbb{C}_I \Downarrow \mathbb{C}_S$.*

Theorem 4. *For any consistent configuration $\mathbb{C}$ which satisfies the barrier condition, for every implementation configuration $\mathbb{C}_I$ such that $\mathbb{C} \to_I^* \mathbb{C}_I$ and every specification configuration $\mathbb{C}_S$ such that $\mathbb{C}_I \Downarrow \mathbb{C}_S$, $\ulcorner\mathbb{C}\urcorner \to_S^* \mathbb{C}_S$.*

In order to prove this theorem, we need the following lemmas:

$$(S, C, P_i[\boldsymbol{E}[x]]) \xrightarrow{(\texttt{rd1}^v_x, i)} (S, C, P_i[\boldsymbol{E}[v]]) \qquad \textit{where } x \in \textit{dom}(C_i) \wedge C_i[x].\textit{val} = v$$
$$(S, C, P_i[\boldsymbol{E}[x]]) \xrightarrow{(\texttt{rd2}^v_x, i)} (S, C, P_i[\boldsymbol{E}[v]]) \qquad \textit{where } x \notin \textit{dom}(C_i) \wedge S(x) = v$$
$$(S, C, P_i[\boldsymbol{E}[x]]) \xrightarrow{(\texttt{rd3}^v_x, i)} (S, C_i[x \leftarrow (v, \texttt{clean})], P_i[\boldsymbol{E}[v]]) \quad \textit{where } x \notin \textit{dom}(C_i) \wedge S(x) = v$$
$$(S, C, P_i[\boldsymbol{E}[x{:=}v]]) \xrightarrow{(\texttt{wr}^v_x, i)} (S, C_i[x \leftarrow (v, \texttt{dirty})], P_i[\boldsymbol{E}[()]])$$

Fig. 7. Implementation Semantics

Lemma 4. *Consider a consistent configuration $\mathbb{C}$, and a configuration $\mathbb{C}_I$ such that $\mathbb{C} \xrightarrow{*}\xrightarrow{(a_0,i_0)} \cdots \xrightarrow{*}\xrightarrow{(a_n,i_n)} \mathbb{C}_I$. If this sequence is multiple race free, then for every $\mathbb{C}_S$ such that $\mathbb{C}_I \Downarrow \mathbb{C}_S$ there exists a sequence $\ulcorner\mathbb{C}\urcorner \xrightarrow{(b_0,j_0)} \cdots \xrightarrow{(b_n,j_n)} \mathbb{C}_S$. Furthermore, the sequence of pairs $\{(b_k, j_k)\}$ is a permutation of the sequence $\{(a_k, i_k)\}$.*

Lemma 5. *For any consistent configuration $\mathbb{C}$ which satisfies the barrier condition, for every implementation configuration $\mathbb{C}_I$ such that $\mathbb{C} \rightarrow^*_I \mathbb{C}_I$ and every specification configuration $\mathbb{C}_S$ such that $\mathbb{C}_I \Downarrow \mathbb{C}_S$, the following hold:*

1. *The sequence $\mathbb{C} \rightarrow^*_I \mathbb{C}_I$ is multiple race free between* `bars`.
2. *$\ulcorner\mathbb{C}\urcorner \rightarrow^*_S \mathbb{C}_S$.*
3. *The sequence $\ulcorner\mathbb{C}\urcorner \rightarrow^*_S \mathbb{C}_S$ is a barrier-bounded permutation of (the program transitions in) $\mathbb{C} \rightarrow^*_I \mathbb{C}_I$.*

6 Modeling Multiprocessors with Caches

This section gives examples of how a multiprocessor system with local caches can be modeled in our framework. The memory M now becomes a tuple (S, C), where S is a store (as in the specification semantics) and C is a set of $|P|$ caches. The caches contain a local copy of a subset of the store. When a variable is written to, the write is to the cache. System transitions are used to update the store and the other caches asynchronously at some later time. A read may also pull a variable into the cache.

If $x \in \textit{dom}(C_n)$ then this means the nth processor has x in its cache. Its value $C_n[x]$ is given by a pair $(\textit{val}, \textit{state})$, where *val* is the ordinary integer value of the variable and *state* may be either `clean` or `dirty`. A variable is `clean` either if it has not been written to by *this* processor, or if its changed value has been written through to the store. Otherwise it is `dirty`. However note that in general, $C_n(x) = (v, \texttt{clean}) \not\Rightarrow S(x) = v$. The system may allow the store to contain a different value if some other processor has updated the store but this cache has not yet been notified. As a notational convenience, we shall write $C_i[x].\textit{val} = v$ and $C_i[x].\textit{state} = s$ when $C_i[x] = (v, s)$.

Figure 7 gives the semantics for $M_i[x]$ and $M_i[x \leftarrow v]$. We express all the possibilities as separate transitions to make it easier to read. There are three transitions for reading a variable but they merely represent the different cases possible for the same label $\texttt{rd}^v_x$. Note also that there are two transitions for

$$(S, C, P) \xrightarrow[i\uparrow]{x} (S, C_i \uparrow x, P) \qquad C_i[x] = (v, \texttt{clean})$$

$$(S, C, P) \xrightarrow[i \to j]{x} (S, C_j[x \leftarrow (v, \texttt{clean})], P)$$
$$x \in dom(C_j) \wedge C_j[x] \neq (v, \texttt{clean}) \wedge C_i[x] = (v, \texttt{dirty})$$

$$(S, C, P) \xrightarrow[i \to S]{x} (S[x \leftarrow v], C_i[x \leftarrow (v, \texttt{clean})], P)$$
$$\forall j : j \neq i \wedge x \in dom(C_j), C_j[x] = (v, \texttt{clean}) \wedge C_i[x] = (v, \texttt{dirty})$$

Fig. 8. System Transitions: Update

$\texttt{rd}_x^v$ when $x \notin dom(C_i)$, corresponding to whether or not x is pulled into the cache. This decision is made non-deterministically, which (along with another transition for *eviction* to be introduced later) makes the model independent of the *cache-replacement* policy used by the actual implementation.

The system transitions are used to propagate writes to other caches and the store. In practice this is usually done either with an *update-based* protocol (where cached copies are updated with the new value) or with an *invalidation-based* protocol (where cached copies are invalidated, effectively removing them from the cache)[5]. We give two sets of system transitions, one for each type of protocol.

This model allows for **W** $\to$ **R** reordering, since a read may be serviced while a previous write (to the cache) has not yet been propagated. **W** $\to$ **W** reorderings are possible because there is no guarantee that writes will be propagated in the order in which they appear. Thus the behaviors described in Fig 5 (a) and (b) in [1] will be exhibited by this model. Further, a processor may see its own writes before any other processor, simply because updates/invalidates haven't occurred yet. Similarly, other processors may see the write at different times, since the updates/invalidates on other caches need not happen all at once.

In [6] we show that this model with an update-based protocol satisfies the constraints in §3.2. This means that the abstract operational description presented earlier is general enough to at least allow these four relaxations.

6.1 Coherence and Consistency

For both protocols, we reformulate the definitions of coherence and consistency. We will show that these *structural* definitions are equivalent to the *operational* definitions given earlier.

Definition 10. *A configuration* $\mathbb{C}$ *is said to be* coherent for x *if* $\exists v : \forall i : x \in dom(C_i) \wedge C_i[x].state = \texttt{dirty} \Rightarrow C_i[x].val = v$.

Definition 11. *A configuration* (S, C, P) *is said to be* consistent for x *if and only if* $\forall i : x \in dom(C_i), C_i[x] = (S(x), \texttt{clean})$.

6.2 Modeling Update-Based Protocols

Figure 8 gives the system transitions used in the update-based model. The transitions are as follows:

1. **Eviction** $\xrightarrow[i\upharpoonright]{x}$: Evict x from C_i. This is only used for the cache replacement policy. We do not need it to achieve a consistent configuration in this model.
2. **Cache update** $\xrightarrow[i\to j]{x}$: Update x in C_j from C_i. This is used to update other caches when a variable is written to in a cache. It can be applied anytime there is some cache whose entry for the variable differs from the "correct" one.
3. **Store update** $\xrightarrow[i\to S]{x}$: Update x in S from C_i. The condition for its application ensures that a store update only happens *after* all caches have been updated and agree on the value of the variable.

As an example of how these transitions work, suppose a write occurs on a processor, and this is the only processor where that variable is `dirty`. An update-based system would execute the cache update transition multiple times to update the value in the other caches, and then a store update to put that value in the store. The $\to$-normal configurations are those that have empty caches.

If $\mathbb{C}$ is coherent for x by the structural definition, then we can see that any $\xrightarrow[i\to S]{x}$ will set $S(x)$ to the same value. Conversely, if $\exists i,j : C_i[x].state = C_j[x].state = \texttt{dirty} \wedge C_i[x].val \neq C_j[x].val$ then depending on whether $\xrightarrow[i\to j]{x}$ or $\xrightarrow[j\to i]{x}$ occurs (one of the two must occur), two distinct store updates are possible. Thus the structural and operational definitions for coherence are equivalent.

Similarly, it is easy to see that if $\mathbb{C}$ is consistent by the structural definition, it is consistent by the operational definition. Conversely, for $\mathbb{C}$ to be consistent for x, $\forall i : x \in dom(C_i), C_i[x].val = S(x)$ due to (b) and (c) of Definition 4. Further, if $\exists i : C_i[x] = (v, \texttt{dirty})$ then for any $w \neq v \wedge j \neq i$, $\mathbb{C}'$ is not coherent for x where $\mathbb{C}'.M = \mathbb{C}.M_j[x \leftarrow w]$, thus violating condition (d) of Definition 4.

This model satisfies all the constraints in §3.2 [6]. We additionally prove that it is possible to achieve a consistent configuration *without* the use of the eviction transition. This models the intended semantics of an update based protocol.

Lemma 6. *For any configuration $\mathbb{C}$ reachable from a consistent configuration, there exists a sequence of system transitions $\xrightarrow{*}$ not involving evictions such that $\mathbb{C} \xrightarrow{*} \mathbb{C}'$ and $\mathbb{C}'$ is a consistent configuration.*

6.3 Relaxing the Unlocking condition

The following lemma holds in the update based model:

Lemma 7. *If $\mathbb{C}$ is consistent for x and $\mathbb{C} \to_{\check{I}}^{*} \mathbb{C}_I$ where $\mathbb{C}_I$ is such that $\forall i$, $C_i[x].state = \texttt{clean}$, then $\mathbb{C}_I$ is also consistent for x (i.e. $\forall i, \mathbb{C}_I.C_i[x].val = S(x)$)*

Using this lemma, we can relax the condition for an $\check{1}$ operation and still ensure that the implementation and specification semantics coincide for WS configurations. Currently, an unlock can only happen if the configuration is consistent, but we can replace the "*configuration is consistent*" condition with the following:

$$\forall x \in dom(C_i), C_i[x].state = \texttt{clean}$$

$$(S, C, P) \xrightarrow[i\uparrow]{x} (S, C_i \uparrow x, P) \qquad C_i[x] = (v, \texttt{clean})$$
$$(S, C, P) \xrightarrow[i \to S]{x} (S[x \leftarrow v], C_i[x \leftarrow (v, \texttt{clean})], P) \qquad C_i[x] = (v, \texttt{dirty})$$

Fig. 9. System Transitions: Invalidation

i.e. there are no `dirty` entries in the current cache. This is a purely *local* condition (i.e. local to the current processor) on the unlock similar to the semantics of the unlock instruction on x86 processors [8].

In a system where Lemma 7 holds, this condition ensures that the configuration is consistent for x after the last unlock $\check{\mathtt{l}}$ in a WS sequence, as used in the proof of Theorem 2. We can modify the abstract semantics to allow local semantics for unlocking $\check{\mathtt{l}}$ by introducing an abstract predicate on M, $\texttt{safe}_i^x$ with the conditions that only a $(\texttt{wr}_x, i)$ destroys $\texttt{safe}_i^x$, and $\forall i\ \texttt{safe}_i^x \Rightarrow$ *consistent for* x. An $\check{\mathtt{l}}$ can then happen only when $\forall x\ \texttt{safe}_i^x$. Then in the cache model $\texttt{safe}_i^x$ is definable as $C_i[x].state = \texttt{clean}$.

Note that with the *global* semantics for locks it may be possible to simulate barriers with locks, but with these local semantics that is no longer true.

6.4 Modeling Invalidation-Based Protocols

Figure 9 gives the system transitions required to model an invalidation based cache consistency protocol. The transitions are as follows:

1. **Eviction** $\xrightarrow[i\uparrow]{x}$**:** This is now used for both cache replacement and cache consistency.
2. **Store update** $\xrightarrow[i \to S]{x}$**:** This can now happen *before* other caches have been notified about a write.

As an example of how these work, suppose a write occurs on a processor, and this is the only processor where that variable is `dirty`. An invalidation-based system would execute $\xrightarrow[j\uparrow]{x}$ on all other caches, and $\xrightarrow[i \to S]{x}$ on this cache (with no restrictions on the order in which these are carried out).

The proof that this model satisfies the constraints in §3.2 is nearly the same as that for the update model. Lemma 7 does *not* hold in this model, so the relaxed unlock condition cannot be used. The reason this lemma does not hold is that the last store update can happen before all caches have been invalidated. Thus some cache may hold a `clean` entry which nevertheless has a wrong value, simply because it has not yet been evicted.

7 Related and Future Work

Our work is complementary to the seminal work of Adve *et al* [1] wherein they present a classification of memory models (from a systems perspective rather than a programming perspective) that examine permissible reorderings of instructions. The notions of Data Race Freedom and weak orderings are also extensively explored by Adve *et al* [2].

Owens *et al* [8] have considered the x86 memory model and shown the correspondence between an axiomatic characterization of the model and an operational one. It would be interesting to relate our work to such concrete instances.

There are several strands of work that we identify for the future. First, the conditions we give are certainly *sufficient* to ensure sequential consistency, but it is not clear whether they are *necessary*. We also plan to investigate other synchronization primitives in a similar manner, in particular atomic *compare-and-swap* instructions for synchronization which are preferred over locks in many processors.

An interesting direction is the development of program analysis tools that will help analyze whether a program satisfies the condition that guarantees sequentially consistent behavior. Finally, we are formalizing the results presented here using the proof assistant Coq.

References

1. Adve, S.V., Gharachorloo, K.: Shared Memory Consistency Models: A Tutorial. Computer 29(12), 66–76 (1996)
2. Adve, S.V., Hill, M.D.: Weak Ordering—A new definition. SIGARCH Comput. Archit. News 18(3a), 2–14 (1990)
3. Arvind, N.N., Maessen, J.-W., Nikhil, R.S., Stoy, J.E.: A Lambda Calculus with Letrecs and Barriers. In: Proceedings of the 16th Conference on Foundations of Software Technology and Theoretical Computer Science, London, UK, pp. 19–36. Springer, Heidelberg (1996)
4. Boudol, G., Petri, G.: Relaxed Memory Models: An Operational Approach. In: POPL '09: Proceedings of the 36th annual ACM SIGPLAN-SIGACT symposium on Principles of Programming Languages, pp. 392–403. ACM, New York (2009)
5. Handy, J.: The Cache Memory Book. Academic Press Professional, Inc., San Diego (1993)
6. Joshi, S., Prasad, S.: An Operational Model for Multiprocessors with Caches. Technical report, Indian Institute of Technology Delhi (2010), `http://cse.iitd.ac.in/~sanjiva/OpCache.pdf`
7. Lamport, L.: How to Make a Multiprocessor Computer That Correctly Executes Multiprocess Programs. IEEE Transactions on Computers 100(28), 690–691 (1979)
8. Owens, S., Sarkar, S., Sewell, P.: A Better x86 Memory Model: x86-TSO. In: Berghofer, S., Nipkow, T., Urban, C., Wenzel, M. (eds.) TPHOL 2009. LNCS, vol. 5674, pp. 391–407. Springer, Heidelberg (2009)
9. Sarkar, S., Sewell, P., Nardelli, F.Z., Owens, S., Ridge, T., Braibant, T., Myreen, M.O., Alglave, J.: The semantics of x86-CC multiprocessor machine code. ACM SIGPLAN Notices 44(1), 379–391 (2009)
10. Wright, A.K., Felleisen, M.: A Syntactic Approach to Type Soundness. Information and Computation 115, 38–94 (1992)

Author Index